Operating
System Concepts
Essentials
Second Edition

Operating System Concepts Essentials

Second Edition

ABRAHAM SILBERSCHATZ
Yale University

PETER BAER GALVIN
Corporate Technologies, Inc.

GREG GAGNE
Westminster College

WILEY

Vice President & Executive Publisher	Don Fowley
Executive Editor	Beth Lang Golub
Executive Marketing Manager	Christopher Ruel
Associate Production Manager	Joyce Poh
Cover designer	Madelyn Lesure

This book was set in Palatino by the author using LaTeX and printed and bound by Courier Kendallville. The cover was printed by Courier Kendallville. This book is printed on acid free paper.

Founded in 1807, John Wiley & Sons, Inc. has been a valued source of knowledge and understanding for more than 200 years, helping people around the world meet their needs and fulfill their aspirations. Our company is built on a foundation of principles that include responsibility to the communities we serve and where we live and work. In 2008, we launched a Corporate Citizenship Initiative, a global effort to address the environmental, social, economic, and ethical challenges we face in our business. Among the issues we are addressing are carbon impact, paper specifications and procurement, ethical conduct within our business and among our vendors, and community and charitable support. For more information, please visit our website: www.wiley.com/go/citizenship.

Printed in the United States of America

10 9 8 7 6 5 4 3 2 1

To my children, Lemor, Sivan, and Aaron
and my Nicolette

Avi Silberschatz

To my wife, Carla,
and my children, Gwen, Owen, and Maddie

Peter Baer Galvin

To my wife, Pat,
and our sons, Tom and Jay

Greg Gagne

Preface

Operating systems are an essential part of any computer system. Similarly, a course on operating systems is an essential part of any computer science education. This field is undergoing rapid change, as computers are now prevalent in virtually every arena of day-to-day life—from embedded devices in automobiles through the most sophisticated planning tools for governments and multinational firms. Yet the fundamental concepts remain fairly clear, and it is on these that we base this book.

We wrote this book as a text for an introductory course in operating systems at the junior or senior undergraduate level or at the first-year graduate level. We hope that practitioners will also find it useful. It provides a clear description of the *concepts* that underlie operating systems. As prerequisites, we assume that the reader is familiar with basic data structures, computer organization, and a high-level language, such as C or Java. The hardware topics required for an understanding of operating systems are covered in Chapter 1. In that chapter, we also include an overview of the fundamental data structures that are prevalent in most operating systems. For code examples, we use predominantly C, with some Java, but the reader can still understand the algorithms without a thorough knowledge of these languages.

Concepts are presented using intuitive descriptions. Important theoretical results are covered, but formal proofs are largely omitted. The bibliographical notes at the end of each chapter contain pointers to research papers in which results were first presented and proved, as well as references to recent material for further reading. In place of proofs, figures and examples are used to suggest why we should expect the result in question to be true.

The fundamental concepts and algorithms covered in the book are often based on those used in both commercial and open-source operating systems. Our aim is to present these concepts and algorithms in a general setting that is not tied to one particular operating system. However, we present a large number of examples that pertain to the most popular and the most innovative operating systems, including Linux, Microsoft Windows, Apple Mac OS X, and Solaris. We also include examples of both Android and iOS, currently the two dominant mobile operating systems.

The organization of the text reflects our many years of teaching courses on operating systems, as well as curriculum guidelines published by the IEEE

Computing Society and the Association for Computing Machinery (ACM). Consideration was also given to the feedback provided by the reviewers of the text, along with the many comments and suggestions we received from readers of our previous editions and from our current and former students.

Content of This Book

The text is organized in six major parts:

- **Overview**. Chapters 1 and 2 explain what operating systems are, what they do, and how they are designed and constructed. These chapters discuss what the common features of an operating system are and what an operating system does for the user. We include coverage of both traditional PC and server operating systems, as well as operating systems for mobile devices. The presentation is motivational and explanatory in nature. We have avoided a discussion of how things are done internally in these chapters. Therefore, they are suitable for individual readers or for students in lower-level classes who want to learn what an operating system is without getting into the details of the internal algorithms.

- **Process management**. Chapters 3 through 6 describe the process concept and concurrency as the heart of modern operating systems. A *process* is the unit of work in a system. Such a system consists of a collection of *concurrently* executing processes, some of which are operating-system processes (those that execute system code) and the rest of which are user processes (those that execute user code). These chapters cover methods for process scheduling, interprocess communication, process synchronization, and deadlock handling. Also included is a discussion of threads, as well as an examination of issues related to multicore systems and parallel programming.

- **Memory management**. Chapters 7 and 8 deal with the management of main memory during the execution of a process. To improve both the utilization of the CPU and the speed of its response to its users, the computer must keep several processes in memory. There are many different memory-management schemes, reflecting various approaches to memory management, and the effectiveness of a particular algorithm depends on the situation.

- **Storage management**. Chapters 9 through 12 describe how mass storage, the file system, and I/O are handled in a modern computer system. The file system provides the mechanism for on-line storage of and access to both data and programs. We describe the classic internal algorithms and structures of storage management and provide a firm practical understanding of the algorithms used—their properties, advantages, and disadvantages. Since the I/O devices that attach to a computer vary widely, the operating system needs to provide a wide range of functionality to applications to allow them to control all aspects of these devices. We discuss system I/O in depth, including I/O system design, interfaces, and internal system structures and functions. In many ways, I/O devices are the slowest major components of the computer. Because they represent a performance bottleneck, we also examine performance issues associated with I/O devices.

- **Protection and security**. Chapters 13 and 14 discuss the mechanisms necessary for the protection and security of computer systems. The processes in an operating system must be protected from one another's activities, and to provide such protection, we must ensure that only processes that have gained proper authorization from the operating system can operate on the files, memory, CPU, and other resources of the system. Protection is a mechanism for controlling the access of programs, processes, or users to computer-system resources. This mechanism must provide a means of specifying the controls to be imposed, as well as a means of enforcement. Security protects the integrity of the information stored in the system (both data and code), as well as the physical resources of the system, from unauthorized access, malicious destruction or alteration, and accidental introduction of inconsistency.

- **Case studies**. Chapter 15 in the text, along with Appendices A and B (which are available on http://www.os-book.com), present detailed case studies of real operating systems, including Linux, FreeBSD, and Mach. Coverage of Linux is presented throughout this text; however, the case studies provide much more detail.

Operating System Essentials

We have based *Operating System Essentials* on the Ninth Edition of *Operating System Concepts*, published in 2012. Our intention behind developing this *Essentials* edition is to provide readers with a textbook that focuses on the core concepts that underlie contemporary operating systems. By focusing on core concepts, we believe students are able to grasp the essential features of a modern operating system more easily and more quickly.

To achieve this, *Operating System Essentials* omits the following coverage from the Ninth Edition of *Operating System Concepts*:

1. We removed Chapter 7—Deadlocks—and instead offer a detailed overview of deadlocks in Chapter 6.

2. We removed Chapter 16—Virtual Machines.

3. We removed Chapter 17—Distributed Systems.

4. We removed Chapter 19—Windows 7.

5. We removed Chapter 20—Influential Operating Systems.

For those that wish to pursue a more comprehensive study of operating systems, we refer you to the Ninth Edition of *Operating System Concepts*, and in the following we describe the changes relevant to that edition.

The Second Edition

As we wrote this Second Edition of *Operating System Concepts Essentials*, we were guided by the recent growth in the following fundamental areas that affect operating systems:

1. Multicore systems

2. Mobile computing

We have integrated relevant coverage throughout this new edition To emphasize these topics. Additionally, we have rewritten material in almost every chapter by bringing older material up to date and removing material that is no longer interesting or relevant.

We have also made substantial organizational changes. For example, we have eliminated the chapter on real-time systems and instead have integrated appropriate coverage of these systems throughout the text. We have reordered the chapters on storage management and have moved up the presentation of process synchronization so that it appears before process scheduling. Most of these organizational changes are based on our experiences while teaching courses on operating systems.

Below, we provide a brief outline of the major changes to the various chapters:

- **Chapter 1, Introduction,** includes updated coverage of multiprocessor and multicore systems, as well as a new section on kernel data structures. Additionally, the coverage of computing environments now includes mobile systems and cloud computing. We also have incorporated an overview of real-time systems.

- **Chapter 2, Operating-System Structures,** provides new coverage of user interfaces for mobile devices, including discussions of iOS and Android, and expanded coverage of Mac OS X as a type of hybrid system.

- **Chapter 3, Processes,** now includes coverage of multitasking in mobile operating systems, support for the multiprocess model in Google's Chrome web browser, and zombie and orphan processes in UNIX.

- **Chapter 4, Threads,** supplies expanded coverage of parallelism and Amdahl's law. It also provides a new section on implicit threading, including OpenMP and Apple's Grand Central Dispatch.

- **Chapter 5, Process Synchronization** (previously Chapter 6), adds a new section on mutex locks as well as coverage of synchronization using OpenMP, as well as functional languages.

- **Chapter 6, CPU Scheduling** (previously Chapter 5), contains new coverage of the Linux CFS scheduler and Windows user-mode scheduling. Coverage of real-time scheduling algorithms ·has also been integrated into this chapter.

- **Chapter 7, Main Memory,** includes new coverage of swapping on mobile systems and Intel 32- and 64-bit architectures. A new section discusses ARM architecture.

- **Chapter 8, Virtual Memory,** updates kernel memory management to include the Linux SLUB and SLOB memory allocators.

- **Chapter 9, Mass-Storage Structure** (previously Chapter 11), adds coverage of solid-state disks.

- **Chapter 10, File-System Interface** (previously Chapter 9), is updated with information about current technologies.

- **Chapter 11, File-System Implementation** (previously Chapter 10), is updated with coverage of current technologies.

- **Chapter 12, I/O,** updates technologies and performance numbers, expands coverage of synchronous/asynchronous and blocking/nonblocking I/O, and adds a section on vectored I/O.

- **Chapter 13, Protection,** has no major changes.

- **Chapter 14, Security,** has a revised cryptography section with modern notation and an improved explanation of various encryption methods and their uses. The chapter also includes new coverage of Windows 7 security.

- **Chapter 15, The Linux System,** has been updated to cover the Linux 3.2 kernel.

Programming Environments

This book uses examples of many real-world operating systems to illustrate fundamental operating-system concepts. Particular attention is paid to Linux and Microsoft Windows, but we also refer to various versions of UNIX (including Solaris, BSD, and Mac OS X).

The text also provides several example programs written in C and Java. These programs are intended to run in the following programming environments:

- **POSIX**. POSIX (which stands for *Portable Operating System Interface*) represents a set of standards implemented primarily for UNIX-based operating systems. Although Windows systems can also run certain POSIX programs, our coverage of POSIX focuses on UNIX and Linux systems. POSIX-compliant systems must implement the POSIX core standard (POSIX.1); Linux, Solaris, and Mac OS X are examples of POSIX-compliant systems. POSIX also defines several extensions to the standards, including real-time extensions (POSIX1.b) and an extension for a threads library (POSIX1.c, better known as Pthreads). We provide several programming examples written in C illustrating the POSIX base API, as well as Pthreads and the extensions for real-time programming. These example programs were tested on Linux 2.6 and 3.2 systems, Mac OS X 10.7, and Solaris 10 using the gcc 4.0 compiler.

- **Java**. Java is a widely used programming language with a rich API and built-in language support for thread creation and management. Java programs run on any operating system supporting a Java virtual machine (or JVM). We illustrate various operating-system and networking concepts with Java programs tested using the Java 1.6 JVM.

- **Windows systems**. The primary programming environment for Windows systems is the Windows API, which provides a comprehensive set of functions for managing processes, threads, memory, and peripheral devices. We supply several C programs illustrating the use of this API. Programs were tested on systems running Windows XP and Windows 7.

We have chosen these three programming environments because we believe that they best represent the two most popular operating-system models —Windows and UNIX/Linux—along with the widely used Java environment. Most programming examples are written in C, and we expect readers to be comfortable with this language. Readers familiar with both the C and Java languages should easily understand most programs provided in this text.

In some instances—such as thread creation—we illustrate a specific concept using all three programming environments, allowing the reader to contrast the three different libraries as they address the same task. In other situations, we may use just one of the APIs to demonstrate a concept. For example, we illustrate shared memory using just the POSIX API; socket programming in TCP/IP is highlighted using the Java API.

Linux Virtual Machine

To help students gain a better understanding of the Linux system, we provide a Linux virtual machine, including the Linux source code, that is available for download from the website supporting this text (http://www.os-book.com). This virtual machine also includes a gcc development environment with compilers and editors. Most of the programming assignments in the book can be completed on this virtual machine, with the exception of assignments that require Java or the Windows API.

We also provide three programming assignments that modify the Linux kernel through kernel modules:

1. Adding a basic kernel module to the Linux kernel.

2. Adding a kernel module that uses various kernel data structures.

3. Adding a kernel module that iterates over tasks in a running Linux system.

Over time it is our intention to add additional kernel module assignments on the supporting website.

Supporting Website

When you visit the website supporting this text at http://www.os-book.com, you can download the following resources:

- Linux virtual machine
- C and Java source code

- Sample syllabi
- Set of Powerpoint slides
- Set of figures and illustrations
- FreeBSD and Mach case studies
- Set of review questions indexed by section
- Solutions to practice exercises
- Study guide for students
- Errata

Notes to Instructors

On the website for this text, we provide several sample syllabi that suggest various approaches for using the text in both introductory and advanced courses. As a general rule, we encourage instructors to progress sequentially through the chapters, as this strategy provides the most thorough study of operating systems. However, by using the sample syllabi, an instructor can select a different ordering of chapters (or subsections of chapters).

In this edition, we have added over sixty new written exercises and over twenty new programming problems and projects. Most of the new programming assignments involve processes, threads, process synchronization, and memory management. Some involve adding kernel modules to the Linux system which requires using either the Linux virtual machine that accompanies this text or another suitable Linux distribution.

Solutions to review questions, written exercises and programming assignments are available to instructors who have adopted this text for their operating-system class. To obtain these restricted supplements, contact your local John Wiley & Sons sales representative. You can find your Wiley representative by going to http://www.wiley.com/college and clicking "Who's my rep?"

Notes to Students

We encourage you to take advantage of the review questions (available online) and practice exercises that appear at the end of each chapter. The review questions as well as solutions to the practice exercises are available for download from the supporting website http://www.os-book.com. We also encourage you to read through the study guide, which was prepared by one of our students. Finally, for students who are unfamiliar with UNIX and Linux systems, we recommend that you download and install the Linux virtual machine that we include on the supporting website. Not only will this provide you with a new computing experience, but the open-source nature of Linux will allow you to easily examine the inner details of this popular operating system.

We wish you the very best of luck in your study of operating systems.

Contacting Us

We have endeavored to eliminate typos, bugs, and the like from the text. But, as in new releases of software, bugs almost surely remain. An up-to-date errata list is accessible from the book's website. We would be grateful if you would notify us of any errors or omissions in the book that are not on the current list of errata.

We would be glad to receive suggestions on improvements to the book. We also welcome any contributions to the book website that could be of use to other readers, such as programming exercises, project suggestions, on-line labs and tutorials, and teaching tips. E-mail should be addressed to os-book-authors@cs.yale.edu.

Acknowledgments

This book is derived from the previous editions, the first three of which were coauthored by James Peterson. Others who helped us with previous editions include Hamid Arabnia, Rida Bazzi, Randy Bentson, David Black, Joseph Boykin, Jeff Brumfield, Gael Buckley, Roy Campbell, P. C. Capon, John Carpenter, Gil Carrick, Thomas Casavant, Bart Childs, Ajoy Kumar Datta, Joe Deck, Sudarshan K. Dhall, Thomas Doeppner, Caleb Drake, M. Racsit Eskicioğlu, Hans Flack, Robert Fowler, G. Scott Graham, Richard Guy, Max Hailperin, Rebecca Hartman, Wayne Hathaway, Christopher Haynes, Don Heller, Bruce Hillyer, Mark Holliday, Dean Hougen, Michael Huang, Ahmed Kamel, Morty Kewstel, Richard Kieburtz, Carol Kroll, Morty Kwestel, Thomas LeBlanc, John Leggett, Jerrold Leichter, Ted Leung, Gary Lippman, Carolyn Miller, Michael Molloy, Euripides Montagne, Yoichi Muraoka, Jim M. Ng, Banu Özden, Ed Posnak, Boris Putanec, Charles Qualline, John Quarterman, Mike Reiter, Gustavo Rodriguez-Rivera, Carolyn J. C. Schauble, Thomas P. Skinner, Yannis Smaragdakis, Jesse St. Laurent, John Stankovic, Adam Stauffer, Steven Stepanek, John Sterling, Hal Stern, Louis Stevens, Pete Thomas, David Umbaugh, Steve Vinoski, Tommy Wagner, Larry L. Wear, John Werth, James M. Westall, J. S. Weston, and Yang Xiang

Robert Love updated both Chapter 15 and the Linux coverage throughout the text, as well as answering many of our Android-related questions. Jonathan Katz contributed to Chapter 14. Salahuddin Khan updated Section 14.9 to provide new coverage of Windows 7 security.

Chapter 15 was derived from an unpublished manuscript by Stephen Tweedie. Cliff Martin helped with updating the UNIX appendix to cover FreeBSD. Some of the exercises and accompanying solutions were supplied by Arvind Krishnamurthy. Andrew DeNicola prepared the student study guide that is available on our website. Some of the slides were prepeared by Marilyn Turnamian.

Mike Shapiro, Bryan Cantrill, and Jim Mauro answered several Solaris-related questions, and Bryan Cantrill from Sun Microsystems helped with the ZFS coverage. Josh Dees and Rob Reynolds contributed coverage of Microsoft's NET. The project for POSIX message queues was contributed by John Trono of Saint Michael's College in Colchester, Vermont.

Judi Paige helped with generating figures and presentation of slides. Thomas Gagne prepared new artwork for this edition. Mark Wogahn has made sure that the software to produce this book (LaTeX and fonts) works properly. Ranjan Kumar Meher rewrote some of the LaTeX software used in the production of this new text.

Our Executive Editor, Beth Lang Golub, provided expert guidance as we prepared this edition. She was assisted by Katherine Willis, who managed many details of the project smoothly. The Senior Production Editor, Joyce Poh, was instrumental in handling all the production details.

The cover illustrator was Susan Cyr, and the cover designer was Madelyn Lesure. Beverly Peavler copy-edited the manuscript. The freelance proofreader was Katrina Avery; the freelance indexer was WordCo, Inc.

Abraham Silberschatz, New Haven, CT, 2013
Peter Baer Galvin, Boston, MA, 2013
Greg Gagne, Salt Lake City, UT, 2013

Contents

Chapter 4   Threads

Chapter 5   Process Synchronization

Chapter 6   CPU Scheduling

PART THREE ■ MEMORY MANAGEMENT

Chapter 7   Main Memory

Chapter 8   Virtual Memory

PART FOUR ■ STORAGE MANAGEMENT

Chapter 9   Mass-Storage Structure

Chapter 10   File-System Interface

Chapter 11   File-System Implementation

Chapter 12   I/O Systems

PART FIVE ■ PROTECTION AND SECURITY

Chapter 13   Protection

Chapter 14   Security

PART SIX   ■   CASE STUDIES

Chapter 15   The Linux System

Appendix A   BSD UNIX (contents online)

Appendix B   The Mach System (contents online)

Part One

Overview

An *operating system* acts as an intermediary between the user of a computer and the computer hardware. The purpose of an operating system is to provide an environment in which a user can execute programs in a *convenient* and *efficient* manner.

An operating system is software that manages the computer hardware. The hardware must provide appropriate mechanisms to ensure the correct operation of the computer system and to prevent user programs from interfering with the proper operation of the system.

Internally, operating systems vary greatly in their makeup, since they are organized along many different lines. The design of a new operating system is a major task. It is important that the goals of the system be well defined before the design begins. These goals form the basis for choices among various algorithms and strategies.

Because an operating system is large and complex, it must be created piece by piece. Each of these pieces should be a well-delineated portion of the system, with carefully defined inputs, outputs, and functions.

Introduction

An **operating system** is a program that manages a computer's hardware. It also provides a basis for application programs and acts as an intermediary between the computer user and the computer hardware. An amazing aspect of operating systems is how they vary in accomplishing these tasks. Mainframe operating systems are designed primarily to optimize utilization of hardware. Personal computer (PC) operating systems support complex games, business applications, and everything in between. Operating systems for mobile computers provide an environment in which a user can easily interface with the computer to execute programs. Thus, some operating systems are designed to be *convenient*, others to be *efficient*, and others to be some combination of the two.

Before we can explore the details of computer system operation, we need to know something about system structure. We thus discuss the basic functions of system startup, I/O, and storage early in this chapter. We also describe the basic computer architecture that makes it possible to write a functional operating system.

Because an operating system is large and complex, it must be created piece by piece. Each of these pieces should be a well-delineated portion of the system, with carefully defined inputs, outputs, and functions. In this chapter, we provide a general overview of the major components of a contemporary computer system as well as the functions provided by the operating system. Additionally, we cover several other topics to help set the stage for the remainder of this text: data structures used in operating systems, computing environments, and open-source operating systems.

CHAPTER OBJECTIVES

- To describe the basic organization of computer systems.
- To provide a grand tour of the major components of operating systems.
- To give an overview of the many types of computing environments.
- To explore several open-source operating systems.

Figure 1.1   Abstract view of the components of a computer system.

1.1   What Operating Systems Do

We begin our discussion by looking at the operating system's role in the overall computer system. A computer system can be divided roughly into four components: the *hardware*, the *operating system*, the *application programs*, and the *users* (Figure 1.1).

The **hardware**—the **central processing unit** (CPU), the **memory**, and the **input/output** (I/O) **devices**—provides the basic computing resources for the system. The **application programs**—such as word processors, spreadsheets, compilers, and Web browsers—define the ways in which these resources are used to solve users' computing problems. The operating system controls the hardware and coordinates its use among the various application programs for the various users.

We can also view a computer system as consisting of hardware, software, and data. The operating system provides the means for proper use of these resources in the operation of the computer system. An operating system is similar to a government. Like a government, it performs no useful function by itself. It simply provides an *environment* within which other programs can do useful work.

To understand more fully the operating system's role, we next explore operating systems from two viewpoints: that of the user and that of the system.

1.1.1   User View

The user's view of the computer varies according to the interface being used. Most computer users sit in front of a PC, consisting of a monitor, keyboard, mouse, and system unit. Such a system is designed for one user to monopolize its resources. The goal is to maximize the work (or play) that the user is performing. In this case, the operating system is designed mostly for **ease of use**, with some attention paid to performance and none paid to **resource utilization**—how various hardware and software resources are shared. Performance is, of course, important to the user; but such systems are optimized for the single-user experience rather than the requirements of multiple users.

In other cases, a user sits at a terminal connected to a **mainframe** or a **minicomputer**. Other users are accessing the same computer through other terminals. These users share resources and may exchange information. The operating system in such cases is designed to maximize resource utilization— to assure that all available CPU time, memory, and I/O are used efficiently and that no individual user takes more than her fair share.

In still other cases, users sit at **workstations** connected to networks of other workstations and **servers**. These users have dedicated resources at their disposal, but they also share resources such as networking and servers, including file, compute, and print servers. Therefore, their operating system is designed to compromise between individual usability and resource utilization.

Recently, many varieties of mobile computers, such as smartphones and tablets, have come into fashion. Most mobile computers are standalone units for individual users. Quite often, they are connected to networks through cellular or other wireless technologies. Increasingly, these mobile devices are replacing desktop and laptop computers for people who are primarily interested in using computers for e-mail and web browsing. The user interface for mobile computers generally features a **touch screen**, where the user interacts with the system by pressing and swiping fingers across the screen rather than using a physical keyboard and mouse.

Some computers have little or no user view. For example, embedded computers in home devices and automobiles may have numeric keypads and may turn indicator lights on or off to show status, but they and their operating systems are designed primarily to run without user intervention.

1.1.2   System View

From the computer's point of view, the operating system is the program most intimately involved with the hardware. In this context, we can view an operating system as a **resource allocator**. A computer system has many resources that may be required to solve a problem: CPU time, memory space, file-storage space, I/O devices, and so on. The operating system acts as the manager of these resources. Facing numerous and possibly conflicting requests for resources, the operating system must decide how to allocate them to specific programs and users so that it can operate the computer system efficiently and fairly. As we have seen, resource allocation is especially important where many users access the same mainframe or minicomputer.

A slightly different view of an operating system emphasizes the need to control the various I/O devices and user programs. An operating system is a control program. A **control program** manages the execution of user programs to prevent errors and improper use of the computer. It is especially concerned with the operation and control of I/O devices.

1.1.3 Defining Operating Systems

By now, you can probably see that the term *operating system* covers many roles and functions. That is the case, at least in part, because of the myriad designs and uses of computers. Computers are present within toasters, cars, ships, spacecraft, homes, and businesses. They are the basis for game machines, music players, cable TV tuners, and industrial control systems. Although computers have a relatively short history, they have evolved rapidly. Computing started as an experiment to determine what could be done and quickly moved to fixed-purpose systems for military uses, such as code breaking and trajectory plotting, and governmental uses, such as census calculation. Those early computers evolved into general-purpose, multifunction mainframes, and that's when operating systems were born. In the 1960s, Moore's Law predicted that the number of transistors on an integrated circuit would double every eighteen months, and that prediction has held true. Computers gained in functionality and shrunk in size, leading to a vast number of uses and a vast number and variety of operating systems.

How, then, can we define what an operating system is? In general, we have no completely adequate definition of an operating system. Operating systems exist because they offer a reasonable way to solve the problem of creating a usable computing system. The fundamental goal of computer systems is to execute user programs and to make solving user problems easier. Computer hardware is constructed toward this goal. Since bare hardware alone is not particularly easy to use, application programs are developed. These programs require certain common operations, such as those controlling the I/O devices. The common functions of controlling and allocating resources are then brought together into one piece of software: the operating system.

In addition, we have no universally accepted definition of what is part of the operating system. A simple viewpoint is that it includes everything a vendor ships when you order "the operating system." The features included, however, vary greatly across systems. Some systems take up less than a megabyte of space and lack even a full-screen editor, whereas others require gigabytes of space and are based entirely on graphical windowing systems. A more common definition, and the one that we usually follow, is that the operating system is the one program running at all times on the computer—usually called the kernel. (Along with the kernel, there are two other types of programs: system programs, which are associated with the operating system but are not necessarily part of the kernel, and application programs, which include all programs not associated with the operation of the system.)

The matter of what constitutes an operating system became increasingly important as personal computers became more widespread and operating systems grew increasingly sophisticated. In 1998, the United States Department of Justice filed suit against Microsoft, in essence claiming that Microsoft included too much functionality in its operating systems and thus prevented application vendors from competing. (For example, a Web browser was an integral part of the operating systems.) As a result, Microsoft was found guilty of using its operating-system monopoly to limit competition.

Today, however, if we look at operating systems for mobile devices, we see that once again the number of features constituting the operating system is increasing. Mobile operating systems often include not only a core kernel but also **middleware**—a set of software frameworks that provide additional services to application developers. For example, each of the two most prominent mobile operating systems—Apple's iOS and Google's Android—features a core kernel along with middleware that supports databases, multimedia, and graphics (to name only a few).

1.2 Computer-System Organization

Before we can explore the details of how computer systems operate, we need general knowledge of the structure of a computer system. In this section, we look at several parts of this structure. The section is mostly concerned with computer-system organization, so you can skim or skip it if you already understand the concepts.

1.2.1 Computer-System Operation

A modern general-purpose computer system consists of one or more CPUs and a number of device controllers connected through a common bus that provides access to shared memory (Figure 1.2). Each device controller is in charge of a specific type of device (for example, disk drives, audio devices, or video displays). The CPU and the device controllers can execute in parallel, competing for memory cycles. To ensure orderly access to the shared memory, a memory controller synchronizes access to the memory.

For a computer to start running—for instance, when it is powered up or rebooted—it needs to have an initial program to run. This initial program, or **bootstrap program**, tends to be simple. Typically, it is stored within the computer hardware in read-only memory (ROM) or electrically erasable programmable read-only memory (EEPROM), known by the general term **firmware**. It initializes all aspects of the system, from CPU registers to device controllers to memory contents. The bootstrap program must know how to load the operating system and how to start executing that system. To accomplish

Figure 1.2 A modern computer system.

CPU   user
       process
       executing

       I/O interrupt
       processing

I/O   idle
device
       transferring

I/O   transfer   I/O   transfer
request done   request done

Figure 1.3   Interrupt timeline for a single process doing output.

this goal, the bootstrap program must locate the operating-system kernel and load it into memory.

Once the kernel is loaded and executing, it can start providing services to the system and its users. Some services are provided outside of the kernel, by system programs that are loaded into memory at boot time to become **system processes**, or **system daemons** that run the entire time the kernel is running. On UNIX, the first system process is "init," and it starts many other daemons. Once this phase is complete, the system is fully booted, and the system waits for some event to occur.

The occurrence of an event is usually signaled by an **interrupt** from either the hardware or the software. Hardware may trigger an interrupt at any time by sending a signal to the CPU, usually by way of the system bus. Software may trigger an interrupt by executing a special operation called a **system call** (also called a **monitor call**).

When the CPU is interrupted, it stops what it is doing and immediately transfers execution to a fixed location. The fixed location usually contains the starting address where the service routine for the interrupt is located. The interrupt service routine executes; on completion, the CPU resumes the interrupted computation. A timeline of this operation is shown in Figure 1.3.

Interrupts are an important part of a computer architecture. Each computer design has its own interrupt mechanism, but several functions are common. The interrupt must transfer control to the appropriate interrupt service routine. The straightforward method for handling this transfer would be to invoke a generic routine to examine the interrupt information. The routine, in turn, would call the interrupt-specific handler. However, interrupts must be handled quickly. Since only a predefined number of interrupts is possible, a table of pointers to interrupt routines can be used instead to provide the necessary speed. The interrupt routine is called indirectly through the table, with no intermediate routine needed. Generally, the table of pointers is stored in low memory (the first hundred or so locations). These locations hold the addresses of the interrupt service routines for the various devices. This array, or **interrupt vector**, of addresses is then indexed by a unique device number, given with the interrupt request, to provide the address of the interrupt service routine for

STORAGE DEFINITIONS AND NOTATION

The basic unit of computer storage is the bit. A bit can contain one of two values, 0 and 1. All other storage in a computer is based on collections of bits. Given enough bits, it is amazing how many things a computer can represent: numbers, letters, images, movies, sounds, documents, and programs, to name a few. A byte is 8 bits, and on most computers it is the smallest convenient chunk of storage. For example, most computers don't have an instruction to move a bit but do have one to move a byte. A less common term is word, which is a given computer architecture's native unit of data. A word is made up of one or more bytes. For example, a computer that has 64-bit registers and 64-bit memory addressing typically has 64-bit (8-byte) words. A computer executes many operations in its native word size rather than a byte at a time.

Computer storage, along with most computer throughput, is generally measured and manipulated in bytes and collections of bytes. A kilobyte, or KB, is 1,024 bytes; a megabyte, or MB, is $1,024^2$ bytes; a gigabyte, or GB, is $1,024^3$ bytes; a terabyte, or TB, is $1,024^4$ bytes; and a petabyte, or PB, is $1,024^5$ bytes. Computer manufacturers often round off these numbers and say that a megabyte is 1 million bytes and a gigabyte is 1 billion bytes. Networking measurements are an exception to this general rule; they are given in bits (because networks move data a bit at a time).

the interrupting device. Operating systems as different as Windows and UNIX dispatch interrupts in this manner.

The interrupt architecture must also save the address of the interrupted instruction. Many old designs simply stored the interrupt address in a fixed location or in a location indexed by the device number. More recent architectures store the return address on the system stack. If the interrupt routine needs to modify the processor state—for instance, by modifying register values—it must explicitly save the current state and then restore that state before returning. After the interrupt is serviced, the saved return address is loaded into the program counter, and the interrupted computation resumes as though the interrupt had not occurred.

1.2.2 Storage Structure

The CPU can load instructions only from memory, so any programs to run must be stored there. General-purpose computers run most of their programs from rewritable memory, called main memory (also called random-access memory, or RAM). Main memory commonly is implemented in a semiconductor technology called dynamic random-access memory (DRAM).

Computers use other forms of memory as well. We have already mentioned read-only memory, ROM) and electrically erasable programmable read-only memory, EEPROM). Because ROM cannot be changed, only static programs, such as the bootstrap program described earlier, are stored there. The immutability of ROM is of use in game cartridges. EEPROM can be changed but cannot be changed frequently and so contains mostly static programs. For example, smartphones have EEPROM to store their factory-installed programs.

All forms of memory provide an array of bytes. Each byte has its own address. Interaction is achieved through a sequence of `load` or `store` instructions to specific memory addresses. The `load` instruction moves a byte or word from main memory to an internal register within the CPU, whereas the `store` instruction moves the content of a register to main memory. Aside from explicit loads and stores, the CPU automatically loads instructions from main memory for execution.

A typical instruction–execution cycle, as executed on a system with a **von Neumann architecture**, first fetches an instruction from memory and stores that instruction in the **instruction register**. The instruction is then decoded and may cause operands to be fetched from memory and stored in some internal register. After the instruction on the operands has been executed, the result may be stored back in memory. Notice that the memory unit sees only a stream of memory addresses. It does not know how they are generated (by the instruction counter, indexing, indirection, literal addresses, or some other means) or what they are for (instructions or data). Accordingly, we can ignore *how* a memory address is generated by a program. We are interested only in the sequence of memory addresses generated by the running program.

Ideally, we want the programs and data to reside in main memory permanently. This arrangement usually is not possible for the following two reasons:

1. Main memory is usually too small to store all needed programs and data permanently.

2. Main memory is a **volatile** storage device that loses its contents when power is turned off or otherwise lost.

Thus, most computer systems provide **secondary storage** as an extension of main memory. The main requirement for secondary storage is that it be able to hold large quantities of data permanently.

The most common secondary-storage device is a **hard disk drive** (HDD), which provides storage for both programs and data. Most programs (system and application) are stored on a disk until they are loaded into memory. Many programs then use the disk as both the source and the destination of their processing. Hence, the proper management of disk storage is of central importance to a computer system, as we discuss in Chapter 9.

In a larger sense, however, the storage structure that we have described —consisting of registers, main memory, and hard disks—is only one of many possible storage systems. Others include cache memory, CD-ROM, magnetic tapes, and so on. Each storage system provides the basic functions of storing a datum and holding that datum until it is retrieved at a later time. The main differences among the various storage systems lie in speed, cost, size, and volatility.

The wide variety of storage systems can be organized in a hierarchy (Figure 1.4) according to speed and cost. The higher levels are expensive, but they are fast. As we move down the hierarchy, the cost per bit generally decreases, whereas the access time generally increases. This trade-off is reasonable; if a given storage system were both faster and less expensive than another—other properties being the same—then there would be no reason to use the slower, more expensive memory. In fact, many early storage devices, including paper

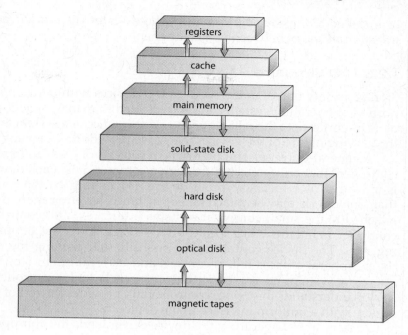

Figure 1.4 Storage-device hierarchy.

tape and core memories, are relegated to museums now that magnetic tape and **semiconductor memory** have become faster and cheaper. The top four levels of memory in Figure 1.4 may be constructed using semiconductor memory.

In addition to differing in speed and cost, the various storage systems are either volatile or nonvolatile. As mentioned earlier, **volatile storage** loses its contents when the power to the device is removed. In the absence of expensive battery and generator backup systems, data must be written to **nonvolatile storage** for safekeeping. In the hierarchy shown in Figure 1.4, the storage systems above the solid-state disk are volatile, whereas those including the solid-state disk and below are nonvolatile.

Solid-state disks have several variants but in general are faster than hard disks and are nonvolatile. One type of solid-state disk stores data in a large DRAM array during normal operation but also contains a hidden hard disk and a battery for backup power. If external power is interrupted, this solid-state disk's controller copies the data from RAM to the hard disk. When external power is restored, the controller copies the data back into RAM. Another form of solid-state disk is flash memory, which is popular in cameras and **personal digital assistants** (PDAs), in robots, and increasingly for storage on general-purpose computers. Flash memory is slower than DRAM but needs no power to retain its contents. Another form of nonvolatile storage is NVRAM, which is DRAM with battery backup power. This memory can be as fast as DRAM and (as long as the battery lasts) is nonvolatile.

The design of a complete memory system must balance all the factors just discussed: it must use only as much expensive memory as necessary while providing as much inexpensive, nonvolatile memory as possible. Caches can be installed to improve performance where a large disparity in access time or transfer rate exists between two components.

1.2.3 I/O Structure

Storage is only one of many types of I/O devices within a computer. A large portion of operating system code is dedicated to managing I/O, both because of its importance to the reliability and performance of a system and because of the varying nature of the devices. Next, we provide an overview of I/O.

A general-purpose computer system consists of CPUs and multiple device controllers that are connected through a common bus. Each device controller is in charge of a specific type of device. Depending on the controller, more than one device may be attached. For instance, seven or more devices can be attached to the **small computer-systems interface** (SCSI) controller. A device controller maintains some local buffer storage and a set of special-purpose registers. The device controller is responsible for moving the data between the peripheral devices that it controls and its local buffer storage. Typically, operating systems have a **device driver** for each device controller. This device driver understands the device controller and provides the rest of the operating system with a uniform interface to the device.

To start an I/O operation, the device driver loads the appropriate registers within the device controller. The device controller, in turn, examines the contents of these registers to determine what action to take (such as "read a character from the keyboard"). The controller starts the transfer of data from the device to its local buffer. Once the transfer of data is complete, the device controller informs the device driver via an interrupt that it has finished its operation. The device driver then returns control to the operating system, possibly returning the data or a pointer to the data if the operation was a read. For other operations, the device driver returns status information.

This form of interrupt-driven I/O is fine for moving small amounts of data but can produce high overhead when used for bulk data movement such as disk I/O. To solve this problem, **direct memory access** (DMA) is used. After setting up buffers, pointers, and counters for the I/O device, the device controller transfers an entire block of data directly to or from its own buffer storage to memory, with no intervention by the CPU. Only one interrupt is generated per block, to tell the device driver that the operation has completed, rather than the one interrupt per byte generated for low-speed devices. While the device controller is performing these operations, the CPU is available to accomplish other work.

Some high-end systems use switch rather than bus architecture. On these systems, multiple components can talk to other components concurrently, rather than competing for cycles on a shared bus. In this case, DMA is even more effective. Figure 1.5 shows the interplay of all components of a computer system.

1.3 Computer-System Architecture

In Section 1.2, we introduced the general structure of a typical computer system. A computer system can be organized in a number of different ways, which we

Figure 1.5 How a modern computer system works.

can categorize roughly according to the number of general-purpose processors used.

1.3.1 Single-Processor Systems

Until recently, most computer systems used a single processor. On a single-processor system, there is one main CPU capable of executing a general-purpose instruction set, including instructions from user processes. Almost all single-processor systems have other special-purpose processors as well. They may come in the form of device-specific processors, such as disk, keyboard, and graphics controllers; or, on mainframes, they may come in the form of more general-purpose processors, such as I/O processors that move data rapidly among the components of the system.

All of these special-purpose processors run a limited instruction set and do not run user processes. Sometimes, they are managed by the operating system, in that the operating system sends them information about their next task and monitors their status. For example, a disk-controller microprocessor receives a sequence of requests from the main CPU and implements its own disk queue and scheduling algorithm. This arrangement relieves the main CPU of the overhead of disk scheduling. PCs contain a microprocessor in the keyboard to convert the keystrokes into codes to be sent to the CPU. In other systems or circumstances, special-purpose processors are low-level components built into the hardware. The operating system cannot communicate with these processors; they do their jobs autonomously. The use of special-purpose microprocessors is common and does not turn a single-processor system into a multiprocessor. If there is only one general-purpose CPU, then the system is a single-processor system.

1.3.2 Multiprocessor Systems

Within the past several years, **multiprocessor systems** (also known as **parallel systems** or **multicore systems**) have begun to dominate the landscape of computing. Such systems have two or more processors in close communication, sharing the computer bus and sometimes the clock, memory, and peripheral devices. Multiprocessor systems first appeared prominently in servers and have since migrated to desktop and laptop systems. Recently, multiple processors have appeared on mobile devices such as smartphones and tablet computers.

Multiprocessor systems have three main advantages:

1. **Increased throughput**. By increasing the number of processors, we expect to get more work done in less time. The speed-up ratio with N processors is not N, however; rather, it is less than N. When multiple processors cooperate on a task, a certain amount of overhead is incurred in keeping all the parts working correctly. This overhead, plus contention for shared resources, lowers the expected gain from additional processors. Similarly, N programmers working closely together do not produce N times the amount of work a single programmer would produce.

2. **Economy of scale**. Multiprocessor systems can cost less than equivalent multiple single-processor systems, because they can share peripherals, mass storage, and power supplies. If several programs operate on the same set of data, it is cheaper to store those data on one disk and to have all the processors share them than to have many computers with local disks and many copies of the data.

3. **Increased reliability**. If functions can be distributed properly among several processors, then the failure of one processor will not halt the system, only slow it down. If we have ten processors and one fails, then each of the remaining nine processors can pick up a share of the work of the failed processor. Thus, the entire system runs only 10 percent slower, rather than failing altogether.

Increased reliability of a computer system is crucial in many applications. The ability to continue providing service proportional to the level of surviving hardware is called **graceful degradation**. Some systems go beyond graceful degradation and are called **fault tolerant**, because they can suffer a failure of any single component and still continue operation. Fault tolerance requires a mechanism to allow the failure to be detected, diagnosed, and, if possible, corrected. The HP NonStop (formerly Tandem) system uses both hardware and software duplication to ensure continued operation despite faults. The system consists of multiple pairs of CPUs, working in lockstep. Both processors in the pair execute each instruction and compare the results. If the results differ, then one CPU of the pair is at fault, and both are halted. The process that was being executed is then moved to another pair of CPUs, and the instruction that failed is restarted. This solution is expensive, since it involves special hardware and considerable hardware duplication.

The multiple-processor systems in use today are of two types. Some systems use **asymmetric multiprocessing,** in which each processor is assigned a specific task. A *boss* processor controls the system; the other processors either look to the boss for instruction or have predefined tasks. This scheme defines a boss–worker relationship. The boss processor schedules and allocates work to the worker processors.

The most common systems use **symmetric multiprocessing (SMP),** in which each processor performs all tasks, including operating system functions and user processes. SMP means that all processors are peers; no boss–worker relationship exists between processors. Figure 1.6 illustrates a typical SMP architecture. Notice that each processor has its own set of registers, as well as a private—or local—cache. However, all processors share physical memory. An example of an SMP system is AIX, a commercial version of UNIX designed by IBM. An AIX system can be configured to employ dozens of processors. The benefit of this model is that many processes can run simultaneously—*N* processes can run if there are *N* CPUs—without causing performance to deteriorate significantly. However, we must carefully control I/O to ensure that the data reach the appropriate processor. Also, since the CPUs are separate, one may be sitting idle while another is overloaded, resulting in inefficiencies. These inefficiencies can be avoided if the processors share certain data structures. A multiprocessor system of this form will allow processes and resources—such as memory—to be shared dynamically among the various processors and can lower the variance among the processors. Such a system must be written carefully, as we shall see in Chapter 5. Virtually all modern operating systems —including Windows, Mac OS X, and Linux—now provide support for SMP.

The difference between symmetric and asymmetric multiprocessing may result from either hardware or software. Special hardware can differentiate the multiple processors, or the software can be written to allow only one boss and multiple workers. For instance, Sun Microsystems' operating system SunOS Version 4 provided asymmetric multiprocessing, whereas Version 5 (Solaris) is symmetric on the same hardware.

Multiprocessing adds CPUs to increase computing power. If the CPU has an integrated memory controller, then adding CPUs can also increase the amount

Figure 1.6   Symmetric multiprocessing architecture.

of memory addressable in the system. Either way, multiprocessing can cause a system to change its memory access model from uniform memory access (UMA) to non-uniform memory access (NUMA). UMA is defined as the situation in which access to any RAM from any CPU takes the same amount of time. With NUMA, some parts of memory may take longer to access than other parts, creating a performance penalty. Operating systems can minimize the NUMA penalty through resource management, as discussed in Section 8.5.4.

A recent trend in CPU design is to include multiple computing **cores** on a single chip. Such multiprocessor systems are termed **multicore**. They can be more efficient than multiple chips with single cores because on-chip communication is faster than between-chip communication. In addition, one chip with multiple cores uses significantly less power than multiple single-core chips.

It is important to note that while multicore systems are multiprocessor systems, not all multiprocessor systems are multicore, as we shall see in Section 1.3.3. In our coverage of multiprocessor systems throughout this text, unless we state otherwise, we generally use the more contemporary term *multicore*, which excludes some multiprocessor systems.

In Figure 1.7, we show a dual-core design with two cores on the same chip. In this design, each core has its own register set as well as its own local cache. Other designs might use a shared cache or a combination of local and shared caches. Aside from architectural considerations, such as cache, memory, and bus contention, these multicore CPUs appear to the operating system as N standard processors. This characteristic puts pressure on operating system designers—and application programmers—to make use of those processing cores.

Finally, **blade servers** are a relatively recent development in which multiple processor boards, I/O boards, and networking boards are placed in the same chassis. The difference between these and traditional multiprocessor systems is that each blade-processor board boots independently and runs its own operating system. Some blade-server boards are multiprocessor as well, which blurs the lines between types of computers. In essence, these servers consist of multiple independent multiprocessor systems.

Figure 1.7   A dual-core design with two cores placed on the same chip.

1.3.3   Clustered Systems

Another type of multiprocessor system is a **clustered system**, which gathers together multiple CPUs. Clustered systems differ from the multiprocessor systems described in Section 1.3.2 in that they are composed of two or more individual systems—or nodes—joined together. Such systems are considered **loosely coupled**. Each node may be a single processor system or a multicore system. We should note that the definition of *clustered* is not concrete; many commercial packages wrestle to define a clustered system and why one form is better than another. The generally accepted definition is that clustered computers share storage and are closely linked via a local-area network LAN or a faster interconnect, such as InfiniBand.

Clustering is usually used to provide **high-availability** service—that is, service will continue even if one or more systems in the cluster fail. Generally, we obtain high availability by adding a level of redundancy in the system. A layer of cluster software runs on the cluster nodes. Each node can monitor one or more of the others (over the LAN). If the monitored machine fails, the monitoring machine can take ownership of its storage and restart the applications that were running on the failed machine. The users and clients of the applications see only a brief interruption of service.

Clustering can be structured asymmetrically or symmetrically. In **asymmetric clustering**, one machine is in **hot-standby mode** while the other is running the applications. The hot-standby host machine does nothing but monitor the active server. If that server fails, the hot-standby host becomes the active server. In **symmetric clustering**, two or more hosts are running applications and are monitoring each other. This structure is obviously more efficient, as it uses all of the available hardware. However it does require that more than one application be available to run.

Since a cluster consists of several computer systems connected via a network, clusters can also be used to provide **high-performance computing** environments. Such systems can supply significantly greater computational power than single-processor or even SMP systems because they can run an application concurrently on all computers in the cluster. The application must have been written specifically to take advantage of the cluster, however. This involves a technique known as **parallelization**, which divides a program into separate components that run in parallel on individual cores in a computer or computers in a cluster. Typically, these applications are designed so that once each computing node in the cluster has solved its portion of the problem, the results from all the nodes are combined into a final solution.

Other forms of clusters include parallel clusters and clustering over a wide-area network (WAN). Parallel clusters allow multiple hosts to access the same data on shared storage. Because most operating systems lack support for simultaneous data access by multiple hosts, parallel clusters usually require the use of special versions of software and special releases of applications. For example, Oracle Real Application Cluster is a version of Oracle's database that has been designed to run on a parallel cluster. Each machine runs Oracle, and a layer of software tracks access to the shared disk. Each machine has full access to all data in the database. To provide this shared access, the system must also supply access control and locking to ensure that no conflicting operations

BEOWULF CLUSTERS

Beowulf clusters are designed to solve high-performance computing tasks. A Beowulf cluster consists of commodity hardware—such as personal computers—connected via a simple local-area network. No single specific software package is required to construct a cluster. Rather, the nodes use a set of open-source software libraries to communicate with one another. Thus, there are a variety of approaches to constructing a Beowulf cluster. Typically, though, Beowulf computing nodes run the Linux operating system. Since Beowulf clusters require no special hardware and operate using open-source software that is available free, they offer a low-cost strategy for building a high-performance computing cluster. In fact, some Beowulf clusters built from discarded personal computers are using hundreds of nodes to solve computationally expensive scientific computing problems.

occur. This function, commonly known as a **distributed lock manager** (DLM), is included in some cluster technology.

Cluster technology is changing rapidly. Some cluster products support dozens of systems in a cluster, as well as clustered nodes that are separated by miles. Many of these improvements are made possible by **storage-area networks** (SANs), as described in Section 9.3.3, which allow many systems to attach to a pool of storage. If the applications and their data are stored on the SAN, then the cluster software can assign the application to run on any host that is attached to the SAN. If the host fails, then any other host can take over. In a database cluster, dozens of hosts can share the same database, greatly increasing performance and reliability. Figure 1.8 depicts the general structure of a clustered system.

Figure 1.8   General structure of a clustered system.

Figure 1.9 Memory layout for a multiprogramming system.

1.4   Operating-System Structure

Now that we have discussed basic computer-system organization and architecture, we are ready to talk about operating systems. An operating system provides the environment within which programs are executed. Internally, operating systems vary greatly in their makeup, since they are organized along many different lines. There are, however, many commonalities, which we consider in this section.

One of the most important aspects of operating systems is the ability to multiprogram. A single program cannot, in general, keep either the CPU or the I/O devices busy at all times. Single users frequently have multiple programs running. **Multiprogramming** increases CPU utilization by organizing jobs (code and data) so that the CPU always has one to execute.

The idea is as follows: The operating system keeps several jobs in memory simultaneously (Figure 1.9). Since, in general, main memory is too small to accommodate all jobs, the jobs are kept initially on the disk in the **job pool**. This pool consists of all processes residing on disk awaiting allocation of main memory.

The set of jobs in memory can be a subset of the jobs kept in the job pool. The operating system picks and begins to execute one of the jobs in memory. Eventually, the job may have to wait for some task, such as an I/O operation, to complete. In a non-multiprogrammed system, the CPU would sit idle. In a multiprogrammed system, the operating system simply switches to, and executes, another job. When *that* job needs to wait, the CPU switches to *another* job, and so on. Eventually, the first job finishes waiting and gets the CPU back. As long as at least one job needs to execute, the CPU is never idle.

This idea is common in other life situations. A lawyer does not work for only one client at a time, for example. While one case is waiting to go to trial or have papers typed, the lawyer can work on another case. If he has enough clients, the lawyer will never be idle for lack of work. (Idle lawyers tend to become politicians, so there is a certain social value in keeping lawyers busy.)

Multiprogrammed systems provide an environment in which the various system resources (for example, CPU, memory, and peripheral devices) are utilized effectively, but they do not provide for user interaction with the computer system. Time sharing (or multitasking) is a logical extension of multiprogramming. In time-sharing systems, the CPU executes multiple jobs by switching among them, but the switches occur so frequently that the users can interact with each program while it is running.

Time sharing requires an interactive computer system, which provides direct communication between the user and the system. The user gives instructions to the operating system or to a program directly, using a input device such as a keyboard, mouse, touch pad, or touch screen, and waits for immediate results on an output device. Accordingly, the response time should be short—typically less than one second.

A time-shared operating system allows many users to share the computer simultaneously. Since each action or command in a time-shared system tends to be short, only a little CPU time is needed for each user. As the system switches rapidly from one user to the next, each user is given the impression that the entire computer system is dedicated to his use, even though it is being shared among many users.

A time-shared operating system uses CPU scheduling and multiprogramming to provide each user with a small portion of a time-shared computer. Each user has at least one separate program in memory. A program loaded into memory is called a process. When a process executes, it typically executes for only a short time before it either finishes or needs to perform I/O. I/O may be interactive; that is, output goes to a display for the user, and input comes from a user keyboard, mouse, or other device. Since interactive I/O typically runs at "people speeds," it may take a long time to complete. Input, for example, may be bounded by the user's typing speed; seven characters per second is fast for people but incredibly slow for computers. Rather than let the CPU sit idle as this interactive input takes place, the operating system will rapidly switch the CPU to the program of some other user.

Time sharing and multiprogramming require that several jobs be kept simultaneously in memory. If several jobs are ready to be brought into memory, and if there is not enough room for all of them, then the system must choose among them. Making this decision involves job scheduling, which we discuss in Chapter 6. When the operating system selects a job from the job pool, it loads that job into memory for execution. Having several programs in memory at the same time requires some form of memory management, which we cover in Chapters 7 and 8. In addition, if several jobs are ready to run at the same time, the system must choose which job will run first. Making this decision is CPU scheduling, which is also discussed in Chapter 6. Finally, running multiple jobs concurrently requires that their ability to affect one another be limited in all phases of the operating system, including process scheduling, disk storage, and memory management. We discuss these considerations throughout the text.

In a time-sharing system, the operating system must ensure reasonable response time. This goal is sometimes accomplished through swapping, whereby processes are swapped in and out of main memory to the disk. A more common method for ensuring reasonable response time is virtual memory, a technique that allows the execution of a process that is not completely in memory (Chapter 8). The main advantage of the virtual-memory scheme is that it enables users to run programs that are larger than actual **physical memory**. Further, it abstracts main memory into a large, uniform array of storage, separating **logical memory** as viewed by the user from physical memory. This arrangement frees programmers from concern over memory-storage limitations.

A time-sharing system must also provide a file system (Chapters 10 and 11). The file system resides on a collection of disks; hence, disk management must be provided (Chapter 9). In addition, a time-sharing system provides a mechanism for protecting resources from inappropriate use (Chapter 13). To ensure orderly execution, the system must provide mechanisms for job synchronization and communication (Chapter 5), and it may ensure that jobs do not get stuck in a deadlock, forever waiting for one another.

1.5   Operating-System Operations

As mentioned earlier, modern operating systems are **interrupt driven**. If there are no processes to execute, no I/O devices to service, and no users to whom to respond, an operating system will sit quietly, waiting for something to happen. Events are almost always signaled by the occurrence of an interrupt or a trap. A **trap** (or an **exception**) is a software-generated interrupt caused either by an error (for example, division by zero or invalid memory access) or by a specific request from a user program that an operating-system service be performed. The interrupt-driven nature of an operating system defines that system's general structure. For each type of interrupt, separate segments of code in the operating system determine what action should be taken. An interrupt service routine is provided to deal with the interrupt.

Since the operating system and the users share the hardware and software resources of the computer system, we need to make sure that an error in a user program could cause problems only for the one program running. With sharing, many processes could be adversely affected by a bug in one program. For example, if a process gets stuck in an infinite loop, this loop could prevent the correct operation of many other processes. More subtle errors can occur in a multiprogramming system, where one erroneous program might modify another program, the data of another program, or even the operating system itself.

Without protection against these sorts of errors, either the computer must execute only one process at a time or all output must be suspect. A properly designed operating system must ensure that an incorrect (or malicious) program cannot cause other programs to execute incorrectly.

1.5.1   Dual-Mode and Multimode Operation

In order to ensure the proper execution of the operating system, we must be able to distinguish between the execution of operating-system code and user-defined code. The approach taken by most computer systems is to provide hardware support that allows us to differentiate among various modes of execution.

Figure 1.10 Transition from user to kernel mode.

At the very least, we need two separate *modes* of operation: **user mode** and **kernel mode** (also called **supervisor mode, system mode,** or **privileged mode**). A bit, called the **mode bit,** is added to the hardware of the computer to indicate the current mode: kernel (0) or user (1). With the mode bit, we can distinguish between a task that is executed on behalf of the operating system and one that is executed on behalf of the user. When the computer system is executing on behalf of a user application, the system is in user mode. However, when a user application requests a service from the operating system (via a system call), the system must transition from user to kernel mode to fulfill the request. This is shown in Figure 1.10. As we shall see, this architectural enhancement is useful for many other aspects of system operation as well.

At system boot time, the hardware starts in kernel mode. The operating system is then loaded and starts user applications in user mode. Whenever a trap or interrupt occurs, the hardware switches from user mode to kernel mode (that is, changes the state of the mode bit to 0). Thus, whenever the operating system gains control of the computer, it is in kernel mode. The system always switches to user mode (by setting the mode bit to 1) before passing control to a user program.

The dual mode of operation provides us with the means for protecting the operating system from errant users—and errant users from one another. We accomplish this protection by designating some of the machine instructions that may cause harm as **privileged instructions.** The hardware allows privileged instructions to be executed only in kernel mode. If an attempt is made to execute a privileged instruction in user mode, the hardware does not execute the instruction but rather treats it as illegal and traps it to the operating system.

The instruction to switch to kernel mode is an example of a privileged instruction. Some other examples include I/O control, timer management, and interrupt management. As we shall see throughout the text, there are many additional privileged instructions.

The concept of modes can be extended beyond two modes (in which case the CPU uses more than one bit to set and test the mode). CPUs that support virtualization frequently have a separate mode to indicate when the **virtual machine manager** (VMM)—and the virtualization management software— is in control of the system. In this mode, the VMM has more privileges than user processes but fewer than the kernel. It needs that level of privilege so it can create and manage virtual machines, changing the CPU state to do so. Sometimes, too, different modes are used by various kernel components. We should note that, as an alternative to modes, the CPU designer may use other methods to differentiate operational privileges. The Intel 64 family of CPUs supports four *privilege levels,* for example, and supports virtualization but does not have a separate mode for virtualization.

We can now see the life cycle of instruction execution in a computer system. Initial control resides in the operating system, where instructions are executed in kernel mode. When control is given to a user application, the mode is set to user mode. Eventually, control is switched back to the operating system via an interrupt, a trap, or a system call.

System calls provide the means for a user program to ask the operating system to perform tasks reserved for the operating system on the user program's behalf. A system call is invoked in a variety of ways, depending on the functionality provided by the underlying processor. In all forms, it is the method used by a process to request action by the operating system. A system call usually takes the form of a trap to a specific location in the interrupt vector. This trap can be executed by a generic trap instruction, although some systems (such as MIPS) have a specific syscall instruction to invoke a system call.

When a system call is executed, it is typically treated by the hardware as a software interrupt. Control passes through the interrupt vector to a service routine in the operating system, and the mode bit is set to kernel mode. The system-call service routine is a part of the operating system. The kernel examines the interrupting instruction to determine what system call has occurred; a parameter indicates what type of service the user program is requesting. Additional information needed for the request may be passed in registers, on the stack, or in memory (with pointers to the memory locations passed in registers). The kernel verifies that the parameters are correct and legal, executes the request, and returns control to the instruction following the system call. We describe system calls more fully in Section 2.3.

The lack of a hardware-supported dual mode can cause serious shortcomings in an operating system. For instance, MS-DOS was written for the Intel 8088 architecture, which has no mode bit and therefore no dual mode. A user program running awry can wipe out the operating system by writing over it with data; and multiple programs are able to write to a device at the same time, with potentially disastrous results. Modern versions of the Intel CPU do provide dual-mode operation. Accordingly, most contemporary operating systems—such as Microsoft Windows 7, as well as Unix and Linux—take advantage of this dual-mode feature and provide greater protection for the operating system.

Once hardware protection is in place, it detects errors that violate modes. These errors are normally handled by the operating system. If a user program fails in some way—such as by making an attempt either to execute an illegal instruction or to access memory that is not in the user's address space—then the hardware traps to the operating system. The trap transfers control through the interrupt vector to the operating system, just as an interrupt does. When a program error occurs, the operating system must terminate the program abnormally. This situation is handled by the same code as a user-requested abnormal termination. An appropriate error message is given, and the memory of the program may be dumped. The memory dump is usually written to a file so that the user or programmer can examine it and perhaps correct it and restart the program.

1.5.2 Timer

We must ensure that the operating system maintains control over the CPU. We cannot allow a user program to get stuck in an infinite loop or to fail to call system services and never return control to the operating system. To accomplish this goal, we can use a timer. A timer can be set to interrupt the computer after a specified period. The period may be fixed (for example, 1/60 second) or variable (for example, from 1 millisecond to 1 second). A variable timer is generally implemented by a fixed-rate clock and a counter. The operating system sets the counter. Every time the clock ticks, the counter is decremented. When the counter reaches 0, an interrupt occurs. For instance, a 10-bit counter with a 1-millisecond clock allows interrupts at intervals from 1 millisecond to 1,024 milliseconds, in steps of 1 millisecond.

Before turning over control to the user, the operating system ensures that the timer is set to interrupt. If the timer interrupts, control transfers automatically to the operating system, which may treat the interrupt as a fatal error or may give the program more time. Clearly, instructions that modify the content of the timer are privileged.

We can use the timer to prevent a user program from running too long. A simple technique is to initialize a counter with the amount of time that a program is allowed to run. A program with a 7-minute time limit, for example, would have its counter initialized to 420. Every second, the timer interrupts, and the counter is decremented by 1. As long as the counter is positive, control is returned to the user program. When the counter becomes negative, the operating system terminates the program for exceeding the assigned time limit.

1.6   Process Management

A program does nothing unless its instructions are executed by a CPU. A program in execution, as mentioned, is a process. A time-shared user program such as a compiler is a process. A word-processing program being run by an individual user on a PC is a process. A system task, such as sending output to a printer, can also be a process (or at least part of one). For now, you can consider a process to be a job or a time-shared program, but later you will learn that the concept is more general. As we shall see in Chapter 3, it is possible to provide system calls that allow processes to create subprocesses to execute concurrently.

A process needs certain resources—including CPU time, memory, files, and I/O devices—to accomplish its task. These resources are either given to the process when it is created or allocated to it while it is running. In addition to the various physical and logical resources that a process obtains when it is created, various initialization data (input) may be passed along. For example, consider a process whose function is to display the status of a file on the screen of a terminal. The process will be given the name of the file as an input and will execute the appropriate instructions and system calls to obtain and display the desired information on the terminal. When the process terminates, the operating system will reclaim any reusable resources.

We emphasize that a program by itself is not a process. A program is a *passive* entity, like the contents of a file stored on disk, whereas a process is an *active* entity. A single-threaded process has one **program counter** specifying the next instruction to execute. (Threads are covered in Chapter 4.) The execution of such a process must be sequential. The CPU executes one instruction of the process after another, until the process completes. Further, at any time, one instruction at most is executed on behalf of the process. Thus, although two processes may be associated with the same program, they are nevertheless considered two separate execution sequences. A multithreaded process has multiple program counters, each pointing to the next instruction to execute for a given thread.

A process is the unit of work in a system. A system consists of a collection of processes, some of which are operating-system processes (those that execute system code) and the rest of which are user processes (those that execute user code). All these processes can potentially execute concurrently—by multiplexing on a single CPU, for example.

The operating system is responsible for the following activities in connection with process management:

- Scheduling processes and threads on the CPUs
- Creating and deleting both user and system processes
- Suspending and resuming processes
- Providing mechanisms for process synchronization
- Providing mechanisms for process communication

We discuss process-management techniques in Chapters 3 through 5.

1.7 Memory Management

As we discussed in Section 1.2.2, the main memory is central to the operation of a modern computer system. Main memory is a large array of bytes, ranging in size from hundreds of thousands to billions. Each byte has its own address. Main memory is a repository of quickly accessible data shared by the CPU and I/O devices. The central processor reads instructions from main memory during the instruction-fetch cycle and both reads and writes data from main memory during the data-fetch cycle (on a von Neumann architecture). As noted earlier, the main memory is generally the only large storage device that the CPU is able to address and access directly. For example, for the CPU to process data from disk, those data must first be transferred to main memory by CPU-generated I/O calls. In the same way, instructions must be in memory for the CPU to execute them.

For a program to be executed, it must be mapped to absolute addresses and loaded into memory. As the program executes, it accesses program instructions and data from memory by generating these absolute addresses. Eventually, the program terminates, its memory space is declared available, and the next program can be loaded and executed.

To improve both the utilization of the CPU and the speed of the computer's response to its users, general-purpose computers must keep several programs in memory, creating a need for memory management. Many different memory-management schemes are used. These schemes reflect various approaches, and the effectiveness of any given algorithm depends on the situation. In selecting a memory-management scheme for a specific system, we must take into account many factors—especially the *hardware* design of the system. Each algorithm requires its own hardware support.

The operating system is responsible for the following activities in connection with memory management:

- Keeping track of which parts of memory are currently being used and who is using them

- Deciding which processes (or parts of processes) and data to move into and out of memory

- Allocating and deallocating memory space as needed

Memory-management techniques are discussed in Chapters 7 and 8.

1.8   Storage Management

To make the computer system convenient for users, the operating system provides a uniform, logical view of information storage. The operating system abstracts from the physical properties of its storage devices to define a logical storage unit, the file. The operating system maps files onto physical media and accesses these files via the storage devices.

1.8.1   File-System Management

File management is one of the most visible components of an operating system. Computers can store information on several different types of physical media. Hard disk, optical disk, and magnetic tape are the most common. Each of these media has its own characteristics and physical organization. Each medium is controlled by a device, such as a disk drive or tape drive, that also has its own unique characteristics. These properties include access speed, capacity, data-transfer rate, and access method (sequential or random).

A file is a collection of related information defined by its creator. Commonly, files represent programs (both source and object forms) and data. Data files may be numeric, alphabetic, alphanumeric, or binary. Files may be free-form (for example, text files), or they may be formatted rigidly (for example, fixed fields). Clearly, the concept of a file is an extremely general one.

The operating system implements the abstract concept of a file by managing mass-storage media, such as tapes and disks, and the devices that control them. In addition, files are normally organized into directories to make them easier to use. Finally, when multiple users have access to files, it may be desirable to control which user may access a file and how that user may access it (for example, read, write, append).

The operating system is responsible for the following activities in connection with file management:

- Creating and deleting files

- Creating and deleting directories to organize files
- Supporting primitives for manipulating files and directories
- Mapping files onto secondary storage
- Backing up files on stable (nonvolatile) storage media

File-management techniques are discussed in Chapters 10 and 11.

1.8.2 Mass-Storage Management

As we have already seen, because main memory is too small to accommodate all data and programs, and because the data that it holds are lost when power is lost, the computer system must provide secondary storage to back up main memory. Most modern computer systems use disks as the principal on-line storage medium for both programs and data. Most programs—including compilers, assemblers, word processors, editors, and formatters—are stored on a disk until loaded into memory. They then use the disk as both the source and destination of their processing. Hence, the proper management of disk storage is of central importance to a computer system. The operating system is responsible for the following activities in connection with disk management:

- Free-space management
- Storage allocation
- Disk scheduling

Because secondary storage is used frequently, it must be used efficiently. The entire speed of operation of a computer may hinge on the speeds of the disk subsystem and the algorithms that manipulate that subsystem.

There are, however, many uses for storage that is slower and lower in cost (and sometimes of higher capacity) than secondary storage. Backups of disk data, storage of seldom-used data, and long-term archival storage are some examples. Magnetic tape drives and their tapes and CD and DVD drives and platters are typical **tertiary storage** devices. The media (tapes and optical platters) vary between WORM (write-once, read-many-times) and RW (read–write) formats.

Tertiary storage is not crucial to system performance, but it still must be managed. Some operating systems take on this task, while others leave tertiary-storage management to application programs. Some of the functions that operating systems can provide include mounting and unmounting media in devices, allocating and freeing the devices for exclusive use by processes, and migrating data from secondary to tertiary storage.

Techniques for secondary and tertiary storage management are discussed in Chapter 9.

1.8.3 Caching

Caching is an important principle of computer systems. Here's how it works. Information is normally kept in some storage system (such as main memory). As it is used, it is copied into a faster storage system—the cache—on a temporary basis. When we need a particular piece of information, we first check whether it is in the cache. If it is, we use the information directly from the cache. If it is not, we use the information from the source, putting a copy in the cache under the assumption that we will need it again soon.

In addition, internal programmable registers, such as index registers, provide a high-speed cache for main memory. The programmer (or compiler) implements the register-allocation and register-replacement algorithms to decide which information to keep in registers and which to keep in main memory.

Other caches are implemented totally in hardware. For instance, most systems have an instruction cache to hold the instructions expected to be executed next. Without this cache, the CPU would have to wait several cycles while an instruction was fetched from main memory. For similar reasons, most systems have one or more high-speed data caches in the memory hierarchy. We are not concerned with these hardware-only caches in this text, since they are outside the control of the operating system.

Because caches have limited size, cache management is an important design problem. Careful selection of the cache size and of a replacement policy can result in greatly increased performance. Figure 1.11 compares storage performance in large workstations and small servers. Various replacement algorithms for software-controlled caches are discussed in Chapter 8.

Main memory can be viewed as a fast cache for secondary storage, since data in secondary storage must be copied into main memory for use and data must be in main memory before being moved to secondary storage for safekeeping. The file-system data, which resides permanently on secondary storage, may appear on several levels in the storage hierarchy. At the highest level, the operating system may maintain a cache of file-system data in main memory. In addition, solid-state disks may be used for high-speed storage that is accessed through the file-system interface. The bulk of secondary storage is on hard disks. The hard-disk storage, in turn, is often backed up onto magnetic tapes or removable disks to protect against data loss in case of a hard-disk failure. Some systems automatically archive old file data from secondary storage to tertiary storage, such as tape jukeboxes, to lower the storage cost (see Chapter 9).

Level	1	2	3	4	5
Name	registers	cache	main memory	solid state disk	hard disk
Typical size	< 1 KB	< 16MB	< 64GB	< 1 TB	< 10 TB
Implementation technology	custom memory with multiple ports CMOS	on-chip or off-chip CMOS SRAM	CMOS SRAM	flash memory	hard disk
Access time (ns)	0.25 - 0.5	0.5 - 25	80 - 250	25,000 - 50,000	5,000,000
Bandwidth (MB/sec)	20,000 - 100,000	5,000 - 10,000	1,000 - 5,000	500	20 - 150
Managed by	compiler	hardware	operating system	operating system	operating system
Backed by	cache	main memory	disk	disk	disk or tape

Figure 1.11 Performance of various levels of storage.

Figure 1.12   Migration of integer A from disk to register.

The movement of information between levels of a storage hierarchy may be either explicit or implicit, depending on the hardware design and the controlling operating-system software. For instance, data transfer from cache to CPU and registers is usually a hardware function, with no operating-system intervention. In contrast, transfer of data from disk to memory is usually controlled by the operating system.

In a hierarchical storage structure, the same data may appear in different levels of the storage system. For example, suppose that an integer A that is to be incremented by 1 is located in file B, and file B resides on hard disk. The increment operation proceeds by first issuing an I/O operation to copy the disk block on which A resides to main memory. This operation is followed by copying A to the cache and to an internal register. Thus, the copy of A appears in several places: on the hard disk, in main memory, in the cache, and in an internal register (see Figure 1.12). Once the increment takes place in the internal register, the value of A differs in the various storage systems. The value of A becomes the same only after the new value of A is written from the internal register back to the hard disk.

In a computing environment where only one process executes at a time, this arrangement poses no difficulties, since an access to integer A will always be to the copy at the highest level of the hierarchy. However, in a multitasking environment, where the CPU is switched back and forth among various processes, extreme care must be taken to ensure that, if several processes wish to access A, then each of these processes will obtain the most recently updated value of A.

The situation becomes more complicated in a multiprocessor environment where, in addition to maintaining internal registers, each of the CPUs also contains a local cache (Figure 1.6). In such an environment, a copy of A may exist simultaneously in several caches. Since the various CPUs can all execute in parallel, we must make sure that an update to the value of A in one cache is immediately reflected in all other caches where A resides. This situation is called **cache coherency**, and it is usually a hardware issue (handled below the operating-system level).

In a distributed environment, the situation becomes even more complex. In this environment, several copies (or replicas) of the same file can be kept on different computers. Since the various replicas may be accessed and updated concurrently, some distributed systems ensure that, when a replica is updated in one place, all other replicas are brought up to date as soon as possible. There are various ways to achieve this guarantee.

1.8.4   I/O Systems

One of the purposes of an operating system is to hide the peculiarities of specific hardware devices from the user. For example, in UNIX, the peculiarities of I/O devices are hidden from the bulk of the operating system itself by the I/O subsystem. The I/O subsystem consists of several components:

- A memory-management component that includes buffering, caching, and spooling
- A general device-driver interface
- Drivers for specific hardware devices

Only the device driver knows the peculiarities of the specific device to which it is assigned.

We discussed in Section 1.2.3 how interrupt handlers and device drivers are used in the construction of efficient I/O subsystems. In Chapter 12, we discuss how the I/O subsystem interfaces to the other system components, manages devices, transfers data, and detects I/O completion.

1.9   Protection and Security

If a computer system has multiple users and allows the concurrent execution of multiple processes, then access to data must be regulated. For that purpose, mechanisms ensure that files, memory segments, CPU, and other resources can be operated on by only those processes that have gained proper authorization from the operating system. For example, memory-addressing hardware ensures that a process can execute only within its own address space. The timer ensures that no process can gain control of the CPU without eventually relinquishing control. Device-control registers are not accessible to users, so the integrity of the various peripheral devices is protected.

Protection, then, is any mechanism for controlling the access of processes or users to the resources defined by a computer system. This mechanism must provide means to specify the controls to be imposed and to enforce the controls.

Protection can improve reliability by detecting latent errors at the interfaces between component subsystems. Early detection of interface errors can often prevent contamination of a healthy subsystem by another subsystem that is malfunctioning. Furthermore, an unprotected resource cannot defend against use (or misuse) by an unauthorized or incompetent user. A protection-oriented system provides a means to distinguish between authorized and unauthorized usage, as we discuss in Chapter 13.

A system can have adequate protection but still be prone to failure and allow inappropriate access. Consider a user whose authentication information (her means of identifying herself to the system) is stolen. Her data could be copied or deleted, even though file and memory protection are working. It is the job of **security** to defend a system from external and internal attacks. Such attacks spread across a huge range and include viruses and worms, denial-of-service attacks (which use all of a system's resources and so keep legitimate users out of the system), identity theft, and theft of service (unauthorized use of a system). Prevention of some of these attacks is considered an operating-system function on some systems, while other systems leave it to policy or additional software. Due to the alarming rise in security incidents, operating-system security features represent a fast-growing area of research and implementation. We discuss security in Chapter 14.

Protection and security require the system to be able to distinguish among all its users. Most operating systems maintain a list of user names and associated **user identifiers** (**user IDs**). In Windows parlance, this is a **security ID** (**SID**). These numerical IDs are unique, one per user. When a user logs in to the system, the authentication stage determines the appropriate user ID for the user. That user ID is associated with all of the user's processes and threads. When an ID needs to be readable by a user, it is translated back to the user name via the user name list.

In some circumstances, we wish to distinguish among sets of users rather than individual users. For example, the owner of a file on a UNIX system may be allowed to issue all operations on that file, whereas a selected set of users may be allowed only to read the file. To accomplish this, we need to define a group name and the set of users belonging to that group. Group functionality can be implemented as a system-wide list of group names and **group identifiers**. A user can be in one or more groups, depending on operating-system design decisions. The user's group IDs are also included in every associated process and thread.

In the course of normal system use, the user ID and group ID for a user are sufficient. However, a user sometimes needs to **escalate privileges** to gain extra permissions for an activity. The user may need access to a device that is restricted, for example. Operating systems provide various methods to allow privilege escalation. On UNIX, for instance, the *setuid* attribute on a program causes that program to run with the user ID of the owner of the file, rather than the current user's ID. The process runs with this **effective UID** until it turns off the extra privileges or terminates.

1.10 Kernel Data Structures

We turn next to a topic central to operating-system implementation: the way data are structured in the system. In this section, we briefly describe several fundamental data structures used extensively in operating systems. Readers who require further details on these structures, as well as others, should consult the bibliography at the end of the chapter.

1.10.1 Lists, Stacks, and Queues

An array is a simple data structure in which each element can be accessed directly. For example, main memory is constructed as an array. If the data item being stored is larger than one byte, then multiple bytes can be allocated to the item, and the item is addressed as item number × item size. But what about storing an item whose size may vary? And what about removing an item if the relative positions of the remaining items must be preserved? In such situations, arrays give way to other data structures.

After arrays, lists are perhaps the most fundamental data structures in computer science. Whereas each item in an array can be accessed directly, the items in a list must be accessed in a particular order. That is, a **list** represents a collection of data values as a sequence. The most common method for

Figure 1.13   Singly linked list.

implementing this structure is a **linked list**, in which items are linked to one another. Linked lists are of several types:

- In a *singly linked list,* each item points to its successor, as illustrated in Figure 1.13.
- In a *doubly linked list,* a given item can refer either to its predecessor or to its successor, as illustrated in Figure 1.14.
- In a *circularly linked list,* the last element in the list refers to the first element, rather than to null, as illustrated in Figure 1.15.

Linked lists accommodate items of varying sizes and allow easy insertion and deletion of items. One potential disadvantage of using a list is that performance for retrieving a specified item in a list of size n is linear — $O(n)$, as it requires potentially traversing all n elements in the worst case. Lists are sometimes used directly by kernel algorithms. Frequently, though, they are used for constructing more powerful data structures, such as stacks and queues.

A **stack** is a sequentially ordered data structure that uses the last in, first out (**LIFO**) principle for adding and removing items, meaning that the last item placed onto a stack is the first item removed. The operations for inserting and removing items from a stack are known as *push* and *pop*, respectively. An operating system often uses a stack when invoking function calls. Parameters, local variables, and the return address are pushed onto the stack when a function is called; returning from the function call pops those items off the stack.

A **queue**, in contrast, is a sequentially ordered data structure that uses the first in, first out (**FIFO**) principle: items are removed from a queue in the order in which they were inserted. There are many everyday examples of queues, including shoppers waiting in a checkout line at a store and cars waiting in line at a traffic signal. Queues are also quite common in operating systems—jobs that are sent to a printer are typically printed in the order in which they were submitted, for example. As we shall see in Chapter 6, tasks that are waiting to be run on an available CPU are often organized in queues.

Figure 1.14   Doubly linked list.

Figure 1.15 Circularly linked list.

1.10.2 Trees

A **tree** is a data structure that can be used to represent data hierarchically. Data values in a tree structure are linked through parent–child relationships. In a **general tree**, a parent may have an unlimited number of children. In a **binary tree**, a parent may have at most two children, which we term the **left child** and the **right child**. A **binary search tree** additionally requires an ordering between the parent's two children in which $left\_child <= right\_child$. Figure 1.16 provides an example of a binary search tree. When we search for an item in a binary search tree, the worst-case performance is $O(n)$ (consider how this can occur). To remedy this situation, we can use an algorithm to create a **balanced binary search tree**. Here, a tree containing n items has at most $lg\ n$ levels, thus ensuring worst-case performance of $O(lg\ n)$. We shall see in Section 6.7.1 that Linux uses a balanced binary search tree as part its CPU-scheduling algorithm.

1.10.3 Hash Functions and Maps

A **hash function** takes data as its input, performs a numeric operation on this data, and returns a numeric value. This numeric value can then be used as an index into a table (typically an array) to quickly retrieve the data. Whereas searching for a data item through a list of size n can require up to $O(n)$ comparisons in the worst case, using a hash function for retrieving data from table can be as good as $O(1)$ in the worst case, depending on implementation details. Because of this performance, hash functions are used extensively in operating systems.

One potential difficulty with hash functions is that two inputs can result in the same output value—that is, they can link to the same table location. We can accommodate this *hash collision* by having a linked list at that table

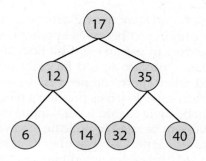

Figure 1.16 Binary search tree.

Figure 1.17 Hash map.

location that contains all of the items with the same hash value. Of course, the more collisions there are, the less efficient the hash function is.

One use of a hash function is to implement a **hash map**, which associates (or *maps*) [key:value] pairs using a hash function. For example, we can map the key *operating* to the value *system*. Once the mapping is established, we can apply the hash function to the key to obtain the value from the hash map (Figure 1.17). For example, suppose that a user name is mapped to a password. Password authentication then proceeds as follows: a user enters his user name and password. The hash function is applied to the user name, which is then used to retrieve the password. The retrieved password is then compared with the password entered by the user for authentication.

1.10.4 Bitmaps

A **bitmap** is a string of n binary digits that can be used to represent the status of n items. For example, suppose we have several resources, and the availability of each resource is indicated by the value of a binary digit: 0 means that the resource is available, while 1 indicates that it is unavailable (or vice-versa). The value of the ith position in the bitmap is associated with the ith resource. As an example, consider the bitmap shown below:

001011101

Resources 2, 4, 5, 6, and 8 are unavailable; resources 0, 1, 3, and 7 are available.

The power of bitmaps becomes apparent when we consider their space efficiency. If we were to use an eight-bit Boolean value instead of a single bit, the resulting data structure would be eight times larger. Thus, bitmaps are commonly used when there is a need to represent the availability of a large number of resources. Disk drives provide a nice illustration. A medium-sized disk drive might be divided into several thousand individual units, called **disk blocks**. A bitmap can be used to indicate the availability of each disk block.

Data structures are pervasive in operating system implementations. Thus, we will see the structures discussed here, along with others, throughout this text as we explore kernel algorithms and their implementations.

LINUX KERNEL DATA STRUCTURES

The data structures used in the Linux kernel are available in the kernel source code. The *include* file <linux/list.h> provides details of the linked-list data structure used throughout the kernel. A queue in Linux is known as a kfifo, and its implementation can be found in the kfifo.c file in the kernel directory of the source code. Linux also provides a balanced binary search tree implementation using *red-black trees*. Details can be found in the include file <linux/rbtree.h>.

1.11 Computing Environments

So far, we have briefly described several aspects of computer systems and the operating systems that manage them. We turn now to a discussion of how operating systems are used in a variety of computing environments.

1.11.1 Traditional Computing

As computing has matured, the lines separating many of the traditional computing environments have blurred. Consider the "typical office environment." Just a few years ago, this environment consisted of PCs connected to a network, with servers providing file and print services. Remote access was awkward, and portability was achieved by use of laptop computers. Terminals attached to mainframes were prevalent at many companies as well, with even fewer remote access and portability options.

The current trend is toward providing more ways to access these computing environments. Web technologies and increasing WAN bandwidth are stretching the boundaries of traditional computing. Companies establish **portals**, which provide Web accessibility to their internal servers. **Network computers** (or **thin clients**)—which are essentially terminals that understand web-based computing—are used in place of traditional workstations where more security or easier maintenance is desired. Mobile computers can synchronize with PCs to allow very portable use of company information. Mobile computers can also connect to **wireless networks** and cellular data networks to use the company's Web portal (as well as the myriad other Web resources).

At home, most users once had a single computer with a slow modem connection to the office, the Internet, or both. Today, network-connection speeds once available only at great cost are relatively inexpensive in many places, giving home users more access to more data. These fast data connections are allowing home computers to serve up Web pages and to run networks that include printers, client PCs, and servers. Many homes use **firewalls** to protect their networks from security breaches.

In the latter half of the 20th century, computing resources were relatively scarce. (Before that, they were nonexistent!) For a period of time, systems were either batch or interactive. Batch systems processed jobs in bulk, with predetermined input from files or other data sources. Interactive systems waited for input from users. To optimize the use of the computing resources, multiple users shared time on these systems. Time-sharing systems used a timer and scheduling algorithms to cycle processes rapidly through the CPU, giving each user a share of the resources.

Today, traditional time-sharing systems are uncommon. The same scheduling technique is still in use on desktop computers, laptops, servers, and even mobile computers, but frequently all the processes are owned by the same user (or a single user and the operating system). User processes, and system processes that provide services to the user, are managed so that each frequently gets a slice of computer time. Consider the windows created while a user is working on a PC, for example, and the fact that they may be performing different tasks at the same time. Even a web browser can be composed of multiple processes, one for each website currently being visited, with time sharing applied to each web browser process.

1.11.2 Mobile Computing

Mobile computing refers to computing on handheld smartphones and tablet computers. These devices share the distinguishing physical features of being portable and lightweight. Historically, compared with desktop and laptop computers, mobile systems gave up screen size, memory capacity, and overall functionality in return for handheld mobile access to services such as e-mail and web browsing. Over the past few years, however, features on mobile devices have become so rich that the distinction in functionality between, say, a consumer laptop and a tablet computer may be difficult to discern. In fact, we might argue that the features of a contemporary mobile device allow it to provide functionality that is either unavailable or impractical on a desktop or laptop computer.

Today, mobile systems are used not only for e-mail and web browsing but also for playing music and video, reading digital books, taking photos, and recording high-definition video. Accordingly, tremendous growth continues in the wide range of applications that run on such devices. Many developers are now designing applications that take advantage of the unique features of mobile devices, such as global positioning system (GPS) chips, accelerometers, and gyroscopes. An embedded GPS chip allows a mobile device to use satellites to determine its precise location on earth. That functionality is especially useful in designing applications that provide navigation—for example, telling users which way to walk or drive or perhaps directing them to nearby services, such as restaurants. An accelerometer allows a mobile device to detect its orientation with respect to the ground and to detect certain other forces, such as tilting and shaking. In several computer games that employ accelerometers, players interface with the system not by using a mouse or a keyboard but rather by tilting, rotating, and shaking the mobile device! Perhaps more a practical use of these features is found in *augmented-reality* applications, which overlay information on a display of the current environment. It is difficult to imagine how equivalent applications could be developed on traditional laptop or desktop computer systems.

To provide access to on-line services, mobile devices typically use either IEEE standard 802.11 wireless or cellular data networks. The memory capacity and processing speed of mobile devices, however, are more limited than those of PCs. Whereas a smartphone or tablet may have 64 GB in storage, it is not uncommon to find 1 TB in storage on a desktop computer. Similarly, because power consumption is such a concern, mobile devices often use processors that are smaller, are slower, and offer fewer processing cores than processors found on traditional desktop and laptop computers.

Two operating systems currently dominate mobile computing: **Apple iOS** and **Google Android**. iOS was designed to run on Apple iPhone and iPad mobile devices. Android powers smartphones and tablet computers available from many manufacturers. We examine these two mobile operating systems in further detail in Chapter 2.

1.11.3   Distributed Systems

A distributed system is a collection of physically separate, possibly heterogeneous, computer systems that are networked to provide users with access to the various resources that the system maintains. Access to a shared resource increases computation speed, functionality, data availability, and reliability. Some operating systems generalize network access as a form of file access, with the details of networking contained in the network interface's device driver. Others make users specifically invoke network functions. Generally, systems contain a mix of the two modes—for example FTP and NFS. The protocols that create a distributed system can greatly affect that system's utility and popularity.

A **network**, in the simplest terms, is a communication path between two or more systems. Distributed systems depend on networking for their functionality. Networks vary by the protocols used, the distances between nodes, and the transport media. TCP/IP is the most common network protocol, and it provides the fundamental architecture of the Internet. Most operating systems support TCP/IP, including all general-purpose ones. Some systems support proprietary protocols to suit their needs. To an operating system, a network protocol simply needs an interface device—a network adapter, for example—with a device driver to manage it, as well as software to handle data. These concepts are discussed throughout this book.

Networks are characterized based on the distances between their nodes. A **local-area network** (**LAN**) connects computers within a room, a building, or a campus. A **wide-area network** (**WAN**) usually links buildings, cities, or countries. A global company may have a WAN to connect its offices worldwide, for example. These networks may run one protocol or several protocols. The continuing advent of new technologies brings about new forms of networks. For example, a **metropolitan-area network** (**MAN**) could link buildings within a city. BlueTooth and 802.11 devices use wireless technology to communicate over a distance of several feet, in essence creating a **personal-area network** (**PAN**) between a phone and a headset or a smartphone and a desktop computer.

The media to carry networks are equally varied. They include copper wires, fiber strands, and wireless transmissions between satellites, microwave dishes, and radios. When computing devices are connected to cellular phones, they create a network. Even very short-range infrared communication can be used for networking. At a rudimentary level, whenever computers communicate, they use or create a network. These networks also vary in their performance and reliability.

Some operating systems have taken the concept of networks and distributed systems further than the notion of providing network connectivity.

A **network operating system** is an operating system that provides features such as file sharing across the network, along with a communication scheme that allows different processes on different computers to exchange messages. A computer running a network operating system acts autonomously from all other computers on the network, although it is aware of the network and is able to communicate with other networked computers. A distributed operating system provides a less autonomous environment. The different computers communicate closely enough to provide the illusion that only a single operating system controls the network.

1.11.4 Client–Server Computing

As PCs have become faster, more powerful, and cheaper, designers have shifted away from centralized system architecture. Terminals connected to centralized systems are now being supplanted by PCs and mobile devices. Correspondingly, user-interface functionality once handled directly by centralized systems is increasingly being handled by PCs, quite often through a web interface. As a result, many of today's systems act as **server systems** to satisfy requests generated by **client systems**. This form of specialized distributed system, called a **client–server** system, has the general structure depicted in Figure 1.18.

Server systems can be broadly categorized as compute servers and file servers:

- The **compute-server system** provides an interface to which a client can send a request to perform an action (for example, read data). In response, the server executes the action and sends the results to the client. A server running a database that responds to client requests for data is an example of such a system.

- The **file-server system** provides a file-system interface where clients can create, update, read, and delete files. An example of such a system is a web server that delivers files to clients running web browsers.

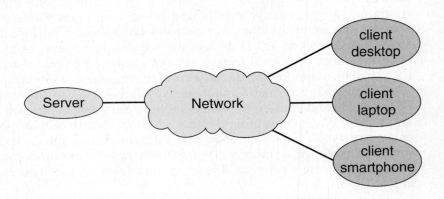

Figure 1.18 General structure of a client–server system.

1.11.5 Peer-to-Peer Computing

Another structure for a distributed system is the peer-to-peer (P2P) system model. In this model, clients and servers are not distinguished from one another. Instead, all nodes within the system are considered peers, and each may act as either a client or a server, depending on whether it is requesting or providing a service. Peer-to-peer systems offer an advantage over traditional client-server systems. In a client-server system, the server is a bottleneck; but in a peer-to-peer system, services can be provided by several nodes distributed throughout the network.

To participate in a peer-to-peer system, a node must first join the network of peers. Once a node has joined the network, it can begin providing services to—and requesting services from—other nodes in the network. Determining what services are available is accomplished in one of two general ways:

- When a node joins a network, it registers its service with a centralized lookup service on the network. Any node desiring a specific service first contacts this centralized lookup service to determine which node provides the service. The remainder of the communication takes place between the client and the service provider.

- An alternative scheme uses no centralized lookup service. Instead, a peer acting as a client must discover what node provides a desired service by broadcasting a request for the service to all other nodes in the network. The node (or nodes) providing that service responds to the peer making the request. To support this approach, a *discovery protocol* must be provided that allows peers to discover services provided by other peers in the network. Figure 1.19 illustrates such a scenario.

Peer-to-peer networks gained widespread popularity in the late 1990s with several file-sharing services, such as Napster and Gnutella, that enabled peers to exchange files with one another. The Napster system used an approach similar to the first type described above: a centralized server maintained an index of all files stored on peer nodes in the Napster network, and the actual

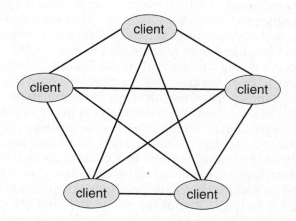

Figure 1.19 Peer-to-peer system with no centralized service.

exchange of files took place between the peer nodes. The Gnutella system used a technique similar to the second type: a client broadcasted file requests to other nodes in the system, and nodes that could service the request responded directly to the client. The future of exchanging files remains uncertain because peer-to-peer networks can be used to exchange copyrighted materials (music, for example) anonymously, and there are laws governing the distribution of copyrighted material. Notably, Napster ran into legal trouble for copyright infringement and its services were shut down in 2001.

Skype is another example of peer-to-peer computing. It allows clients to make voice calls and video calls and to send text messages over the Internet using a technology known as **voice over IP** (**VoIP**). Skype uses a hybrid peer-to-peer approach. It includes a centralized login server, but it also incorporates decentralized peers and allows two peers to communicate.

1.11.6 Virtualization

Virtualization is a technology that allows operating systems to run as applications within other operating systems. At first blush, there seems to be little reason for such functionality. But the virtualization industry is vast and growing, which is a testament to its utility and importance.

Broadly speaking, virtualization is one member of a class of software that also includes emulation. **Emulation** is used when the source CPU type is different from the target CPU type. For example, when Apple switched from the IBM Power CPU to the Intel x86 CPU for its desktop and laptop computers, it included an emulation facility called "Rosetta," which allowed applications compiled for the IBM CPU to run on the Intel CPU. That same concept can be extended to allow an entire operating system written for one platform to run on another. Emulation comes at a heavy price, however. Every machine-level instruction that runs natively on the source system must be translated to the equivalent function on the target system, frequently resulting in several target instructions. If the source and target CPUs have similar performance levels, the emulated code can run much slower than the native code.

A common example of emulation occurs when a computer language is not compiled to native code but instead is either executed in its high-level form or translated to an intermediate form. This is known as **interpretation**. Some languages, such as BASIC, can be either compiled or interpreted. Java, in contrast, is always interpreted. Interpretation is a form of emulation in that the high-level language code is translated to native CPU instructions, emulating not another CPU but a theoretical virtual machine on which that language could run natively. Thus, we can run Java programs on "Java virtual machines," but technically those virtual machines are Java emulators.

With **virtualization**, in contrast, an operating system that is natively compiled for a particular CPU architecture runs within another operating system also native to that CPU. Virtualization first came about on IBM mainframes as a method for multiple users to run tasks concurrently. Running multiple virtual machines allowed (and still allows) many users to run tasks on a system designed for a single user. Later, in response to problems with running multiple Microsoft Windows XP applications on the Intel x86 CPU, VMware created a new virtualization technology in the form of an application that ran on XP. That application ran one or more **guest** copies of Windows or other native

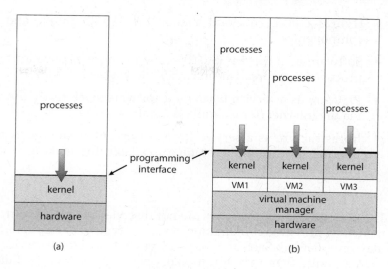

Figure 1.20 VMware.

x86 operating systems, each running its own applications. (See Figure 1.20.) Windows was the **host** operating system, and the VMware application was the VMM. The VMM runs the guest operating systems, manages their resource use, and protects each guest from the others.

Even though modern operating systems are fully capable of running multiple applications reliably, the use of virtualization continues to grow. On laptops and desktops, a VMM allows the user to install multiple operating systems for exploration or to run applications written for operating systems other than the native host. For example, an Apple laptop running Mac OS X on the x86 CPU can run a Windows guest to allow execution of Windows applications. Companies writing software for multiple operating systems can use virtualization to run all of those operating systems on a single physical server for development, testing, and debugging. Within data centers, virtualization has become a common method of executing and managing computing environments. VMMs like VMware ESX, and Citrix XenServer no longer run on host operating systems but rather *are* the hosts.

1.11.7 Cloud Computing

Cloud computing is a type of computing that delivers computing, storage, and even applications as a service across a network. In some ways, it's a logical extension of virtualization, because it uses virtualization as a base for its functionality. For example, the Amazon Elastic Compute Cloud (**EC2**) facility has thousands of servers, millions of virtual machines, and petabytes of storage available for use by anyone on the Internet. Users pay per month based on how much of those resources they use.

There are actually many types of cloud computing, including the following:

- **Public cloud**—a cloud available via the Internet to anyone willing to pay for the services

- **Private cloud**—a cloud run by a company for that company's own use

- **Hybrid cloud**—a cloud that includes both public and private cloud components
- Software as a service (**SaaS**)—one or more applications (such as word processors or spreadsheets) available via the Internet
- Platform as a service (**PaaS**)—a software stack ready for application use via the Internet (for example, a database server)
- Infrastructure as a service (**IaaS**)—servers or storage available over the Internet (for example, storage available for making backup copies of production data)

These cloud-computing types are not discrete, as a cloud computing environment may provide a combination of several types. For example, an organization may provide both SaaS and IaaS as a publicly available service.

Certainly, there are traditional operating systems within many of the types of cloud infrastructure. Beyond those are the VMMs that manage the virtual machines in which the user processes run. At a higher level, the VMMs themselves are managed by cloud management tools, such as Vware vCloud Director and the open-source Eucalyptus toolset. These tools manage the resources within a given cloud and provide interfaces to the cloud components, making a good argument for considering them a new type of operating system.

Figure 1.21 illustrates a public cloud providing IaaS. Notice that both the cloud services and the cloud user interface are protected by a firewall.

Figure 1.21 Cloud computing.

1.11.8 Real-Time Embedded Systems

Embedded computers are the most prevalent form of computers in existence. These devices are found everywhere, from car engines and manufacturing robots to DVDs and microwave ovens. They tend to have very specific tasks. The systems they run on are usually primitive, and so the operating systems provide limited features. Usually, they have little or no user interface, preferring to spend their time monitoring and managing hardware devices, such as automobile engines and robotic arms.

These embedded systems vary considerably. Some are general-purpose computers, running standard operating systems—such as Linux—with special-purpose applications to implement the functionality. Others are hardware devices with a special-purpose embedded operating system providing just the functionality desired. Yet others are hardware devices with application-specific integrated circuits (ASICs) that perform their tasks without an operating system.

The use of embedded systems continues to expand. The power of these devices, both as standalone units and as elements of networks and the web, is sure to increase as well. Even now, entire houses can be computerized, so that a central computer—either a general-purpose computer or an embedded system—can control heating and lighting, alarm systems, and even coffee makers. Web access can enable a home owner to tell the house to heat up before she arrives home. Someday, the refrigerator can notify the grocery store when it notices the milk is gone.

Embedded systems almost always run **real-time operating systems**. A real-time system is used when rigid time requirements have been placed on the operation of a processor or the flow of data; thus, it is often used as a control device in a dedicated application. Sensors bring data to the computer. The computer must analyze the data and possibly adjust controls to modify the sensor inputs. Systems that control scientific experiments, medical imaging systems, industrial control systems, and certain display systems are real-time systems. Some automobile-engine fuel-injection systems, home-appliance controllers, and weapon systems are also real-time systems.

A real-time system has well-defined, fixed time constraints. Processing *must* be done within the defined constraints, or the system will fail. For instance, it would not do for a robot arm to be instructed to halt *after* it had smashed into the car it was building. A real-time system functions correctly only if it returns the correct result within its time constraints. Contrast this system with a time-sharing system, where it is desirable (but not mandatory) to respond quickly, or a batch system, which may have no time constraints at all.

In Chapter 6, we consider the scheduling facility needed to implement real-time functionality in an operating system. In Chapter 8, we describe the design of memory management for real-time computing. Finally, in Chapters 15, we describe the real-time components of the Linux operating system.

1.12 Open-Source Operating Systems

We noted at the beginning of this chapter that the study of operating systems has been made easier by the availability of a vast number of open-source releases. Open-source operating systems are those available in source-code format rather than as compiled binary code. Linux is the most famous open-source operating system, while Microsoft Windows is a well-known example of the opposite closed-source approach. Apple's Mac OS X and iOS operating systems comprise a hybrid approach. They contain an open-source kernel named Darwin yet include proprietary, closed-source components as well.

Starting with the source code allows the programmer to produce binary code that can be executed on a system. Doing the opposite—reverse engineering the source code from the binaries—is quite a lot of work, and useful items such as comments are never recovered. Learning operating systems by examining the source code has other benefits as well. With the source code in hand, a student can modify the operating system and then compile and run the code to try out those changes, which is an excellent learning tool. This text includes projects that involve modifying operating-system source code, while also describing algorithms at a high level to be sure all important operating-system topics are covered. Throughout the text, we provide pointers to examples of open-source code for deeper study.

There are many benefits to open-source operating systems, including a community of interested (and usually unpaid) programmers who contribute to the code by helping to debug it, analyze it, provide support, and suggest changes. Arguably, open-source code is more secure than closed-source code because many more eyes are viewing the code. Certainly, open-source code has bugs, but open-source advocates argue that bugs tend to be found and fixed faster owing to the number of people using and viewing the code. Companies that earn revenue from selling their programs often hesitate to open-source their code, but Red Hat and a myriad of other companies are doing just that and showing that commercial companies benefit, rather than suffer, when they open-source their code. Revenue can be generated through support contracts and the sale of hardware on which the software runs, for example.

1.12.1 History

In the early days of modern computing (that is, the 1950s), a great deal of software was available in open-source format. The original hackers (computer enthusiasts) at MIT's Tech Model Railroad Club left their programs in drawers for others to work on. "Homebrew" user groups exchanged code during their meetings. Later, company-specific user groups, such as Digital Equipment Corporation's DEC, accepted contributions of source-code programs, collected them onto tapes, and distributed the tapes to interested members.

Computer and software companies eventually sought to limit the use of their software to authorized computers and paying customers. Releasing only the binary files compiled from the source code, rather than the source code itself, helped them to achieve this goal, as well as protecting their code and their ideas from their competitors. Another issue involved copyrighted material. Operating systems and other programs can limit the ability to play back movies and music or display electronic books to authorized computers. Such copy protection or digital rights management (DRM) would not be effective if the source code that implemented these limits were published. Laws in many countries, including the U.S. Digital Millennium Copyright Act (DMCA), make it illegal to reverse-engineer DRM code or otherwise try to circumvent copy protection.

To counter the move to limit software use and redistribution, Richard Stallman in 1983 started the GNU project to create a free, open-source, UNIX-compatible operating system. In 1985, he published the GNU Manifesto, which argues that all software should be free and open-sourced. He also formed the **Free Software Foundation (FSF)** with the goal of encouraging the free exchange of software source code and the free use of that software. Rather than copyright its software, the FSF "copylefts" the software to encourage sharing and improvement. The **GNU General Public License (GPL)** codifies copylefting and is a common license under which free software is released. Fundamentally, GPL requires that the source code be distributed with any binaries and that any changes made to the source code be released under the same GPL license.

1.12.2   Linux

As an example of an open-source operating system, consider **GNU/Linux**. The GNU project produced many UNIX-compatible tools, including compilers, editors, and utilities, but never released a kernel. In 1991, a student in Finland, Linus Torvalds, released a rudimentary UNIX-like kernel using the GNU compilers and tools and invited contributions worldwide. The advent of the Internet meant that anyone interested could download the source code, modify it, and submit changes to Torvalds. Releasing updates once a week allowed this so-called Linux operating system to grow rapidly, enhanced by several thousand programmers.

The resulting GNU/Linux operating system has spawned hundreds of unique **distributions**, or custom builds, of the system. Major distributions include Red Hat, SUSE, Fedora, Debian, Slackware, and Ubuntu. Distributions vary in function, utility, installed applications, hardware support, user interface, and purpose. For example, Red Hat Enterprise Linux is geared to large commercial use. PCLinuxOS is a **LiveCD**—an operating system that can be booted and run from a CD-ROM without being installed on a system's boot disk(s). One variant of PCLinuxOS—called "PCLinuxOS Supergamer DVD"—is a **LiveDVD** that includes graphics drivers and games. A gamer can run it on any compatible system simply by booting from the DVD. When the gamer is finished, a reboot of the system resets it to its installed operating system.

You can run Linux on a Windows system using the following simple, free approach:

1. Download the free "VMware Player" tool from

    http://www.vmware.com/download/player/

    and install it on your system.

2. Choose a Linux version from among the hundreds of "appliances," or virtual machine images, available from VMware at

    http://www.vmware.com/appliances/

    These images are preinstalled with operating systems and applications and include many flavors of Linux.

3.   Boot the virtual machine within VMware Player.

With this text, we provide a virtual machine image of Linux running the Debian release. This image contains the Linux source code as well as tools for software development. We cover examples involving that Linux image throughout this text, as well as in a detailed case study in Chapter 15.

1.12.3   BSD UNIX

BSD UNIX has a longer and more complicated history than Linux. It started in 1978 as a derivative of AT&T's UNIX. Releases from the University of California at Berkeley (UCB) came in source and binary form, but they were not open-source because a license from AT&T was required. BSD UNIX's development was slowed by a lawsuit by AT&T, but eventually a fully functional, open-source version, 4.4BSD-lite, was released in 1994.

Just as with Linux, there are many distributions of BSD UNIX, including FreeBSD, NetBSD, OpenBSD, and DragonflyBSD. To explore the source code of FreeBSD, simply download the virtual machine image of the version of interest and boot it within VMware, as described above for Linux. The source code comes with the distribution and is stored in /usr/src/. The kernel source code is in /usr/src/sys. For example, to examine the virtual memory implementation code in the FreeBSD kernel, see the files in /usr/src/sys/vm.

Darwin, the core kernel component of Mac OS X, is based on BSD UNIX and is open-sourced as well. That source code is available from http://www.opensource.apple.com/. Every Mac OS X release has its open-source components posted at that site. The name of the package that contains the kernel begins with "xnu." Apple also provides extensive developer tools, documentation, and support at http://connect.apple.com. For more information, see Appendix A.

1.12.4   Solaris

Solaris is the commercial UNIX-based operating system of Sun Microsystems. Originally, Sun's SunOS operating system was based on BSD UNIX. Sun moved to AT&T's System V UNIX as its base in 1991. In 2005, Sun open-sourced most of the Solaris code as the OpenSolaris project. The purchase of Sun by Oracle in 2009, however, left the state of this project unclear. The source code as it was in 2005 is still available via a source code browser and for download at http://src.opensolaris.org/source.

Several groups interested in using OpenSolaris have started from that base and expanded its features. Their working set is Project Illumos, which has expanded from the OpenSolaris base to include more features and to be the basis for several products. Illumos is available at http://wiki.illumos.org.

1.12.5   Open-Source Systems as Learning Tools

The free software movement is driving legions of programmers to create thousands of open-source projects, including operating systems. Sites like http://freshmeat.net/ and http://distrowatch.com/ provide portals to many of these projects. As we stated earlier, open-source projects enable students to use source code as a learning tool. They can modify programs and test them, help find and fix bugs, and otherwise explore mature, full-featured operating systems, compilers, tools, user interfaces, and other types of programs. The availability of source code for historic projects, such as Multics, can help students to understand those projects and to build knowledge that will help in the implementation of new projects.

GNU/Linux and BSD UNIX are all open-source operating systems, but each has its own goals, utility, licensing, and purpose. Sometimes, licenses are not mutually exclusive and cross-pollination occurs, allowing rapid improvements in operating-system projects. For example, several major components of OpenSolaris have been ported to BSD UNIX. The advantages of free software and open sourcing are likely to increase the number and quality of open-source projects, leading to an increase in the number of individuals and companies that use these projects.

1.13 Summary

An operating system is software that manages the computer hardware, as well as providing an environment for application programs to run. Perhaps the most visible aspect of an operating system is the interface to the computer system it provides to the human user.

For a computer to do its job of executing programs, the programs must be in main memory. Main memory is the only large storage area that the processor can access directly. It is an array of bytes, ranging in size from millions to billions. Each byte in memory has its own address. The main memory is usually a volatile storage device that loses its contents when power is turned off or lost. Most computer systems provide secondary storage as an extension of main memory. Secondary storage provides a form of nonvolatile storage that is capable of holding large quantities of data permanently. The most common secondary-storage device is a hard disk, which provides storage of both programs and data.

The wide variety of storage systems in a computer system can be organized in a hierarchy according to speed and cost. The higher levels are expensive, but they are fast. As we move down the hierarchy, the cost per bit generally decreases, whereas the access time generally increases.

There are several different strategies for designing a computer system. Single-processor systems have only one processor, while multiprocessor systems contain two or more processors that share physical memory and peripheral devices. The most common multiprocessor design is symmetric multiprocessing (or SMP), where all processors are considered peers and run independently of one another. Clustered systems are a specialized form of multiprocessor systems and consist of multiple computer systems connected by a local-area network.

To best utilize the CPU, modern operating systems employ multiprogramming, which allows several jobs to be in memory at the same time, thus ensuring that the CPU always has a job to execute. Time-sharing systems are an extension of multiprogramming wherein CPU scheduling algorithms rapidly switch between jobs, thus providing the illusion that each job is running concurrently.

The operating system must ensure correct operation of the computer system. To prevent user programs from interfering with the proper operation of

THE STUDY OF OPERATING SYSTEMS

There has never been a more interesting time to study operating systems, and it has never been easier. The open-source movement has overtaken operating systems, causing many of them to be made available in both source and binary (executable) format. The list of operating systems available in both formats includes Linux, BSD UNIX, Solaris, and part of Mac OS X. The availability of source code allows us to study operating systems from the inside out. Questions that we could once answer only by looking at documentation or the behavior of an operating system we can now answer by examining the code itself.

Operating systems that are no longer commercially viable have been open-sourced as well, enabling us to study how systems operated in a time of fewer CPU, memory, and storage resources. An extensive but incomplete list of open-source operating-system projects is available from http://dmoz.org/Computers/Software/Operating_Systems/Open_Source/.

In addition, the rise of virtualization as a mainstream (and frequently free) computer function makes it possible to run many operating systems on top of one core system. For example, VMware (http://www.vmware.com) provides a free "player" for Windows on which hundreds of free "virtual appliances" can run. Virtualbox (http://www.virtualbox.com) provides a free, open-source virtual machine manager on many operating systems. Using such tools, students can try out hundreds of operating systems without dedicated hardware.

In some cases, simulators of specific hardware are also available, allowing the operating system to run on "native" hardware, all within the confines of a modern computer and modern operating system. For example, a DECSYSTEM-20 simulator running on Mac OS X can boot TOPS-20, load the source tapes, and modify and compile a new TOPS-20 kernel. An interested student can search the Internet to find the original papers that describe the operating system, as well as the original manuals.

The advent of open-source operating systems has also made it easier to make the move from student to operating-system developer. With some knowledge, some effort, and an Internet connection, a student can even create a new operating-system distribution. Just a few years ago, it was difficult or impossible to get access to source code. Now, such access is limited only by how much interest, time, and disk space a student has.

---

the system, the hardware has two modes: user mode and kernel mode. Various instructions (such as I/O instructions and halt instructions) are privileged and can be executed only in kernel mode. The memory in which the operating system resides must also be protected from modification by the user. A timer prevents infinite loops. These facilities (dual mode, privileged instructions, memory protection, and timer interrupt) are basic building blocks used by operating systems to achieve correct operation.

A process (or job) is the fundamental unit of work in an operating system. Process management includes creating and deleting processes and providing mechanisms for processes to communicate and synchronize with each other.

An operating system manages memory by keeping track of what parts of memory are being used and by whom. The operating system is also responsible for dynamically allocating and freeing memory space. Storage space is also managed by the operating system; this includes providing file systems for representing files and directories and managing space on mass-storage devices.

Operating systems must also be concerned with protecting and securing the operating system and users. Protection measures control the access of processes or users to the resources made available by the computer system. Security measures are responsible for defending a computer system from external or internal attacks.

Several data structures that are fundamental to computer science are widely used in operating systems, including lists, stacks, queues, trees, hash functions, maps, and bitmaps.

Computing takes place in a variety of environments. Traditional computing involves desktop and laptop PCs, usually connected to a computer network. Mobile computing refers to computing on handheld smartphones and tablet computers, which offer several unique features. Distributed systems allow users to share resources on geographically dispersed hosts connected via a computer network. Services may be provided through either the client–server model or the peer-to-peer model. Virtualization involves abstracting a computer's hardware into several different execution environments. Cloud computing uses a distributed system to abstract services into a "cloud," where users may access the services from remote locations. Real-time operating systems are designed for embedded environments, such as consumer devices, automobiles, and robotics.

The free software movement has created thousands of open-source projects, including operating systems. Because of these projects, students are able to use source code as a learning tool. They can modify programs and test them, help find and fix bugs, and otherwise explore mature, full-featured operating systems, compilers, tools, user interfaces, and other types of programs.

GNU/Linux and BSD UNIX are open-source operating systems. The advantages of free software and open sourcing are likely to increase the number and quality of open-source projects, leading to an increase in the number of individuals and companies that use these projects.

Review Questions

Review questions for this chapter can be accessed by visiting our website.

Practice Exercises

Answers for the Practice Exercises can be accceed by visiting our website.

1.1 What are the three main purposes of an operating system?

1.2 We have stressed the need for an operating system to make efficient use of the computing hardware. When is it appropriate for the operating system to forsake this principle and to "waste" resources? Why is such a system not really wasteful?

1.3   What is the main difficulty that a programmer must overcome in writing an operating system for a real-time environment?

1.4   Keeping in mind the various definitions of *operating system,* consider whether the operating system should include applications such as web browsers and mail programs. Argue both that it should and that it should not, and support your answers.

1.5   How does the distinction between kernel mode and user mode function as a rudimentary form of protection (security) system?

1.6   Which of the following instructions should be privileged?

    a.   Set value of timer.

    b.   Read the clock.

    c.   Clear memory.

    d.   Issue a trap instruction.

    e.   Turn off interrupts.

    f.   Modify entries in device-status table.

    g.   Switch from user to kernel mode.

    h.   Access I/O device.

1.7   Some early computers protected the operating system by placing it in a memory partition that could not be modified by either the user job or the operating system itself. Describe two difficulties that you think could arise with such a scheme.

1.8   Some CPUs provide for more than two modes of operation. What are two possible uses of these multiple modes?

1.9   Timers could be used to compute the current time. Provide a short description of how this could be accomplished.

1.10   Give two reasons why caches are useful. What problems do they solve? What problems do they cause? If a cache can be made as large as the device for which it is caching (for instance, a cache as large as a disk), why not make it that large and eliminate the device?

1.11   Distinguish between the client–server and peer-to-peer models of distributed systems.

Exercises

1.12   In a multiprogramming and time-sharing environment, several users share the system simultaneously. This situation can result in various security problems.

    a.   What are two such problems?

    b.   Can we ensure the same degree of security in a time-shared machine as in a dedicated machine? Explain your answer.

1.13   The issue of resource utilization shows up in different forms in different types of operating systems. List what resources must be managed carefully in the following settings:

    a.   Mainframe or minicomputer systems

    b.   Workstations connected to servers

    c.   Mobile computers

1.14   Under what circumstances would a user be better off using a time-sharing system than a PC or a single-user workstation?

1.15   Describe the differences between symmetric and asymmetric multiprocessing. What are three advantages and one disadvantage of multiprocessor systems?

1.16   How do clustered systems differ from multiprocessor systems? What is required for two machines belonging to a cluster to cooperate to provide a highly available service?

1.17   Consider a computing cluster consisting of two nodes running a database. Describe two ways in which the cluster software can manage access to the data on the disk. Discuss the benefits and disadvantages of each.

1.18   How are network computers different from traditional personal computers? Describe some usage scenarios in which it is advantageous to use network computers.

1.19   What is the purpose of interrupts? How does an interrupt differ from a trap? Can traps be generated intentionally by a user program? If so, for what purpose?

1.20   Direct memory access is used for high-speed I/O devices in order to avoid increasing the CPU's execution load.

    a.   How does the CPU interface with the device to coordinate the transfer?

    b.   How does the CPU know when the memory operations are complete?

    c.   The CPU is allowed to execute other programs while the DMA controller is transferring data. Does this process interfere with the execution of the user programs? If so, describe what forms of interference are caused.

1.21   Some computer systems do not provide a privileged mode of operation in hardware. Is it possible to construct a secure operating system for these computer systems? Give arguments both that it is and that it is not possible.

1.22   Many SMP systems have different levels of caches; one level is local to each processing core, and another level is shared among all processing cores. Why are caching systems designed this way?

1.23 Consider an SMP system similar to the one shown in Figure 1.6. Illustrate with an example how data residing in memory could in fact have a different value in each of the local caches.

1.24 Discuss, with examples, how the problem of maintaining coherence of cached data manifests itself in the following processing environments:

    a. Single-processor systems

    b. Multiprocessor systems

    c. Distributed systems

1.25 Describe a mechanism for enforcing memory protection in order to prevent a program from modifying the memory associated with other programs.

1.26 Which network configuration—LAN or WAN—would best suit the following environments?

    a. A campus student union

    b. Several campus locations across a statewide university system

    c. A neighborhood

1.27 Describe some of the challenges of designing operating systems for mobile devices compared with designing operating systems for traditional PCs.

1.28 What are some advantages of peer-to-peer systems over client-server systems?

1.29 Describe some distributed applications that would be appropriate for a peer-to-peer system.

1.30 Identify several advantages and several disadvantages of open-source operating systems. Include the types of people who would find each aspect to be an advantage or a disadvantage.

Bibliographical Notes

[Brookshear (2012)] provides an overview of computer science in general. Thorough coverage of data structures can be found in [Cormen et al. (2009)].

[Russinovich and Solomon (2009)] give an overview of Microsoft Windows and covers considerable technical detail about the system internals and components. [McDougall and Mauro (2007)] cover the internals of the Solaris operating system. Mac OS X internals are discussed in [Singh (2007)]. [Love (2010)] provides an overview of the Linux operating system and great detail about data structures used in the Linux kernel.

Many general textbooks cover operating systems, including [Stallings (2011)], [Deitel et al. (2004)], and [Tanenbaum (2007)]. [Kurose and Ross (2013)] provides a general overview of computer networks, including a discussion of client-server and peer-to-peer systems. [Tarkoma and Lagerspetz (2011)] examines several different mobile operating systems, including Android and iOs.

[Hennessy and Patterson (2012)] provide coverage of I/O systems and buses and of system architecture in general. [Bryant and O'Hallaron (2010)] provide a thorough overview of a computer system from the perspective of a computer programmer. Details of the Intel 64 instruction set and privilege modes can be found in [Intel (2011)].

The history of open sourcing and its benefits and challenges appears in [Raymond (1999)]. The Free Software Foundation has published its philosophy in http://www.gnu.org/philosophy/free-software-for-freedom.html. The open source of Mac OS X are available from http://www.apple.com/opensource/.

Wikipedia has an informative entry about the contributions of Richard Stallman at http://en.wikipedia.org/wiki/Richard_Stallman.

The source code of Multics is available at http://web.mit.edu/multics-history /source/Multics_Internet_Server/Multics_sources.html.

Bibliography

[Brookshear (2012)]   J. G. Brookshear, *Computer Science: An Overview,* Eleventh Edition, Addison-Wesley (2012).

[Bryant and O'Hallaron (2010)]   R. Bryant and D. O'Hallaron, *Computer Systems: A Programmers Perspective,* Second Edition, Addison-Wesley (2010).

[Cormen et al. (2009)]   T. H. Cormen, C. E. Leiserson, R. L. Rivest, and C. Stein, *Introduction to Algorithms,* Third Edition, MIT Press (2009).

[Deitel et al. (2004)]   H. Deitel, P. Deitel, and D. Choffnes, *Operating Systems,* Third Edition, Prentice Hall (2004).

[Hennessy and Patterson (2012)]   J. Hennessy and D. Patterson, *Computer Architecture: A Quantitative Approach,* Fifth Edition, Morgan Kaufmann (2012).

[Intel (2011)]   *Intel 64 and IA-32 Architectures Software Developer's Manual, Combined Volumes: 1, 2A, 2B, 3A and 3B.* Intel Corporation (2011).

[Kurose and Ross (2013)]   J. Kurose and K. Ross, *Computer Networking—A Top–Down Approach,* Sixth Edition, Addison-Wesley (2013).

[Love (2010)]   R. Love, *Linux Kernel Development,* Third Edition, Developer's Library (2010).

[McDougall and Mauro (2007)]   R. McDougall and J. Mauro, *Solaris Internals,* Second Edition, Prentice Hall (2007).

[Raymond (1999)]   E. S. Raymond, *The Cathedral and the Bazaar,* O'Reilly & Associates (1999).

[Russinovich and Solomon (2009)]   M. E. Russinovich and D. A. Solomon, *Windows Internals: Including Windows Server 2008 and Windows Vista,* Fifth Edition, Microsoft Press (2009).

[Singh (2007)]   A. Singh, *Mac OS X Internals: A Systems Approach,* Addison-Wesley (2007).

[Stallings (2011)]   W. Stallings, *Operating Systems,* Seventh Edition, Prentice Hall (2011).

[Tanenbaum (2007)]   A. S. Tanenbaum, *Modern Operating Systems,* Third Edition, Prentice Hall (2007).

[Tarkoma and Lagerspetz (2011)]   S. Tarkoma and E. Lagerspetz, "Arching over the Mobile Computing Chasm: Platforms and Runtimes", *IEEE Computer,* Volume 44, (2011), pages 22–28.

Operating-System Structures

CHAPTER 2

An operating system provides the environment within which programs are executed. Internally, operating systems vary greatly in their makeup, since they are organized along many different lines. The design of a new operating system is a major task. It is important that the goals of the system be well defined before the design begins. These goals form the basis for choices among various algorithms and strategies.

We can view an operating system from several vantage points. One view focuses on the services that the system provides; another, on the interface that it makes available to users and programmers; a third, on its components and their interconnections. In this chapter, we explore all three aspects of operating systems, showing the viewpoints of users, programmers, and operating system designers. We consider what services an operating system provides, how they are provided, how they are debugged, and what the various methodologies are for designing such systems. Finally, we describe how operating systems are created and how a computer starts its operating system.

CHAPTER OBJECTIVES

- To describe the services an operating system provides to users, processes, and other systems.
- To discuss the various ways of structuring an operating system.
- To explain how operating systems are installed and customized and how they boot.

2.1 Operating-System Services

An operating system provides an environment for the execution of programs. It provides certain services to programs and to the users of those programs. The specific services provided, of course, differ from one operating system to another, but we can identify common classes. These operating system services are provided for the convenience of the programmer, to make the programming

Figure 2.1   A view of operating system services.

task easier. Figure 2.1 shows one view of the various operating-system services and how they interrelate.

One set of operating system services provides functions that are helpful to the user.

- **User interface**. Almost all operating systems have a **user interface (UI)**. This interface can take several forms. One is a **command-line interface (CLI)**, which uses text commands and a method for entering them (say, a keyboard for typing in commands in a specific format with specific options). Another is a **batch interface**, in which commands and directives to control those commands are entered into files, and those files are executed. Most commonly, a **graphical user interface (GUI)** is used. Here, the interface is a window system with a pointing device to direct I/O, choose from menus, and make selections and a keyboard to enter text. Some systems provide two or all three of these variations.

- **Program execution**. The system must be able to load a program into memory and to run that program. The program must be able to end its execution, either normally or abnormally (indicating error).

- **I/O operations**. A running program may require I/O, which may involve a file or an I/O device. For specific devices, special functions may be desired (such as recording to a CD or DVD drive or blanking a display screen). For efficiency and protection, users usually cannot control I/O devices directly. Therefore, the operating system must provide a means to do I/O.

- **File-system manipulation**. The file system is of particular interest. Obviously, programs need to read and write files and directories. They also need to create and delete them by name, search for a given file, and list file information. Finally, some operating systems include permissions management to allow or deny access to files or directories based on file ownership. Many operating systems provide a variety of file systems, sometimes to allow personal choice and sometimes to provide specific features or performance characteristics.

- **Communications**. There are many circumstances in which one process needs to exchange information with another process. Such communication may occur between processes that are executing on the same computer or between processes that are executing on different computer systems tied together by a computer network. Communications may be implemented via shared memory, in which two or more processes read and write to a shared section of memory, or message passing, in which packets of information in predefined formats are moved between processes by the operating system.

- **Error detection**. The operating system needs to be detecting and correcting errors constantly. Errors may occur in the CPU and memory hardware (such as a memory error or a power failure), in I/O devices (such as a parity error on disk, a connection failure on a network, or lack of paper in the printer), and in the user program (such as an arithmetic overflow, an attempt to access an illegal memory location, or a too-great use of CPU time). For each type of error, the operating system should take the appropriate action to ensure correct and consistent computing. Sometimes, it has no choice but to halt the system. At other times, it might terminate an error-causing process or return an error code to a process for the process to detect and possibly correct.

Another set of operating system functions exists not for helping the user but rather for ensuring the efficient operation of the system itself. Systems with multiple users can gain efficiency by sharing the computer resources among the users.

- **Resource allocation**. When there are multiple users or multiple jobs running at the same time, resources must be allocated to each of them. The operating system manages many different types of resources. Some (such as CPU cycles, main memory, and file storage) may have special allocation code, whereas others (such as I/O devices) may have much more general request and release code. For instance, in determining how best to use the CPU, operating systems have CPU-scheduling routines that take into account the speed of the CPU, the jobs that must be executed, the number of registers available, and other factors. There may also be routines to allocate printers, USB storage drives, and other peripheral devices.

- **Accounting**. We want to keep track of which users use how much and what kinds of computer resources. This record keeping may be used for accounting (so that users can be billed) or simply for accumulating usage statistics. Usage statistics may be a valuable tool for researchers who wish to reconfigure the system to improve computing services.

- **Protection and security**. The owners of information stored in a multiuser or networked computer system may want to control use of that information. When several separate processes execute concurrently, it should not be possible for one process to interfere with the others or with the operating system itself. Protection involves ensuring that all access to system resources is controlled. Security of the system from outsiders is also important. Such security starts with requiring each user to authenticate himself or herself to the system, usually by means of a password, to gain access to system resources. It extends to defending external I/O devices, including network adapters, from invalid access attempts and to recording all such connections for detection of break-ins. If a system is to be protected and secure, precautions must be instituted throughout it. A chain is only as strong as its weakest link.

2.2 User and Operating-System Interface

We mentioned earlier that there are several ways for users to interface with the operating system. Here, we discuss two fundamental approaches. One provides a command-line interface, or **command interpreter**, that allows users to directly enter commands to be performed by the operating system. The other allows users to interface with the operating system via a graphical user interface, or GUI.

2.2.1 Command Interpreters

Some operating systems include the command interpreter in the kernel. Others, such as Windows and UNIX, treat the command interpreter as a special program that is running when a job is initiated or when a user first logs on (on interactive systems). On systems with multiple command interpreters to choose from, the interpreters are known as **shells**. For example, on UNIX and Linux systems, a user may choose among several different shells, including the *Bourne shell, C shell, Bourne-Again shell, Korn shell*, and others. Third-party shells and free user-written shells are also available. Most shells provide similar functionality, and a user's choice of which shell to use is generally based on personal preference. Figure 2.2 shows the Bourne shell command interpreter being used on Solaris 10.

The main function of the command interpreter is to get and execute the next user-specified command. Many of the commands given at this level manipulate files: create, delete, list, print, copy, execute, and so on. The MS-DOS and UNIX shells operate in this way. These commands can be implemented in two general ways.

In one approach, the command interpreter itself contains the code to execute the command. For example, a command to delete a file may cause the command interpreter to jump to a section of its code that sets up the parameters and makes the appropriate system call. In this case, the number of commands that can be given determines the size of the command interpreter, since each command requires its own implementing code.

An alternative approach—used by UNIX, among other operating systems —implements most commands through system programs. In this case, the command interpreter does not understand the command in any way; it merely uses the command to identify a file to be loaded into memory and executed. Thus, the UNIX command to delete a file

```
rm file.txt
```

would search for a file called `rm`, load the file into memory, and execute it with the parameter `file.txt`. The function associated with the `rm` command would

Figure 2.2 The Bourne shell command interpreter in Solaris 10.

be defined completely by the code in the file rm. In this way, programmers can add new commands to the system easily by creating new files with the proper names. The command-interpreter program, which can be small, does not have to be changed for new commands to be added.

2.2.2 Graphical User Interfaces

A second strategy for interfacing with the operating system is through a user-friendly graphical user interface, or GUI. Here, rather than entering commands directly via a command-line interface, users employ a mouse-based window-and-menu system characterized by a **desktop** metaphor. The user moves the mouse to position its pointer on images, or **icons**, on the screen (the desktop) that represent programs, files, directories, and system functions. Depending on the mouse pointer's location, clicking a button on the mouse can invoke a program, select a file or directory—known as a **folder**—or pull down a menu that contains commands.

Graphical user interfaces first appeared due in part to research taking place in the early 1970s at Xerox PARC research facility. The first GUI appeared on the Xerox Alto computer in 1973. However, graphical interfaces became more widespread with the advent of Apple Macintosh computers in the 1980s. The user interface for the Macintosh operating system (Mac OS) has undergone various changes over the years, the most significant being the adoption of the *Aqua* interface that appeared with Mac OS X. Microsoft's first version of Windows—Version 1.0—was based on the addition of a GUI interface to the MS-DOS operating system. Later versions of Windows have made cosmetic changes in the appearance of the GUI along with several enhancements in its functionality.

Because a mouse is impractical for most mobile systems, smartphones and handheld tablet computers typically use a touchscreen interface. Here, users interact by making gestures on the touchscreen—for example, pressing and swiping fingers across the screen. Figure 2.3 illustrates the touchscreen of the Apple iPad. Whereas earlier smartphones included a physical keyboard, most smartphones now simulate a keyboard on the touchscreen.

Traditionally, UNIX systems have been dominated by command-line interfaces. Various GUI interfaces are available, however. These include the Common Desktop Environment (CDE) and X-Windows systems, which are common on commercial versions of UNIX, such as Solaris and IBM's AIX system. In addition, there has been significant development in GUI designs from various open-source projects, such as *K Desktop Environment* (or *KDE*) and the *GNOME* desktop by the GNU project. Both the KDE and GNOME desktops run on Linux and various UNIX systems and are available under open-source licenses, which means their source code is readily available for reading and for modification under specific license terms.

Figure 2.3   The iPad touchscreen.

2.2.3   Choice of Interface

The choice of whether to use a command-line or GUI interface is mostly one of personal preference. **System administrators** who manage computers and **power users** who have deep knowledge of a system frequently use the command-line interface. For them, it is more efficient, giving them faster access to the activities they need to perform. Indeed, on some systems, only a subset of system functions is available via the GUI, leaving the less common tasks to those who are command-line knowledgeable. Further, command-line interfaces usually make repetitive tasks easier, in part because they have their own programmability. For example, if a frequent task requires a set of command-line steps, those steps can be recorded into a file, and that file can be run just like a program. The program is not compiled into executable code but rather is interpreted by the command-line interface. These **shell scripts** are very common on systems that are command-line oriented, such as UNIX and Linux.

In contrast, most Windows users are happy to use the Windows GUI environment and almost never use the MS-DOS shell interface. The various changes undergone by the Macintosh operating systems provide a nice study in contrast. Historically, Mac OS has not provided a command-line interface, always requiring its users to interface with the operating system using its GUI. However, with the release of Mac OS X (which is in part implemented using a UNIX kernel), the operating system now provides both a Aqua interface and a command-line interface. Figure 2.4 is a screenshot of the Mac OS X GUI.

Figure 2.4   The Mac OS X GUI.

(This an independent publication and it has not been authorized, sponsored, or otherwise approved by Apple Inc.)

The user interface can vary from system to system and even from user to user within a system. It typically is substantially removed from the actual system structure. The design of a useful and friendly user interface is therefore not a direct function of the operating system. In this book, we concentrate on the fundamental problems of providing adequate service to user programs. From the point of view of the operating system, we do not distinguish between user programs and system programs.

2.3 System Calls

System calls provide an interface to the services made available by an operating system. These calls are generally available as routines written in C and C++, although certain low-level tasks (for example, tasks where hardware must be accessed directly) may have to be written using assembly-language instructions.

Before we discuss how an operating system makes system calls available, let's first use an example to illustrate how system calls are used: writing a simple program to read data from one file and copy them to another file. The first input that the program will need is the names of the two files: the input file and the output file. These names can be specified in many ways, depending on the operating-system design. One approach is for the program to ask the user for the names. In an interactive system, this approach will require a sequence of system calls, first to write a prompting message on the screen and then to read from the keyboard the characters that define the two files. On mouse-based and icon-based systems, a menu of file names is usually displayed in a window. The user can then use the mouse to select the source name, and a window can be opened for the destination name to be specified. This sequence requires many I/O system calls.

Once the two file names have been obtained, the program must open the input file and create the output file. Each of these operations requires another system call. Possible error conditions for each operation can require additional system calls. When the program tries to open the input file, for example, it may find that there is no file of that name or that the file is protected against access. In these cases, the program should print a message on the console (another sequence of system calls) and then terminate abnormally (another system call). If the input file exists, then we must create a new output file. We may find that there is already an output file with the same name. This situation may cause the program to abort (a system call), or we may delete the existing file (another system call) and create a new one (yet another system call). Another option, in an interactive system, is to ask the user (via a sequence of system calls to output the prompting message and to read the response from the terminal) whether to replace the existing file or to abort the program.

When both files are set up, we enter a loop that reads from the input file (a system call) and writes to the output file (another system call). Each read and write must return status information regarding various possible error conditions. On input, the program may find that the end of the file has been reached or that there was a hardware failure in the read (such as a parity error). The write operation may encounter various errors, depending on the output device (for example, no more disk space).

Finally, after the entire file is copied, the program may close both files (another system call), write a message to the console or window (more system calls), and finally terminate normally (the final system call). This system-call sequence is shown in Figure 2.5.

As you can see, even simple programs may make heavy use of the operating system. Frequently, systems execute thousands of system calls per second. Most programmers never see this level of detail, however. Typically, application developers design programs according to an **application programming interface** (API). The API specifies a set of functions that are available to an application programmer, including the parameters that are passed to each function and the return values the programmer can expect. Three of the most common APIs available to application programmers are the Windows API for Windows systems, the POSIX API for POSIX-based systems (which include virtually all versions of UNIX, Linux, and Mac OS X), and the Java API for programs that run on the Java virtual machine. A programmer accesses an API via a library of code provided by the operating system. In the case of UNIX and Linux for programs written in the C language, the library is called libc. Note that—unless specified—the system-call names used throughout this text are generic examples. Each operating system has its own name for each system call.

Behind the scenes, the functions that make up an API typically invoke the actual system calls on behalf of the application programmer. For example, the Windows function CreateProcess() (which unsurprisingly is used to create a new process) actually invokes the NTCreateProcess() system call in the Windows kernel.

Why would an application programmer prefer programming according to an API rather than invoking actual system calls? There are several reasons for doing so. One benefit concerns program portability. An application program-

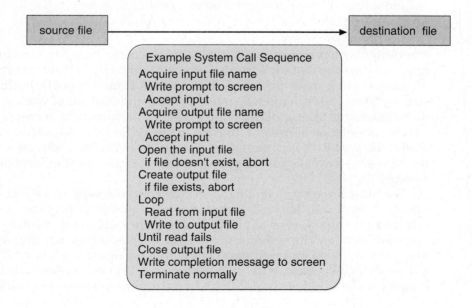

Figure 2.5 Example of how system calls are used.

EXAMPLE OF STANDARD API

As an example of a standard API, consider the `read()` function that is available in UNIX and Linux systems. The API for this function is obtained from the man page by invoking the command

```
man read
```

on the command line. A description of this API appears below:

A program that uses the `read()` function must include the `unistd.h` header file, as this file defines the `ssize_t` and `size_t` data types (among other things). The parameters passed to `read()` are as follows:

- `int fd`—the file descriptor to be read
- `void *buf`—a buffer where the data will be read into
- `size_t count`—the maximum number of bytes to be read into the buffer

On a successful read, the number of bytes read is returned. A return value of 0 indicates end of file. If an error occurs, `read()` returns −1.

mer designing a program using an API can expect her program to compile and run on any system that supports the same API (although, in reality, architectural differences often make this more difficult than it may appear). Furthermore, actual system calls can often be more detailed and difficult to work with than the API available to an application programmer. Nevertheless, there often exists a strong correlation between a function in the API and its associated system call within the kernel. In fact, many of the POSIX and Windows APIs are similar to the native system calls provided by the UNIX, Linux, and Windows operating systems.

For most programming languages, the run-time support system (a set of functions built into libraries included with a compiler) provides a **system-call interface** that serves as the link to system calls made available by the operating system. The system-call interface intercepts function calls in the API and invokes the necessary system calls within the operating system. Typically, a number is associated with each system call, and the system-call interface maintains a table indexed according to these numbers. The system call interface

Figure 2.6   The handling of a user application invoking the open() system call.

then invokes the intended system call in the operating-system kernel and returns the status of the system call and any return values.

The caller need know nothing about how the system call is implemented or what it does during execution. Rather, the caller need only obey the API and understand what the operating system will do as a result of the execution of that system call. Thus, most of the details of the operating-system interface are hidden from the programmer by the API and are managed by the run-time support library. The relationship between an API, the system-call interface, and the operating system is shown in Figure 2.6, which illustrates how the operating system handles a user application invoking the open() system call.

System calls occur in different ways, depending on the computer in use. Often, more information is required than simply the identity of the desired system call. The exact type and amount of information vary according to the particular operating system and call. For example, to get input, we may need to specify the file or device to use as the source, as well as the address and length of the memory buffer into which the input should be read. Of course, the device or file and length may be implicit in the call.

Three general methods are used to pass parameters to the operating system. The simplest approach is to pass the parameters in registers. In some cases, however, there may be more parameters than registers. In these cases, the parameters are generally stored in a block, or table, in memory, and the address of the block is passed as a parameter in a register (Figure 2.7). This is the approach taken by Linux and Solaris. Parameters also can be placed, or **pushed**, onto the **stack** by the program and **popped** off the stack by the operating system. Some operating systems prefer the block or stack method because those approaches do not limit the number or length of parameters being passed.

Figure 2.7   Passing of parameters as a table.

2.4 Types of System Calls

System calls can be grouped roughly into six major categories: **process control**, **file manipulation**, **device manipulation**, **information maintenance**, **communications**, and **protection**. In Sections 2.4.1 through 2.4.6, we briefly discuss the types of system calls that may be provided by an operating system. Most of these system calls support, or are supported by, concepts and functions that are discussed in later chapters. Figure 2.8 summarizes the types of system calls normally provided by an operating system. As mentioned, in this text, we normally refer to the system calls by generic names. Throughout the text, however, we provide examples of the actual counterparts to the system calls for Windows, UNIX, and Linux systems.

2.4.1 Process Control

A running program needs to be able to halt its execution either normally (end()) or abnormally (abort()). If a system call is made to terminate the currently running program abnormally, or if the program runs into a problem and causes an error trap, a dump of memory is sometimes taken and an error message generated. The dump is written to disk and may be examined by a **debugger**—a system program designed to aid the programmer in finding and correcting errors, or **bugs**—to determine the cause of the problem. Under either normal or abnormal circumstances, the operating system must transfer control to the invoking command interpreter. The command interpreter then reads the next command. In an interactive system, the command interpreter simply continues with the next command; it is assumed that the user will issue an appropriate command to respond to any error. In a GUI system, a pop-up window might alert the user to the error and ask for guidance. In a batch system, the command interpreter usually terminates the entire job and continues with the next job. Some systems may allow for special recovery actions in case an error occurs. If the program discovers an error in its input and wants to terminate abnormally, it may also want to define an error level. More severe errors can be indicated by a higher-level error parameter. It is then

- Process control
  - end, abort
  - load, execute
  - create process, terminate process
  - get process attributes, set process attributes
  - wait for time
  - wait event, signal event
  - allocate and free memory
- File management
  - create file, delete file
  - open, close
  - read, write, reposition
  - get file attributes, set file attributes
- Device management
  - request device, release device
  - read, write, reposition
  - get device attributes, set device attributes
  - logically attach or detach devices
- Information maintenance
  - get time or date, set time or date
  - get system data, set system data
  - get process, file, or device attributes
  - set process, file, or device attributes
- Communications
  - create, delete communication connection
  - send, receive messages
  - transfer status information
  - attach or detach remote devices

Figure 2.8 Types of system calls.

possible to combine normal and abnormal termination by defining a normal termination as an error at level 0. The command interpreter or a following program can use this error level to determine the next action automatically.

A process or job executing one program may want to load() and execute() another program. This feature allows the command interpreter to execute a program as directed by, for example, a user command, the click of a

EXAMPLES OF WINDOWS AND UNIX SYSTEM CALLS

	Windows	Unix
Process Control	CreateProcess() ExitProcess() WaitForSingleObject()	fork() exit() wait()
File Manipulation	CreateFile() ReadFile() WriteFile() CloseHandle()	open() read() write() close()
Device Manipulation	SetConsoleMode() ReadConsole() WriteConsole()	ioctl() read() write()
Information Maintenance	GetCurrentProcessID() SetTimer() Sleep()	getpid() alarm() sleep()
Communication	CreatePipe() CreateFileMapping() MapViewOfFile()	pipe() shm_open() mmap()
Protection	SetFileSecurity() InitlializeSecurityDescriptor() SetSecurityDescriptorGroup()	chmod() umask() chown()

mouse, or a batch command. An interesting question is where to return control when the loaded program terminates. This question is related to whether the existing program is lost, saved, or allowed to continue execution concurrently with the new program.

If control returns to the existing program when the new program terminates, we must save the memory image of the existing program; thus, we have effectively created a mechanism for one program to call another program. If both programs continue concurrently, we have created a new job or process to be multiprogrammed. Often, there is a system call specifically for this purpose (create_process() or submit_job()).

If we create a new job or process, or perhaps even a set of jobs or processes, we should be able to control its execution. This control requires the ability to determine and reset the attributes of a job or process, including the job's priority, its maximum allowable execution time, and so on (get_process_attributes() and set_process_attributes()). We may also want to terminate a job or process that we created (terminate_process()) if we find that it is incorrect or is no longer needed.

EXAMPLE OF STANDARD C LIBRARY

The standard C library provides a portion of the system-call interface for many versions of UNIX and Linux. As an example, let's assume a C program invokes the `printf()` statement. The C library intercepts this call and invokes the necessary system call (or calls) in the operating system—in this instance, the `write()` system call. The C library takes the value returned by `write()` and passes it back to the user program. This is shown below:

Having created new jobs or processes, we may need to wait for them to finish their execution. We may want to wait for a certain amount of time to pass (`wait_time()`). More probably, we will want to wait for a specific event to occur (`wait_event()`). The jobs or processes should then signal when that event has occurred (`signal_event()`).

Quite often, two or more processes may share data. To ensure the integrity of the data being shared, operating systems often provide system calls allowing a process to lock shared data. Then, no other process can access the data until the lock is released. Typically, such system calls include `acquire_lock()` and `release_lock()`. System calls of these types, dealing with the coordination of concurrent processes, are discussed in great detail in Chapter 5.

There are so many facets of and variations in process and job control that we next use two examples—one involving a single-tasking system and the other a multitasking system—to clarify these concepts. The MS-DOS operating system is an example of a single-tasking system. It has a command interpreter that is invoked when the computer is started (Figure 2.9(a)). Because MS-DOS is single-tasking, it uses a simple method to run a program and does not create a new process. It loads the program into memory, writing over most of itself to

(a)   (b)

Figure 2.9   MS-DOS execution. (a) At system startup. (b) Running a program.

give the program as much memory as possible (Figure 2.9(b)). Next, it sets the instruction pointer to the first instruction of the program. The program then runs, and either an error causes a trap, or the program executes a system call to terminate. In either case, the error code is saved in the system memory for later use. Following this action, the small portion of the command interpreter that was not overwritten resumes execution. Its first task is to reload the rest of the command interpreter from disk. Then the command interpreter makes the previous error code available to the user or to the next program.

FreeBSD (derived from Berkeley UNIX) is an example of a multitasking system. When a user logs on to the system, the shell of the user's choice is run. This shell is similar to the MS-DOS shell in that it accepts commands and executes programs that the user requests. However, since FreeBSD is a multitasking system, the command interpreter may continue running while another program is executed (Figure 2.10). To start a new process, the shell

Figure 2.10   FreeBSD running multiple programs.

executes a `fork()` system call. Then, the selected program is loaded into memory via an `exec()` system call, and the program is executed. Depending on the way the command was issued, the shell then either waits for the process to finish or runs the process "in the background." In the latter case, the shell immediately requests another command. When a process is running in the background, it cannot receive input directly from the keyboard, because the shell is using this resource. I/O is therefore done through files or through a GUI interface. Meanwhile, the user is free to ask the shell to run other programs, to monitor the progress of the running process, to change that program's priority, and so on. When the process is done, it executes an `exit()` system call to terminate, returning to the invoking process a status code of 0 or a nonzero error code. This status or error code is then available to the shell or other programs. Processes are discussed in Chapter 3 with a program example using the `fork()` and `exec()` system calls.

2.4.2 File Management

The file system is discussed in more detail in Chapter 10 and in Chapter 11. We can, however, identify several common system calls dealing with files.

We first need to be able to `create()` and `delete()` files. Either system call requires the name of the file and perhaps some of the file's attributes. Once the file is created, we need to `open()` it and to use it. We may also `read()`, `write()`, or `reposition()` (rewind or skip to the end of the file, for example). Finally, we need to `close()` the file, indicating that we are no longer using it.

We may need these same sets of operations for directories if we have a directory structure for organizing files in the file system. In addition, for either files or directories, we need to be able to determine the values of various attributes and perhaps to reset them if necessary. File attributes include the file name, file type, protection codes, accounting information, and so on. At least two system calls, `get_file_attributes()` and `set_file_attributes()`, are required for this function. Some operating systems provide many more calls, such as calls for file `move()` and `copy()`. Others might provide an API that performs those operations using code and other system calls, and others might provide system programs to perform those tasks. If the system programs are callable by other programs, then each can be considered an API by other system programs.

2.4.3 Device Management

A process may need several resources to execute—main memory, disk drives, access to files, and so on. If the resources are available, they can be granted, and control can be returned to the user process. Otherwise, the process will have to wait until sufficient resources are available.

The various resources controlled by the operating system can be thought of as devices. Some of these devices are physical devices (for example, disk drives), while others can be thought of as abstract or virtual devices (for example, files). A system with multiple users may require us to first `request()` a device, to ensure exclusive use of it. After we are finished with the device, we `release()` it. These functions are similar to the `open()` and `close()` system calls for files. Other operating systems allow unmanaged access to devices.

The hazard then is the potential for device contention and perhaps deadlock, which are described in Section 5.11.

Once the device has been requested (and allocated to us), we can read(), write(), and (possibly) reposition() the device, just as we can with files. In fact, the similarity between I/O devices and files is so great that many operating systems, including UNIX, merge the two into a combined file–device structure. In this case, a set of system calls is used on both files and devices. Sometimes, I/O devices are identified by special file names, directory placement, or file attributes.

The user interface can also make files and devices appear to be similar, even though the underlying system calls are dissimilar. This is another example of the many design decisions that go into building an operating system and user interface.

2.4.4   Information Maintenance

Many system calls exist simply for the purpose of transferring information between the user program and the operating system. For example, most systems have a system call to return the current time() and date(). Other system calls may return information about the system, such as the number of current users, the version number of the operating system, the amount of free memory or disk space, and so on.

Another set of system calls is helpful in debugging a program. Many systems provide system calls to dump() memory. This provision is useful for debugging. A program trace lists each system call as it is executed. Even microprocessors provide a CPU mode known as **single step**, in which a trap is executed by the CPU after every instruction. The trap is usually caught by a debugger.

Many operating systems provide a time profile of a program to indicate the amount of time that the program executes at a particular location or set of locations. A time profile requires either a tracing facility or regular timer interrupts. At every occurrence of the timer interrupt, the value of the program counter is recorded. With sufficiently frequent timer interrupts, a statistical picture of the time spent on various parts of the program can be obtained.

In addition, the operating system keeps information about all its processes, and system calls are used to access this information. Generally, calls are also used to reset the process information (get_process_attributes() and set_process_attributes()). In Section 3.1.3, we discuss what information is normally kept.

2.4.5   Communication

There are two common models of interprocess communication: the message-passing model and the shared-memory model. In the **message-passing model**, the communicating processes exchange messages with one another to transfer information. Messages can be exchanged between the processes either directly or indirectly through a common mailbox. Before communication can take place, a connection must be opened. The name of the other communicator must be known, be it another process on the same system or a process on another computer connected by a communications network. Each computer in a network has a **host name** by which it is commonly known. A host also has a network identifier, such as an IP address. Similarly, each process has a **process name**, and this name is translated into an identifier by which the operating system can refer to the process. The get_hostid() and get_processid() system calls do this translation. The identifiers are then passed to the general-purpose open() and close() calls provided by the file system or to specific open_connection() and close_connection() system calls, depending on the system's model of communication. The recipient process usually must give its permission for communication to take place with an accept_connection() call. Most processes that will be receiving connections are special-purpose **daemons**, which are system programs provided for that purpose. They execute a wait_for_connection() call and are awakened when a connection is made. The source of the communication, known as the **client**, and the receiving daemon, known as a **server**, then exchange messages by using read_message() and write_message() system calls. The close_connection() call terminates the communication.

In the **shared-memory model**, processes use shared_memory_create() and shared_memory_attach() system calls to create and gain access to regions of memory owned by other processes. Recall that, normally, the operating system tries to prevent one process from accessing another process's memory. Shared memory requires that two or more processes agree to remove this restriction. They can then exchange information by reading and writing data in the shared areas. The form of the data is determined by the processes and is not under the operating system's control. The processes are also responsible for ensuring that they are not writing to the same location simultaneously. Such mechanisms are discussed in Chapter 5. In Chapter 4, we look at a variation of the process scheme—threads—in which memory is shared by default.

Both of the models just discussed are common in operating systems, and most systems implement both. Message passing is useful for exchanging smaller amounts of data, because no conflicts need be avoided. It is also easier to implement than is shared memory for intercomputer communication. Shared memory allows maximum speed and convenience of communication, since it can be done at memory transfer speeds when it takes place within a computer. Problems exist, however, in the areas of protection and synchronization between the processes sharing memory.

2.4.6 Protection

Protection provides a mechanism for controlling access to the resources provided by a computer system. Historically, protection was a concern only on multiprogrammed computer systems with several users. However, with the advent of networking and the Internet, all computer systems, from servers to mobile handheld devices, must be concerned with protection.

Typically, system calls providing protection include set_permission() and get_permission(), which manipulate the permission settings of resources such as files and disks. The allow_user() and deny_user() system calls specify whether particular users can—or cannot—be allowed access to certain resources.

We cover protection in Chapter 13 and the much larger issue of security in Chapter 14.

2.5   System Programs

Another aspect of a modern system is its collection of system programs. Recall Figure 1.1, which depicted the logical computer hierarchy. At the lowest level is hardware. Next is the operating system, then the system programs, and finally the application programs. **System programs**, also known as **system utilities**, provide a convenient environment for program development and execution. Some of them are simply user interfaces to system calls. Others are considerably more complex. They can be divided into these categories:

- **File management**. These programs create, delete, copy, rename, print, dump, list, and generally manipulate files and directories.

- **Status information**. Some programs simply ask the system for the date, time, amount of available memory or disk space, number of users, or similar status information. Others are more complex, providing detailed performance, logging, and debugging information. Typically, these programs format and print the output to the terminal or other output devices or files or display it in a window of the GUI. Some systems also support a **registry**, which is used to store and retrieve configuration information.

- **File modification**. Several text editors may be available to create and modify the content of files stored on disk or other storage devices. There may also be special commands to search contents of files or perform transformations of the text.

- **Programming-language support**. Compilers, assemblers, debuggers, and interpreters for common programming languages (such as C, C++, Java, and PERL) are often provided with the operating system or available as a separate download.

- **Program loading and execution**. Once a program is assembled or compiled, it must be loaded into memory to be executed. The system may provide absolute loaders, relocatable loaders, linkage editors, and overlay loaders. Debugging systems for either higher-level languages or machine language are needed as well.

- **Communications**. These programs provide the mechanism for creating virtual connections among processes, users, and computer systems. They allow users to send messages to one another's screens, to browse Web pages, to send e-mail messages, to log in remotely, or to transfer files from one machine to another.

- **Background services**. All general-purpose systems have methods for launching certain system-program processes at boot time. Some of these processes terminate after completing their tasks, while others continue to run until the system is halted. Constantly running system-program processes are known as **services**, **subsystems**, or daemons. One example is the network daemon discussed in Section 2.4.5. In that example, a system needed a service to listen for network connections in order to connect those requests to the correct processes. Other examples include process schedulers that start processes according to a specified schedule, system error monitoring services, and print servers. Typical systems have dozens of daemons. In addition, operating systems that run important activities in user context rather than in kernel context may use daemons to run these activities.

Along with system programs, most operating systems are supplied with programs that are useful in solving common problems or performing common operations. Such **application programs** include Web browsers, word processors and text formatters, spreadsheets, database systems, compilers, plotting and statistical-analysis packages, and games.

The view of the operating system seen by most users is defined by the application and system programs, rather than by the actual system calls. Consider a user's PC. When a user's computer is running the Mac OS X operating system, the user might see the GUI, featuring a mouse-and-windows interface. Alternatively, or even in one of the windows, the user might have a command-line UNIX shell. Both use the same set of system calls, but the system calls look different and act in different ways. Further confusing the user view, consider the user dual-booting from Mac OS X into Windows. Now the same user on the same hardware has two entirely different interfaces and two sets of applications using the same physical resources. On the same hardware, then, a user can be exposed to multiple user interfaces sequentially or concurrently.

2.6   Operating-System Design and Implementation

In this section, we discuss problems we face in designing and implementing an operating system. There are, of course, no complete solutions to such problems, but there are approaches that have proved successful.

2.6.1   Design Goals

The first problem in designing a system is to define goals and specifications. At the highest level, the design of the system will be affected by the choice of hardware and the type of system: batch, time sharing, single user, multiuser, distributed, real time, or general purpose.

Beyond this highest design level, the requirements may be much harder to specify. The requirements can, however, be divided into two basic groups: **user goals** and **system goals**.

Users want certain obvious properties in a system. The system should be convenient to use, easy to learn and to use, reliable, safe, and fast. Of course, these specifications are not particularly useful in the system design, since there is no general agreement on how to achieve them.

A similar set of requirements can be defined by those people who must design, create, maintain, and operate the system. The system should be easy to design, implement, and maintain; and it should be flexible, reliable, error free, and efficient. Again, these requirements are vague and may be interpreted in various ways.

There is, in short, no unique solution to the problem of defining the requirements for an operating system. The wide range of systems in existence shows that different requirements can result in a large variety of solutions for different environments. For example, the requirements for VxWorks, a real-time operating system for embedded systems, must have been substantially different from those for MVS, a large multiuser, multiaccess operating system for IBM mainframes.

Specifying and designing an operating system is a highly creative task. Although no textbook can tell you how to do it, general principles have been developed in the field of software engineering, and we turn now to a discussion of some of these principles.

2.6.2 Mechanisms and Policies

One important principle is the separation of policy from mechanism. Mechanisms determine *how* to do something; policies determine *what* will be done. For example, the timer construct (see Section 1.5.2) is a mechanism for ensuring CPU protection, but deciding how long the timer is to be set for a particular user is a policy decision.

The separation of policy and mechanism is important for flexibility. Policies are likely to change across places or over time. In the worst case, each change in policy would require a change in the underlying mechanism. A general mechanism insensitive to changes in policy would be more desirable. A change in policy would then require redefinition of only certain parameters of the system. For instance, consider a mechanism for giving priority to certain types of programs over others. If the mechanism is properly separated from policy, it can be used either to support a policy decision that I/O-intensive programs should have priority over CPU-intensive ones or to support the opposite policy.

Microkernel-based operating systems (Section 2.7.3) take the separation of mechanism and policy to one extreme by implementing a basic set of primitive building blocks. These blocks are almost policy free, allowing more advanced mechanisms and policies to be added via user-created kernel modules or user programs themselves. As an example, consider the history of UNIX. At first, it had a time-sharing scheduler. In the latest version of Solaris, scheduling is controlled by loadable tables. Depending on the table currently loaded, the system can be time sharing, batch processing, real time, fair share, or any combination. Making the scheduling mechanism general purpose allows vast policy changes to be made with a single `load-new-table` command. At the other extreme is a system such as Windows, in which both mechanism and policy are encoded in the system to enforce a global look and feel. All applications have similar interfaces, because the interface itself is built into the kernel and system libraries. The Mac OS X operating system has similar functionality.

Policy decisions are important for all resource allocation. Whenever it is necessary to decide whether or not to allocate a resource, a policy decision must be made. Whenever the question is *how* rather than *what*, it is a mechanism that must be determined.

2.6.3 Implementation

Once an operating system is designed, it must be implemented. Because operating systems are collections of many programs, written by many people over a long period of time, it is difficult to make general statements about how they are implemented.

Early operating systems were written in assembly language. Now, although some operating systems are still written in assembly language, most are written in a higher-level language such as C or an even higher-level language such as C++. Actually, an operating system can be written in more than one language. The lowest levels of the kernel might be assembly language. Higher-level routines might be in C, and system programs might be in C or C++, in interpreted scripting languages like PERL or Python, or in shell scripts. In fact, a given Linux distribution probably includes programs written in all of those languages.

The first system that was not written in assembly language was probably the Master Control Program (MCP) for Burroughs computers. MCP was written in a variant of ALGOL. MULTICS, developed at MIT, was written mainly in the system programming language PL/1. The Linux and Windows operating system kernels are written mostly in C, although there are some small sections of assembly code for device drivers and for saving and restoring the state of registers.

The advantages of using a higher-level language, or at least a systems-implementation language, for implementing operating systems are the same as those gained when the language is used for application programs: the code can be written faster, is more compact, and is easier to understand and debug. In addition, improvements in compiler technology will improve the generated code for the entire operating system by simple recompilation. Finally, an operating system is far easier to **port**—to move to some other hardware— if it is written in a higher-level language. For example, MS-DOS was written in Intel 8088 assembly language. Consequently, it runs natively only on the Intel x86 family of CPUs. (Note that although MS-DOS runs natively only on Intel x86, emulators of the x86 instruction set allow the operating system to run on other CPUs—but more slowly, and with higher resource use. As we mentioned in Chapter 1, **emulators** are programs that duplicate the functionality of one system on another system.) The Linux operating system, in contrast, is written mostly in C and is available natively on a number of different CPUs, including Intel x86, Oracle SPARC, and IBM PowerPC.

The only possible disadvantages of implementing an operating system in a higher-level language are reduced speed and increased storage requirements. This, however, is no longer a major issue in today's systems. Although an expert assembly-language programmer can produce efficient small routines, for large programs a modern compiler can perform complex analysis and apply sophisticated optimizations that produce excellent code. Modern processors have deep pipelining and multiple functional units that can handle the details of complex dependencies much more easily than can the human mind.

As is true in other systems, major performance improvements in operating systems are more likely to be the result of better data structures and algorithms than of excellent assembly-language code. In addition, although operating systems are large, only a small amount of the code is critical to high performance; the interrupt handler, I/O manager, memory manager, and CPU scheduler are probably the most critical routines. After the system is written and is working correctly, bottleneck routines can be identified and can be replaced with assembly-language equivalents.

2.7   Operating-System Structure

A system as large and complex as a modern operating system must be engineered carefully if it is to function properly and be modified easily. A common approach is to partition the task into small components, or modules, rather than have one **monolithic** system. Each of these modules should be a well-defined portion of the system, with carefully defined inputs, outputs, and functions. We have already discussed briefly in Chapter 1 the common components of operating systems. In this section, we discuss how these components are interconnected and melded into a kernel.

2.7.1   Simple Structure

Many operating systems do not have well-defined structures. Frequently, such systems started as small, simple, and limited systems and then grew beyond their original scope. MS-DOS is an example of such a system. It was originally designed and implemented by a few people who had no idea that it would become so popular. It was written to provide the most functionality in the least space, so it was not carefully divided into modules. Figure 2.11 shows its structure.

In MS-DOS, the interfaces and levels of functionality are not well separated. For instance, application programs are able to access the basic I/O routines to write directly to the display and disk drives. Such freedom leaves MS-DOS vulnerable to errant (or malicious) programs, causing entire system crashes when user programs fail. Of course, MS-DOS was also limited by the hardware of its era. Because the Intel 8088 for which it was written provides no dual mode and no hardware protection, the designers of MS-DOS had no choice but to leave the base hardware accessible.

Another example of limited structuring is the original UNIX operating system. Like MS-DOS, UNIX initially was limited by hardware functionality. It consists of two separable parts: the kernel and the system programs. The kernel

Figure 2.11   MS-DOS layer structure.

Figure 2.12 Traditional UNIX system structure.

is further separated into a series of interfaces and device drivers, which have been added and expanded over the years as UNIX has evolved. We can view the traditional UNIX operating system as being layered to some extent, as shown in Figure 2.12. Everything below the system-call interface and above the physical hardware is the kernel. The kernel provides the file system, CPU scheduling, memory management, and other operating-system functions through system calls. Taken in sum, that is an enormous amount of functionality to be combined into one level. This monolithic structure was difficult to implement and maintain. It had a distinct performance advantage, however: there is very little overhead in the system call interface or in communication within the kernel. We still see evidence of this simple, monolithic structure in the UNIX, Linux, and Windows operating systems.

2.7.2 Layered Approach

With proper hardware support, operating systems can be broken into pieces that are smaller and more appropriate than those allowed by the original MS-DOS and UNIX systems. The operating system can then retain much greater control over the computer and over the applications that make use of that computer. Implementers have more freedom in changing the inner workings of the system and in creating modular operating systems. Under a top-down approach, the overall functionality and features are determined and are separated into components. Information hiding is also important, because it leaves programmers free to implement the low-level routines as they see fit, provided that the external interface of the routine stays unchanged and that the routine itself performs the advertised task.

A system can be made modular in many ways. One method is the **layered approach**, in which the operating system is broken into a number of layers (levels). The bottom layer (layer 0) is the hardware; the highest (layer N) is the user interface. This layering structure is depicted in Figure 2.13.

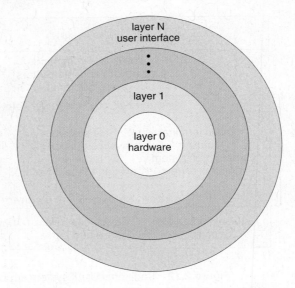

Figure 2.13 A layered operating system.

An operating-system layer is an implementation of an abstract object made up of data and the operations that can manipulate those data. A typical operating-system layer—say, layer M—consists of data structures and a set of routines that can be invoked by higher-level layers. Layer M, in turn, can invoke operations on lower-level layers.

The main advantage of the layered approach is simplicity of construction and debugging. The layers are selected so that each uses functions (operations) and services of only lower-level layers. This approach simplifies debugging and system verification. The first layer can be debugged without any concern for the rest of the system, because, by definition, it uses only the basic hardware (which is assumed correct) to implement its functions. Once the first layer is debugged, its correct functioning can be assumed while the second layer is debugged, and so on. If an error is found during the debugging of a particular layer, the error must be on that layer, because the layers below it are already debugged. Thus, the design and implementation of the system are simplified.

Each layer is implemented only with operations provided by lower-level layers. A layer does not need to know how these operations are implemented; it needs to know only what these operations do. Hence, each layer hides the existence of certain data structures, operations, and hardware from higher-level layers.

The major difficulty with the layered approach involves appropriately defining the various layers. Because a layer can use only lower-level layers, careful planning is necessary. For example, the device driver for the backing store (disk space used by virtual-memory algorithms) must be at a lower level than the memory-management routines, because memory management requires the ability to use the backing store.

Other requirements may not be so obvious. The backing-store driver would normally be above the CPU scheduler, because the driver may need to wait for I/O and the CPU can be rescheduled during this time. However, on a large system, the CPU scheduler may have more information about all the active processes than can fit in memory. Therefore, this information may need to be swapped in and out of memory, requiring the backing-store driver routine to be below the CPU scheduler.

A final problem with layered implementations is that they tend to be less efficient than other types. For instance, when a user program executes an I/O operation, it executes a system call that is trapped to the I/O layer, which calls the memory-management layer, which in turn calls the CPU-scheduling layer, which is then passed to the hardware. At each layer, the parameters may be modified, data may need to be passed, and so on. Each layer adds overhead to the system call. The net result is a system call that takes longer than does one on a nonlayered system.

These limitations have caused a small backlash against layering in recent years. Fewer layers with more functionality are being designed, providing most of the advantages of modularized code while avoiding the problems of layer definition and interaction.

2.7.3 Microkernels

We have already seen that as UNIX expanded, the kernel became large and difficult to manage. In the mid-1980s, researchers at Carnegie Mellon University developed an operating system called **Mach** that modularized the kernel using the **microkernel** approach. This method structures the operating system by removing all nonessential components from the kernel and implementing them as system and user-level programs. The result is a smaller kernel. There is little consensus regarding which services should remain in the kernel and which should be implemented in user space. Typically, however, microkernels provide minimal process and memory management, in addition to a communication facility. Figure 2.14 illustrates the architecture of a typical microkernel.

The main function of the microkernel is to provide communication between the client program and the various services that are also running in user space. Communication is provided through **message passing**, which was described in Section 2.4.5. For example, if the client program wishes to access a file, it

Figure 2.14 Architecture of a typical microkernel.

must interact with the file server. The client program and service never interact directly. Rather, they communicate indirectly by exchanging messages with the microkernel.

One benefit of the microkernel approach is that it makes extending the operating system easier. All new services are added to user space and consequently do not require modification of the kernel. When the kernel does have to be modified, the changes tend to be fewer, because the microkernel is a smaller kernel. The resulting operating system is easier to port from one hardware design to another. The microkernel also provides more security and reliability, since most services are running as user—rather than kernel—processes. If a service fails, the rest of the operating system remains untouched.

Some contemporary operating systems have used the microkernel approach. Tru64 UNIX (formerly Digital UNIX) provides a UNIX interface to the user, but it is implemented with a Mach kernel. The Mach kernel maps UNIX system calls into messages to the appropriate user-level services. The Mac OS X kernel (also known as **Darwin**) is also partly based on the Mach microkernel.

Another example is QNX, a real-time operating system for embedded systems. The QNX Neutrino microkernel provides services for message passing and process scheduling. It also handles low-level network communication and hardware interrupts. All other services in QNX are provided by standard processes that run outside the kernel in user mode.

Unfortunately, the performance of microkernels can suffer due to increased system-function overhead. Consider the history of Windows NT. The first release had a layered microkernel organization. This version's performance was low compared with that of Windows 95. Windows NT 4.0 partially corrected the performance problem by moving layers from user space to kernel space and integrating them more closely. By the time Windows XP was designed, Windows architecture had become more monolithic than microkernel.

2.7.4 Modules

Perhaps the best current methodology for operating-system design involves using **loadable kernel modules**. Here, the kernel has a set of core components and links in additional services via modules, either at boot time or during run time. This type of design is common in modern implementations of UNIX, such as Solaris, Linux, and Mac OS X, as well as Windows.

The idea of the design is for the kernel to provide core services while other services are implemented dynamically, as the kernel is running. Linking services dynamically is preferable to adding new features directly to the kernel, which would require recompiling the kernel every time a change was made. Thus, for example, we might build CPU scheduling and memory management algorithms directly into the kernel and then add support for different file systems by way of loadable modules.

The overall result resembles a layered system in that each kernel section has defined, protected interfaces; but it is more flexible than a layered system, because any module can call any other module. The approach is also similar to the microkernel approach in that the primary module has only core functions and knowledge of how to load and communicate with other modules; but it

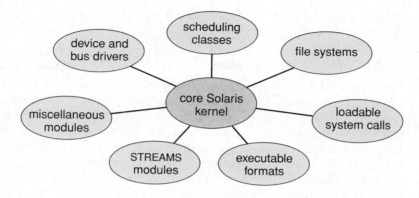

Figure 2.15   Solaris loadable modules.

is more efficient, because modules do not need to invoke message passing in order to communicate.

The Solaris operating system structure, shown in Figure 2.15, is organized around a core kernel with seven types of loadable kernel modules:

1. Scheduling classes

2. File systems

3. Loadable system calls

4. Executable formats

5. STREAMS modules

6. Miscellaneous

7. Device and bus drivers

Linux also uses loadable kernel modules, primarily for supporting device drivers and file systems. We cover creating loadable kernel modules in Linux as a programming exercise at the end of this chapter.

2.7.5   Hybrid Systems

In practice, very few operating systems adopt a single, strictly defined structure. Instead, they combine different structures, resulting in hybrid systems that address performance, security, and usability issues. For example, both Linux and Solaris are monolithic, because having the operating system in a single address space provides very efficient performance. However, they are also modular, so that new functionality can be dynamically added to the kernel. Windows is largely monolithic as well (again primarily for performance reasons), but it retains some behavior typical of microkernel systems, including providing support for separate subsystems (known as operating-system *personalities*) that run as user-mode processes. Windows systems also provide support for dynamically loadable kernel modules. We provide a case study of Linux in Chapter 15. In the remainder of this section, we explore the structure of three hybrid systems: the Apple Mac OS X operating system and the two most prominent mobile operating systems—iOS and Android.

2.7.5.1   Mac OS X

The Apple Mac OS X operating system uses a hybrid structure. As shown in Figure 2.16, it is a layered system. The top layers include the *Aqua* user interface (Figure 2.4) and a set of application environments and services. Notably, the Cocoa environment specifies an API for the Objective-C programming language, which is used for writing Mac OS X applications. Below these layers is the *kernel environment*, which consists primarily of the Mach microkernel and the BSD UNIX kernel. Mach provides memory management; support for remote procedure calls (RPCs) and interprocess communication (IPC) facilities, including message passing; and thread scheduling. The BSD component provides a BSD command-line interface, support for networking and file systems, and an implementation of POSIX APIs, including Pthreads. In addition to Mach and BSD, the kernel environment provides an I/O kit for development of device drivers and dynamically loadable modules (which Mac OS X refers to as **kernel extensions**). As shown in Figure 2.16, the BSD application environment can make use of BSD facilities directly.

2.7.5.2   iOS

iOS is a mobile operating system designed by Apple to run its smartphone, the *iPhone*, as well as its tablet computer, the *iPad*. iOS is structured on the Mac OS X operating system, with added functionality pertinent to mobile devices, but does not directly run Mac OS X applications. The structure of iOS appears in Figure 2.17.

Cocoa Touch is an API for Objective-C that provides several frameworks for developing applications that run on iOS devices. The fundamental difference between Cocoa, mentioned earlier, and Cocoa Touch is that the latter provides support for hardware features unique to mobile devices, such as touch screens. The media services layer provides services for graphics, audio, and video.

Figure 2.16   The Mac OS X structure.

Figure 2.17 Architecture of Apple's iOS.

The **core services** layer provides a variety of features, including support for cloud computing and databases. The bottom layer represents the core operating system, which is based on the kernel environment shown in Figure 2.16.

2.7.5.3 Android

The Android operating system was designed by the Open Handset Alliance (led primarily by Google) and was developed for Android smartphones and tablet computers. Whereas iOS is designed to run on Apple mobile devices and is close-sourced, Android runs on a variety of mobile platforms and is open-sourced, partly explaining its rapid rise in popularity. The structure of Android appears in Figure 2.18.

Android is similar to iOS in that it is a layered stack of software that provides a rich set of frameworks for developing mobile applications. At the bottom of this software stack is the Linux kernel, although it has been modified by Google and is currently outside the normal distribution of Linux releases.

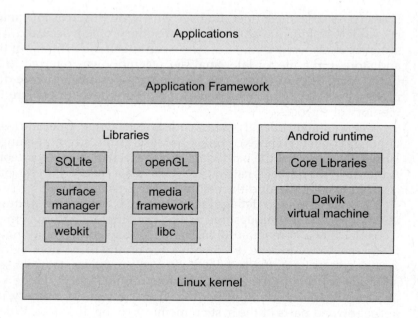

Figure 2.18 Architecture of Google's Android.

Linux is used primarily for process, memory, and device-driver support for hardware and has been expanded to include power management. The Android runtime environment includes a core set of libraries as well as the Dalvik virtual machine. Software designers for Android devices develop applications in the Java language. However, rather than using the standard Java API, Google has designed a separate Android API for Java development. The Java class files are first compiled to Java bytecode and then translated into an executable file that runs on the Dalvik virtual machine. The Dalvik virtual machine was designed for Android and is optimized for mobile devices with limited memory and CPU processing capabilities.

The set of libraries available for Android applications includes frameworks for developing web browsers (webkit), database support (SQLite), and multimedia. The libc library is similar to the standard C library but is much smaller and has been designed for the slower CPUs that characterize mobile devices.

2.8 Operating-System Debugging

We have mentioned debugging frequently in this chapter. Here, we take a closer look. Broadly, **debugging** is the activity of finding and fixing errors in a system, both in hardware and in software. Performance problems are considered bugs, so debugging can also include **performance tuning**, which seeks to improve performance by removing processing **bottlenecks**. In this section, we explore debugging process and kernel errors and performance problems. Hardware debugging is outside the scope of this text.

2.8.1 Failure Analysis

If a process fails, most operating systems write the error information to a **log file** to alert system operators or users that the problem occurred. The operating system can also take a **core dump**—a capture of the memory of the process—and store it in a file for later analysis. (Memory was referred to as the "core" in the early days of computing.) Running programs and core dumps can be probed by a debugger, which allows a programmer to explore the code and memory of a process.

Debugging user-level process code is a challenge. Operating-system kernel debugging is even more complex because of the size and complexity of the kernel, its control of the hardware, and the lack of user-level debugging tools. A failure in the kernel is called a **crash**. When a crash occurs, error information is saved to a log file, and the memory state is saved to a **crash dump**.

Operating-system debugging and process debugging frequently use different tools and techniques due to the very different nature of these two tasks. Consider that a kernel failure in the file-system code would make it risky for the kernel to try to save its state to a file on the file system before rebooting. A common technique is to save the kernel's memory state to a section of disk set aside for this purpose that contains no file system. If the kernel detects an unrecoverable error, it writes the entire contents of memory, or at least the kernel-owned parts of the system memory, to the disk area. When the system reboots, a process runs to gather the data from that area and write it to a crash

Kernighan's Law

"Debugging is twice as hard as writing the code in the first place. Therefore, if you write the code as cleverly as possible, you are, by definition, not smart enough to debug it."

dump file within a file system for analysis. Obviously, such strategies would be unnecessary for debugging ordinary user-level processes.

2.8.2   Performance Tuning

We mentioned earlier that performance tuning seeks to improve performance by removing processing bottlenecks. To identify bottlenecks, we must be able to monitor system performance. Thus, the operating system must have some means of computing and displaying measures of system behavior. In a number of systems, the operating system does this by producing *trace listings* of system behavior. All interesting events are logged with their time and important parameters and are written to a file. Later, an analysis program can process the log file to determine system performance and to identify bottlenecks and inefficiencies. These same traces can be run as input for a simulation of a suggested improved system. Traces also can help people to find errors in operating-system behavior.

Another approach to performance tuning uses single-purpose, interactive tools that allow users and administrators to question the state of various system components to look for bottlenecks. One such tool employs the UNIX command top to display the resources used on the system, as well as a sorted list of the "top" resource-using processes. Other tools display the state of disk I/O, memory allocation, and network traffic.

The **Windows Task Manager** is a similar tool for Windows systems. The task manager includes information for current applications as well as processes, CPU and memory usage, and networking statistics. A screen shot of the task manager appears in Figure 2.19.

Making operating systems easier to understand, debug, and tune as they run is an active area of research and implementation. A new generation of kernel-enabled performance analysis tools has made significant improvements in how this goal can be achieved. Next, we discuss a leading example of such a tool: the Solaris 10 DTrace dynamic tracing facility.

2.8.3   DTrace

DTrace is a facility that dynamically adds probes to a running system, both in user processes and in the kernel. These probes can be queried via the D programming language to determine an astonishing amount about the kernel, the system state, and process activities. For example, Figure 2.20 follows an application as it executes a system call (ioctl()) and shows the functional calls within the kernel as they execute to perform the system call. Lines ending with "U" are executed in user mode, and lines ending in "K" in kernel mode.

Figure 2.19   The Windows task manager.

Debugging the interactions between user-level and kernel code is nearly impossible without a toolset that understands both sets of code and can instrument the interactions. For that toolset to be truly useful, it must be able to debug any area of a system, including areas that were not written with debugging in mind, and do so without affecting system reliability. This tool must also have a minimum performance impact—ideally it should have no impact when not in use and a proportional impact during use. The DTrace tool meets these requirements and provides a dynamic, safe, low-impact debugging environment.

Until the DTrace framework and tools became available with Solaris 10, kernel debugging was usually shrouded in mystery and accomplished via happenstance and archaic code and tools. For example, CPUs have a breakpoint feature that will halt execution and allow a debugger to examine the state of the system. Then execution can continue until the next breakpoint or termination. This method cannot be used in a multiuser operating-system kernel without negatively affecting all of the users on the system. **Profiling**, which periodically samples the instruction pointer to determine which code is being executed, can show statistical trends but not individual activities. Code can be included in the kernel to emit specific data under specific circumstances, but that code slows down the kernel and tends not to be included in the part of the kernel where the specific problem being debugged is occurring.

```
# ./all.d 'pgrep xclock' XEventsQueued
dtrace: script './all.d' matched 52377 probes
CPU FUNCTION
  0  -> XEventsQueued                         U
  0     -> _XEventsQueued                     U
  0        -> _X11TransBytesReadable          U
  0        <- _X11TransBytesReadable          U
  0        -> _X11TransSocketBytesReadable    U
  0        <- _X11TransSocketBytesreadable    U
  0        -> ioctl                           U
  0           -> ioctl                        K
  0              -> getf                      K
  0                 -> set_active_fd          K
  0                 <- set_active_fd          K
  0              <- getf                      K
  0              -> get_udatamodel            K
  0              <- get_udatamodel            K
...
  0              -> releasef                  K
  0                 -> clear_active_fd        K
  0                 <- clear_active_fd        K
  0                 -> cv_broadcast           K
  0                 <- cv_broadcast           K
  0              <- releasef                  K
  0           <- ioctl                        K
  0        <- ioctl                           U
  0     <- _XEventsQueued                     U
  0  <- XEventsQueued                         U
```

Figure 2.20   Solaris 10 `dtrace` follows a system call within the kernel.

In contrast, DTrace runs on production systems—systems that are running important or critical applications—and causes no harm to the system. It slows activities while enabled, but after execution it resets the system to its pre-debugging state. It is also a broad and deep tool. It can broadly debug everything happening in the system (both at the user and kernel levels and between the user and kernel layers). It can also delve deep into code, showing individual CPU instructions or kernel subroutine activities.

DTrace is composed of a compiler, a framework, **providers** of **probes** written within that framework, and **consumers** of those probes. DTrace providers create probes. Kernel structures exist to keep track of all probes that the providers have created. The probes are stored in a hash-table data structure that is hashed by name and indexed according to unique probe identifiers. When a probe is enabled, a bit of code in the area to be probed is rewritten to call `dtrace_probe(probe identifier)` and then continue with the code's original operation. Different providers create different kinds of probes. For example, a kernel system-call probe works differently from a user-process probe, and that is different from an I/O probe.

DTrace features a compiler that generates a byte code that is run in the kernel. This code is assured to be "safe" by the compiler. For example, no loops are allowed, and only specific kernel state modifications are allowed when specifically requested. Only users with DTrace "privileges" (or "root" users) are allowed to use DTrace, as it can retrieve private kernel data (and modify data if requested). The generated code runs in the kernel and enables probes. It also enables consumers in user mode and enables communications between the two.

A DTrace consumer is code that is interested in a probe and its results. A consumer requests that the provider create one or more probes. When a probe fires, it emits data that are managed by the kernel. Within the kernel, actions called **enabling control blocks**, or ECBs, are performed when probes fire. One probe can cause multiple ECBs to execute if more than one consumer is interested in that probe. Each ECB contains a predicate ("if statement") that can filter out that ECB. Otherwise, the list of actions in the ECB is executed. The most common action is to capture some bit of data, such as a variable's value at that point of the probe execution. By gathering such data, a complete picture of a user or kernel action can be built. Further, probes firing from both user space and the kernel can show how a user-level action caused kernel-level reactions. Such data are invaluable for performance monitoring and code optimization.

Once the probe consumer terminates, its ECBs are removed. If there are no ECBs consuming a probe, the probe is removed. That involves rewriting the code to remove the `dtrace_probe()` call and put back the original code. Thus, before a probe is created and after it is destroyed, the system is exactly the same, as if no probing occurred.

DTrace takes care to assure that probes do not use too much memory or CPU capacity, which could harm the running system. The buffers used to hold the probe results are monitored for exceeding default and maximum limits. CPU time for probe execution is monitored as well. If limits are exceeded, the consumer is terminated, along with the offending probes. Buffers are allocated per CPU to avoid contention and data loss.

An example of D code and its output shows some of its utility. The following program shows the DTrace code to enable scheduler probes and record the amount of CPU time of each process running with user ID 101 while those probes are enabled (that is, while the program runs):

```
sched:::on-cpu
uid == 101
{
    self->ts = timestamp;
}

sched:::off-cpu
self->ts
{
    @time[execname] = sum(timestamp - self->ts);
    self->ts = 0;
}
```

The output of the program, showing the processes and how much time (in nanoseconds) they spend running on the CPUs, is shown in Figure 2.21.

Because DTrace is part of the open-source OpenSolaris version of the Solaris 10 operating system, it has been added to other operating systems when those

```
# dtrace -s sched.d
dtrace: script 'sched.d' matched 6 probes
^C
        gnome-settings-d                    142354
        gnome-vfs-daemon                    158243
        dsdm                                189804
        wnck-applet                         200030
        gnome-panel                         277864
        clock-applet                        374916
        mapping-daemon                      385475
        xscreensaver                        514177
        metacity                            539281
        Xorg                               2579646
        gnome-terminal                     5007269
        mixer_applet2                      7388447
        java                              10769137
```

Figure 2.21   Output of the D code.

systems do not have conflicting license agreements. For example, DTrace has been added to Mac OS X and FreeBSD and will likely spread further due to its unique capabilities. Other operating systems, especially the Linux derivatives, are adding kernel-tracing functionality as well. Still other operating systems are beginning to include performance and tracing tools fostered by research at various institutions, including the Paradyn project.

2.9   Operating-System Generation

It is possible to design, code, and implement an operating system specifically for one machine at one site. More commonly, however, operating systems are designed to run on any of a class of machines at a variety of sites with a variety of peripheral configurations. The system must then be configured or generated for each specific computer site, a process sometimes known as **system generation** (SYSGEN).

The operating system is normally distributed on disk, on CD-ROM or DVD-ROM, or as an "ISO" image, which is a file in the format of a CD-ROM or DVD-ROM. To generate a system, we use a special program. This SYSGEN program reads from a given file, or asks the operator of the system for information concerning the specific configuration of the hardware system, or probes the hardware directly to determine what components are there. The following kinds of information must be determined.

- What CPU is to be used? What options (extended instruction sets, floating-point arithmetic, and so on) are installed? For multiple CPU systems, each CPU may be described.

- How will the boot disk be formatted? How many sections, or "partitions," will it be separated into, and what will go into each partition?

- How much memory is available? Some systems will determine this value themselves by referencing memory location after memory location until an "illegal address" fault is generated. This procedure defines the final legal address and hence the amount of available memory.

- What devices are available? The system will need to know how to address each device (the device number), the device interrupt number, the device's type and model, and any special device characteristics.

- What operating-system options are desired, or what parameter values are to be used? These options or values might include how many buffers of which sizes should be used, what type of CPU-scheduling algorithm is desired, what the maximum number of processes to be supported is, and so on.

Once this information is determined, it can be used in several ways. At one extreme, a system administrator can use it to modify a copy of the source code of the operating system. The operating system then is completely compiled. Data declarations, initializations, and constants, along with conditional compilation, produce an output-object version of the operating system that is tailored to the system described.

At a slightly less tailored level, the system description can lead to the creation of tables and the selection of modules from a precompiled library. These modules are linked together to form the generated operating system. Selection allows the library to contain the device drivers for all supported I/O devices, but only those needed are linked into the operating system. Because the system is not recompiled, system generation is faster, but the resulting system may be overly general.

At the other extreme, it is possible to construct a system that is completely table driven. All the code is always part of the system, and selection occurs at execution time, rather than at compile or link time. System generation involves simply creating the appropriate tables to describe the system.

The major differences among these approaches are the size and generality of the generated system and the ease of modifying it as the hardware configuration changes. Consider the cost of modifying the system to support a newly acquired graphics terminal or another disk drive. Balanced against that cost, of course, is the frequency (or infrequency) of such changes.

2.10   System Boot

After an operating system is generated, it must be made available for use by the hardware. But how does the hardware know where the kernel is or how to load that kernel? The procedure of starting a computer by loading the kernel is known as booting the system. On most computer systems, a small piece of code known as the bootstrap program or bootstrap loader locates the kernel, loads it into main memory, and starts its execution. Some computer systems, such as PCs, use a two-step process in which a simple bootstrap loader fetches a more complex boot program from disk, which in turn loads the kernel.

When a CPU receives a reset event—for instance, when it is powered up or rebooted—the instruction register is loaded with a predefined memory location, and execution starts there. At that location is the initial bootstrap program. This program is in the form of read-only memory (ROM), because the RAM is in an unknown state at system startup. ROM is convenient because it needs no initialization and cannot easily be infected by a computer virus.

The bootstrap program can perform a variety of tasks. Usually, one task is to run diagnostics to determine the state of the machine. If the diagnostics pass, the program can continue with the booting steps. It can also initialize all aspects of the system, from CPU registers to device controllers and the contents of main memory. Sooner or later, it starts the operating system.

Some systems—such as cellular phones, tablets, and game consoles—store the entire operating system in ROM. Storing the operating system in ROM is suitable for small operating systems, simple supporting hardware, and rugged operation. A problem with this approach is that changing the bootstrap code requires changing the ROM hardware chips. Some systems resolve this problem by using **erasable programmable read-only memory** (EPROM), which is read-only except when explicitly given a command to become writable. All forms of ROM are also known as **firmware**, since their characteristics fall somewhere between those of hardware and those of software. A problem with firmware in general is that executing code there is slower than executing code in RAM. Some systems store the operating system in firmware and copy it to RAM for fast execution. A final issue with firmware is that it is relatively expensive, so usually only small amounts are available.

For large operating systems (including most general-purpose operating systems like Windows, Mac OS X, and UNIX) or for systems that change frequently, the bootstrap loader is stored in firmware, and the operating system is on disk. In this case, the bootstrap runs diagnostics and has a bit of code that can read a single block at a fixed location (say block zero) from disk into memory and execute the code from that **boot block**. The program stored in the boot block may be sophisticated enough to load the entire operating system into memory and begin its execution. More typically, it is simple code (as it fits in a single disk block) and knows only the address on disk and length of the remainder of the bootstrap program. **GRUB** is an example of an open-source bootstrap program for Linux systems. All of the disk-bound bootstrap, and the operating system itself, can be easily changed by writing new versions to disk. A disk that has a boot partition (more on that in Section 9.5.1) is called a **boot disk** or **system disk**.

Now that the full bootstrap program has been loaded, it can traverse the file system to find the operating system kernel, load it into memory, and start its execution. It is only at this point that the system is said to be **running**.

2.11 Summary

Operating systems provide a number of services. At the lowest level, system calls allow a running program to make requests from the operating system directly. At a higher level, the command interpreter or shell provides a mechanism for a user to issue a request without writing a program. Commands may come from files during batch-mode execution or directly from a terminal or desktop GUI when in an interactive or time-shared mode. System programs are provided to satisfy many common user requests.

The types of requests vary according to level. The system-call level must provide the basic functions, such as process control and file and device manipulation. Higher-level requests, satisfied by the command interpreter or system programs, are translated into a sequence of system calls. System services can be classified into several categories: program control, status requests, and I/O requests. Program errors can be considered implicit requests for service.

The design of a new operating system is a major task. It is important that the goals of the system be well defined before the design begins. The type of system desired is the foundation for choices among various algorithms and strategies that will be needed.

Throughout the entire design cycle, we must be careful to separate policy decisions from implementation details (mechanisms). This separation allows maximum flexibility if policy decisions are to be changed later.

Once an operating system is designed, it must be implemented. Operating systems today are almost always written in a systems-implementation language or in a higher-level language. This feature improves their implementation, maintenance, and portability.

A system as large and complex as a modern operating system must be engineered carefully. Modularity is important. Designing a system as a sequence of layers or using a microkernel is considered a good technique. Many operating systems now support dynamically loaded modules, which allow adding functionality to an operating system while it is executing. Generally, operating systems adopt a hybrid approach that combines several different types of structures.

Debugging process and kernel failures can be accomplished through the use of debuggers and other tools that analyze core dumps. Tools such as DTrace analyze production systems to find bottlenecks and understand other system behavior.

To create an operating system for a particular machine configuration, we must perform system generation. For the computer system to begin running, the CPU must initialize and start executing the bootstrap program in firmware. The bootstrap can execute the operating system directly if the operating system is also in the firmware, or it can complete a sequence in which it loads progressively smarter programs from firmware and disk until the operating system itself is loaded into memory and executed.

Review Questions

Review questions for this chapter can be accessed by visiting our website.

Practice Exercises

Answers for the Practice Exercises can be accceed by visiting our website.

2.1   What is the purpose of system calls?

2.2   What are the five major activities of an operating system with regard to process management?

2.3   What are the three major activities of an operating system with regard to memory management?

2.4 What are the three major activities of an operating system with regard to secondary-storage management?

2.5 What is the purpose of the command interpreter? Why is it usually separate from the kernel?

2.6 What system calls have to be executed by a command interpreter or shell in order to start a new process?

2.7 What is the purpose of system programs?

2.8 What is the main advantage of the layered approach to system design? What are the disadvantages of the layered approach?

2.9 List five services provided by an operating system, and explain how each creates convenience for users. In which cases would it be impossible for user-level programs to provide these services? Explain your answer.

2.10 Why do some systems store the operating system in firmware, while others store it on disk?

2.11 How could a system be designed to allow a choice of operating systems from which to boot? What would the bootstrap program need to do?

Exercises

2.12 The services and functions provided by an operating system can be divided into two main categories. Briefly describe the two categories, and discuss how they differ.

2.13 Describe three general methods for passing parameters to the operating system.

2.14 Describe how you could obtain a statistical profile of the amount of time spent by a program executing different sections of its code. Discuss the importance of obtaining such a statistical profile.

2.15 What are the five major activities of an operating system with regard to file management?

2.16 What are the advantages and disadvantages of using the same system-call interface for manipulating both files and devices?

2.17 Would it be possible for the user to develop a new command interpreter using the system-call interface provided by the operating system?

2.18 What are the two models of interprocess communication? What are the strengths and weaknesses of the two approaches?

2.19 Why is the separation of mechanism and policy desirable?

2.20 It is sometimes difficult to achieve a layered approach if two components of the operating system are dependent on each other. Identify a scenario in which it is unclear how to layer two system components that require tight coupling of their functionalities.

2.21 What is the main advantage of the microkernel approach to system design? How do user programs and system services interact in a microkernel architecture? What are the disadvantages of using the microkernel approach?

2.22 What are the advantages of using loadable kernel modules?

2.23 How are iOS and Android similar? How are they different?

2.24 Explain why Java programs running on Android systems do not use the standard Java API and virtual machine.

2.25 The experimental Synthesis operating system has an assembler incorporated in the kernel. To optimize system-call performance, the kernel assembles routines within kernel space to minimize the path that the system call must take through the kernel. This approach is the antithesis of the layered approach, in which the path through the kernel is extended to make building the operating system easier. Discuss the pros and cons of the Synthesis approach to kernel design and system-performance optimization.

Programming Problems

2.26 In Section 2.3, we described a program that copies the contents of one file to a destination file. This program works by first prompting the user for the name of the source and destination files. Write this program using either the Windows or POSIX API. Be sure to include all necessary error checking, including ensuring that the source file exists.

Once you have correctly designed and tested the program, if you used a system that supports it, run the program using a utility that traces system calls. Linux systems provide the `strace` utility, and Solaris and Mac OS X systems use the `dtrace` command. As Windows systems do not provide such features, you will have to trace through the Windows version of this program using a debugger.

Programming Projects

Linux Kernel Modules

In this project, you will learn how to create a kernel module and load it into the Linux kernel. The project can be completed using the Linux virtual machine that is available with this text. Although you may use an editor to write these C programs, you will have to use the *terminal* application to compile the programs, and you will have to enter commands on the command line to manage the modules in the kernel.

As you'll discover, the advantage of developing kernel modules is that it is a relatively easy method of interacting with the kernel, thus allowing you to write programs that directly invoke kernel functions. It is important for you to keep in mind that you are indeed writing *kernel code* that directly interacts with the kernel. That normally means that any errors in the code could crash the system! However, since you will be using a virtual machine, any failures will at worst only require rebooting the system.

Part I—Creating Kernel Modules

The first part of this project involves following a series of steps for creating and inserting a module into the Linux kernel.

You can list all kernel modules that are currently loaded by entering the command

```
lsmod
```

This command will list the current kernel modules in three columns: name, size, and where the module is being used.

The following program (named simple.c and available with the source code for this text) illustrates a very basic kernel module that prints appropriate messages when the kernel module is loaded and unloaded.

```
#include <linux/init.h>
#include <linux/kernel.h>
#include <linux/module.h>

/* This function is called when the module is loaded. */
int simple_init(void)
{
   printk(KERN_INFO "Loading Module\n");

   return 0;
}

/* This function is called when the module is removed. */
void simple_exit(void)
{
   printk(KERN_INFO "Removing Module\n");
}

/* Macros for registering module entry and exit points. */
module_init(simple_init);
module_exit(simple_exit);

MODULE_LICENSE("GPL");
MODULE_DESCRIPTION("Simple Module");
MODULE_AUTHOR("SGG");
```

The function simple_init() is the **module entry point**, which represents the function that is invoked when the module is loaded into the kernel. Similarly, the simple_exit() function is the **module exit point**—the function that is called when the module is removed from the kernel.

The module entry point function must return an integer value, with 0 representing success and any other value representing failure. The module exit point function returns void. Neither the module entry point nor the module exit point is passed any parameters. The two following macros are used for registering the module entry and exit points with the kernel:

```
module_init()
```

```
module_exit()
```

Notice how both the module entry and exit point functions make calls to the printk() function. printk() is the kernel equivalent of printf(), yet its output is sent to a kernel log buffer whose contents can be read by the dmesg command. One difference between printf() and printk() is that printk() allows us to specify a priority flag whose values are given in the <linux/printk.h> include file. In this instance, the priority is KERN_INFO, which is defined as an *informational* message.

The final lines—MODULE_LICENSE(), MODULE_DESCRIPTION(), and MODULE_AUTHOR()—represent details regarding the software license, description of the module, and author. For our purposes, we do not depend on this information, but we include it because it is standard practice in developing kernel modules.

This kernel module simple.c is compiled using the Makefile accompanying the source code with this project. To compile the module, enter the following on the command line:

```
make
```

The compilation produces several files. The file simple.ko represents the compiled kernel module. The following step illustrates inserting this module into the Linux kernel.

Loading and Removing Kernel Modules

Kernel modules are loaded using the insmod command, which is run as follows:

```
sudo insmod simple.ko
```

To check whether the module has loaded, enter the lsmod command and search for the module simple. Recall that the module entry point is invoked when the module is inserted into the kernel. To check the contents of this message in the kernel log buffer, enter the command

```
dmesg
```

You should see the message "Loading Module." Removing the kernel module involves invoking the rmmod command (notice that the .ko suffix is unnecessary):

```
sudo rmmod simple
```

Be sure to check with the dmesg command to ensure the module has been removed.

Because the kernel log buffer can fill up quickly, it often makes sense to clear the buffer periodically. This can be accomplished as follows:

```
sudo dmesg -c
```

Part I Assignment

Proceed through the steps described above to create the kernel module and to load and unload the module. Be sure to check the contents of the kernel log buffer using dmesg to ensure you have properly followed the steps.

Part II—Kernel Data Structures

The second part of this project involves modifying the kernel module so that it uses the kernel linked-list data structure.

In Section 1.10, we covered various data structures that are common in operating systems. The Linux kernel provides several of these structures. Here, we explore using the circular, doubly linked list that is available to kernel developers. Much of what we discuss is available in the Linux source code— in this instance, the include file <linux/list.h>—and we recommend that you examine this file as you proceed through the following steps.

Initially, you must define a struct containing the elements that are to be inserted in the linked list. The following C struct defines birthdays:

```
struct birthday {
    int day;
    int month;
    int year;
    struct list_head list;
}
```

Notice the member struct list_head list. The list_head structure is defined in the include file <linux/types.h>. Its intention is to embed the linked list within the nodes that comprise the list. This list_head structure is quite simple—it merely holds two members, next and prev, that point to the next and previous entries in the list. By embedding the linked list within the structure, Linux makes it possible to manage the data structure with a series of *macro* functions.

Inserting Elements into the Linked List

We can declare a list_head object, which we use as a reference to the head of the list by using the LIST_HEAD() macro

```
static LIST_HEAD(birthday_list);
```

This macro defines and initializes the variable birthday_list, which is of type struct list_head.

We create and initialize instances of struct birthday as follows:

```
struct birthday *person;

person = kmalloc(sizeof(*person), GFP_KERNEL);
person->day = 2;
person->month= 8;
person->year = 1995;
INIT_LIST_HEAD(&person->list);
```

The kmalloc() function is the kernel equivalent of the user-level malloc() function for allocating memory, except that kernel memory is being allocated. (The *GFP_KERNEL* flag indicates routine kernel memory allocation.) The macro INIT_LIST_HEAD() initializes the list member in struct birthday. We can then add this instance to the end of the linked list using the list_add_tail() macro:

```
list_add_tail(&person->list, &birthday_list);
```

Traversing the Linked List

Traversing the list involves using the list_for_each_entry() Macro, which accepts three parameters:

- A pointer to the structure being iterated over
- A pointer to the head of the list being iterated over
- The name of the variable containing the list_head structure

The following code illustrates this macro:

```
struct birthday *ptr;

list_for_each_entry(ptr, &birthday_list, list) {
    /* on each iteration ptr points */
    /* to the next birthday struct */
}
```

Removing Elements from the Linked List

Removing elements from the list involves using the list_del() macro, which is passed a pointer to struct list_head

```
list_del(struct list_head *element)
```

This removes *element* from the list while maintaining the structure of the remainder of the list.

Perhaps the simplest approach for removing all elements from a linked list is to remove each element as you traverse the list. The macro list_for_each_entry_safe() behaves much like list_for_each_entry()

except that it is passed an additional argument that maintains the value of the next pointer of the item being deleted. (This is necessary for preserving the structure of the list.) The following code example illustrates this macro:

```
struct birthday *ptr, *next

list_for_each_entry_safe(ptr,next,&birthday_list,list) {
    /* on each iteration ptr points */
    /* to the next birthday struct */
    list_del(&ptr->list);
    kfree(ptr);
}
```

Notice that after deleting each element, we return memory that was previously allocated with kmalloc() back to the kernel with the call to kfree(). Careful memory management—which includes releasing memory to prevent *memory leaks*—is crucial when developing kernel-level code.

Part II Assignment

In the module entry point, create a linked list containing five struct birthday elements. Traverse the linked list and output its contents to the kernel log buffer. Invoke the dmesg command to ensure the list is properly constructed once the kernel module has been loaded.

In the module exit point, delete the elements from the linked list and return the free memory back to the kernel. Again, invoke the dmesg command to check that the list has been removed once the kernel module has been unloaded.

Bibliographical Notes

[Dijkstra (1968)] advocated the layered approach to operating-system design. [Brinch-Hansen (1970)] was an early proponent of constructing an operating system as a kernel (or nucleus) on which more complete systems could be built. [Tarkoma and Lagerspetz (2011)] provide an overview of various mobile operating systems, including Android and iOS.

MS-DOS, Version 3.1, is described in [Microsoft (1986)]. Windows NT and Windows 2000 are described by [Solomon (1998)] and [Solomon and Russinovich (2000)]. Windows XP internals are described in [Russinovich and Solomon (2009)]. [Hart (2005)] covers Windows systems programming in detail. BSD UNIX is described in [McKusick et al. (1996)]. [Love (2010)] and [Mauerer (2008)] thoroughly discuss the Linux kernel. In particular, [Love (2010)] covers Linux kernel modules as well as kernel data structures. Several UNIX systems—including Mach—are treated in detail in [Vahalia (1996)]. Mac OS X is presented at http://www.apple.com/macosx and in [Singh (2007)]. Solaris is fully described in [McDougall and Mauro (2007)].

DTrace is discussed in [Gregg and Mauro (2011)]. The DTrace source code is available at http://src.opensolaris.org/source/.

Bibliography

[Brinch-Hansen (1970)]   P. Brinch-Hansen, "The Nucleus of a Multiprogramming System", *Communications of the ACM*, Volume 13, Number 4 (1970), pages 238–241 and 250.

[Dijkstra (1968)]   E. W. Dijkstra, "The Structure of the THE Multiprogramming System", *Communications of the ACM,* Volume 11, Number 5 (1968), pages 341–346.

[Gregg and Mauro (2011)]   B. Gregg and J. Mauro, *DTrace—Dynamic Tracing in Oracle Solaris, Mac OS X, and FreeBSD*, Prentice Hall (2011).

[Hart (2005)]   J. M. Hart, *Windows System Programming,* Third Edition, Addison-Wesley (2005).

[Love (2010)]   R. Love, *Linux Kernel Development*, Third Edition, Developer's Library (2010).

[Mauerer (2008)]   W. Mauerer, *Professional Linux Kernel Architecture*, John Wiley and Sons (2008).

[McDougall and Mauro (2007)]   R. McDougall and J. Mauro, *Solaris Internals*, Second Edition, Prentice Hall (2007).

[McKusick et al. (1996)]   M. K. McKusick, K. Bostic, and M. J. Karels, *The Design and Implementation of the 4.4 BSD UNIX Operating System*, John Wiley and Sons (1996).

[Microsoft (1986)]   *Microsoft MS-DOS User's Reference and Microsoft MS-DOS Programmer's Reference.* Microsoft Press (1986).

[Russinovich and Solomon (2009)]   M. E. Russinovich and D. A. Solomon, *Windows Internals: Including Windows Server 2008 and Windows Vista,* Fifth Edition, Microsoft Press (2009).

[Singh (2007)]   A. Singh, *Mac OS X Internals: A Systems Approach*, Addison-Wesley (2007).

[Solomon (1998)]   D. A. Solomon, *Inside Windows NT,* Second Edition, Microsoft Press (1998).

[Solomon and Russinovich (2000)]   D. A. Solomon and M. E. Russinovich, *Inside Microsoft Windows 2000*, Third Edition, Microsoft Press (2000).

[Tarkoma and Lagerspetz (2011)]   S. Tarkoma and E. Lagerspetz, "Arching over the Mobile Computing Chasm: Platforms and Runtimes", *IEEE Computer*, Volume 44, (2011), pages 22–28.

[Vahalia (1996)]   U. Vahalia, *Unix Internals: The New Frontiers*, Prentice Hall (1996).

Part Two

Process Management

A *process* can be thought of as a program in execution. A process will need certain resources—such as CPU time, memory, files, and I/O devices—to accomplish its task. These resources are allocated to the process either when it is created or while it is executing.

A process is the unit of work in most systems. Systems consist of a collection of processes: operating-system processes execute system code, and user processes execute user code. All these processes may execute concurrently.

Although traditionally a process contained only a single *thread* of control as it ran, most modern operating systems now support processes that have multiple threads.

The operating system is responsible for several important aspects of process and thread management: the creation and deletion of both user and system processes; the scheduling of processes; and the provision of mechanisms for synchronization, communication, and deadlock handling for processes.

Processes

Early computers allowed only one program to be executed at a time. This program had complete control of the system and had access to all the system's resources. In contrast, contemporary computer systems allow multiple programs to be loaded into memory and executed concurrently. This evolution required firmer control and more compartmentalization of the various programs; and these needs resulted in the notion of a **process**, which is a program in execution. A process is the unit of work in a modern time-sharing system.

The more complex the operating system is, the more it is expected to do on behalf of its users. Although its main concern is the execution of user programs, it also needs to take care of various system tasks that are better left outside the kernel itself. A system therefore consists of a collection of processes: operating-system processes executing system code and user processes executing user code. Potentially, all these processes can execute concurrently, with the CPU (or CPUs) multiplexed among them. By switching the CPU between processes, the operating system can make the computer more productive. In this chapter, you will read about what processes are and how they work.

CHAPTER OBJECTIVES

- To introduce the notion of a process — a program in execution, which forms the basis of all computation.
- To describe the various features of processes, including scheduling, creation, and termination.
- To explore interprocess communication using shared memory and message passing.
- To describe communication in client–server systems.

3.1 Process Concept

A question that arises in discussing operating systems involves what to call all the CPU activities. A batch system executes **jobs**, whereas a time-shared system has **user programs**, or **tasks**. Even on a single-user system, a user may be able to run several programs at one time: a word processor, a Web browser, and an e-mail package. And even if a user can execute only one program at a time, such as on an embedded device that does not support multitasking, the operating system may need to support its own internal programmed activities, such as memory management. In many respects, all these activities are similar, so we call all of them **processes**.

The terms *job* and *process* are used almost interchangeably in this text. Although we personally prefer the term *process*, much of operating-system theory and terminology was developed during a time when the major activity of operating systems was job processing. It would be misleading to avoid the use of commonly accepted terms that include the word *job* (such as *job scheduling*) simply because *process* has superseded *job.*

3.1.1   The Process

Informally, as mentioned earlier, a process is a program in execution. A process is more than the program code, which is sometimes known as the **text section**. It also includes the current activity, as represented by the value of the **program counter** and the contents of the processor's registers. A process generally also includes the process **stack**, which contains temporary data (such as function parameters, return addresses, and local variables), and a **data section**, which contains global variables. A process may also include a **heap**, which is memory that is dynamically allocated during process run time. The structure of a process in memory is shown in Figure 3.1.

We emphasize that a program by itself is not a process. A program is a *passive* entity, such as a file containing a list of instructions stored on disk (often called an **executable file**). In contrast, a process is an *active* entity, with a program counter specifying the next instruction to execute and a set of associated resources. A program becomes a process when an executable file is loaded into memory. Two common techniques for loading executable files

Figure 3.1   Process in memory.

are double-clicking an icon representing the executable file and entering the name of the executable file on the command line (as in `prog.exe` or `a.out`).

Although two processes may be associated with the same program, they are nevertheless considered two separate execution sequences. For instance, several users may be running different copies of the mail program, or the same user may invoke many copies of the web browser program. Each of these is a separate process; and although the text sections are equivalent, the data, heap, and stack sections vary. It is also common to have a process that spawns many processes as it runs. We discuss such matters in Section 3.4.

Note that a process itself can be an execution environment for other code. The Java programming environment provides a good example. In most circumstances, an executable Java program is executed within the Java virtual machine (JVM). The JVM executes as a process that interprets the loaded Java code and takes actions (via native machine instructions) on behalf of that code. For example, to run the compiled Java program `Program.class`, we would enter

```
java Program
```

The command `java` runs the JVM as an ordinary process, which in turns executes the Java program `Program` in the virtual machine. The concept is the same as simulation, except that the code, instead of being written for a different instruction set, is written in the Java language.

3.1.2 Process State

As a process executes, it changes **state**. The state of a process is defined in part by the current activity of that process. A process may be in one of the following states:

- **New**. The process is being created.
- **Running**. Instructions are being executed.
- **Waiting**. The process is waiting for some event to occur (such as an I/O completion or reception of a signal).
- **Ready**. The process is waiting to be assigned to a processor.
- **Terminated**. The process has finished execution.

These names are arbitrary, and they vary across operating systems. The states that they represent are found on all systems, however. Certain operating systems also more finely delineate process states. It is important to realize that only one process can be *running* on any processor at any instant. Many processes may be *ready* and *waiting*, however. The state diagram corresponding to these states is presented in Figure 3.2.

3.1.3 Process Control Block

Each process is represented in the operating system by a **process control block** (**PCB**)—also called a **task control block**. A PCB is shown in Figure 3.3. It contains many pieces of information associated with a specific process, including these:

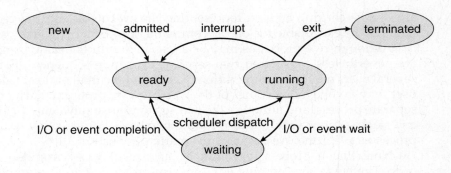

Figure 3.2   Diagram of process state.

- **Process state**. The state may be new, ready, running, waiting, halted, and so on.

- **Program counter**. The counter indicates the address of the next instruction to be executed for this process.

- **CPU registers**. The registers vary in number and type, depending on the computer architecture. They include accumulators, index registers, stack pointers, and general-purpose registers, plus any condition-code information. Along with the program counter, this state information must be saved when an interrupt occurs, to allow the process to be continued correctly afterward (Figure 3.4).

- **CPU-scheduling information**. This information includes a process priority, pointers to scheduling queues, and any other scheduling parameters. (Chapter 6 describes process scheduling.)

- **Memory-management information**. This information may include such items as the value of the base and limit registers and the page tables, or the segment tables, depending on the memory system used by the operating system (Chapter 7).

Figure 3.3   Process control block (PCB).

Figure 3.4 Diagram showing CPU switch from process to process.

- **Accounting information**. This information includes the amount of CPU and real time used, time limits, account numbers, job or process numbers, and so on.

- **I/O status information**. This information includes the list of I/O devices allocated to the process, a list of open files, and so on.

In brief, the PCB simply serves as the repository for any information that may vary from process to process.

3.1.4 Threads

The process model discussed so far has implied that a process is a program that performs a single **thread** of execution. For example, when a process is running a word-processor program, a single thread of instructions is being executed. This single thread of control allows the process to perform only one task at a time. The user cannot simultaneously type in characters and run the spell checker within the same process, for example. Most modern operating systems have extended the process concept to allow a process to have multiple threads of execution and thus to perform more than one task at a time. This feature is especially beneficial on multicore systems, where multiple threads can run in parallel. On a system that supports threads, the PCB is expanded to include information for each thread. Other changes throughout the system are also needed to support threads. Chapter 4 explores threads in detail.

PROCESS REPRESENTATION IN LINUX

The process control block in the Linux operating system is represented by the C structure task_struct, which is found in the <linux/sched.h> include file in the kernel source-code directory. This structure contains all the necessary information for representing a process, including the state of the process, scheduling and memory-management information, list of open files, and pointers to the process's parent and a list of its children and siblings. (A process's parent is the process that created it; its children are any processes that it creates. Its siblings are children with the same parent process.) Some of these fields include:

```
long state; /* state of the process */
struct sched_entity se; /* scheduling information */
struct task_struct *parent; /* this process's parent */
struct list_head children; /* this process's children */
struct files_struct *files; /* list of open files */
struct mm_struct *mm; /* address space of this process */
```

For example, the state of a process is represented by the field long state in this structure. Within the Linux kernel, all active processes are represented using a doubly linked list of task_struct. The kernel maintains a pointer—current—to the process currently executing on the system, as shown below:

current
(currently executing proccess)

As an illustration of how the kernel might manipulate one of the fields in the task_struct for a specified process, let's assume the system would like to change the state of the process currently running to the value new_state. If current is a pointer to the process currently executing, its state is changed with the following:

```
current->state = new_state;
```

3.2 Process Scheduling

The objective of multiprogramming is to have some process running at all times, to maximize CPU utilization. The objective of time sharing is to switch the CPU among processes so frequently that users can interact with each program

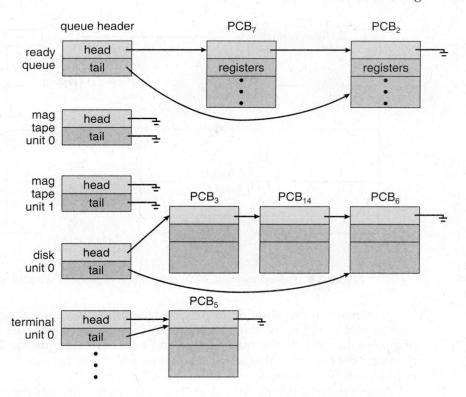

Figure 3.5 The ready queue and various I/O device queues.

while it is running. To meet these objectives, the **process scheduler** selects an available process (possibly from a set of several available processes) for program execution on the CPU. For a single-processor system, there will never be more than one running process. If there are more processes, the rest will have to wait until the CPU is free and can be rescheduled.

3.2.1 Scheduling Queues

As processes enter the system, they are put into a **job queue**, which consists of all processes in the system. The processes that are residing in main memory and are ready and waiting to execute are kept on a list called the **ready queue**. This queue is generally stored as a linked list. A ready-queue header contains pointers to the first and final PCBs in the list. Each PCB includes a pointer field that points to the next PCB in the ready queue.

The system also includes other queues. When a process is allocated the CPU, it executes for a while and eventually quits, is interrupted, or waits for the occurrence of a particular event, such as the completion of an I/O request. Suppose the process makes an I/O request to a shared device, such as a disk. Since there are many processes in the system, the disk may be busy with the I/O request of some other process. The process therefore may have to wait for the disk. The list of processes waiting for a particular I/O device is called a **device queue**. Each device has its own device queue (Figure 3.5).

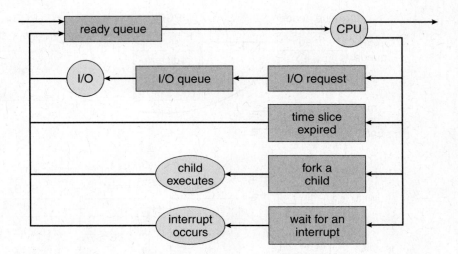

Figure 3.6   Queueing-diagram representation of process scheduling.

A common representation of process scheduling is a **queueing diagram,** such as that in Figure 3.6. Each rectangular box represents a queue. Two types of queues are present: the ready queue and a set of device queues. The circles represent the resources that serve the queues, and the arrows indicate the flow of processes in the system.

A new process is initially put in the ready queue. It waits there until it is selected for execution, or **dispatched.** Once the process is allocated the CPU and is executing, one of several events could occur:

- The process could issue an I/O request and then be placed in an I/O queue.

- The process could create a new child process and wait for the child's termination.

- The process could be removed forcibly from the CPU, as a result of an interrupt, and be put back in the ready queue.

In the first two cases, the process eventually switches from the waiting state to the ready state and is then put back in the ready queue. A process continues this cycle until it terminates, at which time it is removed from all queues and has its PCB and resources deallocated.

3.2.2   Schedulers

A process migrates among the various scheduling queues throughout its lifetime. The operating system must select, for scheduling purposes, processes from these queues in some fashion. The selection process is carried out by the appropriate **scheduler.**

Often, in a batch system, more processes are submitted than can be executed immediately. These processes are spooled to a mass-storage device (typically a disk), where they are kept for later execution. The **long-term scheduler,** or **job scheduler,** selects processes from this pool and loads them into memory for execution. The short-term scheduler, or CPU scheduler, selects from among the processes that are ready to execute and allocates the CPU to one of them.

The primary distinction between these two schedulers lies in frequency of execution. The short-term scheduler must select a new process for the CPU frequently. A process may execute for only a few milliseconds before waiting for an I/O request. Often, the short-term scheduler executes at least once every 100 milliseconds. Because of the short time between executions, the short-term scheduler must be fast. If it takes 10 milliseconds to decide to execute a process for 100 milliseconds, then $10/(100 + 10) = 9$ percent of the CPU is being used (wasted) simply for scheduling the work.

The long-term scheduler executes much less frequently; minutes may separate the creation of one new process and the next. The long-term scheduler controls the degree of multiprogramming (the number of processes in memory). If the degree of multiprogramming is stable, then the average rate of process creation must be equal to the average departure rate of processes leaving the system. Thus, the long-term scheduler may need to be invoked only when a process leaves the system. Because of the longer interval between executions, the long-term scheduler can afford to take more time to decide which process should be selected for execution.

It is important that the long-term scheduler make a careful selection. In general, most processes can be described as either I/O bound or CPU bound. An I/O-bound process is one that spends more of its time doing I/O than it spends doing computations. A CPU-bound process, in contrast, generates I/O requests infrequently, using more of its time doing computations. It is important that the long-term scheduler select a good *process mix* of I/O-bound and CPU-bound processes. If all processes are I/O bound, the ready queue will almost always be empty, and the short-term scheduler will have little to do. If all processes are CPU bound, the I/O waiting queue will almost always be empty, devices will go unused, and again the system will be unbalanced. The system with the best performance will thus have a combination of CPU-bound and I/O-bound processes.

On some systems, the long-term scheduler may be absent or minimal. For example, time-sharing systems such as UNIX and Microsoft Windows systems often have no long-term scheduler but simply put every new process in memory for the short-term scheduler. The stability of these systems depends either on a physical limitation (such as the number of available terminals) or on the self-adjusting nature of human users. If performance declines to unacceptable levels on a multiuser system, some users will simply quit.

Some operating systems, such as time-sharing systems, may introduce an additional, intermediate level of scheduling. This medium-term scheduler is diagrammed in Figure 3.7. The key idea behind a medium-term scheduler is that sometimes it can be advantageous to remove a process from memory (and from active contention for the CPU) and thus reduce the degree of multiprogramming. Later, the process can be reintroduced into memory, and its execution can be continued where it left off. This scheme is called swapping. The process is swapped out, and is later swapped in, by the medium-term scheduler. Swapping may be necessary to improve the process mix or because a change in memory requirements has overcommitted available memory, requiring memory to be freed up. Swapping is discussed in Chapter 7.

Figure 3.7   Addition of medium-term scheduling to the queueing diagram.

3.2.3 Context Switch

As mentioned in Section 1.2.1, interrupts cause the operating system to change a CPU from its current task and to run a kernel routine. Such operations happen frequently on general-purpose systems. When an interrupt occurs, the system needs to save the current **context** of the process running on the CPU so that it can restore that context when its processing is done, essentially suspending the process and then resuming it. The context is represented in the PCB of the process. It includes the value of the CPU registers, the process state (see Figure 3.2), and memory-management information. Generically, we perform a **state save** of the current state of the CPU, be it in kernel or user mode, and then a **state restore** to resume operations.

Switching the CPU to another process requires performing a state save of the current process and a state restore of a different process. This task is known as a **context switch**. When a context switch occurs, the kernel saves the context of the old process in its PCB and loads the saved context of the new process scheduled to run. Context-switch time is pure overhead, because the system does no useful work while switching. Switching speed varies from machine to machine, depending on the memory speed, the number of registers that must be copied, and the existence of special instructions (such as a single instruction to load or store all registers). A typical speed is a few milliseconds.

Context-switch times are highly dependent on hardware support. For instance, some processors (such as the Sun UltraSPARC) provide multiple sets of registers. A context switch here simply requires changing the pointer to the current register set. Of course, if there are more active processes than there are register sets, the system resorts to copying register data to and from memory, as before. Also, the more complex the operating system, the greater the amount of work that must be done during a context switch. As we will see in Chapter 7, advanced memory-management techniques may require that extra data be switched with each context. For instance, the address space of the current process must be preserved as the space of the next task is prepared for use. How the address space is preserved, and what amount of work is needed to preserve it, depend on the memory-management method of the operating system.

MULTITASKING IN MOBILE SYSTEMS

Because of the constraints imposed on mobile devices, early versions of iOS did not provide user-application multitasking; only one application runs in the foreground and all other user applications are suspended. Operating-system tasks were multitasked because they were written by Apple and well behaved. However, beginning with iOS 4, Apple now provides a limited form of multitasking for user applications, thus allowing a single foreground application to run concurrently with multiple background applications. (On a mobile device, the foreground application is the application currently open and appearing on the display. The background application remains in memory, but does not occupy the display screen.) The iOS 4 programming API provides support for multitasking, thus allowing a process to run in the background without being suspended. However, it is limited and only available for a limited number of application types, including applications

- running a single, finite-length task (such as completing a download of content from a network);

- receiving notifications of an event occurring (such as a new email message);

- with long-running background tasks (such as an audio player.)

Apple probably limits multitasking due to battery life and memory use concerns. The CPU certainly has the features to support multitasking, but Apple chooses to not take advantage of some of them in order to better manage resource use.

Android does not place such constraints on the types of applications that can run in the background. If an application requires processing while in the background, the application must use a service, a separate application component that runs on behalf of the background process. Consider a streaming audio application: if the application moves to the background, the service continues to send audio files to the audio device driver on behalf of the background application. In fact, the service will continue to run even if the background application is suspended. Services do not have a user interface and have a small memory footprint, thus providing an efficient technique for multitasking in a mobile environment.

3.3   Operations on Processes

The processes in most systems can execute concurrently, and they may be created and deleted dynamically. Thus, these systems must provide a mechanism for process creation and termination. In this section, we explore the mechanisms involved in creating processes and illustrate process creation on UNIX and Windows systems.

3.3.1 Process Creation

During the course of execution, a process may create several new processes. As mentioned earlier, the creating process is called a parent process, and the new processes are called the children of that process. Each of these new processes may in turn create other processes, forming a **tree** of processes.

Most operating systems (including UNIX, Linux, and Windows) identify processes according to a unique **process identifier** (or **pid**), which is typically an integer number. The pid provides a unique value for each process in the system, and it can be used as an index to access various attributes of a process within the kernel.

Figure 3.8 illustrates a typical process tree for the Linux operating system, showing the name of each process and its pid. (We use the term *process* rather loosely, as Linux prefers the term *task* instead.) The init process (which always has a pid of 1) serves as the root parent process for all user processes. Once the system has booted, the init process can also create various user processes, such as a web or print server, an ssh server, and the like. In Figure 3.8, we see two children of init—kthreadd and sshd. The kthreadd process is responsible for creating additional processes that perform tasks on behalf of the kernel (in this situation, khelper and pdflush). The sshd process is responsible for managing clients that connect to the system by using ssh (which is short for *secure shell*). The login process is responsible for managing clients that directly log onto the system. In this example, a client has logged on and is using the bash shell, which has been assigned pid 8416. Using the bash command-line interface, this user has created the process ps as well as the emacs editor.

On UNIX and Linux systems, we can obtain a listing of processes by using the ps command. For example, the command

```
ps -el
```

will list complete information for all processes currently active in the system. It is easy to construct a process tree similar to the one shown in Figure 3.8 by recursively tracing parent processes all the way to the init process.

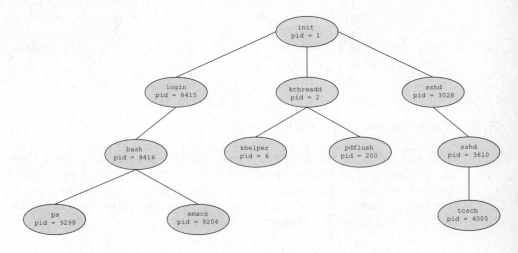

Figure 3.8   A tree of processes on a typical Linux system.

In general, when a process creates a child process, that child process will need certain resources (CPU time, memory, files, I/O devices) to accomplish its task. A child process may be able to obtain its resources directly from the operating system, or it may be constrained to a subset of the resources of the parent process. The parent may have to partition its resources among its children, or it may be able to share some resources (such as memory or files) among several of its children. Restricting a child process to a subset of the parent's resources prevents any process from overloading the system by creating too many child processes.

In addition to supplying various physical and logical resources, the parent process may pass along initialization data (input) to the child process. For example, consider a process whose function is to display the contents of a file —say, image.jpg—on the screen of a terminal. When the process is created, it will get, as an input from its parent process, the name of the file *image.jpg*. Using that file name, it will open the file and write the contents out. It may also get the name of the output device. Alternatively, some operating systems pass resources to child processes. On such a system, the new process may get two open files, image.jpg and the terminal device, and may simply transfer the datum between the two.

When a process creates a new process, two possibilities for execution exist:

1. The parent continues to execute concurrently with its children.

2. The parent waits until some or all of its children have terminated.

There are also two address-space possibilities for the new process:

1. The child process is a duplicate of the parent process (it has the same program and data as the parent).

2. The child process has a new program loaded into it.

To illustrate these differences, let's first consider the UNIX operating system. In UNIX, as we've seen, each process is identified by its process identifier, which is a unique integer. A new process is created by the fork() system call. The new process consists of a copy of the address space of the original process. This mechanism allows the parent process to communicate easily with its child process. Both processes (the parent and the child) continue execution at the instruction after the fork(), with one difference: the return code for the fork() is zero for the new (child) process, whereas the (nonzero) process identifier of the child is returned to the parent.

After a fork() system call, one of the two processes typically uses the exec() system call to replace the process's memory space with a new program. The exec() system call loads a binary file into memory (destroying the memory image of the program containing the exec() system call) and starts its execution. In this manner, the two processes are able to communicate and then go their separate ways. The parent can then create more children; or, if it has nothing else to do while the child runs, it can issue a wait() system call to move itself off the ready queue until the termination of the child. Because the

```
#include <sys/types.h>
#include <stdio.h>
#include <unistd.h>

int main()
{
pid_t pid;

    /* fork a child process */
    pid = fork();

    if (pid < 0) { /* error occurred */
       fprintf(stderr, "Fork Failed");
       return 1;
    }
    else if (pid == 0) { /* child process */
       execlp("/bin/ls","ls",NULL);
    }
    else { /* parent process */
       /* parent will wait for the child to complete */
       wait(NULL);
       printf("Child Complete");
    }

    return 0;
}
```

Figure 3.9   Creating a separate process using the UNIX fork() system call.

call to exec() overlays the process's address space with a new program, the call to exec() does not return control unless an error occurs.

The C program shown in Figure 3.9 illustrates the UNIX system calls previously described. We now have two different processes running copies of the same program. The only difference is that the value of pid (the process identifier) for the child process is zero, while that for the parent is an integer value greater than zero (in fact, it is the actual pid of the child process). The child process inherits privileges and scheduling attributes from the parent, as well certain resources, such as open files. The child process then overlays its address space with the UNIX command /bin/ls (used to get a directory listing) using the execlp() system call (execlp() is a version of the exec() system call). The parent waits for the child process to complete with the wait() system call. When the child process completes (by either implicitly or explicitly invoking exit()), the parent process resumes from the call to wait(), where it completes using the exit() system call. This is also illustrated in Figure 3.10.

Of course, there is nothing to prevent the child from *not* invoking exec() and instead continuing to execute as a copy of the parent process. In this scenario, the parent and child are concurrent processes running the same code

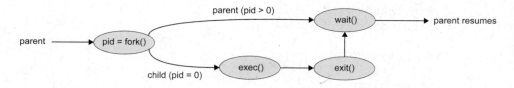

Figure 3.10   Process creation using the `fork()` system call.

instructions. Because the child is a copy of the parent, each process has its own copy of any data.

As an alternative example, we next consider process creation in Windows. Processes are created in the Windows API using the `CreateProcess()` function, which is similar to `fork()` in that a parent creates a new child process. However, whereas `fork()` has the child process inheriting the address space of its parent, `CreateProcess()` requires loading a specified program into the address space of the child process at process creation. Furthermore, whereas `fork()` is passed no parameters, `CreateProcess()` expects no fewer than ten parameters.

The C program shown in Figure 3.11 illustrates the `CreateProcess()` function, which creates a child process that loads the application mspaint.exe. We opt for many of the default values of the ten parameters passed to `CreateProcess()`. Readers interested in pursuing the details of process creation and management in the Windows API are encouraged to consult the bibliographical notes at the end of this chapter.

The two parameters passed to the `CreateProcess()` function are instances of the STARTUPINFO and PROCESS_INFORMATION structures. STARTUPINFO specifies many properties of the new process, such as window size and appearance and handles to standard input and output files. The PRO-CESS_INFORMATION structure contains a handle and the identifiers to the newly created process and its thread. We invoke the `ZeroMemory()` function to allocate memory for each of these structures before proceeding with `CreateProcess()`.

The first two parameters passed to `CreateProcess()` are the application name and command-line parameters. If the application name is NULL (as it is in this case), the command-line parameter specifies the application to load. In this instance, we are loading the Microsoft Windows mspaint.exe application. Beyond these two initial parameters, we use the default parameters for inheriting process and thread handles as well as specifying that there will be no creation flags. We also use the parent's existing environment block and starting directory. Last, we provide two pointers to the STARTUPINFO and PROCESS_-INFORMATION structures created at the beginning of the program. In Figure 3.9, the parent process waits for the child to complete by invoking the `wait()` system call. The equivalent of this in Windows is `WaitForSingleObject()`, which is passed a handle of the child process—pi.hProcess—and waits for this process to complete. Once the child process exits, control returns from the `WaitForSingleObject()` function in the parent process.

```
#include <stdio.h>
#include <windows.h>

int main(VOID)
{
STARTUPINFO si;
PROCESS_INFORMATION pi;

    /* allocate memory */
    ZeroMemory(&si, sizeof(si));
    si.cb = sizeof(si);
    ZeroMemory(&pi, sizeof(pi));

    /* create child process */
    if (!CreateProcess(NULL, /* use command line */
     "C:\\WINDOWS\\system32\\mspaint.exe", /* command */
     NULL, /* don't inherit process handle */
     NULL, /* don't inherit thread handle */
     FALSE, /* disable handle inheritance */
     0, /* no creation flags */
     NULL, /* use parent's environment block */
     NULL, /* use parent's existing directory */
     &si,
     &pi))
    {
      fprintf(stderr, "Create Process Failed");
      return -1;
    }
    /* parent will wait for the child to complete */
    WaitForSingleObject(pi.hProcess, INFINITE);
    printf("Child Complete");

    /* close handles */
    CloseHandle(pi.hProcess);
    CloseHandle(pi.hThread);
}
```

Figure 3.11   Creating a separate process using the Windows API.

3.3.2 Process Termination

A process terminates when it finishes executing its final statement and asks the operating system to delete it by using the exit() system call. At that point, the process may return a status value (typically an integer) to its parent process (via the wait() system call). All the resources of the process—including physical and virtual memory, open files, and I/O buffers—are deallocated by the operating system.

Termination can occur in other circumstances as well. A process can cause the termination of another process via an appropriate system call (for example, TerminateProcess() in Windows). Usually, such a system call can be invoked only by the parent of the process that is to be terminated. Otherwise, users could arbitrarily kill each other's jobs. Note that a parent needs to know the identities of its children if it is to terminate them. Thus, when one process creates a new process, the identity of the newly created process is passed to the parent.

A parent may terminate the execution of one of its children for a variety of reasons, such as these:

- The child has exceeded its usage of some of the resources that it has been allocated. (To determine whether this has occurred, the parent must have a mechanism to inspect the state of its children.)

- The task assigned to the child is no longer required.

- The parent is exiting, and the operating system does not allow a child to continue if its parent terminates.

Some systems do not allow a child to exist if its parent has terminated. In such systems, if a process terminates (either normally or abnormally), then all its children must also be terminated. This phenomenon, referred to as cascading termination, is normally initiated by the operating system.

To illustrate process execution and termination, consider that, in Linux and UNIX systems, we can terminate a process by using the exit() system call, providing an exit status as a parameter:

```
/* exit with status 1 */
exit(1);
```

In fact, under normal termination, exit() may be called either directly (as shown above) or indirectly (by a return statement in main()).

A parent process may wait for the termination of a child process by using the wait() system call. The wait() system call is passed a parameter that allows the parent to obtain the exit status of the child. This system call also returns the process identifier of the terminated child so that the parent can tell which of its children has terminated:

```
pid_t pid;
int status;

pid = wait(&status);
```

When a process terminates, its resources are deallocated by the operating system. However, its entry in the process table must remain there until the parent calls wait(), because the process table contains the process's exit status. A process that has terminated, but whose parent has not yet called wait(), is known as a zombie process. All processes transition to this state when they terminate, but generally they exist as zombies only briefly. Once the parent calls wait(), the process identifier of the zombie process and its entry in the process table are released.

Now consider what would happen if a parent did not invoke wait() and instead terminated, thereby leaving its child processes as orphans. Linux and UNIX address this scenario by assigning the init process as the new parent to orphan processes. (Recall from Figure 3.8 that the `init` process is the root of the process hierarchy in UNIX and Linux systems.) The `init` process periodically invokes `wait()`, thereby allowing the exit status of any orphaned process to be collected and releasing the orphan's process identifier and process-table entry.

3.4   Interprocess Communication

Processes executing concurrently in the operating system may be either independent processes or cooperating processes. A process is *independent* if it cannot affect or be affected by the other processes executing in the system. Any process that does not share data with any other process is independent. A process is *cooperating* if it can affect or be affected by the other processes executing in the system. Clearly, any process that shares data with other processes is a cooperating process.

There are several reasons for providing an environment that allows process cooperation:

- **Information sharing**. Since several users may be interested in the same piece of information (for instance, a shared file), we must provide an environment to allow concurrent access to such information.

- **Computation speedup**. If we want a particular task to run faster, we must break it into subtasks, each of which will be executing in parallel with the others. Notice that such a speedup can be achieved only if the computer has multiple processing cores.

- **Modularity**. We may want to construct the system in a modular fashion, dividing the system functions into separate processes or threads, as we discussed in Chapter 2.

- **Convenience**. Even an individual user may work on many tasks at the same time. For instance, a user may be editing, listening to music, and compiling in parallel.

Cooperating processes require an **interprocess communication (IPC)** mechanism that will allow them to exchange data and information. There are two fundamental models of interprocess communication: **shared memory** and **message passing**. In the shared-memory model, a region of memory that is shared by cooperating processes is established. Processes can then exchange information by reading and writing data to the shared region. In the message-passing model, communication takes place by means of messages exchanged between the cooperating processes. The two communications models are contrasted in Figure 3.12.

Both of the models just mentioned are common in operating systems, and many systems implement both. Message passing is useful for exchanging smaller amounts of data, because no conflicts need be avoided. Message passing is also easier to implement in a distributed system than shared memory. (Although there are systems that provide distributed shared memory, we do not consider them in this text.) Shared memory can be faster than message passing, since message-passing systems are typically implemented using system calls

MULTIPROCESS ARCHITECTURE—CHROME BROWSER

Many websites contain active content such as JavaScript, Flash, and HTML5 to provide a rich and dynamic web-browsing experience. Unfortunately, these web applications may also contain bugs, which can result in sluggish response times and can even cause the web browser to crash. This isn't a big problem in a web browser that displays content from only one website. But most contemporary web browsers provide tabbed browsing, which allows a single instance of a web browser application to open several websites at the same time, with each site in a separate tab. To switch between the different sites, a user need only click on the appropriate tab. This arrangement is illustrated below:

(Chrome is a registered trademark of Google, Inc. used with permission)

A problem with this approach is that if a web application in any tab crashes, the entire process—including all other tabs displaying additional websites—crashes as well.

Google's Chrome web browser was designed to address this issue by using a multiprocess architecture. Chrome identifies three different types of processes: browser, renderers, and plug-ins.

- The browser process is responsible for managing the user interface as well as disk and network I/O. A new browser process is created when Chrome is started. Only one browser process is created.

- Renderer processes contain logic for rendering web pages. Thus, they contain the logic for handling HTML, Javascript, images, and so forth. As a general rule, a new renderer process is created for each website opened in a new tab, and so several renderer processes may be active at the same time.

- A plug-in process is created for each type of plug-in (such as Flash or QuickTime) in use. Plug-in processes contain the code for the plug-in as well as additional code that enables the plug-in to communicate with associated renderer processes and the browser process.

The advantage of the multiprocess approach is that websites run in isolation from one another. If one website crashes, only its renderer process is affected; all other processes remain unharmed. Furthermore, renderer processes run in a sandbox, which means that access to disk and network I/O is restricted, minimizing the effects of any security exploits.

and thus require the more time-consuming task of kernel intervention. In shared-memory systems, system calls are required only to establish shared-

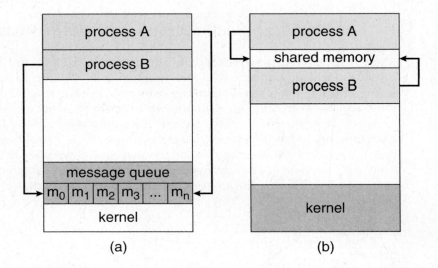

Figure 3.12   Communications models. (a) Message passing. (b) Shared memory.

memory regions. Once shared memory is established, all accesses are treated as routine memory accesses, and no assistance from the kernel is required.

Recent research on systems with several processing cores indicates that message passing provides better performance than shared memory on such systems. Shared memory suffers from cache coherency issues, which arise because shared data migrate among the several caches. As the number of processing cores on systems increases, it is possible that we will see message passing as the preferred mechanism for IPC.

In the remainder of this section, we explore shared-memory and message-passing systems in more detail.

3.4.1   Shared-Memory Systems

Interprocess communication using shared memory requires communicating processes to establish a region of shared memory. Typically, a shared-memory region resides in the address space of the process creating the shared-memory segment. Other processes that wish to communicate using this shared-memory segment must attach it to their address space. Recall that, normally, the operating system tries to prevent one process from accessing another process's memory. Shared memory requires that two or more processes agree to remove this restriction. They can then exchange information by reading and writing data in the shared areas. The form of the data and the location are determined by these processes and are not under the operating system's control. The processes are also responsible for ensuring that they are not writing to the same location simultaneously.

To illustrate the concept of cooperating processes, let's consider the producer–consumer problem, which is a common paradigm for cooperating processes. A **producer** process produces information that is consumed by a **consumer** process. For example, a compiler may produce assembly code that is consumed by an assembler. The assembler, in turn, may produce object modules that are consumed by the loader. The producer–consumer problem

```
item next_produced;

while (true) {
        /* produce an item in next_produced */

        while (((in + 1) % BUFFER_SIZE) == out)
          ; /* do nothing */

        buffer[in] = next_produced;
        in = (in + 1) % BUFFER_SIZE;
}
```

Figure 3.13   The producer process using shared memory.

also provides a useful metaphor for the client–server paradigm. We generally think of a server as a producer and a client as a consumer. For example, a web server produces (that is, provides) HTML files and images, which are consumed (that is, read) by the client web browser requesting the resource.

One solution to the producer–consumer problem uses shared memory. To allow producer and consumer processes to run concurrently, we must have available a buffer of items that can be filled by the producer and emptied by the consumer. This buffer will reside in a region of memory that is shared by the producer and consumer processes. A producer can produce one item while the consumer is consuming another item. The producer and consumer must be synchronized, so that the consumer does not try to consume an item that has not yet been produced.

Two types of buffers can be used. The **unbounded buffer** places no practical limit on the size of the buffer. The consumer may have to wait for new items, but the producer can always produce new items. The **bounded buffer** assumes a fixed buffer size. In this case, the consumer must wait if the buffer is empty, and the producer must wait if the buffer is full.

Let's look more closely at how the bounded buffer illustrates interprocess communication using shared memory. The following variables reside in a region of memory shared by the producer and consumer processes:

```
#define BUFFER_SIZE 10

typedef struct {
        . . .
}item;

item buffer[BUFFER_SIZE];
int in = 0;
int out = 0;
```

The shared buffer is implemented as a circular array with two logical pointers: in and out. The variable in points to the next free position in the buffer; out points to the first full position in the buffer. The buffer is empty when in == out; the buffer is full when ((in + 1) % BUFFER_SIZE) == out.

The code for the producer process is shown in Figure 3.13, and the code for the consumer process is shown in Figure 3.14. The producer process has a

```
          item next_consumed;

      while (true) {
          while (in == out)
             ; /* do nothing */

          next_consumed = buffer[out];
          out = (out + 1) % BUFFER_SIZE;

          /* consume the item in next_consumed */
      }
```

Figure 3.14   The consumer process using shared memory.

local variable next_produced in which the new item to be produced is stored. The consumer process has a local variable next_consumed in which the item to be consumed is stored.

This scheme allows at most BUFFER_SIZE − 1 items in the buffer at the same time. We leave it as an exercise for you to provide a solution in which BUFFER_SIZE items can be in the buffer at the same time. In Section 3.5.1, we illustrate the POSIX API for shared memory.

One issue this illustration does not address concerns the situation in which both the producer process and the consumer process attempt to access the shared buffer concurrently. In Chapter 5, we discuss how synchronization among cooperating processes can be implemented effectively in a shared-memory environment.

3.4.2   Message-Passing Systems

In Section 3.4.1, we showed how cooperating processes can communicate in a shared-memory environment. The scheme requires that these processes share a region of memory and that the code for accessing and manipulating the shared memory be written explicitly by the application programmer. Another way to achieve the same effect is for the operating system to provide the means for cooperating processes to communicate with each other via a message-passing facility.

Message passing provides a mechanism to allow processes to communicate and to synchronize their actions without sharing the same address space. It is particularly useful in a distributed environment, where the communicating processes may reside on different computers connected by a network. For example, an Internet chat program could be designed so that chat participants communicate with one another by exchanging messages.

A message-passing facility provides at least two operations:

```
      send(message)          receive(message)
```

Messages sent by a process can be either fixed or variable in size. If only fixed-sized messages can be sent, the system-level implementation is straight-forward. This restriction, however, makes the task of programming more difficult. Conversely, variable-sized messages require a more complex system-level implementation, but the programming task becomes simpler. This is a common kind of tradeoff seen throughout operating-system design.

If processes P and Q want to communicate, they must send messages to and receive messages from each other: a *communication link* must exist between them. This link can be implemented in a variety of ways. We are concerned here not with the link's physical implementation (such as shared memory, hardware bus, or network), but rather with its logical implementation. Here are several methods for logically implementing a link and the `send()`/`receive()` operations:

- Direct or indirect communication

- Synchronous or asynchronous communication

- Automatic or explicit buffering

We look at issues related to each of these features next.

3.4.2.1   Naming

Processes that want to communicate must have a way to refer to each other. They can use either direct or indirect communication.

Under **direct communication**, each process that wants to communicate must explicitly name the recipient or sender of the communication. In this scheme, the `send()` and `receive()` primitives are defined as:

- `send(P, message)` —Send a message to process P.

- `receive(Q, message)` —Receive a message from process Q.

A communication link in this scheme has the following properties:

- A link is established automatically between every pair of processes that want to communicate. The processes need to know only each other's identity to communicate.

- A link is associated with exactly two processes.

- Between each pair of processes, there exists exactly one link.

This scheme exhibits *symmetry* in addressing; that is, both the sender process and the receiver process must name the other to communicate. A variant of this scheme employs *asymmetry* in addressing. Here, only the sender names the recipient; the recipient is not required to name the sender. In this scheme, the `send()` and `receive()` primitives are defined as follows:

- `send(P, message)` —Send a message to process P.

- `receive(id, message)` —Receive a message from any process. The variable `id` is set to the name of the process with which communication has taken place.

The disadvantage in both of these schemes (symmetric and asymmetric) is the limited modularity of the resulting process definitions. Changing the identifier of a process may necessitate examining all other process definitions. All references to the old identifier must be found, so that they can be modified to the new identifier. In general, any such *hard-coding* techniques, where identifiers must be explicitly stated, are less desirable than techniques involving indirection, as described next.

With *indirect communication*, the messages are sent to and received from *mailboxes*, or *ports*. A mailbox can be viewed abstractly as an object into which messages can be placed by processes and from which messages can be removed. Each mailbox has a unique identification. For example, POSIX message queues use an integer value to identify a mailbox. A process can communicate with another process via a number of different mailboxes, but two processes can communicate only if they have a shared mailbox. The `send()` and `receive()` primitives are defined as follows:

- `send(A, message)` —Send a message to mailbox A.

- `receive(A, message)` —Receive a message from mailbox A.

In this scheme, a communication link has the following properties:

- A link is established between a pair of processes only if both members of the pair have a shared mailbox.

- A link may be associated with more than two processes.

- Between each pair of communicating processes, a number of different links may exist, with each link corresponding to one mailbox.

Now suppose that processes P_1, P_2, and P_3 all share mailbox A. Process P_1 sends a message to A, while both P_2 and P_3 execute a `receive()` from A. Which process will receive the message sent by P_1? The answer depends on which of the following methods we choose:

- Allow a link to be associated with two processes at most.

- Allow at most one process at a time to execute a `receive()` operation.

- Allow the system to select arbitrarily which process will receive the message (that is, either P_2 or P_3, but not both, will receive the message). The system may define an algorithm for selecting which process will receive the message (for example, *round robin*, where processes take turns receiving messages). The system may identify the receiver to the sender.

A mailbox may be owned either by a process or by the operating system. If the mailbox is owned by a process (that is, the mailbox is part of the address space of the process), then we distinguish between the owner (which can only receive messages through this mailbox) and the user (which can only send messages to the mailbox). Since each mailbox has a unique owner, there can be no confusion about which process should receive a message sent to this mailbox. When a process that owns a mailbox terminates, the mailbox disappears. Any process that subsequently sends a message to this mailbox must be notified that the mailbox no longer exists.

In contrast, a mailbox that is owned by the operating system has an existence of its own. It is independent and is not attached to any particular process. The operating system then must provide a mechanism that allows a process to do the following:

- Create a new mailbox.
- Send and receive messages through the mailbox.
- Delete a mailbox.

The process that creates a new mailbox is that mailbox's owner by default. Initially, the owner is the only process that can receive messages through this mailbox. However, the ownership and receiving privilege may be passed to other processes through appropriate system calls. Of course, this provision could result in multiple receivers for each mailbox.

3.4.2.2   Synchronization

Communication between processes takes place through calls to `send()` and `receive()` primitives. There are different design options for implementing each primitive. Message passing may be either **blocking** or **nonblocking**— also known as **synchronous** and **asynchronous**. (Throughout this text, you will encounter the concepts of synchronous and asynchronous behavior in relation to various operating-system algorithms.)

- **Blocking send**. The sending process is blocked until the message is received by the receiving process or by the mailbox.
- **Nonblocking send**. The sending process sends the message and resumes operation.
- **Blocking receive**. The receiver blocks until a message is available.
- **Nonblocking receive**. The receiver retrieves either a valid message or a null.

Different combinations of `send()` and `receive()` are possible. When both `send()` and `receive()` are blocking, we have a **rendezvous** between the sender and the receiver. The solution to the producer–consumer problem becomes trivial when we use blocking `send()` and `receive()` statements. The producer merely invokes the blocking `send()` call and waits until the message is delivered to either the receiver or the mailbox. Likewise, when the consumer invokes `receive()`, it blocks until a message is available. This is illustrated in Figures 3.15 and 3.16.

3.4.2.3   Buffering

Whether communication is direct or indirect, messages exchanged by communicating processes reside in a temporary queue. Basically, such queues can be implemented in three ways:

```
message next_produced;

while (true) {
    /* produce an item in next_produced */

    send(next_produced);
}
```

Figure 3.15   The producer process using message passing.

- **Zero capacity**. The queue has a maximum length of ze̶
  cannot have any messages waiting in it. In this case, th̶
  until the recipient receives the message.

- **Bounded capacity**. The queue has finite length n; thus,
  can reside in it. If the queue is not full when a new n̶
  message is placed in the queue (either the message is
  to the message is kept), and the sender can continue
  waiting. The link's capacity is finite, however. If the lin̶
  must block until space is available in the queue.

- **Unbounded capacity**. The queue's length is potentially
  number of messages can wait in it. The sender never bl̶

The zero-capacity case is sometimes referred to as a messa̶
buffering. The other cases are referred to as systems with au̶

3.5   Examples of IPC Systems

In this section, we explore three different IPC systems. We fir̶
API for shared memory and then discuss message passing in th̶
system. We conclude with Windows, which interestingly use̶
as a mechanism for providing certain types of message passi̶

3.5.1   An Example: POSIX Shared Memory

Several IPC mechanisms are available for POSIX systems, including shared
memory and message passing. Here, we explore the POSIX API for shared
memory.

POSIX shared memory is organized using memory-mapped files, which
associate the region of shared memory with a file. A process must first create

```
message next_consumed;

while (true) {
    receive(next_consumed);

    /* consume the item in next_consumed */
}
```

Figure 3.16   The consumer process using message passing.

a shared-memory object using the shm_open() system call, as follows:

```
shm_fd = shm_open(name, O_CREAT | O_RDWR, 0666);
```

The first parameter specifies the name of the shared-memory object. Processes that wish to access this shared memory must refer to the object by this name. The subsequent parameters specify that the shared-memory object is to be created if it does not yet exist (O_CREAT) and that the object is open for reading and writing (O_RDWR). The last parameter establishes the directory permissions of the shared-memory object. A successful call to shm_open() returns an integer file descriptor for the shared-memory object.

Once the object is established, the ftruncate() function is used to configure the size of the object in bytes. The call

```
ftruncate(shm_fd, 4096);
```

sets the size of the object to 4,096 bytes.

Finally, the mmap() function establishes a memory-mapped file containing the shared-memory object. It also returns a pointer to the memory-mapped file that is used for accessing the shared-memory object.

The programs shown in Figures 3.17 and 3.18 use the producer–consumer model in implementing shared memory. The producer establishes a shared-memory object and writes to shared memory, and the consumer reads from shared memory.

The producer, shown in Figure 3.17, creates a shared-memory object named OS and writes the infamous string "Hello World!" to shared memory. The program memory-maps a shared-memory object of the specified size and allows writing to the object. (Obviously, only writing is necessary for the producer.) The flag MAP_SHARED specifies that changes to the shared-memory object will be visible to all processes sharing the object. Notice that we write to the shared-memory object by calling the sprintf() function and writing the formatted string to the pointer ptr. After each write, we must increment the pointer by the number of bytes written.

The consumer process, shown in Figure 3.18, reads and outputs the contents of the shared memory. The consumer also invokes the shm_unlink() function, which removes the shared-memory segment after the consumer has accessed it. We provide further exercises using the POSIX shared-memory API in the programming exercises at the end of this chapter. Additionally, we provide more detailed coverage of memory mapping in Section 8.7.

3.5.2 An Example: Mach

As an example of message passing, we next consider the Mach operating system. You may recall that we introduced Mach in Chapter 2 as part of the Mac OS X operating system. The Mach kernel supports the creation and destruction of multiple tasks, which are similar to processes but have multiple threads of control and fewer associated resources. Most communication in Mach—including all intertask information—is carried out by **messages**. Messages are sent to and received from mailboxes, called **ports** in Mach.

```
#include <stdio.h>
#include <stdlib.h>
#include <string.h>
#include <fcntl.h>
#include <sys/shm.h>
#include <sys/stat.h>

int main()
{
/* the size (in bytes) of shared memory object */
const int SIZE = 4096;
/* name of the shared memory object */
const char *name = "OS";
/* strings written to shared memory */
const char *message_0 = "Hello";
const char *message_1 = "World!";

/* shared memory file descriptor */
int shm_fd;
/* pointer to shared memory obect */
void *ptr;

    /* create the shared memory object */
    shm_fd = shm_open(name, O_CREAT | O_RDWR, 0666);

    /* configure the size of the shared memory object */
    ftruncate(shm_fd, SIZE);

    /* memory map the shared memory object */
    ptr = mmap(0, SIZE, PROT_WRITE, MAP_SHARED, shm_fd, 0);

    /* write to the shared memory object */
    sprintf(ptr,"%s",message_0);
    ptr += strlen(message_0);
    sprintf(ptr,"%s",message_1);
    ptr += strlen(message_1);

    return 0;
}
```

Figure 3.17 Producer process illustrating POSIX shared-memory API.

Even system calls are made by messages. When a task is created, two special mailboxes—the Kernel mailbox and the Notify mailbox—are also created. The kernel uses the Kernel mailbox to communicate with the task and sends notification of event occurrences to the Notify port. Only three system calls are needed for message transfer. The msg_send() call sends a message to a mailbox. A message is received via msg_receive(). Remote procedure calls (RPCs) are executed via msg_rpc(), which sends a message and waits for exactly one return message from the sender. In this way, the RPC models a

```
#include <stdio.h>
#include <stdlib.h>
#include <fcntl.h>
#include <sys/shm.h>
#include <sys/stat.h>

int main()
{
/* the size (in bytes) of shared memory object */
const int SIZE = 4096;
/* name of the shared memory object */
const char *name = "OS";
/* shared memory file descriptor */
int shm_fd;
/* pointer to shared memory obect */
void *ptr;

    /* open the shared memory object */
    shm_fd = shm_open(name, O_RDONLY, 0666);

    /* memory map the shared memory object */
    ptr = mmap(0, SIZE, PROT_READ, MAP_SHARED, shm_fd, 0);

    /* read from the shared memory object */
    printf("%s",(char *)ptr);

    /* remove the shared memory object */
    shm_unlink(name);

    return 0;
}
```

Figure 3.18 Consumer process illustrating POSIX shared-memory API.

typical subroutine procedure call but can work between systems—hence the term *remote*. Remote procedure calls are covered in detail in Section 3.6.2.

The port_allocate() system call creates a new mailbox and allocates space for its queue of messages. The maximum size of the message queue defaults to eight messages. The task that creates the mailbox is that mailbox's owner. The owner is also allowed to receive from the mailbox. Only one task at a time can either own or receive from a mailbox, but these rights can be sent to other tasks.

The mailbox's message queue is initially empty. As messages are sent to the mailbox, the messages are copied into the mailbox. All messages have the same priority. Mach guarantees that multiple messages from the same sender are queued in first-in, first-out (FIFO) order but does not guarantee an absolute ordering. For instance, messages from two senders may be queued in any order.

The messages themselves consist of a fixed-length header followed by a variable-length data portion. The header indicates the length of the message and includes two mailbox names. One mailbox name specifies the mailbox to which the message is being sent. Commonly, the sending thread expects a reply, so the mailbox name of the sender is passed on to the receiving task, which can use it as a "return address."

The variable part of a message is a list of typed data items. Each entry in the list has a type, size, and value. The type of the objects specified in the message is important, since objects defined by the operating system—such as ownership or receive access rights, task states, and memory segments—may be sent in messages.

The send and receive operations themselves are flexible. For instance, when a message is sent to a mailbox, the mailbox may be full. If the mailbox is not full, the message is copied to the mailbox, and the sending thread continues. If the mailbox is full, the sending thread has four options:

1. Wait indefinitely until there is room in the mailbox.

2. Wait at most n milliseconds.

3. Do not wait at all but rather return immediately.

4. Temporarily cache a message. Here, a message is given to the operating system to keep, even though the mailbox to which that message is being sent is full. When the message can be put in the mailbox, a message is sent back to the sender. Only one message to a full mailbox can be pending at any time for a given sending thread.

The final option is meant for server tasks, such as a line-printer driver. After finishing a request, such tasks may need to send a one-time reply to the task that requested service, but they must also continue with other service requests, even if the reply mailbox for a client is full.

The receive operation must specify the mailbox or mailbox set from which a message is to be received. A **mailbox set** is a collection of mailboxes, as declared by the task, which can be grouped together and treated as one mailbox for the purposes of the task. Threads in a task can receive only from a mailbox or mailbox set for which the task has receive access. A port_status() system call returns the number of messages in a given mailbox. The receive operation attempts to receive from (1) any mailbox in a mailbox set or (2) a specific (named) mailbox. If no message is waiting to be received, the receiving thread can either wait at most n milliseconds or not wait at all.

The Mach system was especially designed for distributed systems, but Mach was shown to be suitable for systems with fewer processing cores, as evidenced by its inclusion in the Mac OS X system. The major problem with message systems has generally been poor performance caused by double copying of messages: the message is copied first from the sender to the mailbox and then from the mailbox to the receiver. The Mach message system attempts to avoid double-copy operations by using virtual-memory-management techniques (Chapter 8). Essentially, Mach maps the address space containing the sender's message into the receiver's address space. The message itself is never actually copied. This message-management technique provides a large performance boost but works for only intrasystem messages. The Mach operating system is discussed in more detail in the online Appendix B.

3.5.3   An Example: Windows

The Windows operating system is an example of modern design that employs modularity to increase functionality and decrease the time needed to implement new features. Windows provides support for multiple operating environments, or *subsystems.* Application programs communicate with these subsystems via a message-passing mechanism. Thus, application programs can be considered clients of a subsystem server.

The message-passing facility in Windows is called the advanced local procedure call (ALPC) facility. It is used for communication between two processes on the same machine. It is similar to the standard remote procedure call (RPC) mechanism that is widely used, but it is optimized for and specific to Windows. (Remote procedure calls are covered in detail in Section 3.6.2.) Like Mach, Windows uses a port object to establish and maintain a connection between two processes. Windows uses two types of ports: connection ports and communication ports.

Server processes publish connection-port objects that are visible to all processes. When a client wants services from a subsystem, it opens a handle to the server's connection-port object and sends a connection request to that port. The server then creates a channel and returns a handle to the client. The channel consists of a pair of private communication ports: one for client—server messages, the other for server—client messages. Additionally, communication channels support a callback mechanism that allows the client and server to accept requests when they would normally be expecting a reply.

When an ALPC channel is created, one of three message-passing techniques is chosen:

1. For small messages (up to 256 bytes), the port's message queue is used as intermediate storage, and the messages are copied from one process to the other.

2. Larger messages must be passed through a section object, which is a region of shared memory associated with the channel.

3. When the amount of data is too large to fit into a section object, an API is available that allows server processes to read and write directly into the address space of a client.

The client has to decide when it sets up the channel whether it will need to send a large message. If the client determines that it does want to send large messages, it asks for a section object to be created. Similarly, if the server decides that replies will be large, it creates a section object. So that the section object can be used, a small message is sent that contains a pointer and size information about the section object. This method is more complicated than the first method listed above, but it avoids data copying. The structure of advanced local procedure calls in Windows is shown in Figure 3.19.

It is important to note that the ALPC facility in Windows is not part of the Windows API and hence is not visible to the application programmer. Rather, applications using the Windows API invoke standard remote procedure calls. When the RPC is being invoked on a process on the same system, the RPC is handled indirectly through an ALPC. procedure call. Additionally, many kernel services use ALPC to communicate with client processes.

Figure 3.19   Advanced local procedure calls in Windows.

3.6   Communication in Client–Server Systems

In Section 3.4, we described how processes can communicate using shared memory and message passing. These techniques can be used for communication in client–server systems (Section 1.11.4) as well. In this section, we explore three other strategies for communication in client–server systems: sockets, remote procedure calls (RPCs), and pipes.

3.6.1 Sockets

A socket is defined as an endpoint for communication. A pair of processes communicating over a network employs a pair of sockets—one for each process. A socket is identified by an IP address concatenated with a port number. In general, sockets use a client–server architecture. The server waits for incoming client requests by listening to a specified port. Once a request is received, the server accepts a connection from the client socket to complete the connection. Servers implementing specific services (such as telnet, FTP, and HTTP) listen to well-known ports (a telnet server listens to port 23; an FTP server listens to port 21; and a web, or HTTP, server listens to port 80). All ports below 1024 are considered *well known;* we can use them to implement standard services.

When a client process initiates a request for a connection, it is assigned a port by its host computer. This port has some arbitrary number greater than 1024. For example, if a client on host X with IP address 146.86.5.20 wishes to establish a connection with a web server (which is listening on port 80) at address 161.25.19.8, host X may be assigned port 1625. The connection will consist of a pair of sockets: (146.86.5.20:1625) on host X and (161.25.19.8:80) on the web server. This situation is illustrated in Figure 3.20. The packets traveling between the hosts are delivered to the appropriate process based on the destination port number.

All connections must be unique. Therefore, if another process also on host X wished to establish another connection with the same web server, it would be assigned a port number greater than 1024 and not equal to 1625. This ensures that all connections consist of a unique pair of sockets.

host *X*
(146.86.5.20)

socket
(146.86.5.20:1625)

web server
(161.25.19.8)

socket
(161.25.19.8:80)

Figure 3.20 Communication using sockets.

Although most program examples in this text use C, we will illustrate sockets using Java, as it provides a much easier interface to sockets and has a rich library for networking utilities. Those interested in socket programming in C or C++ should consult the bibliographical notes at the end of the chapter.

Java provides three different types of sockets. **Connection-oriented (TCP)** sockets are implemented with the Socket class. **Connectionless (UDP)** sockets use the DatagramSocket class. Finally, the MulticastSocket class is a subclass of the DatagramSocket class. A multicast socket allows data to be sent to multiple recipients.

Our example describes a date server that uses connection-oriented TCP sockets. The operation allows clients to request the current date and time from the server. The server listens to port 6013, although the port could have any arbitrary number greater than 1024. When a connection is received, the server returns the date and time to the client.

The date server is shown in Figure 3.21. The server creates a ServerSocket that specifies that it will listen to port 6013. The server then begins listening to the port with the accept() method. The server blocks on the accept() method waiting for a client to request a connection. When a connection request is received, accept() returns a socket that the server can use to communicate with the client.

The details of how the server communicates with the socket are as follows. The server first establishes a PrintWriter object that it will use to communicate with the client. A PrintWriter object allows the server to write to the socket using the routine print() and println() methods for output. The server process sends the date to the client, calling the method println(). Once it has written the date to the socket, the server closes the socket to the client and resumes listening for more requests.

A client communicates with the server by creating a socket and connecting to the port on which the server is listening. We implement such a client in the Java program shown in Figure 3.22. The client creates a Socket and requests a connection with the server at IP address 127.0.0.1 on port 6013. Once the connection is made, the client can read from the socket using normal stream I/O statements. After it has received the date from the server, the client closes

```java
import java.net.*;
import java.io.*;

public class DateServer
{
   public static void main(String[] args) {
      try {
         ServerSocket sock = new ServerSocket(6013);

         /* now listen for connections */
         while (true) {
            Socket client = sock.accept();

            PrintWriter pout = new
             PrintWriter(client.getOutputStream(), true);

            /* write the Date to the socket */
            pout.println(new java.util.Date().toString());

            /* close the socket and resume */
            /* listening for connections */
            client.close();
         }
      }
      catch (IOException ioe) {
         System.err.println(ioe);
      }
   }
}
```

Figure 3.21   Date server.

the socket and exits. The IP address 127.0.0.1 is a special IP address known as the **loopback**. When a computer refers to IP address 127.0.0.1, it is referring to itself. This mechanism allows a client and server on the same host to communicate using the TCP/IP protocol. The IP address 127.0.0.1 could be replaced with the IP address of another host running the date server. In addition to an IP address, an actual host name, such as www.westminstercollege.edu, can be used as well.

Communication using sockets—although common and efficient—is considered a low-level form of communication between distributed processes. One reason is that sockets allow only an unstructured stream of bytes to be exchanged between the communicating threads. It is the responsibility of the client or server application to impose a structure on the data. In the next two subsections, we look at two higher-level methods of communication: remote procedure calls (RPCs) and pipes.

3.6.2   Remote Procedure Calls

One of the most common forms of remote service is the RPC paradigm, which we discussed briefly in Section 3.5.2. The RPC was designed as a way to

```
import java.net.*;
import java.io.*;

public class DateClient
{
  public static void main(String[] args) {
    try {
      /* make connection to server socket */
      Socket sock = new Socket("127.0.0.1",6013);

      InputStream in = sock.getInputStream();
      BufferedReader bin = new
        BufferedReader(new InputStreamReader(in));

      /* read the date from the socket */
      String line;
      while ( (line = bin.readLine()) != null)
        System.out.println(line);

      /* close the socket connection*/
      sock.close();
    }
    catch (IOException ioe) {
      System.err.println(ioe);
    }
  }
}
```

Figure 3.22 Date client.

abstract the procedure-call mechanism for use between systems with network connections. It is similar in many respects to the IPC mechanism described in Section 3.4, and it is usually built on top of such a system. Here, however, because we are dealing with an environment in which the processes are executing on separate systems, we must use a message-based communication scheme to provide remote service.

In contrast to IPC messages, the messages exchanged in RPC communication are well structured and are thus no longer just packets of data. Each message is addressed to an RPC daemon listening to a port on the remote system, and each contains an identifier specifying the function to execute and the parameters to pass to that function. The function is then executed as requested, and any output is sent back to the requester in a separate message.

A **port** is simply a number included at the start of a message packet. Whereas a system normally has one network address, it can have many ports within that address to differentiate the many network services it supports. If a remote process needs a service, it addresses a message to the proper port. For instance, if a system wished to allow other systems to be able to list its current users, it would have a daemon supporting such an RPC attached to a port—say, port 3027. Any remote system could obtain the needed information (that is, the list of current users) by sending an RPC message to port 3027 on the server. The data would be received in a reply message.

The semantics of RPCs allows a client to invoke a procedure on a remote host as it would invoke a procedure locally. The RPC system hides the details that allow communication to take place by providing a stub on the client side. Typically, a separate stub exists for each separate remote procedure. When the client invokes a remote procedure, the RPC system calls the appropriate stub, passing it the parameters provided to the remote procedure. This stub locates the port on the server and marshals the parameters. Parameter marshalling involves packaging the parameters into a form that can be transmitted over a network. The stub then transmits a message to the server using message passing. A similar stub on the server side receives this message and invokes the procedure on the server. If necessary, return values are passed back to the client using the same technique. On Windows systems, stub code is compiled from a specification written in the Microsoft Interface Definition Language (MIDL), which is used for defining the interfaces between client and server programs.

One issue that must be dealt with concerns differences in data representation on the client and server machines. Consider the representation of 32-bit integers. Some systems (known as big-endian) store the most significant byte first, while other systems (known as little-endian) store the least significant byte first. Neither order is "better" per se; rather, the choice is arbitrary within a computer architecture. To resolve differences like this, many RPC systems define a machine-independent representation of data. One such representation is known as external data representation (XDR). On the client side, parameter marshalling involves converting the machine-dependent data into XDR before they are sent to the server. On the server side, the XDR data are unmarshalled and converted to the machine-dependent representation for the server.

Another important issue involves the semantics of a call. Whereas local procedure calls fail only under extreme circumstances, RPCs can fail, or be duplicated and executed more than once, as a result of common network errors. One way to address this problem is for the operating system to ensure that messages are acted on *exactly once*, rather than *at most once*. Most local procedure calls have the "exactly once" functionality, but it is more difficult to implement.

First, consider "at most once." This semantic can be implemented by attaching a timestamp to each message. The server must keep a history of all the timestamps of messages it has already processed or a history large enough to ensure that repeated messages are detected. Incoming messages that have a timestamp already in the history are ignored. The client can then send a message one or more times and be assured that it only executes once.

For "exactly once," we need to remove the risk that the server will never receive the request. To accomplish this, the server must implement the "at most once" protocol described above but must also acknowledge to the client that the RPC call was received and executed. These ACK messages are common throughout networking. The client must resend each RPC call periodically until it receives the ACK for that call.

Yet another important issue concerns the communication between a server and a client. With standard procedure calls, some form of binding takes place during link, load, or execution time (Chapter 7) so that a procedure call's name

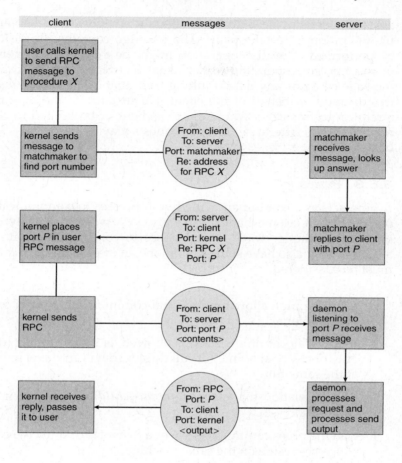

Figure 3.23 Execution of a remote procedure call (RPC).

is replaced by the memory address of the procedure call. The RPC scheme requires a similar binding of the client and the server port, but how does a client know the port numbers on the server? Neither system has full information about the other, because they do not share memory.

Two approaches are common. First, the binding information may be predetermined, in the form of fixed port addresses. At compile time, an RPC call has a fixed port number associated with it. Once a program is compiled, the server cannot change the port number of the requested service. Second, binding can be done dynamically by a rendezvous mechanism. Typically, an operating system provides a rendezvous (also called a **matchmaker**) daemon on a fixed RPC port. A client then sends a message containing the name of the RPC to the rendezvous daemon requesting the port address of the RPC it needs to execute. The port number is returned, and the RPC calls can be sent to that port until the process terminates (or the server crashes). This method requires the extra overhead of the initial request but is more flexible than the first approach. Figure 3.23 shows a sample interaction.

The RPC scheme is useful in implementing a distributed file system. Such a system can be implemented as a set of RPC daemons and clients. The messages are addressed to the distributed file system port on a server on which a file operation is to take place. The message contains the disk operation to be performed. The disk operation might be read, write, rename, delete, or status, corresponding to the usual file-related system calls. The return message contains any data resulting from that call, which is executed by the DFS daemon on behalf of the client. For instance, a message might contain a request to transfer a whole file to a client or be limited to a simple block request. In the latter case, several requests may be needed if a whole file is to be transferred.

3.6.3 Pipes

A pipe acts as a conduit allowing two processes to communicate. Pipes were one of the first IPC mechanisms in early UNIX systems. They typically provide one of the simpler ways for processes to communicate with one another, although they also have some limitations. In implementing a pipe, four issues must be considered:

1. Does the pipe allow bidirectional communication, or is communication unidirectional?

2. If two-way communication is allowed, is it half duplex (data can travel only one way at a time) or full duplex (data can travel in both directions at the same time)?

3. Must a relationship (such as *parent–child*) exist between the communicating processes?

4. Can the pipes communicate over a network, or must the communicating processes reside on the same machine?

In the following sections, we explore two common types of pipes used on both UNIX and Windows systems: ordinary pipes and named pipes.

3.6.3.1 Ordinary Pipes

Ordinary pipes allow two processes to communicate in standard producer–consumer fashion: the producer writes to one end of the pipe (the write-end) and the consumer reads from the other end (the read-end). As a result, ordinary pipes are unidirectional, allowing only one-way communication. If two-way communication is required, two pipes must be used, with each pipe sending data in a different direction. We next illustrate constructing ordinary pipes on both UNIX and Windows systems. In both program examples, one process writes the message Greetings to the pipe, while the other process reads this message from the pipe.

On UNIX systems, ordinary pipes are constructed using the function

```
pipe(int fd[])
```

This function creates a pipe that is accessed through the int fd[] file descriptors: fd[0] is the read-end of the pipe, and fd[1] is the write-end.

Figure 3.24   File descriptors for an ordinary pipe.

UNIX treats a pipe as a special type of file. Thus, pipes can be accessed using ordinary `read()` and `write()` system calls.

An ordinary pipe cannot be accessed from outside the process that created it. Typically, a parent process creates a pipe and uses it to communicate with a child process that it creates via `fork()`. Recall from Section 3.3.1 that a child process inherits open files from its parent. Since a pipe is a special type of file, the child inherits the pipe from its parent process. Figure 3.24 illustrates the relationship of the file descriptor `fd` to the parent and child processes.

In the UNIX program shown in Figure 3.25, the parent process creates a pipe and then sends a `fork()` call creating the child process. What occurs after the `fork()` call depends on how the data are to flow through the pipe. In this instance, the parent writes to the pipe, and the child reads from it. It is important to notice that both the parent process and the child process initially close their unused ends of the pipe. Although the program shown in Figure 3.25 does not require this action, it is an important step to ensure that a process reading from the pipe can detect end-of-file (`read()` returns 0) when the writer has closed its end of the pipe.

Ordinary pipes on Windows systems are termed **anonymous pipes**, and they behave similarly to their UNIX counterparts: they are unidirectional and

```
#include <sys/types.h>
#include <stdio.h>
#include <string.h>
#include <unistd.h>

#define BUFFER_SIZE 25
#define READ_END 0
#define WRITE_END 1

int main(void)
{
char write_msg[BUFFER_SIZE] = "Greetings";
char read_msg[BUFFER_SIZE];
int fd[2];
pid_t pid;
```

/* Program continues in Figure 3.26 */

Figure 3.25   Ordinary pipe in UNIX.

```
                  /* create the pipe */
                  if (pipe(fd) == -1) {
                     fprintf(stderr,"Pipe failed");
                     return 1;
                  }

                  /* fork a child process */
                  pid = fork();

                  if (pid < 0) { /* error occurred */
                     fprintf(stderr, "Fork Failed");
                     return 1;
                  }

                  if (pid > 0) { /* parent process */
                     /* close the unused end of the pipe */
                     close(fd[READ_END]);

                     /* write to the pipe */
                     write(fd[WRITE_END], write_msg, strlen(write_msg)+1);

                     /* close the write end of the pipe */
                     close(fd[WRITE_END]);
                  }
                  else { /* child process */
                     /* close the unused end of the pipe */
                     close(fd[WRITE_END]);

                     /* read from the pipe */
                     read(fd[READ_END], read_msg, BUFFER_SIZE);
                     printf("read %s",read_msg);

                     /* close the read end of the pipe */
                     close(fd[READ_END]);
                  }

                  return 0;
               }
```

Figure 3.26   Figure 3.25, continued.

employ parent–child relationships between the communicating processes. In addition, reading and writing to the pipe can be accomplished with the ordinary ReadFile() and WriteFile() functions. The Windows API for creating pipes is the CreatePipe() function, which is passed four parameters. The parameters provide separate handles for (1) reading and (2) writing to the pipe, as well as (3) an instance of the STARTUPINFO structure, which is used to specify that the child process is to inherit the handles of the pipe. Furthermore, (4) the size of the pipe (in bytes) may be specified.

Figure 3.27 illustrates a parent process creating an anonymous pipe for communicating with its child. Unlike UNIX systems, in which a child process

```
#include <stdio.h>
#include <stdlib.h>
#include <windows.h>

#define BUFFER_SIZE 25

int main(VOID)
{
HANDLE ReadHandle, WriteHandle;
STARTUPINFO si;
PROCESS_INFORMATION pi;
char message[BUFFER_SIZE] = "Greetings";
DWORD written;
```

/* Program continues in Figure 3.28 */

Figure 3.27 Windows anonymous pipe — parent process.

automatically inherits a pipe created by its parent, Windows requires the programmer to specify which attributes the child process will inherit. This is accomplished by first initializing the SECURITY_ATTRIBUTES structure to allow handles to be inherited and then redirecting the child process's handles for standard input or standard output to the read or write handle of the pipe. Since the child will be reading from the pipe, the parent must redirect the child's standard input to the read handle of the pipe. Furthermore, as the pipes are half duplex, it is necessary to prohibit the child from inheriting the write-end of the pipe. The program to create the child process is similar to the program in Figure 3.11, except that the fifth parameter is set to TRUE, indicating that the child process is to inherit designated handles from its parent. Before writing to the pipe, the parent first closes its unused read end of the pipe. The child process that reads from the pipe is shown in Figure 3.29. Before reading from the pipe, this program obtains the read handle to the pipe by invoking GetStdHandle().

Note that ordinary pipes require a parent–child relationship between the communicating processes on both UNIX and Windows systems. This means that these pipes can be used only for communication between processes on the same machine.

3.6.3.2   Named Pipes

Ordinary pipes provide a simple mechanism for allowing a pair of processes to communicate. However, ordinary pipes exist only while the processes are communicating with one another. On both UNIX and Windows systems, once the processes have finished communicating and have terminated, the ordinary pipe ceases to exist.

Named pipes provide a much more powerful communication tool. Communication can be bidirectional, and no parent–child relationship is required. Once a named pipe is established, several processes can use it for communication. In fact, in a typical scenario, a named pipe has several writers. Additionally, named pipes continue to exist after communicating processes have

```
/* set up security attributes allowing pipes to be inherited */
SECURITY_ATTRIBUTES sa = {sizeof(SECURITY_ATTRIBUTES),NULL,TRUE};
/* allocate memory */
ZeroMemory(&pi, sizeof(pi));

/* create the pipe */
if (!CreatePipe(&ReadHandle, &WriteHandle, &sa, 0)) {
  fprintf(stderr, "Create Pipe Failed");
  return 1;
}

/* establish the START_INFO structure for the child process */
GetStartupInfo(&si);
si.hStdOutput = GetStdHandle(STD_OUTPUT_HANDLE);

/* redirect standard input to the read end of the pipe */
si.hStdInput = ReadHandle;
si.dwFlags = STARTF_USESTDHANDLES;

/* don't allow the child to inherit the write end of pipe */
SetHandleInformation(WriteHandle, HANDLE_FLAG_INHERIT, 0);

/* create the child process */
CreateProcess(NULL, "child.exe", NULL, NULL,
  TRUE, /* inherit handles */
  0, NULL, NULL, &si, &pi);

/* close the unused end of the pipe */
CloseHandle(ReadHandle);

/* the parent writes to the pipe */
if (!WriteFile(WriteHandle, message,BUFFER_SIZE,&written,NULL))
  fprintf(stderr, "Error writing to pipe.");

/* close the write end of the pipe */
CloseHandle(WriteHandle);

/* wait for the child to exit */
WaitForSingleObject(pi.hProcess, INFINITE);
CloseHandle(pi.hProcess);
CloseHandle(pi.hThread);
return 0;
}
```

Figure 3.28   Figure 3.27, continued.

finished. Both UNIX and Windows systems support named pipes, although the details of implementation differ greatly. Next, we explore named pipes in each of these systems.

```
#include <stdio.h>
#include <windows.h>

#define BUFFER_SIZE 25

int main(VOID)
{
HANDLE Readhandle;
CHAR buffer[BUFFER_SIZE];
DWORD read;

    /* get the read handle of the pipe */
    ReadHandle = GetStdHandle(STD_INPUT_HANDLE);

    /* the child reads from the pipe */
    if (ReadFile(ReadHandle, buffer, BUFFER_SIZE, &read, NULL))
      printf("child read %s",buffer);
    else
      fprintf(stderr, "Error reading from pipe");

    return 0;
}
```

Figure 3.29 Windows anonymous pipes — child process.

Named pipes are referred to as FIFOs in UNIX systems. Once created, they appear as typical files in the file system. A FIFO is created with the `mkfifo()` system call and manipulated with the ordinary `open()`, `read()`, `write()`, and `close()` system calls. It will continue to exist until it is explicitly deleted from the file system. Although FIFOs allow bidirectional communication, only half-duplex transmission is permitted. If data must travel in both directions, two FIFOs are typically used. Additionally, the communicating processes must reside on the same machine. If intermachine communication is required, sockets (Section 3.6.1) must be used.

Named pipes on Windows systems provide a richer communication mechanism than their UNIX counterparts. Full-duplex communication is allowed, and the communicating processes may reside on either the same or different machines. Additionally, only byte-oriented data may be transmitted across a UNIX FIFO, whereas Windows systems allow either byte- or message-oriented data. Named pipes are created with the `CreateNamedPipe()` function, and a client can connect to a named pipe using `ConnectNamedPipe()`. Communication over the named pipe can be accomplished using the `ReadFile()` and `WriteFile()` functions.

3.7   Summary

A process is a program in execution. As a process executes, it changes state. The state of a process is defined by that process's current activity. Each process may be in one of the following states: new, ready, running, waiting, or terminated.

PIPES IN PRACTICE

Pipes are used quite often in the UNIX command-line environment for situations in which the output of one command serves as input to another. For example, the UNIX `ls` command produces a directory listing. For especially long directory listings, the output may scroll through several screens. The command `more` manages output by displaying only one screen of output at a time; the user must press the space bar to move from one screen to the next. Setting up a pipe between the `ls` and `more` commands (which are running as individual processes) allows the output of `ls` to be delivered as the input to `more`, enabling the user to display a large directory listing a screen at a time. A pipe can be constructed on the command line using the | character. The complete command is

```
ls | more
```

In this scenario, the `ls` command serves as the producer, and its output is consumed by the `more` command.

Windows systems provide a `more` command for the DOS shell with functionality similar to that of its UNIX counterpart. The DOS shell also uses the | character for establishing a pipe. The only difference is that to get a directory listing, DOS uses the `dir` command rather than `ls`, as shown below:

```
dir | more
```

Each process is represented in the operating system by its own process control block (PCB).

A process, when it is not executing, is placed in some waiting queue. There are two major classes of queues in an operating system: I/O request queues and the ready queue. The ready queue contains all the processes that are ready to execute and are waiting for the CPU. Each process is represented by a PCB.

The operating system must select processes from various scheduling queues. Long-term (job) scheduling is the selection of processes that will be allowed to contend for the CPU. Normally, long-term scheduling is heavily influenced by resource-allocation considerations, especially memory management. Short-term (CPU) scheduling is the selection of one process from the ready queue.

Operating systems must provide a mechanism for parent processes to create new child processes. The parent may wait for its children to terminate before proceeding, or the parent and children may execute concurrently. There are several reasons for allowing concurrent execution: information sharing, computation speedup, modularity, and convenience.

The processes executing in the operating system may be either independent processes or cooperating processes. Cooperating processes require an interprocess communication mechanism to communicate with each other. Principally, communication is achieved through two schemes: shared memory and message passing. The shared-memory method requires communicating processes to share some variables. The processes are expected to exchange information through the use of these shared variables. In a shared-memory system, the responsibility for providing communication rests with the application programmers; the operating system needs to provide only the shared memory. The message-passing method allows the processes to exchange messages. The responsibility for providing communication may rest with the operating system itself. These two schemes are not mutually exclusive and can be used simultaneously within a single operating system.

Communication in client–server systems may use (1) sockets, (2) remote procedure calls (RPCs), or (3) pipes. A socket is defined as an endpoint for communication. A connection between a pair of applications consists of a pair of sockets, one at each end of the communication channel. RPCs are another form of distributed communication. An RPC occurs when a process (or thread) calls a procedure on a remote application. Pipes provide a relatively simple ways for processes to communicate with one another. Ordinary pipes allow communication between parent and child processes, while named pipes permit unrelated processes to communicate.

Review Questions

Review questions for this chapter can be accessed by visiting our website.

Practice Exercises

Answers for the Practice Exercises can be accceed by visiting our website.

3.1 Using the program shown in Figure 3.30, explain what the output will be at LINE A.

3.2 Including the initial parent process, how many processes are created by the program shown in Figure 3.31?

3.3 Original versions of Apple's mobile iOS operating system provided no means of concurrent processing. Discuss three major complications that concurrent processing adds to an operating system.

3.4 The Sun UltraSPARC processor has multiple register sets. Describe what happens when a context switch occurs if the new context is already loaded into one of the register sets. What happens if the new context is in memory rather than in a register set and all the register sets are in use?

3.5 When a process creates a new process using the fork() operation, which of the following states is shared between the parent process and the child process?

a. Stack

b. Heap

c. Shared memory segments

```
#include <sys/types.h>
#include <stdio.h>
#include <unistd.h>

int value = 5;

int main()
{
pid_t pid;

   pid = fork();

   if (pid == 0) { /* child process */
      value += 15;
      return 0;
   }
   else if (pid > 0) { /* parent process */
      wait(NULL);
      printf("PARENT: value = %d",value); /* LINE A */
      return 0;
   }
}
```

Figure 3.30   What output will be at Line A?

3.6   Consider the "exactly once"semantic with respect to the RPC mechanism. Does the algorithm for implementing this semantic execute correctly even if the ACK message sent back to the client is lost due to a network problem? Describe the sequence of messages, and discuss whether "exactly once" is still preserved.

```
#include <stdio.h>
#include <unistd.h>

int main()
{
    /* fork a child process */
    fork();

    /* fork another child process */
    fork();

    /* and fork another */
    fork();

    return 0;
}
```

Figure 3.31   How many processes are created?

```
#include <stdio.h>
#include <unistd.h>

int main()
{
    int i;

    for (i = 0; i < 4; i++)
        fork();

    return 0;
}
```

Figure 3.32 How many processes are created?

3.7 Assume that a distributed system is susceptible to server failure. What mechanisms would be required to guarantee the "exactly once" semantic for execution of RPCs?

Exercises

3.8 Describe the differences among short-term, medium-term, and long-term scheduling.

3.9 Describe the actions taken by a kernel to context-switch between processes.

3.10 Construct a process tree similar to Figure 3.8. To obtain process information for the UNIX or Linux system, use the command ps -ael. Use the command man ps to get more information about the ps command. The task manager on Windows systems does not provide the parent process ID, but the *process monitor* tool, available from tech-net.microsoft.com, provides a process-tree tool.

3.11 Explain the role of the init process on UNIX and Linux systems in regard to process termination.

3.12 Including the initial parent process, how many processes are created by the program shown in Figure 3.32?

3.13 Explain the circumstances under which the line of code marked printf("LINE J") in Figure 3.33 will be reached.

3.14 Using the program in Figure 3.34, identify the values of pid at lines A, B, C, and D. (Assume that the actual pids of the parent and child are 2600 and 2603, respectively.)

3.15 Give an example of a situation in which ordinary pipes are more suitable than named pipes and an example of a situation in which named pipes are more suitable than ordinary pipes.

3.16 Consider the RPC mechanism. Describe the undesirable consequences that could arise from not enforcing either the "at most once" or "exactly

```
#include <sys/types.h>
#include <stdio.h>
#include <unistd.h>

int main()
{
pid_t pid;

    /* fork a child process */
    pid = fork();

    if (pid < 0) { /* error occurred */
      fprintf(stderr, "Fork Failed");
      return 1;
    }
    else if (pid == 0) { /* child process */
      execlp("/bin/ls","ls",NULL);
      printf("LINE J");
    }
    else { /* parent process */
      /* parent will wait for the child to complete */
      wait(NULL);
      printf("Child Complete");
    }

    return 0;
}
```

Figure 3.33 When will LINE J be reached?

once" semantic. Describe possible uses for a mechanism that has neither of these guarantees.

3.17 Using the program shown in Figure 3.35, explain what the output will be at lines X and Y.

3.18 What are the benefits and the disadvantages of each of the following? Consider both the system level and the programmer level.

   a. Synchronous and asynchronous communication

   b. Automatic and explicit buffering

   c. Send by copy and send by reference

   d. Fixed-sized and variable-sized messages

Programming Problems

3.19 Using either a UNIX or a Linux system, write a C program that forks a child process that ultimately becomes a zombie process. This zombie

```c
#include <sys/types.h>
#include <stdio.h>
#include <unistd.h>

int main()
{
pid_t pid, pid1;

    /* fork a child process */
    pid = fork();

    if (pid < 0) { /* error occurred */
       fprintf(stderr, "Fork Failed");
       return 1;
    }
    else if (pid == 0) { /* child process */
       pid1 = getpid();
       printf("child: pid = %d",pid); /* A */
       printf("child: pid1 = %d",pid1); /* B */
    }
    else { /* parent process */
       pid1 = getpid();
       printf("parent: pid = %d",pid); /* C */
       printf("parent: pid1 = %d",pid1); /* D */
       wait(NULL);
    }

    return 0;
}
```

Figure 3.34 What are the pid values?

process must remain in the system for at least 10 seconds. Process states can be obtained from the command

```
ps -l
```

The process states are shown below the S column; processes with a state of Z are zombies. The process identifier (pid) of the child process is listed in the PID column, and that of the parent is listed in the PPID column.

Perhaps the easiest way to determine that the child process is indeed a zombie is to run the program that you have written in the background (using the &) and then run the command ps -l to determine whether the child is a zombie process. Because you do not want too many zombie processes existing in the system, you will need to remove the one that you have created. The easiest way to do that is to terminate the parent process using the kill command. For example, if the process id of the parent is 4884, you would enter

```
kill -9 4884
```

```
#include <sys/types.h>
#include <stdio.h>
#include <unistd.h>

#define SIZE 5

int nums[SIZE] = {0,1,2,3,4};

int main()
{
int i;
pid_t pid;

    pid = fork();

    if (pid == 0) {
        for (i = 0; i < SIZE; i++) {
            nums[i] *= -i;
            printf("CHILD: %d ",nums[i]); /* LINE X */
        }
    }
    else if (pid > 0) {
        wait(NULL);
        for (i = 0; i < SIZE; i++)
            printf("PARENT: %d ",nums[i]); /* LINE Y */
    }

    return 0;
}
```

Figure 3.35   What output will be at Line X and Line Y?

3.20 An operating system's **pid manager** is responsible for managing process identifiers. When a process is first created, it is assigned a unique pid by the pid manager. The pid is returned to the pid manager when the process completes execution, and the manager may later reassign this pid. Process identifiers are discussed more fully in Section 3.3.1. What is most important here is to recognize that process identifiers must be unique; no two active processes can have the same pid.

Use the following constants to identify the range of possible pid values:

```
#define MIN_PID 300
#define MAX_PID 5000
```

You may use any data structure of your choice to represent the availability of process identifiers. One strategy is to adopt what Linux has done and use a bitmap in which a value of 0 at position i indicates that a process id of value i is available and a value of 1 indicates that the process id is currently in use.

Implement the following API for obtaining and releasing a pid:

- `int allocate_map(void)`—Creates and initializes a data structure for representing pids; returns —1 if unsuccessful, 1 if successful

- `int allocate_pid(void)`—Allocates and returns a pid; returns —1 if unable to allocate a pid (all pids are in use)

- `void release_pid(int pid)`—Releases a pid

This programming problem will be modified later on in Chapter 4 and in Chapter 5.

3.21 The Collatz conjecture concerns what happens when we take any positive integer n and apply the following algorithm:

$$n = \begin{cases} n/2, & \text{if n is even} \\ 3 \times n + 1, & \text{if n is odd} \end{cases}$$

The conjecture states that when this algorithm is continually applied, all positive integers will eventually reach 1. For example, if $n = 35$, the sequence is

$$35, 106, 53, 160, 80, 40, 20, 10, 5, 16, 8, 4, 2, 1$$

Write a C program using the `fork()` system call that generates this sequence in the child process. The starting number will be provided from the command line. For example, if 8 is passed as a parameter on the command line, the child process will output 8, 4, 2, 1. Because the parent and child processes have their own copies of the data, it will be necessary for the child to output the sequence. Have the parent invoke the `wait()` call to wait for the child process to complete before exiting the program. Perform necessary error checking to ensure that a positive integer is passed on the command line.

3.22 In Exercise 3.21, the child process must output the sequence of numbers generated from the algorithm specified by the Collatz conjecture because the parent and child have their own copies of the data. Another approach to designing this program is to establish a shared-memory object between the parent and child processes. This technique allows the child to write the contents of the sequence to the shared-memory object. The parent can then output the sequence when the child completes. Because the memory is shared, any changes the child makes will be reflected in the parent process as well.

This program will be structured using POSIX shared memory as described in Section 3.5.1. The parent process will progress through the following steps:

a. Establish the shared-memory object (`shm_open()`, `ftruncate()`, and `mmap()`).

b. Create the child process and wait for it to terminate.

    c.   Output the contents of shared memory.

    d.   Remove the shared-memory object.

One area of concern with cooperating processes involves synchronization issues. In this exercise, the parent and child processes must be coordinated so that the parent does not output the sequence until the child finishes execution. These two processes will be synchronized using the `wait()` system call: the parent process will invoke `wait()`, which will suspend it until the child process exits.

3.23   Section 3.6.1 describes port numbers below 1024 as being well known—that is, they provide standard services. Port 17 is known as the *quote-of-the-day* service. When a client connects to port 17 on a server, the server responds with a quote for that day.

Modify the date server shown in Figure 3.21 so that it delivers a quote of the day rather than the current date. The quotes should be printable ASCII characters and should contain fewer than 512 characters, although multiple lines are allowed. Since port 17 is well known and therefore unavailable, have your server listen to port 6017. The date client shown in Figure 3.22 can be used to read the quotes returned by your server.

3.24   A haiku is a three-line poem in which the first line contains five syllables, the second line contains seven syllables, and the third line contains five syllables. Write a haiku server that listens to port 5575. When a client connects to this port, the server responds with a haiku. The date client shown in Figure 3.22 can be used to read the quotes returned by your haiku server.

3.25   An echo server echoes back whatever it receives from a client. For example, if a client sends the server the string `Hello there!`, the server will respond with `Hello there!`

Write an echo server using the Java networking API described in Section 3.6.1. This server will wait for a client connection using the `accept()` method. When a client connection is received, the server will loop, performing the following steps:

- Read data from the socket into a buffer.

- Write the contents of the buffer back to the client.

The server will break out of the loop only when it has determined that the client has closed the connection.

Consider again the date server shown in Figure 3.21, which uses the `java.io.BufferedReader` class. `BufferedReader` extends the `java.io.Reader` class, which is used for reading character streams. However, the echo server cannot guarantee that it will read characters from clients; it may receive binary data as well. The class `java.io.InputStream` deals with data at the byte level rather than the character level. Thus, your echo server must use an object that extends `java.io.InputStream`. The `read()` method in the `java.io.InputStream` class returns −1 when the client has closed its end of the socket connection.

3.26 Design a program using ordinary pipes in which one process sends a string message to a second process, and the second process reverses the case of each character in the message and sends it back to the first process. For example, if the first process sends the message Hi There, the second process will return hI tHERE. This will require using two pipes, one for sending the original message from the first to the second process and the other for sending the modified message from the second to the first process. You can write this program using either UNIX or Windows pipes.

3.27 Design a file-copying program named filecopy using ordinary pipes. This program will be passed two parameters: the name of the file to be copied and the name of the copied file. The program will then create an ordinary pipe and write the contents of the file to be copied to the pipe. The child process will read this file from the pipe and write it to the destination file. For example, if we invoke the program as follows:

```
filecopy input.txt copy.txt
```

the file input.txt will be written to the pipe. The child process will read the contents of this file and write it to the destination file copy.txt. You may write this program using either UNIX or Windows pipes.

Programming Projects

Project 1—UNIX Shell and History Feature

This project consists of designing a C program to serve as a shell interface that accepts user commands and then executes each command in a separate process. This project can be completed on any Linux, UNIX, or Mac OS X system.

A shell interface gives the user a prompt, after which the next command is entered. The example below illustrates the prompt osh> and the user's next command: cat prog.c. (This command displays the file prog.c on the terminal using the UNIX cat command.)

```
osh> cat prog.c
```

One technique for implementing a shell interface is to have the parent process first read what the user enters on the command line (in this case, cat prog.c), and then create a separate child process that performs the command. Unless otherwise specified, the parent process waits for the child to exit before continuing. This is similar in functionality to the new process creation illustrated in Figure 3.10. However, UNIX shells typically also allow the child process to run in the background, or concurrently. To accomplish this, we add an ampersand (&) at the end of the command. Thus, if we rewrite the above command as

```
osh> cat prog.c &
```

the parent and child processes will run concurrently.

```
#include <stdio.h>
#include <unistd.h>

#define MAX_LINE 80 /* The maximum length command */

int main(void)
{
char *args[MAX_LINE/2 + 1]; /* command line arguments */
int should_run = 1; /* flag to determine when to exit program */

    while (should_run) {
        printf("osh>");
        fflush(stdout);

        /**
         * After reading user input, the steps are:
         * (1) fork a child process using fork()
         * (2) the child process will invoke execvp()
         * (3) if command included &, parent will invoke wait()
         */
    }

    return 0;
}
```

Figure 3.36 Outline of simple shell.

The separate child process is created using the fork() system call, and the user's command is executed using one of the system calls in the exec() family (as described in Section 3.3.1).

A C program that provides the general operations of a command-line shell is supplied in Figure 3.36. The main() function presents the prompt osh-> and outlines the steps to be taken after input from the user has been read. The main() function continually loops as long as should_run equals 1; when the user enters exit at the prompt, your program will set should_run to 0 and terminate.

This project is organized into two parts: (1) creating the child process and executing the command in the child, and (2) modifying the shell to allow a history feature.

Part I— Creating a Child Process

The first task is to modify the main() function in Figure 3.36 so that a child process is forked and executes the command specified by the user. This will require parsing what the user has entered into separate tokens and storing the tokens in an array of character strings (args in Figure 3.36). For example, if the user enters the command ps -ael at the osh> prompt, the values stored in the args array are:

```
args[0] = "ps"
args[1] = "-ael"
args[2] = NULL
```

This `args` array will be passed to the `execvp()` function, which has the following prototype:

```
execvp(char *command, char *params[]);
```

Here, `command` represents the command to be performed and `params` stores the parameters to this command. For this project, the `execvp()` function should be invoked as `execvp(args[0], args)`. Be sure to check whether the user included an & to determine whether or not the parent process is to wait for the child to exit.

Part II—Creating a History Feature

The next task is to modify the shell interface program so that it provides a *history* feature that allows the user to access the most recently entered commands. The user will be able to access up to 10 commands by using the feature. The commands will be consecutively numbered starting at 1, and the numbering will continue past 10. For example, if the user has entered 35 commands, the 10 most recent commands will be numbered 26 to 35.

The user will be able to list the command history by entering the command

```
history
```

at the osh> prompt. As an example, assume that the history consists of the commands (from most to least recent):

```
ps, ls -l, top, cal, who, date
```

The command `history` will output:

```
6 ps
5 ls -l
4 top
3 cal
2 who
1 date
```

Your program should support two techniques for retrieving commands from the command history:

1. When the user enters `!!`, the most recent command in the history is executed.

2. When the user enters a single `!` followed by an integer N, the Nth command in the history is executed.

Continuing our example from above, if the user enters `!!`, the ps command will be performed; if the user enters `!3`, the command `cal` will be executed. Any command executed in this fashion should be echoed on the user's screen. The command should also be placed in the history buffer as the next command.

The program should also manage basic error handling. If there are no commands in the history, entering !! should result in a message "No commands in history." If there is no command corresponding to the number entered with the single !, the program should output "No such command in history."

Project 2—Linux Kernel Module for Listing Tasks

In this project, you will write a kernel module that lists all current tasks in a Linux system. Be sure to review the programming project in Chapter 2, which deals with creating Linux kernel modules, before you begin this project. The project can be completed using the Linux virtual machine provided with this text.

Part I—Iterating over Tasks Linearly

As illustrated in Section 3.1, the PCB in Linux is represented by the structure task_struct, which is found in the <linux/sched.h> include file. In Linux, the for_each_process() macro easily allows iteration over all current tasks in the system:

```
#include <linux/sched.h>

struct task_struct *task;

for_each_process(task) {
   /* on each iteration task points to the next task */
}
```

The various fields in task_struct can then be displayed as the program loops through the for_each_process() macro.

Part I Assignment

Design a kernel module that iterates through all tasks in the system using the for_each_process() macro. In particular, output the task name (known as *executable name*), state, and process id of each task. (You will probably have to read through the task_struct structure in <linux/sched.h> to obtain the names of these fields.) Write this code in the module entry point so that its contents will appear in the kernel log buffer, which can be viewed using the dmesg command. To verify that your code is working correctly, compare the contents of the kernel log buffer with the output of the following command, which lists all tasks in the system:

```
ps -el
```

The two values should be very similar. Because tasks are dynamic, however, it is possible that a few tasks may appear in one listing but not the other.

Part II—Iterating over Tasks with a Depth-First Search Tree

The second portion of this project involves iterating over all tasks in the system using a depth-first search (DFS) tree. (As an example: the DFS iteration of the processes in Figure 3.8 is 1, 8415, 8416, 9298, 9204, 2, 6, 200, 3028, 3610, 4005.)

Linux maintains its process tree as a series of lists. Examining the task_struct in <linux/sched.h>, we see two struct list_head objects:

    children

and

    sibling

These objects are pointers to a list of the task's children, as well as its siblings. Linux also maintains references to the init task (struct task_struct init_task). Using this information as well as macro operations on lists, we can iterate over the children of init as follows:

```
struct task_struct *task;
struct list_head *list;

list_for_each(list, &init_task->children) {
    task = list_entry(list, struct task_struct, sibling);
    /* task points to the next child in the list */
}
```

The list_for_each() macro is passed two parameters, both of type struct list_head:

- A pointer to the head of the list to be traversed
- A pointer to the head node of the list to be traversed

At each iteration of list_for_each(), the first parameter is set to the list structure of the next child. We then use this value to obtain each structure in the list using the list_entry() macro.

Part II Assignment

Beginning from the init task, design a kernel module that iterates over all tasks in the system using a DFS tree. Just as in the first part of this project, output the name, state, and pid of each task. Perform this iteration in the kernel entry module so that its output appears in the kernel log buffer.

If you output all tasks in the system, you may see many more tasks than appear with the ps -ael command. This is because some threads appear as children but do not show up as ordinary processes. Therefore, to check the output of the DFS tree, use the command

    ps -eLf

Bibliographical Notes

Process creation, management, and IPC in UNIX and Windows systems, respectively, are discussed in [Robbins and Robbins (2003)] and [Russinovich and Solomon (2009)]. [Love (2010)] covers support for processes in the Linux kernel, and [Hart (2005)] covers Windows systems programming in detail. Coverage of the multiprocess model used in Google's Chrome can be found at http://blog.chromium.org/2008/09/multi-process-architecture.html.

Message passing for multicore systems is discussed in [Holland and Seltzer (2011)]. [Baumann et al. (2009)] describe performance issues in shared-memory and message-passing systems. [Vahalia (1996)] describes interprocess communication in the Mach system.

The implementation of RPCs is discussed by [Birrell and Nelson (1984)]. [Staunstrup (1982)] discusses procedure calls versus message-passing communication. [Harold (2005)] provides coverage of socket programming.

[Hart (2005)] and [Robbins and Robbins (2003)] cover pipes in Windows and UNIX systems, respectively.

Bibliography

[Baumann et al. (2009)]   A. Baumann, P. Barham, P.-E. Dagand, T. Harris, R. Isaacs, P. Simon, T. Roscoe, A. Schüpbach, and A. Singhania, "The multikernel: a new OS architecture for scalable multicore systems" (2009), pages 29–44.

[Birrell and Nelson (1984)]   A. D. Birrell and B. J. Nelson, "Implementing Remote Procedure Calls", *ACM Transactions on Computer Systems*, Volume 2, Number 1 (1984), pages 39–59.

[Harold (2005)]   E. R. Harold, *Java Network Programming*, Third Edition, O'Reilly & Associates (2005).

[Hart (2005)]   J. M. Hart, *Windows System Programming*, Third Edition, Addison-Wesley (2005).

[Holland and Seltzer (2011)]   D. Holland and M. Seltzer, "Multicore OSes: looking forward from 1991, er, 2011", *Proceedings of the 13th USENIX conference on Hot topics in operating systems* (2011), pages 33–33.

[Love (2010)]   R. Love, *Linux Kernel Development*, Third Edition, Developer's Library (2010).

[Robbins and Robbins (2003)]   K. Robbins and S. Robbins, *Unix Systems Programming: Communication, Concurrency and Threads*, Second Edition, Prentice Hall (2003).

[Russinovich and Solomon (2009)]   M. E. Russinovich and D. A. Solomon, *Windows Internals: Including Windows Server 2008 and Windows Vista*, Fifth Edition, Microsoft Press (2009).

[Staunstrup (1982)]   J. Staunstrup, "Message Passing Communication Versus Procedure Call Communication", *Software—Practice and Experience*, Volume 12, Number 3 (1982), pages 223–234.

[Vahalia (1996)]   U. Vahalia, *Unix Internals: The New Frontiers*, Prentice Hall (1996).

CHAPTER 4

Threads

The process model introduced in Chapter 3 assumed that a process was an executing program with a single thread of control. Virtually all modern operating systems, however, provide features enabling a process to contain multiple threads of control. In this chapter, we introduce many concepts associated with multithreaded computer systems, including a discussion of the APIs for the Pthreads, Windows, and Java thread libraries. We look at a number of issues related to multithreaded programming and its effect on the design of operating systems. Finally, we explore how the Windows and Linux operating systems support threads at the kernel level.

CHAPTER OBJECTIVES

- To introduce the notion of a thread — a fundamental unit of CPU utilization that forms the basis of multithreaded computer systems.
- To discuss the APIs for the Pthreads, Windows, and Java thread libraries.
- To explore several strategies that provide implicit threading.
- To examine issues related to multithreaded programming.
- To cover operating system support for threads in Windows and Linux.

4.1 Overview

A thread is a basic unit of CPU utilization; it comprises a thread ID, a program counter, a register set, and a stack. It shares with other threads belonging to the same process its code section, data section, and other operating-system resources, such as open files and signals. A traditional (or *heavyweight*) process has a single thread of control. If a process has multiple threads of control, it can perform more than one task at a time. Figure 4.1 illustrates the difference between a traditional single-threaded process and a multithreaded process.

4.1.1 Motivation

Most software applications that run on modern computers are multithreaded. An application typically is implemented as a separate process with several

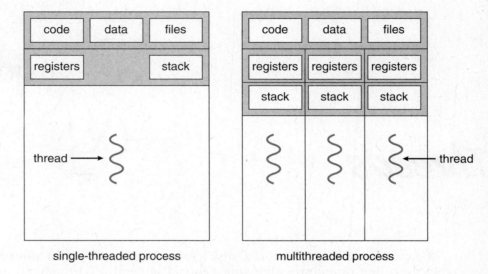

Figure 4.1   Single-threaded and multithreaded processes.

threads of control. A web browser might have one thread display images or text while another thread retrieves data from the network, for example. A word processor may have a thread for displaying graphics, another thread for responding to keystrokes from the user, and a third thread for performing spelling and grammar checking in the background. Applications can also be designed to leverage processing capabilities on multicore systems. Such applications can perform several CPU-intensive tasks in parallel across the multiple computing cores.

In certain situations, a single application may be required to perform several similar tasks. For example, a web server accepts client requests for web pages, images, sound, and so forth. A busy web server may have several (perhaps thousands of) clients concurrently accessing it. If the web server ran as a traditional single-threaded process, it would be able to service only one client at a time, and a client might have to wait a very long time for its request to be serviced.

One solution is to have the server run as a single process that accepts requests. When the server receives a request, it creates a separate process to service that request. In fact, this process-creation method was in common use before threads became popular. Process creation is time consuming and resource intensive, however. If the new process will perform the same tasks as the existing process, why incur all that overhead? It is generally more efficient to use one process that contains multiple threads. If the web-server process is multithreaded, the server will create a separate thread that listens for client requests. When a request is made, rather than creating another process, the server creates a new thread to service the request and resume listening for additional requests. This is illustrated in Figure 4.2.

Threads also play a vital role in remote procedure call (RPC) systems. Recall from Chapter 3 that RPCs allow interprocess communication by providing a communication mechanism similar to ordinary function or procedure calls. Typically, RPC servers are multithreaded. When a server receives a message, it

(1) request

(2) create new
thread to service
the request

(3) resume listening
for additional
client requests

Figure 4.2 Multithreaded server architecture.

services the message using a separate thread. This allows the server to service several concurrent requests.

Finally, most operating-system kernels are now multithreaded. Several threads operate in the kernel, and each thread performs a specific task, such as managing devices, managing memory, or interrupt handling. For example, Solaris has a set of threads in the kernel specifically for interrupt handling; Linux uses a kernel thread for managing the amount of free memory in the system.

4.1.2 Benefits

The benefits of multithreaded programming can be broken down into four major categories:

1. **Responsiveness**. Multithreading an interactive application may allow a program to continue running even if part of it is blocked or is performing a lengthy operation, thereby increasing responsiveness to the user. This quality is especially useful in designing user interfaces. For instance, consider what happens when a user clicks a button that results in the performance of a time-consuming operation. A single-threaded application would be unresponsive to the user until the operation had completed. In contrast, if the time-consuming operation is performed in a separate thread, the application remains responsive to the user.

2. **Resource sharing**. Processes can only share resources through techniques such as shared memory and message passing. Such techniques must be explicitly arranged by the programmer. However, threads share the memory and the resources of the process to which they belong by default. The benefit of sharing code and data is that it allows an application to have several different threads of activity within the same address space.

3. **Economy**. Allocating memory and resources for process creation is costly. Because threads share the resources of the process to which they belong, it is more economical to create and context-switch threads. Empirically gauging the difference in overhead can be difficult, but in general it is significantly more time consuming to create and manage processes than threads. In Solaris, for example, creating a process is about thirty times

Figure 4.3   Concurrent execution on a single-core system.

slower than is creating a thread, and context switching is about five times slower.

4. **Scalability.** The benefits of multithreading can be even greater in a multiprocessor architecture, where threads may be running in parallel on different processing cores. A single-threaded process can run on only one processor, regardless how many are available. We explore this issue further in the following section.

4.2 Multicore Programming

Earlier in the history of computer design, in response to the need for more computing performance, single-CPU systems evolved into multi-CPU systems. A more recent, similar trend in system design is to place multiple computing cores on a single chip. Each core appears as a separate processor to the operating system (Section 1.3.2). Whether the cores appear across CPU chips or within CPU chips, we call these systems **multicore** or **multiprocessor** systems. Multithreaded programming provides a mechanism for more efficient use of these multiple computing cores and improved concurrency. Consider an application with four threads. On a system with a single computing core, concurrency merely means that the execution of the threads will be interleaved over time (Figure 4.3), because the processing core is capable of executing only one thread at a time. On a system with multiple cores, however, concurrency means that the threads can run in parallel, because the system can assign a separate thread to each core (Figure 4.4).

Notice the distinction between *parallelism* and *concurrency* in this discussion. A system is parallel if it can perform more than one task simultaneously. In contrast, a concurrent system supports more than one task by allowing all the tasks to make progress. Thus, it is possible to have concurrency without parallelism. Before the advent of SMP and multicore architectures, most computer systems had only a single processor. CPU schedulers were designed to provide the illusion of parallelism by rapidly switching between processes in

Figure 4.4   Parallel execution on a multicore system.

AMDAHL'S LAW

Amdahl's Law is a formula that identifies potential performance gains from adding additional computing cores to an application that has both serial (nonparallel) and parallel components. If S is the portion of the application that must be performed serially on a system with N processing cores, the formula appears as follows:

$$speedup \leq \frac{1}{S + \frac{(1-S)}{N}}$$

As an example, assume we have an application that is 75 percent parallel and 25 percent serial. If we run this application on a system with two processing cores, we can get a speedup of 1.6 times. If we add two additional cores (for a total of four), the speedup is 2.28 times.

One interesting fact about Amdahl's Law is that as N approaches infinity, the speedup converges to $1/S$. For example, if 40 percent of an application is performed serially, the maximum speedup is 2.5 times, regardless of the number of processing cores we add. This is the fundamental principle behind Amdahl's Law: the serial portion of an application can have a disproportionate effect on the performance we gain by adding additional computing cores.

Some argue that Amdahl's Law does not take into account the hardware performance enhancements used in the design of contemporary multicore systems. Such arguments suggest Amdahl's Law may cease to be applicable as the number of processing cores continues to increase on modern computer systems.

the system, thereby allowing each process to make progress. Such processes were running concurrently, but not in parallel.

As systems have grown from tens of threads to thousands of threads, CPU designers have improved system performance by adding hardware to improve thread performance. Modern Intel CPUs frequently support two threads per core, while the Oracle T4 CPU supports eight threads per core. This support means that multiple threads can be loaded into the core for fast switching. Multicore computers will no doubt continue to increase in core counts and hardware thread support.

4.2.1 Programming Challenges

The trend towards multicore systems continues to place pressure on system designers and application programmers to make better use of the multiple computing cores. Designers of operating systems must write scheduling algorithms that use multiple processing cores to allow the parallel execution shown in Figure 4.4. For application programmers, the challenge is to modify existing programs as well as design new programs that are multithreaded.

In general, five areas present challenges in programming for multicore systems:

1. **Identifying tasks**. This involves examining applications to find areas that can be divided into separate, concurrent tasks. Ideally, tasks are independent of one another and thus can run in parallel on individual cores.

2. **Balance**. While identifying tasks that can run in parallel, programmers must also ensure that the tasks perform equal work of equal value. In some instances, a certain task may not contribute as much value to the overall process as other tasks. Using a separate execution core to run that task may not be worth the cost.

3. **Data splitting**. Just as applications are divided into separate tasks, the data accessed and manipulated by the tasks must be divided to run on separate cores.

4. **Data dependency**. The data accessed by the tasks must be examined for dependencies between two or more tasks. When one task depends on data from another, programmers must ensure that the execution of the tasks is synchronized to accommodate the data dependency. We examine such strategies in Chapter 5.

5. **Testing and debugging**. When a program is running in parallel on multiple cores, many different execution paths are possible. Testing and debugging such concurrent programs is inherently more difficult than testing and debugging single-threaded applications.

Because of these challenges, many software developers argue that the advent of multicore systems will require an entirely new approach to designing software systems in the future. (Similarly, many computer science educators believe that software development must be taught with increased emphasis on parallel programming.)

4.2.2 Types of Parallelism

In general, there are two types of parallelism: data parallelism and task parallelism. Data parallelism focuses on distributing subsets of the same data across multiple computing cores and performing the same operation on each core. Consider, for example, summing the contents of an array of size N. On a single-core system, one thread would simply sum the elements $[0] \ldots [N-1]$. On a dual-core system, however, thread A, running on core 0, could sum the elements $[0] \ldots [N/2-1]$ while thread B, running on core 1, could sum the elements $[N/2] \ldots [N-1]$. The two threads would be running in parallel on separate computing cores.

Task parallelism involves distributing not data but tasks (threads) across multiple computing cores. Each thread is performing a unique operation. Different threads may be operating on the same data, or they may be operating on different data. Consider again our example above. In contrast to that situation, an example of task parallelism might involve two threads, each performing a unique statistical operation on the array of elements. The threads again are operating in parallel on separate computing cores, but each is performing a unique operation.

Fundamentally, then, data parallelism involves the distribution of data across multiple cores and task parallelism on the distribution of tasks across multiple cores. In practice, however, few applications strictly follow either data or task parallelism. In most instances, applications use a hybrid of these two strategies.

4.3   Multithreading Models

Our discussion so far has treated threads in a generic sense. However, support for threads may be provided either at the user level, for **user threads**, or by the kernel, for **kernel threads**. User threads are supported above the kernel and are managed without kernel support, whereas kernel threads are supported and managed directly by the operating system. Virtually all contemporary operating systems—including Windows, Linux, Mac OS X, and Solaris—support kernel threads.

Ultimately, a relationship must exist between user threads and kernel threads. In this section, we look at three common ways of establishing such a relationship: the many-to-one model, the one-to-one model, and the many-to-many model.

4.3.1   Many-to-One Model

The many-to-one model (Figure 4.5) maps many user-level threads to one kernel thread. Thread management is done by the thread library in user space, so it is efficient (we discuss thread libraries in Section 4.4). However, the entire process will block if a thread makes a blocking system call. Also, because only one thread can access the kernel at a time, multiple threads are unable to run in parallel on multicore systems. **Green threads**—a thread library available for Solaris systems and adopted in early versions of Java—used the many-to-one model. However, very few systems continue to use the model because of its inability to take advantage of multiple processing cores.

Figure 4.5   Many-to-one model.

Figure 4.6   One-to-one model.

4.3.2   One-to-One Model

The one-to-one model (Figure 4.6) maps each user thread to a kernel thread. It provides more concurrency than the many-to-one model by allowing another thread to run when a thread makes a blocking system call. It also allows multiple threads to run in parallel on multiprocessors. The only drawback to this model is that creating a user thread requires creating the corresponding kernel thread. Because the overhead of creating kernel threads can burden the performance of an application, most implementations of this model restrict the number of threads supported by the system. Linux, along with the family of Windows operating systems, implement the one-to-one model.

4.3.3   Many-to-Many Model

The many-to-many model (Figure 4.7) multiplexes many user-level threads to a smaller or equal number of kernel threads. The number of kernel threads may be specific to either a particular application or a particular machine (an application may be allocated more kernel threads on a multiprocessor than on a single processor).

Let's consider the effect of this design on concurrency. Whereas the many-to-one model allows the developer to create as many user threads as she wishes, it does not result in true concurrency, because the kernel can schedule only one thread at a time. The one-to-one model allows greater concurrency, but the developer has to be careful not to create too many threads within an application (and in some instances may be limited in the number of threads she can

Figure 4.7   Many-to-many model.

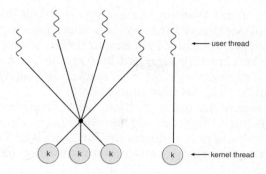

Figure 4.8 Two-level model.

create). The many-to-many model suffers from neither of these shortcomings: developers can create as many user threads as necessary, and the corresponding kernel threads can run in parallel on a multiprocessor. Also, when a thread performs a blocking system call, the kernel can schedule another thread for execution.

One variation on the many-to-many model still multiplexes many user-level threads to a smaller or equal number of kernel threads but also allows a user-level thread to be bound to a kernel thread. This variation is sometimes referred to as the **two-level model** (Figure 4.8). The Solaris operating system supported the two-level model in versions older than Solaris 9. However, beginning with Solaris 9, this system uses the one-to-one model.

4.4 Thread Libraries

A **thread library** provides the programmer with an API for creating and managing threads. There are two primary ways of implementing a thread library. The first approach is to provide a library entirely in user space with no kernel support. All code and data structures for the library exist in user space. This means that invoking a function in the library results in a local function call in user space and not a system call.

The second approach is to implement a kernel-level library supported directly by the operating system. In this case, code and data structures for the library exist in kernel space. Invoking a function in the API for the library typically results in a system call to the kernel.

Three main thread libraries are in use today: POSIX Pthreads, Windows, and Java. Pthreads, the threads extension of the POSIX standard, may be provided as either a user-level or a kernel-level library. The Windows thread library is a kernel-level library available on Windows systems. The Java thread API allows threads to be created and managed directly in Java programs. However, because in most instances the JVM is running on top of a host operating system, the Java thread API is generally implemented using a thread library available on the host system. This means that on Windows systems, Java threads are typically implemented using the Windows API; UNIX and Linux systems often use Pthreads.

For POSIX and Windows threading, any data declared globally—that is, declared outside of any function—are shared among all threads belonging to the same process. Because Java has no notion of global data, access to shared data must be explicitly arranged between threads. Data declared local to a function are typically stored on the stack. Since each thread has its own stack, each thread has its own copy of local data.

In the remainder of this section, we describe basic thread creation using these three thread libraries. As an illustrative example, we design a multithreaded program that performs the summation of a non-negative integer in a separate thread using the well-known summation function:

$$sum = \sum_{i=0}^{N} i$$

For example, if N were 5, this function would represent the summation of integers from 0 to 5, which is 15. Each of the three programs will be run with the upper bounds of the summation entered on the command line. Thus, if the user enters 8, the summation of the integer values from 0 to 8 will be output.

Before we proceed with our examples of thread creation, we introduce two general strategies for creating multiple threads: asynchronous threading and synchronous threading. With asynchronous threading, once the parent creates a child thread, the parent resumes its execution, so that the parent and child execute concurrently. Each thread runs independently of every other thread, and the parent thread need not know when its child terminates. Because the threads are independent, there is typically little data sharing between threads. Asynchronous threading is the strategy used in the multithreaded server illustrated in Figure 4.2.

Synchronous threading occurs when the parent thread creates one or more children and then must wait for all of its children to terminate before it resumes —the so-called *fork-join* strategy. Here, the threads created by the parent perform work concurrently, but the parent cannot continue until this work has been completed. Once each thread has finished its work, it terminates and joins with its parent. Only after all of the children have joined can the parent resume execution. Typically, synchronous threading involves significant data sharing among threads. For example, the parent thread may combine the results calculated by its various children. All of the following examples use synchronous threading.

4.4.1 Pthreads

Pthreads refers to the POSIX standard (IEEE 1003.1c) defining an API for thread creation and synchronization. This is a *specification* for thread behavior, not an *implementation*. Operating-system designers may implement the specification in any way they wish. Numerous systems implement the Pthreads specification; most are UNIX-type systems, including Linux, Mac OS X, and Solaris. Although Windows doesn't support Pthreads natively, some third-party implementations for Windows are available.

The C program shown in Figure 4.9 demonstrates the basic Pthreads API for constructing a multithreaded program that calculates the summation of a non-negative integer in a separate thread. In a Pthreads program, separate threads

```
#include <pthread.h>
#include <stdio.h>

int sum; /* this data is shared by the thread(s) */
void *runner(void *param); /* threads call this function */

int main(int argc, char *argv[])
{
   pthread_t tid; /* the thread identifier */
   pthread_attr_t attr; /* set of thread attributes */

   if (argc != 2) {
      fprintf(stderr,"usage: a.out <integer value>\n");
      return -1;
   }
   if (atoi(argv[1]) < 0) {
      fprintf(stderr,"%d must be >= 0\n",atoi(argv[1]));
      return -1;
   }

   /* get the default attributes */
   pthread_attr_init(&attr);
   /* create the thread */
   pthread_create(&tid,&attr,runner,argv[1]);
   /* wait for the thread to exit */
   pthread_join(tid,NULL);

   printf("sum = %d\n",sum);
}

/* The thread will begin control in this function */
void *runner(void *param)
{
   int i, upper = atoi(param);
   sum = 0;

   for (i = 1; i <= upper; i++)
      sum += i;

   pthread_exit(0);
}
```

Figure 4.9 Multithreaded C program using the Pthreads API.

begin execution in a specified function. In Figure 4.9, this is the runner()
function. When this program begins, a single thread of control begins in
main(). After some initialization, main() creates a second thread that begins
control in the runner() function. Both threads share the global data sum.

Let's look more closely at this program. All Pthreads programs must
include the pthread.h header file. The statement pthread_t tid declares

```
#define NUM_THREADS 10

/* an array of threads to be joined upon */
pthread_t workers[NUM_THREADS];

for (int i = 0; i < NUM_THREADS; i++)
   pthread_join(workers[i], NULL);
```

Figure 4.10   Pthread code for joining ten threads.

the identifier for the thread we will create. Each thread has a set of attributes, including stack size and scheduling information. The pthread_attr_t attr declaration represents the attributes for the thread. We set the attributes in the function call pthread_attr_init(&attr). Because we did not explicitly set any attributes, we use the default attributes provided. (In Chapter 6, we discuss some of the scheduling attributes provided by the Pthreads API.) A separate thread is created with the pthread_create() function call. In addition to passing the thread identifier and the attributes for the thread, we also pass the name of the function where the new thread will begin execution—in this case, the runner() function. Last, we pass the integer parameter that was provided on the command line, argv[1].

At this point, the program has two threads: the initial (or parent) thread in main() and the summation (or child) thread performing the summation operation in the runner() function. This program follows the fork-join strategy described earlier: after creating the summation thread, the parent thread will wait for it to terminate by calling the pthread_join() function. The summation thread will terminate when it calls the function pthread_exit(). Once the summation thread has returned, the parent thread will output the value of the shared data sum.

This example program creates only a single thread. With the growing dominance of multicore systems, writing programs containing several threads has become increasingly common. A simple method for waiting on several threads using the pthread_join() function is to enclose the operation within a simple for loop. For example, you can join on ten threads using the Pthread code shown in Figure 4.10.

4.4.2   Windows Threads

The technique for creating threads using the Windows thread library is similar to the Pthreads technique in several ways. We illustrate the Windows thread API in the C program shown in Figure 4.11. Notice that we must include the windows.h header file when using the Windows API.

Just as in the Pthreads version shown in Figure 4.9, data shared by the separate threads—in this case, Sum—are declared globally (the DWORD data type is an unsigned 32-bit integer). We also define the Summation() function that is to be performed in a separate thread. This function is passed a pointer to a void, which Windows defines as LPVOID. The thread performing this function sets the global data Sum to the value of the summation from 0 to the parameter passed to Summation().

```
#include <windows.h>
#include <stdio.h>
DWORD Sum; /* data is shared by the thread(s) */

/* the thread runs in this separate function */
DWORD WINAPI Summation(LPVOID Param)
{
   DWORD Upper = *(DWORD*)Param;
   for (DWORD i = 0; i <= Upper; i++)
     Sum += i;
   return 0;
}

int main(int argc, char *argv[])
{
   DWORD ThreadId;
   HANDLE ThreadHandle;
   int Param;

   if (argc != 2) {
     fprintf(stderr,"An integer parameter is required\n");
     return -1;
   }
   Param = atoi(argv[1]);
   if (Param < 0) {
     fprintf(stderr,"An integer >= 0 is required\n");
     return -1;
   }

   /* create the thread */
   ThreadHandle = CreateThread(
     NULL, /* default security attributes */
     0, /* default stack size */
     Summation, /* thread function */
     &Param, /* parameter to thread function */
     0, /* default creation flags */
     &ThreadId); /* returns the thread identifier */

   if (ThreadHandle != NULL) {
      /* now wait for the thread to finish */
     WaitForSingleObject(ThreadHandle,INFINITE);

     /* close the thread handle */
     CloseHandle(ThreadHandle);

     printf("sum = %d\n",Sum);
   }
}
```

Figure 4.11   Multithreaded C program using the Windows API.

Threads are created in the Windows API using the CreateThread() function, and—just as in Pthreads—a set of attributes for the thread is passed to this function. These attributes include security information, the size of the stack, and a flag that can be set to indicate if the thread is to start in a suspended state. In this program, we use the default values for these attributes. (The default values do not initially set the thread to a suspended state and instead make it eligible to be run by the CPU scheduler.) Once the summation thread is created, the parent must wait for it to complete before outputting the value of Sum, as the value is set by the summation thread. Recall that the Pthread program (Figure 4.9) had the parent thread wait for the summation thread using the pthread_join() statement. We perform the equivalent of this in the Windows API using the WaitForSingleObject() function, which causes the creating thread to block until the summation thread has exited.

In situations that require waiting for multiple threads to complete, the WaitForMultipleObjects() function is used. This function is passed four parameters:

1. The number of objects to wait for

2. A pointer to the array of objects

3. A flag indicating whether all objects have been signaled

4. A timeout duration (or INFINITE)

For example, if THandles is an array of thread HANDLE objects of size N, the parent thread can wait for all its child threads to complete with this statement:

```
WaitForMultipleObjects(N, THandles, TRUE, INFINITE);
```

4.4.3 Java Threads

Threads are the fundamental model of program execution in a Java program, and the Java language and its API provide a rich set of features for the creation and management of threads. All Java programs comprise at least a single thread of control—even a simple Java program consisting of only a main() method runs as a single thread in the JVM. Java threads are available on any system that provides a JVM including Windows, Linux, and Mac OS X. The Java thread API is available for Android applications as well.

There are two techniques for creating threads in a Java program. One approach is to create a new class that is derived from the Thread class and to override its run() method. An alternative—and more commonly used—technique is to define a class that implements the Runnable interface. The Runnable interface is defined as follows:

```
public interface Runnable
{
    public abstract void run();
}
```

When a class implements Runnable, it must define a run() method. The code implementing the run() method is what runs as a separate thread.

Figure 4.12 shows the Java version of a multithreaded program that determines the summation of a non-negative integer. The Summation class implements the Runnable interface. Thread creation is performed by creating an object instance of the Thread class and passing the constructor a Runnable object.

Creating a Thread object does not specifically create the new thread; rather, the start() method creates the new thread. Calling the start() method for the new object does two things:

1. It allocates memory and initializes a new thread in the JVM.

2. It calls the run() method, making the thread eligible to be run by the JVM. (Note again that we never call the run() method directly. Rather, we call the start() method, and it calls the run() method on our behalf.)

When the summation program runs, the JVM creates two threads. The first is the parent thread, which starts execution in the main() method. The second thread is created when the start() method on the Thread object is invoked. This child thread begins execution in the run() method of the Summation class. After outputting the value of the summation, this thread terminates when it exits from its run() method.

Data sharing between threads occurs easily in Windows and Pthreads, since shared data are simply declared globally. As a pure object-oriented language, Java has no such notion of global data. If two or more threads are to share data in a Java program, the sharing occurs by passing references to the shared object to the appropriate threads. In the Java program shown in Figure 4.12, the main thread and the summation thread share the object instance of the Sum class. This shared object is referenced through the appropriate getSum() and setSum() methods. (You might wonder why we don't use an Integer object rather than designing a new sum class. The reason is that the Integer class is *immutable*—that is, once its value is set, it cannot change.)

Recall that the parent threads in the Pthreads and Windows libraries use pthread_join() and WaitForSingleObject() (respectively) to wait for the summation threads to finish before proceeding. The join() method in Java provides similar functionality. (Notice that join() can throw an InterruptedException, which we choose to ignore.) If the parent must wait for several threads to finish, the join() method can be enclosed in a for loop similar to that shown for Pthreads in Figure 4.10.

4.5   Implicit Threading

With the continued growth of multicore processing, applications containing hundreds—or even thousands—of threads are looming on the horizon. Designing such applications is not a trivial undertaking: programmers must address not only the challenges outlined in Section 4.2 but additional difficulties as well. These difficulties, which relate to program correctness, are covered in Chapter 5.

One way to address these difficulties and better support the design of multithreaded applications is to transfer the creation and management of

```java
class Sum
{
  private int sum;

  public int getSum() {
    return sum;
  }

  public void setSum(int sum) {
    this.sum = sum;
  }
}

class Summation implements Runnable
{
  private int upper;
  private Sum sumValue;

  public Summation(int upper, Sum sumValue) {
    this.upper = upper;
    this.sumValue = sumValue;
  }

  public void run() {
    int sum = 0;
    for (int i = 0; i <= upper; i++)
      sum += i;
    sumValue.setSum(sum);
  }
}

public class Driver
{
  public static void main(String[] args) {
    if (args.length > 0) {
      if (Integer.parseInt(args[0]) < 0)
      System.err.println(args[0] + " must be >= 0.");
      else {
      Sum sumObject = new Sum();
      int upper = Integer.parseInt(args[0]);
      Thread thrd = new Thread(new Summation(upper, sumObject));
      thrd.start();
      try {
         thrd.join();
         System.out.println
                 ("The sum of "+upper+" is "+sumObject.getSum());
      } catch (InterruptedException ie) { }
      }
    }
    else
      System.err.println("Usage: Summation <integer value>"); }
}
```

Figure 4.12 Java program for the summation of a non-negative integers.

THE JVM AND THE HOST OPERATING SYSTEM

The JVM is typically implemented on top of a host operating system. This setup allows the JVM to hide the implementation details of the underlying operating system and to provide a consistent, abstract environment that allows Java programs to operate on any platform that supports a JVM. The specification for the JVM does not indicate how Java threads are to be mapped to the underlying operating system, instead leaving that decision to the particular implementation of the JVM. For example, the Windows XP operating system uses the one-to-one model; therefore, each Java thread for a JVM running on such a system maps to a kernel thread. On operating systems that use the many-to-many model (such as Tru64 UNIX), a Java thread is mapped according to the many-to-many model. Solaris initially implemented the JVM using the many-to-one model (the green threads library, mentioned earlier). Later releases of the JVM were implemented using the many-to-many model. Beginning with Solaris 9, Java threads were mapped using the one-to-one model. In addition, there may be a relationship between the Java thread library and the thread library on the host operating system. For example, implementations of a JVM for the Windows family of operating systems might use the Windows API when creating Java threads; Linux, Solaris, and Mac OS X systems might use the Pthreads API.

---

threading from application developers to compilers and run-time libraries. This strategy, termed **implicit threading**, is a popular trend today. In this section, we explore three alternative approaches for designing multithreaded programs that can take advantage of multicore processors through implicit threading.

4.5.1 Thread Pools

In Section 4.1, we described a multithreaded web server. In this situation, whenever the server receives a request, it creates a separate thread to service the request. Whereas creating a separate thread is certainly superior to creating a separate process, a multithreaded server nonetheless has potential problems. The first issue concerns the amount of time required to create the thread, together with the fact that the thread will be discarded once it has completed its work. The second issue is more troublesome. If we allow all concurrent requests to be serviced in a new thread, we have not placed a bound on the number of threads concurrently active in the system. Unlimited threads could exhaust system resources, such as CPU time or memory. One solution to this problem is to use a **thread pool**.

The general idea behind a thread pool is to create a number of threads at process startup and place them into a pool, where they sit and wait for work. When a server receives a request, it awakens a thread from this pool—if one is available—and passes it the request for service. Once the thread completes its service, it returns to the pool and awaits more work. If the pool contains no available thread, the server waits until one becomes free.

Thread pools offer these benefits:

1. Servicing a request with an existing thread is faster than waiting to create a thread.

2. A thread pool limits the number of threads that exist at any one point. This is particularly important on systems that cannot support a large number of concurrent threads.

3. Separating the task to be performed from the mechanics of creating the task allows us to use different strategies for running the task. For example, the task could be scheduled to execute after a time delay or to execute periodically.

The number of threads in the pool can be set heuristically based on factors such as the number of CPUs in the system, the amount of physical memory, and the expected number of concurrent client requests. More sophisticated thread-pool architectures can dynamically adjust the number of threads in the pool according to usage patterns. Such architectures provide the further benefit of having a smaller pool—thereby consuming less memory—when the load on the system is low. We discuss one such architecture, Apple's Grand Central Dispatch, later in this section.

The Windows API provides several functions related to thread pools. Using the thread pool API is similar to creating a thread with the `Thread_Create()` function, as described in Section 4.4.2. Here, a function that is to run as a separate thread is defined. Such a function may appear as follows:

```
DWORD WINAPI PoolFunction(AVOID Param) {
    /*
    * this function runs as a separate thread.
    */
}
```

A pointer to `PoolFunction()` is passed to one of the functions in the thread pool API, and a thread from the pool executes this function. One such member in the thread pool API is the `QueueUserWorkItem()` function, which is passed three parameters:

- `LPTHREAD_START_ROUTINE Function`—a pointer to the function that is to run as a separate thread

- `PVOID Param`—the parameter passed to `Function`

- `ULONG Flags`—flags indicating how the thread pool is to create and manage execution of the thread

An example of invoking a function is the following:

```
QueueUserWorkItem(&PoolFunction, NULL, 0);
```

This causes a thread from the thread pool to invoke `PoolFunction()` on behalf of the programmer. In this instance, we pass no parameters to PoolFunction(). Because we specify 0 as a flag, we provide the thread pool with no special instructions for thread creation.

Other members in the Windows thread pool API include utilities that invoke functions at periodic intervals or when an asynchronous I/O request completes. The java.util.concurrent package in the Java API provides a thread-pool utility as well.

4.5.2 OpenMP

OpenMP is a set of compiler directives as well as an API for programs written in C, C++, or FORTRAN that provides support for parallel programming in shared-memory environments. OpenMP identifies **parallel regions** as blocks of code that may run in parallel. Application developers insert compiler directives into their code at parallel regions, and these directives instruct the OpenMP run-time library to execute the region in parallel. The following C program illustrates a compiler directive above the parallel region containing the printf() statement:

```
#include <omp.h>
#include <stdio.h>

int main(int argc, char *argv[])
{
    /* sequential code */

    #pragma omp parallel
    {
        printf("I am a parallel region.");
    }

    /* sequential code */

    return 0;
}
```

When OpenMP encounters the directive

```
#pragma omp parallel
```

it creates as many threads as there are processing cores in the system. Thus, for a dual-core system, two threads are created, for a quad-core system, four are created; and so forth. All the threads then simultaneously execute the parallel region. As each thread exits the parallel region, it is terminated.

OpenMP provides several additional directives for running code regions in parallel, including parallelizing loops. For example, assume we have two arrays a and b of size N. We wish to sum their contents and place the results in array c. We can have this task run in parallel by using the following code segment, which contains the compiler directive for parallelizing for loops:

```
#pragma omp parallel for
for (i = 0; i < N; i++) {
    c[i] = a[i] + b[i];
}
```

OpenMP divides the work contained in the `for` loop among the threads it has created in response to the directive

```
#pragma omp parallel for
```

In addition to providing directives for parallelization, OpenMP allows developers to choose among several levels of parallelism. For example, they can set the number of threads manually. It also allows developers to identify whether data are shared between threads or are private to a thread. OpenMP is available on several open-source and commercial compilers for Linux, Windows, and Mac OS X systems. We encourage readers interested in learning more about OpenMP to consult the bibliography at the end of the chapter.

4.5.3 Grand Central Dispatch

Grand Central Dispatch (GCD)—a technology for Apple's Mac OS X and iOS operating systems—is a combination of extensions to the C language, an API, and a run-time library that allows application developers to identify sections of code to run in parallel. Like OpenMP, GCD manages most of the details of threading.

GCD identifies extensions to the C and C++ languages known as **blocks**. A block is simply a self-contained unit of work. It is specified by a caret ˆ inserted in front of a pair of braces { }. A simple example of a block is shown below:

```
^{ printf("I am a block"); }
```

GCD schedules blocks for run-time execution by placing them on a **dispatch queue**. When it removes a block from a queue, it assigns the block to an available thread from the thread pool it manages. GCD identifies two types of dispatch queues: *serial* and *concurrent*.

Blocks placed on a serial queue are removed in FIFO order. Once a block has been removed from the queue, it must complete execution before another block is removed. Each process has its own serial queue (known as its **main queue**). Developers can create additional serial queues that are local to particular processes. Serial queues are useful for ensuring the sequential execution of several tasks.

Blocks placed on a concurrent queue are also removed in FIFO order, but several blocks may be removed at a time, thus allowing multiple blocks to execute in parallel. There are three system-wide concurrent dispatch queues, and they are distinguished according to priority: low, default, and high. Priorities represent an approximation of the relative importance of blocks. Quite simply, blocks with a higher priority should be placed on the high-priority dispatch queue.

The following code segment illustrates obtaining the default-priority concurrent queue and submitting a block to the queue using the `dispatch_async()` function:

```
dispatch_queue_t queue = dispatch_get_global_queue
   (DISPATCH_QUEUE_PRIORITY_DEFAULT, 0);

dispatch_async(queue, ^{ printf("I am a block."); });
```

Internally, GCD's thread pool is composed of POSIX threads. GCD actively manages the pool, allowing the number of threads to grow and shrink according to application demand and system capacity.

4.5.4 Other Approaches

Thread pools, OpenMP, and Grand Central Dispatch are just a few of many emerging technologies for managing multithreaded applications. Other commercial approaches include parallel and concurrent libraries, such as Intel's Threading Building Blocks (TBB) and several products from Microsoft. The Java language and API have seen significant movement toward supporting concurrent programming as well. A notable example is the java.util.concurrent package, which supports implicit thread creation and management.

4.6 Threading Issues

In this section, we discuss some of the issues to consider in designing multithreaded programs.

4.6.1 The fork() and exec() System Calls

In Chapter 3, we described how the fork() system call is used to create a separate, duplicate process. The semantics of the fork() and exec() system calls change in a multithreaded program.

If one thread in a program calls fork(), does the new process duplicate all threads, or is the new process single-threaded? Some UNIX systems have chosen to have two versions of fork(), one that duplicates all threads and another that duplicates only the thread that invoked the fork() system call.

The exec() system call typically works in the same way as described in Chapter 3. That is, if a thread invokes the exec() system call, the program specified in the parameter to exec() will replace the entire process—including all threads.

Which of the two versions of fork() to use depends on the application. If exec() is called immediately after forking, then duplicating all threads is unnecessary, as the program specified in the parameters to exec() will replace the process. In this instance, duplicating only the calling thread is appropriate. If, however, the separate process does not call exec() after forking, the separate process should duplicate all threads.

4.6.2 Signal Handling

A **signal** is used in UNIX systems to notify a process that a particular event has occurred. A signal may be received either synchronously or asynchronously, depending on the source of and the reason for the event being signaled. All signals, whether synchronous or asynchronous, follow the same pattern:

1. A signal is generated by the occurrence of a particular event.

2. The signal is delivered to a process.

3. Once delivered, the signal must be handled.

Examples of synchronous signal include illegal memory access and division by 0. If a running program performs either of these actions, a signal is generated. Synchronous signals are delivered to the same process that performed the operation that caused the signal (that is the reason they are considered synchronous).

When a signal is generated by an event external to a running process, that process receives the signal asynchronously. Examples of such signals include terminating a process with specific keystrokes (such as <control><C>) and having a timer expire. Typically, an asynchronous signal is sent to another process.

A signal may be *handled* by one of two possible handlers:

1. A default signal handler

2. A user-defined signal handler

Every signal has a **default signal handler** that the kernel runs when handling that signal. This default action can be overridden by a **user-defined signal handler** that is called to handle the signal. Signals are handled in different ways. Some signals (such as changing the size of a window) are simply ignored; others (such as an illegal memory access) are handled by terminating the program.

Handling signals in single-threaded programs is straightforward: signals are always delivered to a process. However, delivering signals is more complicated in multithreaded programs, where a process may have several threads. Where, then, should a signal be delivered?

In general, the following options exist:

1. Deliver the signal to the thread to which the signal applies.

2. Deliver the signal to every thread in the process.

3. Deliver the signal to certain threads in the process.

4. Assign a specific thread to receive all signals for the process.

The method for delivering a signal depends on the type of signal generated. For example, synchronous signals need to be delivered to the thread causing the signal and not to other threads in the process. However, the situation with asynchronous signals is not as clear. Some asynchronous signals—such as a signal that terminates a process (<control><C>, for example)—should be sent to all threads.

The standard UNIX function for delivering a signal is

```
kill(pid_t pid, int signal)
```

This function specifies the process (pid) to which a particular signal (signal) is to be delivered. Most multithreaded versions of UNIX allow a thread to specify which signals it will accept and which it will block. Therefore, in some cases, an asynchronous signal may be delivered only to those threads that are not blocking it. However, because signals need to be handled only once, a signal is typically delivered only to the first thread found that is not blocking it. POSIX Pthreads provides the following function, which allows a signal to be delivered to a specified thread (tid):

```
pthread_kill(pthread_t tid, int signal)
```

Although Windows does not explicitly provide support for signals, it allows us to emulate them using **asynchronous procedure calls (APCs)**. The APC facility enables a user thread to specify a function that is to be called when the user thread receives notification of a particular event. As indicated by its name, an APC is roughly equivalent to an asynchronous signal in UNIX. However, whereas UNIX must contend with how to deal with signals in a multithreaded environment, the APC facility is more straightforward, since an APC is delivered to a particular thread rather than a process.

4.6.3 Thread Cancellation

Thread cancellation involves terminating a thread before it has completed. For example, if multiple threads are concurrently searching through a database and one thread returns the result, the remaining threads might be canceled. Another situation might occur when a user presses a button on a web browser that stops a web page from loading any further. Often, a web page loads using several threads—each image is loaded in a separate thread. When a user presses the stop button on the browser, all threads loading the page are canceled.

A thread that is to be canceled is often referred to as the **target thread**. Cancellation of a target thread may occur in two different scenarios:

1. **Asynchronous cancellation**. One thread immediately terminates the target thread.

2. **Deferred cancellation**. The target thread periodically checks whether it should terminate, allowing it an opportunity to terminate itself in an orderly fashion.

The difficulty with cancellation occurs in situations where resources have been allocated to a canceled thread or where a thread is canceled while in the midst of updating data it is sharing with other threads. This becomes especially troublesome with asynchronous cancellation. Often, the operating system will reclaim system resources from a canceled thread but will not reclaim all resources. Therefore, canceling a thread asynchronously may not free a necessary system-wide resource.

With deferred cancellation, in contrast, one thread indicates that a target thread is to be canceled, but cancellation occurs only after the target thread has checked a flag to determine whether or not it should be canceled. The thread can perform this check at a point at which it can be canceled safely.

In Pthreads, thread cancellation is initiated using the pthread_cancel() function. The identifier of the target thread is passed as a parameter to the function. The following code illustrates creating—and then canceling— a thread:

```
pthread_t tid;

/* create the thread */
pthread_create(&tid, 0, worker, NULL);

. . .

/* cancel the thread */
pthread_cancel(tid);
```

Invoking pthread_cancel() indicates only a request to cancel the target thread, however; actual cancellation depends on how the target thread is set up to handle the request. Pthreads supports three cancellation modes. Each mode is defined as a state and a type, as illustrated in the table below. A thread may set its cancellation state and type using an API.

Mode	State	Type
Off	Disabled	–
Deferred	Enabled	Deferred
Asynchronous	Enabled	Asynchronous

As the table illustrates, Pthreads allows threads to disable or enable cancellation. Obviously, a thread cannot be canceled if cancellation is disabled. However, cancellation requests remain pending, so the thread can later enable cancellation and respond to the request.

The default cancellation type is deferred cancellation. Here, cancellation occurs only when a thread reaches a **cancellation point**. One technique for establishing a cancellation point is to invoke the pthread_testcancel() function. If a cancellation request is found to be pending, a function known as a **cleanup handler** is invoked. This function allows any resources a thread may have acquired to be released before the thread is terminated.

The following code illustrates how a thread may respond to a cancellation request using deferred cancellation:

```
while (1) {
    /* do some work for awhile */
    /* . . . */

    /* check if there is a cancellation request */
    pthread_testcancel();
}
```

Because of the issues described earlier, asynchronous cancellation is not recommended in Pthreads documentation. Thus, we do not cover it here. An interesting note is that on Linux systems, thread cancellation using the Pthreads API is handled through signals (Section 4.6.2).

4.6.4 Thread-Local Storage

Threads belonging to a process share the data of the process. Indeed, this data sharing provides one of the benefits of multithreaded programming. However, in some circumstances, each thread might need its own copy of certain data. We will call such data **thread-local storage** (or TLS.) For example, in a transaction-processing system, we might service each transaction in a separate thread. Furthermore, each transaction might be assigned a unique identifier. To associate each thread with its unique identifier, we could use thread-local storage.

It is easy to confuse TLS with local variables. However, local variables are visible only during a single function invocation, whereas TLS data are visible across function invocations. In some ways, TLS is similar to `static` data. The difference is that TLS data are unique to each thread. Most thread libraries—including Windows and Pthreads—provide some form of support for thread-local storage; Java provides support as well.

4.6.5 Scheduler Activations

A final issue to be considered with multithreaded programs concerns communication between the kernel and the thread library, which may be required by the many-to-many and two-level models discussed in Section 4.3.3. Such coordination allows the number of kernel threads to be dynamically adjusted to help ensure the best performance.

Many systems implementing either the many-to-many or the two-level model place an intermediate data structure between the user and kernel threads. This data structure—typically known as a **lightweight process**, or LWP—is shown in Figure 4.13. To the user-thread library, the LWP appears to be a virtual processor on which the application can schedule a user thread to run. Each LWP is attached to a kernel thread, and it is kernel threads that the

Figure 4.13 Lightweight process (LWP).

operating system schedules to run on physical processors. If a kernel thread blocks (such as while waiting for an I/O operation to complete), the LWP blocks as well. Up the chain, the user-level thread attached to the LWP also blocks.

An application may require any number of LWPs to run efficiently. Consider a CPU-bound application running on a single processor. In this scenario, only one thread can run at a time, so one LWP is sufficient. An application that is I/O-intensive may require multiple LWPs to execute, however. Typically, an LWP is required for each concurrent blocking system call. Suppose, for example, that five different file-read requests occur simultaneously. Five LWPs are needed, because all could be waiting for I/O completion in the kernel. If a process has only four LWPs, then the fifth request must wait for one of the LWPs to return from the kernel.

One scheme for communication between the user-thread library and the kernel is known as **scheduler activation**. It works as follows: The kernel provides an application with a set of virtual processors (LWPs), and the application can schedule user threads onto an available virtual processor. Furthermore, the kernel must inform an application about certain events. This procedure is known as an **upcall**. Upcalls are handled by the thread library with an **upcall handler**, and upcall handlers must run on a virtual processor. One event that triggers an upcall occurs when an application thread is about to block. In this scenario, the kernel makes an upcall to the application informing it that a thread is about to block and identifying the specific thread. The kernel then allocates a new virtual processor to the application. The application runs an upcall handler on this new virtual processor, which saves the state of the blocking thread and relinquishes the virtual processor on which the blocking thread is running. The upcall handler then schedules another thread that is eligible to run on the new virtual processor. When the event that the blocking thread was waiting for occurs, the kernel makes another upcall to the thread library informing it that the previously blocked thread is now eligible to run. The upcall handler for this event also requires a virtual processor, and the kernel may allocate a new virtual processor or preempt one of the user threads and run the upcall handler on its virtual processor. After marking the unblocked thread as eligible to run, the application schedules an eligible thread to run on an available virtual processor.

4.7   Operating-System Examples

At this point, we have examined a number of concepts and issues related to threads. We conclude the chapter by exploring how threads are implemented in Windows and Linux systems.

4.7.1   Windows Threads

Windows implements the Windows API, which is the primary API for the family of Microsoft operating systems (Windows 98, NT, 2000, and XP, as well as Windows 7). Indeed, much of what is mentioned in this section applies to this entire family of operating systems.

A Windows application runs as a separate process, and each process may contain one or more threads. The Windows API for creating threads is covered in

Section 4.4.2. Additionally, Windows uses the one-to-one mapping described in Section 4.3.2, where each user-level thread maps to an associated kernel thread.

The general components of a thread include:

- A thread ID uniquely identifying the thread

- A register set representing the status of the processor

- A user stack, employed when the thread is running in user mode, and a kernel stack, employed when the thread is running in kernel mode

- A private storage area used by various run-time libraries and dynamic link libraries (DLLs)

The register set, stacks, and private storage area are known as the **context** of the thread.

The primary data structures of a thread include:

- ETHREAD—executive thread block

- KTHREAD—kernel thread block

- TEB—thread environment block

The key components of the ETHREAD include a pointer to the process to which the thread belongs and the address of the routine in which the thread starts control. The ETHREAD also contains a pointer to the corresponding KTHREAD.

The KTHREAD includes scheduling and synchronization information for the thread. In addition, the KTHREAD includes the kernel stack (used when the thread is running in kernel mode) and a pointer to the TEB.

The ETHREAD and the KTHREAD exist entirely in kernel space; this means that only the kernel can access them. The TEB is a user-space data structure that is accessed when the thread is running in user mode. Among other fields, the TEB contains the thread identifier, a user-mode stack, and an array for thread-local storage. The structure of a Windows thread is illustrated in Figure 4.14.

4.7.2 Linux Threads

Linux provides the fork() system call with the traditional functionality of duplicating a process, as described in Chapter 3. Linux also provides the ability to create threads using the clone() system call. However, Linux does not distinguish between processes and threads. In fact, Linux uses the term *task* —rather than *process* or *thread*— when referring to a flow of control within a program.

When clone() is invoked, it is passed a set of flags that determine how much sharing is to take place between the parent and child tasks. Some of these flags are listed in Figure 4.15. For example, suppose that clone() is passed the flags CLONE_FS, CLONE_VM, CLONE_SIGHAND, and CLONE_FILES. The parent and child tasks will then share the same file-system information (such as the current working directory), the same memory space, the same signal handlers,

Figure 4.14 Data structures of a Windows thread.

and the same set of open files. Using `clone()` in this fashion is equivalent to creating a thread as described in this chapter, since the parent task shares most of its resources with its child task. However, if none of these flags is set when `clone()` is invoked, no sharing takes place, resulting in functionality similar to that provided by the `fork()` system call.

The varying level of sharing is possible because of the way a task is represented in the Linux kernel. A unique kernel data structure (specifically, `struct task_struct`) exists for each task in the system. This data structure, instead of storing data for the task, contains pointers to other data structures where these data are stored—for example, data structures that represent the list of open files, signal-handling information, and virtual memory. When `fork()` is invoked, a new task is created, along with a *copy* of all the associated data

flag	meaning
`CLONE_FS`	File-system information is shared.
`CLONE_VM`	The same memory space is shared.
`CLONE_SIGHAND`	Signal handlers are shared.
`CLONE_FILES`	The set of open files is shared.

Figure 4.15 Some of the flags passed when `clone()` is invoked.

structures of the parent process. A new task is also created when the `clone()` system call is made. However, rather than copying all data structures, the new task *points* to the data structures of the parent task, depending on the set of flags passed to `clone()`.

4.8 Summary

A thread is a flow of control within a process. A multithreaded process contains several different flows of control within the same address space. The benefits of multithreading include increased responsiveness to the user, resource sharing within the process, economy, and scalability factors, such as more efficient use of multiple processing cores.

User-level threads are threads that are visible to the programmer and are unknown to the kernel. The operating-system kernel supports and manages kernel-level threads. In general, user-level threads are faster to create and manage than are kernel threads, because no intervention from the kernel is required.

Three different types of models relate user and kernel threads. The many-to-one model maps many user threads to a single kernel thread. The one-to-one model maps each user thread to a corresponding kernel thread. The many-to-many model multiplexes many user threads to a smaller or equal number of kernel threads.

Most modern operating systems provide kernel support for threads. These include Windows, Mac OS X, Linux, and Solaris.

Thread libraries provide the application programmer with an API for creating and managing threads. Three primary thread libraries are in common use: POSIX Pthreads, Windows threads, and Java threads.

In addition to explicitly creating threads using the API provided by a library, we can use implicit threading, in which the creation and management of threading is transferred to compilers and run-time libraries. Strategies for implicit threading include thread pools, OpenMP, and Grand Central Dispatch.

Multithreaded programs introduce many challenges for programmers, including the semantics of the `fork()` and `exec()` system calls. Other issues include signal handling, thread cancellation, thread-local storage, and scheduler activations.

Review Questions

Review questions for this chapter can be accessed by visiting our website.

Practice Exercises

Answers for the Practice Exercises can be accceed by visiting our website.

4.1 Provide two programming examples in which multithreading provides better performance than a single-threaded solution.

4.2   What are two differences between user-level threads and kernel-level threads? Under what circumstances is one type better than the other?

4.3   Describe the actions taken by a kernel to context-switch between kernel-level threads.

4.4   What resources are used when a thread is created? How do they differ from those used when a process is created?

4.5   Assume that an operating system maps user-level threads to the kernel using the many-to-many model and that the mapping is done through LWPs. Furthermore, the system allows developers to create real-time threads for use in real-time systems. Is it necessary to bind a real-time thread to an LWP? Explain.

Exercises

4.6   Provide two programming examples in which multithreading does *not* provide better performance than a single-threaded solution.

4.7   Under what circumstances does a multithreaded solution using multiple kernel threads provide better performance than a single-threaded solution on a single-processor system?

4.8   Which of the following components of program state are shared across threads in a multithreaded process?

a.   Register values

b.   Heap memory

c.   Global variables

d.   Stack memory

4.9   Can a multithreaded solution using multiple user-level threads achieve better performance on a multiprocessor system than on a single-processor system? Explain.

4.10   In Chapter 3, we discussed Google's Chrome browser and its practice of opening each new website in a separate process. Would the same benefits have been achieved if instead Chrome had been designed to open each new website in a separate thread? Explain.

4.11   Is it possible to have concurrency but not parallelism? Explain.

4.12   Using Amdahl's Law, calculate the speedup gain of an application that has a 60 percent parallel component for (a) two processing cores and (b) four processing cores.

4.13   Determine if the following problems exhibit task or data parallelism:

• The multithreaded statistical program described in Exercise 4.21

• The multithreaded Sudoku validator described in Project 1 in this chapter

- The multithreaded sorting program described in Project 2 in this chapter

- The multithreaded web server described in Section 4.1

4.14 A system with two dual-core processors has four processors available for scheduling. A CPU-intensive application is running on this system. All input is performed at program start-up, when a single file must be opened. Similarly, all output is performed just before the program terminates, when the program results must be written to a single file. Between startup and termination, the program is entirely CPU-bound. Your task is to improve the performance of this application by multithreading it. The application runs on a system that uses the one-to-one threading model (each user thread maps to a kernel thread).

- How many threads will you create to perform the input and output? Explain.

- How many threads will you create for the CPU-intensive portion of the application? Explain.

4.15 Consider the following code segment:

```
pid_t pid;

pid = fork();
if (pid == 0) { /* child process */
    fork();
    thread_create( . . .);
}
fork();
```

   a.   How many unique processes are created?

   b.   How many unique threads are created?

4.16 As described in Section 4.7.2, Linux does not distinguish between processes and threads. Instead, Linux treats both in the same way, allowing a task to be more akin to a process or a thread depending on the set of flags passed to the clone() system call. However, other operating systems, such as Windows, treat processes and threads differently. Typically, such systems use a notation in which the data structure for a process contains pointers to the separate threads belonging to the process. Contrast these two approaches for modeling processes and threads within the kernel.

4.17 The program shown in Figure 4.16 uses the Pthreads API. What would be the output from the program at LINE C and LINE P?

4.18 Consider a multicore system and a multithreaded program written using the many-to-many threading model. Let the number of user-level threads in the program be greater than the number of processing cores

```
#include <pthread.h>
#include <stdio.h>

int value = 0;
void *runner(void *param); /* the thread */

int main(int argc, char *argv[])
{
pid_t pid;
pthread_t tid;
pthread_attr_t attr;

   pid = fork();

   if (pid == 0) { /* child process */
      pthread_attr_init(&attr);
      pthread_create(&tid,&attr,runner,NULL);
      pthread_join(tid,NULL);
      printf("CHILD: value = %d",value); /* LINE C */
   }
   else if (pid > 0) { /* parent process */
      wait(NULL);
      printf("PARENT: value = %d",value); /* LINE P */
   }
}

void *runner(void *param) {
   value = 5;
   pthread_exit(0);
}
```

Figure 4.16   C program for Exercise 4.17.

in the system. Discuss the performance implications of the following scenarios.

a.   The number of kernel threads allocated to the program is less than the number of processing cores.

b.   The number of kernel threads allocated to the program is equal to the number of processing cores.

c.   The number of kernel threads allocated to the program is greater than the number of processing cores but less than the number of user-level threads.

4.19   Pthreads provides an API for managing thread cancellation. The pthread_setcancelstate() function is used to set the cancellation state. Its prototype appears as follows:

```
pthread_setcancelstate(int state, int *oldstate)
```

```
int oldstate;

pthread_setcancelstate(PTHREAD_CANCEL_DISABLE, &oldstate);

/* What operations would be performed here? */

pthread_setcancelstate(PTHREAD_CANCEL_ENABLE, &oldstate);
```

Figure 4.17   C program for Exercise 4.19.

The two possible values for the state are PTHREAD_CANCEL_ENABLE and PTHREAD_CANCEL_DISABLE.

Using the code segment shown in Figure 4.17, provide examples of two operations that would be suitable to perform between the calls to disable and enable thread cancellation.

Programming Problems

4.20 Modify programming problem Exercise 3.20 from Chapter 3, which asks you to design a pid manager. This modification will consist of writing a multithreaded program that tests your solution to Exercise 3.20. You will create a number of threads—for example, 100—and each thread will request a pid, sleep for a random period of time, and then release the pid. (Sleeping for a random period of time approximates the typical pid usage in which a pid is assigned to a new process, the process executes and then terminates, and the pid is released on the process's termination.) On UNIX and Linux systems, sleeping is accomplished through the sleep() function, which is passed an integer value representing the number of seconds to sleep. This problem will be modified in Chapter 5.

4.21 Write a multithreaded program that calculates various statistical values for a list of numbers. This program will be passed a series of numbers on the command line and will then create three separate worker threads. One thread will determine the average of the numbers, the second will determine the maximum value, and the third will determine the minimum value. For example, suppose your program is passed the integers

90 81 78 95 79 72 85

The program will report

```
The average value is 82
The minimum value is 72
The maximum value is 95
```

The variables representing the average, minimum, and maximum values will be stored globally. The worker threads will set these values, and the parent thread will output the values once the workers have exited. (We

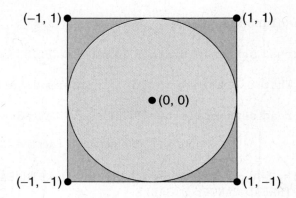

Figure 4.18   Monte Carlo technique for calculating pi.

could obviously expand this program by creating additional threads that determine other statistical values, such as median and standard deviation.)

4.22   An interesting way of calculating π is to use a technique known as *Monte Carlo,* which involves randomization. This technique works as follows: Suppose you have a circle inscribed within a square, as shown in Figure 4.18. (Assume that the radius of this circle is 1.) First, generate a series of random points as simple (x, y) coordinates. These points must fall within the Cartesian coordinates that bound the square. Of the total number of random points that are generated, some will occur within the circle. Next, estimate π by performing the following calculation:

$$\pi = 4 \times \textit{(number of points in circle)} \, / \, \textit{(total number of points)}$$

Write a multithreaded version of this algorithm that creates a separate thread to generate a number of random points. The thread will count the number of points that occur within the circle and store that result in a global variable. When this thread has exited, the parent thread will calculate and output the estimated value of π. It is worth experimenting with the number of random points generated. As a general rule, the greater the number of points, the closer the approximation to π.

In the source-code download for this text, we provide a sample program that provides a technique for generating random numbers, as well as determining if the random (x, y) point occurs within the circle.

Readers interested in the details of the Monte Carlo method for estimating π should consult the bibliography at the end of this chapter. In Chapter 5, we modify this exercise using relevant material from that chapter.

4.23   Repeat Exercise 4.22, but instead of using a separate thread to generate random points, use OpenMP to parallelize the generation of points. Be careful not to place the calculcation of π in the parallel region, since you want to calculcate π only once.

4.24   Write a multithreaded program that outputs prime numbers. This program should work as follows: The user will run the program and will enter a number on the command line. The program will then create a separate thread that outputs all the prime numbers less than or equal to the number entered by the user.

4.25 Modify the socket-based date server (Figure 3.21) in Chapter 3 so that the server services each client request in a separate thread.

4.26 The Fibonacci sequence is the series of numbers $0, 1, 1, 2, 3, 5, 8, \ldots$. Formally, it can be expressed as:

$$fib_0 = 0$$
$$fib_1 = 1$$
$$fib_n = fib_{n-1} + fib_{n-2}$$

Write a multithreaded program that generates the Fibonacci sequence. This program should work as follows: On the command line, the user will enter the number of Fibonacci numbers that the program is to generate. The program will then create a separate thread that will generate the Fibonacci numbers, placing the sequence in data that can be shared by the threads (an array is probably the most convenient data structure). When the thread finishes execution, the parent thread will output the sequence generated by the child thread. Because the parent thread cannot begin outputting the Fibonacci sequence until the child thread finishes, the parent thread will have to wait for the child thread to finish. Use the techniques described in Section 4.4 to meet this requirement.

4.27 Exercise 3.25 in Chapter 3 involves designing an echo server using the Java threading API. This server is single-threaded, meaning that the server cannot respond to concurrent echo clients until the current client exits. Modify the solution to Exercise 3.25 so that the echo server services each client in a separate request.

Programming Projects

Project 1—Sudoku Solution Validator

A *Sudoku* puzzle uses a 9×9 grid in which each column and row, as well as each of the nine 3×3 subgrids, must contain all of the digits $1 \cdots 9$. Figure 4.19 presents an example of a valid Sudoku puzzle. This project consists of designing a multithreaded application that determines whether the solution to a Sudoku puzzle is valid.

There are several different ways of multithreading this application. One suggested strategy is to create threads that check the following criteria:

- A thread to check that each column contains the digits 1 through 9
- A thread to check that each row contains the digits 1 through 9

6	2	4	5	3	9	1	8	7
5	1	9	7	2	8	6	3	4
8	3	7	6	1	4	2	9	5
1	4	3	8	6	5	7	2	9
9	5	8	2	4	7	3	6	1
7	6	2	3	9	1	4	5	8
3	7	1	9	5	6	8	4	2
4	9	6	1	8	2	5	7	3
2	8	5	4	7	3	9	1	6

Figure 4.19   Solution to a 9 × 9 Sudoku puzzle.

- Nine threads to check that each of the 3 × 3 subgrids contains the digits 1 through 9

This would result in a total of eleven separate threads for validating a Sudoku puzzle. However, you are welcome to create even more threads for this project. For example, rather than creating one thread that checks all nine columns, you could create nine separate threads and have each of them check one column.

Passing Parameters to Each Thread

The parent thread will create the worker threads, passing each worker the location that it must check in the Sudoku grid. This step will require passing several parameters to each thread. The easiest approach is to create a data structure using a struct. For example, a structure to pass the row and column where a thread must begin validating would appear as follows:

```
/* structure for passing data to threads */
typedef struct
{
    int row;
    int column;
} parameters;
```

Both Pthreads and Windows programs will create worker threads using a strategy similar to that shown below:

```
parameters *data = (parameters *) malloc(sizeof(parameters));
data->row = 1;
data->column = 1;
/* Now create the thread passing it data as a parameter */
```

Figure 4.20   Multithreaded sorting.

The data pointer will be passed to either the pthread_create() (Pthreads) function or the CreateThread() (Windows) function, which in turn will pass it as a parameter to the function that is to run as a separate thread.

Returning Results to the Parent Thread

Each worker thread is assigned the task of determining the validity of a particular region of the Sudoku puzzle. Once a worker has performed this check, it must pass its results back to the parent. One good way to handle this is to create an array of integer values that is visible to each thread. The ith index in this array corresponds to the ith worker thread. If a worker sets its corresponding value to 1, it is indicating that its region of the Sudoku puzzle is valid. A value of 0 would indicate otherwise. When all worker threads have completed, the parent thread checks each entry in the result array to determine if the Sudoku puzzle is valid.

Project 2—Multithreaded Sorting Application

Write a multithreaded sorting program that works as follows: A list of integers is divided into two smaller lists of equal size. Two separate threads (which we will term *sorting threads*) sort each sublist using a sorting algorithm of your choice. The two sublists are then merged by a third thread—a *merging thread* —which merges the two sublists into a single sorted list.

Because global data are shared across all threads, perhaps the easiest way to set up the data is to create a global array. Each sorting thread will work on one half of this array. A second global array of the same size as the unsorted integer array will also be established. The merging thread will then merge the two sublists into this second array. Graphically, this program is structured according to Figure 4.20.

This programming project will require passing parameters to each of the sorting threads. In particular, it will be necessary to identify the starting index from which each thread is to begin sorting. Refer to the instructions in Project 1 for details on passing parameters to a thread.

The parent thread will output the sorted array once all sorting threads have exited.

Bibliographical Notes

Threads have had a long evolution, starting as "cheap concurrency" in programming languages and moving to "lightweight processes," with early examples that included the Thoth system ([Cheriton et al. (1979)]) and the Pilot system ([Redell et al. (1980)]). [Binding (1985)] described moving threads into the UNIX kernel. Mach ([Accetta et al. (1986)], [Tevanian et al. (1987)]), and V ([Cheriton (1988)]) made extensive use of threads, and eventually almost all major operating systems implemented them in some form or another.

[Vahalia (1996)] covers threading in several versions of UNIX. [McDougall and Mauro (2007)] describes developments in threading the Solaris kernel. [Russinovich and Solomon (2009)] discuss threading in the Windows operating system family. [Mauerer (2008)] and [Love (2010)] explain how Linux handles threading, and [Singh (2007)] covers threads in Mac OS X.

Information on Pthreads programming is given in [Lewis and Berg (1998)] and [Butenhof (1997)]. [Oaks and Wong (1999)] and [Lewis and Berg (2000)] discuss multithreading in Java. [Goetz et al. (2006)] present a detailed discussion of concurrent programming in Java. [Hart (2005)] describes multithreading using Windows. Details on using OpenMP can be found at http://openmp.org.

An analysis of an optimal thread-pool size can be found in [Ling et al. (2000)]. Scheduler activations were first presented in [Anderson et al. (1991)], and [Williams (2002)] discusses scheduler activations in the NetBSD system.

[Breshears (2009)] and [Pacheco (2011)] cover parallel programming in detail. [Hill and Marty (2008)] examine Amdahl's Law with respect to multicore systems. The Monte Carlo technique for estimating π is further discussed in http://math.fullerton.edu/mathews/n2003/montecarlopimod.html.

Bibliography

[Accetta et al. (1986)]   M. Accetta, R. Baron, W. Bolosky, D. B. Golub, R. Rashid, A. Tevanian, and M. Young, "Mach: A New Kernel Foundation for UNIX Development", *Proceedings of the Summer USENIX Conference* (1986), pages 93–112.

[Anderson et al. (1991)]   T. E. Anderson, B. N. Bershad, E. D. Lazowska, and H. M. Levy, "Scheduler Activations: Effective Kernel Support for the User-Level Management of Parallelism", *Proceedings of the ACM Symposium on Operating Systems Principles* (1991), pages 95–109.

[Binding (1985)]   C. Binding, "Cheap Concurrency in C", *SIGPLAN Notices*, Volume 20, Number 9 (1985), pages 21–27.

[Breshears (2009)]   C. Breshears, *The Art of Concurrency*, O'Reilly & Associates (2009).

[Butenhof (1997)]   D. Butenhof, *Programming with POSIX Threads*, Addison-Wesley (1997).

[Cheriton (1988)]   D. Cheriton, "The V Distributed System", *Communications of the ACM*, Volume 31, Number 3 (1988), pages 314–333.

[Cheriton et al. (1979)]   D. R. Cheriton, M. A. Malcolm, L. S. Melen, and G. R. Sager, "Thoth, a Portable Real-Time Operating System", *Communications of the ACM*, Volume 22, Number 2 (1979), pages 105–115.

[Goetz et al. (2006)]   B. Goetz, T. Peirls, J. Bloch, J. Bowbeer, D. Holmes, and D. Lea, *Java Concurrency in Practice*, Addison-Wesley (2006).

[Hart (2005)]   J. M. Hart, *Windows System Programming*, Third Edition, Addison-Wesley (2005).

[Hill and Marty (2008)]   M. Hill and M. Marty, "Amdahl's Law in the Multicore Era", *IEEE Computer*, Volume 41, Number 7 (2008), pages 33–38.

[Lewis and Berg (1998)]   B. Lewis and D. Berg, *Multithreaded Programming with Pthreads*, Sun Microsystems Press (1998).

[Lewis and Berg (2000)]   B. Lewis and D. Berg, *Multithreaded Programming with Java Technology*, Sun Microsystems Press (2000).

[Ling et al. (2000)]   Y. Ling, T. Mullen, and X. Lin, "Analysis of Optimal Thread Pool Size", *Operating System Review*, Volume 34, Number 2 (2000), pages 42–55.

[Love (2010)]   R. Love, *Linux Kernel Development*, Third Edition, Developer's Library (2010).

[Mauerer (2008)]   W. Mauerer, *Professional Linux Kernel Architecture*, John Wiley and Sons (2008).

[McDougall and Mauro (2007)]   R. McDougall and J. Mauro, *Solaris Internals*, Second Edition, Prentice Hall (2007).

[Oaks and Wong (1999)]   S. Oaks and H. Wong, *Java Threads*, Second Edition, O'Reilly & Associates (1999).

[Pacheco (2011)]   P. S. Pacheco, *An Introduction to Parallel Programming*, Morgan Kaufmann (2011).

[Redell et al. (1980)]   D. D. Redell, Y. K. Dalal, T. R. Horsley, H. C. Lauer, W. C. Lynch, P. R. McJones, H. G. Murray, and S. P. Purcell, "Pilot: An Operating System for a Personal Computer", *Communications of the ACM*, Volume 23, Number 2 (1980), pages 81–92.

[Russinovich and Solomon (2009)]   M. E. Russinovich and D. A. Solomon, *Windows Internals: Including Windows Server 2008 and Windows Vista*, Fifth Edition, Microsoft Press (2009).

[Singh (2007)]   A. Singh, *Mac OS X Internals: A Systems Approach*, Addison-Wesley (2007).

[Tevanian et al. (1987)]   A. Tevanian, Jr., R. F. Rashid, D. B. Golub, D. L. Black, E. Cooper, and M. W. Young, "Mach Threads and the Unix Kernel: The Battle for Control", *Proceedings of the Summer USENIX Conference* (1987).

[Vahalia (1996)]   U. Vahalia, *Unix Internals: The New Frontiers*, Prentice Hall (1996).

[Williams (2002)]   N. Williams, "An Implementation of Scheduler Activations on the NetBSD Operating System", *2002 USENIX Annual Technical Conference, FREENIX Track* (2002).

CHAPTER 5

Process Synchronization

A **cooperating process** is one that can affect or be affected by other processes executing in the system. Cooperating processes can either directly share a logical address space (that is, both code and data) or be allowed to share data only through files or messages. The former case is achieved through the use of threads, discussed in Chapter 4. Concurrent access to shared data may result in data inconsistency, however. In this chapter, we discuss various mechanisms to ensure the orderly execution of cooperating processes that share a logical address space, so that data consistency is maintained.

CHAPTER OBJECTIVES

- To introduce the critical-section problem, whose solutions can be used to ensure the consistency of shared data.
- To present both software and hardware solutions of the critical-section problem.
- To examine several classical process-synchronization problems.
- To explore several tools that are used to solve process synchronization problems.

5.1 Background

We've already seen that processes can execute concurrently or in parallel. Section 3.2.2 introduced the role of process scheduling and described how the CPU scheduler switches rapidly between processes to provide concurrent execution. This means that one process may only partially complete execution before another process is scheduled. In fact, a process may be interrupted at any point in its instruction stream, and the processing core may be assigned to execute instructions of another process. Additionally, Section 4.2 introduced parallel execution, in which two instruction streams (representing different processes) execute simultaneously on separate processing cores. In this chapter,

203

we explain how concurrent or parallel execution can contribute to issues involving the integrity of data shared by several processes.

Let's consider an example of how this can happen. In Chapter 3, we developed a model of a system consisting of cooperating sequential processes or threads, all running asynchronously and possibly sharing data. We illustrated this model with the producer–consumer problem, which is representative of operating systems. Specifically, in Section 3.4.1, we described how a bounded buffer could be used to enable processes to share memory.

We now return to our consideration of the bounded buffer. As we pointed out, our original solution allowed at most BUFFER_SIZE − 1 items in the buffer at the same time. Suppose we want to modify the algorithm to remedy this deficiency. One possibility is to add an integer variable counter, initialized to 0. counter is incremented every time we add a new item to the buffer and is decremented every time we remove one item from the buffer. The code for the producer process can be modified as follows:

```
while (true) {
      /* produce an item in next_produced */

      while (counter == BUFFER_SIZE)
         ; /* do nothing */

      buffer[in] = next_produced;
      in = (in + 1) % BUFFER_SIZE;
      counter++;
}
```

The code for the consumer process can be modified as follows:

```
while (true) {
      while (counter == 0)
         ; /* do nothing */

      next_consumed = buffer[out];
      out = (out + 1) % BUFFER_SIZE;
      counter--;

      /* consume the item in next_consumed */
}
```

Although the producer and consumer routines shown above are correct separately, they may not function correctly when executed concurrently. As an illustration, suppose that the value of the variable counter is currently 5 and that the producer and consumer processes concurrently execute the statements "counter++" and "counter--". Following the execution of these two statements, the value of the variable counter may be 4, 5, or 6! The only correct result, though, is counter == 5, which is generated correctly if the producer and consumer execute separately.

We can show that the value of counter may be incorrect as follows. Note that the statement "counter++" may be implemented in machine language (on a typical machine) as follows:

$$register_1 = \text{counter}$$
$$register_1 = register_1 + 1$$
$$\text{counter} = register_1$$

where $register_1$ is one of the local CPU registers. Similarly, the statement "counter--" is implemented as follows:

$$register_2 = \text{counter}$$
$$register_2 = register_2 - 1$$
$$\text{counter} = register_2$$

where again $register_2$ is one of the local CPU registers. Even though $register_1$ and $register_2$ may be the same physical register (an accumulator, say), remember that the contents of this register will be saved and restored by the interrupt handler (Section 1.2.3).

The concurrent execution of "counter++" and "counter--" is equivalent to a sequential execution in which the lower-level statements presented previously are interleaved in some arbitrary order (but the order within each high-level statement is preserved). One such interleaving is the following:

T_0:	producer	execute	$register_1 = \text{counter}$	$\{register_1 = 5\}$
T_1:	producer	execute	$register_1 = register_1 + 1$	$\{register_1 = 6\}$
T_2:	consumer	execute	$register_2 = \text{counter}$	$\{register_2 = 5\}$
T_3:	consumer	execute	$register_2 = register_2 - 1$	$\{register_2 = 4\}$
T_4:	producer	execute	$\text{counter} = register_1$	$\{counter = 6\}$
T_5:	consumer	execute	$\text{counter} = register_2$	$\{counter = 4\}$

Notice that we have arrived at the incorrect state "counter == 4", indicating that four buffers are full, when, in fact, five buffers are full. If we reversed the order of the statements at T_4 and T_5, we would arrive at the incorrect state "counter == 6".

We would arrive at this incorrect state because we allowed both processes to manipulate the variable counter concurrently. A situation like this, where several processes access and manipulate the same data concurrently and the outcome of the execution depends on the particular order in which the access takes place, is called a **race condition**. To guard against the race condition above, we need to ensure that only one process at a time can be manipulating the variable counter. To make such a guarantee, we require that the processes be synchronized in some way.

Situations such as the one just described occur frequently in operating systems as different parts of the system manipulate resources. Furthermore, as we have emphasized in earlier chapters, the growing importance of multicore systems has brought an increased emphasis on developing multithreaded applications. In such applications, several threads—which are quite possibly sharing data—are running in parallel on different processing cores. Clearly, do {

entry section

critical section

exit section

remainder section

} while (true);

Figure 5.1   General structure of a typical process P_i.

we want any changes that result from such activities not to interfere with one another. Because of the importance of this issue, we devote a major portion of this chapter to process synchronization and coordination among cooperating processes.

5.2   The Critical-Section Problem

We begin our consideration of process synchronization by discussing the so-called critical-section problem. Consider a system consisting of n processes $\{P_0, P_1, ..., P_{n-1}\}$. Each process has a segment of code, called a critical section, in which the process may be changing common variables, updating a table, writing a file, and so on. The important feature of the system is that, when one process is executing in its critical section, no other process is allowed to execute in its critical section. That is, no two processes are executing in their critical sections at the same time. The *critical-section problem* is to design a protocol that the processes can use to cooperate. Each process must request permission to enter its critical section. The section of code implementing this request is the entry section. The critical section may be followed by an exit section. The remaining code is the remainder section. The general structure of a typical process P_i is shown in Figure 5.1. The entry section and exit section are enclosed in boxes to highlight these important segments of code.

A solution to the critical-section problem must satisfy the following three requirements:

1. **Mutual exclusion**. If process P_i is executing in its critical section, then no other processes can be executing in their critical sections.

2. **Progress**. If no process is executing in its critical section and some processes wish to enter their critical sections, then only those processes that are not executing in their remainder sections can participate in deciding which will enter its critical section next, and this selection cannot be postponed indefinitely.

3. **Bounded waiting**. There exists a bound, or limit, on the number of times that other processes are allowed to enter their critical sections after a

process has made a request to enter its critical section and before that request is granted.

We assume that each process is executing at a nonzero speed. However, we can make no assumption concerning the relative speed of the n processes.

At a given point in time, many kernel-mode processes may be active in the operating system. As a result, the code implementing an operating system (*kernel code*) is subject to several possible race conditions. Consider as an example a kernel data structure that maintains a list of all open files in the system. This list must be modified when a new file is opened or closed (adding the file to the list or removing it from the list). If two processes were to open files simultaneously, the separate updates to this list could result in a race condition. Other kernel data structures that are prone to possible race conditions include structures for maintaining memory allocation, for maintaining process lists, and for interrupt handling. It is up to kernel developers to ensure that the operating system is free from such race conditions.

Two general approaches are used to handle critical sections in operating systems: preemptive kernels and nonpreemptive kernels. A preemptive kernel allows a process to be preempted while it is running in kernel mode. A nonpreemptive kernel does not allow a process running in kernel mode to be preempted; a kernel-mode process will run until it exits kernel mode, blocks, or voluntarily yields control of the CPU.

Obviously, a nonpreemptive kernel is essentially free from race conditions on kernel data structures, as only one process is active in the kernel at a time. We cannot say the same about preemptive kernels, so they must be carefully designed to ensure that shared kernel data are free from race conditions. Preemptive kernels are especially difficult to design for SMP architectures, since in these environments it is possible for two kernel-mode processes to run simultaneously on different processors.

Why, then, would anyone favor a preemptive kernel over a nonpreemptive one? A preemptive kernel may be more responsive, since there is less risk that a kernel-mode process will run for an arbitrarily long period before relinquishing the processor to waiting processes. (Of course, this risk can also be minimized by designing kernel code that does not behave in this way.) Furthermore, a preemptive kernel is more suitable for real-time programming, as it will allow a real-time process to preempt a process currently running in the kernel. Later in this chapter, we explore how various operating systems manage preemption within the kernel.

5.3 Peterson's Solution

Next, we illustrate a classic software-based solution to the critical-section problem known as Peterson's solution. Because of the way modern computer architectures perform basic machine-language instructions, such as `load` and `store`, there are no guarantees that Peterson's solution will work correctly on such architectures. However, we present the solution because it provides a good algorithmic description of solving the critical-section problem and illustrates some of the complexities involved in designing software that addresses the requirements of mutual exclusion, progress, and bounded waiting.

```
do {
```

```
flag[i] = true;
turn = j;
while (flag[j] && turn == j);
```

critical section

```
flag[i] = false;
```

remainder section

```
} while (true);
```

Figure 5.2   The structure of process P_i in Peterson's solution.

Peterson's solution is restricted to two processes that alternate execution between their critical sections and remainder sections. The processes are numbered P_0 and P_1. For convenience, when presenting P_i, we use P_j to denote the other process; that is, j equals $1 - $ i.

Peterson's solution requires the two processes to share two data items:

```
int turn;
boolean flag[2];
```

The variable turn indicates whose turn it is to enter its critical section. That is, if turn == i, then process P_i is allowed to execute in its critical section. The flag array is used to indicate if a process is ready to enter its critical section. For example, if flag[i] is true, this value indicates that P_i is ready to enter its critical section. With an explanation of these data structures complete, we are now ready to describe the algorithm shown in Figure 5.2.

To enter the critical section, process P_i first sets flag[i] to be true and then sets turn to the value j, thereby asserting that if the other process wishes to enter the critical section, it can do so. If both processes try to enter at the same time, turn will be set to both i and j at roughly the same time. Only one of these assignments will last; the other will occur but will be overwritten immediately. The eventual value of turn determines which of the two processes is allowed to enter its critical section first.

We now prove that this solution is correct. We need to show that:

1. Mutual exclusion is preserved.

2. The progress requirement is satisfied.

3. The bounded-waiting requirement is met.

To prove property 1, we note that each P_i enters its critical section only if either flag[j] == false or turn == i. Also note that, if both processes can be executing in their critical sections at the same time, then flag[0] == flag[1] == true. These two observations imply that P_0 and P_1 could not have successfully executed their while statements at about the same time, since the value of turn can be either 0 or 1 but cannot be both. Hence, one of the processes —say, P_j—must have successfully executed the while statement, whereas P_i had to execute at least one additional statement ("turn == j"). However, at that time, flag[j] == true and turn == j, and this condition will persist as long as P_j is in its critical section; as a result, mutual exclusion is preserved.

To prove properties 2 and 3, we note that a process P_i can be prevented from entering the critical section only if it is stuck in the while loop with the condition flag[j] == true and turn == j; this loop is the only one possible. If P_j is not ready to enter the critical section, then flag[j] == false, and P_i can enter its critical section. If P_j has set flag[j] to true and is also executing in its while statement, then either turn == i or turn == j. If turn == i, then P_i will enter the critical section. If turn == j, then P_j will enter the critical section. However, once P_j exits its critical section, it will reset flag[j] to false, allowing P_i to enter its critical section. If P_j resets flag[j] to true, it must also set turn to i. Thus, since P_i does not change the value of the variable turn while executing the while statement, P_i will enter the critical section (progress) after at most one entry by P_j (bounded waiting).

5.4 Synchronization Hardware

We have just described one software-based solution to the critical-section problem. However, as mentioned, software-based solutions such as Peterson's are not guaranteed to work on modern computer architectures. In the following discussions, we explore several more solutions to the critical-section problem using techniques ranging from hardware to software-based APIs available to both kernel developers and application programmers. All these solutions are based on the premise of locking —that is, protecting critical regions through the use of locks. As we shall see, the designs of such locks can be quite sophisticated.

We start by presenting some simple hardware instructions that are available on many systems and showing how they can be used effectively in solving the critical-section problem. Hardware features can make any programming task easier and improve system efficiency.

The critical-section problem could be solved simply in a single-processor environment if we could prevent interrupts from occurring while a shared variable was being modified. In this way, we could be sure that the current sequence of instructions would be allowed to execute in order without pre-emption. No other instructions would be run, so no unexpected modifications could be made to the shared variable. This is often the approach taken by nonpreemptive kernels.

```
boolean test_and_set(boolean *target) {
    boolean rv = *target;
    *target = true;

    return rv;
}
```

Figure 5.3 The definition of the test_and_set() instruction.

```
do {
    while (test_and_set(&lock))
    ; /* do nothing */

    /* critical section */

    lock = false;

    /* remainder section */
} while (true);
```

Figure 5.4   Mutual-exclusion implementation with `test_and_set()`.

Unfortunately, this solution is not as feasible in a multiprocessor environment. Disabling interrupts on a multiprocessor can be time consuming, since the message is passed to all the processors. This message passing delays entry into each critical section, and system efficiency decreases. Also consider the effect on a system's clock if the clock is kept updated by interrupts.

Many modern computer systems therefore provide special hardware instructions that allow us either to test and modify the content of a word or to swap the contents of two words **atomically**—that is, as one uninterruptible unit. We can use these special instructions to solve the critical-section problem in a relatively simple manner. Rather than discussing one specific instruction for one specific machine, we abstract the main concepts behind these types of instructions by describing the `test_and_set()` and `compare_and_swap()` instructions.

The `test_and_set()` instruction can be defined as shown in Figure 5.3. The important characteristic of this instruction is that it is executed atomically. Thus, if two `test_and_set()` instructions are executed simultaneously (each on a different CPU), they will be executed sequentially in some arbitrary order. If the machine supports the `test_and_set()` instruction, then we can implement mutual exclusion by declaring a boolean variable `lock`, initialized to `false`. The structure of process P_i is shown in Figure 5.4.

The `compare_and_swap()` instruction, in contrast to the `test_and_set()` instruction, operates on three operands; it is defined in Figure 5.5. The operand `value` is set to `new_value` only if the expression (`*value == expected`) is true. Regardless, `compare_and_swap()` always returns the original value of the variable `value`. Like the `test_and_set()` instruction, `compare_and_swap()` is

```
int compare_and_swap(int *value, int expected, int new_value) {
    int temp = *value;

    if (*value == expected)
        *value = new_value;

    return temp;
}
```

Figure 5.5   The definition of the `compare_and_swap()` instruction.

```
do {
    while (compare_and_swap(&lock, 0, 1) != 0)
        ; /* do nothing */

        /* critical section */

    lock = 0;

        /* remainder section */
} while (true);
```

Figure 5.6 Mutual-exclusion implementation with the compare_and_swap() instruction.

executed atomically. Mutual exclusion can be provided as follows: a global variable (lock) is declared and is initialized to 0. The first process that invokes compare_and_swap() will set lock to 1. It will then enter its critical section, because the original value of lock was equal to the expected value of 0. Subsequent calls to compare_and_swap() will not succeed, because lock now is not equal to the expected value of 0. When a process exits its critical section, it sets lock back to 0, which allows another process to enter its critical section. The structure of process P_i is shown in Figure 5.6.

Although these algorithms satisfy the mutual-exclusion requirement, they do not satisfy the bounded-waiting requirement. In Figure 5.7, we present another algorithm using the test_and_set() instruction that satisfies all the critical-section requirements. The common data structures are

```
do {
    waiting[i] = true;
    key = true;
    while (waiting[i] && key)
        key = test_and_set(&lock);
    waiting[i] = false;

        /* critical section */

    j = (i + 1) % n;
    while ((j != i) && !waiting[j])
        j = (j + 1) % n;

    if (j == i)
        lock = false;
    else
        waiting[j] = false;

        /* remainder section */
} while (true);
```

Figure 5.7 Bounded-waiting mutual exclusion with test_and_set().

```
boolean waiting[n];
boolean lock;
```

These data structures are initialized to false. To prove that the mutual-exclusion requirement is met, we note that process P_i can enter its critical section only if either waiting[i] == false or key == false. The value of key can become false only if the test_and_set() is executed. The first process to execute the test_and_set() will find key == false; all others must wait. The variable waiting[i] can become false only if another process leaves its critical section; only one waiting[i] is set to false, maintaining the mutual-exclusion requirement.

To prove that the progress requirement is met, we note that the arguments presented for mutual exclusion also apply here, since a process exiting the critical section either sets lock to false or sets waiting[j] to false. Both allow a process that is waiting to enter its critical section to proceed.

To prove that the bounded-waiting requirement is met, we note that, when a process leaves its critical section, it scans the array waiting in the cyclic ordering $(i + 1, i + 2, ..., n - 1, 0, ..., i - 1)$. It designates the first process in this ordering that is in the entry section (waiting[j] == true) as the next one to enter the critical section. Any process waiting to enter its critical section will thus do so within $n - 1$ turns.

Details describing the implementation of the atomic test_and_set() and compare_and_swap() instructions are discussed more fully in books on computer architecture.

5.5 Mutex Locks

The hardware-based solutions to the critical-section problem presented in Section 5.4 are complicated as well as generally inaccessible to application programmers. Instead, operating-systems designers build software tools to solve the critical-section problem. The simplest of these tools is the mutex lock. (In fact, the term *mutex* is short for *mut*ual *ex*clusion.) We use the mutex lock to protect critical regions and thus prevent race conditions. That is, a process must acquire the lock before entering a critical section; it releases the lock when it exits the critical section. The acquire() function acquires the lock, and the release() function releases the lock, as illustrated in Figure 5.8.

A mutex lock has a boolean variable available whose value indicates if the lock is available or not. If the lock is available, a call to acquire() succeeds, and the lock is then considered unavailable. A process that attempts to acquire an unavailable lock is blocked until the lock is released.

The definition of acquire() is as follows:

```
acquire() {
    while (!available)
        ; /* busy wait */
    available = false;
}
```

do {

acquire lock

critical section

release lock

remainder section

} while (true);

Figure 5.8 Solution to the critical-section problem using mutex locks.

The definition of `release()` is as follows:

```
release() {
    available = true;
}
```

Calls to either `acquire()` or `release()` must be performed atomically. Thus, mutex locks are often implemented using one of the hardware mechanisms described in Section 5.4, and we leave the description of this technique as an exercise.

The main disadvantage of the implementation given here is that it requires busy waiting. While a process is in its critical section, any other process that tries to enter its critical section must loop continuously in the call to `acquire()`. In fact, this type of mutex lock is also called a spinlock because the process "spins" while waiting for the lock to become available. (We see the same issue with the code examples illustrating the `test_and_set()` instruction and the `compare_and_swap()` instruction.) This continual looping is clearly a problem in a real multiprogramming system, where a single CPU is shared among many processes. Busy waiting wastes CPU cycles that some other process might be able to use productively.

Spinlocks do have an advantage, however, in that no context switch is required when a process must wait on a lock, and a context switch may take considerable time. Thus, when locks are expected to be held for short times, spinlocks are useful. They are often employed on multiprocessor systems where one thread can "spin" on one processor while another thread performs its critical section on another processor.

Later in this chapter (Section 5.7), we examine how mutex locks can be used to solve classical synchronization problems. We also discuss how these locks are used in several operating systems, as well as in Pthreads.

5.6   Semaphores

Mutex locks, as we mentioned earlier, are generally considered the simplest of synchronization tools. In this section, we examine a more robust tool that can behave similarly to a mutex lock but can also provide more sophisticated ways for processes to synchronize their activities.

A semaphore S is an integer variable that, apart from initialization, is accessed only through two standard atomic operations: wait() and signal(). The wait() operation was originally termed P (from the Dutch *proberen,* "to test"); signal() was originally called V (from *verhogen,* "to increment"). The definition of wait() is as follows:

```
wait(S) {
    while (S <= 0)
        ; // busy wait
    S--;
}
```

The definition of signal() is as follows:

```
signal(S) {
    S++;
}
```

All modifications to the integer value of the semaphore in the wait() and signal() operations must be executed indivisibly. That is, when one process modifies the semaphore value, no other process can simultaneously modify that same semaphore value. In addition, in the case of wait(S), the testing of the integer value of S ($S \leq 0$), as well as its possible modification (S--), must be executed without interruption. We shall see how these operations can be implemented in Section 5.6.2. First, let's see how semaphores can be used.

5.6.1 Semaphore Usage

Operating systems often distinguish between counting and binary semaphores. The value of a counting semaphore can range over an unrestricted domain. The value of a binary semaphore can range only between 0 and 1. Thus, binary semaphores behave similarly to mutex locks. In fact, on systems that do not provide mutex locks, binary semaphores can be used instead for providing mutual exclusion.

Counting semaphores can be used to control access to a given resource consisting of a finite number of instances. The semaphore is initialized to the number of resources available. Each process that wishes to use a resource performs a wait() operation on the semaphore (thereby decrementing the count). When a process releases a resource, it performs a signal() operation (incrementing the count). When the count for the semaphore goes to 0, all resources are being used. After that, processes that wish to use a resource will block until the count becomes greater than 0.

We can also use semaphores to solve various synchronization problems. For example, consider two concurrently running processes: P_1 with a statement S_1 and P_2 with a statement S_2. Suppose we require that S_2 be executed only after S_1 has completed. We can implement this scheme readily by letting P_1 and P_2 share a common semaphore synch, initialized to 0. In process P_1, we insert the statements

$$S_1;$$
$$\text{signal(synch)};$$

In process P_2, we insert the statements

$$\text{wait(synch)};$$
$$S_2;$$

Because synch is initialized to 0, P_2 will execute S_2 only after P_1 has invoked signal(synch), which is after statement S_1 has been executed.

5.6.2 Semaphore Implementation

Recall that the implementation of mutex locks discussed in Section 5.5 suffers from busy waiting. The definitions of the wait() and signal() semaphore operations just described present the same problem. To overcome the need for busy waiting, we can modify the definition of the wait() and signal() operations as follows: When a process executes the wait() operation and finds that the semaphore value is not positive, it must wait. However, rather than engaging in busy waiting, the process can block itself. The block operation places a process into a waiting queue associated with the semaphore, and the state of the process is switched to the waiting state. Then control is transferred to the CPU scheduler, which selects another process to execute.

A process that is blocked, waiting on a semaphore S, should be restarted when some other process executes a signal() operation. The process is restarted by a wakeup() operation, which changes the process from the waiting state to the ready state. The process is then placed in the ready queue. (The CPU may or may not be switched from the running process to the newly ready process, depending on the CPU-scheduling algorithm.)

To implement semaphores under this definition, we define a semaphore as follows:

```
typedef struct {
    int value;
    struct process *list;
} semaphore;
```

Each semaphore has an integer value and a list of processes list. When a process must wait on a semaphore, it is added to the list of processes. A signal() operation removes one process from the list of waiting processes and awakens that process.

Now, the wait() semaphore operation can be defined as

```
wait(semaphore *S) {
    S->value--;
    if (S->value < 0) {
        add this process to S->list;
        block();
    }
}
```

and the `signal()` semaphore operation can be defined as

```
signal(semaphore *S) {
        S->value++;
        if (S->value <= 0) {
                remove a process P from S->list;
                wakeup(P);
        }
}
```

The `block()` operation suspends the process that invokes it. The `wakeup(P)` operation resumes the execution of a blocked process P. These two operations are provided by the operating system as basic system calls.

Note that in this implementation, semaphore values may be negative, whereas semaphore values are never negative under the classical definition of semaphores with busy waiting. If a semaphore value is negative, its magnitude is the number of processes waiting on that semaphore. This fact results from switching the order of the decrement and the test in the implementation of the `wait()` operation.

The list of waiting processes can be easily implemented by a link field in each process control block (PCB). Each semaphore contains an integer value and a pointer to a list of PCBs. One way to add and remove processes from the list so as to ensure bounded waiting is to use a FIFO queue, where the semaphore contains both head and tail pointers to the queue. In general, however, the list can use any queueing strategy. Correct usage of semaphores does not depend on a particular queueing strategy for the semaphore lists.

It is critical that semaphore operations be executed atomically. We must guarantee that no two processes can execute `wait()` and `signal()` operations on the same semaphore at the same time. This is a critical-section problem; and in a single-processor environment, we can solve it by simply inhibiting interrupts during the time the `wait()` and `signal()` operations are executing. This scheme works in a single-processor environment because, once interrupts are inhibited, instructions from different processes cannot be interleaved. Only the currently running process executes until interrupts are reenabled and the scheduler can regain control.

In a multiprocessor environment, interrupts must be disabled on every processor. Otherwise, instructions from different processes (running on different processors) may be interleaved in some arbitrary way. Disabling interrupts on every processor can be a difficult task and furthermore can seriously diminish performance. Therefore, SMP systems must provide alternative locking techniques—such as `compare_and_swap()` or spinlocks—to ensure that `wait()` and `signal()` are performed atomically.

It is important to admit that we have not completely eliminated busy waiting with this definition of the `wait()` and `signal()` operations. Rather, we have moved busy waiting from the entry section to the critical sections of application programs. Furthermore, we have limited busy waiting to the critical sections of the `wait()` and `signal()` operations, and these sections are short (if properly coded, they should be no more than about ten instructions). Thus, the critical section is almost never occupied, and busy waiting occurs rarely, and then for only a short time. An entirely different situation exists with application programs whose critical sections may be long (minutes or even hours) or may almost always be occupied. In such cases, busy waiting is extremely inefficient.

5.6.3 Deadlocks and Starvation

The implementation of a semaphore with a waiting queue may result in a situation where two or more processes are waiting indefinitely for an event that can be caused only by one of the waiting processes. The event in question is the execution of a `signal()` operation. When such a state is reached, these processes are said to be **deadlocked**.

To illustrate this, consider a system consisting of two processes, P_0 and P_1, each accessing two semaphores, S and Q, set to the value 1:

P_0	P_1
`wait(S);`	`wait(Q);`
`wait(Q);`	`wait(S);`
.	.
.	.
.	.
`signal(S);`	`signal(Q);`
`signal(Q);`	`signal(S);`

Suppose that P_0 executes `wait(S)` and then P_1 executes `wait(Q)`. When P_0 executes `wait(Q)`, it must wait until P_1 executes `signal(Q)`. Similarly, when P_1 executes `wait(S)`, it must wait until P_0 executes `signal(S)`. Since these `signal()` operations cannot be executed, P_0 and P_1 are deadlocked.

We say that a set of processes is in a deadlocked state when every process in the set is waiting for an event that can be caused only by another process in the set. The events with which we are mainly concerned here are resource acquisition and release. However, other types of events may result in deadlocks, which we discuss in Section 5.11.

Another problem related to deadlocks is **indefinite blocking** or **starvation**, a situation in which processes wait indefinitely within the semaphore. Indefinite blocking may occur if we remove processes from the list associated with a semaphore in LIFO (last-in, first-out) order.

5.6.4 Priority Inversion

A scheduling challenge arises when a higher-priority process needs to read or modify kernel data that are currently being accessed by a lower-priority process—or a chain of lower-priority processes. Since kernel data are typically protected with a lock, the higher-priority process will have to wait for a lower-priority one to finish with the resource. The situation becomes more complicated if the lower-priority process is preempted in favor of another process with a higher priority.

As an example, assume we have three processes—L, M, and H—whose priorities follow the order $L < M < H$. Assume that process H requires resource R, which is currently being accessed by process L. Ordinarily, process

> ## PRIORITY INVERSION AND THE MARS PATHFINDER
>
> Priority inversion can be more than a scheduling inconvenience. On systems with tight time constraints—such as real-time systems—priority inversion can cause a process to take longer than it should to accomplish a task. When that happens, other failures can cascade, resulting in system failure.
>
> Consider the Mars Pathfinder, a NASA space probe that landed a robot, the Sojourner rover, on Mars in 1997 to conduct experiments. Shortly after the Sojourner began operating, it started to experience frequent computer resets. Each reset reinitialized all hardware and software, including communications. If the problem had not been solved, the Sojourner would have failed in its mission.
>
> The problem was caused by the fact that one high-priority task, "bc_dist," was taking longer than expected to complete its work. This task was being forced to wait for a shared resource that was held by the lower-priority "ASI/MET" task, which in turn was preempted by multiple medium-priority tasks. The "bc_dist" task would stall waiting for the shared resource, and ultimately the "bc_sched" task would discover the problem and perform the reset. The Sojourner was suffering from a typical case of priority inversion.
>
> The operating system on the Sojourner was the VxWorks real-time operating system, which had a global variable to enable priority inheritance on all semaphores. After testing, the variable was set on the Sojourner (on Mars!), and the problem was solved.
>
> A full description of the problem, its detection, and its solution was written by the software team lead and is available at http://research.microsoft.com/en-us/um/people/mbj/mars_pathfinder/authoritative_account.html.

H would wait for L to finish using resource R. However, now suppose that process M becomes runnable, thereby preempting process L. Indirectly, a process with a lower priority—process M—has affected how long process H must wait for L to relinquish resource R.

This problem is known as priority inversion. It occurs only in systems with more than two priorities, so one solution is to have only two priorities. That is insufficient for most general-purpose operating systems, however. Typically these systems solve the problem by implementing a priority-inheritance protocol. According to this protocol, all processes that are accessing resources needed by a higher-priority process inherit the higher priority until they are finished with the resources in question. When they are finished, their priorities revert to their original values. In the example above, a priority-inheritance protocol would allow process L to temporarily inherit the priority of process H, thereby preventing process M from preempting its execution. When process L had finished using resource R, it would relinquish its inherited priority from H and assume its original priority. Because resource R would now be available, process H—not M—would run next.

```
do {
      . . .
   /* produce an item in next_produced */
      . . .
   wait(empty);
   wait(mutex);
      . . .
   /* add next_produced to the buffer */
      . . .
   signal(mutex);
   signal(full);
} while (true);
```

Figure 5.9 The structure of the producer process.

5.7 Classic Problems of Synchronization

In this section, we present a number of synchronization problems as examples of a large class of concurrency-control problems. These problems are used for testing nearly every newly proposed synchronization scheme. In our solutions to the problems, we use semaphores for synchronization, since that is the traditional way to present such solutions. However, actual implementations of these solutions could use mutex locks in place of binary semaphores.

5.7.1 The Bounded-Buffer Problem

The *bounded-buffer problem* was introduced in Section 5.1; it is commonly used to illustrate the power of synchronization primitives. Here, we present a general structure of this scheme without committing ourselves to any particular implementation. We provide a related programming project in the exercises at the end of the chapter.

In our problem, the producer and consumer processes share the following data structures:

```
int n;
semaphore mutex = 1;
semaphore empty = n;
semaphore full = 0
```

We assume that the pool consists of n buffers, each capable of holding one item. The mutex semaphore provides mutual exclusion for accesses to the buffer pool and is initialized to the value 1. The empty and full semaphores count the number of empty and full buffers. The semaphore empty is initialized to the value n; the semaphore full is initialized to the value 0.

The code for the producer process is shown in Figure 5.9, and the code for the consumer process is shown in Figure 5.10. Note the symmetry between the producer and the consumer. We can interpret this code as the producer producing full buffers for the consumer or as the consumer producing empty buffers for the producer.

```
do {
   wait(full);
   wait(mutex);
      . . .
   /* remove an item from buffer to next_consumed */
      . . .
   signal(mutex);
   signal(empty);
      . . .
   /* consume the item in next_consumed */
      . . .
} while (true);
```

Figure 5.10   The structure of the consumer process.

5.7.2   The Readers–Writers Problem

Suppose that a database is to be shared among several concurrent processes. Some of these processes may want only to read the database, whereas others may want to update (that is, to read and write) the database. We distinguish between these two types of processes by referring to the former as *readers* and to the latter as *writers*. Obviously, if two readers access the shared data simultaneously, no adverse effects will result. However, if a writer and some other process (either a reader or a writer) access the database simultaneously, chaos may ensue.

To ensure that these difficulties do not arise, we require that the writers have exclusive access to the shared database while writing to the database. This synchronization problem is referred to as the **readers–writers problem**. Since it was originally stated, it has been used to test nearly every new synchronization primitive. The readers–writers problem has several variations, all involving priorities. The simplest one, referred to as the *first* readers–writers problem, requires that no reader be kept waiting unless a writer has already obtained permission to use the shared object. In other words, no reader should wait for other readers to finish simply because a writer is waiting. The *second* readers –writers problem requires that, once a writer is ready, that writer perform its write as soon as possible. In other words, if a writer is waiting to access the object, no new readers may start reading.

A solution to either problem may result in starvation. In the first case, writers may starve; in the second case, readers may starve. For this reason, other variants of the problem have been proposed. Next, we present a solution to the first readers–writers problem. See the bibliographical notes at the end of the chapter for references describing starvation-free solutions to the second readers–writers problem.

In the solution to the first readers–writers problem, the reader processes share the following data structures:

```
semaphore rw_mutex = 1;
semaphore mutex = 1;
int read_count = 0;
```

The semaphores mutex and rw_mutex are initialized to 1; read_count is initialized to 0. The semaphore rw_mutex is common to both reader and writer

```
do {
  wait(rw_mutex);
    . . .
  /* writing is performed */
    . . .
  signal(rw_mutex);
} while (true);
```

Figure 5.11   The structure of a writer process.

processes. The mutex semaphore is used to ensure mutual exclusion when the variable read_count is updated. The read_count variable keeps track of how many processes are currently reading the object. The semaphore rw_mutex functions as a mutual exclusion semaphore for the writers. It is also used by the first or last reader that enters or exits the critical section. It is not used by readers who enter or exit while other readers are in their critical sections.

The code for a writer process is shown in Figure 5.11; the code for a reader process is shown in Figure 5.12. Note that, if a writer is in the critical section and n readers are waiting, then one reader is queued on rw_mutex, and $n - 1$ readers are queued on mutex. Also observe that, when a writer executes signal(rw_mutex), we may resume the execution of either the waiting readers or a single waiting writer. The selection is made by the scheduler.

The readers–writers problem and its solutions have been generalized to provide **reader–writer** locks on some systems. Acquiring a reader–writer lock requires specifying the mode of the lock: either *read* or *write* access. When a process wishes only to read shared data, it requests the reader–writer lock in read mode. A process wishing to modify the shared data must request the lock in write mode. Multiple processes are permitted to concurrently acquire a reader–writer lock in read mode, but only one process may acquire the lock for writing, as exclusive access is required for writers.

Reader–writer locks are most useful in the following situations:

```
do {
  wait(mutex);
  read_count++;
  if (read_count == 1)
    wait(rw_mutex);
  signal(mutex);
    . . .
  /* reading is performed */
    . . .
  wait(mutex);
  read_count--;
  if (read_count == 0)
    signal(rw_mutex);
  signal(mutex);
} while (true);
```

Figure 5.12   The structure of a reader process.

Figure 5.13   The situation of the dining philosophers.

- In applications where it is easy to identify which processes only read shared data and which processes only write shared data.

- In applications that have more readers than writers. This is because reader–writer locks generally require more overhead to establish than semaphores or mutual-exclusion locks. The increased concurrency of allowing multiple readers compensates for the overhead involved in setting up the reader–writer lock.

5.7.3 The Dining-Philosophers Problem

Consider five philosophers who spend their lives thinking and eating. The philosophers share a circular table surrounded by five chairs, each belonging to one philosopher. In the center of the table is a bowl of rice, and the table is laid with five single chopsticks (Figure 5.13). When a philosopher thinks, she does not interact with her colleagues. From time to time, a philosopher gets hungry and tries to pick up the two chopsticks that are closest to her (the chopsticks that are between her and her left and right neighbors). A philosopher may pick up only one chopstick at a time. Obviously, she cannot pick up a chopstick that is already in the hand of a neighbor. When a hungry philosopher has both her chopsticks at the same time, she eats without releasing the chopsticks. When she is finished eating, she puts down both chopsticks and starts thinking again.

The **dining-philosophers problem** is considered a classic synchronization problem neither because of its practical importance nor because computer scientists dislike philosophers but because it is an example of a large class of concurrency-control problems. It is a simple representation of the need to allocate several resources among several processes in a deadlock-free and starvation-free manner.

One simple solution is to represent each chopstick with a semaphore. A philosopher tries to grab a chopstick by executing a wait() operation on that semaphore. She releases her chopsticks by executing the signal() operation on the appropriate semaphores. Thus, the shared data are

```
semaphore chopstick[5];
```

```
do {
   wait(chopstick[i]);
   wait(chopstick[(i+1) % 5]);
      . . .
   /* eat for awhile */
      . . .
   signal(chopstick[i]);
   signal(chopstick[(i+1) % 5]);
      . . .
   /* think for awhile */
      . . .
} while (true);
```

Figure 5.14 The structure of philosopher i.

where all the elements of chopstick are initialized to 1. The structure of philosopher i is shown in Figure 5.14.

Although this solution guarantees that no two neighbors are eating simultaneously, it nevertheless must be rejected because it could create a deadlock. Suppose that all five philosophers become hungry at the same time and each grabs her left chopstick. All the elements of chopstick will now be equal to 0. When each philosopher tries to grab her right chopstick, she will be delayed forever.

Several possible remedies to the deadlock problem are replaced by:

- Allow at most four philosophers to be sitting simultaneously at the table.

- Allow a philosopher to pick up her chopsticks only if both chopsticks are available (to do this, she must pick them up in a critical section).

- Use an asymmetric solution—that is, an odd-numbered philosopher picks up first her left chopstick and then her right chopstick, whereas an even-numbered philosopher picks up her right chopstick and then her left chopstick.

In Section 5.8, we present a solution to the dining-philosophers problem that ensures freedom from deadlocks. Note, however, that any satisfactory solution to the dining-philosophers problem must guard against the possibility that one of the philosophers will starve to death. A deadlock-free solution does not necessarily eliminate the possibility of starvation.

5.8 Monitors

Although semaphores provide a convenient and effective mechanism for process synchronization, using them incorrectly can result in timing errors that are difficult to detect, since these errors happen only if particular execution sequences take place and these sequences do not always occur.

We have seen an example of such errors in the use of counters in our solution to the producer–consumer problem (Section 5.1). In that example, the timing problem happened only rarely, and even then the counter value appeared to be reasonable—off by only 1. Nevertheless, the solution is obviously not an acceptable one. It is for this reason that semaphores were introduced in the first place.

Unfortunately, such timing errors can still occur when semaphores are used. To illustrate how, we review the semaphore solution to the critical-section problem. All processes share a semaphore variable `mutex`, which is initialized to 1. Each process must execute `wait(mutex)` before entering the critical section and `signal(mutex)` afterward. If this sequence is not observed, two processes may be in their critical sections simultaneously. Next, we examine the various difficulties that may result. Note that these difficulties will arise even if a *single* process is not well behaved. This situation may be caused by an honest programming error or an uncooperative programmer.

- Suppose that a process interchanges the order in which the `wait()` and `signal()` operations on the semaphore `mutex` are executed, resulting in the following execution:

  ```
  signal(mutex);
      ...
  critical section
      ...
  wait(mutex);
  ```

  In this situation, several processes may be executing in their critical sections simultaneously, violating the mutual-exclusion requirement. This error may be discovered only if several processes are simultaneously active in their critical sections. Note that this situation may not always be reproducible.

- Suppose that a process replaces `signal(mutex)` with `wait(mutex)`. That is, it executes

  ```
  wait(mutex);
      ...
  critical section
      ...
  wait(mutex);
  ```

  In this case, a deadlock will occur.

- Suppose that a process omits the `wait(mutex)`, or the `signal(mutex)`, or both. In this case, either mutual exclusion is violated or a deadlock will occur.

These examples illustrate that various types of errors can be generated easily when programmers use semaphores incorrectly to solve the critical-section problem. Similar problems may arise in the other synchronization models discussed in Section 5.7.

To deal with such errors, researchers have developed high-level language constructs. In this section, we describe one fundamental high-level synchronization construct—the **monitor** type.

```
monitor monitor name
{
    /* shared variable declarations */

    function P1 ( . . . ) {
        . . .
    }

    function P2 ( . . . ) {
        . . .
    }

            .
            .
            .

    function Pn ( . . . ) {
        . . .
    }

    initialization_code ( . . . ) {
        . . .
    }
}
```

Figure 5.15 Syntax of a monitor.

5.8.1 Monitor Usage

An abstract data type—or ADT—encapsulates data with a set of functions to operate on that data that are independent of any specific implementation of the ADT. A *monitor type* is an ADT that includes a set of programmer-defined operations that are provided with mutual exclusion within the monitor. The monitor type also declares the variables whose values define the state of an instance of that type, along with the bodies of functions that operate on those variables. The syntax of a monitor type is shown in Figure 5.15. The representation of a monitor type cannot be used directly by the various processes. Thus, a function defined within a monitor can access only those variables declared locally within the monitor and its formal parameters. Similarly, the local variables of a monitor can be accessed by only the local functions.

The monitor construct ensures that only one process at a time is active within the monitor. Consequently, the programmer does not need to code this synchronization constraint explicitly (Figure 5.16). However, the monitor construct, as defined so far, is not sufficiently powerful for modeling some synchronization schemes. For this purpose, we need to define additional synchronization mechanisms. These mechanisms are provided by the condition construct. A programmer who needs to write a tailor-made synchronization scheme can define one or more variables of type *condition*:

```
condition x, y;
```

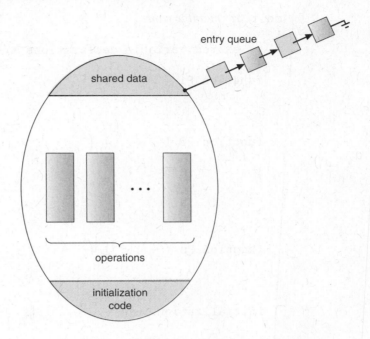

Figure 5.16   Schematic view of a monitor.

The only operations that can be invoked on a condition variable are `wait()` and `signal()`. The operation

$$\texttt{x.wait();}$$

means that the process invoking this operation is suspended until another process invokes

$$\texttt{x.signal();}$$

The `x.signal()` operation resumes exactly one suspended process. If no process is suspended, then the `signal()` operation has no effect; that is, the state of `x` is the same as if the operation had never been executed (Figure 5.17). Contrast this operation with the `signal()` operation associated with semaphores, which always affects the state of the semaphore.

Now suppose that, when the `x.signal()` operation is invoked by a process *P*, there exists a suspended process *Q* associated with condition x. Clearly, if the suspended process *Q* is allowed to resume its execution, the signaling process *P* must wait. Otherwise, both *P* and *Q* would be active simultaneously within the monitor. Note, however, that conceptually both processes can continue with their execution. Two possibilities exist:

1. **Signal and wait**. *P* either waits until *Q* leaves the monitor or waits for another condition.

2. **Signal and continue**. *Q* either waits until *P* leaves the monitor or waits for another condition.

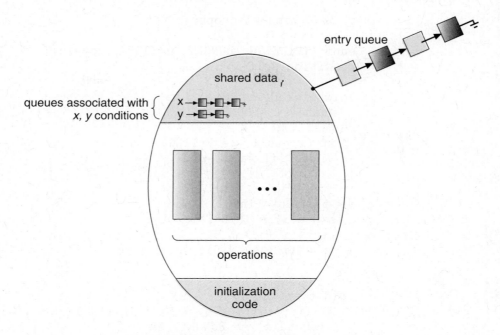

Figure 5.17 Monitor with condition variables.

There are reasonable arguments in favor of adopting either option. On the one hand, since P was already executing in the monitor, the **signal-and-continue** method seems more reasonable. On the other, if we allow thread P to continue, then by the time Q is resumed, the logical condition for which Q was waiting may no longer hold. A compromise between these two choices was adopted in the language Concurrent Pascal. When thread P executes the signal operation, it immediately leaves the monitor. Hence, Q is immediately resumed.

Many programming languages have incorporated the idea of the monitor as described in this section, including Java and C# (pronounced "C-sharp"). Other languages—such as Erlang—provide some type of concurrency support using a similar mechanism.

5.8.2 Dining-Philosophers Solution Using Monitors

Next, we illustrate monitor concepts by presenting a deadlock-free solution to the dining-philosophers problem. This solution imposes the restriction that a philosopher may pick up her chopsticks only if both of them are available. To code this solution, we need to distinguish among three states in which we may find a philosopher. For this purpose, we introduce the following data structure:

```
enum {THINKING, HUNGRY, EATING} state[5];
```

Philosopher i can set the variable `state[i] = EATING` only if her two neighbors are not eating: `(state[(i+4) % 5] != EATING)` and `(state[(i+1) % 5] != EATING)`.

```
monitor DiningPhilosophers
{
    enum {THINKING, HUNGRY, EATING} state[5];
    condition self[5];

    void pickup(int i) {
        state[i] = HUNGRY;
        test(i);
        if (state[i] != EATING)
            self[i].wait();
    }

    void putdown(int i) {
        state[i] = THINKING;
        test((i + 4) % 5);
        test((i + 1) % 5);
    }

    void test(int i) {
        if ((state[(i + 4) % 5] != EATING) &&
          (state[i] == HUNGRY) &&
          (state[(i + 1) % 5] != EATING)) {
            state[i] = EATING;
            self[i].signal();
        }
    }

    initialization_code() {
        for (int i = 0; i < 5; i++)
            state[i] = THINKING;
    }
}
```

Figure 5.18 A monitor solution to the dining-philosopher problem.

We also need to declare

```
condition self[5];
```

This allows philosopher *i* to delay herself when she is hungry but is unable to obtain the chopsticks she needs.

We are now in a position to describe our solution to the dining-philosophers problem. The distribution of the chopsticks is controlled by the monitor DiningPhilosophers, whose definition is shown in Figure 5.18. Each philosopher, before starting to eat, must invoke the operation pickup(). This act may result in the suspension of the philosopher process. After the successful completion of the operation, the philosopher may eat. Following this, the philosopher invokes the putdown() operation. Thus, philosopher *i* must invoke the operations pickup() and putdown() in the following sequence:

```
DiningPhilosophers.pickup(i);
                ...
                eat
                ...
DiningPhilosophers.putdown(i);
```

It is easy to show that this solution ensures that no two neighbors are eating simultaneously and that no deadlocks will occur. We note, however, that it is possible for a philosopher to starve to death. We do not present a solution to this problem but rather leave it as an exercise for you.

5.8.3 Implementing a Monitor Using Semaphores

We now consider a possible implementation of the monitor mechanism using semaphores. For each monitor, a semaphore mutex (initialized to 1) is provided. A process must execute wait(mutex) before entering the monitor and must execute signal(mutex) after leaving the monitor.

Since a signaling process must wait until the resumed process either leaves or waits, an additional semaphore, next, is introduced, initialized to 0. The signaling processes can use next to suspend themselves. An integer variable next_count is also provided to count the number of processes suspended on next. Thus, each external function F is replaced by

```
wait(mutex);
    ...
    body of F
    ...
if (next_count > 0)
    signal(next);
else
    signal(mutex);
```

Mutual exclusion within a monitor is ensured.

We can now describe how condition variables are implemented as well. For each condition x, we introduce a semaphore x_sem and an integer variable x_count, both initialized to 0. The operation x.wait() can now be implemented as

```
x_count++;
if (next_count > 0)
    signal(next);
else
    signal(mutex);
wait(x_sem);
x_count--;
```

The operation x.signal() can be implemented as

```
if (x_count > 0) {
    next_count++;
    signal(x_sem);
    wait(next);
    next_count--;
}
```

This implementation is applicable to the definitions of monitors given by both Hoare and Brinch-Hansen (see the bibliographical notes at the end of the chapter). In some cases, however, the generality of the implementation is unnecessary, and a significant improvement in efficiency is possible. We leave this problem to you in Exercise 5.32.

5.8.4 Resuming Processes within a Monitor

We turn now to the subject of process-resumption order within a monitor. If several processes are suspended on condition x, and an x.signal() operation is executed by some process, then how do we determine which of the suspended processes should be resumed next? One simple solution is to use a first-come, first-served (FCFS) ordering, so that the process that has been waiting the longest is resumed first. In many circumstances, however, such a simple scheduling scheme is not adequate. For this purpose, the **conditional-wait** construct can be used. This construct has the form

$$x.\text{wait}(c);$$

where c is an integer expression that is evaluated when the wait() operation is executed. The value of c, which is called a **priority number**, is then stored with the name of the process that is suspended. When x.signal() is executed, the process with the smallest priority number is resumed next.

To illustrate this new mechanism, consider the ResourceAllocator monitor shown in Figure 5.19, which controls the allocation of a single resource among competing processes. Each process, when requesting an allocation of this resource, specifies the maximum time it plans to use the resource. The monitor allocates the resource to the process that has the shortest time-allocation request. A process that needs to access the resource in question must observe the following sequence:

```
R.acquire(t);
    ...
access the resource;
    ...
R.release();
```

where R is an instance of type ResourceAllocator.

Unfortunately, the monitor concept cannot guarantee that the preceding access sequence will be observed. In particular, the following problems can occur:

- A process might access a resource without first gaining access permission to the resource.

```
monitor ResourceAllocator
{
    boolean busy;
    condition x;

    void acquire(int time) {
        if (busy)
            x.wait(time);
        busy = true;
    }

    void release() {
        busy = false;
        x.signal();
    }

    initialization_code() {
        busy = false;
    }
}
```

Figure 5.19 A monitor to allocate a single resource.

- A process might never release a resource once it has been granted access to the resource.

- A process might attempt to release a resource that it never requested.

- A process might request the same resource twice (without first releasing the resource).

The same difficulties are encountered with the use of semaphores, and these difficulties are similar in nature to those that encouraged us to develop the monitor constructs in the first place. Previously, we had to worry about the correct use of semaphores. Now, we have to worry about the correct use of higher-level programmer-defined operations, with which the compiler can no longer assist us.

One possible solution to the current problem is to include the resource-access operations within the ResourceAllocator monitor. However, using this solution will mean that scheduling is done according to the built-in monitor-scheduling algorithm rather than the one we have coded.

To ensure that the processes observe the appropriate sequences, we must inspect all the programs that make use of the ResourceAllocator monitor and its managed resource. We must check two conditions to establish the correctness of this system. First, user processes must always make their calls on the monitor in a correct sequence. Second, we must be sure that an uncooperative process does not simply ignore the mutual-exclusion gateway provided by the monitor and try to access the shared resource directly, without using the access protocols. Only if these two conditions can be ensured can we guarantee that no time-dependent errors will occur and that the scheduling algorithm will not be defeated.

JAVA MONITORS

Java provides a monitor-like concurrency mechanism for thread synchronization. Every object in Java has associated with it a single lock. When a method is declared to be synchronized, calling the method requires owning the lock for the object. We declare a synchronized method by placing the synchronized keyword in the method definition. The following defines safeMethod() as synchronized, for example:

```
public class SimpleClass {
    . . .
    public synchronized void safeMethod() {
        . . .
        /* Implementation of safeMethod() */
        . . .
    }
}
```

Next, we create an object instance of SimpleClass, such as the following:

```
SimpleClass sc = new SimpleClass();
```

Invoking sc.safeMethod() method requires owning the lock on the object instance sc. If the lock is already owned by another thread, the thread calling the synchronized method blocks and is placed in the *entry set* for the object's lock. The entry set represents the set of threads waiting for the lock to become available. If the lock is available when a synchronized method is called, the calling thread becomes the owner of the object's lock and can enter the method. The lock is released when the thread exits the method. A thread from the entry set is then selected as the new owner of the lock.

Java also provides wait() and notify() methods, which are similar in function to the wait() and signal() statements for a monitor. The Java API provides support for semaphores, condition variables, and mutex locks (among other concurrency mechanisms) in the java.util.concurrent package.

Although this inspection may be possible for a small, static system, it is not reasonable for a large system or a dynamic system. This access-control problem can be solved only through the use of the additional mechanisms that are described in Chapter 13.

5.9 Synchronization Examples

We next describe the synchronization mechanisms provided by the Windows, Linux, and Solaris operating systems, as well as the Pthreads API. We have chosen these three operating systems because they provide good examples of different approaches to synchronizing the kernel, and we have included the

Pthreads API because it is widely used for thread creation and synchronization by developers on UNIX and Linux systems. As you will see in this section, the synchronization methods available in these differing systems vary in subtle and significant ways.

5.9.1 Synchronization in Windows

The Windows operating system is a multithreaded kernel that provides support for real-time applications and multiple processors. When the Windows kernel accesses a global resource on a single-processor system, it temporarily masks interrupts for all interrupt handlers that may also access the global resource. On a multiprocessor system, Windows protects access to global resources using spinlocks, although the kernel uses spinlocks only to protect short code segments. Furthermore, for reasons of efficiency, the kernel ensures that a thread will never be preempted while holding a spinlock.

For thread synchronization outside the kernel, Windows provides **dispatcher objects**. Using a dispatcher object, threads synchronize according to several different mechanisms, including mutex locks, semaphores, events, and timers. The system protects shared data by requiring a thread to gain ownership of a mutex to access the data and to release ownership when it is finished. Semaphores behave as described in Section 5.6. **Events** are similar to condition variables; that is, they may notify a waiting thread when a desired condition occurs. Finally, timers are used to notify one (or more than one) thread that a specified amount of time has expired.

Dispatcher objects may be in either a signaled state or a nonsignaled state. An object in a **signaled state** is available, and a thread will not block when acquiring the object. An object in a **nonsignaled state** is not available, and a thread will block when attempting to acquire the object. We illustrate the state transitions of a mutex lock dispatcher object in Figure 5.20.

A relationship exists between the state of a dispatcher object and the state of a thread. When a thread blocks on a nonsignaled dispatcher object, its state changes from ready to waiting, and the thread is placed in a waiting queue for that object. When the state for the dispatcher object moves to signaled, the kernel checks whether any threads are waiting on the object. If so, the kernel moves one thread—or possibly more—from the waiting state to the ready state, where they can resume executing. The number of threads the kernel selects from the waiting queue depends on the type of dispatcher object for which it is waiting. The kernel will select only one thread from the waiting queue for a mutex, since a mutex object may be "owned" by only a single

Figure 5.20 Mutex dispatcher object.

thread. For an event object, the kernel will select all threads that are waiting for the event.

We can use a mutex lock as an illustration of dispatcher objects and thread states. If a thread tries to acquire a mutex dispatcher object that is in a nonsignaled state, that thread will be suspended and placed in a waiting queue for the mutex object. When the mutex moves to the signaled state (because another thread has released the lock on the mutex), the thread waiting at the front of the queue will be moved from the waiting state to the ready state and will acquire the mutex lock.

A critical-section object is a user-mode mutex that can often be acquired and released without kernel intervention. On a multiprocessor system, a critical-section object first uses a spinlock while waiting for the other thread to release the object. If it spins too long, the acquiring thread will then allocate a kernel mutex and yield its CPU. Critical-section objects are particularly efficient because the kernel mutex is allocated only when there is contention for the object. In practice, there is very little contention, so the savings are significant.

We provide a programming project at the end of this chapter that uses mutex locks and semaphores in the Windows API.

5.9.2 Synchronization in Linux

Prior to Version 2.6, Linux was a nonpreemptive kernel, meaning that a process running in kernel mode could not be preempted—even if a higher-priority process became available to run. Now, however, the Linux kernel is fully preemptive, so a task can be preempted when it is running in the kernel.

Linux provides several different mechanisms for synchronization in the kernel. As most computer architectures provide instructions for atomic versions of simple math operations, the simplest synchronization technique within the Linux kernel is an atomic integer, which is represented using the opaque data type atomic_t. As the name implies, all math operations using atomic integers are performed without interruption. The following code illustrates declaring an atomic integer counter and then performing various atomic operations:

```
atomic_t counter;
int value;

atomic_set(&counter,5); /* counter = 5 */
atomic_add(10, &counter); /* counter = counter + 10 */
atomic_sub(4, &counter); /* counter = counter - 4 */
atomic_inc(&counter); /* counter = counter + 1 */
value = atomic_read(&counter); /* value = 12 */
```

Atomic integers are particularly efficient in situations where an integer variable —such as a counter—needs to be updated, since atomic operations do not require the overhead of locking mechanisms. However, their usage is limited to these sorts of scenarios. In situations where there are several variables contributing to a possible race condition, more sophisticated locking tools must be used.

Mutex locks are available in Linux for protecting critical sections within the kernel. Here, a task must invoke the mutex_lock() function prior to entering a critical section and the `mutex_unlock()` function after exiting the critical section. If the mutex lock is unavailable, a task calling `mutex_lock()` is put into a sleep state and is awakened when the lock's owner invokes `mutex_unlock()`.

Linux also provides spinlocks and semaphores (as well as reader–writer versions of these two locks) for locking in the kernel. On SMP machines, the fundamental locking mechanism is a spinlock, and the kernel is designed so that the spinlock is held only for short durations. On single-processor machines, such as embedded systems with only a single processing core, spinlocks are inappropriate for use and are replaced by enabling and disabling kernel preemption. That is, on single-processor systems, rather than holding a spinlock, the kernel disables kernel preemption; and rather than releasing the spinlock, it enables kernel preemption. This is summarized below:

single processor	multiple processors
Disable kernel preemption.	Acquire spin lock.
Enable kernel preemption.	Release spin lock.

Linux uses an interesting approach to disable and enable kernel preemption. It provides two simple system calls—`preempt_disable()` and `preempt_enable()`—for disabling and enabling kernel preemption. The kernel is not preemptible, however, if a task running in the kernel is holding a lock. To enforce this rule, each task in the system has a `thread-info` structure containing a counter, `preempt_count`, to indicate the number of locks being held by the task. When a lock is acquired, `preempt_count` is incremented. It is decremented when a lock is released. If the value of `preempt_count` for the task currently running in the kernel is greater than 0, it is not safe to preempt the kernel, as this task currently holds a lock. If the count is 0, the kernel can safely be interrupted (assuming there are no outstanding calls to `preempt_disable()`).

Spinlocks—along with enabling and disabling kernel preemption—are used in the kernel only when a lock (or disabling kernel preemption) is held for a short duration. When a lock must be held for a longer period, semaphores or mutex locks are appropriate for use.

5.9.3 Synchronization in Solaris

To control access to critical sections, Solaris provides adaptive mutex locks, condition variables, semaphores, reader–writer locks, and turnstiles. Solaris implements semaphores and condition variables essentially as they are presented in Sections 5.6 and 5.7 In this section, we describe adaptive mutex locks, reader–writer locks, and turnstiles.

An **adaptive mutex** protects access to every critical data item. On a multiprocessor system, an adaptive mutex starts as a standard semaphore implemented as a spinlock. If the data are locked and therefore already in use, the adaptive mutex does one of two things. If the lock is held by a thread that is currently running on another CPU, the thread spins while waiting for the lock to become available, because the thread holding the lock is likely to finish soon. If the thread holding the lock is not currently in run state, the thread blocks, going to sleep until it is awakened by the release of the lock. It is put to sleep so that it will not spin while waiting, since the lock will not be freed very soon. A lock held by a sleeping thread is likely to be in this category. On a single-processor system, the thread holding the lock is never running if the lock is being tested by another thread, because only one thread can run at a time. Therefore, on this type of system, threads always sleep rather than spin if they encounter a lock.

Solaris uses the adaptive-mutex method to protect only data that are accessed by short code segments. That is, a mutex is used if a lock will be held for less than a few hundred instructions. If the code segment is longer than that, the spin-waiting method is exceedingly inefficient. For these longer code segments, condition variables and semaphores are used. If the desired lock is already held, the thread issues a wait and sleeps. When a thread frees the lock, it issues a signal to the next sleeping thread in the queue. The extra cost of putting a thread to sleep and waking it, and of the associated context switches, is less than the cost of wasting several hundred instructions waiting in a spinlock.

Reader–writer locks are used to protect data that are accessed frequently but are usually accessed in a read-only manner. In these circumstances, reader–writer locks are more efficient than semaphores, because multiple threads can read data concurrently, whereas semaphores always serialize access to the data. Reader–writer locks are relatively expensive to implement, so again they are used only on long sections of code.

Solaris uses turnstiles to order the list of threads waiting to acquire either an adaptive mutex or a reader–writer lock. A **turnstile** is a queue structure containing threads blocked on a lock. For example, if one thread currently owns the lock for a synchronized object, all other threads trying to acquire the lock will block and enter the turnstile for that lock. When the lock is released, the kernel selects a thread from the turnstile as the next owner of the lock. Each synchronized object with at least one thread blocked on the object's lock requires a separate turnstile. However, rather than associating a turnstile with each synchronized object, Solaris gives each kernel thread its own turnstile. Because a thread can be blocked only on one object at a time, this is more efficient than having a turnstile for each object.

The turnstile for the first thread to block on a synchronized object becomes the turnstile for the object itself. Threads subsequently blocking on the lock will be added to this turnstile. When the initial thread ultimately releases the lock, it gains a new turnstile from a list of free turnstiles maintained by the kernel. To prevent a priority inversion, turnstiles are organized according to a **priority-inheritance protocol**. This means that if a lower-priority thread currently holds a lock on which a higher-priority thread is blocked, the thread with the lower priority will temporarily inherit the priority of the higher-priority thread. Upon releasing the lock, the thread will revert to its original priority.

Note that the locking mechanisms used by the kernel are implemented for user-level threads as well, so the same types of locks are available inside and outside the kernel. A crucial implementation difference is the priority-inheritance protocol. Kernel-locking routines adhere to the kernel priority-inheritance methods used by the scheduler, as described in Section 5.6.4. User-level thread-locking mechanisms do not provide this functionality.

To optimize Solaris performance, developers have refined and fine-tuned the locking methods. Because locks are used frequently and typically are used for crucial kernel functions, tuning their implementation and use can produce great performance gains.

5.9.4   Pthreads Synchronization

Although the locking mechanisms used in Solaris are available to user-level threads as well as kernel threads, basically the synchronization methods discussed thus far pertain to synchronization within the kernel. In contrast, the Pthreads API is available for programmers at the user level and is not part of any particular kernel. This API provides mutex locks, condition variables, and read–write locks for thread synchronization.

Mutex locks represent the fundamental synchronization technique used with Pthreads. A mutex lock is used to protect critical sections of code—that is, a thread acquires the lock before entering a critical section and releases it upon exiting the critical section. Pthreads uses the `pthread_mutex_t` data type for mutex locks. A mutex is created with the `pthread_mutex_init()` function. The first parameter is a pointer to the mutex. By passing NULL as a second parameter, we initialize the mutex to its default attributes. This is illustrated below:

```
#include <pthread.h>

pthread_mutex_t mutex;

/* create the mutex lock */
pthread_mutex_init(&mutex,NULL);
```

The mutex is acquired and released with the `pthread_mutex_lock()` and `pthread_mutex_unlock()` functions. If the mutex lock is unavailable when `pthread_mutex_lock()` is invoked, the calling thread is blocked until the owner invokes `pthread_mutex_unlock()`. The following code illustrates protecting a critical section with mutex locks:

```
/* acquire the mutex lock */
pthread_mutex_lock(&mutex);

/* critical section */

/* release the mutex lock */
pthread_mutex_unlock(&mutex);
```

All mutex functions return a value of 0 with correct operation; if an error occurs, these functions return a nonzero error code. Condition variables and read–write locks behave similarly to the way they are described in Section 5.8 and Section 5.7.2, respectively.

Many systems that implement Pthreads also provide semaphores, although semaphores are not part of the Pthreads standard and instead belong to the POSIX SEM extension. POSIX specifies two types of semaphores—**named** and unnamed. The fundamental distinction between the two is that a named semaphore has an actual name in the file system and can be shared by multiple unrelated processes. Unnamed semaphores can be used only by threads belonging to the same process. In this section, we describe unnamed semaphores.

The code below illustrates the sem_init() function for creating and initializing an unnamed semaphore:

```
#include <semaphore.h>
sem_t sem;

/* Create the semaphore and initialize it to 1 */
sem_init(&sem, 0, 1);
```

The sem_init() function is passed three parameters:

1. A pointer to the semaphore

2. A flag indicating the level of sharing

3. The semaphore's initial value

In this example, by passing the flag 0, we are indicating that this semaphore can be shared only by threads belonging to the process that created the semaphore. A nonzero value would allow other processes to access the semaphore as well. In addition, we initialize the semaphore to the value 1.

In Section 5.6, we described the classical wait() and signal() semaphore operations. Pthreads names these operations sem_wait() and sem_post(), respectively. The following code sample illustrates protecting a critical section using the semaphore created above:

```
/* acquire the semaphore */
sem_wait(&sem);

/* critical section */

/* release the semaphore */
sem_post(&sem);
```

Just like mutex locks, all semaphore functions return 0 when successful, and nonzero when an error condition occurs.

There are other extensions to the Pthreads API — including spinlocks — but it is important to note that not all extensions are considered portable from one implementation to another. We provide several programming problems and projects at the end of this chapter that use Pthreads mutex locks and condition variables as well as POSIX semaphores.

5.10 Alternative Approaches

With the emergence of multicore systems has come increased pressure to develop multithreaded applications that take advantage of multiple processing cores. However, multithreaded applications present an increased risk of race conditions and deadlocks. Traditionally, techniques such as mutex locks, semaphores, and monitors have been used to address these issues, but as the number of processing cores increases, it becomes increasingly difficult to design multithreaded applications that are free from race conditions and deadlocks.

In this section, we explore various features provided in both programming languages and hardware that support designing thread-safe concurrent applications.

5.10.1 Transactional Memory

Quite often in computer science, ideas from one area of study can be used to solve problems in other areas. The concept of **transactional memory** originated in database theory, for example, yet it provides a strategy for process synchronization. A **memory transaction** is a sequence of memory read–write operations that are atomic. If all operations in a transaction are completed, the memory transaction is committed. Otherwise, the operations must be aborted and rolled back. The benefits of transactional memory can be obtained through features added to a programming language.

Consider an example. Suppose we have a function update() that modifies shared data. Traditionally, this function would be written using mutex locks (or semaphores) such as the following:

```
void update ()
{
   acquire();

   /* modify shared data */

   release();
}
```

However, using synchronization mechanisms such as mutex locks and semaphores involves many potential problems, including deadlock. Additionally, as the number of threads increases, traditional locking scales less well, because the level of contention among threads for lock ownership becomes very high.

As an alternative to traditional locking methods, new features that take advantage of transactional memory can be added to a programming language. In our example, suppose we add the construct atomic{S}, which ensures that the operations in S execute as a transaction. This allows us to rewrite the update() function as follows:

```
void update ()
{
   atomic {
      /* modify shared data */
   }
}
```

The advantage of using such a mechanism rather than locks is that the transactional memory system—not the developer—is responsible for guaranteeing atomicity. Additionally, because no locks are involved, deadlock is not possible. Furthermore, a transactional memory system can identify which statements in atomic blocks can be executed concurrently, such as concurrent read access to a shared variable. It is, of course, possible for a programmer to identify these situations and use reader–writer locks, but the task becomes increasingly difficult as the number of threads within an application grows.

Transactional memory can be implemented in either software or hardware. **Software transactional memory** (STM), as the name suggests, implements transactional memory exclusively in software—no special hardware is needed. STM works by inserting instrumentation code inside transaction blocks. The code is inserted by a compiler and manages each transaction by examining where statements may run concurrently and where specific low-level locking is required. **Hardware transactional memory** (HTM) uses hardware cache hierarchies and cache coherency protocols to manage and resolve conflicts involving shared data residing in separate processors' caches. HTM requires no special code instrumentation and thus has less overhead than STM. However, HTM does require that existing cache hierarchies and cache coherency protocols be modified to support transactional memory.

Transactional memory has existed for several years without widespread implementation. However, the growth of multicore systems and the associated emphasis on concurrent and parallel programming have prompted a significant amount of research in this area on the part of both academics and commercial software and hardware vendors.

5.10.2 OpenMP

In Section 4.5.2, we provided an overview of OpenMP and its support of parallel programming in a shared-memory environment. Recall that OpenMP includes a set of compiler directives and an API. Any code following the compiler directive `#pragma omp parallel` is identified as a parallel region and is performed by a number of threads equal to the number of processing cores in the system. The advantage of OpenMP (and similar tools) is that thread creation and management are handled by the OpenMP library and are not the responsibility of application developers.

Along with its `#pragma omp parallel` compiler directive, OpenMP provides the compiler directive `#pragma omp critical`, which specifies the code region following the directive as a critical section in which only one thread may be active at a time. In this way, OpenMP provides support for ensuring that threads do not generate race conditions.

As an example of the use of the critical-section compiler directive, first assume that the shared variable `counter` can be modified in the `update()` function as follows:

```
void update(int value)
{
    counter += value;
}
```

If the `update()` function can be part of—or invoked from—a parallel region, a race condition is possible on the variable `counter`.

The critical-section compiler directive can be used to remedy this race condition and is coded as follows:

```
void update(int value)
{
    #pragma omp critical
    {
        counter += value;
    }
}
```

The critical-section compiler directive behaves much like a binary semaphore or mutex lock, ensuring that only one thread at a time is active in the critical section. If a thread attempts to enter a critical section when another thread is currently active in that section (that is, *owns* the section), the calling thread is blocked until the owner thread exits. If multiple critical sections must be used, each critical section can be assigned a separate name, and a rule can specify that no more than one thread may be active in a critical section of the same name simultaneously.

An advantage of using the critical-section compiler directive in OpenMP is that it is generally considered easier to use than standard mutex locks. However, a disadvantage is that application developers must still identify possible race conditions and adequately protect shared data using the compiler directive. Additionally, because the critical-section compiler directive behaves much like a mutex lock, deadlock is still possible when two or more critical sections are identified.

5.10.3 Functional Programming Languages

Most well-known programming languages—such as C, C++, Java, and C#—are known as imperative (or procedural) languages. Imperative languages are used for implementing algorithms that are state-based. In these languages, the flow of the algorithm is crucial to its correct operation, and state is represented with variables and other data structures. Of course, program state is mutable, as variables may be assigned different values over time.

With the current emphasis on concurrent and parallel programming for multicore systems, there has been greater focus on functional programming languages, which follow a programming paradigm much different from that offered by imperative languages. The fundamental difference between imperative and functional languages is that functional languages do not maintain state. That is, once a variable has been defined and assigned a value, its value is immutable—it cannot change. Because functional languages disallow mutable state, they need not be concerned with issues such as race conditions and deadlocks. Essentially, most of the problems addressed in this chapter are nonexistent in functional languages.

Several functional languages are presently in use, and we briefly mention two of them here: Erlang and Scala. The Erlang language has gained significant attention because of its support for concurrency and the ease with which it can be used to develop applications that run on parallel systems. Scala is a functional language that is also object-oriented. In fact, much of the syntax of Scala is similar to the popular object-oriented languages Java and C#. Readers interested in Erlang and Scala, and in further details about functional languages in general, are encouraged to consult the bibliography at the end of this chapter for additional references.

5.11   Deadlocks

In a multiprogramming environment, several processes may compete for a finite number of resources. A process requests resources; if the resources are not available at that time, the process enters a waiting state. Sometimes, a waiting process is never again able to change state, because the resources it has requested are held by other waiting processes. This situation is called a **deadlock**. We discussed this issue briefly in Section 5.6.3 in connection with semaphores, although we will see that deadlocks can occur with many other types of resources available in a computer system.

Perhaps the best illustration of a deadlock can be drawn from a law passed by the Kansas legislature early in the 20th century. It said, in part: "When two trains approach each other at a crossing, both shall come to a full stop and neither shall start up again until the other has gone."

5.11.1   System Model

A system consists of a finite number of resources to be distributed among a number of competing processes. The resources are partitioned into several types, each consisting of some number of identical instances. Memory space, CPU cycles, files, and I/O devices (such as printers and DVD drives) are examples of resource types. If a system has two CPUs, then the resource type *CPU* has two instances. Similarly, the resource type *printer* may have five instances.

If a process requests an instance of a resource type, the allocation of *any* instance of the type will satisfy the request. If it will not, then the instances are not identical, and the resource type classes have not been defined properly. For example, a system may have two printers. These two printers may be defined to be in the same resource class if no one cares which printer prints which output. However, if one printer is on the ninth floor and the other is in the basement, then people on the ninth floor may not see both printers as equivalent, and separate resource classes may need to be defined for each printer.

A process must request a resource before using it and must release the resource after using it. A process may request as many resources as it requires to carry out its designated task. Obviously, the number of resources requested may not exceed the total number of resources available in the system. In other words, a process cannot request three printers if the system has only two.

Under the normal mode of operation, a process may utilize a resource in only the following sequence:

1. **Request**. The process requests the resource. If the request cannot be granted immediately (for example, if the resource is being used by another process), then the requesting process must wait until it can acquire the resource.

2. **Use**. The process can operate on the resource (for example, if the resource is a printer, the process can print on the printer).

3. **Release**. The process releases the resource.

The request and release of resources are system calls, as explained in Chapter 2. Examples are the request() and release() device, open() and close() file, and allocate() and free() memory system calls. Request and release of resources that are not managed by the operating system can be accomplished through the wait() and signal() operations on semaphores or through acquisition and release of a mutex lock. For each use of a kernel-managed resource by a process or thread, the operating system checks to make sure that the process has requested and has been allocated the resource. A system table records whether each resource is free or allocated; for each resource that is allocated, the table also records the process to which it is allocated. If a process requests a resource that is currently allocated to another process, it can be added to a queue of processes waiting for this resource.

A set of processes is in a deadlocked state when every process in the set is waiting for an event that can be caused only by another process in the set. The events with which we are mainly concerned here are resource acquisition and release. The resources may be either physical resources (for example, printers, tape drives, memory space, and CPU cycles) or logical resources (for example, files, semaphores, and monitors). However, other types of events may result in deadlocks (for example, the IPC facilities discussed in Chapter 3).

To illustrate a deadlocked state, consider a system with three CD RW drives. Suppose each of three processes holds one of these drives. If each process now requests another drive, the three processes will be in a deadlocked state. Each is waiting for the event "CD RW is released," which can be caused only by one of the other waiting processes. This example illustrates a deadlock involving the same resource type.

Deadlocks may also involve different resource types. For example, consider a system with one printer and one DVD drive. Suppose that process P_i is holding the DVD and process P_j is holding the printer. If P_i requests the printer and P_j requests the DVD drive, a deadlock occurs.

A programmer who is developing multithreaded applications must pay particular attention to this problem. Multithreaded programs are good candidates for deadlock because multiple threads can compete for shared resources.

5.11.2 Deadlock Characterization

In a deadlock, processes never finish executing, and system resources are tied up, preventing other jobs from starting. Before we discuss the various methods for dealing with the deadlock problem, we look more closely at features that characterize deadlocks.

5.11.2.1 Necessary Conditions

A deadlock situation can arise if the following four conditions hold simultaneously in a system:

1. **Mutual exclusion**. At least one resource must be held in a nonsharable mode; that is, only one process at a time can use the resource. If another process requests that resource, the requesting process must be delayed until the resource has been released.

2. **Hold and wait**. A process must be holding at least one resource and waiting to acquire additional resources that are currently being held by other processes.

3. **No preemption**. Resources cannot be preempted; that is, a resource can be released only voluntarily by the process holding it, after that process has completed its task.

4. **Circular wait**. A set $\{P_0, P_1, ..., P_n\}$ of waiting processes must exist such that P_0 is waiting for a resource held by P_1, P_1 is waiting for a resource held by P_2, ..., P_{n-1} is waiting for a resource held by P_n, and P_n is waiting for a resource held by P_0.

We emphasize that all four conditions must hold for a deadlock to occur. The circular-wait condition implies the hold-and-wait condition, so the four conditions are not completely independent.

5.11.2.2   Resource-Allocation Graph

Deadlocks can be described more precisely in terms of a directed graph called a **system resource-allocation graph**. This graph consists of a set of vertices V and a set of edges E. The set of vertices V is partitioned into two different types of nodes: $P = \{P_1, P_2, ..., P_n\}$, the set consisting of all the active processes in the system, and $R = \{R_1, R_2, ..., R_m\}$, the set consisting of all resource types in the system.

DEADLOCK WITH MUTEX LOCKS

Let's see how deadlock can occur in a multithreaded Pthread program using mutex locks. The pthread_mutex_init() function initializes an unlocked mutex. Mutex locks are acquired and released using pthread_mutex_lock() and pthread_mutex_unlock(), respectively. If a thread attempts to acquire a locked mutex, the call to pthread_mutex_lock() blocks the thread until the owner of the mutex lock invokes pthread_mutex_unlock().

Two mutex locks are created in the following code example:

```
/* Create and initialize the mutex locks */
pthread_mutex_t first_mutex;
pthread_mutex_t second_mutex;

pthread_mutex_init(&first_mutex,NULL);
pthread_mutex_init(&second_mutex,NULL);
```

Next, two threads—thread_one and thread_two—are created, and both these threads have access to both mutex locks. thread_one and thread_two run in the functions do_work_one() and do_work_two(), respectively, as shown in Figure 5.21.

(continued on following page.)

DEADLOCK WITH MUTEX LOCKS (continued)

```
/* thread_one runs in this function */
void *do_work_one(void *param)
{
    pthread_mutex_lock(&first_mutex);
    pthread_mutex_lock(&second_mutex);
    /**
     * Do some work
     */
    pthread_mutex_unlock(&second_mutex);
    pthread_mutex_unlock(&first_mutex);

    pthread_exit(0);
}

/* thread_two runs in this function */
void *do_work_two(void *param)
{
    pthread_mutex_lock(&second_mutex);
    pthread_mutex_lock(&first_mutex);
    /**
     * Do some work
     */
    pthread_mutex_unlock(&first_mutex);
    pthread_mutex_unlock(&second_mutex);

    pthread_exit(0);
}
```

Figure 5.21   Deadlock example.

In this example, thread_one attempts to acquire the mutex locks in the order (1) first_mutex, (2) second_mutex, while thread_two attempts to acquire the mutex locks in the order (1) second_mutex, (2) first_mutex. Deadlock is possible if thread_one acquires first_mutex while thread_two aacquites second_mutex.

Note that, even though deadlock is possible, it will not occur if thread_one is able to acquire and release the mutex locks for first_mutex and second_mutex before thread_two attempts to acquire the locks. This example illustrates a problem with handling deadlocks: it is difficult to identify and test for deadlocks that may occur only under certain circumstances.

A directed edge from process P_i to resource type R_j is denoted by $P_i \rightarrow R_j$; it signifies that process P_i has requested an instance of resource type R_j and is currently waiting for that resource. A directed edge from resource type R_j to process P_i is denoted by $R_j \rightarrow P_i$; it signifies that an instance of resource type R_j has been allocated to process P_i. A directed edge $P_i \rightarrow R_j$ is called a **request edge**; a directed edge $R_j \rightarrow P_i$ is called an **assignment edge**.

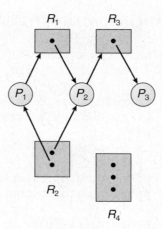

Figure 5.22   Resource-allocation graph.

Pictorially, we represent each process P_i as a circle and each resource type R_j as a rectangle. Since resource type R_j may have more than one instance, we represent each such instance as a dot within the rectangle. Note that a request edge points to only the rectangle R_j, whereas an assignment edge must also designate one of the dots in the rectangle.

When process P_i requests an instance of resource type R_j, a request edge is inserted in the resource-allocation graph. When this request can be fulfilled, the request edge is ***instantaneously*** transformed to an assignment edge. When the process no longer needs access to the resource, it releases the resource; as a result, the assignment edge is deleted.

The resource-allocation graph shown in Figure 5.22 depicts the following situation.

- The sets P, R, and E:
  - $P = \{P_1, P_2, P_3\}$
  - $R = \{R_1, R_2, R_3, R_4\}$
  - $E = \{P_1 \rightarrow R_1, P_2 \rightarrow R_3, R_1 \rightarrow P_2, R_2 \rightarrow P_2, R_2 \rightarrow P_1, R_3 \rightarrow P_3\}$
- Resource instances:
  - One instance of resource type R_1
  - Two instances of resource type R_2
  - One instance of resource type R_3
  - Three instances of resource type R_4
- Process states:
  - Process P_1 is holding an instance of resource type R_2 and is waiting for an instance of resource type R_1.
  - Process P_2 is holding an instance of R_1 and an instance of R_2 and is waiting for an instance of R_3.

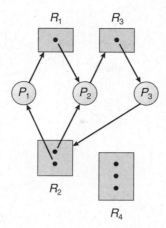

Figure 5.23 Resource-allocation graph with a deadlock.

○ Process P_3 is holding an instance of R_3.

Given the definition of a resource-allocation graph, it can be shown that, if the graph contains no cycles, then no process in the system is deadlocked. If the graph does contain a cycle, then a deadlock may exist.

If each resource type has exactly one instance, then a cycle implies that a deadlock has occurred. If the cycle involves only a set of resource types, each of which has only a single instance, then a deadlock has occurred. Each process involved in the cycle is deadlocked. In this case, a cycle in the graph is both a necessary and a sufficient condition for the existence of deadlock.

If each resource type has several instances, then a cycle does not necessarily imply that a deadlock has occurred. In this case, a cycle in the graph is a necessary but not a sufficient condition for the existence of deadlock.

To illustrate this concept, we return to the resource-allocation graph depicted in Figure 5.22. Suppose that process P_3 requests an instance of resource type R_2. Since no resource instance is currently available, a request edge $P_3 \rightarrow R_2$ is added to the graph (Figure 5.23). At this point, two minimal cycles exist in the system:

$$P_1 \rightarrow R_1 \rightarrow P_2 \rightarrow R_3 \rightarrow P_3 \rightarrow R_2 \rightarrow P_1$$
$$P_2 \rightarrow R_3 \rightarrow P_3 \rightarrow R_2 \rightarrow P_2$$

Processes P_1, P_2, and P_3 are deadlocked. Process P_2 is waiting for the resource R_3, which is held by process P_3. Process P_3 is waiting for either process P_1 or process P_2 to release resource R_2. In addition, process P_1 is waiting for process P_2 to release resource R_1.

Now consider the resource-allocation graph in Figure 5.24. In this example, we also have a cycle:

$$P_1 \rightarrow R_1 \rightarrow P_3 \rightarrow R_2 \rightarrow P_1$$

However, there is no deadlock. Observe that process P_4 may release its instance of resource type R_2. That resource can then be allocated to P_3, breaking the cycle.

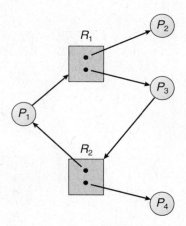

Figure 5.24 Resource-allocation graph with a cycle but no deadlock.

In summary, if a resource-allocation graph does not have a cycle, then the system is *not* in a deadlocked state. If there is a cycle, then the system may or may not be in a deadlocked state. This observation is important when we deal with the deadlock problem.

5.11.3 Methods for Handling Deadlocks

Generally speaking, we can deal with the deadlock problem in one of three ways:

- We can use a protocol to prevent or avoid deadlocks, ensuring that the system will *never* enter a deadlocked state.

- We can allow the system to enter a deadlocked state, detect it, and recover.

- We can ignore the problem altogether and pretend that deadlocks never occur in the system.

The third solution is the one used by most operating systems, including UNIX and Windows; it is then up to the application developer to write programs that handle deadlocks.

Next, we elaborate briefly on each of the three methods for handling deadlocks. Before proceeding, we should mention that some researchers have argued that none of the basic approaches alone is appropriate for the entire spectrum of resource-allocation problems in operating systems. The basic approaches can be combined, however, allowing us to select an optimal approach for each class of resources in a system.

To ensure that deadlocks never occur, the system can use either a deadlock-prevention or a deadlock-avoidance scheme. **Deadlock prevention** provides a set of methods for ensuring that at least one of the necessary conditions (Section 5.11.2.1) cannot hold. These methods prevent deadlocks by constraining how requests for resources can be made.

Deadlock avoidance requires that the operating system be given in advance additional information concerning which resources a process will request and use during its lifetime. With this additional knowledge, it can decide for each request whether or not the process should wait. To decide whether the current request can be satisfied or must be delayed, the system must consider the resources currently available, the resources currently allocated to each process, and the future requests and releases of each process.

If a system does not employ either a deadlock-prevention or a deadlock-avoidance algorithm, then a deadlock situation may arise. In this environment, the system can provide an algorithm that examines the state of the system to determine whether a deadlock has occurred and an algorithm to recover from the deadlock (if a deadlock has indeed occurred).

In the absence of algorithms to detect and recover from deadlocks, we may arrive at a situation in which the system is in a deadlock state yet has no way of recognizing what has happened. In this case, the undetected deadlock will result in deterioration of the system's performance, because resources are being held by processes that cannot run and because more and more processes, as they make requests for resources, will enter a deadlocked state. Eventually, the system will stop functioning and will need to be restarted manually.

Although this method may not seem to be a viable approach to the deadlock problem, it is nevertheless used in most operating systems, as mentioned earlier. In many systems, deadlocks occur infrequently (say, once per year); thus, this method is cheaper than the prevention, avoidance, or detection and recovery methods, which must be used constantly. Also, in some circumstances, a system is in a frozen state but not in a deadlocked state. We see this situation, for example, with a real-time process running at the highest priority (or any process running on a nonpreemptive scheduler) and never returning control to the operating system. The system must have manual recovery methods for such conditions and may simply use those techniques for deadlock recovery.

5.12 Summary

Given a collection of cooperating sequential processes that share data, mutual exclusion must be provided to ensure that a critical section of code is used by only one process or thread at a time. Typically, computer hardware provides several operations that ensure mutual exclusion. However, such hardware-based solutions are too complicated for most developers to use. Mutex locks and semaphores overcome this obstacle. Both tools can be used to solve various synchronization problems and can be implemented efficiently, especially if hardware support for atomic operations is available.

Various synchronization problems (such as the bounded-buffer problem, the readers–writers problem, and the dining-philosophers problem) are important mainly because they are examples of a large class of concurrency-control problems. These problems are used to test nearly every newly proposed synchronization scheme.

The operating system must provide the means to guard against timing errors, and several language constructs have been proposed to deal with these problems. Monitors provide a synchronization mechanism for sharing abstract data types. A condition variable provides a method by which a monitor function can block its execution until it is signaled to continue.

Operating systems also provide support for synchronization. For example, Windows, Linux, and Solaris provide mechanisms such as semaphores, mutex locks, spinlocks, and condition variables to control access to shared data. The Pthreads API provides support for mutex locks and semaphores, as well as condition variables.

Several alternative approaches focus on synchronization for multicore systems. One approach uses transactional memory, which may address synchronization issues using either software or hardware techniques. Another approach uses the compiler extensions offered by OpenMP. Finally, functional programming languages address synchronization issues by disallowing mutability.

A deadlocked state occurs when two or more processes are waiting indefinitely for an event that can be caused only by one of the waiting processes. There are three principal methods for dealing with deadlocks:

- Use some protocol to prevent or avoid deadlocks, ensuring that the system will never enter a deadlocked state.

- Allow the system to enter a deadlocked state, detect it, and then recover.

- Ignore the problem altogether and pretend that deadlocks never occur in the system.

The third solution is the one used by most operating systems, including UNIX and Windows.

A deadlock can occur only if four necessary conditions hold simultaneously in the system: mutual exclusion, hold and wait, no preemption, and circular wait. To prevent deadlocks, we can ensure that at least one of the necessary conditions never holds.

Review Questions

Review questions for this chapter can be accessed by visiting our website.

Practice Exercises

Answers for the Practice Exercises can be accceed by visiting our website.

5.1   In Section 5.4, we mentioned that disabling interrupts frequently can affect the system's clock. Explain why this can occur and how such effects can be minimized.

5.2   Explain why Windows, Linux, and Solaris implement multiple locking mechanisms. Describe the circumstances under which they use spinlocks, mutex locks, semaphores, adaptive mutex locks, and condition variables. In each case, explain why the mechanism is needed.

5.3   What is the meaning of the term *busy waiting*? What other kinds of waiting are there in an operating system? Can busy waiting be avoided altogether? Explain your answer.

5.4 Explain why spinlocks are not appropriate for single-processor systems yet are often used in multiprocessor systems.

5.5 Show that, if the `wait()` and `signal()` semaphore operations are not executed atomically, then mutual exclusion may be violated.

5.6 Illustrate how a binary semaphore can be used to implement mutual exclusion among n processes.

5.7 List three examples of deadlocks that are not related to a computer-system environment.

5.8 Is it possible to have a deadlock involving only a single process? Explain your answer.

Exercises

5.9 Race conditions are possible in many computer systems. Consider a banking system that maintains an account balance with two functions: `deposit(amount)` and `withdraw(amount)`. These two functions are passed the amount that is to be deposited or withdrawn from the bank account balance. Assume that a husband and wife share a bank account. Concurrently, the husband calls the `withdraw()` function and the wife calls `deposit()`. Describe how a race condition is possible and what might be done to prevent the race condition from occurring.

5.10 The first known correct software solution to the critical-section problem for two processes was developed by Dekker. The two processes, P_0 and P_1, share the following variables:

```
boolean flag[2]; /* initially false */
int turn;
```

The structure of process P_i (i == 0 or 1) is shown in Figure 5.25. The other process is P_j (j == 1 or 0). Prove that the algorithm satisfies all three requirements for the critical-section problem.

5.11 The first known correct software solution to the critical-section problem for n processes with a lower bound on waiting of $n - 1$ turns was presented by Eisenberg and McGuire. The processes share the following variables:

```
enum pstate {idle, want_in, in_cs};
pstate flag[n];
int turn;
```

All the elements of `flag` are initially `idle`. The initial value of `turn` is immaterial (between 0 and n-1). The structure of process P_i is shown in Figure 5.26. Prove that the algorithm satisfies all three requirements for the critical-section problem.

```
                    do {
                        flag[i] = true;

                        while (flag[j]) {
                            if (turn == j) {
                                flag[i] = false;
                                while (turn == j)
                                    ; /* do nothing */
                                flag[i] = true;
                            }
                        }

                        /* critical section */

                        turn = j;
                        flag[i] = false;

                        /* remainder section */
                    } while (true);
```

Figure 5.25 The structure of process P_i in Dekker's algorithm.

5.12 Explain why implementing synchronization primitives by disabling interrupts is not appropriate in a single-processor system if the synchronization primitives are to be used in user-level programs.

5.13 Explain why interrupts are not appropriate for implementing synchronization primitives in multiprocessor systems.

5.14 The Linux kernel has a policy that a process cannot hold a spinlock while attempting to acquire a semaphore. Explain why this policy is in place.

5.15 Describe two kernel data structures in which race conditions are possible. Be sure to include a description of how a race condition can occur.

5.16 Describe how the compare_and_swap() instruction can be used to provide mutual exclusion that satisfies the bounded-waiting requirement.

5.17 Consider how to implement a mutex lock using an atomic hardware instruction. Assume that the following structure defining the mutex lock is available:

```
                        typedef struct {
                            int available;
                        } lock;
```

(available == 0) indicates that the lock is available, and a value of 1 indicates that the lock is unavailable. Using this struct, illustrate how the following functions can be implemented using the test_and_set() and compare_and_swap() instructions:

- void acquire(lock *mutex)
- void release(lock *mutex)

```
do {
  while (true) {
    flag[i] = want_in;
    j = turn;

    while (j != i) {
       if (flag[j] != idle) {
          j = turn;
       else
          j = (j + 1) % n;
    }

    flag[i] = in_cs;
    j = 0;

    while ( (j < n) && (j == i || flag[j] != in_cs))
      j++;

    if ( (j >= n) && (turn == i || flag[turn] == idle))
      break;
  }

    /* critical section */

  j = (turn + 1) % n;

  while (flag[j] == idle)
    j = (j + 1) % n;

  turn = j;
  flag[i] = idle;

    /* remainder section */
} while (true);
```

Figure 5.26 The structure of process P_i in Eisenberg and McGuire's algorithm.

Be sure to include any initialization that may be necessary.

5.18 The implementation of mutex locks provided in Section 5.5 suffers from busy waiting. Describe what changes would be necessary so that a process waiting to acquire a mutex lock would be blocked and placed into a waiting queue until the lock became available.

5.19 Assume that a system has multiple processing cores. For each of the following scenarios, describe which is a better locking mechanism—a spinlock or a mutex lock where waiting processes sleep while waiting for the lock to become available:

- The lock is to be held for a short duration.

- The lock is to be held for a long duration.

- A thread may be put to sleep while holding the lock.

5.20 Assume that a context switch takes T time. Suggest an upper bound (in terms of T) for holding a spinlock. If the spinlock is held for any longer, a mutex lock (where waiting threads are put to sleep) is a better alternative.

5.21 A multithreaded web server wishes to keep track of the number of requests it services (known as *hits*). Consider the two following strategies to prevent a race condition on the variable hits. The first strategy is to use a basic mutex lock when updating hits:

```
int hits;
mutex_lock hit_lock;

hit_lock.acquire();
hits++;
hit_lock.release();
```

A second strategy is to use an atomic integer:

```
atomic_t hits;
atomic_inc(&hits);
```

Explain which of these two strategies is more efficient.

5.22 Consider the code example for allocating and releasing processes shown in Figure 5.27.

  a. Identify the race condition(s).

  b. Assume you have a mutex lock named mutex with the operations acquire() and release(). Indicate where the locking needs to be placed to prevent the race condition(s).

  c. Could we replace the integer variable

```
int number_of_processes = 0
```

  with the atomic integer

```
atomic_t number_of_processes = 0
```

  to prevent the race condition(s)?

5.23 Servers can be designed to limit the number of open connections. For example, a server may wish to have only N socket connections at any point in time. As soon as N connections are made, the server will not accept another incoming connection until an existing connection is released. Explain how semaphores can be used by a server to limit the number of concurrent connections.

5.24 Windows Vista provides a lightweight synchronization tool called slim reader–writer locks. Whereas most implementations of reader–writer locks favor either readers or writers, or perhaps order waiting threads using a FIFO policy, slim reader–writer locks favor neither readers nor

```
#define MAX_PROCESSES 255
int number_of_processes = 0;

/* the implementation of fork() calls this function */
int allocate_process() {
int new_pid;

    if (number_of_processes == MAX_PROCESSES)
        return -1;
    else {
        /* allocate necessary process resources */
        ++number_of_processes;

        return new_pid;
    }
}

/* the implementation of exit() calls this function */
void release_process() {
    /* release process resources */
    --number_of_processes;
}
```

Figure 5.27 Allocating and releasing processes.

writers, nor are waiting threads ordered in a FIFO queue. Explain the benefits of providing such a synchronization tool.

5.25 Show how to implement the wait() and signal() semaphore operations in multiprocessor environments using the test_and_set() instruction. The solution should exhibit minimal busy waiting.

5.26 Exercise 4.26 requires the parent thread to wait for the child thread to finish its execution before printing out the computed values. If we let the parent thread access the Fibonacci numbers as soon as they have been computed by the child thread—rather than waiting for the child thread to terminate—what changes would be necessary to the solution for this exercise? Implement your modified solution.

5.27 Demonstrate that monitors and semaphores are equivalent insofar as they can be used to implement solutions to the same types of synchronization problems.

5.28 Design an algorithm for a bounded-buffer monitor in which the buffers (portions) are embedded within the monitor itself.

5.29 The strict mutual exclusion within a monitor makes the bounded-buffer monitor of Exercise 5.28 mainly suitable for small portions.

    a.   Explain why this is true.

    b.   Design a new scheme that is suitable for larger portions.

5.30 Discuss the tradeoff between fairness and throughput of operations in the readers–writers problem. Propose a method for solving the readers–writers problem without causing starvation.

5.31 How does the `signal()` operation associated with monitors differ from the corresponding operation defined for semaphores?

5.32 Suppose the `signal()` statement can appear only as the last statement in a monitor function. Suggest how the implementation described in Section 5.8 can be simplified in this situation.

5.33 Consider a system consisting of processes P_1, P_2, ..., P_n, each of which has a unique priority number. Write a monitor that allocates three identical printers to these processes, using the priority numbers for deciding the order of allocation.

5.34 A file is to be shared among different processes, each of which has a unique number. The file can be accessed simultaneously by several processes, subject to the following constraint: the sum of all unique numbers associated with all the processes currently accessing the file must be less than n. Write a monitor to coordinate access to the file.

5.35 When a signal is performed on a condition inside a monitor, the signaling process can either continue its execution or transfer control to the process that is signaled. How would the solution to the preceding exercise differ with these two different ways in which signaling can be performed?

5.36 Suppose we replace the `wait()` and `signal()` operations of monitors with a single construct `await(B)`, where B is a general Boolean expression that causes the process executing it to wait until B becomes `true`.

   a. Write a monitor using this scheme to implement the readers–writers problem.

   b. Explain why, in general, this construct cannot be implemented efficiently.

   c. What restrictions need to be put on the `await` statement so that it can be implemented efficiently? (Hint: Restrict the generality of B; see [Kessels (1977)].)

5.37 Design an algorithm for a monitor that implements an *alarm clock* that enables a calling program to delay itself for a specified number of time units (*ticks*). You may assume the existence of a real hardware clock that invokes a function `tick()` in your monitor at regular intervals.

5.38 Consider the traffic deadlock depicted in Figure 5.28.

   a. Show that the four necessary conditions for deadlock hold in this example.

   b. State a simple rule for avoiding deadlocks in this system.

5.39 Consider the deadlock situation that can occur in the dining-philosophers problem when the philosophers obtain the chopsticks one at a time. Discuss how the four necessary conditions for deadlock hold

Figure 5.28   Traffic deadlock for Exercise 5.38.

in this setting. Discuss how deadlocks could be avoided by eliminating any one of the four necessary conditions.

Programming Problems

5.40   Programming Exercise 3.20 required you to design a PID manager that allocated a unique process identifier to each process. Exercise 4.20 required you to modify your solution to Exercise 3.20 by writing a program that created a number of threads that requested and released process identifiers. Now modify your solution to Exercise 4.20 by ensuring that the data structure used to represent the availability of process identifiers is safe from race conditions. Use Pthreads mutex locks, described in Section 5.9.4.

5.41   Assume that a finite number of resources of a single resource type must be managed. Processes may ask for a number of these resources and will return them once finished. As an example, many commercial software packages provide a given number of *licenses*, indicating the number of applications that may run concurrently. When the application is started, the license count is decremented. When the application is terminated, the license count is incremented. If all licenses are in use, requests to start the application are denied. Such requests will only be granted when an existing license holder terminates the application and a license is returned.

The following program segment is used to manage a finite number of instances of an available resource. The maximum number of resources and the number of available resources are declared as follows:

```
#define MAX_RESOURCES 5
int available_resources = MAX_RESOURCES;
```

When a process wishes to obtain a number of resources, it invokes the `decrease_count()` function:

```
/* decrease available_resources by count resources */
/* return 0 if sufficient resources available, */
/* otherwise return -1 */
int decrease_count(int count) {
  if (available_resources < count)
    return -1;
  else {
    available_resources -= count;

    return 0;
  }
}
```

When a process wants to return a number of resources, it calls the `increase_count()` function:

```
/* increase available_resources by count */
int increase_count(int count) {
  available_resources += count;

  return 0;
}
```

The preceding program segment produces a race condition. Do the following:

a. Identify the data involved in the race condition.

b. Identify the location (or locations) in the code where the race condition occurs.

c. Using a semaphore or mutex lock, fix the race condition. It is permissible to modify the `decrease_count()` function so that the calling process is blocked until sufficient resources are available.

5.42 The `decrease_count()` function in the previous exercise currently returns 0 if sufficient resources are available and −1 otherwise. This leads to awkward programming for a process that wishes to obtain a number of resources:

```
while (decrease_count(count) == -1)
  ;
```

Rewrite the resource-manager code segment using a monitor and condition variables so that the `decrease_count()` function suspends the process until sufficient resources are available. This will allow a process to invoke `decrease_count()` by simply calling

        decrease_count(count);

The process will return from this function call only when sufficient resources are available.

5.43 Exercise 4.22 asked you to design a multithreaded program that estimated π using the Monte Carlo technique. In that exercise, you were asked to create a single thread that generated random points, storing the result in a global variable. Once that thread exited, the parent thread performed the calcuation that estimated the value of π. Modify that program so that you create several threads, each of which generates random points and determines if the points fall within the circle. Each thread will have to update the global count of all points that fall within the circle. Protect against race conditions on updates to the shared global variable by using mutex locks.

5.44 Exercise 4.23 asked you to design a program using OpenMP that estimated π using the Monte Carlo technique. Examine your solution to that program looking for any possible race conditions. If you identify a race condition, protect against it using the strategy outlined in Section 5.10.2.

5.45 A barrier is a tool for synchronizing the activity of a number of threads. When a thread reaches a barrier point, it cannot proceed until all other threads have reached this point as well. When the last thread reaches the barrier point, all threads are released and can resume concurrent execution.
Assume that the barrier is initialized to N—the number of threads that must wait at the barrier point:

        init(N);

Each thread then performs some work until it reaches the barrier point:

        /* do some work for awhile */

        barrier_point();

        /* do some work for awhile */

Using synchronization tools described in this chapter, construct a barrier that implements the following API:

- `int init(int n)`—Initializes the barrier to the specified size.
- `int barrier_point(void)`—Identifies the barrier point. All threads are released from the barrier when the last thread reaches this point.

The return value of each function is used to identify error conditions. Each function will return 0 under normal operation and will return −1 if an error occurs. A testing harness is provided in the source code download to test your implementation of the barrier.

Programming Projects

Project 1—The Sleeping Teaching Assistant

A university computer science department has a teaching assistant (TA) who helps undergraduate students with their programming assignments during regular office hours. The TA's office is rather small and has room for only one desk with a chair and computer. There are three chairs in the hallway outside the office where students can sit and wait if the TA is currently helping another student. When there are no students who need help during office hours, the TA sits at the desk and takes a nap. If a student arrives during office hours and finds the TA sleeping, the student must awaken the TA to ask for help. If a student arrives and finds the TA currently helping another student, the student sits on one of the chairs in the hallway and waits. If no chairs are available, the student will come back at a later time.

Using POSIX threads, mutex locks, and semaphores, implement a solution that coordinates the activities of the TA and the students. Details for this assignment are provided below.

The Students and the TA

Using Pthreads (Section 4.4.1), begin by creating n students. Each will run as a separate thread. The TA will run as a separate thread as well. Student threads will alternate between programming for a period of time and seeking help from the TA. If the TA is available, they will obtain help. Otherwise, they will either sit in a chair in the hallway or, if no chairs are available, will resume programming and will seek help at a later time. If a student arrives and notices that the TA is sleeping, the student must notify the TA using a semaphore. When the TA finishes helping a student, the TA must check to see if there are students waiting for help in the hallway. If so, the TA must help each of these students in turn. If no students are present, the TA may return to napping.

Perhaps the best option for simulating students programming—as well as the TA providing help to a student—is to have the appropriate threads sleep for a random period of time.

POSIX Synchronization

Coverage of POSIX mutex locks and semaphores is provided in Section 5.9.4. Consult that section for details.

Project 2—The Dining Philosophers Problem

In Section 5.7.3, we provide an outline of a solution to the dining-philosophers problem using monitors. This problem will require implementing a solution using Pthreads mutex locks and condition variables.

The Philosophers

Begin by creating five philosophers, each identified by a number 0 . . 4. Each philosopher will run as a separate thread. Thread creation using Pthreads is covered in Section 4.4.1. Philosophers alternate between thinking and eating. To simulate both activities, have the thread sleep for a random period between one and three seconds. When a philosopher wishes to eat, she invokes the function

```
pickup_forks(int philosopher_number)
```

where `philosopher_number` identifies the number of the philosopher wishing to eat. When a philosopher finishes eating, she invokes

```
return_forks(int philosopher_number)
```

Pthreads Condition Variables

Condition variables in Pthreads behave similarly to those described in Section 5.8. However, in that section, condition variables are used within the context of a monitor, which provides a locking mechanism to ensure data integrity. Since Pthreads is typically used in C programs—and since C does not have a monitor— we accomplish locking by associating a condition variable with a mutex lock. Pthreads mutex locks are covered in Section 5.9.4. We cover Pthreads condition variables here.

Condition variables in Pthreads use the `pthread_cond_t` data type and are initialized using the `pthread_cond_init()` function. The following code creates and initializes a condition variable as well as its associated mutex lock:

```
pthread_mutex_t mutex;
pthread_cond_t cond_var;

pthread_mutex_init(&mutex,NULL);
pthread_cond_init(&cond_var,NULL);
```

The `pthread_cond_wait()` function is used for waiting on a condition variable. The following code illustrates how a thread can wait for the condition `a == b` to become true using a Pthread condition variable:

```
pthread_mutex_lock(&mutex);
while (a != b)
    pthread_cond_wait(&mutex, &cond_var);

pthread_mutex_unlock(&mutex);
```

The mutex lock associated with the condition variable must be locked before the `pthread_cond_wait()` function is called, since it is used to protect the data in the conditional clause from a possible race condition. Once this lock is acquired, the thread can check the condition. If the condition is not true, the thread then invokes `pthread_cond_wait()`, passing the mutex lock and the condition variable as parameters. Calling `pthread_cond_wait()` releases the mutex lock, thereby allowing another thread to access the shared data and possibly update its value so that the condition clause evaluates to true. (To protect against program errors, it is important to place the conditional clause within a loop so that the condition is rechecked after being signaled.)

A thread that modifies the shared data can invoke the `pthread_cond_signal()` function, thereby signaling one thread waiting on the condition variable. This is illustrated below:

```
pthread_mutex_lock(&mutex);
a = b;
pthread_cond_signal(&cond_var);
pthread_mutex_unlock(&mutex);
```

It is important to note that the call to `pthread_cond_signal()` does not release the mutex lock. It is the subsequent call to `pthread_mutex_unlock()` that releases the mutex. Once the mutex lock is released, the signaled thread becomes the owner of the mutex lock and returns control from the call to `pthread_cond_wait()`.

Project 3—Producer–Consumer Problem

In Section 5.7.1, we presented a semaphore-based solution to the producer–consumer problem using a bounded buffer. In this project, you will design a programming solution to the bounded-buffer problem using the producer and consumer processes shown in Figures 5.9 and 5.10. The solution presented in Section 5.7.1 uses three semaphores: `empty` and `full`, which count the number of empty and full slots in the buffer, and `mutex`, which is a binary (or mutual-exclusion) semaphore that protects the actual insertion or removal of items in the buffer. For this project, you will use standard counting semaphores for `empty` and `full` and a mutex lock, rather than a binary semaphore, to represent `mutex`. The producer and consumer—running as separate threads—will move items to and from a buffer that is synchronized with the `empty`, `full`, and `mutex` structures. You can solve this problem using either Pthreads or the Windows API.

The Buffer

Internally, the buffer will consist of a fixed-size array of type `buffer_item` (which will be defined using a `typedef`). The array of `buffer_item` objects will be manipulated as a circular queue. The definition of `buffer_item`, along with the size of the buffer, can be stored in a header file such as the following:

```
/* buffer.h */
typedef int buffer_item;
#define BUFFER_SIZE 5
```

The buffer will be manipulated with two functions, `insert_item()` and `remove_item()`, which are called by the producer and consumer threads, respectively. A skeleton outlining these functions appears in Figure 5.29.

```
#include "buffer.h"

/* the buffer */
buffer_item buffer[BUFFER_SIZE];

int insert_item(buffer_item item) {
   /* insert item into buffer
    return 0 if successful, otherwise
    return -1 indicating an error condition */
}

int remove_item(buffer_item *item) {
   /* remove an object from buffer
    placing it in item
    return 0 if successful, otherwise
    return -1 indicating an error condition */
}
```

Figure 5.29 Outline of buffer operations.

The `insert_item()` and `remove_item()` functions will synchronize the producer and consumer using the algorithms outlined in Figures 5.9 and 5.10. The buffer will also require an initialization function that initializes the mutual-exclusion object `mutex` along with the `empty` and `full` semaphores.

The `main()` function will initialize the buffer and create the separate producer and consumer threads. Once it has created the producer and consumer threads, the `main()` function will sleep for a period of time and, upon awakening, will terminate the application. The `main()` function will be passed three parameters on the command line:

1. How long to sleep before terminating
2. The number of producer threads
3. The number of consumer threads

A skeleton for this function appears in Figure 5.30.

```
#include "buffer.h"

int main(int argc, char *argv[]) {
   /* 1. Get command line arguments argv[1],argv[2],argv[3] */
   /* 2. Initialize buffer */
   /* 3. Create producer thread(s) */
   /* 4. Create consumer thread(s) */
   /* 5. Sleep */
   /* 6. Exit */
}
```

Figure 5.30 Outline of skeleton program.

```
#include <stdlib.h> /* required for rand() */
#include "buffer.h"

void *producer(void *param) {
  buffer_item item;

  while (true) {
    /* sleep for a random period of time */
    sleep(...);
    /* generate a random number */
    item = rand();
    if (insert_item(item))
      fprintf("report error condition");
    else
      printf("producer produced %d\n",item);
  }
}

void *consumer(void *param) {
  buffer_item item;

  while (true) {
    /* sleep for a random period of time */
    sleep(...);
    if (remove_item(&item))
      fprintf("report error condition");
    else
      printf("consumer consumed %d\n",item);
  }
}
```

Figure 5.31   An outline of the producer and consumer threads.

The Producer and Consumer Threads

The producer thread will alternate between sleeping for a random period of time and inserting a random integer into the buffer. Random numbers will be produced using the rand() function, which produces random integers between 0 and RAND_MAX. The consumer will also sleep for a random period of time and, upon awakening, will attempt to remove an item from the buffer. An outline of the producer and consumer threads appears in Figure 5.31.

As noted earlier, you can solve this problem using either Pthreads or the Windows API. In the following sections, we supply more information on each of these choices.

Pthreads Thread Creation and Synchronization

Creating threads using the Pthreads API is discussed in Section 4.4.1. Coverage of mutex locks and semaphores using Pthreads is provided in Section 5.9.4. Refer to those sections for specific instructions on Pthreads thread creation and synchronization.

Windows

Section 4.4.2 discusses thread creation using the Windows API. Refer to that section for specific instructions on creating threads.

Windows Mutex Locks

Mutex locks are a type of dispatcher object, as described in Section 5.9.1. The following illustrates how to create a mutex lock using the `CreateMutex()` function:

```
#include <windows.h>

HANDLE Mutex;
Mutex = CreateMutex(NULL, FALSE, NULL);
```

The first parameter refers to a security attribute for the mutex lock. By setting this attribute to NULL, we disallow any children of the process creating this mutex lock to inherit the handle of the lock. The second parameter indicates whether the creator of the mutex lock is the lock's initial owner. Passing a value of FALSE indicates that the thread creating the mutex is not the initial owner. (We shall soon see how mutex locks are acquired.) The third parameter allows us to name the mutex. However, because we provide a value of NULL, we do not name the mutex. If successful, `CreateMutex()` returns a HANDLE to the mutex lock; otherwise, it returns NULL.

In Section 5.9.1, we identified dispatcher objects as being either *signaled* or *nonsignaled*. A signaled dispatcher object (such as a mutex lock) is available for ownership. Once it is acquired, it moves to the nonsignaled state. When it is released, it returns to signaled.

Mutex locks are acquired by invoking the `WaitForSingleObject()` function. The function is passed the HANDLE to the lock along with a flag indicating how long to wait. The following code demonstrates how the mutex lock created above can be acquired:

```
WaitForSingleObject(Mutex, INFINITE);
```

The parameter value INFINITE indicates that we will wait an infinite amount of time for the lock to become available. Other values could be used that would allow the calling thread to time out if the lock did not become available within a specified time. If the lock is in a signaled state, `WaitForSingleObject()` returns immediately, and the lock becomes nonsignaled. A lock is released (moves to the signaled state) by invoking `ReleaseMutex()` —for example, as follows:

```
ReleaseMutex(Mutex);
```

Windows Semaphores

Semaphores in the Windows API are dispatcher objects and thus use the same signaling mechanism as mutex locks. Semaphores are created as follows:

```
#include <windows.h>

HANDLE Sem;
Sem = CreateSemaphore(NULL, 1, 5, NULL);
```

The first and last parameters identify a security attribute and a name for the semaphore, similar to what we described for mutex locks. The second and third parameters indicate the initial value and maximum value of the semaphore. In this instance, the initial value of the semaphore is 1, and its maximum value is 5. If successful, CreateSemaphore() returns a HANDLE to the mutex lock; otherwise, it returns NULL.

Semaphores are acquired with the same WaitForSingleObject() function as mutex locks. We acquire the semaphore Sem created in this example by using the following statement:

```
WaitForSingleObject(Sem, INFINITE);
```

If the value of the semaphore is > 0, the semaphore is in the signaled state and thus is acquired by the calling thread. Otherwise, the calling thread blocks indefinitely—as we are specifying INFINITE—until the semaphore returns to the signaled state.

The equivalent of the signal() operation for Windows semaphores is the ReleaseSemaphore() function. This function is passed three parameters:

1. The HANDLE of the semaphore

2. How much to increase the value of the semaphore

3. A pointer to the previous value of the semaphore

We can use the following statement to increase Sem by 1:

```
ReleaseSemaphore(Sem, 1, NULL);
```

Both ReleaseSemaphore() and ReleaseMutex() return a nonzero value if successful and 0 otherwise.

Bibliographical Notes

The mutual-exclusion problem was first discussed in a classic paper by [Dijkstra (1965)]. Dekker's algorithm (Exercise 5.10)—the first correct software solution to the two-process mutual-exclusion problem—was developed by the Dutch mathematician T. Dekker. This algorithm also was discussed by [Dijkstra (1965)]. A simpler solution to the two-process mutual-exclusion problem has since been presented by [Peterson (1981)] (Figure 5.2). The semaphore concept was suggested by [Dijkstra (1965)].

The classic process-coordination problems that we have described are paradigms for a large class of concurrency-control problems. The bounded-buffer problem and the dining-philosophers problem were suggested in

[Dijkstra (1965)] and [Dijkstra (1971)]. The readers–writers problem was suggested by [Courtois et al. (1971)].

The critical-region concept was suggested by [Hoare (1972)] and by [Brinch-Hansen (1972)]. The monitor concept was developed by [Brinch-Hansen (1973)]. [Hoare (1974)] gave a complete description of the monitor.

Some details of the locking mechanisms used in Solaris were presented in [Mauro and McDougall (2007)]. As noted earlier, the locking mechanisms used by the kernel are implemented for user-level threads as well, so the same types of locks are available inside and outside the kernel. Details of Windows 2000 synchronization can be found in [Solomon and Russinovich (2000)]. [Love (2010)] describes synchronization in the Linux kernel.

Information on Pthreads programming can be found in [Lewis and Berg (1998)] and [Butenhof (1997)]. [Hart (2005)] describes thread synchronization using Windows. [Goetz et al. (2006)] present a detailed discussion of concurrent programming in Java as well as the `java.util.concurrent` package. [Breshears (2009)] and [Pacheco (2011)] provide detailed coverage of synchronization issues in relation to parallel programming. [Lu et al. (2008)] provide a study of concurrency bugs in real-world applications.

[Adl-Tabatabai et al. (2007)] discuss transactional memory. Details on using OpenMP can be found at http://openmp.org. Functional programming using Erlang and Scala is covered in [Armstrong (2007)] and [Odersky et al. (2006)] respectively.

[Dijkstra (1965)] was one of the first and most influential contributors in the deadlock area. A study of deadlock handling is provided in [Levine (2003)].

Bibliography

[Adl-Tabatabai et al. (2007)]   A.-R. Adl-Tabatabai, C. Kozyrakis, and B. Saha, "Unlocking Concurrency", *Queue*, Volume 4, Number 10 (2007), pages 24–33.

[Armstrong (2007)]   J. Armstrong, *Programming Erlang Software for a Concurrent World*, The Pragmatic Bookshelf (2007).

[Breshears (2009)]   C. Breshears, *The Art of Concurrency*, O'Reilly & Associates (2009).

[Brinch-Hansen (1972)]   P. Brinch-Hansen, "Structured Multiprogramming", *Communications of the ACM*, Volume 15, Number 7 (1972), pages 574–578.

[Brinch-Hansen (1973)]   P. Brinch-Hansen, *Operating System Principles*, Prentice Hall (1973).

[Butenhof (1997)]   D. Butenhof, *Programming with POSIX Threads*, Addison-Wesley (1997).

[Courtois et al. (1971)]   P. J. Courtois, F. Heymans, and D. L. Parnas, "Concurrent Control with 'Readers' and 'Writers'", *Communications of the ACM*, Volume 14, Number 10 (1971), pages 667–668.

[Dijkstra (1965)]   E. W. Dijkstra, "Cooperating Sequential Processes", Technical report, Technological University, Eindhoven, the Netherlands (1965).

[Dijkstra (1971)]   E. W. Dijkstra, "Hierarchical Ordering of Sequential Processes", *Acta Informatica*, Volume 1, Number 2 (1971), pages 115–138.

[Goetz et al. (2006)]   B. Goetz, T. Peirls, J. Bloch, J. Bowbeer, D. Holmes, and D. Lea, *Java Concurrency in Practice*, Addison-Wesley (2006).

[Hart (2005)]   J. M. Hart, *Windows System Programming*, Third Edition, Addison-Wesley (2005).

[Hoare (1972)]   C. A. R. Hoare, "Towards a Theory of Parallel Programming", in **[Hoare and Perrott 1972]** (1972), pages 61–71.

[Hoare (1974)]   C. A. R. Hoare, "Monitors: An Operating System Structuring Concept", *Communications of the ACM*, Volume 17, Number 10 (1974), pages 549–557.

[Kessels (1977)]   J. L. W. Kessels, "An Alternative to Event Queues for Synchronization in Monitors", *Communications of the ACM*, Volume 20, Number 7 (1977), pages 500–503.

[Levine (2003)]   G. Levine, "Defining Deadlock", *Operating Systems Review*, Volume 37, Number 1 (2003).

[Lewis and Berg (1998)]   B. Lewis and D. Berg, *Multithreaded Programming with Pthreads*, Sun Microsystems Press (1998).

[Love (2010)]   R. Love, *Linux Kernel Development*, Third Edition, Developer's Library (2010).

[Lu et al. (2008)]   S. Lu, S. Park, E. Seo, and Y. Zhou, "Learning from mistakes: a comprehensive study on real world concurrency bug characteristics", *SIGPLAN Notices*, Volume 43, Number 3 (2008), pages 329–339.

[Mauro and McDougall (2007)]   J. Mauro and R. McDougall, *Solaris Internals: Core Kernel Architecture*, Prentice Hall (2007).

[Odersky et al. (2006)]   M. Odersky, V. Cremet, I. Dragos, G. Dubochet, B. Emir, S. Mcdirmid, S. Micheloud, N. Mihaylov, M. Schinz, E. Stenman, L. Spoon, and M. Zenger, "An overview of the Scala programming language", *EPFL* (2006).

[Pacheco (2011)]   P. S. Pacheco, *An Introduction to Parallel Programming*, Morgan Kaufmann (2011).

[Peterson (1981)]   G. L. Peterson, "Myths About the Mutual Exclusion Problem", *Information Processing Letters*, Volume 12, Number 3 (1981).

[Solomon and Russinovich (2000)]   D. A. Solomon and M. E. Russinovich, *Inside Microsoft Windows 2000*, Third Edition, Microsoft Press (2000).

CHAPTER 6

CPU Scheduling

CPU scheduling is the basis of multiprogrammed operating systems. By switching the CPU among processes, the operating system can make the computer more productive. In this chapter, we introduce basic CPU-scheduling concepts and present several CPU-scheduling algorithms. We also consider the problem of selecting an algorithm for a particular system.

In Chapter 4, we introduced threads to the process model. On operating systems that support them, it is kernel-level threads—not processes—that are in fact being scheduled by the operating system. However, the terms "process scheduling" and "thread scheduling" are often used interchangeably. In this chapter, we use *process scheduling* when discussing general scheduling concepts and *thread scheduling* to refer to thread-specific ideas.

CHAPTER OBJECTIVES

- To introduce CPU scheduling, which is the basis for multiprogrammed operating systems.
- To describe various CPU-scheduling algorithms.
- To discuss evaluation criteria for selecting a CPU-scheduling algorithm for a particular system.
- To examine the scheduling algorithms of several operating systems.

6.1 Basic Concepts

In a single-processor system, only one process can run at a time. Others must wait until the CPU is free and can be rescheduled. The objective of multiprogramming is to have some process running at all times, to maximize CPU utilization. The idea is relatively simple. A process is executed until it must wait, typically for the completion of some I/O request. In a simple computer system, the CPU then just sits idle. All this waiting time is wasted; no useful work is accomplished. With multiprogramming, we try to use this time productively. Several processes are kept in memory at one time. When

Figure 6.1   Alternating sequence of CPU and I/O bursts.

one process has to wait, the operating system takes the CPU away from that process and gives the CPU to another process. This pattern continues. Every time one process has to wait, another process can take over use of the CPU.

Scheduling of this kind is a fundamental operating-system function. Almost all computer resources are scheduled before use. The CPU is, of course, one of the primary computer resources. Thus, its scheduling is central to operating-system design.

6.1.1   CPU–I/O Burst Cycle

The success of CPU scheduling depends on an observed property of processes: process execution consists of a cycle of CPU execution and I/O wait. Processes alternate between these two states. Process execution begins with a CPU burst That is followed by an I/O burst, which is followed by another CPU burst, then another I/O burst, and so on. Eventually, the final CPU burst ends with a system request to terminate execution (Figure 6.1).

The durations of CPU bursts have been measured extensively. Although they vary greatly from process to process and from computer to computer, they tend to have a frequency curve similar to that shown in Figure 6.2. The curve is generally characterized as exponential or hyperexponential, with a large number of short CPU bursts and a small number of long CPU bursts.

Figure 6.2 Histogram of CPU-burst durations.

An I/O-bound program typically has many short CPU bursts. A CPU-bound program might have a few long CPU bursts. This distribution can be important in the selection of an appropriate CPU-scheduling algorithm.

6.1.2 CPU Scheduler

Whenever the CPU becomes idle, the operating system must select one of the processes in the ready queue to be executed. The selection process is carried out by the **short-term scheduler**, or CPU scheduler. The scheduler selects a process from the processes in memory that are ready to execute and allocates the CPU to that process.

Note that the ready queue is not necessarily a first-in, first-out (FIFO) queue. As we shall see when we consider the various scheduling algorithms, a ready queue can be implemented as a FIFO queue, a priority queue, a tree, or simply an unordered linked list. Conceptually, however, all the processes in the ready queue are lined up waiting for a chance to run on the CPU. The records in the queues are generally process control blocks (PCBs) of the processes.

6.1.3 Preemptive Scheduling

CPU-scheduling decisions may take place under the following four circumstances:

1. When a process switches from the running state to the waiting state (for example, as the result of an I/O request or an invocation of `wait()` for the termination of a child process)

2. When a process switches from the running state to the ready state (for example, when an interrupt occurs)

3. When a process switches from the waiting state to the ready state (for example, at completion of I/O)

4. When a process terminates

For situations 1 and 4, there is no choice in terms of scheduling. A new process (if one exists in the ready queue) must be selected for execution. There is a choice, however, for situations 2 and 3.

When scheduling takes place only under circumstances 1 and 4, we say that the scheduling scheme is **nonpreemptive** or **cooperative**. Otherwise, it is **preemptive**. Under nonpreemptive scheduling, once the CPU has been allocated to a process, the process keeps the CPU until it releases the CPU either by terminating or by switching to the waiting state. This scheduling method was used by Microsoft Windows 3.x. Windows 95 introduced preemptive scheduling, and all subsequent versions of Windows operating systems have used preemptive scheduling. The Mac OS X operating system for the Macintosh also uses preemptive scheduling; previous versions of the Macintosh operating system relied on cooperative scheduling. Cooperative scheduling is the only method that can be used on certain hardware platforms, because it does not require the special hardware (for example, a timer) needed for preemptive scheduling.

Unfortunately, preemptive scheduling can result in race conditions when data are shared among several processes. Consider the case of two processes that share data. While one process is updating the data, it is preempted so that the second process can run. The second process then tries to read the data, which are in an inconsistent state. This issue was explored in detail in Chapter 5.

Preemption also affects the design of the operating-system kernel. During the processing of a system call, the kernel may be busy with an activity on behalf of a process. Such activities may involve changing important kernel data (for instance, I/O queues). What happens if the process is preempted in the middle of these changes and the kernel (or the device driver) needs to read or modify the same structure? Chaos ensues. Certain operating systems, including most versions of UNIX, deal with this problem by waiting either for a system call to complete or for an I/O block to take place before doing a context switch. This scheme ensures that the kernel structure is simple, since the kernel will not preempt a process while the kernel data structures are in an inconsistent state. Unfortunately, this kernel-execution model is a poor one for supporting real-time computing where tasks must complete execution within a given time frame. In Section 6.6, we explore scheduling demands of real-time systems.

Because interrupts can, by definition, occur at any time, and because they cannot always be ignored by the kernel, the sections of code affected by interrupts must be guarded from simultaneous use. The operating system needs to accept interrupts at almost all times. Otherwise, input might be lost or output overwritten. So that these sections of code are not accessed concurrently by several processes, they disable interrupts at entry and reenable interrupts at exit. It is important to note that sections of code that disable interrupts do not occur very often and typically contain few instructions.

6.1.4 Dispatcher

Another component involved in the CPU-scheduling function is the **dispatcher**. The dispatcher is the module that gives control of the CPU to the process selected by the short-term scheduler. This function involves the following:

- Switching context
- Switching to user mode
- Jumping to the proper location in the user program to restart that program

The dispatcher should be as fast as possible, since it is invoked during every process switch. The time it takes for the dispatcher to stop one process and start another running is known as the **dispatch latency**.

6.2 Scheduling Criteria

Different CPU-scheduling algorithms have different properties, and the choice of a particular algorithm may favor one class of processes over another. In choosing which algorithm to use in a particular situation, we must consider the properties of the various algorithms.

Many criteria have been suggested for comparing CPU-scheduling algorithms. Which characteristics are used for comparison can make a substantial difference in which algorithm is judged to be best. The criteria include the following:

- **CPU utilization**. We want to keep the CPU as busy as possible. Conceptually, CPU utilization can range from 0 to 100 percent. In a real system, it should range from 40 percent (for a lightly loaded system) to 90 percent (for a heavily loaded system).

- **Throughput**. If the CPU is busy executing processes, then work is being done. One measure of work is the number of processes that are completed per time unit, called **throughput**. For long processes, this rate may be one process per hour; for short transactions, it may be ten processes per second.

- **Turnaround time**. From the point of view of a particular process, the important criterion is how long it takes to execute that process. The interval from the time of submission of a process to the time of completion is the turnaround time. Turnaround time is the sum of the periods spent waiting to get into memory, waiting in the ready queue, executing on the CPU, and doing I/O.

- **Waiting time**. The CPU-scheduling algorithm does not affect the amount of time during which a process executes or does I/O. It affects only the amount of time that a process spends waiting in the ready queue. Waiting time is the sum of the periods spent waiting in the ready queue.

- **Response time**. In an interactive system, turnaround time may not be the best criterion. Often, a process can produce some output fairly early and can continue computing new results while previous results are being output to the user. Thus, another measure is the time from the submission of a request until the first response is produced. This measure, called response time, is the time it takes to start responding, not the time it takes to output the response. The turnaround time is generally limited by the speed of the output device.

It is desirable to maximize CPU utilization and throughput and to minimize turnaround time, waiting time, and response time. In most cases, we optimize the average measure. However, under some circumstances, we prefer to optimize the minimum or maximum values rather than the average. For example, to guarantee that all users get good service, we may want to minimize the maximum response time.

Investigators have suggested that, for interactive systems (such as desktop systems), it is more important to minimize the variance in the response time than to minimize the average response time. A system with reasonable and predictable response time may be considered more desirable than a system that is faster on the average but is highly variable. However, little work has been done on CPU-scheduling algorithms that minimize variance.

As we discuss various CPU-scheduling algorithms in the following section, we illustrate their operation. An accurate illustration should involve many processes, each a sequence of several hundred CPU bursts and I/O bursts. For simplicity, though, we consider only one CPU burst (in milliseconds) per process in our examples. Our measure of comparison is the average waiting time. More elaborate evaluation mechanisms are discussed in Section 6.8.

6.3 Scheduling Algorithms

CPU scheduling deals with the problem of deciding which of the processes in the ready queue is to be allocated the CPU. There are many different CPU-scheduling algorithms. In this section, we describe several of them.

6.3.1 First-Come, First-Served Scheduling

By far the simplest CPU-scheduling algorithm is the **first-come, first-served (FCFS)** scheduling algorithm. With this scheme, the process that requests the CPU first is allocated the CPU first. The implementation of the FCFS policy is easily managed with a FIFO queue. When a process enters the ready queue, its PCB is linked onto the tail of the queue. When the CPU is free, it is allocated to the process at the head of the queue. The running process is then removed from the queue. The code for FCFS scheduling is simple to write and understand.

On the negative side, the average waiting time under the FCFS policy is often quite long. Consider the following set of processes that arrive at time 0, with the length of the CPU burst given in milliseconds:

Process	Burst Time
P_1	24
P_2	3
P_3	3

If the processes arrive in the order P_1, P_2, P_3, and are served in FCFS order, we get the result shown in the following Gantt chart, which is a bar chart that illustrates a particular schedule, including the start and finish times of each of the participating processes:

The waiting time is 0 milliseconds for process P_1, 24 milliseconds for process P_2, and 27 milliseconds for process P_3. Thus, the average waiting time is (0 + 24 + 27)/3 = 17 milliseconds. If the processes arrive in the order P_2, P_3, P_1, however, the results will be as shown in the following Gantt chart:

The average waiting time is now (6 + 0 + 3)/3 = 3 milliseconds. This reduction is substantial. Thus, the average waiting time under an FCFS policy is generally not minimal and may vary substantially if the processes' CPU burst times vary greatly.

In addition, consider the performance of FCFS scheduling in a dynamic situation. Assume we have one CPU-bound process and many I/O-bound processes. As the processes flow around the system, the following scenario may result. The CPU-bound process will get and hold the CPU. During this time, all the other processes will finish their I/O and will move into the ready queue, waiting for the CPU. While the processes wait in the ready queue, the I/O devices are idle. Eventually, the CPU-bound process finishes its CPU burst and moves to an I/O device. All the I/O-bound processes, which have short CPU bursts, execute quickly and move back to the I/O queues. At this point, the CPU sits idle. The CPU-bound process will then move back to the ready queue and be allocated the CPU. Again, all the I/O processes end up waiting in the ready queue until the CPU-bound process is done. There is a convoy effect as all the other processes wait for the one big process to get off the CPU. This effect results in lower CPU and device utilization than might be possible if the shorter processes were allowed to go first.

Note also that the FCFS scheduling algorithm is nonpreemptive. Once the CPU has been allocated to a process, that process keeps the CPU until it releases the CPU, either by terminating or by requesting I/O. The FCFS algorithm is thus particularly troublesome for time-sharing systems, where it is important that each user get a share of the CPU at regular intervals. It would be disastrous to allow one process to keep the CPU for an extended period.

6.3.2 Shortest-Job-First Scheduling

A different approach to CPU scheduling is the shortest-job-first (SJF) scheduling algorithm. This algorithm associates with each process the length of the process's next CPU burst. When the CPU is available, it is assigned to the process that has the smallest next CPU burst. If the next CPU bursts of two processes are the same, FCFS scheduling is used to break the tie. Note that a more appropriate term for this scheduling method would be the *shortest-next-CPU-burst* algorithm, because scheduling depends on the length of the next CPU burst of a process, rather than its total length. We use the term SJF because most people and textbooks use this term to refer to this type of scheduling.

As an example of SJF scheduling, consider the following set of processes, with the length of the CPU burst given in milliseconds:

Process	Burst Time
P_1	6
P_2	8
P_3	7
P_4	3

Using SJF scheduling, we would schedule these processes according to the following Gantt chart:

The waiting time is 3 milliseconds for process P_1, 16 milliseconds for process P_2, 9 milliseconds for process P_3, and 0 milliseconds for process P_4. Thus, the average waiting time is $(3 + 16 + 9 + 0)/4 = 7$ milliseconds. By comparison, if we were using the FCFS scheduling scheme, the average waiting time would be 10.25 milliseconds.

The SJF scheduling algorithm is provably optimal, in that it gives the minimum average waiting time for a given set of processes. Moving a short process before a long one decreases the waiting time of the short process more than it increases the waiting time of the long process. Consequently, the average waiting time decreases.

The real difficulty with the SJF algorithm is knowing the length of the next CPU request. For long-term (job) scheduling in a batch system, we can use the process time limit that a user specifies when he submits the job. In this situation, users are motivated to estimate the process time limit accurately, since a lower value may mean faster response but too low a value will cause a time-limit-exceeded error and require resubmission. SJF scheduling is used frequently in long-term scheduling.

Although the SJF algorithm is optimal, it cannot be implemented at the level of short-term CPU scheduling. With short-term scheduling, there is no way to know the length of the next CPU burst. One approach to this problem is to try to approximate SJF scheduling. We may not know the length of the next CPU burst, but we may be able to predict its value. We expect that the next CPU burst will be similar in length to the previous ones. By computing an approximation of the length of the next CPU burst, we can pick the process with the shortest predicted CPU burst.

The next CPU burst is generally predicted as an *exponential average* of the measured lengths of previous CPU bursts. We can define the exponential

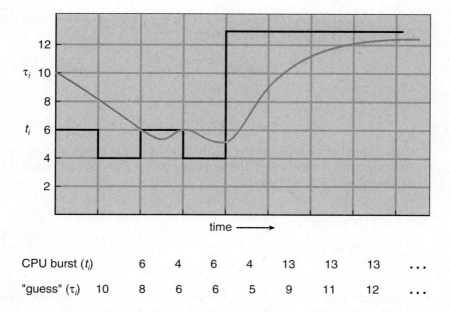

CPU burst (t_i)		6	4	6	4	13	13	13	...
"guess" (τ_i)	10	8	6	6	5	9	11	12	...

Figure 6.3 Prediction of the length of the next CPU burst.

average with the following formula. Let t_n be the length of the nth CPU burst, and let τ_{n+1} be our predicted value for the next CPU burst. Then, for α, $0 \le \alpha \le 1$, define

$$\tau_{n+1} = \alpha\, t_n + (1 - \alpha)\tau_n.$$

The value of t_n contains our most recent information, while τ_n stores the past history. The parameter α controls the relative weight of recent and past history in our prediction. If $\alpha = 0$, then $\tau_{n+1} = \tau_n$, and recent history has no effect (current conditions are assumed to be transient). If $\alpha = 1$, then $\tau_{n+1} = t_n$, and only the most recent CPU burst matters (history is assumed to be old and irrelevant). More commonly, $\alpha = 1/2$, so recent history and past history are equally weighted. The initial τ_0 can be defined as a constant or as an overall system average. Figure 6.3 shows an exponential average with $\alpha = 1/2$ and $\tau_0 = 10$.

To understand the behavior of the exponential average, we can expand the formula for τ_{n+1} by substituting for τ_n to find

$$\tau_{n+1} = \alpha t_n + (1 - \alpha)\alpha t_{n-1} + \cdots + (1 - \alpha)^j \alpha t_{n-j} + \cdots + (1 - \alpha)^{n+1}\tau_0.$$

Typically, α is less than 1. As a result, $(1 - \alpha)$ is also less than 1, and each successive term has less weight than its predecessor.

The SJF algorithm can be either preemptive or nonpreemptive. The choice arises when a new process arrives at the ready queue while a previous process is still executing. The next CPU burst of the newly arrived process may be shorter than what is left of the currently executing process. A preemptive SJF algorithm will preempt the currently executing process, whereas a nonpreemptive SJF algorithm will allow the currently running process to finish its CPU burst. Preemptive SJF scheduling is sometimes called shortest-remaining-time-first scheduling.

As an example, consider the following four processes, with the length of the CPU burst given in milliseconds:

Process	Arrival Time	Burst Time
P_1	0	8
P_2	1	4
P_3	2	9
P_4	3	5

If the processes arrive at the ready queue at the times shown and need the indicated burst times, then the resulting preemptive SJF schedule is as depicted in the following Gantt chart:

Process P_1 is started at time 0, since it is the only process in the queue. Process P_2 arrives at time 1. The remaining time for process P_1 (7 milliseconds) is larger than the time required by process P_2 (4 milliseconds), so process P_1 is preempted, and process P_2 is scheduled. The average waiting time for this example is $[(10 - 1) + (1 - 1) + (17 - 2) + (5 - 3)]/4 = 26/4 = 6.5$ milliseconds. Nonpreemptive SJF scheduling would result in an average waiting time of 7.75 milliseconds.

6.3.3 Priority Scheduling

The SJF algorithm is a special case of the general priority-scheduling algorithm. A priority is associated with each process, and the CPU is allocated to the process with the highest priority. Equal-priority processes are scheduled in FCFS order. An SJF algorithm is simply a priority algorithm where the priority (p) is the inverse of the (predicted) next CPU burst. The larger the CPU burst, the lower the priority, and vice versa.

Note that we discuss scheduling in terms of *high* priority and *low* priority. Priorities are generally indicated by some fixed range of numbers, such as 0 to 7 or 0 to 4,095. However, there is no general agreement on whether 0 is the highest or lowest priority. Some systems use low numbers to represent low priority; others use low numbers for high priority. This difference can lead to confusion. In this text, we assume that low numbers represent high priority.

As an example, consider the following set of processes, assumed to have arrived at time 0 in the order P_1, P_2, $\cdots$, P_5, with the length of the CPU burst given in milliseconds:

Process	Burst Time	Priority
P_1	10	3
P_2	1	1
P_3	2	4
P_4	1	5
P_5	5	2

Using priority scheduling, we would schedule these processes according to the following Gantt chart:

The average waiting time is 8.2 milliseconds.

Priorities can be defined either internally or externally. Internally defined priorities use some measurable quantity or quantities to compute the priority of a process. For example, time limits, memory requirements, the number of open files, and the ratio of average I/O burst to average CPU burst have been used in computing priorities. External priorities are set by criteria outside the operating system, such as the importance of the process, the type and amount of funds being paid for computer use, the department sponsoring the work, and other, often political, factors.

Priority scheduling can be either preemptive or nonpreemptive. When a process arrives at the ready queue, its priority is compared with the priority of the currently running process. A preemptive priority scheduling algorithm will preempt the CPU if the priority of the newly arrived process is higher than the priority of the currently running process. A nonpreemptive priority scheduling algorithm will simply put the new process at the head of the ready queue.

A major problem with priority scheduling algorithms is **indefinite blocking**, or **starvation**. A process that is ready to run but waiting for the CPU can be considered blocked. A priority scheduling algorithm can leave some low-priority processes waiting indefinitely. In a heavily loaded computer system, a steady stream of higher-priority processes can prevent a low-priority process from ever getting the CPU. Generally, one of two things will happen. Either the process will eventually be run (at 2 A.M. Sunday, when the system is finally lightly loaded), or the computer system will eventually crash and lose all unfinished low-priority processes. (Rumor has it that when they shut down the IBM 7094 at MIT in 1973, they found a low-priority process that had been submitted in 1967 and had not yet been run.)

A solution to the problem of indefinite blockage of low-priority processes is **aging**. Aging involves gradually increasing the priority of processes that wait in the system for a long time. For example, if priorities range from 127 (low) to 0 (high), we could increase the priority of a waiting process by 1 every 15 minutes. Eventually, even a process with an initial priority of 127 would have the highest priority in the system and would be executed. In fact, it would take no more than 32 hours for a priority-127 process to age to a priority-0 process.

6.3.4 Round-Robin Scheduling

The **round-robin (RR)** scheduling algorithm is designed especially for time-sharing systems. It is similar to FCFS scheduling, but preemption is added to enable the system to switch between processes. A small unit of time, called a **time quantum** or **time slice**, is defined. A time quantum is generally from 10 to 100 milliseconds in length. The ready queue is treated as a circular queue.

The CPU scheduler goes around the ready queue, allocating the CPU to each process for a time interval of up to 1 time quantum.

To implement RR scheduling, we again treat the ready queue as a FIFO queue of processes. New processes are added to the tail of the ready queue. The CPU scheduler picks the first process from the ready queue, sets a timer to interrupt after 1 time quantum, and dispatches the process.

One of two things will then happen. The process may have a CPU burst of less than 1 time quantum. In this case, the process itself will release the CPU voluntarily. The scheduler will then proceed to the next process in the ready queue. If the CPU burst of the currently running process is longer than 1 time quantum, the timer will go off and will cause an interrupt to the operating system. A context switch will be executed, and the process will be put at the tail of the ready queue. The CPU scheduler will then select the next process in the ready queue.

The average waiting time under the RR policy is often long. Consider the following set of processes that arrive at time 0, with the length of the CPU burst given in milliseconds:

Process	Burst Time
P_1	24
P_2	3
P_3	3

If we use a time quantum of 4 milliseconds, then process P_1 gets the first 4 milliseconds. Since it requires another 20 milliseconds, it is preempted after the first time quantum, and the CPU is given to the next process in the queue, process P_2. Process P_2 does not need 4 milliseconds, so it quits before its time quantum expires. The CPU is then given to the next process, process P_3. Once each process has received 1 time quantum, the CPU is returned to process P_1 for an additional time quantum. The resulting RR schedule is as follows:

Let's calculate the average waiting time for this schedule. P_1 waits for 6 milliseconds (10 - 4), P_2 waits for 4 milliseconds, and P_3 waits for 7 milliseconds. Thus, the average waiting time is 17/3 = 5.66 milliseconds.

In the RR scheduling algorithm, no process is allocated the CPU for more than 1 time quantum in a row (unless it is the only runnable process). If a process's CPU burst exceeds 1 time quantum, that process is preempted and is put back in the ready queue. The RR scheduling algorithm is thus preemptive.

If there are n processes in the ready queue and the time quantum is q, then each process gets $1/n$ of the CPU time in chunks of at most q time units. Each process must wait no longer than $(n - 1) \times q$ time units until its next time quantum. For example, with five processes and a time quantum of 20 milliseconds, each process will get up to 20 milliseconds every 100 milliseconds.

The performance of the RR algorithm depends heavily on the size of the time quantum. At one extreme, if the time quantum is extremely large, the RR policy

Figure 6.4   How a smaller time quantum increases context switches.

is the same as the FCFS policy. In contrast, if the time quantum is extremely small (say, 1 millisecond), the RR approach can result in a large number of context switches. Assume, for example, that we have only one process of 10 time units. If the quantum is 12 time units, the process finishes in less than 1 time quantum, with no overhead. If the quantum is 6 time units, however, the process requires 2 quanta, resulting in a context switch. If the time quantum is 1 time unit, then nine context switches will occur, slowing the execution of the process accordingly (Figure 6.4).

Thus, we want the time quantum to be large with respect to the context-switch time. If the context-switch time is approximately 10 percent of the time quantum, then about 10 percent of the CPU time will be spent in context switching. In practice, most modern systems have time quanta ranging from 10 to 100 milliseconds. The time required for a context switch is typically less than 10 microseconds; thus, the context-switch time is a small fraction of the time quantum.

Turnaround time also depends on the size of the time quantum. As we can see from Figure 6.5, the average turnaround time of a set of processes does not necessarily improve as the time-quantum size increases. In general, the average turnaround time can be improved if most processes finish their next CPU burst in a single time quantum. For example, given three processes of 10 time units each and a quantum of 1 time unit, the average turnaround time is 29. If the time quantum is 10, however, the average turnaround time drops to 20. If context-switch time is added in, the average turnaround time increases even more for a smaller time quantum, since more context switches are required.

Although the time quantum should be large compared with the context-switch time, it should not be too large. As we pointed out earlier, if the time quantum is too large, RR scheduling degenerates to an FCFS policy. A rule of thumb is that 80 percent of the CPU bursts should be shorter than the time quantum.

6.3.5   Multilevel Queue Scheduling

Another class of scheduling algorithms has been created for situations in which processes are easily classified into different groups. For example, a

process	time
P_1	6
P_2	3
P_3	1
P_4	7

Figure 6.5   How turnaround time varies with the time quantum.

common division is made between **foreground** (interactive) processes and **background** (batch) processes. These two types of processes have different response-time requirements and so may have different scheduling needs. In addition, foreground processes may have priority (externally defined) over background processes.

A **multilevel queue** scheduling algorithm partitions the ready queue into several separate queues (Figure 6.6). The processes are permanently assigned to one queue, generally based on some property of the process, such as memory size, process priority, or process type. Each queue has its own scheduling algorithm. For example, separate queues might be used for foreground and background processes. The foreground queue might be scheduled by an RR algorithm, while the background queue is scheduled by an FCFS algorithm.

In addition, there must be scheduling among the queues, which is commonly implemented as fixed-priority preemptive scheduling. For example, the foreground queue may have absolute priority over the background queue.

Let's look at an example of a multilevel queue scheduling algorithm with five queues, listed below in order of priority:

1. System processes
2. Interactive processes
3. Interactive editing processes
4. Batch processes
5. Student processes

highest priority

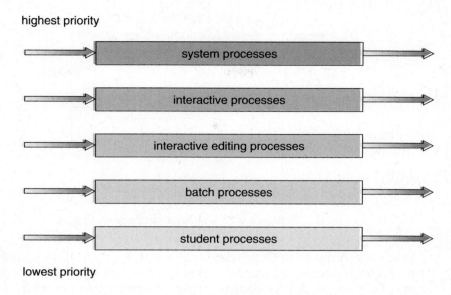

lowest priority

Figure 6.6 Multilevel queue scheduling.

Each queue has absolute priority over lower-priority queues. No process in the batch queue, for example, could run unless the queues for system processes, interactive processes, and interactive editing processes were all empty. If an interactive editing process entered the ready queue while a batch process was running, the batch process would be preempted.

Another possibility is to time-slice among the queues. Here, each queue gets a certain portion of the CPU time, which it can then schedule among its various processes. For instance, in the foreground–background queue example, the foreground queue can be given 80 percent of the CPU time for RR scheduling among its processes, while the background queue receives 20 percent of the CPU to give to its processes on an FCFS basis.

6.3.6 Multilevel Feedback Queue Scheduling

Normally, when the multilevel queue scheduling algorithm is used, processes are permanently assigned to a queue when they enter the system. If there are separate queues for foreground and background processes, for example, processes do not move from one queue to the other, since processes do not change their foreground or background nature. This setup has the advantage of low scheduling overhead, but it is inflexible.

The multilevel feedback queue scheduling algorithm, in contrast, allows a process to move between queues. The idea is to separate processes according to the characteristics of their CPU bursts. If a process uses too much CPU time, it will be moved to a lower-priority queue. This scheme leaves I/O-bound and interactive processes in the higher-priority queues. In addition, a process that waits too long in a lower-priority queue may be moved to a higher-priority queue. This form of aging prevents starvation.

For example, consider a multilevel feedback queue scheduler with three queues, numbered from 0 to 2 (Figure 6.7). The scheduler first executes all

Figure 6.7   Multilevel feedback queues.

processes in queue 0. Only when queue 0 is empty will it execute processes in queue 1. Similarly, processes in queue 2 will be executed only if queues 0 and 1 are empty. A process that arrives for queue 1 will preempt a process in queue 2. A process in queue 1 will in turn be preempted by a process arriving for queue 0.

A process entering the ready queue is put in queue 0. A process in queue 0 is given a time quantum of 8 milliseconds. If it does not finish within this time, it is moved to the tail of queue 1. If queue 0 is empty, the process at the head of queue 1 is given a quantum of 16 milliseconds. If it does not complete, it is preempted and is put into queue 2. Processes in queue 2 are run on an FCFS basis but are run only when queues 0 and 1 are empty.

This scheduling algorithm gives highest priority to any process with a CPU burst of 8 milliseconds or less. Such a process will quickly get the CPU, finish its CPU burst, and go off to its next I/O burst. Processes that need more than 8 but less than 24 milliseconds are also served quickly, although with lower priority than shorter processes. Long processes automatically sink to queue 2 and are served in FCFS order with any CPU cycles left over from queues 0 and 1.

In general, a multilevel feedback queue scheduler is defined by the following parameters:

- The number of queues
- The scheduling algorithm for each queue
- The method used to determine when to upgrade a process to a higher-priority queue
- The method used to determine when to demote a process to a lower-priority queue
- The method used to determine which queue a process will enter when that process needs service

The definition of a multilevel feedback queue scheduler makes it the most general CPU-scheduling algorithm. It can be configured to match a specific system under design. Unfortunately, it is also the most complex algorithm, since defining the best scheduler requires some means by which to select values for all the parameters.

6.4 Thread Scheduling

In Chapter 4, we introduced threads to the process model, distinguishing between *user-level* and *kernel-level* threads. On operating systems that support them, it is kernel-level threads—not processes—that are being scheduled by the operating system. User-level threads are managed by a thread library, and the kernel is unaware of them. To run on a CPU, user-level threads must ultimately be mapped to an associated kernel-level thread, although this mapping may be indirect and may use a lightweight process (LWP). In this section, we explore scheduling issues involving user-level and kernel-level threads and offer specific examples of scheduling for Pthreads.

6.4.1 Contention Scope

One distinction between user-level and kernel-level threads lies in how they are scheduled. On systems implementing the many-to-one (Section 4.3.1) and many-to-many (Section 4.3.3) models, the thread library schedules user-level threads to run on an available LWP. This scheme is known as **process-contention scope** (PCS), since competition for the CPU takes place among threads belonging to the same process. (When we say the thread library *schedules* user threads onto available LWPs, we do not mean that the threads are actually running on a CPU. That would require the operating system to schedule the kernel thread onto a physical CPU.) To decide which kernel-level thread to schedule onto a CPU, the kernel uses **system-contention scope** (SCS). Competition for the CPU with SCS scheduling takes place among all threads in the system. Systems using the one-to-one model (Section 4.3.2), such as Windows, Linux, and Solaris, schedule threads using only SCS.

Typically, PCS is done according to priority—the scheduler selects the runnable thread with the highest priority to run. User-level thread priorities are set by the programmer and are not adjusted by the thread library, although some thread libraries may allow the programmer to change the priority of a thread. It is important to note that PCS will typically preempt the thread currently running in favor of a higher-priority thread; however, there is no guarantee of time slicing (Section 6.3.4) among threads of equal priority.

6.4.2 Pthread Scheduling

We provided a sample POSIX Pthread program in Section 4.4.1, along with an introduction to thread creation with Pthreads. Now, we highlight the POSIX Pthread API that allows specifying PCS or SCS during thread creation. Pthreads identifies the following contention scope values:

- PTHREAD_SCOPE_PROCESS schedules threads using PCS scheduling.
- PTHREAD_SCOPE_SYSTEM schedules threads using SCS scheduling.

On systems implementing the many-to-many model, the PTHREAD_SCOPE_PROCESS policy schedules user-level threads onto available LWPs. The number of LWPs is maintained by the thread library, perhaps using scheduler activations (Section 4.6.5). The PTHREAD_SCOPE_SYSTEM scheduling policy will create and bind an LWP for each user-level thread on many-to-many systems, effectively mapping threads using the one-to-one policy.

The Pthread IPC (Interprocess Communication) provides two functions for getting—and setting—the contention scope policy:

- `pthread_attr_setscope(pthread_attr_t *attr, int scope)`
- `pthread_attr_getscope(pthread_attr_t *attr, int *scope)`

The first parameter for both functions contains a pointer to the attribute set for the thread. The second parameter for the `pthread_attr_setscope()` function is passed either the PTHREAD_SCOPE_SYSTEM or the PTHREAD_SCOPE_PROCESS value, indicating how the contention scope is to be set. In the case of `pthread_attr_getscope()`, this second parameter contains a pointer to an `int` value that is set to the current value of the contention scope. If an error occurs, each of these functions returns a nonzero value.

In Figure 6.8, we illustrate a Pthread scheduling API. The program first determines the existing contention scope and sets it to PTHREAD_SCOPE_SYSTEM. It then creates five separate threads that will run using the SCS scheduling policy. Note that on some systems, only certain contention scope values are allowed. For example, Linux and Mac OS X systems allow only PTHREAD_SCOPE_SYSTEM.

6.5 Multiple-Processor Scheduling

Our discussion thus far has focused on the problems of scheduling the CPU in a system with a single processor. If multiple CPUs are available, load sharing becomes possible—but scheduling problems become correspondingly more complex. Many possibilities have been tried; and as we saw with single-processor CPU scheduling, there is no one best solution.

Here, we discuss several concerns in multiprocessor scheduling. We concentrate on systems in which the processors are identical—homogeneous —in terms of their functionality. We can then use any available processor to run any process in the queue. Note, however, that even with homogeneous multiprocessors, there are sometimes limitations on scheduling. Consider a system with an I/O device attached to a private bus of one processor. Processes that wish to use that device must be scheduled to run on that processor.

6.5.1 Approaches to Multiple-Processor Scheduling

One approach to CPU scheduling in a multiprocessor system has all scheduling decisions, I/O processing, and other system activities handled by a single processor—the master server. The other processors execute only user code. This asymmetric multiprocessing is simple because only one processor accesses the system data structures, reducing the need for data sharing.

```c
#include <pthread.h>
#include <stdio.h>
#define NUM_THREADS 5

int main(int argc, char *argv[])
{
  int i, scope;
  pthread_t tid[NUM_THREADS];
  pthread_attr_t attr;

  /* get the default attributes */
  pthread_attr_init(&attr);

  /* first inquire on the current scope */
  if (pthread_attr_getscope(&attr, &scope) != 0)
    fprintf(stderr, "Unable to get scheduling scope\n");
  else {
    if (scope == PTHREAD_SCOPE_PROCESS)
      printf("PTHREAD_SCOPE_PROCESS");
    else if (scope == PTHREAD_SCOPE_SYSTEM)
      printf("PTHREAD_SCOPE_SYSTEM");
    else
      fprintf(stderr, "Illegal scope value.\n");
  }

  /* set the scheduling algorithm to PCS or SCS */
  pthread_attr_setscope(&attr, PTHREAD_SCOPE_SYSTEM);

  /* create the threads */
  for (i = 0; i < NUM_THREADS; i++)
    pthread_create(&tid[i],&attr,runner,NULL);

  /* now join on each thread */
  for (i = 0; i < NUM_THREADS; i++)
    pthread_join(tid[i], NULL);
}

/* Each thread will begin control in this function */
void *runner(void *param)
{
  /* do some work ... */

  pthread_exit(0);
}
```

Figure 6.8   Pthread scheduling API.

A second approach uses **symmetric multiprocessing (SMP)**, where each processor is self-scheduling. All processes may be in a common ready queue, or each processor may have its own private queue of ready processes. Regardless, scheduling proceeds by having the scheduler for each processor examine the ready queue and select a process to execute. As we saw in Chapter 5, if we have multiple processors trying to access and update a common data structure, the scheduler must be programmed carefully. We must ensure that two separate processors do not choose to schedule the same process and that processes are not lost from the queue. Virtually all modern operating systems support SMP, including Windows, Linux, and Mac OS X. In the remainder of this section, we discuss issues concerning SMP systems.

6.5.2 Processor Affinity

Consider what happens to cache memory when a process has been running on a specific processor. The data most recently accessed by the process populate the cache for the processor. As a result, successive memory accesses by the process are often satisfied in cache memory. Now consider what happens if the process migrates to another processor. The contents of cache memory must be invalidated for the first processor, and the cache for the second processor must be repopulated. Because of the high cost of invalidating and repopulating caches, most SMP systems try to avoid migration of processes from one processor to another and instead attempt to keep a process running on the same processor. This is known as **processor affinity**—that is, a process has an affinity for the processor on which it is currently running.

Processor affinity takes several forms. When an operating system has a policy of attempting to keep a process running on the same processor—but not guaranteeing that it will do so—we have a situation known as **soft affinity**. Here, the operating system will attempt to keep a process on a single processor, but it is possible for a process to migrate between processors. In contrast, some systems provide system calls that support **hard affinity**, thereby allowing a process to specify a subset of processors on which it may run. Many systems provide both soft and hard affinity. For example, Linux implements soft affinity, but it also provides the sched_setaffinity() system call, which supports hard affinity.

The main-memory architecture of a system can affect processor affinity issues. Figure 6.9 illustrates an architecture featuring non-uniform memory access (NUMA), in which a CPU has faster access to some parts of main memory than to other parts. Typically, this occurs in systems containing combined CPU and memory boards. The CPUs on a board can access the memory on that board faster than they can access memory on other boards in the system. If the operating system's CPU scheduler and memory-placement algorithms work together, then a process that is assigned affinity to a particular CPU can be allocated memory on the board where that CPU resides. This example also shows that operating systems are frequently not as cleanly defined and implemented as described in operating-system textbooks. Rather, the "solid lines" between sections of an operating system are frequently only "dotted lines," with algorithms creating connections in ways aimed at optimizing performance and reliability.

6.5.3 Load Balancing

On SMP systems, it is important to keep the workload balanced among all processors to fully utilize the benefits of having more than one processor.

Figure 6.9 NUMA and CPU scheduling.

Otherwise, one or more processors may sit idle while other processors have high workloads, along with lists of processes awaiting the CPU. **Load balancing** attempts to keep the workload evenly distributed across all processors in an SMP system. It is important to note that load balancing is typically necessary only on systems where each processor has its own private queue of eligible processes to execute. On systems with a common run queue, load balancing is often unnecessary, because once a processor becomes idle, it immediately extracts a runnable process from the common run queue. It is also important to note, however, that in most contemporary operating systems supporting SMP, each processor does have a private queue of eligible processes.

There are two general approaches to load balancing: **push migration** and **pull migration**. With push migration, a specific task periodically checks the load on each processor and—if it finds an imbalance—evenly distributes the load by moving (or pushing) processes from overloaded to idle or less-busy processors. Pull migration occurs when an idle processor pulls a waiting task from a busy processor. Push and pull migration need not be mutually exclusive and are in fact often implemented in parallel on load-balancing systems. For example, the Linux scheduler (described in Section 6.7.1) and the ULE scheduler available for FreeBSD systems implement both techniques.

Interestingly, load balancing often counteracts the benefits of processor affinity, discussed in Section 6.5.2. That is, the benefit of keeping a process running on the same processor is that the process can take advantage of its data being in that processor's cache memory. Either pulling or pushing a process from one processor to another removes this benefit. As is often the case in systems engineering, there is no absolute rule concerning what policy is best. Thus, in some systems, an idle processor always pulls a process from a non-idle processor. In other systems, processes are moved only if the imbalance exceeds a certain threshold.

6.5.4 Multicore Processors

Traditionally, SMP systems have allowed several threads to run concurrently by providing multiple physical processors. However, a recent practice in computer

Figure 6.10   Memory stall.

hardware has been to place multiple processor cores on the same physical chip, resulting in a **multicore processor**. Each core maintains its architectural state and thus appears to the operating system to be a separate physical processor. SMP systems that use multicore processors are faster and consume less power than systems in which each processor has its own physical chip.

Multicore processors may complicate scheduling issues. Let's consider how this can happen. Researchers have discovered that when a processor accesses memory, it spends a significant amount of time waiting for the data to become available. This situation, known as a **memory stall**, may occur for various reasons, such as a cache miss (accessing data that are not in cache memory). Figure 6.10 illustrates a memory stall. In this scenario, the processor can spend up to 50 percent of its time waiting for data to become available from memory. To remedy this situation, many recent hardware designs have implemented multithreaded processor cores in which two (or more) hardware threads are assigned to each core. That way, if one thread stalls while waiting for memory, the core can switch to another thread. Figure 6.11 illustrates a dual-threaded processor core on which the execution of thread 0 and the execution of thread 1 are interleaved. From an operating-system perspective, each hardware thread appears as a logical processor that is available to run a software thread. Thus, on a dual-threaded, dual-core system, four logical processors are presented to the operating system. The UltraSPARC T3 CPU has sixteen cores per chip and eight hardware threads per core. From the perspective of the operating system, there appear to be 128 logical processors.

In general, there are two ways to multithread a processing core: **coarse-grained** and **fine-grained** multithreading. With coarse-grained multithreading, a thread executes on a processor until a long-latency event such as a memory stall occurs. Because of the delay caused by the long-latency event, the processor must switch to another thread to begin execution. However, the cost of switching between threads is high, since the instruction pipeline must

Figure 6.11   Multithreaded multicore system.

be flushed before the other thread can begin execution on the processor core. Once this new thread begins execution, it begins filling the pipeline with its instructions. Fine-grained (or interleaved) multithreading switches between threads at a much finer level of granularity—typically at the boundary of an instruction cycle. However, the architectural design of fine-grained systems includes logic for thread switching. As a result, the cost of switching between threads is small.

Notice that a multithreaded multicore processor actually requires two different levels of scheduling. On one level are the scheduling decisions that must be made by the operating system as it chooses which software thread to run on each hardware thread (logical processor). For this level of scheduling, the operating system may choose any scheduling algorithm, such as those described in Section 6.3. A second level of scheduling specifies how each core decides which hardware thread to run. There are several strategies to adopt in this situation. The UltraSPARC T3, mentioned earlier, uses a simple round-robin algorithm to schedule the eight hardware threads to each core. Another example, the Intel Itanium, is a dual-core processor with two hardware-managed threads per core. Assigned to each hardware thread is a dynamic *urgency* value ranging from 0 to 7, with 0 representing the lowest urgency and 7 the highest. The Itanium identifies five different events that may trigger a thread switch. When one of these events occurs, the thread-switching logic compares the urgency of the two threads and selects the thread with the highest urgency value to execute on the processor core.

6.6 Real-Time CPU Scheduling

CPU scheduling for real-time operating systems involves special issues. In general, we can distinguish between soft real-time systems and hard real-time systems. Soft real-time systems provide no guarantee as to when a critical real-time process will be scheduled. They guarantee only that the process will be given preference over noncritical processes. Hard real-time systems have stricter requirements. A task must be serviced by its deadline; service after the deadline has expired is the same as no service at all. In this section, we explore several issues related to process scheduling in both soft and hard real-time operating systems.

6.6.1 Minimizing Latency

Consider the event-driven nature of a real-time system. The system is typically waiting for an event in real time to occur. Events may arise either in software —as when a timer expires—or in hardware—as when a remote-controlled vehicle detects that it is approaching an obstruction. When an event occurs, the system must respond to and service it as quickly as possible. We refer to event latency as the amount of time that elapses from when an event occurs to when it is serviced (Figure 6.12).

Usually, different events have different latency requirements. For example, the latency requirement for an antilock brake system might be 3 to 5 milliseconds. That is, from the time a wheel first detects that it is sliding, the system controlling the antilock brakes has 3 to 5 milliseconds to respond to and control

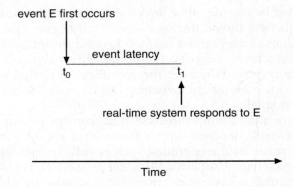

Figure 6.12   Event latency.

the situation. Any response that takes longer might result in the automobile's veering out of control. In contrast, an embedded system controlling radar in an airliner might tolerate a latency period of several seconds.

Two types of latencies affect the performance of real-time systems:

1. Interrupt latency

2. Dispatch latency

Interrupt latency refers to the period of time from the arrival of an interrupt at the CPU to the start of the routine that services the interrupt. When an interrupt occurs, the operating system must first complete the instruction it is executing and determine the type of interrupt that occurred. It must then save the state of the current process before servicing the interrupt using the specific interrupt service routine (ISR). The total time required to perform these tasks is the interrupt latency (Figure 6.13). Obviously, it is crucial for real-

Figure 6.13   Interrupt latency.

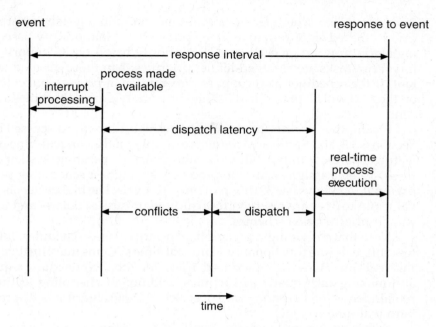

Figure 6.14   Dispatch latency.

time operating systems to minimize interrupt latency to ensure that real-time tasks receive immediate attention. Indeed, for hard real-time systems, interrupt latency must not simply be minimized, it must be bounded to meet the strict requirements of these systems.

One important factor contributing to interrupt latency is the amount of time interrupts may be disabled while kernel data structures are being updated. Real-time operating systems require that interrupts be disabled for only very short periods of time.

The amount of time required for the scheduling dispatcher to stop one process and start another is known as dispatch latency. Providing real-time tasks with immediate access to the CPU mandates that real-time operating systems minimize this latency as well. The most effective technique for keeping dispatch latency low is to provide preemptive kernels.

In Figure 6.14, we diagram the makeup of dispatch latency. The **conflict phase** of dispatch latency has two components:

1. Preemption of any process running in the kernel

2. Release by low-priority processes of resources needed by a high-priority process

As an example, in Solaris, the dispatch latency with preemption disabled is over a hundred milliseconds. With preemption enabled, it is reduced to less than a millisecond.

6.6.2   Priority-Based Scheduling

The most important feature of a real-time operating system is to respond immediately to a real-time process as soon as that process requires the CPU.

As a result, the scheduler for a real-time operating system must support a priority-based algorithm with preemption. Recall that priority-based scheduling algorithms assign each process a priority based on its importance; more important tasks are assigned higher priorities than those deemed less important. If the scheduler also supports preemption, a process currently running on the CPU will be preempted if a higher-priority process becomes available to run.

Preemptive, priority-based scheduling algorithms are discussed in detail in Section 6.3.3, and Section 6.7 presents examples of the soft real-time scheduling features of the Linux, Windows, and Solaris operating systems. Each of these systems assigns real-time processes the highest scheduling priority. For example, Windows has 32 different priority levels. The highest levels—priority values 16 to 31—are reserved for real-time processes. Solaris and Linux have similar prioritization schemes.

Note that providing a preemptive, priority-based scheduler only guarantees soft real-time functionality. Hard real-time systems must further guarantee that real-time tasks will be serviced in accord with their deadline requirements, and making such guarantees requires additional scheduling features. In the remainder of this section, we cover scheduling algorithms appropriate for hard real-time systems.

Before we proceed with the details of the individual schedulers, however, we must define certain characteristics of the processes that are to be scheduled. First, the processes are considered periodic That is, they require the CPU at constant intervals (periods). Once a periodic process has acquired the CPU, it has a fixed processing time t, a deadline d by which it must be serviced by the CPU, and a period p. The relationship of the processing time, the deadline, and the period can be expressed as $0 \leq t \leq d \leq p$. The rate of a periodic task is $1/p$. Figure 6.15 illustrates the execution of a periodic process over time. Schedulers can take advantage of these characteristics and assign priorities according to a process's deadline or rate requirements.

What is unusual about this form of scheduling is that a process may have to announce its deadline requirements to the scheduler. Then, using a technique known as an admission-control algorithm, the scheduler does one of two things. It either admits the process, guaranteeing that the process will complete on time, or rejects the request as impossible if it cannot guarantee that the task will be serviced by its deadline.

Figure 6.15   Periodic task.

Figure 6.16 Scheduling of tasks when P_2 has a higher priority than P_1.

6.6.3 Rate-Monotonic Scheduling

The **rate-monotonic** scheduling algorithm schedules periodic tasks using a static priority policy with preemption. If a lower-priority process is running and a higher-priority process becomes available to run, it will preempt the lower-priority process. Upon entering the system, each periodic task is assigned a priority inversely based on its period. The shorter the period, the higher the priority; the longer the period, the lower the priority. The rationale behind this policy is to assign a higher priority to tasks that require the CPU more often. Furthermore, rate-monotonic scheduling assumes that the processing time of a periodic process is the same for each CPU burst. That is, every time a process acquires the CPU, the duration of its CPU burst is the same.

Let's consider an example. We have two processes, P_1 and P_2. The periods for P_1 and P_2 are 50 and 100, respectively—that is, $p_1 = 50$ and $p_2 = 100$. The processing times are $t_1 = 20$ for P_1 and $t_2 = 35$ for P_2. The deadline for each process requires that it complete its CPU burst by the start of its next period.

We must first ask ourselves whether it is possible to schedule these tasks so that each meets its deadlines. If we measure the CPU utilization of a process P_i as the ratio of its burst to its period—t_i/p_i—the CPU utilization of P_1 is $20/50 = 0.40$ and that of P_2 is $35/100 = 0.35$, for a total CPU utilization of 75 percent. Therefore, it seems we can schedule these tasks in such a way that both meet their deadlines and still leave the CPU with available cycles.

Suppose we assign P_2 a higher priority than P_1. The execution of P_1 and P_2 in this situation is shown in Figure 6.16. As we can see, P_2 starts execution first and completes at time 35. At this point, P_1 starts; it completes its CPU burst at time 55. However, the first deadline for P_1 was at time 50, so the scheduler has caused P_1 to miss its deadline.

Now suppose we use rate-monotonic scheduling, in which we assign P_1 a higher priority than P_2 because the period of P_1 is shorter than that of P_2. The execution of these processes in this situation is shown in Figure 6.17. P_1 starts first and completes its CPU burst at time 20, thereby meeting its first deadline. P_2 starts running at this point and runs until time 50. At this time, it is preempted by P_1, although it still has 5 milliseconds remaining in its CPU burst. P_1 completes its CPU burst at time 70, at which point the scheduler resumes

Figure 6.17 Rate-monotonic scheduling.

P_2. P_2 completes its CPU burst at time 75, also meeting its first deadline. The system is idle until time 100, when P_1 is scheduled again.

Rate-monotonic scheduling is considered optimal in that if a set of processes cannot be scheduled by this algorithm, it cannot be scheduled by any other algorithm that assigns static priorities. Let's next examine a set of processes that cannot be scheduled using the rate-monotonic algorithm.

Assume that process P_1 has a period of $p_1 = 50$ and a CPU burst of $t_1 = 25$. For P_2, the corresponding values are $p_2 = 80$ and $t_2 = 35$. Rate-monotonic scheduling would assign process P_1 a higher priority, as it has the shorter period. The total CPU utilization of the two processes is $(25/50)+(35/80) = 0.94$, and it therefore seems logical that the two processes could be scheduled and still leave the CPU with 6 percent available time. Figure 6.18 shows the scheduling of processes P_1 and P_2. Initially, P_1 runs until it completes its CPU burst at time 25. Process P_2 then begins running and runs until time 50, when it is preempted by P_1. At this point, P_2 still has 10 milliseconds remaining in its CPU burst. Process P_1 runs until time 75; consequently, P2 finishes its burst at time 85, after the deadline for completion of its CPU burst at time 80.

Despite being optimal, then, rate-monotonic scheduling has a limitation: CPU utilization is bounded, and it is not always possible fully to maximize CPU resources. The worst-case CPU utilization for scheduling N processes is

$$N(2^{1/N} - 1).$$

With one process in the system, CPU utilization is 100 percent, but it falls to approximately 69 percent as the number of processes approaches infinity. With two processes, CPU utilization is bounded at about 83 percent. Combined CPU utilization for the two processes scheduled in Figure 6.16 and Figure 6.17 is 75 percent; therefore, the rate-monotonic scheduling algorithm is guaranteed to schedule them so that they can meet their deadlines. For the two processes scheduled in Figure 6.18, combined CPU utilization is approximately 94 percent; therefore, rate-monotonic scheduling cannot guarantee that they can be scheduled so that they meet their deadlines.

6.6.4 Earliest-Deadline-First Scheduling

Earliest-deadline-first (EDF) scheduling dynamically assigns priorities according to deadline. The earlier the deadline, the higher the priority; the later the deadline, the lower the priority. Under the EDF policy, when a process becomes runnable, it must announce its deadline requirements to the system. Priorities may have to be adjusted to reflect the deadline of the newly runnable process. Note how this differs from rate-monotonic scheduling, where priorities are fixed.

Figure 6.18   Missing deadlines with rate-monotonic scheduling.

Figure 6.19 Earliest-deadline-first scheduling.

To illustrate EDF scheduling, we again schedule the processes shown in Figure 6.18, which failed to meet deadline requirements under rate-monotonic scheduling. Recall that P_1 has values of $p_1 = 50$ and $t_1 = 25$ and that P_2 has values of $p_2 = 80$ and $t_2 = 35$. The EDF scheduling of these processes is shown in Figure 6.19. Process P_1 has the earliest deadline, so its initial priority is higher than that of process P_2. Process P_2 begins running at the end of the CPU burst for P_1. However, whereas rate-monotonic scheduling allows P_1 to preempt P_2 at the beginning of its next period at time 50, EDF scheduling allows process P_2 to continue running. P_2 now has a higher priority than P_1 because its next deadline (at time 80) is earlier than that of P_1 (at time 100). Thus, both P_1 and P_2 meet their first deadlines. Process P_1 again begins running at time 60 and completes its second CPU burst at time 85, also meeting its second deadline at time 100. P_2 begins running at this point, only to be preempted by P_1 at the start of its next period at time 100. P_2 is preempted because P_1 has an earlier deadline (time 150) than P_2 (time 160). At time 125, P_1 completes its CPU burst and P_2 resumes execution, finishing at time 145 and meeting its deadline as well. The system is idle until time 150, when P_1 is scheduled to run once again.

Unlike the rate-monotonic algorithm, EDF scheduling does not require that processes be periodic, nor must a process require a constant amount of CPU time per burst. The only requirement is that a process announce its deadline to the scheduler when it becomes runnable. The appeal of EDF scheduling is that it is theoretically optimal—theoretically, it can schedule processes so that each process can meet its deadline requirements and CPU utilization will be 100 percent. In practice, however, it is impossible to achieve this level of CPU utilization due to the cost of context switching between processes and interrupt handling.

6.6.5 Proportional Share Scheduling

Proportional share schedulers operate by allocating T shares among all applications. An application can receive N shares of time, thus ensuring that the application will have N/T of the total processor time. As an example, assume that a total of $T = 100$ shares is to be divided among three processes, A, B, and C. A is assigned 50 shares, B is assigned 15 shares, and C is assigned 20 shares. This scheme ensures that A will have 50 percent of total processor time, B will have 15 percent, and C will have 20 percent.

Proportional share schedulers must work in conjunction with an admission-control policy to guarantee that an application receives its allocated shares of time. An admission-control policy will admit a client requesting a particular number of shares only if sufficient shares are available. In our current example, we have allocated $50 + 15 + 20 = 85$ shares of the total of

100 shares. If a new process D requested 30 shares, the admission controller would deny D entry into the system.

6.6.6 POSIX Real-Time Scheduling

The POSIX standard also provides extensions for real-time computing—POSIX.1b. Here, we cover some of the POSIX API related to scheduling real-time threads. POSIX defines two scheduling classes for real-time threads:

- SCHED_FIFO
- SCHED_RR

SCHED_FIFO schedules threads according to a first-come, first-served policy using a FIFO queue as outlined in Section 6.3.1. However, there is no time slicing among threads of equal priority. Therefore, the highest-priority real-time thread at the front of the FIFO queue will be granted the CPU until it terminates or blocks. SCHED_RR uses a round-robin policy. It is similar to SCHED_FIFO except that it provides time slicing among threads of equal priority. POSIX provides an additional scheduling class—SCHED_OTHER—but its implementation is undefined and system specific; it may behave differently on different systems.

The POSIX API specifies the following two functions for getting and setting the scheduling policy:

- `pthread_attr_getsched_policy(pthread_attr_t *attr, int *policy)`
- `pthread_attr_setsched_policy(pthread_attr_t *attr, int policy)`

The first parameter to both functions is a pointer to the set of attributes for the thread. The second parameter is either (1) a pointer to an integer that is set to the current scheduling policy (for `pthread_attr_getsched_policy()`) or (2) an integer value (SCHED_FIFO, SCHED_RR, or SCHED_OTHER) for the `pthread_attr_setsched_policy()` function. Both functions return nonzero values if an error occurs.

In Figure 6.20, we illustrate a POSIX Pthread program using this API. This program first determines the current scheduling policy and then sets the scheduling algorithm to SCHED_FIFO.

6.7 Operating-System Examples

We turn next to a description of the scheduling policies of the Linux, Windows, and Solaris operating systems. It is important to note that we use the term *process scheduling* in a general sense here. In fact, we are describing the scheduling of *kernel threads* with Solaris and Windows systems and of *tasks* with the Linux scheduler.

6.7.1 Example: Linux Scheduling

Process scheduling in Linux has had an interesting history. Prior to Version 2.5, the Linux kernel ran a variation of the traditional UNIX scheduling algorithm.

```c
#include <pthread.h>
#include <stdio.h>
#define NUM_THREADS 5

int main(int argc, char *argv[])
{
  int i, policy;
  pthread_t tid[NUM_THREADS];
  pthread_attr_t attr;

  /* get the default attributes */
  pthread_attr_init(&attr);

  /* get the current scheduling policy */
  if (pthread_attr_getschedpolicy(&attr, &policy) != 0)
    fprintf(stderr, "Unable to get policy.\n");
  else {
    if (policy == SCHED_OTHER)
      printf("SCHED_OTHER\n");
    else if (policy == SCHED_RR)
      printf("SCHED_RR\n");
    else if (policy == SCHED_FIFO)
      printf("SCHED_FIFO\n");
  }

  /* set the scheduling policy - FIFO, RR, or OTHER */
  if (pthread_attr_setschedpolicy(&attr, SCHED_FIFO) != 0)
    fprintf(stderr, "Unable to set policy.\n");

  /* create the threads */
  for (i = 0; i < NUM_THREADS; i++)
    pthread_create(&tid[i],&attr,runner,NULL);

  /* now join on each thread */
  for (i = 0; i < NUM_THREADS; i++)
    pthread_join(tid[i], NULL);
}

/* Each thread will begin control in this function */
void *runner(void *param)
{
  /* do some work ... */

  pthread_exit(0);
}
```

Figure 6.20 POSIX real-time scheduling API.

However, as this algorithm was not designed with SMP systems in mind, it did not adequately support systems with multiple processors. In addition, it resulted in poor performance for systems with a large number of runnable processes. With Version 2.5 of the kernel, the scheduler was overhauled to include a scheduling algorithm—known as $O(1)$—that ran in constant time regardless of the number of tasks in the system. The $O(1)$ scheduler also provided increased support for SMP systems, including processor affinity and load balancing between processors. However, in practice, although the $O(1)$ scheduler delivered excellent performance on SMP systems, it led to poor response times for the interactive processes that are common on many desktop computer systems. During development of the 2.6 kernel, the scheduler was again revised; and in release 2.6.23 of the kernel, the *Completely Fair Scheduler* (CFS) became the default Linux scheduling algorithm.

Scheduling in the Linux system is based on **scheduling classes**. Each class is assigned a specific priority. By using different scheduling classes, the kernel can accommodate different scheduling algorithms based on the needs of the system and its processes. The scheduling criteria for a Linux server, for example, may be different from those for a mobile device running Linux. To decide which task to run next, the scheduler selects the highest-priority task belonging to the highest-priority scheduling class. Standard Linux kernels implement two scheduling classes: (1) a default scheduling class using the CFS scheduling algorithm and (2) a real-time scheduling class. We discuss each of these classes here. New scheduling classes can, of course, be added.

Rather than using strict rules that associate a relative priority value with the length of a time quantum, the CFS scheduler assigns a proportion of CPU processing time to each task. This proportion is calculated based on the **nice value** assigned to each task. Nice values range from −20 to +19, where a numerically lower nice value indicates a higher relative priority. Tasks with lower nice values receive a higher proportion of CPU processing time than tasks with higher nice values. The default nice value is 0. (The term *nice* comes from the idea that if a task increases its nice value from, say, 0 to +10, it is being nice to other tasks in the system by lowering its relative priority.) CFS doesn't use discrete values of time slices and instead identifies a **targeted latency**, which is an interval of time during which every runnable task should run at least once. Proportions of CPU time are allocated from the value of targeted latency. In addition to having default and minimum values, targeted latency can increase if the number of active tasks in the system grows beyond a certain threshold.

The CFS scheduler doesn't directly assign priorities. Rather, it records how long each task has run by maintaining the **virtual run time** of each task using the per-task variable vruntime. The virtual run time is associated with a decay factor based on the priority of a task: lower-priority tasks have higher rates of decay than higher-priority tasks. For tasks at normal priority (nice values of 0), virtual run time is identical to actual physical run time. Thus, if a task with default priority runs for 200 milliseconds, its vruntime will also be 200 milliseconds. However, if a lower-priority task runs for 200 milliseconds, its vruntime will be higher than 200 milliseconds. Similarly, if a higher-priority task runs for 200 milliseconds, its vruntime will be less than 200 milliseconds. To decide which task to run next, the scheduler simply selects the task that has the smallest vruntime value. In addition, a higher-priority task that becomes available to run can preempt a lower-priority task.

CFS PERFORMANCE

The Linux CFS scheduler provides an efficient algorithm for selecting which task to run next. Each runnable task is placed in a red-black tree—a balanced binary search tree whose key is based on the value of vruntime. This tree is shown below:

When a task becomes runnable, it is added to the tree. If a task on the tree is not runnable (for example, if it is blocked while waiting for I/O), it is removed. Generally speaking, tasks that have been given less processing time (smaller values of vruntime) are toward the left side of the tree, and tasks that have been given more processing time are on the right side. According to the properties of a binary search tree, the leftmost node has the smallest key value, which for the sake of the CFS scheduler means that it is the task with the highest priority. Because the red-black tree is balanced, navigating it to discover the leftmost node will require $O(lg N)$ operations (where N is the number of nodes in the tree). However, for efficiency reasons, the Linux scheduler caches this value in the variable rb_leftmost, and thus determining which task to run next requires only retrieving the cached value.

Let's examine the CFS scheduler in action: Assume that two tasks have the same nice values. One task is I/O-bound and the other is CPU-bound. Typically, the I/O-bound task will run only for short periods before blocking for additional I/O, and the CPU-bound task will exhaust its time period whenever it has an opportunity to run on a processor. Therefore, the value of vruntime will eventually be lower for the I/O-bound task than for the CPU-bound task, giving the I/O-bound task higher priority than the CPU-bound task. At that point, if the CPU-bound task is executing when the I/O-bound task becomes eligible to run (for example, when I/O the task is waiting for becomes available), the I/O-bound task will preempt the CPU-bound task.

Linux also implements real-time scheduling using the POSIX standard as described in Section 6.6.6. Any task scheduled using either the SCHED_FIFO or the SCHED_RR real-time policy runs at a higher priority than normal (non-real-

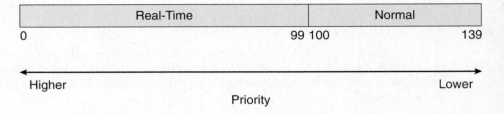

Figure 6.21   Scheduling priorities on a Linux system.

time) tasks. Linux uses two separate priority ranges, one for real-time tasks and a second for normal tasks. Real-time tasks are assigned static priorities within the range of 0 to 99, and normal (i.e. non real-time) tasks are assigned priorities from 100 to 139. These two ranges map into a global priority scheme wherein numerically lower values indicate higher relative priorities. Normal tasks are assigned a priority based on their nice values, where a value of −20 maps to priority 100 and a nice value of +19 maps to 139. This scheme is shown in Figure 6.21.

6.7.2   Example: Windows Scheduling

Windows schedules threads using a priority-based, preemptive scheduling algorithm. The Windows scheduler ensures that the highest-priority thread will always run. The portion of the Windows kernel that handles scheduling is called the **dispatcher**. A thread selected to run by the dispatcher will run until it is preempted by a higher-priority thread, until it terminates, until its time quantum ends, or until it calls a blocking system call, such as for I/O. If a higher-priority real-time thread becomes ready while a lower-priority thread is running, the lower-priority thread will be preempted. This preemption gives a real-time thread preferential access to the CPU when the thread needs such access.

The dispatcher uses a 32-level priority scheme to determine the order of thread execution. Priorities are divided into two classes. The **variable class** contains threads having priorities from 1 to 15, and the **real-time class** contains threads with priorities ranging from 16 to 31. (There is also a thread running at priority 0 that is used for memory management.) The dispatcher uses a queue for each scheduling priority and traverses the set of queues from highest to lowest until it finds a thread that is ready to run. If no ready thread is found, the dispatcher will execute a special thread called the **idle thread**.

There is a relationship between the numeric priorities of the Windows kernel and the Windows API. The Windows API identifies the following six priority classes to which a process can belong:

- IDLE_PRIORITY_CLASS
- BELOW_NORMAL_PRIORITY_CLASS
- NORMAL_PRIORITY_CLASS
- ABOVE_NORMAL_PRIORITY_CLASS

- HIGH_PRIORITY_CLASS

- REALTIME_PRIORITY_CLASS

Processes are typically members of the NORMAL_PRIORITY_CLASS. A process belongs to this class unless the parent of the process was a member of the IDLE_PRIORITY_CLASS or unless another class was specified when the process was created. Additionally, the priority class of a process can be altered with the SetPriorityClass() function in the Windows API. Priorities in all classes except the REALTIME_PRIORITY_CLASS are variable, meaning that the priority of a thread belonging to one of these classes can change.

A thread within a given priority class also has a relative priority. The values for relative priorities include:

- IDLE

- LOWEST

- BELOW_NORMAL

- NORMAL

- ABOVE_NORMAL

- HIGHEST

- TIME_CRITICAL

The priority of each thread is based on both the priority class it belongs to and its relative priority within that class. This relationship is shown in Figure 6.22. The values of the priority classes appear in the top row. The left column contains the values for the relative priorities. For example, if the relative priority of a thread in the ABOVE_NORMAL_PRIORITY_CLASS is NORMAL, the numeric priority of that thread is 10.

Furthermore, each thread has a base priority representing a value in the priority range for the class to which the thread belongs. By default, the base

	real-time	high	above normal	normal	below normal	idle priority
time-critical	31	15	15	15	15	15
highest	26	15	12	10	8	6
above normal	25	14	11	9	7	5
normal	24	13	10	8	6	4
below normal	23	12	9	7	5	3
lowest	22	11	8	6	4	2
idle	16	1	1	1	1	1

Figure 6.22 Windows thread priorities.

priority is the value of the NORMAL relative priority for that class. The base priorities for each priority class are as follows:

- REALTIME_PRIORITY_CLASS—24
- HIGH_PRIORITY_CLASS—13
- ABOVE_NORMAL_PRIORITY_CLASS—10
- NORMAL_PRIORITY_CLASS—8
- BELOW_NORMAL_PRIORITY_CLASS—6
- IDLE_PRIORITY_CLASS—4

The initial priority of a thread is typically the base priority of the process the thread belongs to, although the SetThreadPriority() function in the Windows API can also be used to modify a thread's base priority.

When a thread's time quantum runs out, that thread is interrupted. If the thread is in the variable-priority class, its priority is lowered. The priority is never lowered below the base priority, however. Lowering the priority tends to limit the CPU consumption of compute-bound threads. When a variable-priority thread is released from a wait operation, the dispatcher boosts the priority. The amount of the boost depends on what the thread was waiting for. For example, a thread waiting for keyboard I/O would get a large increase, whereas a thread waiting for a disk operation would get a moderate one. This strategy tends to give good response times to interactive threads that are using the mouse and windows. It also enables I/O-bound threads to keep the I/O devices busy while permitting compute-bound threads to use spare CPU cycles in the background. This strategy is used by several time-sharing operating systems, including UNIX. In addition, the window with which the user is currently interacting receives a priority boost to enhance its response time.

When a user is running an interactive program, the system needs to provide especially good performance. For this reason, Windows has a special scheduling rule for processes in the NORMAL_PRIORITY_CLASS. Windows distinguishes between the **foreground process** that is currently selected on the screen and the **background processes** that are not currently selected. When a process moves into the foreground, Windows increases the scheduling quantum by some factor—typically by 3. This increase gives the foreground process three times longer to run before a time-sharing preemption occurs.

Windows 7 introduced **user-mode scheduling (UMS)**, which allows applications to create and manage threads independently of the kernel. Thus, an application can create and schedule multiple threads without involving the Windows kernel scheduler. For applications that create a large number of threads, scheduling threads in user mode is much more efficient than kernel-mode thread scheduling, as no kernel intervention is necessary.

Earlier versions of Windows provided a similar feature known as **fibers**, which allowed several user-mode threads (fibers) to be mapped to a single kernel thread. However, fibers were of limited practical use. A fiber was unable to make calls to the Windows API because all fibers had to share the thread environment block (TEB) of the thread on which they were running. This presented a problem if a Windows API function placed state information into the TEB for one fiber, only to have the information overwritten by a different fiber. UMS overcomes this obstacle by providing each user-mode thread with its own thread context.

In addition, unlike fibers, UMS is not intended to be used directly by the programmer. The details of writing user-mode schedulers can be very challenging, and UMS does not include such a scheduler. Rather, the schedulers come from programming language libraries that build on top of UMS. For example, Microsoft provides Concurrency Runtime (ConcRT), a concurrent programming framework for C++ that is designed for task-based parallelism (Section 4.2) on multicore processors. ConcRT provides a user-mode scheduler together with facilities for decomposing programs into tasks, which can then be scheduled on the available processing cores.

6.7.3 Example: Solaris Scheduling

Solaris uses priority-based thread scheduling. Each thread belongs to one of six classes:

1. Time sharing (TS)

2. Interactive (IA)

3. Real time (RT)

4. System (SYS)

5. Fair share (FSS)

6. Fixed priority (FP)

Within each class there are different priorities and different scheduling algorithms.

The default scheduling class for a process is time sharing. The scheduling policy for the time-sharing class dynamically alters priorities and assigns time slices of different lengths using a multilevel feedback queue. By default, there is an inverse relationship between priorities and time slices. The higher the priority, the smaller the time slice; and the lower the priority, the larger the time slice. Interactive processes typically have a higher priority; CPU-bound processes, a lower priority. This scheduling policy gives good response time for interactive processes and good throughput for CPU-bound processes. The interactive class uses the same scheduling policy as the time-sharing class, but it gives windowing applications—such as those created by the KDE or GNOME window managers—a higher priority for better performance.

Figure 6.23 shows the dispatch table for scheduling time-sharing and interactive threads. These two scheduling classes include 60 priority levels, but for brevity, we display only a handful. The dispatch table shown in Figure 6.23 contains the following fields:

- **Priority**. The class-dependent priority for the time-sharing and interactive classes. A higher number indicates a higher priority.

priority	time quantum	time quantum expired	return from sleep
0	200	0	50
5	200	0	50
10	160	0	51
15	160	5	51
20	120	10	52
25	120	15	52
30	80	20	53
35	80	25	54
40	40	30	55
45	40	35	56
50	40	40	58
55	40	45	58
59	20	49	59

Figure 6.23 Solaris dispatch table for time-sharing and interactive threads.

- **Time quantum.** The time quantum for the associated priority. This illustrates the inverse relationship between priorities and time quanta: the lowest priority (priority 0) has the highest time quantum (200 milliseconds), and the highest priority (priority 59) has the lowest time quantum (20 milliseconds).

- **Time quantum expired.** The new priority of a thread that has used its entire time quantum without blocking. Such threads are considered CPU-intensive. As shown in the table, these threads have their priorities lowered.

- **Return from sleep.** The priority of a thread that is returning from sleeping (such as from waiting for I/O). As the table illustrates, when I/O is available for a waiting thread, its priority is boosted to between 50 and 59, supporting the scheduling policy of providing good response time for interactive processes.

Threads in the real-time class are given the highest priority. A real-time process will run before a process in any other class. This assignment allows a real-time process to have a guaranteed response from the system within a bounded period of time. In general, however, few processes belong to the real-time class.

Solaris uses the system class to run kernel threads, such as the scheduler and paging daemon. Once the priority of a system thread is established, it does not change. The system class is reserved for kernel use (user processes running in kernel mode are not in the system class).

The fixed-priority and fair-share classes were introduced with Solaris 9. Threads in the fixed-priority class have the same priority range as those in the time-sharing class; however, their priorities are not dynamically adjusted. The fair-share scheduling class uses CPU **shares** instead of priorities to make scheduling decisions. CPU shares indicate entitlement to available CPU resources and are allocated to a set of processes (known as a **project**).

Each scheduling class includes a set of priorities. However, the scheduler converts the class-specific priorities into global priorities and selects the thread with the highest global priority to run. The selected thread runs on the CPU until it (1) blocks, (2) uses its time slice, or (3) is preempted by a higher-priority thread. If there are multiple threads with the same priority, the scheduler uses a round-robin queue. Figure 6.24 illustrates how the six scheduling classes relate to one another and how they map to global priorities. Notice that the kernel maintains ten threads for servicing interrupts. These threads do not belong to any scheduling class and execute at the highest priority (160–169). As mentioned, Solaris has traditionally used the many-to-many model (Section 4.3.3) but switched to the one-to-one model (Section 4.3.2) beginning with Solaris 9.

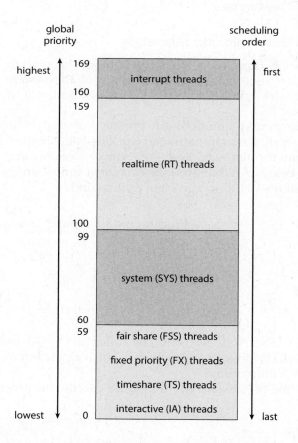

Figure 6.24 Solaris scheduling.

6.8   Algorithm Evaluation

How do we select a CPU-scheduling algorithm for a particular system? As we saw in Section 6.3, there are many scheduling algorithms, each with its own parameters. As a result, selecting an algorithm can be difficult.

The first problem is defining the criteria to be used in selecting an algorithm. As we saw in Section 6.2, criteria are often defined in terms of CPU utilization, response time, or throughput. To select an algorithm, we must first define the relative importance of these elements. Our criteria may include several measures, such as these:

- Maximizing CPU utilization under the constraint that the maximum response time is 1 second

- Maximizing throughput such that turnaround time is (on average) linearly proportional to total execution time

Once the selection criteria have been defined, we want to evaluate the algorithms under consideration. We next describe the various evaluation methods we can use.

6.8.1   Deterministic Modeling

One major class of evaluation methods is **analytic evaluation**. Analytic evaluation uses the given algorithm and the system workload to produce a formula or number to evaluate the performance of the algorithm for that workload.

Deterministic modeling is one type of analytic evaluation. This method takes a particular predetermined workload and defines the performance of each algorithm for that workload. For example, assume that we have the workload shown below. All five processes arrive at time 0, in the order given, with the length of the CPU burst given in milliseconds:

Process	Burst Time
P_1	10
P_2	29
P_3	3
P_4	7
P_5	12

Consider the FCFS, SJF, and RR (quantum = 10 milliseconds) scheduling algorithms for this set of processes. Which algorithm would give the minimum average waiting time?

For the FCFS algorithm, we would execute the processes as

The waiting time is 0 milliseconds for process P_1, 10 milliseconds for process P_2, 39 milliseconds for process P_3, 42 milliseconds for process P_4, and 49 milliseconds for process P_5. Thus, the average waiting time is $(0 + 10 + 39 + 42 + 49)/5 = 28$ milliseconds.

With nonpreemptive SJF scheduling, we execute the processes as

The waiting time is 10 milliseconds for process P_1, 32 milliseconds for process P_2, 0 milliseconds for process P_3, 3 milliseconds for process P_4, and 20 milliseconds for process P_5. Thus, the average waiting time is $(10 + 32 + 0 + 3 + 20)/5 = 13$ milliseconds.

With the RR algorithm, we execute the processes as

The waiting time is 0 milliseconds for process P_1, 32 milliseconds for process P_2, 20 milliseconds for process P_3, 23 milliseconds for process P_4, and 40 milliseconds for process P_5. Thus, the average waiting time is $(0 + 32 + 20 + 23 + 40)/5 = 23$ milliseconds.

We can see that, in this case, the average waiting time obtained with the SJF policy is less than half that obtained with FCFS scheduling; the RR algorithm gives us an intermediate value.

Deterministic modeling is simple and fast. It gives us exact numbers, allowing us to compare the algorithms. However, it requires exact numbers for input, and its answers apply only to those cases. The main uses of deterministic modeling are in describing scheduling algorithms and providing examples. In cases where we are running the same program over and over again and can measure the program's processing requirements exactly, we may be able to use deterministic modeling to select a scheduling algorithm. Furthermore, over a set of examples, deterministic modeling may indicate trends that can then be analyzed and proved separately. For example, it can be shown that, for the environment described (all processes and their times available at time 0), the SJF policy will always result in the minimum waiting time.

6.8.2 Queueing Models

On many systems, the processes that are run vary from day to day, so there is no static set of processes (or times) to use for deterministic modeling. What can be determined, however, is the distribution of CPU and I/O bursts. These distributions can be measured and then approximated or simply estimated. The result is a mathematical formula describing the probability of a particular CPU burst. Commonly, this distribution is exponential and is described by its mean. Similarly, we can describe the distribution of times when processes arrive in the system (the arrival-time distribution). From these two distributions, it is possible to compute the average throughput, utilization, waiting time, and so on for most algorithms.

The computer system is described as a network of servers. Each server has a queue of waiting processes. The CPU is a server with its ready queue, as is the I/O system with its device queues. Knowing arrival rates and service rates, we can compute utilization, average queue length, average wait time, and so on. This area of study is called **queueing-network analysis**.

As an example, let n be the average queue length (excluding the process being serviced), let W be the average waiting time in the queue, and let λ be the average arrival rate for new processes in the queue (such as three processes per second). We expect that during the time W that a process waits, $\lambda \times W$ new processes will arrive in the queue. If the system is in a steady state, then the number of processes leaving the queue must be equal to the number of processes that arrive. Thus,

$$n = \lambda \times W.$$

This equation, known as **Little's formula**, is particularly useful because it is valid for any scheduling algorithm and arrival distribution.

We can use Little's formula to compute one of the three variables if we know the other two. For example, if we know that 7 processes arrive every second (on average) and that there are normally 14 processes in the queue, then we can compute the average waiting time per process as 2 seconds.

Queueing analysis can be useful in comparing scheduling algorithms, but it also has limitations. At the moment, the classes of algorithms and distributions that can be handled are fairly limited. The mathematics of complicated algorithms and distributions can be difficult to work with. Thus, arrival and service distributions are often defined in mathematically tractable —but unrealistic—ways. It is also generally necessary to make a number of independent assumptions, which may not be accurate. As a result of these difficulties, queueing models are often only approximations of real systems, and the accuracy of the computed results may be questionable.

6.8.3 Simulations

To get a more accurate evaluation of scheduling algorithms, we can use simulations. Running simulations involves programming a model of the computer system. Software data structures represent the major components of the system. The simulator has a variable representing a clock. As this variable's value is increased, the simulator modifies the system state to reflect the activities of the devices, the processes, and the scheduler. As the simulation executes, statistics that indicate algorithm performance are gathered and printed.

The data to drive the simulation can be generated in several ways. The most common method uses a random-number generator that is programmed to generate processes, CPU burst times, arrivals, departures, and so on, according to probability distributions. The distributions can be defined mathematically (uniform, exponential, Poisson) or empirically. If a distribution is to be defined empirically, measurements of the actual system under study are taken. The results define the distribution of events in the real system; this distribution can then be used to drive the simulation.

Figure 6.25 Evaluation of CPU schedulers by simulation.

A distribution-driven simulation may be inaccurate, however, because of relationships between successive events in the real system. The frequency distribution indicates only how many instances of each event occur; it does not indicate anything about the order of their occurrence. To correct this problem, we can use **trace tapes**. We create a trace tape by monitoring the real system and recording the sequence of actual events (Figure 6.25). We then use this sequence to drive the simulation. Trace tapes provide an excellent way to compare two algorithms on exactly the same set of real inputs. This method can produce accurate results for its inputs.

Simulations can be expensive, often requiring hours of computer time. A more detailed simulation provides more accurate results, but it also takes more computer time. In addition, trace tapes can require large amounts of storage space. Finally, the design, coding, and debugging of the simulator can be a major task.

6.8.4 Implementation

Even a simulation is of limited accuracy. The only completely accurate way to evaluate a scheduling algorithm is to code it up, put it in the operating system, and see how it works. This approach puts the actual algorithm in the real system for evaluation under real operating conditions.

The major difficulty with this approach is the high cost. The expense is incurred not only in coding the algorithm and modifying the operating system to support it (along with its required data structures) but also in the reaction of the users to a constantly changing operating system. Most users are not interested in building a better operating system; they merely want to get their processes executed and use their results. A constantly changing operating system does not help the users to get their work done.

Another difficulty is that the environment in which the algorithm is used will change. The environment will change not only in the usual way, as new programs are written and the types of problems change, but also as a result of the performance of the scheduler. If short processes are given priority, then users may break larger processes into sets of smaller processes. If interactive processes are given priority over noninteractive processes, then users may switch to interactive use.

For example, researchers designed one system that classified interactive and noninteractive processes automatically by looking at the amount of terminal I/O. If a process did not input or output to the terminal in a 1-second interval, the process was classified as noninteractive and was moved to a lower-priority queue. In response to this policy, one programmer modified his programs to write an arbitrary character to the terminal at regular intervals of less than 1 second. The system gave his programs a high priority, even though the terminal output was completely meaningless.

The most flexible scheduling algorithms are those that can be altered by the system managers or by the users so that they can be tuned for a specific application or set of applications. A workstation that performs high-end graphical applications, for instance, may have scheduling needs different from those of a Web server or file server. Some operating systems— particularly several versions of UNIX—allow the system manager to fine-tune the scheduling parameters for a particular system configuration. For example, Solaris provides the dispadmin command to allow the system administrator to modify the parameters of the scheduling classes described in Section 6.7.3.

Another approach is to use APIs that can modify the priority of a process or thread. The Java, POSIX, and Windows API provide such functions. The downfall of this approach is that performance-tuning a system or application most often does not result in improved performance in more general situations.

6.9 Summary

CPU scheduling is the task of selecting a waiting process from the ready queue and allocating the CPU to it. The CPU is allocated to the selected process by the dispatcher.

First-come, first-served (FCFS) scheduling is the simplest scheduling algorithm, but it can cause short processes to wait for very long processes. Shortest-job-first (SJF) scheduling is provably optimal, providing the shortest average waiting time. Implementing SJF scheduling is difficult, however, because predicting the length of the next CPU burst is difficult. The SJF algorithm is a special case of the general priority scheduling algorithm, which simply allocates the CPU to the highest-priority process. Both priority and SJF scheduling may suffer from starvation. Aging is a technique to prevent starvation.

Round-robin (RR) scheduling is more appropriate for a time-shared (interactive) system. RR scheduling allocates the CPU to the first process in the ready queue for q time units, where q is the time quantum. After q time units, if the process has not relinquished the CPU, it is preempted, and the process is put at the tail of the ready queue. The major problem is the selection of the time quantum. If the quantum is too large, RR scheduling degenerates to FCFS scheduling. If the quantum is too small, scheduling overhead in the form of context-switch time becomes excessive.

The FCFS algorithm is nonpreemptive; the RR algorithm is preemptive. The SJF and priority algorithms may be either preemptive or nonpreemptive.

Multilevel queue algorithms allow different algorithms to be used for different classes of processes. The most common model includes a foreground interactive queue that uses RR scheduling and a background batch queue that uses FCFS scheduling. Multilevel feedback queues allow processes to move from one queue to another.

Many contemporary computer systems support multiple processors and allow each processor to schedule itself independently. Typically, each processor maintains its own private queue of processes (or threads), all of which are available to run. Additional issues related to multiprocessor scheduling include processor affinity, load balancing, and multicore processing.

A real-time computer system requires that results arrive within a deadline period; results arriving after the deadline has passed are useless. Hard real-time systems must guarantee that real-time tasks are serviced within their deadline periods. Soft real-time systems are less restrictive, assigning real-time tasks higher scheduling priority than other tasks.

Real-time scheduling algorithms include rate-monotonic and earliest-deadline-first scheduling. Rate-monotonic scheduling assigns tasks that require the CPU more often a higher priority than tasks that require the CPU less often. Earliest-deadline-first scheduling assigns priority according to upcoming deadlines—the earlier the deadline, the higher the priority. Proportional share scheduling divides up processor time into shares and assigning each process a number of shares, thus guaranteeing each process a proportional share of CPU time. The POSIX Pthread API provides various features for scheduling real-time threads as well.

Operating systems supporting threads at the kernel level must schedule threads—not processes—for execution. This is the case with Solaris and Windows. Both of these systems schedule threads using preemptive, priority-based scheduling algorithms, including support for real-time threads. The Linux process scheduler uses a priority-based algorithm with real-time support as well. The scheduling algorithms for these three operating systems typically favor interactive over CPU-bound processes.

The wide variety of scheduling algorithms demands that we have methods to select among algorithms. Analytic methods use mathematical analysis to determine the performance of an algorithm. Simulation methods determine performance by imitating the scheduling algorithm on a "representative" sample of processes and computing the resulting performance. However, simulation can at best provide an approximation of actual system performance. The only reliable technique for evaluating a scheduling algorithm is to implement the algorithm on an actual system and monitor its performance in a "real-world" environment.

Review Questions

Review questions for this chapter can be accessed by visiting our website.

Practice Exercises

Answers for the Practice Exercises can be accceed by visiting our website.

6.1   A CPU-scheduling algorithm determines an order for the execution of its scheduled processes. Given n processes to be scheduled on one processor, how many different schedules are possible? Give a formula in terms of n.

6.2   Explain the difference between preemptive and nonpreemptive scheduling.

6.3   Suppose that the following processes arrive for execution at the times indicated. Each process will run for the amount of time listed. In answering the questions, use nonpreemptive scheduling, and base all decisions on the information you have at the time the decision must be made.

Process	Arrival Time	Burst Time
P_1	0.0	8
P_2	0.4	4
P_3	1.0	1

a.   What is the average turnaround time for these processes with the FCFS scheduling algorithm?

b.   What is the average turnaround time for these processes with the SJF scheduling algorithm?

c.   The SJF algorithm is supposed to improve performance, but notice that we chose to run process P_1 at time 0 because we did not know that two shorter processes would arrive soon. Compute what the average turnaround time will be if the CPU is left idle for the first 1 unit and then SJF scheduling is used. Remember that processes P_1 and P_2 are waiting during this idle time, so their waiting time may increase. This algorithm could be called future-knowledge scheduling.

6.4   What advantage is there in having different time-quantum sizes at different levels of a multilevel queueing system?

6.5   Many CPU-scheduling algorithms are parameterized. For example, the RR algorithm requires a parameter to indicate the time slice. Multilevel feedback queues require parameters to define the number of queues, the scheduling algorithm for each queue, the criteria used to move processes between queues, and so on.

These algorithms are thus really sets of algorithms (for example, the set of RR algorithms for all time slices, and so on). One set of algorithms may include another (for example, the FCFS algorithm is the RR algorithm with an infinite time quantum). What (if any) relation holds between the following pairs of algorithm sets?

a. Priority and SJF

b. Multilevel feedback queues and FCFS

c. Priority and FCFS

d. RR and SJF

6.6 Suppose that a scheduling algorithm (at the level of short-term CPU scheduling) favors those processes that have used the least processor time in the recent past. Why will this algorithm favor I/O-bound programs and yet not permanently starve CPU-bound programs?

6.7 Distinguish between PCS and SCS scheduling.

6.8 Assume that an operating system maps user-level threads to the kernel using the many-to-many model and that the mapping is done through the use of LWPs. Furthermore, the system allows program developers to create real-time threads. Is it necessary to bind a real-time thread to an LWP?

6.9 The traditional UNIX scheduler enforces an inverse relationship between priority numbers and priorities: the higher the number, the lower the priority. The scheduler recalculates process priorities once per second using the following function:

Priority = (recent CPU usage / 2) + base

where base = 60 and *recent CPU usage* refers to a value indicating how often a process has used the CPU since priorities were last recalculated.

Assume that recent CPU usage is 40 for process P_1, 18 for process P_2, and 10 for process P_3. What will be the new priorities for these three processes when priorities are recalculated? Based on this information, does the traditional UNIX scheduler raise or lower the relative priority of a CPU-bound process?

Exercises

6.10 Why is it important for the scheduler to distinguish I/O-bound programs from CPU-bound programs?

6.11 Discuss how the following pairs of scheduling criteria conflict in certain settings.

a. CPU utilization and response time

b. Average turnaround time and maximum waiting time

c. I/O device utilization and CPU utilization

6.12 One technique for implementing lottery scheduling works by assigning processes lottery tickets, which are used for allocating CPU time. Whenever a scheduling decision has to be made, a lottery ticket is chosen at random, and the process holding that ticket gets the CPU. The BTV operating system implements lottery scheduling by holding a lottery 50 times each second, with each lottery winner getting 20 milliseconds of CPU time (20 milliseconds × 50 = 1 second). Describe how the BTV scheduler can ensure that higher-priority threads receive more attention from the CPU than lower-priority threads.

6.13   In Chapter 5, we discussed possible race conditions on various kernel data structures. Most scheduling algorithms maintain a **run queue**, which lists processes eligible to run on a processor. On multicore systems, there are two general options: (1) each processing core has its own run queue, or (2) a single run queue is shared by all processing cores. What are the advantages and disadvantages of each of these approaches?

6.14   Consider the exponential average formula used to predict the length of the next CPU burst. What are the implications of assigning the following values to the parameters used by the algorithm?

   a. $\alpha = 0$ and $\tau_0 = 100$ milliseconds

   b. $\alpha = 0.99$ and $\tau_0 = 10$ milliseconds

6.15   A variation of the round-robin scheduler is the **regressive round-robin** scheduler. This scheduler assigns each process a time quantum and a priority. The initial value of a time quantum is 50 milliseconds. However, every time a process has been allocated the CPU and uses its entire time quantum (does not block for I/O), 10 milliseconds is added to its time quantum, and its priority level is boosted. (The time quantum for a process can be increased to a maximum of 100 milliseconds.) When a process blocks before using its entire time quantum, its time quantum is reduced by 5 milliseconds, but its priority remains the same. What type of process (CPU-bound or I/O-bound) does the regressive round-robin scheduler favor? Explain.

6.16   Consider the following set of processes, with the length of the CPU burst given in milliseconds:

Process	Burst Time	Priority
P_1	2	2
P_2	1	1
P_3	8	4
P_4	4	2
P_5	5	3

The processes are assumed to have arrived in the order P_1, P_2, P_3, P_4, P_5, all at time 0.

   a.   Draw four Gantt charts that illustrate the execution of these processes using the following scheduling algorithms: FCFS, SJF, nonpreemptive priority (a larger priority number implies a higher priority), and RR (quantum = 2).

   b.   What is the turnaround time of each process for each of the scheduling algorithms in part a?

   c.   What is the waiting time of each process for each of these scheduling algorithms?

    d.   Which of the algorithms results in the minimum average waiting time (over all processes)?

6.17 The following processes are being scheduled using a preemptive, round-robin scheduling algorithm. Each process is assigned a numerical priority, with a higher number indicating a higher relative priority. In addition to the processes listed below, the system also has an *idle task* (which consumes no CPU resources and is identified as P_{idle}). This task has priority 0 and is scheduled whenever the system has no other available processes to run. The length of a time quantum is 10 units. If a process is preempted by a higher-priority process, the preempted process is placed at the end of the queue.

Thread	Priority	Burst	Arrival
P_1	40	20	0
P_2	30	25	25
P_3	30	25	30
P_4	35	15	60
P_5	5	10	100
P_6	10	10	105

    a.   Show the scheduling order of the processes using a Gantt chart.

    b.   What is the turnaround time for each process?

    c.   What is the waiting time for each process?

    d.   What is the CPU utilization rate?

6.18 The `nice` command is used to set the nice value of a process on Linux, as well as on other UNIX systems. Explain why some systems may allow any user to assign a process a nice value >= 0 yet allow only the root user to assign nice values < 0.

6.19 Which of the following scheduling algorithms could result in starvation?

    a.   First-come, first-served

    b.   Shortest job first

    c.   Round robin

    d.   Priority

6.20 Consider a variant of the RR scheduling algorithm in which the entries in the ready queue are pointers to the PCBs.

    a.   What would be the effect of putting two pointers to the same process in the ready queue?

    b.   What would be two major advantages and two disadvantages of this scheme?

    c.   How would you modify the basic RR algorithm to achieve the same effect without the duplicate pointers?

6.21   Consider a system running ten I/O-bound tasks and one CPU-bound task. Assume that the I/O-bound tasks issue an I/O operation once for every millisecond of CPU computing and that each I/O operation takes 10 milliseconds to complete. Also assume that the context-switching overhead is 0.1 millisecond and that all processes are long-running tasks. Describe the CPU utilization for a round-robin scheduler when:

   a.   The time quantum is 1 millisecond

   b.   The time quantum is 10 milliseconds

6.22   Consider a system implementing multilevel queue scheduling. What strategy can a computer user employ to maximize the amount of CPU time allocated to the user's process?

6.23   Consider a preemptive priority scheduling algorithm based on dynamically changing priorities. Larger priority numbers imply higher priority. When a process is waiting for the CPU (in the ready queue, but not running), its priority changes at a rate α. When it is running, its priority changes at a rate β. All processes are given a priority of 0 when they enter the ready queue. The parameters α and β can be set to give many different scheduling algorithms.

   a.   What is the algorithm that results from $\beta > \alpha > 0$?

   b.   What is the algorithm that results from $\alpha < \beta < 0$?

6.24   Explain the differences in how much the following scheduling algorithms discriminate in favor of short processes:

   a.   FCFS

   b.   RR

   c.   Multilevel feedback queues

6.25   Using the Windows scheduling algorithm, determine the numeric priority of each of the following threads.

   a.   A thread in the REALTIME_PRIORITY_CLASS with a relative priority of NORMAL

   b.   A thread in the ABOVE_NORMAL_PRIORITY_CLASS with a relative priority of HIGHEST

   c.   A thread in the BELOW_NORMAL_PRIORITY_CLASS with a relative priority of ABOVE_NORMAL

6.26   Assuming that no threads belong to the REALTIME_PRIORITY_CLASS and that none may be assigned a TIME_CRITICAL priority, what combination of priority class and priority corresponds to the highest possible relative priority in Windows scheduling?

6.27   Consider the scheduling algorithm in the Solaris operating system for time-sharing threads.

   a.   What is the time quantum (in milliseconds) for a thread with priority 15? With priority 40?

b.   Assume that a thread with priority 50 has used its entire time quantum without blocking. What new priority will the scheduler assign this thread?

c.   Assume that a thread with priority 20 blocks for I/O before its time quantum has expired. What new priority will the scheduler assign this thread?

6.28   Assume that two tasks A and B are running on a Linux system. The nice values of A and B are -5 and $+5$, respectively. Using the CFS scheduler as a guide, describe how the respective values of vruntime vary between the two processes given each of the following scenarios:

- Both A and B are CPU-bound.

- A is I/O-bound, and B is CPU-bound.

- A is CPU-bound, and B is I/O-bound.

6.29   Discuss ways in which the priority inversion problem could be addressed in a real-time system. Also discuss whether the solutions could be implemented within the context of a proportional share scheduler.

6.30   Under what circumstances is rate-monotonic scheduling inferior to earliest-deadline-first scheduling in meeting the deadlines associated with processes?

6.31   Consider two processes, P_1 and P_2, where $p_1 = 50$, $t_1 = 25$, $p_2 = 75$, and $t_2 = 30$.

a.   Can these two processes be scheduled using rate-monotonic scheduling? Illustrate your answer using a Gantt chart such as the ones in Figure 6.16–Figure 6.19.

b.   Illustrate the scheduling of these two processes using earliest-deadline-first (EDF) scheduling.

6.32   Explain why interrupt and dispatch latency times must be bounded in a hard real-time system.

Bibliographical Notes

Feedback queues were originally implemented on the CTSS system described in [Corbato et al. (1962)]. This feedback queue scheduling system was analyzed by [Schrage (1967)]. The preemptive priority scheduling algorithm of Exercise 6.23 was suggested by [Kleinrock (1975)]. The scheduling algorithms for hard real-time systems, such as rate monotonic scheduling and earliest-deadline-first scheduling, are presented in [Liu and Layland (1973)].

[Anderson et al. (1989)], [Lewis and Berg (1998)], and [Philbin et al. (1996)] discuss thread scheduling. Multicore scheduling is examined in [McNairy and Bhatia (2005)] and [Kongetira et al. (2005)].

[Fisher (1981)], [Hall et al. (1996)], and [Lowney et al. (1993)] describe scheduling techniques that take into account information regarding process execution times from previous runs.

Fair-share schedulers are covered by [Henry (1984)], [Woodside (1986)], and [Kay and Lauder (1988)].

Scheduling policies used in the UNIX V operating system are described by [Bach (1987)]; those for UNIX FreeBSD 5.2 are presented by [McKusick and Neville-Neil (2005)]; and those for the Mach operating system are discussed by [Black (1990)]. [Love (2010)] and [Mauerer (2008)] cover scheduling in Linux. [Faggioli et al. (2009)] discuss adding an EDF scheduler to the Linux kernel. Details of the ULE scheduler can be found in [Roberson (2003)]. Solaris scheduling is described by [Mauro and McDougall (2007)]. [Russinovich and Solomon (2009)] discusses scheduling in Windows internals. [Butenhof (1997)] and [Lewis and Berg (1998)] describe scheduling in Pthreads systems. [Siddha et al. (2007)] discuss scheduling challenges on multicore systems.

Bibliography

[Anderson et al. (1989)]   T. E. Anderson, E. D. Lazowska, and H. M. Levy, "The Performance Implications of Thread Management Alternatives for Shared-Memory Multiprocessors", *IEEE Transactions on Computers*, Volume 38, Number 12 (1989), pages 1631–1644.

[Bach (1987)]   M. J. Bach, *The Design of the UNIX Operating System*, Prentice Hall (1987).

[Black (1990)]   D. L. Black, "Scheduling Support for Concurrency and Parallelism in the Mach Operating System", *IEEE Computer*, Volume 23, Number 5 (1990), pages 35–43.

[Butenhof (1997)]   D. Butenhof, *Programming with POSIX Threads*, Addison-Wesley (1997).

[Corbato et al. (1962)]   F. J. Corbato, M. Merwin-Daggett, and R. C. Daley, "An Experimental Time-Sharing System", *Proceedings of the AFIPS Fall Joint Computer Conference* (1962), pages 335–344.

[Faggioli et al. (2009)]   D. Faggioli, F. Checconi, M. Trimarchi, and C. Scordino, "An EDF scheduling class for the Linux kernel", *Proceedings of the 11th Real-Time Linux Workshop* (2009).

[Fisher (1981)]   J. A. Fisher, "Trace Scheduling: A Technique for Global Microcode Compaction", *IEEE Transactions on Computers*, Volume 30, Number 7 (1981), pages 478–490.

[Hall et al. (1996)]   L. Hall, D. Shmoys, and J. Wein, "Scheduling To Minimize Average Completion Time: Off-line and On-line Algorithms", *SODA: ACM-SIAM Symposium on Discrete Algorithms* (1996).

[Henry (1984)]   G. Henry, "The Fair Share Scheduler", *AT&T Bell Laboratories Technical Journal* (1984).

[Kay and Lauder (1988)]   J. Kay and P. Lauder, "A Fair Share Scheduler", *Communications of the ACM*, Volume 31, Number 1 (1988), pages 44–55.

[Kleinrock (1975)]   L. Kleinrock, *Queueing Systems, Volume II: Computer Applications*, Wiley-Interscience (1975).

[Kongetira et al. (2005)]   P. Kongetira, K. Aingaran, and K. Olukotun, "Niagara: A 32-Way Multithreaded SPARC Processor", *IEEE Micro Magazine*, Volume 25, Number 2 (2005), pages 21–29.

[Lewis and Berg (1998)]   B. Lewis and D. Berg, *Multithreaded Programming with Pthreads*, Sun Microsystems Press (1998).

[Liu and Layland (1973)]   C. L. Liu and J. W. Layland, "Scheduling Algorithms for Multiprogramming in a Hard Real-Time Environment", *Communications of the ACM*, Volume 20, Number 1 (1973), pages 46–61.

[Love (2010)]   R. Love, *Linux Kernel Development*, Third Edition, Developer's Library (2010).

[Lowney et al. (1993)]   P. G. Lowney, S. M. Freudenberger, T. J. Karzes, W. D. Lichtenstein, R. P. Nix, J. S. O'Donnell, and J. C. Ruttenberg, "The Multiflow Trace Scheduling Compiler", *Journal of Supercomputing*, Volume 7, Number 1-2 (1993), pages 51–142.

[Mauerer (2008)]   W. Mauerer, *Professional Linux Kernel Architecture*, John Wiley and Sons (2008).

[Mauro and McDougall (2007)]   J. Mauro and R. McDougall, *Solaris Internals: Core Kernel Architecture*, Prentice Hall (2007).

[McKusick and Neville-Neil (2005)]   M. K. McKusick and G. V. Neville-Neil, *The Design and Implementation of the FreeBSD UNIX Operating System*, Addison Wesley (2005).

[McNairy and Bhatia (2005)]   C. McNairy and R. Bhatia, "Montecito: A Dual–Core, Dual-Threaded Itanium Processor", *IEEE Micro Magazine*, Volume 25, Number 2 (2005), pages 10–20.

[Philbin et al. (1996)]   J. Philbin, J. Edler, O. J. Anshus, C. C. Douglas, and K. Li, "Thread Scheduling for Cache Locality", *Architectural Support for Programming Languages and Operating Systems* (1996), pages 60–71.

[Roberson (2003)]   J. Roberson, "ULE: A Modern Scheduler For FreeBSD", *Proceedings of the USENIX BSDCon Conference* (2003), pages 17–28.

[Russinovich and Solomon (2009)]   M. E. Russinovich and D. A. Solomon, *Windows Internals: Including Windows Server 2008 and Windows Vista*, Fifth Edition, Microsoft Press (2009).

[Schrage (1967)]   L. E. Schrage, "The Queue M/G/I with Feedback to Lower Priority Queues", *Management Science*, Volume 13, (1967), pages 466–474.

[Siddha et al. (2007)]   S. Siddha, V. Pallipadi, and A. Mallick, "Process Scheduling Challenges in the Era of Multi-Core Processors", *Intel Technology Journal*, Volume 11, Number 4 (2007).

[Woodside (1986)]   C. Woodside, "Controllability of Computer Performance Tradeoffs Obtained Using Controlled-Share Queue Schedulers", *IEEE Transactions on Software Engineering*, Volume SE-12, Number 10 (1986), pages 1041–1048.

Part Three

Memory Management

The main purpose of a computer system is to execute programs. These programs, together with the data they access, must be at least partially in main memory during execution.

To improve both the utilization of the CPU and the speed of its response to users, a general-purpose computer must keep several processes in memory. Many memory-management schemes exist, reflecting various approaches, and the effectiveness of each algorithm depends on the situation. Selection of a memory-management scheme for a system depends on many factors, especially on the *hardware* design of the system. Most algorithms require hardware support.

CHAPTER 7

Main Memory

In Chapter 6, we showed how the CPU can be shared by a set of processes. As a result of CPU scheduling, we can improve both the utilization of the CPU and the speed of the computer's response to its users. To realize this increase in performance, however, we must keep several processes in memory—that is, we must share memory.

In this chapter, we discuss various ways to manage memory. The memory-management algorithms vary from a primitive bare-machine approach to paging and segmentation strategies. Each approach has its own advantages and disadvantages. Selection of a memory-management method for a specific system depends on many factors, especially on the hardware design of the system. As we shall see, many algorithms require hardware support, leading many systems to have closely integrated hardware and operating-system memory management.

CHAPTER OBJECTIVES

- To provide a detailed description of various ways of organizing memory hardware.
- To explore various techniques of allocating memory to processes.
- To discuss in detail how paging works in contemporary computer systems.

7.1 Background

As we saw in Chapter 1, memory is central to the operation of a modern computer system. Memory consists of a large array of bytes, each with its own address. The CPU fetches instructions from memory according to the value of the program counter. These instructions may cause additional loading from and storing to specific memory addresses.

A typical instruction-execution cycle, for example, first fetches an instruction from memory. The instruction is then decoded and may cause operands to be fetched from memory. After the instruction has been executed on the operands, results may be stored back in memory. The memory unit sees only a stream of memory addresses; it does not know how they are generated (by the instruction counter, indexing, indirection, literal addresses, and so on) or what they are for (instructions or data). Accordingly, we can ignore *how* a program generates a memory address. We are interested only in the sequence of memory addresses generated by the running program.

We begin our discussion by covering several issues that are pertinent to managing memory: basic hardware, the binding of symbolic memory addresses to actual physical addresses, and the distinction between logical and physical addresses. We conclude the section with a discussion of dynamic linking and shared libraries.

7.1.1 Basic Hardware

Main memory and the registers built into the processor itself are the only general-purpose storage that the CPU can access directly. There are machine instructions that take memory addresses as arguments, but none that take disk addresses. Therefore, any instructions in execution, and any data being used by the instructions, must be in one of these direct-access storage devices. If the data are not in memory, they must be moved there before the CPU can operate on them.

Registers that are built into the CPU are generally accessible within one cycle of the CPU clock. Most CPUs can decode instructions and perform simple operations on register contents at the rate of one or more operations per clock tick. The same cannot be said of main memory, which is accessed via a transaction on the memory bus. Completing a memory access may take many cycles of the CPU clock. In such cases, the processor normally needs to stall, since it does not have the data required to complete the instruction that it is executing. This situation is intolerable because of the frequency of memory accesses. The remedy is to add fast memory between the CPU and main memory, typically on the CPU chip for fast access. Such a cache was described in Section 1.8.3. To manage a cache built into the CPU, the hardware automatically speeds up memory access without any operating-system control.

Not only are we concerned with the relative speed of accessing physical memory, but we also must ensure correct operation. For proper system operation we must protect the operating system from access by user processes. On multiuser systems, we must additionally protect user processes from one another. This protection must be provided by the hardware because the operating system doesn't usually intervene between the CPU and its memory accesses (because of the resulting performance penalty). Hardware implements this production in several different ways, as we show throughout the chapter. Here, we outline one possible implementation.

We first need to make sure that each process has a separate memory space. Separate per-process memory space protects the processes from each other and is fundamental to having multiple processes loaded in memory for concurrent execution. To separate memory spaces, we need the ability to determine the range of legal addresses that the process may access and to ensure that the process can access only these legal addresses. We can provide this protection by using two registers, usually a base and a limit, as illustrated in Figure 7.1. The base register holds the smallest legal physical memory address; the limit register specifies the size of the range. For example, if the base register holds

Figure 7.1 A base and a limit register define a logical address space.

300040 and the limit register is 120900, then the program can legally access all addresses from 300040 through 420939 (inclusive).

Protection of memory space is accomplished by having the CPU hardware compare every address generated in user mode with the registers. Any attempt by a program executing in user mode to access operating-system memory or other users' memory results in a trap to the operating system, which treats the attempt as a fatal error (Figure 7.2). This scheme prevents a user program from (accidentally or deliberately) modifying the code or data structures of either the operating system or other users.

The base and limit registers can be loaded only by the operating system, which uses a special privileged instruction. Since privileged instructions can be executed only in kernel mode, and since only the operating system executes in kernel mode, only the operating system can load the base and limit registers.

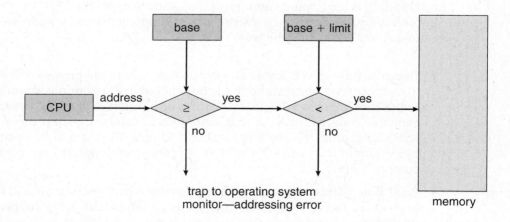

Figure 7.2 Hardware address protection with base and limit registers.

This scheme allows the operating system to change the value of the registers but prevents user programs from changing the registers' contents.

The operating system, executing in kernel mode, is given unrestricted access to both operating-system memory and users' memory. This provision allows the operating system to load users' programs into users' memory, to dump out those programs in case of errors, to access and modify parameters of system calls, to perform I/O to and from user memory, and to provide many other services. Consider, for example, that an operating system for a multiprocessing system must execute context switches, storing the state of one process from the registers into main memory before loading the next process's context from main memory into the registers.

7.1.2 Address Binding

Usually, a program resides on a disk as a binary executable file. To be executed, the program must be brought into memory and placed within a process. Depending on the memory management in use, the process may be moved between disk and memory during its execution. The processes on the disk that are waiting to be brought into memory for execution form the **input queue**.

The normal single-tasking procedure is to select one of the processes in the input queue and to load that process into memory. As the process is executed, it accesses instructions and data from memory. Eventually, the process terminates, and its memory space is declared available.

Most systems allow a user process to reside in any part of the physical memory. Thus, although the address space of the computer may start at 00000, the first address of the user process need not be 00000. You will see later how a user program actually places a process in physical memory.

In most cases, a user program goes through several steps—some of which may be optional—before being executed (Figure 7.3). Addresses may be represented in different ways during these steps. Addresses in the source program are generally symbolic (such as the variable count). A compiler typically **binds** these symbolic addresses to relocatable addresses (such as "14 bytes from the beginning of this module"). The linkage editor or loader in turn binds the relocatable addresses to absolute addresses (such as 74014). Each binding is a mapping from one address space to another.

Classically, the binding of instructions and data to memory addresses can be done at any step along the way:

- **Compile time**. If you know at compile time where the process will reside in memory, then **absolute code** can be generated. For example, if you know that a user process will reside starting at location R, then the generated compiler code will start at that location and extend up from there. If, at some later time, the starting location changes, then it will be necessary to recompile this code. The MS-DOS .COM-format programs are bound at compile time.

- **Load time**. If it is not known at compile time where the process will reside in memory, then the compiler must generate **relocatable code**. In this case, final binding is delayed until load time. If the starting address changes, we need only reload the user code to incorporate this changed value.

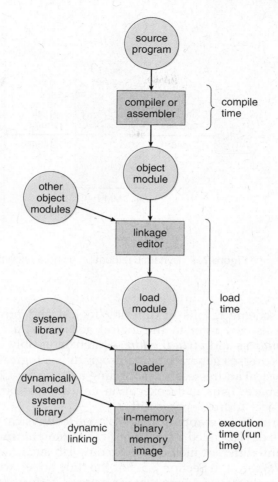

Figure 7.3 Multistep processing of a user program.

- **Execution time**. If the process can be moved during its execution from one memory segment to another, then binding must be delayed until run time. Special hardware must be available for this scheme to work, as will be discussed in Section 7.1.3. Most general-purpose operating systems use this method.

A major portion of this chapter is devoted to showing how these various bindings can be implemented effectively in a computer system and to discussing appropriate hardware support.

7.1.3   Logical Versus Physical Address Space

An address generated by the CPU is commonly referred to as a **logical address**, whereas an address seen by the memory unit—that is, the one loaded into the **memory-address register** of the memory—is commonly referred to as a **physical address**.

The compile-time and load-time address-binding methods generate identical logical and physical addresses. However, the execution-time address-

Figure 7.4 Dynamic relocation using a relocation register.

binding scheme results in differing logical and physical addresses. In this case, we usually refer to the logical address as a **virtual address**. We use *logical address* and *virtual address* interchangeably in this text. The set of all logical addresses generated by a program is a **logical address space**. The set of all physical addresses corresponding to these logical addresses is a **physical address space**. Thus, in the execution-time address-binding scheme, the logical and physical address spaces differ.

The run-time mapping from virtual to physical addresses is done by a hardware device called the **memory-management unit (MMU)**. We can choose from many different methods to accomplish such mapping, as we discuss in Section 7.3 through Section 7.5. For the time being, we illustrate this mapping with a simple MMU scheme that is a generalization of the base-register scheme described in Section 7.1.1. The base register is now called a **relocation register**. The value in the relocation register is added to every address generated by a user process at the time the address is sent to memory (see Figure 7.4). For example, if the base is at 14000, then an attempt by the user to address location 0 is dynamically relocated to location 14000; an access to location 346 is mapped to location 14346.

The user program never sees the real physical addresses. The program can create a pointer to location 346, store it in memory, manipulate it, and compare it with other addresses—all as the number 346. Only when it is used as a memory address (in an indirect load or store, perhaps) is it relocated relative to the base register. The user program deals with logical addresses. The memory-mapping hardware converts logical addresses into physical addresses. This form of execution-time binding was discussed in Section 7.1.2. The final location of a referenced memory address is not determined until the reference is made.

We now have two different types of addresses: logical addresses (in the range 0 to *max*) and physical addresses (in the range $R + 0$ to $R + max$ for a base value R). The user program generates only logical addresses and thinks that the process runs in locations 0 to *max*. However, these logical addresses must be mapped to physical addresses before they are used. The concept of a logical address space that is bound to a separate physical address space is central to proper memory management.

7.1.4   Dynamic Loading

In our discussion so far, it has been necessary for the entire program and all data of a process to be in physical memory for the process to execute. The size of a process has thus been limited to the size of physical memory. To obtain better memory-space utilization, we can use **dynamic loading**. With dynamic loading, a routine is not loaded until it is called. All routines are kept on disk in a relocatable load format. The main program is loaded into memory and is executed. When a routine needs to call another routine, the calling routine first checks to see whether the other routine has been loaded. If it has not, the relocatable linking loader is called to load the desired routine into memory and to update the program's address tables to reflect this change. Then control is passed to the newly loaded routine.

The advantage of dynamic loading is that a routine is loaded only when it is needed. This method is particularly useful when large amounts of code are needed to handle infrequently occurring cases, such as error routines. In this case, although the total program size may be large, the portion that is used (and hence loaded) may be much smaller.

Dynamic loading does not require special support from the operating system. It is the responsibility of the users to design their programs to take advantage of such a method. Operating systems may help the programmer, however, by providing library routines to implement dynamic loading.

7.1.5   Dynamic Linking and Shared Libraries

Dynamically linked libraries are system libraries that are linked to user programs when the programs are run (refer back to Figure 7.3). Some operating systems support only **static linking**, in which system libraries are treated like any other object module and are combined by the loader into the binary program image. Dynamic linking, in contrast, is similar to dynamic loading. Here, though, linking, rather than loading, is postponed until execution time. This feature is usually used with system libraries, such as language subroutine libraries. Without this facility, each program on a system must include a copy of its language library (or at least the routines referenced by the program) in the executable image. This requirement wastes both disk space and main memory.

With dynamic linking, a **stub** is included in the image for each library-routine reference. The stub is a small piece of code that indicates how to locate the appropriate memory-resident library routine or how to load the library if the routine is not already present. When the stub is executed, it checks to see whether the needed routine is already in memory. If it is not, the program loads the routine into memory. Either way, the stub replaces itself with the address of the routine and executes the routine. Thus, the next time that particular code segment is reached, the library routine is executed directly, incurring no cost for dynamic linking. Under this scheme, all processes that use a language library execute only one copy of the library code.

This feature can be extended to library updates (such as bug fixes). A library may be replaced by a new version, and all programs that reference the library will automatically use the new version. Without dynamic linking, all such programs would need to be relinked to gain access to the new library. So that programs will not accidentally execute new, incompatible versions of libraries, version information is included in both the program and the library. More than one version of a library may be loaded into memory, and each program uses its version information to decide which copy of the library to use. Versions with minor changes retain the same version number, whereas versions with major changes increment the number. Thus, only programs that are compiled with the new library version are affected by any incompatible changes incorporated in it. Other programs linked before the new library was installed will continue using the older library. This system is also known as **shared libraries**.

Unlike dynamic loading, dynamic linking and shared libraries generally require help from the operating system. If the processes in memory are protected from one another, then the operating system is the only entity that can check to see whether the needed routine is in another process's memory space or that can allow multiple processes to access the same memory addresses. We elaborate on this concept when we discuss paging in Section 7.5.4.

7.2 Swapping

A process must be in memory to be executed. A process, however, can be **swapped** temporarily out of memory to a **backing store** and then brought back into memory for continued execution (Figure 7.5). Swapping makes it possible for the total physical address space of all processes to exceed the real physical memory of the system, thus increasing the degree of multiprogramming in a system.

7.2.1 Standard Swapping

Standard swapping involves moving processes between main memory and a backing store. The backing store is commonly a fast disk. It must be large

Figure 7.5 Swapping of two processes using a disk as a backing store.

enough to accommodate copies of all memory images for all users, and it must provide direct access to these memory images. The system maintains a ready queue consisting of all processes whose memory images are on the backing store or in memory and are ready to run. Whenever the CPU scheduler decides to execute a process, it calls the dispatcher. The dispatcher checks to see whether the next process in the queue is in memory. If it is not, and if there is no free memory region, the dispatcher swaps out a process currently in memory and swaps in the desired process. It then reloads registers and transfers control to the selected process.

The context-switch time in such a swapping system is fairly high. To get an idea of the context-switch time, let's assume that the user process is 100 MB in size and the backing store is a standard hard disk with a transfer rate of 50 MB per second. The actual transfer of the 100-MB process to or from main memory takes

$$100 \text{ MB}/50 \text{ MB per second} = 2 \text{ seconds}$$

The swap time is 2000 milliseconds. Since we must swap both out and in, the total swap time is about 4,000 milliseconds. (Here, we are ignoring other disk performance aspects, which we cover in Chapter 9.)

Notice that the major part of the swap time is transfer time. The total transfer time is directly proportional to the amount of memory swapped. If we have a computer system with 4 GB of main memory and a resident operating system taking 1 GB, the maximum size of the user process is 3 GB. However, many user processes may be much smaller than this—say, 100 MB. A 100-MB process could be swapped out in 2 seconds, compared with the 60 seconds required for swapping 3 GB. Clearly, it would be useful to know exactly how much memory a user process *is* using, not simply how much it *might* be using. Then we would need to swap only what is actually used, reducing swap time. For this method to be effective, the user must keep the system informed of any changes in memory requirements. Thus, a process with dynamic memory requirements will need to issue system calls (request_memory() and release_memory()) to inform the operating system of its changing memory needs.

Swapping is constrained by other factors as well. If we want to swap a process, we must be sure that it is completely idle. Of particular concern is any pending I/O. A process may be waiting for an I/O operation when we want to swap that process to free up memory. However, if the I/O is asynchronously accessing the user memory for I/O buffers, then the process cannot be swapped. Assume that the I/O operation is queued because the device is busy. If we were to swap out process P_1 and swap in process P_2, the I/O operation might then attempt to use memory that now belongs to process P_2. There are two main solutions to this problem: never swap a process with pending I/O, or execute I/O operations only into operating-system buffers. Transfers between operating-system buffers and process memory then occur only when the process is swapped in. Note that this double buffering itself adds overhead. We now need to copy the data again, from kernel memory to user memory, before the user process can access it.

Standard swapping is not used in modern operating systems. It requires too much swapping time and provides too little execution time to be a reasonable memory-management solution. Modified versions of swapping, however, are found on many systems, including UNIX, Linux, and Windows. In one common variation, swapping is normally disabled but will start if the amount of free memory (unused memory available for the operating system or processes to use) falls below a threshold amount. Swapping is halted when the amount of free memory increases. Another variation involves swapping portions of processes—rather than entire processes—to decrease swap time. Typically, these modified forms of swapping work in conjunction with virtual memory, which we cover in Chapter 8.

7.2.2 Swapping on Mobile Systems

Although most operating systems for PCs and servers support some modified version of swapping, mobile systems typically do not support swapping in any form. Mobile devices generally use flash memory rather than more spacious hard disks as their persistent storage. The resulting space constraint is one reason why mobile operating-system designers avoid swapping. Other reasons include the limited number of writes that flash memory can tolerate before it becomes unreliable and the poor throughput between main memory and flash memory in these devices.

Instead of using swapping, when free memory falls below a certain threshold, Apple's iOS *asks* applications to voluntarily relinquish allocated memory. Read-only data (such as code) are removed from the system and later reloaded from flash memory if necessary. Data that have been modified (such as the stack) are never removed. However, any applications that fail to free up sufficient memory may be terminated by the operating system.

Android does not support swapping and adopts a strategy similar to that used by iOS. It may terminate a process if insufficient free memory is available. However, before terminating a process, Android writes its application state to flash memory so that it can be quickly restarted.

Because of these restrictions, developers for mobile systems must carefully allocate and release memory to ensure that their applications do not use too much memory or suffer from memory leaks. Note that both iOS and Android support paging, so they do have memory-management abilities. We discuss paging later in this chapter.

7.3   Contiguous Memory Allocation

The main memory must accommodate both the operating system and the various user processes. We therefore need to allocate main memory in the most efficient way possible. This section explains one early method, contiguous memory allocation.

The memory is usually divided into two partitions: one for the resident operating system and one for the user processes. We can place the operating system in either low memory or high memory. The major factor affecting this decision is the location of the interrupt vector. Since the interrupt vector is often in low memory, programmers usually place the operating system in low memory as well. Thus, in this text, we discuss only the situation in which the operating system resides in low memory. The development of the other situation is similar.

We usually want several user processes to reside in memory at the same time. We therefore need to consider how to allocate available memory to the processes that are in the input queue waiting to be brought into memory. In **contiguous memory allocation**, each process is contained in a single section of memory that is contiguous to the section containing the next process.

7.3.1   Memory Protection

Before discussing memory allocation further, we must discuss the issue of memory protection. We can prevent a process from accessing memory it does not own by combining two ideas previously discussed. If we have a system with a relocation register (Section 7.1.3), together with a limit register (Section 7.1.1), we accomplish our goal. The relocation register contains the value of the smallest physical address; the limit register contains the range of logical addresses (for example, relocation = 100040 and limit = 74600). Each logical address must fall within the range specified by the limit register. The MMU maps the logical address dynamically by adding the value in the relocation register. This mapped address is sent to memory (Figure 7.6).

When the CPU scheduler selects a process for execution, the dispatcher loads the relocation and limit registers with the correct values as part of the context switch. Because every address generated by a CPU is checked against these registers, we can protect both the operating system and the other users' programs and data from being modified by this running process.

The relocation-register scheme provides an effective way to allow the operating system's size to change dynamically. This flexibility is desirable in many situations. For example, the operating system contains code and buffer space for device drivers. If a device driver (or other operating-system service) is not commonly used, we do not want to keep the code and data in memory, as we might be able to use that space for other purposes. Such code is sometimes called **transient** operating-system code; it comes and goes as needed. Thus, using this code changes the size of the operating system during program execution.

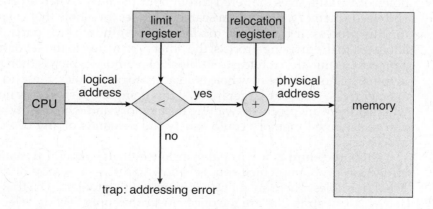

Figure 7.6   Hardware support for relocation and limit registers.

7.3.2 Memory Allocation

Now we are ready to turn to memory allocation. One of the simplest methods for allocating memory is to divide memory into several fixed-sized **partitions**. Each partition may contain exactly one process. Thus, the degree of multiprogramming is bound by the number of partitions. In this **multiple-partition method**, when a partition is free, a process is selected from the input queue and is loaded into the free partition. When the process terminates, the partition becomes available for another process. This method was originally used by the IBM OS/360 operating system (called MFT) but is no longer in use. The method described next is a generalization of the fixed-partition scheme (called MVT); it is used primarily in batch environments. Many of the ideas presented here are also applicable to a time-sharing environment in which pure segmentation is used for memory management (Section 7.4).

In the **variable-partition** scheme, the operating system keeps a table indicating which parts of memory are available and which are occupied. Initially, all memory is available for user processes and is considered one large block of available memory, a **hole**. Eventually, as you will see, memory contains a set of holes of various sizes.

As processes enter the system, they are put into an input queue. The operating system takes into account the memory requirements of each process and the amount of available memory space in determining which processes are allocated memory. When a process is allocated space, it is loaded into memory, and it can then compete for CPU time. When a process terminates, it releases its memory, which the operating system may then fill with another process from the input queue.

At any given time, then, we have a list of available block sizes and an input queue. The operating system can order the input queue according to a scheduling algorithm. Memory is allocated to processes until, finally, the memory requirements of the next process cannot be satisfied—that is, no available block of memory (or hole) is large enough to hold that process. The operating system can then wait until a large enough block is available, or it can skip down the input queue to see whether the smaller memory requirements of some other process can be met.

In general, as mentioned, the memory blocks available comprise a *set* of holes of various sizes scattered throughout memory. When a process arrives and needs memory, the system searches the set for a hole that is large enough for this process. If the hole is too large, it is split into two parts. One part is allocated to the arriving process; the other is returned to the set of holes. When a process terminates, it releases its block of memory, which is then placed back in the set of holes. If the new hole is adjacent to other holes, these adjacent holes are merged to form one larger hole. At this point, the system may need to check whether there are processes waiting for memory and whether this newly freed and recombined memory could satisfy the demands of any of these waiting processes.

This procedure is a particular instance of the general **dynamic storage-allocation problem**, which concerns how to satisfy a request of size n from a list of free holes. There are many solutions to this problem. The **first-fit**, **best-fit**, and **worst-fit** strategies are the ones most commonly used to select a free hole from the set of available holes.

- **First fit**. Allocate the first hole that is big enough. Searching can start either at the beginning of the set of holes or at the location where the previous first-fit search ended. We can stop searching as soon as we find a free hole that is large enough.

- **Best fit**. Allocate the smallest hole that is big enough. We must search the entire list, unless the list is ordered by size. This strategy produces the smallest leftover hole.

- **Worst fit**. Allocate the largest hole. Again, we must search the entire list, unless it is sorted by size. This strategy produces the largest leftover hole, which may be more useful than the smaller leftover hole from a best-fit approach.

Simulations have shown that both first fit and best fit are better than worst fit in terms of decreasing time and storage utilization. Neither first fit nor best fit is clearly better than the other in terms of storage utilization, but first fit is generally faster.

7.3.3 Fragmentation

Both the first-fit and best-fit strategies for memory allocation suffer from external fragmentation. As processes are loaded and removed from memory, the free memory space is broken into little pieces. External fragmentation exists when there is enough total memory space to satisfy a request but the available spaces are not contiguous: storage is fragmented into a large number of small holes. This fragmentation problem can be severe. In the worst case, we could have a block of free (or wasted) memory between every two processes. If all these small pieces of memory were in one big free block instead, we might be able to run several more processes.

Whether we are using the first-fit or best-fit strategy can affect the amount of fragmentation. (First fit is better for some systems, whereas best fit is better for others.) Another factor is which end of a free block is allocated. (Which is the leftover piece—the one on the top or the one on the bottom?) No matter which algorithm is used, however, external fragmentation will be a problem.

Depending on the total amount of memory storage and the average process size, external fragmentation may be a minor or a major problem. Statistical analysis of first fit, for instance, reveals that, even with some optimization, given N allocated blocks, another 0.5 N blocks will be lost to fragmentation. That is, one-third of memory may be unusable! This property is known as the 50-percent rule.

Memory fragmentation can be internal as well as external. Consider a multiple-partition allocation scheme with a hole of 18,464 bytes. Suppose that the next process requests 18,462 bytes. If we allocate exactly the requested block, we are left with a hole of 2 bytes. The overhead to keep track of this hole will be substantially larger than the hole itself. The general approach to avoiding this problem is to break the physical memory into fixed-sized blocks and allocate memory in units based on block size. With this approach, the memory allocated to a process may be slightly larger than the requested memory. The difference between these two numbers is internal fragmentation—unused memory that is internal to a partition.

One solution to the problem of external fragmentation is compaction. The goal is to shuffle the memory contents so as to place all free memory together in one large block. Compaction is not always possible, however. If relocation is static and is done at assembly or load time, compaction cannot be done. It is possible only if relocation is dynamic and is done at execution time. If addresses are relocated dynamically, relocation requires only moving the program and data and then changing the base register to reflect the new base address. When compaction is possible, we must determine its cost. The simplest compaction algorithm is to move all processes toward one end of memory; all holes move in the other direction, producing one large hole of available memory. This scheme can be expensive.

Another possible solution to the external-fragmentation problem is to permit the logical address space of the processes to be noncontiguous, thus allowing a process to be allocated physical memory wherever such memory is available. Two complementary techniques achieve this solution: segmentation (Section 7.4) and paging (Section 7.5). These techniques can also be combined.

Fragmentation is a general problem in computing that can occur wherever we must manage blocks of data. We discuss the topic further in the storage management chapters (Chapter 9 through Chapter 11.)

7.4   Segmentation

As we've already seen, the user's view of memory is not the same as the actual physical memory. This is equally true of the programmer's view of memory. Indeed, dealing with memory in terms of its physical properties is inconvenient to both the operating system and the programmer. What if the hardware could provide a memory mechanism that mapped the programmer's view to the actual physical memory? The system would have more freedom to manage memory, while the programmer would have a more natural programming environment. Segmentation provides such a mechanism.

7.4.1   Basic Method

Do programmers think of memory as a linear array of bytes, some containing instructions and others containing data? Most programmers would say "no." Rather, they prefer to view memory as a collection of variable-sized segments, with no necessary ordering among the segments (Figure 7.7).

When writing a program, a programmer thinks of it as a main program with a set of methods, procedures, or functions. It may also include various data structures: objects, arrays, stacks, variables, and so on. Each of these modules or data elements is referred to by name. The programmer talks about "the stack," "the math library," and "the main program" without caring what addresses in memory these elements occupy. She is not concerned with whether the stack is stored before or after the Sqrt() function. Segments vary in length, and the length of each is intrinsically defined by its purpose in the program. Elements within a segment are identified by their offset from the beginning of the segment: the first statement of the program, the seventh stack frame entry in the stack, the fifth instruction of the Sqrt(), and so on.

Segmentation is a memory-management scheme that supports this programmer view of memory. A logical address space is a collection of segments.

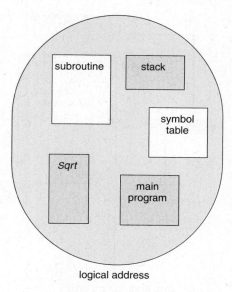

logical address

Figure 7.7 Programmer's view of a program.

Each segment has a name and a length. The addresses specify both the segment name and the offset within the segment. The programmer therefore specifies each address by two quantities: a segment name and an offset.

For simplicity of implementation, segments are numbered and are referred to by a segment number, rather than by a segment name. Thus, a logical address consists of a *two tuple*:

$$<\text{segment-number, offset}>.$$

Normally, when a program is compiled, the compiler automatically constructs segments reflecting the input program.

A C compiler might create separate segments for the following:

1. The code
2. Global variables
3. The heap, from which memory is allocated
4. The stacks used by each thread
5. The standard C library

Libraries that are linked in during compile time might be assigned separate segments. The loader would take all these segments and assign them segment numbers.

7.4.2 Segmentation Hardware

Although the programmer can now refer to objects in the program by a two-dimensional address, the actual physical memory is still, of course, a one-dimensional sequence of bytes. Thus, we must define an implementation to map two-dimensional programmer-defined addresses into one-dimensional

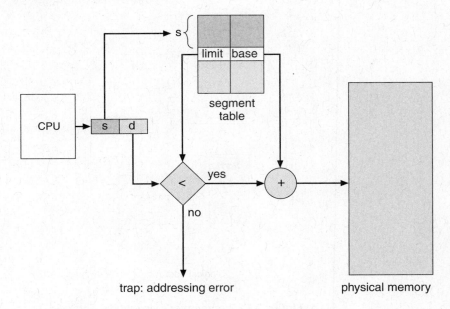

Figure 7.8 Segmentation hardware.

physical addresses. This mapping is effected by a **segment table**. Each entry in the segment table has a **segment base** and a **segment limit**. The segment base contains the starting physical address where the segment resides in memory, and the segment limit specifies the length of the segment.

The use of a segment table is illustrated in Figure 7.8. A logical address consists of two parts: a segment number, s, and an offset into that segment, d. The segment number is used as an index to the segment table. The offset d of the logical address must be between 0 and the segment limit. If it is not, we trap to the operating system (logical addressing attempt beyond end of segment). When an offset is legal, it is added to the segment base to produce the address in physical memory of the desired byte. The segment table is thus essentially an array of base–limit register pairs.

As an example, consider the situation shown in Figure 7.9. We have five segments numbered from 0 through 4. The segments are stored in physical memory as shown. The segment table has a separate entry for each segment, giving the beginning address of the segment in physical memory (or base) and the length of that segment (or limit). For example, segment 2 is 400 bytes long and begins at location 4300. Thus, a reference to byte 53 of segment 2 is mapped onto location 4300 + 53 = 4353. A reference to segment 3, byte 852, is mapped to 3200 (the base of segment 3) + 852 = 4052. A reference to byte 1222 of segment 0 would result in a trap to the operating system, as this segment is only 1000 bytes long.

7.5 Paging

Segmentation permits the physical address space of a process to be non-contiguous. **Paging** is another memory-management scheme that offers this advantage. However, paging avoids external fragmentation and the need for

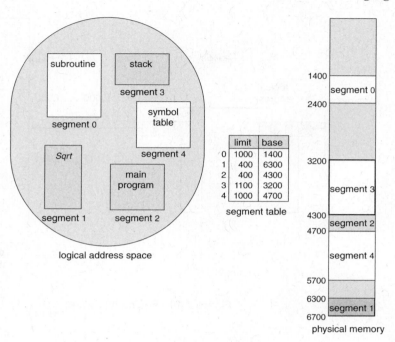

Figure 7.9 Example of segmentation.

compaction, whereas segmentation does not. It also solves the considerable problem of fitting memory chunks of varying sizes onto the backing store. Most memory-management schemes used before the introduction of paging suffered from this problem. The problem arises because, when code fragments or data residing in main memory need to be swapped out, space must be found on the backing store. The backing store has the same fragmentation problems discussed in connection with main memory, but access is much slower, so compaction is impossible. Because of its advantages over earlier methods, paging in its various forms is used in most operating systems, from those for mainframes through those for smartphones. Paging is implemented through cooperation between the operating system and the computer hardware.

7.5.1 Basic Method

The basic method for implementing paging involves breaking physical memory into fixed-sized blocks called **frames** and breaking logical memory into blocks of the same size called **pages**. When a process is to be executed, its pages are loaded into any available memory frames from their source (a file system or the backing store). The backing store is divided into fixed-sized blocks that are the same size as the memory frames or clusters of multiple frames. This rather simple idea has great functionality and wide ramifications. For example, the logical address space is now totally separate from the physical address space, so a process can have a logical 64-bit address space even though the system has less than 2^{64} bytes of physical memory.

The hardware support for paging is illustrated in Figure 7.10. Every address generated by the CPU is divided into two parts: a **page number (p)** and a **page**

Figure 7.10   Paging hardware.

offset (d). The page number is used as an index into a page table. The page table contains the base address of each page in physical memory. This base address is combined with the page offset to define the physical memory address that is sent to the memory unit. The paging model of memory is shown in Figure 7.11.

Figure 7.11   Paging model of logical and physical memory.

The page size (like the frame size) is defined by the hardware. The size of a page is a power of 2, varying between 512 bytes and 1 GB per page, depending on the computer architecture. The selection of a power of 2 as a page size makes the translation of a logical address into a page number and page offset particularly easy. If the size of the logical address space is 2^m, and a page size is 2^n bytes, then the high-order $m - n$ bits of a logical address designate the page number, and the n low-order bits designate the page offset. Thus, the logical address is as follows:

page number	page offset
p	d
$m - n$	n

where p is an index into the page table and d is the displacement within the page.

As a concrete (although minuscule) example, consider the memory in Figure 7.12. Here, in the logical address, $n = 2$ and $m = 4$. Using a page size of 4 bytes and a physical memory of 32 bytes (8 pages), we show how the programmer's view of memory can be mapped into physical memory. Logical address 0 is page 0, offset 0. Indexing into the page table, we find that page 0

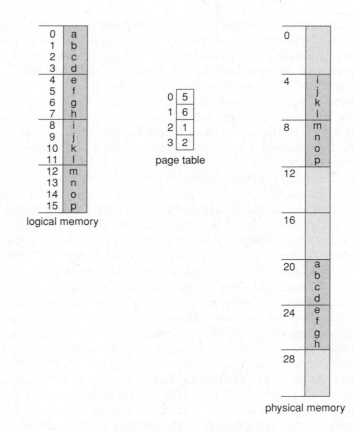

Figure 7.12 Paging example for a 32-byte memory with 4-byte pages.

OBTAINING THE PAGE SIZE ON LINUX SYSTEMS

On a Linux system, the page size varies according to architecture, and there are several ways of obtaining the page size. One approach is to use the getpagesize() system call. Another strategy is to enter the following command on the command line:

    getconf PAGESIZE

Each of these techniques returns the page size as a number of bytes.

is in frame 5. Thus, logical address 0 maps to physical address 20 [= (5 × 4) + 0]. Logical address 3 (page 0, offset 3) maps to physical address 23 [= (5 × 4) + 3]. Logical address 4 is page 1, offset 0; according to the page table, page 1 is mapped to frame 6. Thus, logical address 4 maps to physical address 24 [= (6 × 4) + 0]. Logical address 13 maps to physical address 9.

You may have noticed that paging itself is a form of dynamic relocation. Every logical address is bound by the paging hardware to some physical address. Using paging is similar to using a table of base (or relocation) registers, one for each frame of memory.

When we use a paging scheme, we have no external fragmentation: any free frame can be allocated to a process that needs it. However, we may have some internal fragmentation. Notice that frames are allocated as units. If the memory requirements of a process do not happen to coincide with page boundaries, the last frame allocated may not be completely full. For example, if page size is 2,048 bytes, a process of 72,766 bytes will need 35 pages plus 1,086 bytes. It will be allocated 36 frames, resulting in internal fragmentation of 2,048 − 1,086 = 962 bytes. In the worst case, a process would need n pages plus 1 byte. It would be allocated n + 1 frames, resulting in internal fragmentation of almost an entire frame.

If process size is independent of page size, we expect internal fragmentation to average one-half page per process. This consideration suggests that small page sizes are desirable. However, overhead is involved in each page-table entry, and this overhead is reduced as the size of the pages increases. Also, disk I/O is more efficient when the amount of data being transferred is larger (Chapter 9). Generally, page sizes have grown over time as processes, data sets, and main memory have become larger. Today, pages typically are between 4 KB and 8 KB in size, and some systems support even larger page sizes. Some CPUs and kernels even support multiple page sizes. For instance, Solaris uses page sizes of 8 KB and 4 MB, depending on the data stored by the pages. Researchers are now developing support for variable on-the-fly page size.

Frequently, on a 32-bit CPU, each page-table entry is 4 bytes long, but that size can vary as well. A 32-bit entry can point to one of 2^{32} physical page frames. If frame size is 4 KB (2^{12}), then a system with 4-byte entries can address 2^{44} bytes (or 16 TB) of physical memory. We should note here that the size of physical memory in a paged memory system is different from the maximum logical size of a process. As we further explore paging, we introduce other information that must be kept in the page-table entries. That information reduces the number

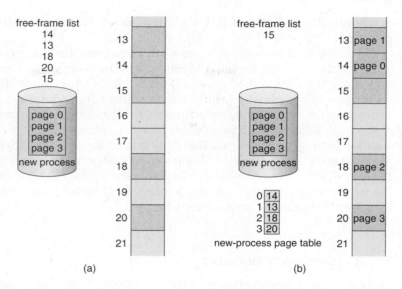

Figure 7.13 Free frames (a) before allocation and (b) after allocation.

of bits available to address page frames. Thus, a system with 32-bit page-table entries may address less physical memory than the possible maximum. A 32-bit CPU uses 32-bit addresses, meaning that a given process space can only be 2^{32} bytes (4 GB). Therefore, paging lets us use physical memory that is larger than what can be addressed by the CPU's address pointer length.

When a process arrives in the system to be executed, its size, expressed in pages, is examined. Each page of the process needs one frame. Thus, if the process requires n pages, at least n frames must be available in memory. If n frames are available, they are allocated to this arriving process. The first page of the process is loaded into one of the allocated frames, and the frame number is put in the page table for this process. The next page is loaded into another frame, its frame number is put into the page table, and so on (Figure 7.13).

An important aspect of paging is the clear separation between the programmer's view of memory and the actual physical memory. The programmer views memory as one single space, containing only this one program. In fact, the user program is scattered throughout physical memory, which also holds other programs. The difference between the programmer's view of memory and the actual physical memory is reconciled by the address-translation hardware. The logical addresses are translated into physical addresses. This mapping is hidden from the programmer and is controlled by the operating system. Notice that the user process by definition is unable to access memory it does not own. It has no way of addressing memory outside of its page table, and the table includes only those pages that the process owns.

Since the operating system is managing physical memory, it must be aware of the allocation details of physical memory—which frames are allocated, which frames are available, how many total frames there are, and so on. This information is generally kept in a data structure called a **frame table**. The frame table has one entry for each physical page frame, indicating whether the latter is free or allocated and, if it is allocated, to which page of which process or processes.

In addition, the operating system must be aware that user processes operate in user space, and all logical addresses must be mapped to produce physical addresses. If a user makes a system call (to do I/O, for example) and provides an address as a parameter (a buffer, for instance), that address must be mapped to produce the correct physical address. The operating system maintains a copy of the page table for each process, just as it maintains a copy of the instruction counter and register contents. This copy is used to translate logical addresses to physical addresses whenever the operating system must map a logical address to a physical address manually. It is also used by the CPU dispatcher to define the hardware page table when a process is to be allocated the CPU. Paging therefore increases the context-switch time.

7.5.2 Hardware Support

Each operating system has its own methods for storing page tables. Some allocate a page table for each process. A pointer to the page table is stored with the other register values (like the instruction counter) in the process control block. When the dispatcher is told to start a process, it must reload the user registers and define the correct hardware page-table values from the stored user page table. Other operating systems provide one or at most a few page tables, which decreases the overhead involved when processes are context-switched.

The hardware implementation of the page table can be done in several ways. In the simplest case, the page table is implemented as a set of dedicated **registers**. These registers should be built with very high-speed logic to make the paging-address translation efficient. Every access to memory must go through the paging map, so efficiency is a major consideration. The CPU dispatcher reloads these registers, just as it reloads the other registers. Instructions to load or modify the page-table registers are, of course, privileged, so that only the operating system can change the memory map. The DEC PDP-11 is an example of such an architecture. The address consists of 16 bits, and the page size is 8 KB. The page table thus consists of eight entries that are kept in fast registers.

The use of registers for the page table is satisfactory if the page table is reasonably small (for example, 256 entries). Most contemporary computers, however, allow the page table to be very large (for example, 1 million entries). For these machines, the use of fast registers to implement the page table is not feasible. Rather, the page table is kept in main memory, and a **page-table base register** (PTBR) points to the page table. Changing page tables requires changing only this one register, substantially reducing context-switch time.

The problem with this approach is the time required to access a user memory location. If we want to access location i, we must first index into the page table, using the value in the PTBR offset by the page number for i. This task requires a memory access. It provides us with the frame number, which is combined with the page offset to produce the actual address. We can then access the desired place in memory. With this scheme, *two* memory accesses are needed to access a byte (one for the page-table entry, one for the byte). Thus, memory access is slowed by a factor of 2. This delay would be intolerable under most circumstances. We might as well resort to swapping!

The standard solution to this problem is to use a special, small, fast-lookup hardware cache called a translation look-aside buffer (TLB). The TLB is associative, high-speed memory. Each entry in the TLB consists of two parts: a key (or tag) and a value. When the associative memory is presented with an item, the item is compared with all keys simultaneously. If the item is found, the corresponding value field is returned. The search is fast; a TLB lookup in modern hardware is part of the instruction pipeline, essentially adding no performance penalty. To be able to execute the search within a pipeline step, however, the TLB must be kept small. It is typically between 32 and 1,024 entries in size. Some CPUs implement separate instruction and data address TLBs. That can double the number of TLB entries available, because those lookups occur in different pipeline steps. We can see in this development an example of the evolution of CPU technology: systems have evolved from having no TLBs to having multiple levels of TLBs, just as they have multiple levels of caches.

The TLB is used with page tables in the following way. The TLB contains only a few of the page-table entries. When a logical address is generated by the CPU, its page number is presented to the TLB. If the page number is found, its frame number is immediately available and is used to access memory. As just mentioned, these steps are executed as part of the instruction pipeline within the CPU, adding no performance penalty compared with a system that does not implement paging.

If the page number is not in the TLB (known as a TLB miss), a memory reference to the page table must be made. Depending on the CPU, this may be done automatically in hardware or via an interrupt to the operating system. When the frame number is obtained, we can use it to access memory (Figure 7.14). In addition, we add the page number and frame number to the TLB, so

Figure 7.14 Paging hardware with TLB.

that they will be found quickly on the next reference. If the TLB is already full of entries, an existing entry must be selected for replacement. Replacement policies range from least recently used (LRU) through round-robin to random. Some CPUs allow the operating system to participate in LRU entry replacement, while others handle the matter themselves. Furthermore, some TLBs allow certain entries to be wired down, meaning that they cannot be removed from the TLB. Typically, TLB entries for key kernel code are wired down.

Some TLBs store address-space identifiers (ASIDs) in each TLB entry. An ASID uniquely identifies each process and is used to provide address-space protection for that process. When the TLB attempts to resolve virtual page numbers, it ensures that the ASID for the currently running process matches the ASID associated with the virtual page. If the ASIDs do not match, the attempt is treated as a TLB miss. In addition to providing address-space protection, an ASID allows the TLB to contain entries for several different processes simultaneously. If the TLB does not support separate ASIDs, then every time a new page table is selected (for instance, with each context switch), the TLB must be flushed (or erased) to ensure that the next executing process does not use the wrong translation information. Otherwise, the TLB could include old entries that contain valid virtual addresses but have incorrect or invalid physical addresses left over from the previous process.

The percentage of times that the page number of interest is found in the TLB is called the hit ratio. An 80-percent hit ratio, for example, means that we find the desired page number in the TLB 80 percent of the time. If it takes 100 nanoseconds to access memory, then a mapped-memory access takes 100 nanoseconds when the page number is in the TLB. If we fail to find the page number in the TLB then we must first access memory for the page table and frame number (100 nanoseconds) and then access the desired byte in memory (100 nanoseconds), for a total of 200 nanoseconds. (We are assuming that a page-table lookup takes only one memory access, but it can take more, as we shall see.) To find the effective memory-access time, we weight the case by its probability:

$$\text{effective access time} = 0.80 \times 100 + 0.20 \times 200$$
$$= 120 \text{ nanoseconds}$$

In this example, we suffer a 20-percent slowdown in average memory-access time (from 100 to 120 nanoseconds).

For a 99-percent hit ratio, which is much more realistic, we have

$$\text{effective access time} = 0.99 \times 100 + 0.01 \times 200$$
$$= 101 \text{ nanoseconds}$$

This increased hit rate produces only a 1 percent slowdown in access time.

As we noted earlier, CPUs today may provide multiple levels of TLBs. Calculating memory access times in modern CPUs is therefore much more complicated than shown in the example above. For instance, the Intel Core i7 CPU has a 128-entry L1 instruction TLB and a 64-entry L1 data TLB. In the case of a miss at L1, it takes the CPU six cycles to check for the entry in the L2 512-entry TLB. A miss in L2 means that the CPU must either walk through the page-table entries in memory to find the associated frame address, which can take hundreds of cycles, or interrupt to the operating system to have it do the work.

A complete performance analysis of paging overhead in such a system would require miss-rate information about each TLB tier. We can see from the general information above, however, that hardware features can have a significant effect on memory performance and that operating-system improvements (such as paging) can result in and, in turn, be affected by hardware changes (such as TLBs). We will further explore the impact of the hit ratio on the TLB in Chapter 8.

TLBs are a hardware feature and therefore would seem to be of little concern to operating systems and their designers. But the designer needs to understand the function and features of TLBs, which vary by hardware platform. For optimal operation, an operating-system design for a given platform must implement paging according to the platform's TLB design. Likewise, a change in the TLB design (for example, between generations of Intel CPUs) may necessitate a change in the paging implementation of the operating systems that use it.

7.5.3 Protection

Memory protection in a paged environment is accomplished by protection bits associated with each frame. Normally, these bits are kept in the page table.

One bit can define a page to be read–write or read-only. Every reference to memory goes through the page table to find the correct frame number. At the same time that the physical address is being computed, the protection bits can be checked to verify that no writes are being made to a read-only page. An attempt to write to a read-only page causes a hardware trap to the operating system (or memory-protection violation).

We can easily expand this approach to provide a finer level of protection. We can create hardware to provide read-only, read–write, or execute-only protection; or, by providing separate protection bits for each kind of access, we can allow any combination of these accesses. Illegal attempts will be trapped to the operating system.

One additional bit is generally attached to each entry in the page table: a valid–invalid bit. When this bit is set to *valid*, the associated page is in the process's logical address space and is thus a legal (or valid) page. When the bit is set to *invalid*, the page is not in the process's logical address space. Illegal addresses are trapped by use of the valid–invalid bit. The operating system sets this bit for each page to allow or disallow access to the page.

Suppose, for example, that in a system with a 14-bit address space (0 to 16383), we have a program that should use only addresses 0 to 10468. Given a page size of 2 KB, we have the situation shown in Figure 7.15. Addresses in pages 0, 1, 2, 3, 4, and 5 are mapped normally through the page table. Any attempt to generate an address in pages 6 or 7, however, will find that the valid–invalid bit is set to invalid, and the computer will trap to the operating system (invalid page reference).

Notice that this scheme has created a problem. Because the program extends only to address 10468, any reference beyond that address is illegal. However, references to page 5 are classified as valid, so accesses to addresses up to 12287 are valid. Only the addresses from 12288 to 16383 are invalid. This

Figure 7.15   Valid (v) or invalid (i) bit in a page table.

problem is a result of the 2-KB page size and reflects the internal fragmentation of paging.

Rarely does a process use all its address range. In fact, many processes use only a small fraction of the address space available to them. It would be wasteful in these cases to create a page table with entries for every page in the address range. Most of this table would be unused but would take up valuable memory space. Some systems provide hardware, in the form of a **page-table length register** (PTLR), to indicate the size of the page table. This value is checked against every logical address to verify that the address is in the valid range for the process. Failure of this test causes an error trap to the operating system.

7.5.4   Shared Pages

An advantage of paging is the possibility of *sharing* common code. This consideration is particularly important in a time-sharing environment. Consider a system that supports 40 users, each of whom executes a text editor. If the text editor consists of 150 KB of code and 50 KB of data space, we need 8,000 KB to support the 40 users. If the code is **reentrant code** (or **pure code**), however, it can be shared, as shown in Figure 7.16. Here, we see three processes sharing a three-page editor—each page 50 KB in size (the large page size is used to simplify the figure). Each process has its own data page.

Reentrant code is non-self-modifying code: it never changes during execution. Thus, two or more processes can execute the same code at the same time.

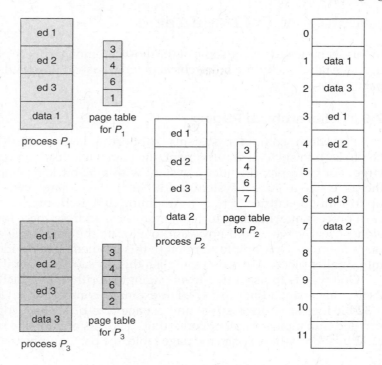

Figure 7.16 Sharing of code in a paging environment.

Each process has its own copy of registers and data storage to hold the data for the process's execution. The data for two different processes will, of course, be different.

Only one copy of the editor need be kept in physical memory. Each user's page table maps onto the same physical copy of the editor, but data pages are mapped onto different frames. Thus, to support 40 users, we need only one copy of the editor (150 KB), plus 40 copies of the 50 KB of data space per user. The total space required is now 2,150 KB instead of 8,000 KB—a significant savings.

Other heavily used programs can also be shared—compilers, window systems, run-time libraries, database systems, and so on. To be sharable, the code must be reentrant. The read-only nature of shared code should not be left to the correctness of the code; the operating system should enforce this property.

The sharing of memory among processes on a system is similar to the sharing of the address space of a task by threads, described in Chapter 4. Furthermore, recall that in Chapter 3 we described shared memory as a method of interprocess communication. Some operating systems implement shared memory using shared pages.

Organizing memory according to pages provides numerous benefits in addition to allowing several processes to share the same physical pages. We cover several other benefits in Chapter 8.

7.6   Structure of the Page Table

In this section, we explore some of the most common techniques for structuring the page table, including hierarchical paging, hashed page tables, and inverted page tables.

7.6.1   Hierarchical Paging

Most modern computer systems support a large logical address space (2^{32} to 2^{64}). In such an environment, the page table itself becomes excessively large. For example, consider a system with a 32-bit logical address space. If the page size in such a system is 4 KB (2^{12}), then a page table may consist of up to 1 million entries ($2^{32}/2^{12}$). Assuming that each entry consists of 4 bytes, each process may need up to 4 MB of physical address space for the page table alone. Clearly, we would not want to allocate the page table contiguously in main memory. One simple solution to this problem is to divide the page table into smaller pieces. We can accomplish this division in several ways.

One way is to use a two-level paging algorithm, in which the page table itself is also paged (Figure 7.17). For example, consider again the system with a 32-bit logical address space and a page size of 4 KB. A logical address is divided into a page number consisting of 20 bits and a page offset consisting of 12 bits. Because we page the page table, the page number is further divided

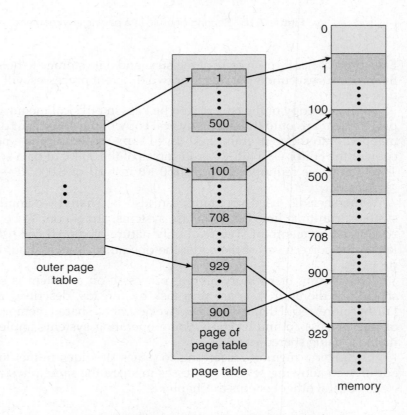

Figure 7.17 A two-level page-table scheme.

logical address

Figure 7.18   Address translation for a two-level 32-bit paging architecture.

into a 10-bit page number and a 10-bit page offset. Thus, a logical address is as follows:

page number		page offset
p_1	p_2	d
10	10	12

where p_1 is an index into the outer page table and p_2 is the displacement within the page of the inner page table. The address-translation method for this architecture is shown in Figure 7.18. Because address translation works from the outer page table inward, this scheme is also known as a **forward-mapped page table**.

Consider the memory management of one of the classic systems, the VAX minicomputer from **Digital Equipment Corporation** (DEC). The VAX was the most popular minicomputer of its time and was sold from 1977 through 2000. The VAX architecture supported a variation of two-level paging. The VAX is a 32-bit machine with a page size of 512 bytes. The logical address space of a process is divided into four equal sections, each of which consists of 2^{30} bytes. Each section represents a different part of the logical address space of a process. The first 2 high-order bits of the logical address designate the appropriate section. The next 21 bits represent the logical page number of that section, and the final 9 bits represent an offset in the desired page. By partitioning the page table in this manner, the operating system can leave partitions unused until a process needs them. Entire sections of virtual address space are frequently unused, and multilevel page tables have no entries for these spaces, greatly decreasing the amount of memory needed to store virtual memory data structures.

An address on the VAX architecture is as follows:

section	page	offset
s	p	d
2	21	9

where s designates the section number, p is an index into the page table, and d is the displacement within the page. Even when this scheme is used, the size of a one-level page table for a VAX process using one section is 2^{21} bits $* 4$

bytes per entry = 8 MB. To further reduce main-memory use, the VAX pages the user-process page tables.

For a system with a 64-bit logical address space, a two-level paging scheme is no longer appropriate. To illustrate this point, let's suppose that the page size in such a system is 4 KB (2^{12}). In this case, the page table consists of up to 2^{52} entries. If we use a two-level paging scheme, then the inner page tables can conveniently be one page long, or contain 2^{10} 4-byte entries. The addresses look like this:

outer page	inner page	offset
p_1	p_2	d
42	10	12

The outer page table consists of 2^{42} entries, or 2^{44} bytes. The obvious way to avoid such a large table is to divide the outer page table into smaller pieces. (This approach is also used on some 32-bit processors for added flexibility and efficiency.)

We can divide the outer page table in various ways. For example, we can page the outer page table, giving us a three-level paging scheme. Suppose that the outer page table is made up of standard-size pages (2^{10} entries, or 2^{12} bytes). In this case, a 64-bit address space is still daunting:

2nd outer page	outer page	inner page	offset
p_1	p_2	p_3	d
32	10	10	12

The outer page table is still 2^{34} bytes (16 GB) in size.

The next step would be a four-level paging scheme, where the second-level outer page table itself is also paged, and so forth. The 64-bit UltraSPARC would require seven levels of paging—a prohibitive number of memory accesses— to translate each logical address. You can see from this example why, for 64-bit architectures, hierarchical page tables are generally considered inappropriate.

7.6.2 Hashed Page Tables

A common approach for handling address spaces larger than 32 bits is to use a **hashed page table**, with the hash value being the virtual page number. Each entry in the hash table contains a linked list of elements that hash to the same location (to handle collisions). Each element consists of three fields: (1) the virtual page number, (2) the value of the mapped page frame, and (3) a pointer to the next element in the linked list.

The algorithm works as follows: The virtual page number in the virtual address is hashed into the hash table. The virtual page number is compared with field 1 in the first element in the linked list. If there is a match, the corresponding page frame (field 2) is used to form the desired physical address. If there is no match, subsequent entries in the linked list are searched for a matching virtual page number. This scheme is shown in Figure 7.19.

A variation of this scheme that is useful for 64-bit address spaces has been proposed. This variation uses **clustered page tables**, which are similar to

Figure 7.19 Hashed page table.

hashed page tables except that each entry in the hash table refers to several pages (such as 16) rather than a single page. Therefore, a single page-table entry can store the mappings for multiple physical-page frames. Clustered page tables are particularly useful for sparse address spaces, where memory references are noncontiguous and scattered throughout the address space.

7.6.3 Inverted Page Tables

Usually, each process has an associated page table. The page table has one entry for each page that the process is using (or one slot for each virtual address, regardless of the latter's validity). This table representation is a natural one, since processes reference pages through the pages' virtual addresses. The operating system must then translate this reference into a physical memory address. Since the table is sorted by virtual address, the operating system is able to calculate where in the table the associated physical address entry is located and to use that value directly. One of the drawbacks of this method is that each page table may consist of millions of entries. These tables may consume large amounts of physical memory just to keep track of how other physical memory is being used.

To solve this problem, we can use an inverted page table. An inverted page table has one entry for each real page (or frame) of memory. Each entry consists of the virtual address of the page stored in that real memory location, with information about the process that owns the page. Thus, only one page table is in the system, and it has only one entry for each page of physical memory. Figure 7.20 shows the operation of an inverted page table. Compare it with Figure 7.10, which depicts a standard page table in operation. Inverted page tables often require that an address-space identifier (Section 7.5.2) be stored in each entry of the page table, since the table usually contains several different address spaces mapping physical memory. Storing the address-space identifier ensures that a logical page for a particular process is mapped to the corresponding physical page frame. Examples of systems using inverted page tables include the 64-bit UltraSPARC and PowerPC.

Figure 7.20 Inverted page table.

To illustrate this method, we describe a simplified version of the inverted page table used in the *IBM RT*. IBM was the first major company to use inverted page tables, starting with the IBM System 38 and continuing through the RS/6000 and the current IBM Power CPUs. For the IBM RT, each virtual address in the system consists of a triple:

<process-id, page-number, offset>.

Each inverted page-table entry is a pair <process-id, page-number> where the process-id assumes the role of the address-space identifier. When a memory reference occurs, part of the virtual address, consisting of <process-id, page-number>, is presented to the memory subsystem. The inverted page table is then searched for a match. If a match is found—say, at entry *i*—then the physical address <*i*, offset> is generated. If no match is found, then an illegal address access has been attempted.

Although this scheme decreases the amount of memory needed to store each page table, it increases the amount of time needed to search the table when a page reference occurs. Because the inverted page table is sorted by physical address, but lookups occur on virtual addresses, the whole table might need to be searched before a match is found. This search would take far too long. To alleviate this problem, we use a hash table, as described in Section 7.6.2, to limit the search to one—or at most a few—page-table entries. Of course, each access to the hash table adds a memory reference to the procedure, so one virtual memory reference requires at least two real memory reads—one for the hash-table entry and one for the page table. (Recall that the TLB is searched first, before the hash table is consulted, offering some performance improvement.)

Systems that use inverted page tables have difficulty implementing shared memory. Shared memory is usually implemented as multiple virtual addresses (one for each process sharing the memory) that are mapped to one physical address. This standard method cannot be used with inverted page tables; because there is only one virtual page entry for every physical page, one physical page cannot have two (or more) shared virtual addresses. A simple technique for addressing this issue is to allow the page table to contain only one mapping of a virtual address to the shared physical address. This means that references to virtual addresses that are not mapped result in page faults.

7.6.4   Oracle SPARC Solaris

Consider as a final example a modern 64-bit CPU and operating system that are tightly integrated to provide low-overhead virtual memory. Solaris running on the SPARC CPU is a fully 64-bit operating system and as such has to solve the problem of virtual memory without using up all of its physical memory by keeping multiple levels of page tables. Its approach is a bit complex but solves the problem efficiently using hashed page tables. There are two hash tables—one for the kernel and one for all user processes. Each maps memory addresses from virtual to physical memory. Each hash-table entry represents a contiguous area of mapped virtual memory, which is more efficient than having a separate hash-table entry for each page. Each entry has a base address and a span indicating the number of pages the entry represents.

Virtual-to-physical translation would take too long if each address required searching through a hash table, so the CPU implements a TLB that holds translation table entries (TTEs) for fast hardware lookups. A cache of these TTEs reside in a translation storage buffer (TSB), which includes an entry per recently accessed page. When a virtual address reference occurs, the hardware searches the TLB for a translation. If none is found, the hardware walks through the in-memory TSB looking for the TTE that corresponds to the virtual address that caused the lookup. This TLB walk functionality is found on many modern CPUs. If a match is found in the TSB, the CPU copies the TSB entry into the TLB, and the memory translation completes. If no match is found in the TSB, the kernel is interrupted to search the hash table. The kernel then creates a TTE from the appropriate hash table and stores it in the TSB for automatic loading into the TLB by the CPU memory-management unit. Finally, the interrupt handler returns control to the MMU, which completes the address translation and retrieves the requested byte or word from main memory.

7.7   Example: Intel 32 and 64-bit Architectures

The architecture of Intel chips has dominated the personal computer landscape for several years. The 16-bit Intel 8086 appeared in the late 1970s and was soon followed by another 16-bit chip—the Intel 8088—which was notable for being the chip used in the original IBM PC. Both the 8086 chip and the 8088 chip were based on a segmented architecture. Intel later produced a series of 32-bit chips —the IA-32—which included the family of 32-bit Pentium processors. The IA-32 architecture supported both paging and segmentation. More recently, Intel has produced a series of 64-bit chips based on the x86-64 architecture. Currently, all the most popular PC operating systems run on Intel chips, including Windows, Mac OS X, and Linux (although Linux, of course, runs on several other architectures as well). Notably, however, Intel's dominance has not spread to mobile systems, where the ARM architecture currently enjoys considerable success (see Section 7.8).

Figure 7.21   Logical to physical address translation in IA-32.

In this section, we examine address translation for both IA-32 and x86-64 architectures. Before we proceed, however, it is important to note that because Intel has released several versions—as well as variations—of its architectures over the years, we cannot provide a complete description of the memory-management structure of all its chips. Nor can we provide all of the CPU details, as that information is best left to books on computer architecture. Rather, we present the major memory-management concepts of these Intel CPUs.

7.7.1 IA-32 Architecture

Memory management in IA-32 systems is divided into two components— segmentation and paging—and works as follows: The CPU generates logical addresses, which are given to the segmentation unit. The segmentation unit produces a linear address for each logical address. The linear address is then given to the paging unit, which in turn generates the physical address in main memory. Thus, the segmentation and paging units form the equivalent of the memory-management unit (MMU). This scheme is shown in Figure 7.21.

7.7.1.1 IA-32 Segmentation

The IA-32 architecture allows a segment to be as large as 4 GB, and the maximum number of segments per process is 16 K. The logical address space of a process is divided into two partitions. The first partition consists of up to 8 K segments that are private to that process. The second partition consists of up to 8 K segments that are shared among all the processes. Information about the first partition is kept in the **local descriptor table** (LDT); information about the second partition is kept in the **global descriptor table** (GDT). Each entry in the LDT and GDT consists of an 8-byte segment descriptor with detailed information about a particular segment, including the base location and limit of that segment.

The logical address is a pair (selector, offset), where the selector is a 16-bit number:

s	g	p
13	1	2

in which s designates the segment number, g indicates whether the segment is in the GDT or LDT, and p deals with protection. The offset is a 32-bit number specifying the location of the byte within the segment in question.

The machine has six segment registers, allowing six segments to be addressed at any one time by a process. It also has six 8-byte microprogram registers to hold the corresponding descriptors from either the LDT or GDT. This cache lets the Pentium avoid having to read the descriptor from memory for every memory reference.

Figure 7.22   IA-32 segmentation.

The linear address on the IA-32 is 32 bits long and is formed as follows. The segment register points to the appropriate entry in the LDT or GDT. The base and limit information about the segment in question is used to generate a **linear address**. First, the limit is used to check for address validity. If the address is not valid, a memory fault is generated, resulting in a trap to the operating system. If it is valid, then the value of the offset is added to the value of the base, resulting in a 32-bit linear address. This is shown in Figure 7.22. In the following section, we discuss how the paging unit turns this linear address into a physical address.

7.7.1.2   IA-32 Paging

The IA-32 architecture allows a page size of either 4 KB or 4 MB. For 4-KB pages, IA-32 uses a two-level paging scheme in which the division of the 32-bit linear address is as follows:

page number		page offset
p_1	p_2	d
10	10	12

The address-translation scheme for this architecture is similar to the scheme shown in Figure 7.18. The IA-32 address translation is shown in more detail in Figure 7.23. The 10 high-order bits reference an entry in the outermost page table, which IA-32 terms the **page directory**. (The CR3 register points to the page directory for the current process.) The page directory entry points to an inner page table that is indexed by the contents of the innermost 10 bits in the linear address. Finally, the low-order bits 0–11 refer to the offset in the 4-KB page pointed to in the page table.

One entry in the page directory is the Page_Size flag, which—if set— indicates that the size of the page frame is 4 MB and not the standard 4 KB. If this flag is set, the page directory points directly to the 4-MB page frame, bypassing the inner page table; and the 22 low-order bits in the linear address refer to the offset in the 4-MB page frame.

Figure 7.23   Paging in the IA-32 architecture.

To improve the efficiency of physical memory use, IA-32 page tables can be swapped to disk. In this case, an invalid bit is used in the page directory entry to indicate whether the table to which the entry is pointing is in memory or on disk. If the table is on disk, the operating system can use the other 31 bits to specify the disk location of the table. The table can then be brought into memory on demand.

As software developers began to discover the 4-GB memory limitations of 32-bit architectures, Intel adopted a **page address extension** (PAE), which allows 32-bit processors to access a physical address space larger than 4 GB. The fundamental difference introduced by PAE support was that paging went from a two-level scheme (as shown in Figure 7.23) to a three-level scheme, where the top two bits refer to a **page directory pointer table**. Figure 7.24 illustrates a PAE system with 4-KB pages. (PAE also supports 2-MB pages.)

Figure 7.24   Page address extensions.

unused	page map level 4	page directory pointer table	page directory	page table	offset
63 48	47 39	38 30	29 21	20 12	11 0

Figure 7.25 x86-64 linear address.

PAE also increased the page-directory and page-table entries from 32 to 64 bits in size, which allowed the base address of page tables and page frames to extend from 20 to 24 bits. Combined with the 12-bit offset, adding PAE support to IA-32 increased the address space to 36 bits, which supports up to 64 GB of physical memory. It is important to note that operating system support is required to use PAE. Both Linux and Mac OS X support PAE. However, 32-bit versions of Windows desktop operating systems still provide support for only 4 GB of physical memory, even if PAE is enabled.

7.7.2 x86-64

Intel has had an interesting history of developing 64-bit architectures. Its initial entry was the IA-64 (later named **Itanium**) architecture, but that architecture was not widely adopted. Meanwhile, another chip manufacturer— AMD — began developing a 64-bit architecture known as x86-64 that was based on extending the existing IA-32 instruction set. The x86-64 supported much larger logical and physical address spaces, as well as several other architectural advances. Historically, AMD had often developed chips based on Intel's architecture, but now the roles were reversed as Intel adopted AMD's x86-64 architecture. In discussing this architecture, rather than using the commercial names AMD64 and Intel 64, we will use the more general term x86-64.

Support for a 64-bit address space yields an astonishing 2^{64} bytes of addressable memory—a number greater than 16 quintillion (or 16 exabytes). However, even though 64-bit systems can potentially address this much memory, in practice far fewer than 64 bits are used for address representation in current designs. The x86-64 architecture currently provides a 48-bit virtual address with support for page sizes of 4 KB, 2 MB, or 1 GB using four levels of paging hierarchy. The representation of the linear address appears in Figure 7.25. Because this addressing scheme can use PAE, virtual addresses are 48 bits in size but support 52-bit physical addresses (4096 terabytes).

64-BIT COMPUTING

History has taught us that even though memory capacities, CPU speeds, and similar computer capabilities seem large enough to satisfy demand for the foreseeable future, the growth of technology ultimately absorbs available capacities, and we find ourselves in need of additional memory or processing power, often sooner than we think. What might the future of technology bring that would make a 64-bit address space seem too small?

7.8   Example: ARM Architecture

Although Intel chips have dominated the personal computer market for over 30 years, chips for mobile devices such as smartphones and tablet computers often instead run on 32-bit ARM processors. Interestingly, whereas Intel both designs and manufactures chips, ARM only designs them. It then licenses its designs to chip manufacturers. Apple has licensed the ARM design for its iPhone and iPad mobile devices, and several Android-based smartphones use ARM processors as well.

The 32-bit ARM architecture supports the following page sizes:

1.   4-KB and 16-KB pages

2.   1-MB and 16-MB pages (termed **sections**)

The paging system in use depends on whether a page or a section is being referenced. One-level paging is used for 1-MB and 16-MB sections; two-level paging is used for 4-KB and 16-KB pages. Address translation with the ARM MMU is shown in Figure 7.26.

The ARM architecture also supports two levels of TLBs. At the outer level are two **micro TLBs**—a separate TLB for data and another for instructions. The micro TLB supports ASIDs as well. At the inner level is a single **main TLB**. Address translation begins at the micro TLB level. In the case of a miss, the main TLB is then checked. If both TLBs yield misses, a page table walk must be performed in hardware.

Figure 7.26   Logical address translation in ARM.

7.9 Summary

Memory-management algorithms for multiprogrammed operating systems range from the simple single-user system approach to segmentation and paging. The most important determinant of the method used in a particular system is the hardware provided. Every memory address generated by the CPU must be checked for legality and possibly mapped to a physical address. The checking cannot be implemented (efficiently) in software. Hence, we are constrained by the hardware available.

The various memory-management algorithms (contiguous allocation, paging, segmentation, and combinations of paging and segmentation) differ in many aspects. In comparing different memory-management strategies, we use the following considerations:

- **Hardware support**. A simple base register or a base–limit register pair is sufficient for the single- and multiple-partition schemes, whereas paging and segmentation need mapping tables to define the address map.

- **Performance**. As the memory-management algorithm becomes more complex, the time required to map a logical address to a physical address increases. For the simple systems, we need only compare or add to the logical address—operations that are fast. Paging and segmentation can be as fast if the mapping table is implemented in fast registers. If the table is in memory, however, user memory accesses can be degraded substantially. A TLB can reduce the performance degradation to an acceptable level.

- **Fragmentation**. A multiprogrammed system will generally perform more efficiently if it has a higher level of multiprogramming. For a given set of processes, we can increase the multiprogramming level only by packing more processes into memory. To accomplish this task, we must reduce memory waste, or fragmentation. Systems with fixed-sized allocation units, such as the single-partition scheme and paging, suffer from internal fragmentation. Systems with variable-sized allocation units, such as the multiple-partition scheme and segmentation, suffer from external fragmentation.

- **Relocation**. One solution to the external-fragmentation problem is compaction. Compaction involves shifting a program in memory in such a way that the program does not notice the change. This consideration requires that logical addresses be relocated dynamically, at execution time. If addresses are relocated only at load time, we cannot compact storage.

- **Swapping**. Swapping can be added to any algorithm. At intervals determined by the operating system, usually dictated by CPU-scheduling policies, processes are copied from main memory to a backing store and later are copied back to main memory. This scheme allows more processes to be run than can be fit into memory at one time. In general, PC operating systems support paging, and operating systems for mobile devices do not.

- **Sharing**. Another means of increasing the multiprogramming level is to share code and data among different processes. Sharing generally requires that either paging or segmentation be used to provide small packets of information (pages or segments) that can be shared. Sharing is a means of running many processes with a limited amount of memory, but shared programs and data must be designed carefully.

- **Protection**. If paging or segmentation is provided, different sections of a user program can be declared execute-only, read-only, or read–write. This restriction is necessary with shared code or data and is generally useful in any case to provide simple run-time checks for common programming errors.

Review Questions

Review questions for this chapter can be accessed by visiting our website.

Practice Exercises

Answers for the Practice Exercises can be accceed by visiting our website.

7.1 Name two differences between logical and physical addresses.

7.2 Consider a system in which a program can be separated into two parts: code and data. The CPU knows whether it wants an instruction (instruction fetch) or data (data fetch or store). Therefore, two base–limit register pairs are provided: one for instructions and one for data. The instruction base–limit register pair is automatically read-only, so programs can be shared among different users. Discuss the advantages and disadvantages of this scheme.

7.3 Why are page sizes always powers of 2?

7.4 Consider a logical address space of 64 pages of 1,024 words each, mapped onto a physical memory of 32 frames.

   a.   How many bits are there in the logical address?

   b.   How many bits are there in the physical address?

7.5 What is the effect of allowing two entries in a page table to point to the same page frame in memory? Explain how this effect could be used to decrease the amount of time needed to copy a large amount of memory from one place to another. What effect would updating some byte on the one page have on the other page?

7.6 Describe a mechanism by which one segment could belong to the address space of two different processes.

7.7 Sharing segments among processes without requiring that they have the same segment number is possible in a dynamically linked segmentation system.

   a.   Define a system that allows static linking and sharing of segments without requiring that the segment numbers be the same.

   b.   Describe a paging scheme that allows pages to be shared without requiring that the page numbers be the same.

7.8 In the IBM/370, memory protection is provided through the use of keys. A key is a 4-bit quantity. Each 2-K block of memory has a key (the storage key) associated with it. The CPU also has a key (the protection key) associated with it. A store operation is allowed only if both keys are equal or if either is 0. Which of the following memory-management schemes could be used successfully with this hardware?

   a.   Bare machine

   b.   Single-user system

   c.   Multiprogramming with a fixed number of processes

   d.   Multiprogramming with a variable number of processes

   e.   Paging

   f.   Segmentation

Exercises

7.9 Explain the difference between internal and external fragmentation.

7.10 Consider the following process for generating binaries. A compiler is used to generate the object code for individual modules, and a linkage editor is used to combine multiple object modules into a single program binary. How does the linkage editor change the binding of instructions and data to memory addresses? What information needs to be passed from the compiler to the linkage editor to facilitate the memory-binding tasks of the linkage editor?

7.11 Given six memory partitions of 300 KB, 600 KB, 350 KB, 200 KB, 750 KB, and 125 KB (in order), how would the first-fit, best-fit, and worst-fit algorithms place processes of size 115 KB, 500 KB, 358 KB, 200 KB, and 375 KB (in order)? Rank the algorithms in terms of how efficiently they use memory.

7.12 Most systems allow a program to allocate more memory to its address space during execution. Allocation of data in the heap segments of programs is an example of such allocated memory. What is required to support dynamic memory allocation in the following schemes?

   a.   Contiguous memory allocation

   b.   Pure segmentation

   c.   Pure paging

7.13 Compare the memory organization schemes of contiguous memory allocation, pure segmentation, and pure paging with respect to the following issues:

   a.   External fragmentation

   b.   Internal fragmentation

   c.   Ability to share code across processes

7.14   On a system with paging, a process cannot access memory that it does not own. Why? How could the operating system allow access to other memory? Why should it or should it not?

7.15   Explain why mobile operating systems such as iOS and Android do not support swapping.

7.16   Although Android does not support swapping on its boot disk, it is possible to set up a swap space using a separate SD nonvolatile memory card. Why would Android disallow swapping on its boot disk yet allow it on a secondary disk?

7.17   Compare paging with segmentation with respect to how much memory the address translation structures require to convert virtual addresses to physical addresses.

7.18   Explain why address space identifiers (ASIDs) are used.

7.19   Program binaries in many systems are typically structured as follows. Code is stored starting with a small, fixed virtual address, such as 0. The code segment is followed by the data segment that is used for storing the program variables. When the program starts executing, the stack is allocated at the other end of the virtual address space and is allowed to grow toward lower virtual addresses. What is the significance of this structure for the following schemes?

   a.   Contiguous memory allocation

   b.   Pure segmentation

   c.   Pure paging

7.20   Assuming a 1-KB page size, what are the page numbers and offsets for the following address references (provided as decimal numbers):

   a.   3085

   b.   42095

   c.   215201

   d.   650000

   e.   2000001

7.21   The BTV operating system has a 21-bit virtual address, yet on certain embedded devices, it has only a 16-bit physical address. It also has a 2-KB page size. How many entries are there in each of the following?

   a.   A conventional, single-level page table

   b.   An inverted page table

7.22   What is the maximum amount of physical memory?

7.23   Consider a logical address space of 256 pages with a 4-KB page size, mapped onto a physical memory of 64 frames.

a. How many bits are required in the logical address?

b. How many bits are required in the physical address?

7.24 Consider a computer system with a 32-bit logical address and 4-KB page size. The system supports up to 512 MB of physical memory. How many entries are there in each of the following?

a. A conventional single-level page table

b. An inverted page table

7.25 Consider a paging system with the page table stored in memory.

a. If a memory reference takes 50 nanoseconds, how long does a paged memory reference take?

b. If we add TLBs, and 75 percent of all page-table references are found in the TLBs, what is the effective memory reference time? (Assume that finding a page-table entry in the TLBs takes 2 nanoseconds, if the entry is present.)

7.26 Why are segmentation and paging sometimes combined into one scheme?

7.27 Explain why sharing a reentrant module is easier when segmentation is used than when pure paging is used.

7.28 Consider the following segment table:

Segment	Base	Length
0	219	600
1	2300	14
2	90	100
3	1327	580
4	1952	96

What are the physical addresses for the following logical addresses?

a. 0,430

b. 1,10

c. 2,500

d. 3,400

e. 4,112

7.29 What is the purpose of paging the page tables?

7.30 Consider the hierarchical paging scheme used by the VAX architecture. How many memory operations are performed when a user program executes a memory-load operation?

7.31 Compare the segmented paging scheme with the hashed page table scheme for handling large address spaces. Under what circumstances is one scheme preferable to the other?

7.32 Consider the Intel address-translation scheme shown in Figure 7.22.

a. Describe all the steps taken by the Intel Pentium in translating a logical address into a physical address.

b. What are the advantages to the operating system of hardware that provides such complicated memory translation?

c. Are there any disadvantages to this address-translation system? If so, what are they? If not, why is this scheme not used by every manufacturer?

Programming Problems

7.33   Assume that a system has a 32-bit virtual address with a 4-KB page size. Write a C program that is passed a virtual address (in decimal) on the command line and have it output the page number and offset for the given address. As an example, your program would run as follows:

```
./a.out 19986
```

Your program would output:

```
The address 19986 contains:
page number = 4
offset = 3602
```

Writing this program will require using the appropriate data type to store 32 bits. We encourage you to use unsigned data types as well.

Bibliographical Notes

Dynamic storage allocation was discussed by [Knuth (1973)] (Section 2.5), who found through simulation that first fit is generally superior to best fit. [Knuth (1973)] also discussed the 50-percent rule.

The concept of paging can be credited to the designers of the Atlas system, which has been described by [Kilburn et al. (1961)] and by [Howarth et al. (1961)]. The concept of segmentation was first discussed by [Dennis (1965)]. Paged segmentation was first supported in the GE 645, on which MULTICS was originally implemented ([Organick (1972)] and [Daley and Dennis (1967)]).

Inverted page tables are discussed in an article about the IBM RT storage manager by [Chang and Mergen (1988)].

[Hennessy and Patterson (2012)] explains the hardware aspects of TLBs, caches, and MMUs. [Talluri et al. (1995)] discusses page tables for 64-bit address spaces. [Jacob and Mudge (2001)] describes techniques for managing the TLB. [Fang et al. (2001)] evaluates support for large pages.

http://msdn.microsoft.com/en-us/library/windows/hardware/gg487512. aspx discusses PAE support for Windows systems.

http://www.intel.com/content/www/us/en/processors/architectures-software-developer-manuals.html provides various manuals for Intel 64 and IA-32 architectures.

http://www.arm.com/products/processors/cortex-a/cortex-a9.php provides an overview of the ARM architecture.

Bibliography

[Chang and Mergen (1988)]   A. Chang and M. F. Mergen, "801 Storage: Architecture and Programming", *ACM Transactions on Computer Systems*, Volume 6, Number 1 (1988), pages 28–50.

[Daley and Dennis (1967)]   R. C. Daley and J. B. Dennis, "Virtual Memory, Processes, and Sharing in Multics", *Proceedings of the ACM Symposium on Operating Systems Principles* (1967), pages 121–128.

[Dennis (1965)]   J. B. Dennis, "Segmentation and the Design of Multiprogrammed Computer Systems", *Communications of the ACM*, Volume 8, Number 4 (1965), pages 589–602.

[Fang et al. (2001)]   Z. Fang, L. Zhang, J. B. Carter, W. C. Hsieh, and S. A. McKee, "Reevaluating Online Superpage Promotion with Hardware Support", *Proceedings of the International Symposium on High-Performance Computer Architecture*, Volume 50, Number 5 (2001).

[Hennessy and Patterson (2012)]   J. Hennessy and D. Patterson, *Computer Architecture: A Quantitative Approach*, Fifth Edition, Morgan Kaufmann (2012).

[Howarth et al. (1961)]   D. J. Howarth, R. B. Payne, and F. H. Sumner, "The Manchester University Atlas Operating System, Part II: User's Description", *Computer Journal*, Volume 4, Number 3 (1961), pages 226–229.

[Jacob and Mudge (2001)]   B. Jacob and T. Mudge, "Uniprocessor Virtual Memory Without TLBs", *IEEE Transactions on Computers*, Volume 50, Number 5 (2001).

[Kilburn et al. (1961)]   T. Kilburn, D. J. Howarth, R. B. Payne, and F. H. Sumner, "The Manchester University Atlas Operating System, Part I: Internal Organization", *Computer Journal*, Volume 4, Number 3 (1961), pages 222–225.

[Knuth (1973)]   D. E. Knuth, *The Art of Computer Programming, Volume 1: Fundamental Algorithms*, Second Edition, Addison-Wesley (1973).

[Organick (1972)]   E. I. Organick, *The Multics System: An Examination of Its Structure*, MIT Press (1972).

[Talluri et al. (1995)]   M. Talluri, M. D. Hill, and Y. A. Khalidi, "A New Page Table for 64-bit Address Spaces", *Proceedings of the ACM Symposium on Operating Systems Principles* (1995), pages 184–200.

Virtual Memory

CHAPTER

8

In Chapter 7, we discussed various memory-management strategies used in computer systems. All these strategies have the same goal: to keep many processes in memory simultaneously to allow multiprogramming. However, they tend to require that an entire process be in memory before it can execute.

Virtual memory is a technique that allows the execution of processes that are not completely in memory. One major advantage of this scheme is that programs can be larger than physical memory. Further, virtual memory abstracts main memory into an extremely large, uniform array of storage, separating logical memory as viewed by the user from physical memory. This technique frees programmers from the concerns of memory-storage limitations. Virtual memory also allows processes to share files easily and to implement shared memory. In addition, it provides an efficient mechanism for process creation. Virtual memory is not easy to implement, however, and may substantially decrease performance if it is used carelessly. In this chapter, we discuss virtual memory in the form of demand paging and examine its complexity and cost.

CHAPTER OBJECTIVES

- To describe the benefits of a virtual memory system.
- To explain the concepts of demand paging, page-replacement algorithms, and allocation of page frames.
- To discuss the principles of the working-set model.
- To examine the relationship between shared memory and memory-mapped files.
- To explore how kernel memory is managed.

8.1 Background

The memory-management algorithms outlined in Chapter 7 are necessary because of one basic requirement: The instructions being executed must be

371

in physical memory. The first approach to meeting this requirement is to place the entire logical address space in physical memory. Dynamic loading can help to ease this restriction, but it generally requires special precautions and extra work by the programmer.

The requirement that instructions must be in physical memory to be executed seems both necessary and reasonable; but it is also unfortunate, since it limits the size of a program to the size of physical memory. In fact, an examination of real programs shows us that, in many cases, the entire program is not needed. For instance, consider the following:

- Programs often have code to handle unusual error conditions. Since these errors seldom, if ever, occur in practice, this code is almost never executed.

- Arrays, lists, and tables are often allocated more memory than they actually need. An array may be declared 100 by 100 elements, even though it is seldom larger than 10 by 10 elements. An assembler symbol table may have room for 3,000 symbols, although the average program has less than 200 symbols.

- Certain options and features of a program may be used rarely. For instance, the routines on U.S. government computers that balance the budget have not been used in many years.

Even in those cases where the entire program is needed, it may not all be needed at the same time.

The ability to execute a program that is only partially in memory would confer many benefits:

- A program would no longer be constrained by the amount of physical memory that is available. Users would be able to write programs for an extremely large *virtual* address space, simplifying the programming task.

- Because each user program could take less physical memory, more programs could be run at the same time, with a corresponding increase in CPU utilization and throughput but with no increase in response time or turnaround time.

- Less I/O would be needed to load or swap user programs into memory, so each user program would run faster.

Thus, running a program that is not entirely in memory would benefit both the system and the user.

Virtual memory involves the separation of logical memory as perceived by users from physical memory. This separation allows an extremely large virtual memory to be provided for programmers when only a smaller physical memory is available (Figure 8.1). Virtual memory makes the task of programming much easier, because the programmer no longer needs to worry about the amount of physical memory available; she can concentrate instead on the problem to be programmed.

The **virtual address space** of a process refers to the logical (or virtual) view of how a process is stored in memory. Typically, this view is that a process begins at a certain logical address—say, address 0—and exists in contiguous memory, as shown in Figure 8.2. Recall from Chapter 7, though, that in fact

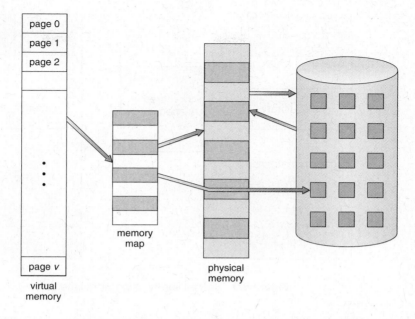

Figure 8.1   Diagram showing virtual memory that is larger than physical memory.

physical memory may be organized in page frames and that the physical page frames assigned to a process may not be contiguous. It is up to the memory-management unit (MMU) to map logical pages to physical page frames in memory.

Note in Figure 8.2 that we allow the heap to grow upward in memory as it is used for dynamic memory allocation. Similarly, we allow for the stack to

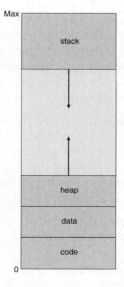

Figure 8.2   Virtual address space.

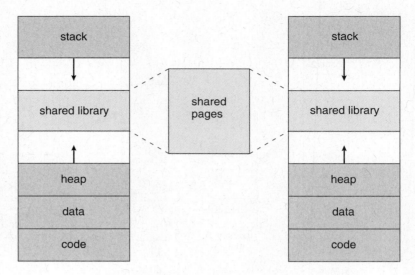

Figure 8.3 Shared library using virtual memory.

grow downward in memory through successive function calls. The large blank space (or hole) between the heap and the stack is part of the virtual address space but will require actual physical pages only if the heap or stack grows. Virtual address spaces that include holes are known as sparse address spaces. Using a sparse address space is beneficial because the holes can be filled as the stack or heap segments grow or if we wish to dynamically link libraries (or possibly other shared objects) during program execution.

In addition to separating logical memory from physical memory, virtual memory allows files and memory to be shared by two or more processes through page sharing (Section 7.5.4). This leads to the following benefits:

- System libraries can be shared by several processes through mapping of the shared object into a virtual address space. Although each process considers the libraries to be part of its virtual address space, the actual pages where the libraries reside in physical memory are shared by all the processes (Figure 8.3). Typically, a library is mapped read-only into the space of each process that is linked with it.

- Similarly, processes can share memory. Recall from Chapter 3 that two or more processes can communicate through the use of shared memory. Virtual memory allows one process to create a region of memory that it can share with another process. Processes sharing this region consider it part of their virtual address space, yet the actual physical pages of memory are shared, much as is illustrated in Figure 8.3.

- Pages can be shared during process creation with the fork() system call, thus speeding up process creation.

We further explore these—and other—benefits of virtual memory later in this chapter. First, though, we discuss implementing virtual memory through demand paging.

8.2   Demand Paging

Consider how an executable program might be loaded from disk into memory. One option is to load the entire program in physical memory at program execution time. However, a problem with this approach is that we may not initially *need* the entire program in memory. Suppose a program starts with a list of available options from which the user is to select. Loading the entire program into memory results in loading the executable code for *all* options, regardless of whether or not an option is ultimately selected by the user. An alternative strategy is to load pages only as they are needed. This technique is known as **demand paging** and is commonly used in virtual memory systems. With demand-paged virtual memory, pages are loaded only when they are demanded during program execution. Pages that are never accessed are thus never loaded into physical memory.

A demand-paging system is similar to a paging system with swapping (Figure 8.4) where processes reside in secondary memory (usually a disk). When we want to execute a process, we swap it into memory. Rather than swapping the entire process into memory, though, we use a **lazy swapper**. A lazy swapper never swaps a page into memory unless that page will be needed. In the context of a demand-paging system, use of the term "swapper" is technically incorrect. A swapper manipulates entire processes, whereas a **pager** is concerned with the individual pages of a process. We thus use "pager," rather than "swapper," in connection with demand paging.

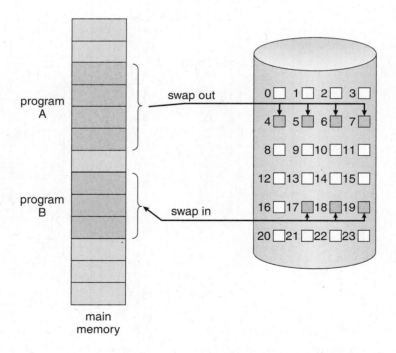

Figure 8.4   Transfer of a paged memory to contiguous disk space.

8.2.1 Basic Concepts

When a process is to be swapped in, the pager guesses which pages will be used before the process is swapped out again. Instead of swapping in a whole process, the pager brings only those pages into memory. Thus, it avoids reading into memory pages that will not be used anyway, decreasing the swap time and the amount of physical memory needed.

With this scheme, we need some form of hardware support to distinguish between the pages that are in memory and the pages that are on the disk. The valid–invalid bit scheme described in Section 7.5.3 can be used for this purpose. This time, however, when this bit is set to "valid," the associated page is both legal and in memory. If the bit is set to "invalid," the page either is not valid (that is, not in the logical address space of the process) or is valid but is currently on the disk. The page-table entry for a page that is brought into memory is set as usual, but the page-table entry for a page that is not currently in memory is either simply marked invalid or contains the address of the page on disk. This situation is depicted in Figure 8.5.

Notice that marking a page invalid will have no effect if the process never attempts to access that page. Hence, if we guess right and page in all pages that are actually needed and only those pages, the process will run exactly as though we had brought in all pages. While the process executes and accesses pages that are **memory resident**, execution proceeds normally.

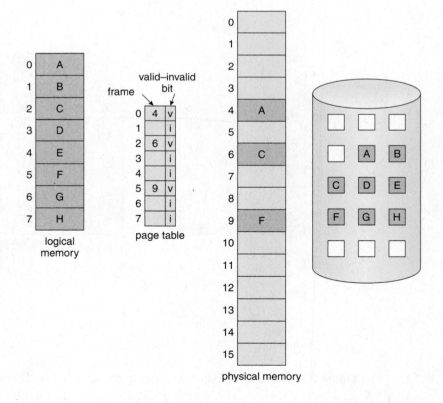

Figure 8.5   Page table when some pages are not in main memory.

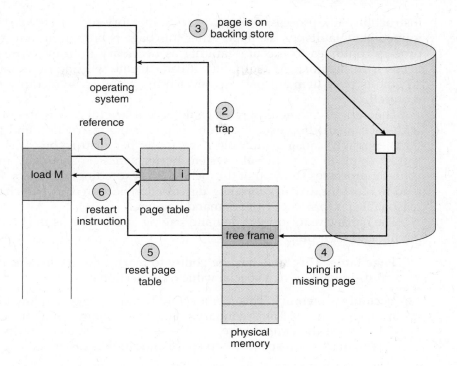

Figure 8.6 Steps in handling a page fault.

But what happens if the process tries to access a page that was not brought into memory? Access to a page marked invalid causes a **page fault**. The paging hardware, in translating the address through the page table, will notice that the invalid bit is set, causing a trap to the operating system. This trap is the result of the operating system's failure to bring the desired page into memory. The procedure for handling this page fault is straightforward (Figure 8.6):

1. We check an internal table (usually kept with the process control block) for this process to determine whether the reference was a valid or an invalid memory access.

2. If the reference was invalid, we terminate the process. If it was valid but we have not yet brought in that page, we now page it in.

3. We find a free frame (by taking one from the free-frame list, for example).

4. We schedule a disk operation to read the desired page into the newly allocated frame.

5. When the disk read is complete, we modify the internal table kept with the process and the page table to indicate that the page is now in memory.

6. We restart the instruction that was interrupted by the trap. The process can now access the page as though it had always been in memory.

In the extreme case, we can start executing a process with *no* pages in memory. When the operating system sets the instruction pointer to the first instruction of the process, which is on a non-memory-resident page, the process immediately faults for the page. After this page is brought into memory, the process continues to execute, faulting as necessary until every page that it needs is in memory. At that point, it can execute with no more faults. This scheme is **pure demand paging**: never bring a page into memory until it is required.

Theoretically, some programs could access several new pages of memory with each instruction execution (one page for the instruction and many for data), possibly causing multiple page faults per instruction. This situation would result in unacceptable system performance. Fortunately, analysis of running processes shows that this behavior is exceedingly unlikely. Programs tend to have **locality of reference**, described in Section 8.6.1, which results in reasonable performance from demand paging.

The hardware to support demand paging is the same as the hardware for paging and swapping:

- **Page table**. This table has the ability to mark an entry invalid through a valid–invalid bit or a special value of protection bits.

- **Secondary memory**. This memory holds those pages that are not present in main memory. The secondary memory is usually a high-speed disk. It is known as the swap device, and the section of disk used for this purpose is known as **swap space**. Swap-space allocation is discussed in Chapter 9.

A crucial requirement for demand paging is the ability to restart any instruction after a page fault. Because we save the state (registers, condition code, instruction counter) of the interrupted process when the page fault occurs, we must be able to restart the process in *exactly* the same place and state, except that the desired page is now in memory and is accessible. In most cases, this requirement is easy to meet. A page fault may occur at any memory reference. If the page fault occurs on the instruction fetch, we can restart by fetching the instruction again. If a page fault occurs while we are fetching an operand, we must fetch and decode the instruction again and then fetch the operand.

As a worst-case example, consider a three-address instruction such as ADD the content of A to B, placing the result in C. These are the steps to execute this instruction:

1. Fetch and decode the instruction (ADD).

2. Fetch A.

3. Fetch B.

4. Add A and B.

5. Store the sum in C.

If we fault when we try to store in C (because C is in a page not currently in memory), we will have to get the desired page, bring it in, correct the page table, and restart the instruction. The restart will require fetching the instruction again, decoding it again, fetching the two operands again, and then adding again. However, there is not much repeated work (less than one complete instruction), and the repetition is necessary only when a page fault occurs.

The major difficulty arises when one instruction may modify several different locations. For example, consider the IBM System 360/370 MVC (move character) instruction, which can move up to 256 bytes from one location to another (possibly overlapping) location. If either block (source or destination) straddles a page boundary, a page fault might occur after the move is partially done. In addition, if the source and destination blocks overlap, the source block may have been modified, in which case we cannot simply restart the instruction.

This problem can be solved in two different ways. In one solution, the microcode computes and attempts to access both ends of both blocks. If a page fault is going to occur, it will happen at this step, before anything is modified. The move can then take place; we know that no page fault can occur, since all the relevant pages are in memory. The other solution uses temporary registers to hold the values of overwritten locations. If there is a page fault, all the old values are written back into memory before the trap occurs. This action restores memory to its state before the instruction was started, so that the instruction can be repeated.

This is by no means the only architectural problem resulting from adding paging to an existing architecture to allow demand paging, but it illustrates some of the difficulties involved. Paging is added between the CPU and the memory in a computer system. It should be entirely transparent to the user process. Thus, people often assume that paging can be added to any system. Although this assumption is true for a non-demand-paging environment, where a page fault represents a fatal error, it is not true where a page fault means only that an additional page must be brought into memory and the process restarted.

8.2.2   Performance of Demand Paging

Demand paging can significantly affect the performance of a computer system. To see why, let's compute the **effective access time** for a demand-paged memory. For most computer systems, the memory-access time, denoted ma, ranges from 10 to 200 nanoseconds. As long as we have no page faults, the effective access time is equal to the memory access time. If, however, a page fault occurs, we must first read the relevant page from disk and then access the desired word.

Let p be the probability of a page fault ($0 \le p \le 1$). We would expect p to be close to zero—that is, we would expect to have only a few page faults. The **effective access time** is then

$$\text{effective access time} = (1 - p) \times ma + p \times \text{page fault time}.$$

To compute the effective access time, we must know how much time is needed to service a page fault. A page fault causes the following sequence to occur:

1. Trap to the operating system.

2. Save the user registers and process state.

3. Determine that the interrupt was a page fault.

4. Check that the page reference was legal and determine the location of the page on the disk.

5. Issue a read from the disk to a free frame:

   a. Wait in a queue for this device until the read request is serviced.

   b. Wait for the device seek and/or latency time.

   c. Begin the transfer of the page to a free frame.

6. While waiting, allocate the CPU to some other user (CPU scheduling, optional).

7. Receive an interrupt from the disk I/O subsystem (I/O completed).

8. Save the registers and process state for the other user (if step 6 is executed).

9. Determine that the interrupt was from the disk.

10. Correct the page table and other tables to show that the desired page is now in memory.

11. Wait for the CPU to be allocated to this process again.

12. Restore the user registers, process state, and new page table, and then resume the interrupted instruction.

Not all of these steps are necessary in every case. For example, we are assuming that, in step 6, the CPU is allocated to another process while the I/O occurs. This arrangement allows multiprogramming to maintain CPU utilization but requires additional time to resume the page-fault service routine when the I/O transfer is complete.

In any case, we are faced with three major components of the page-fault service time:

1. Service the page-fault interrupt.

2. Read in the page.

3. Restart the process.

The first and third tasks can be reduced, with careful coding, to several hundred instructions. These tasks may take from 1 to 100 microseconds each. The page-switch time, however, will probably be close to 8 milliseconds. (A typical hard disk has an average latency of 3 milliseconds, a seek of 5 milliseconds, and a transfer time of 0.05 milliseconds. Thus, the total paging time is about 8 milliseconds, including hardware and software time.) Remember also that we are looking at only the device-service time. If a queue of processes is waiting for the device, we have to add device-queueing time as we wait for the paging device to be free to service our request, increasing even more the time to swap.

With an average page-fault service time of 8 milliseconds and a memory-access time of 200 nanoseconds, the effective access time in nanoseconds is

$$\text{effective access time} = (1 - p) \times (200) + p \,(8 \text{ milliseconds})$$
$$= (1 - p) \times 200 + p \times 8,000,000$$
$$= 200 + 7,999,800 \times p.$$

We see, then, that the effective access time is directly proportional to the page-fault rate. If one access out of 1,000 causes a page fault, the effective access time is 8.2 microseconds. The computer will be slowed down by a factor of 40 because of demand paging! If we want performance degradation to be less than 10 percent, we need to keep the probability of page faults at the following level:

$$220 > 200 + 7,999,800 \times p,$$
$$20 > 7,999,800 \times p,$$
$$p < 0.0000025.$$

That is, to keep the slowdown due to paging at a reasonable level, we can allow fewer than one memory access out of 399,990 to page-fault. In sum, it is important to keep the page-fault rate low in a demand-paging system. Otherwise, the effective access time increases, slowing process execution dramatically.

An additional aspect of demand paging is the handling and overall use of swap space. Disk I/O to swap space is generally faster than that to the file system. It is a faster file system because swap space is allocated in much larger blocks, and file lookups and indirect allocation methods are not used (Chapter 9). The system can therefore gain better paging throughput by copying an entire file image into the swap space at process startup and then performing demand paging from the swap space. Another option is to demand pages from the file system initially but to write the pages to swap space as they are replaced. This approach will ensure that only needed pages are read from the file system but that all subsequent paging is done from swap space.

Some systems attempt to limit the amount of swap space used through demand paging of binary files. Demand pages for such files are brought directly from the file system. However, when page replacement is called for, these frames can simply be overwritten (because they are never modified), and the pages can be read in from the file system again if needed. Using this approach, the file system itself serves as the backing store. However, swap space must still be used for pages not associated with a file (known as anonymous memory); these pages include the stack and heap for a process. This method appears to be a good compromise and is used in several systems, including Solaris and BSD UNIX.

Mobile operating systems typically do not support swapping. Instead, these systems demand-page from the file system and reclaim read-only pages (such as code) from applications if memory becomes constrained. Such data can be demand-paged from the file system if it is later needed. Under iOS, anonymous memory pages are never reclaimed from an application unless the application is terminated or explicitly releases the memory.

8.3 Copy-on-Write

In Section 8.2, we illustrated how a process can start quickly by demand-paging in the page containing the first instruction. However, process creation using the fork() system call may initially bypass the need for demand paging by using a technique similar to page sharing (covered in Section 7.5.4). This technique provides rapid process creation and minimizes the number of new pages that must be allocated to the newly created process.

Recall that the fork() system call creates a child process that is a duplicate of its parent. Traditionally, fork() worked by creating a copy of the parent's address space for the child, duplicating the pages belonging to the parent. However, considering that many child processes invoke the exec() system call immediately after creation, the copying of the parent's address space may be unnecessary. Instead, we can use a technique known as **copy-on-write**, which works by allowing the parent and child processes initially to share the same pages. These shared pages are marked as copy-on-write pages, meaning that if either process writes to a shared page, a copy of the shared page is created. Copy-on-write is illustrated in Figures 8.7 and 8.8, which show the contents of the physical memory before and after process 1 modifies page C.

For example, assume that the child process attempts to modify a page containing portions of the stack, with the pages set to be copy-on-write. The operating system will create a copy of this page, mapping it to the address space of the child process. The child process will then modify its copied page and not the page belonging to the parent process. Obviously, when the copy-on-write technique is used, only the pages that are modified by either process are copied; all unmodified pages can be shared by the parent and child processes. Note, too, that only pages that can be modified need be marked as copy-on-write. Pages that cannot be modified (pages containing executable code) can be shared by the parent and child. Copy-on-write is a common technique used by several operating systems, including Windows XP, Linux, and Solaris.

When it is determined that a page is going to be duplicated using copy-on-write, it is important to note the location from which the free page will be allocated. Many operating systems provide a **pool** of free pages for such requests. These free pages are typically allocated when the stack or heap for a process must expand or when there are copy-on-write pages to be managed.

Figure 8.7   Before process 1 modifies page C.

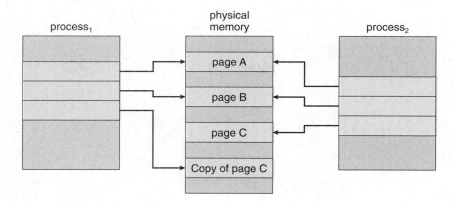

Figure 8.8   After process 1 modifies page C.

Operating systems typically allocate these pages using a technique known as **zero-fill-on-demand**. Zero-fill-on-demand pages have been zeroed-out before being allocated, thus erasing the previous contents.

Several versions of UNIX (including Solaris and Linux) provide a variation of the fork() system call—vfork() (for **virtual memory fork**)—that operates differently from fork() with copy-on-write. With vfork(), the parent process is suspended, and the child process uses the address space of the parent. Because vfork() does not use copy-on-write, if the child process changes any pages of the parent's address space, the altered pages will be visible to the parent once it resumes. Therefore, vfork() must be used with caution to ensure that the child process does not modify the address space of the parent. vfork() is intended to be used when the child process calls exec() immediately after creation. Because no copying of pages takes place, vfork() is an extremely efficient method of process creation and is sometimes used to implement UNIX command-line shell interfaces.

8.4   Page Replacement

In our earlier discussion of the page-fault rate, we assumed that each page faults at most once, when it is first referenced. This representation is not strictly accurate, however. If a process of ten pages actually uses only half of them, then demand paging saves the I/O necessary to load the five pages that are never used. We could also increase our degree of multiprogramming by running twice as many processes. Thus, if we had forty frames, we could run eight processes, rather than the four that could run if each required ten frames (five of which were never used).

If we increase our degree of multiprogramming, we are **over-allocating** memory. If we run six processes, each of which is ten pages in size but actually uses only five pages, we have higher CPU utilization and throughput, with ten frames to spare. It is possible, however, that each of these processes, for a particular data set, may suddenly try to use all ten of its pages, resulting in a need for sixty frames when only forty are available.

Further, consider that system memory is not used only for holding program pages. Buffers for I/O also consume a considerable amount of memory. This use

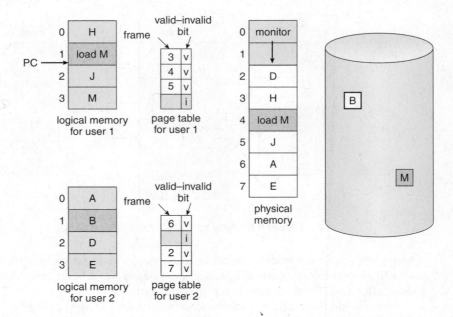

Figure 8.9 Need for page replacement.

can increase the strain on memory-placement algorithms. Deciding how much memory to allocate to I/O and how much to program pages is a significant challenge. Some systems allocate a fixed percentage of memory for I/O buffers, whereas others allow both user processes and the I/O subsystem to compete for all system memory.

Over-allocation of memory manifests itself as follows. While a user process is executing, a page fault occurs. The operating system determines where the desired page is residing on the disk but then finds that there are *no* free frames on the free-frame list; all memory is in use (Figure 8.9).

The operating system has several options at this point. It could terminate the user process. However, demand paging is the operating system's attempt to improve the computer system's utilization and throughput. Users should not be aware that their processes are running on a paged system—paging should be logically transparent to the user. So this option is not the best choice.

The operating system could instead swap out a process, freeing all its frames and reducing the level of multiprogramming. This option is a good one in certain circumstances, and we consider it further in Section 8.6. Here, we discuss the most common solution: **page replacement**.

8.4.1 Basic Page Replacement

Page replacement takes the following approach. If no frame is free, we find one that is not currently being used and free it. We can free a frame by writing its contents to swap space and changing the page table (and all other tables) to indicate that the page is no longer in memory (Figure 8.10). We can now use the freed frame to hold the page for which the process faulted. We modify the page-fault service routine to include page replacement:

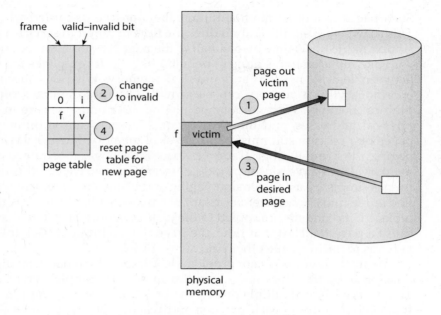

Figure 8.10 Page replacement.

1. Find the location of the desired page on the disk.
2. Find a free frame:
   a. If there is a free frame, use it.
   b. If there is no free frame, use a page-replacement algorithm to select a **victim frame**.
   c. Write the victim frame to the disk; change the page and frame tables accordingly.
3. Read the desired page into the newly freed frame; change the page and frame tables.
4. Continue the user process from where the page fault occurred.

Notice that, if no frames are free, *two* page transfers (one out and one in) are required. This situation effectively doubles the page-fault service time and increases the effective access time accordingly.

We can reduce this overhead by using a **modify bit** (or **dirty bit**). When this scheme is used, each page or frame has a modify bit associated with it in the hardware. The modify bit for a page is set by the hardware whenever any byte in the page is written into, indicating that the page has been modified. When we select a page for replacement, we examine its modify bit. If the bit is set, we know that the page has been modified since it was read in from the disk. In this case, we must write the page to the disk. If the modify bit is not set, however, the page has *not* been modified since it was read into memory. In this case, we need not write the memory page to the disk: it is already there. This technique also applies to read-only pages (for example, pages of binary code).

Such pages cannot be modified; thus, they may be discarded when desired. This scheme can significantly reduce the time required to service a page fault, since it reduces I/O time by one-half *if* the page has not been modified.

Page replacement is basic to demand paging. It completes the separation between logical memory and physical memory. With this mechanism, an enormous virtual memory can be provided for programmers on a smaller physical memory. With no demand paging, user addresses are mapped into physical addresses, and the two sets of addresses can be different. All the pages of a process still must be in physical memory, however. With demand paging, the size of the logical address space is no longer constrained by physical memory. If we have a user process of twenty pages, we can execute it in ten frames simply by using demand paging and using a replacement algorithm to find a free frame whenever necessary. If a page that has been modified is to be replaced, its contents are copied to the disk. A later reference to that page will cause a page fault. At that time, the page will be brought back into memory, perhaps replacing some other page in the process.

We must solve two major problems to implement demand paging: we must develop a **frame-allocation algorithm** and a **page-replacement algorithm**. That is, if we have multiple processes in memory, we must decide how many frames to allocate to each process; and when page replacement is required, we must select the frames that are to be replaced. Designing appropriate algorithms to solve these problems is an important task, because disk I/O is so expensive. Even slight improvements in demand-paging methods yield large gains in system performance.

There are many different page-replacement algorithms. Every operating system probably has its own replacement scheme. How do we select a particular replacement algorithm? In general, we want the one with the lowest page-fault rate.

We evaluate an algorithm by running it on a particular string of memory references and computing the number of page faults. The string of memory references is called a **reference string**. We can generate reference strings artificially (by using a random-number generator, for example), or we can trace a given system and record the address of each memory reference. The latter choice produces a large number of data (on the order of 1 million addresses per second). To reduce the number of data, we use two facts.

First, for a given page size (and the page size is generally fixed by the hardware or system), we need to consider only the page number, rather than the entire address. Second, if we have a reference to a page p, then any references to page p that *immediately* follow will never cause a page fault. Page p will be in memory after the first reference, so the immediately following references will not fault.

For example, if we trace a particular process, we might record the following address sequence:

0100, 0432, 0101, 0612, 0102, 0103, 0104, 0101, 0611, 0102, 0103,
0104, 0101, 0610, 0102, 0103, 0104, 0101, 0609, 0102, 0105

At 100 bytes per page, this sequence is reduced to the following reference string:

1, 4, 1, 6, 1, 6, 1, 6, 1, 6, 1

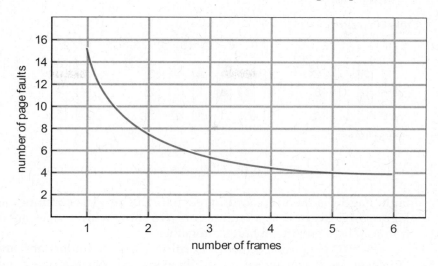

Figure 8.11 Graph of page faults versus number of frames.

To determine the number of page faults for a particular reference string and page-replacement algorithm, we also need to know the number of page frames available. Obviously, as the number of frames available increases, the number of page faults decreases. For the reference string considered previously, for example, if we had three or more frames, we would have only three faults— one fault for the first reference to each page. In contrast, with only one frame available, we would have a replacement with every reference, resulting in eleven faults. In general, we expect a curve such as that in Figure 8.11. As the number of frames increases, the number of page faults drops to some minimal level. Of course, adding physical memory increases the number of frames.

We next illustrate several page-replacement algorithms. In doing so, we use the reference string

$$7, 0, 1, 2, 0, 3, 0, 4, 2, 3, 0, 3, 2, 1, 2, 0, 1, 7, 0, 1$$

for a memory with three frames.

8.4.2 FIFO Page Replacement

The simplest page-replacement algorithm is a first-in, first-out (FIFO) algorithm. A FIFO replacement algorithm associates with each page the time when that page was brought into memory. When a page must be replaced, the oldest page is chosen. Notice that it is not strictly necessary to record the time when a page is brought in. We can create a FIFO queue to hold all pages in memory. We replace the page at the head of the queue. When a page is brought into memory, we insert it at the tail of the queue.

For our example reference string, our three frames are initially empty. The first three references (7, 0, 1) cause page faults and are brought into these empty frames. The next reference (2) replaces page 7, because page 7 was brought in first. Since 0 is the next reference and 0 is already in memory, we have no fault for this reference. The first reference to 3 results in replacement of page 0, since it is now first in line. Because of this replacement, the next reference, to 0, will

reference string

7 0 1 2 0 3 0 4 2 3 0 3 2 1 2 0 1 7 0 1

page frames

Figure 8.12   FIFO page-replacement algorithm.

fault. Page 1 is then replaced by page 0. This process continues as shown in Figure 8.12. Every time a fault occurs, we show which pages are in our three frames. There are fifteen faults altogether.

The FIFO page-replacement algorithm is easy to understand and program. However, its performance is not always good. On the one hand, the page replaced may be an initialization module that was used a long time ago and is no longer needed. On the other hand, it could contain a heavily used variable that was initialized early and is in constant use.

Notice that, even if we select for replacement a page that is in active use, everything still works correctly. After we replace an active page with a new one, a fault occurs almost immediately to retrieve the active page. Some other page must be replaced to bring the active page back into memory. Thus, a bad replacement choice increases the page-fault rate and slows process execution. It does not, however, cause incorrect execution.

To illustrate the problems that are possible with a FIFO page-replacement algorithm, consider the following reference string:

$$1, 2, 3, 4, 1, 2, 5, 1, 2, 3, 4, 5$$

Figure 8.13 shows the curve of page faults for this reference string versus the number of available frames. Notice that the number of faults for four frames (ten) is *greater* than the number of faults for three frames (nine)! This most unexpected result is known as **Belady's anomaly**: for some page-replacement algorithms, the page-fault rate may *increase* as the number of allocated frames increases. We would expect that giving more memory to a process would improve its performance. In some early research, investigators noticed that this assumption was not always true. Belady's anomaly was discovered as a result.

8.4.3   Optimal Page Replacement

One result of the discovery of Belady's anomaly was the search for an **optimal page-replacement algorithm**—the algorithm that has the lowest page-fault rate of all algorithms and will never suffer from Belady's anomaly. Such an algorithm does exist and has been called OPT or MIN. It is simply this:

Replace the page that will not be used for the longest period of time.

Use of this page-replacement algorithm guarantees the lowest possible page-fault rate for a fixed number of frames.

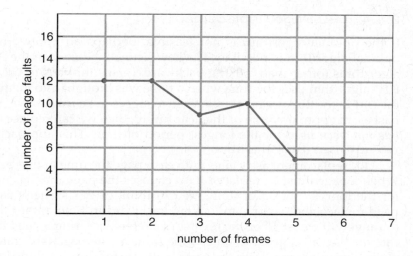

Figure 8.13   Page-fault curve for FIFO replacement on a reference string.

For example, on our sample reference string, the optimal page-replacement algorithm would yield nine page faults, as shown in Figure 8.14. The first three references cause faults that fill the three empty frames. The reference to page 2 replaces page 7, because page 7 will not be used until reference 18, whereas page 0 will be used at 5, and page 1 at 14. The reference to page 3 replaces page 1, as page 1 will be the last of the three pages in memory to be referenced again. With only nine page faults, optimal replacement is much better than a FIFO algorithm, which results in fifteen faults. (If we ignore the first three, which all algorithms must suffer, then optimal replacement is twice as good as FIFO replacement.) In fact, no replacement algorithm can process this reference string in three frames with fewer than nine faults.

Unfortunately, the optimal page-replacement algorithm is difficult to implement, because it requires future knowledge of the reference string. (We encountered a similar situation with the SJF CPU-scheduling algorithm in Section 6.3.2.) As a result, the optimal algorithm is used mainly for comparison studies. For instance, it may be useful to know that, although a new algorithm is not optimal, it is within 12.3 percent of optimal at worst and within 4.7 percent on average.

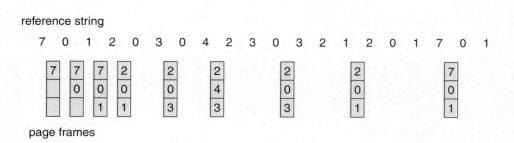

Figure 8.14   Optimal page-replacement algorithm.

8.4.4 LRU Page Replacement

If the optimal algorithm is not feasible, perhaps an approximation of the optimal algorithm is possible. The key distinction between the FIFO and OPT algorithms (other than looking backward versus forward in time) is that the FIFO algorithm uses the time when a page was brought into memory, whereas the OPT algorithm uses the time when a page is to be *used*. If we use the recent past as an approximation of the near future, then we can replace the page that *has not been used* for the longest period of time. This approach is the least recently used (LRU) algorithm.

LRU replacement associates with each page the time of that page's last use. When a page must be replaced, LRU chooses the page that has not been used for the longest period of time. We can think of this strategy as the optimal page-replacement algorithm looking backward in time, rather than forward. (Strangely, if we let S^R be the reverse of a reference string S, then the page-fault rate for the OPT algorithm on S is the same as the page-fault rate for the OPT algorithm on S^R. Similarly, the page-fault rate for the LRU algorithm on S is the same as the page-fault rate for the LRU algorithm on S^R.)

The result of applying LRU replacement to our example reference string is shown in Figure 8.15. The LRU algorithm produces twelve faults. Notice that the first five faults are the same as those for optimal replacement. When the reference to page 4 occurs, however, LRU replacement sees that, of the three frames in memory, page 2 was used least recently. Thus, the LRU algorithm replaces page 2, not knowing that page 2 is about to be used. When it then faults for page 2, the LRU algorithm replaces page 3, since it is now the least recently used of the three pages in memory. Despite these problems, LRU replacement with twelve faults is much better than FIFO replacement with fifteen.

The LRU policy is often used as a page-replacement algorithm and is considered to be good. The major problem is *how* to implement LRU replacement. An LRU page-replacement algorithm may require substantial hardware assistance. The problem is to determine an order for the frames defined by the time of last use. Two implementations are feasible:

- **Counters.** In the simplest case, we associate with each page-table entry a time-of-use field and add to the CPU a logical clock or counter. The clock is incremented for every memory reference. Whenever a reference to a page is made, the contents of the clock register are copied to the time-of-use field in the page-table entry for that page. In this way, we always have

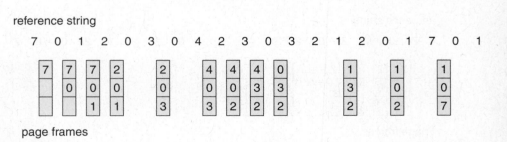

Figure 8.15 LRU page-replacement algorithm.

the "time" of the last reference to each page. We replace the page with the smallest time value. This scheme requires a search of the page table to find the LRU page and a write to memory (to the time-of-use field in the page table) for each memory access. The times must also be maintained when page tables are changed (due to CPU scheduling). Overflow of the clock must be considered.

- **Stack**. Another approach to implementing LRU replacement is to keep a stack of page numbers. Whenever a page is referenced, it is removed from the stack and put on the top. In this way, the most recently used page is always at the top of the stack and the least recently used page is always at the bottom (Figure 8.16). Because entries must be removed from the middle of the stack, it is best to implement this approach by using a doubly linked list with a head pointer and a tail pointer. Removing a page and putting it on the top of the stack then requires changing six pointers at worst. Each update is a little more expensive, but there is no search for a replacement; the tail pointer points to the bottom of the stack, which is the LRU page. This approach is particularly appropriate for software or microcode implementations of LRU replacement.

Like optimal replacement, LRU replacement does not suffer from Belady's anomaly. Both belong to a class of page-replacement algorithms, called **stack algorithms**, that can never exhibit Belady's anomaly. A stack algorithm is an algorithm for which it can be shown that the set of pages in memory for n frames is always a *subset* of the set of pages that would be in memory with n + 1 frames. For LRU replacement, the set of pages in memory would be the n most recently referenced pages. If the number of frames is increased, these n pages will still be the most recently referenced and so will still be in memory.

Note that neither implementation of LRU would be conceivable without hardware assistance beyond the standard TLB registers. The updating of the clock fields or stack must be done for *every* memory reference. If we were to use an interrupt for every reference to allow software to update such data structures, it would slow every memory reference by a factor of at least ten,

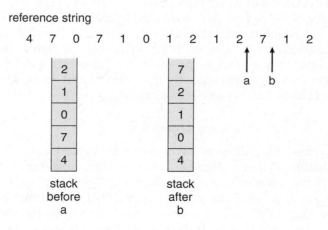

Figure 8.16 Use of a stack to record the most recent page references.

hence slowing every user process by a factor of ten. Few systems could tolerate that level of overhead for memory management.

8.4.5 LRU-Approximation Page Replacement

Few computer systems provide sufficient hardware support for true LRU page replacement. In fact, some systems provide no hardware support, and other page-replacement algorithms (such as a FIFO algorithm) must be used. Many systems provide some help, however, in the form of a reference bit. The reference bit for a page is set by the hardware whenever that page is referenced (either a read or a write to any byte in the page). Reference bits are associated with each entry in the page table.

Initially, all bits are cleared (to 0) by the operating system. As a user process executes, the bit associated with each page referenced is set (to 1) by the hardware. After some time, we can determine which pages have been used and which have not been used by examining the reference bits, although we do not know the *order* of use. This information is the basis for many page-replacement algorithms that approximate LRU replacement.

8.4.5.1 Additional-Reference-Bits Algorithm

We can gain additional ordering information by recording the reference bits at regular intervals. We can keep an 8-bit byte for each page in a table in memory. At regular intervals (say, every 100 milliseconds), a timer interrupt transfers control to the operating system. The operating system shifts the reference bit for each page into the high-order bit of its 8-bit byte, shifting the other bits right by 1 bit and discarding the low-order bit. These 8-bit shift registers contain the history of page use for the last eight time periods. If the shift register contains 00000000, for example, then the page has not been used for eight time periods. A page that is used at least once in each period has a shift register value of 11111111. A page with a history register value of 11000100 has been used more recently than one with a value of 01110111. If we interpret these 8-bit bytes as unsigned integers, the page with the lowest number is the LRU page, and it can be replaced. Notice that the numbers are not guaranteed to be unique, however. We can either replace (swap out) all pages with the smallest value or use the FIFO method to choose among them.

The number of bits of history included in the shift register can be varied, of course, and is selected (depending on the hardware available) to make the updating as fast as possible. In the extreme case, the number can be reduced to zero, leaving only the reference bit itself. This algorithm is called the second-chance page-replacement algorithm.

8.4.5.2 Second-Chance Algorithm

The basic algorithm of second-chance replacement is a FIFO replacement algorithm. When a page has been selected, however, we inspect its reference bit. If the value is 0, we proceed to replace this page; but if the reference bit is set to 1, we give the page a second chance and move on to select the next FIFO page. When a page gets a second chance, its reference bit is cleared, and its arrival time is reset to the current time. Thus, a page that is given a second chance will not be replaced until all other pages have been replaced (or given

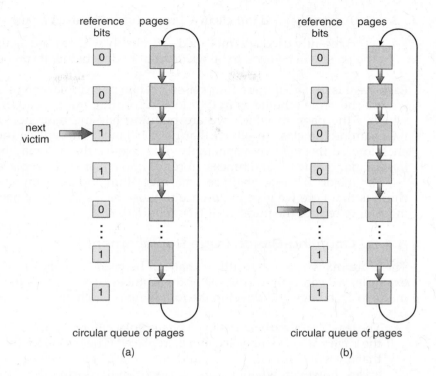

Figure 8.17   Second-chance (clock) page-replacement algorithm.

second chances). In addition, if a page is used often enough to keep its reference bit set, it will never be replaced.

One way to implement the second-chance algorithm (sometimes referred to as the **clock** algorithm) is as a circular queue. A pointer (that is, a hand on the clock) indicates which page is to be replaced next. When a frame is needed, the pointer advances until it finds a page with a 0 reference bit. As it advances, it clears the reference bits (Figure 8.17). Once a victim page is found, the page is replaced, and the new page is inserted in the circular queue in that position. Notice that, in the worst case, when all bits are set, the pointer cycles through the whole queue, giving each page a second chance. It clears all the reference bits before selecting the next page for replacement. Second-chance replacement degenerates to FIFO replacement if all bits are set.

8.4.5.3   Enhanced Second-Chance Algorithm

We can enhance the second-chance algorithm by considering the reference bit and the modify bit (described in Section 8.4.1) as an ordered pair. With these two bits, we have the following four possible classes:

1. (0, 0) neither recently used nor modified—best page to replace

2. (0, 1) not recently used but modified—not quite as good, because the page will need to be written out before replacement

3. (1, 0) recently used but clean—probably will be used again soon

4. (1, 1) recently used and modified—probably will be used again soon, and the page will be need to be written out to disk before it can be replaced

Each page is in one of these four classes. When page replacement is called for, we use the same scheme as in the clock algorithm; but instead of examining whether the page to which we are pointing has the reference bit set to 1, we examine the class to which that page belongs. We replace the first page encountered in the lowest nonempty class. Notice that we may have to scan the circular queue several times before we find a page to be replaced.

The major difference between this algorithm and the simpler clock algorithm is that here we give preference to those pages that have been modified in order to reduce the number of I/Os required.

8.4.6 Counting-Based Page Replacement

There are many other algorithms that can be used for page replacement. For example, we can keep a counter of the number of references that have been made to each page and develop the following two schemes.

- The **least frequently used** (LFU) page-replacement algorithm requires that the page with the smallest count be replaced. The reason for this selection is that an actively used page should have a large reference count. A problem arises, however, when a page is used heavily during the initial phase of a process but then is never used again. Since it was used heavily, it has a large count and remains in memory even though it is no longer needed. One solution is to shift the counts right by 1 bit at regular intervals, forming an exponentially decaying average usage count.

- The **most frequently used** (MFU) page-replacement algorithm is based on the argument that the page with the smallest count was probably just brought in and has yet to be used.

As you might expect, neither MFU nor LFU replacement is common. The implementation of these algorithms is expensive, and they do not approximate OPT replacement well.

8.4.7 Page-Buffering Algorithms

Other procedures are often used in addition to a specific page-replacement algorithm. For example, systems commonly keep a pool of free frames. When a page fault occurs, a victim frame is chosen as before. However, the desired page is read into a free frame from the pool before the victim is written out. This procedure allows the process to restart as soon as possible, without waiting for the victim page to be written out. When the victim is later written out, its frame is added to the free-frame pool.

An expansion of this idea is to maintain a list of modified pages. Whenever the paging device is idle, a modified page is selected and is written to the disk. Its modify bit is then reset. This scheme increases the probability that a page will be clean when it is selected for replacement and will not need to be written out.

Another modification is to keep a pool of free frames but to remember which page was in each frame. Since the frame contents are not modified when a frame is written to the disk, the old page can be reused directly from the free-frame pool if it is needed before that frame is reused. No I/O is needed in this case. When a page fault occurs, we first check whether the desired page is in the free-frame pool. If it is not, we must select a free frame and read into it.

This technique is used in the VAX/VMS system along with a FIFO replacement algorithm. When the FIFO replacement algorithm mistakenly replaces a page that is still in active use, that page is quickly retrieved from the free-frame pool, and no I/O is necessary. The free-frame buffer provides protection against the relatively poor, but simple, FIFO replacement algorithm. This method is necessary because the early versions of VAX did not implement the reference bit correctly.

Some versions of the UNIX system use this method in conjunction with the second-chance algorithm. It can be a useful augmentation to any page-replacement algorithm, to reduce the penalty incurred if the wrong victim page is selected.

8.4.8 Applications and Page Replacement

In certain cases, applications accessing data through the operating system's virtual memory perform worse than if the operating system provided no buffering at all. A typical example is a database, which provides its own memory management and I/O buffering. Applications like this understand their memory use and disk use better than does an operating system that is implementing algorithms for general-purpose use. If the operating system is buffering I/O and the application is doing so as well, however, then twice the memory is being used for a set of I/O.

In another example, data warehouses frequently perform massive sequential disk reads, followed by computations and writes. The LRU algorithm would be removing old pages and preserving new ones, while the application would more likely be reading older pages than newer ones (as it starts its sequential reads again). Here, MFU would actually be more efficient than LRU.

Because of such problems, some operating systems give special programs the ability to use a disk partition as a large sequential array of logical blocks, without any file-system data structures. This array is sometimes called the **raw disk**, and I/O to this array is termed raw I/O. Raw I/O bypasses all the file-system services, such as file I/O demand paging, file locking, prefetching, space allocation, file names, and directories. Note that although certain applications are more efficient when implementing their own special-purpose storage services on a raw partition, most applications perform better when they use the regular file-system services.

8.5 Allocation of Frames

We turn next to the issue of allocation. How do we allocate the fixed amount of free memory among the various processes? If we have 93 free frames and two processes, how many frames does each process get?

The simplest case is the single-user system. Consider a single-user system with 128 KB of memory composed of pages 1 KB in size. This system has 128 frames. The operating system may take 35 KB, leaving 93 frames for the user process. Under pure demand paging, all 93 frames would initially be put on the free-frame list. When a user process started execution, it would generate a sequence of page faults. The first 93 page faults would all get free frames from the free-frame list. When the free-frame list was exhausted, a page-replacement algorithm would be used to select one of the 93 in-memory pages to be replaced with the 94th, and so on. When the process terminated, the 93 frames would once again be placed on the free-frame list.

There are many variations on this simple strategy. We can require that the operating system allocate all its buffer and table space from the free-frame list. When this space is not in use by the operating system, it can be used to support user paging. We can try to keep three free frames reserved on the free-frame list at all times. Thus, when a page fault occurs, there is a free frame available to page into. While the page swap is taking place, a replacement can be selected, which is then written to the disk as the user process continues to execute. Other variants are also possible, but the basic strategy is clear: the user process is allocated any free frame.

8.5.1   Minimum Number of Frames

Our strategies for the allocation of frames are constrained in various ways. We cannot, for example, allocate more than the total number of available frames (unless there is page sharing). We must also allocate at least a minimum number of frames. Here, we look more closely at the latter requirement.

One reason for allocating at least a minimum number of frames involves performance. Obviously, as the number of frames allocated to each process decreases, the page-fault rate increases, slowing process execution. In addition, remember that, when a page fault occurs before an executing instruction is complete, the instruction must be restarted. Consequently, we must have enough frames to hold all the different pages that any single instruction can reference.

For example, consider a machine in which all memory-reference instructions may reference only one memory address. In this case, we need at least one frame for the instruction and one frame for the memory reference. In addition, if one-level indirect addressing is allowed (for example, a `load` instruction on page 16 can refer to an address on page 0, which is an indirect reference to page 23), then paging requires at least three frames per process. Think about what might happen if a process had only two frames.

The minimum number of frames is defined by the computer architecture. For example, the move instruction for the PDP-11 includes more than one word for some addressing modes, and thus the instruction itself may straddle two pages. In addition, each of its two operands may be indirect references, for a total of six frames. Another example is the IBM 370 MVC instruction. Since the instruction is from storage location to storage location, it takes 6 bytes and can straddle two pages. The block of characters to move and the area to which it is to be moved can each also straddle two pages. This situation would require six frames. The worst case occurs when the MVC instruction is the operand of an EXECUTE instruction that straddles a page boundary; in this case, we need eight frames.

The worst-case scenario occurs in computer architectures that allow multiple levels of indirection (for example, each 16-bit word could contain a 15-bit address plus a 1-bit indirect indicator). Theoretically, a simple load instruction could reference an indirect address that could reference an indirect address (on another page) that could also reference an indirect address (on yet another page), and so on, until every page in virtual memory had been touched. Thus, in the worst case, the entire virtual memory must be in physical memory. To overcome this difficulty, we must place a limit on the levels of indirection (for example, limit an instruction to at most 16 levels of indirection). When the first indirection occurs, a counter is set to 16; the counter is then decremented for each successive indirection for this instruction. If the counter is decremented to 0, a trap occurs (excessive indirection). This limitation reduces the maximum number of memory references per instruction to 17, requiring the same number of frames.

Whereas the minimum number of frames per process is defined by the architecture, the maximum number is defined by the amount of available physical memory. In between, we are still left with significant choice in frame allocation.

8.5.2 Allocation Algorithms

The easiest way to split m frames among n processes is to give everyone an equal share, m/n frames (ignoring frames needed by the operating system for the moment). For instance, if there are 93 frames and five processes, each process will get 18 frames. The three leftover frames can be used as a free-frame buffer pool. This scheme is called **equal allocation**.

An alternative is to recognize that various processes will need differing amounts of memory. Consider a system with a 1-KB frame size. If a small student process of 10 KB and an interactive database of 127 KB are the only two processes running in a system with 62 free frames, it does not make much sense to give each process 31 frames. The student process does not need more than 10 frames, so the other 21 are, strictly speaking, wasted.

To solve this problem, we can use **proportional allocation**, in which we allocate available memory to each process according to its size. Let the size of the virtual memory for process p_i be s_i, and define

$$S = \sum s_i.$$

Then, if the total number of available frames is m, we allocate a_i frames to process p_i, where a_i is approximately

$$a_i = s_i / S \times m.$$

Of course, we must adjust each a_i to be an integer that is greater than the minimum number of frames required by the instruction set, with a sum not exceeding m.

With proportional allocation, we would split 62 frames between two processes, one of 10 pages and one of 127 pages, by allocating 4 frames and 57 frames, respectively, since

$$10/137 \times 62 \approx 4, \text{ and}$$
$$127/137 \times 62 \approx 57.$$

In this way, both processes share the available frames according to their "needs," rather than equally.

In both equal and proportional allocation, of course, the allocation may vary according to the multiprogramming level. If the multiprogramming level is increased, each process will lose some frames to provide the memory needed for the new process. Conversely, if the multiprogramming level decreases, the frames that were allocated to the departed process can be spread over the remaining processes.

Notice that, with either equal or proportional allocation, a high-priority process is treated the same as a low-priority process. By its definition, however, we may want to give the high-priority process more memory to speed its execution, to the detriment of low-priority processes. One solution is to use a proportional allocation scheme wherein the ratio of frames depends not on the relative sizes of processes but rather on the priorities of processes or on a combination of size and priority.

8.5.3   Global versus Local Allocation

Another important factor in the way frames are allocated to the various processes is page replacement. With multiple processes competing for frames, we can classify page-replacement algorithms into two broad categories: **global replacement** and **local replacement**. Global replacement allows a process to select a replacement frame from the set of all frames, even if that frame is currently allocated to some other process; that is, one process can take a frame from another. Local replacement requires that each process select from only its own set of allocated frames.

For example, consider an allocation scheme wherein we allow high-priority processes to select frames from low-priority processes for replacement. A process can select a replacement from among its own frames or the frames of any lower-priority process. This approach allows a high-priority process to increase its frame allocation at the expense of a low-priority process. With a local replacement strategy, the number of frames allocated to a process does not change. With global replacement, a process may happen to select only frames allocated to other processes, thus increasing the number of frames allocated to it (assuming that other processes do not choose *its* frames for replacement).

One problem with a global replacement algorithm is that a process cannot control its own page-fault rate. The set of pages in memory for a process depends not only on the paging behavior of that process but also on the paging behavior of other processes. Therefore, the same process may perform quite differently (for example, taking 0.5 seconds for one execution and 10.3 seconds for the next execution) because of totally external circumstances. Such is not the case with a local replacement algorithm. Under local replacement, the set of pages in memory for a process is affected by the paging behavior of only that process. Local replacement might hinder a process, however, by not making available to it other, less used pages of memory. Thus, global replacement generally results in greater system throughput and is therefore the more commonly used method.

8.5.4   Non-Uniform Memory Access

Thus far in our coverage of virtual memory, we have assumed that all main memory is created equal—or at least that it is accessed equally. On many computer systems, that is not the case. Often, in systems with multiple CPUs (Section 1.3.2), a given CPU can access some sections of main memory faster than it can access others. These performance differences are caused by how CPUs and memory are interconnected in the system. Frequently, such a system is made up of several system boards, each containing multiple CPUs and some memory. The system boards are interconnected in various ways, ranging from system buses to high-speed network connections like InfiniBand. As you might expect, the CPUs on a particular board can access the memory on that board with less delay than they can access memory on other boards in the system. Systems in which memory access times vary significantly are known collectively as **non-uniform memory access (NUMA)** systems, and without exception, they are slower than systems in which memory and CPUs are located on the same motherboard.

Managing which page frames are stored at which locations can significantly affect performance in NUMA systems. If we treat memory as uniform in such a system, CPUs may wait significantly longer for memory access than if we modify memory allocation algorithms to take NUMA into account. Similar changes must be made to the scheduling system. The goal of these changes is to have memory frames allocated "as close as possible" to the CPU on which the process is running. The definition of "close" is "with minimum latency," which typically means on the same system board as the CPU.

The algorithmic changes consist of having the scheduler track the last CPU on which each process ran. If the scheduler tries to schedule each process onto its previous CPU, and the memory-management system tries to allocate frames for the process close to the CPU on which it is being scheduled, then improved cache hits and decreased memory access times will result.

The picture is more complicated once threads are added. For example, a process with many running threads may end up with those threads scheduled on many different system boards. How is the memory to be allocated in this case? Solaris solves the problem by creating **lgroups** (for "latency groups") in the kernel. Each lgroup gathers together close CPUs and memory. In fact, there is a hierarchy of lgroups based on the amount of latency between the groups. Solaris tries to schedule all threads of a process and allocate all memory of a process within an lgroup. If that is not possible, it picks nearby lgroups for the rest of the resources needed. This practice minimizes overall memory latency and maximizes CPU cache hit rates.

8.6 Thrashing

If the number of frames allocated to a low-priority process falls below the minimum number required by the computer architecture, we must suspend that process's execution. We should then page out its remaining pages, freeing all its allocated frames. This provision introduces a swap-in, swap-out level of intermediate CPU scheduling.

In fact, look at any process that does not have "enough" frames. If the process does not have the number of frames it needs to support pages in active use, it will quickly page-fault. At this point, it must replace some page. However, since all its pages are in active use, it must replace a page that will be needed again right away. Consequently, it quickly faults again, and again, and again, replacing pages that it must bring back in immediately.

This high paging activity is called **thrashing**. A process is thrashing if it is spending more time paging than executing.

8.6.1   Cause of Thrashing

Thrashing results in severe performance problems. Consider the following scenario, which is based on the actual behavior of early paging systems.

The operating system monitors CPU utilization. If CPU utilization is too low, we increase the degree of multiprogramming by introducing a new process to the system. A global page-replacement algorithm is used; it replaces pages without regard to the process to which they belong. Now suppose that a process enters a new phase in its execution and needs more frames. It starts faulting and taking frames away from other processes. These processes need those pages, however, and so they also fault, taking frames from other processes. These faulting processes must use the paging device to swap pages in and out. As they queue up for the paging device, the ready queue empties. As processes wait for the paging device, CPU utilization decreases.

The CPU scheduler sees the decreasing CPU utilization and *increases* the degree of multiprogramming as a result. The new process tries to get started by taking frames from running processes, causing more page faults and a longer queue for the paging device. As a result, CPU utilization drops even further, and the CPU scheduler tries to increase the degree of multiprogramming even more. Thrashing has occurred, and system throughput plunges. The page-fault rate increases tremendously. As a result, the effective memory-access time increases. No work is getting done, because the processes are spending all their time paging.

This phenomenon is illustrated in Figure 8.18, in which CPU utilization is plotted against the degree of multiprogramming. As the degree of multi-programming increases, CPU utilization also increases, although more slowly, until a maximum is reached. If the degree of multiprogramming is increased even further, thrashing sets in, and CPU utilization drops sharply. At this point, to increase CPU utilization and stop thrashing, we must *decrease* the degree of multiprogramming.

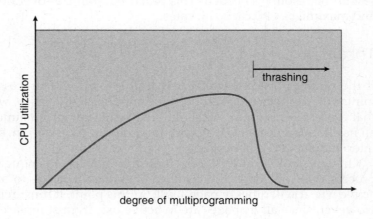

Figure 8.18   Thrashing.

We can limit the effects of thrashing by using a **local replacement algorithm** (or **priority replacement algorithm**). With local replacement, if one process starts thrashing, it cannot steal frames from another process and cause the latter to thrash as well. However, the problem is not entirely solved. If processes are thrashing, they will be in the queue for the paging device most of the time. The average service time for a page fault will increase because of the longer average queue for the paging device. Thus, the effective access time will increase even for a process that is not thrashing.

To prevent thrashing, we must provide a process with as many frames as it needs. But how do we know how many frames it "needs"? There are several techniques. The working-set strategy (Section 8.6.2) starts by looking at how many frames a process is actually using. This approach defines the **locality model** of process execution.

The locality model states that, as a process executes, it moves from locality to locality. A locality is a set of pages that are actively used together (Figure 8.19). A program is generally composed of several different localities, which may overlap.

For example, when a function is called, it defines a new locality. In this locality, memory references are made to the instructions of the function call, its local variables, and a subset of the global variables. When we exit the function, the process leaves this locality, since the local variables and instructions of the function are no longer in active use. We may return to this locality later.

Thus, we see that localities are defined by the program structure and its data structures. The locality model states that all programs will exhibit this basic memory reference structure. Note that the locality model is the unstated principle behind the caching discussions so far in this book. If accesses to any types of data were random rather than patterned, caching would be useless.

Suppose we allocate enough frames to a process to accommodate its current locality. It will fault for the pages in its locality until all these pages are in memory; then, it will not fault again until it changes localities. If we do not allocate enough frames to accommodate the size of the current locality, the process will thrash, since it cannot keep in memory all the pages that it is actively using.

8.6.2   Working-Set Model

As mentioned, the **working-set model** is based on the assumption of locality. This model uses a parameter, Δ, to define the **working-set window**. The idea is to examine the most recent Δ page references. The set of pages in the most recent Δ page references is the **working set** (Figure 8.20). If a page is in active use, it will be in the working set. If it is no longer being used, it will drop from the working set Δ time units after its last reference. Thus, the working set is an approximation of the program's locality.

For example, given the sequence of memory references shown in Figure 8.20, if $\Delta = 10$ memory references, then the working set at time t_1 is $\{1, 2, 5, 6, 7\}$. By time t_2, the working set has changed to $\{3, 4\}$.

The accuracy of the working set depends on the selection of Δ. If Δ is too small, it will not encompass the entire locality; if Δ is too large, it may overlap several localities. In the extreme, if Δ is infinite, the working set is the set of pages touched during the process execution.

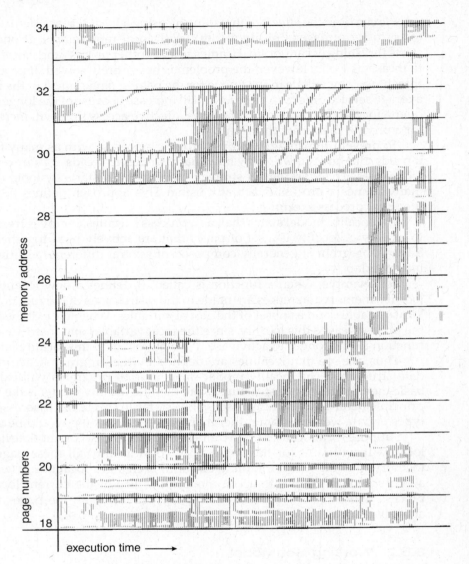

Figure 8.19 Locality in a memory-reference pattern.

The most important property of the working set, then, is its size. If we compute the working-set size, WSS_i, for each process in the system, we can then consider that

$$D = \sum WSS_i,$$

where D is the total demand for frames. Each process is actively using the pages in its working set. Thus, process i needs WSS_i frames. If the total demand is greater than the total number of available frames $(D > m)$, thrashing will occur, because some processes will not have enough frames.

Once Δ has been selected, use of the working-set model is simple. The operating system monitors the working set of each process and allocates to

page reference table

...2 6 1 5 7 7 7 7 5 1 6 2 3 4 1 2 3 4 4 4 3 4 3 4 4 4 1 3 2 3 4 4 4 3 4 4 4 ...

t_1

t_2

WS(t_1) = {1,2,5,6,7}

WS(t_2) = {3,4}

Figure 8.20 Working-set model.

that working set enough frames to provide it with its working-set size. If there are enough extra frames, another process can be initiated. If the sum of the working-set sizes increases, exceeding the total number of available frames, the operating system selects a process to suspend. The process's pages are written out (swapped), and its frames are reallocated to other processes. The suspended process can be restarted later.

This working-set strategy prevents thrashing while keeping the degree of multiprogramming as high as possible. Thus, it optimizes CPU utilization. The difficulty with the working-set model is keeping track of the working set. The working-set window is a moving window. At each memory reference, a new reference appears at one end, and the oldest reference drops off the other end. A page is in the working set if it is referenced anywhere in the working-set window.

We can approximate the working-set model with a fixed-interval timer interrupt and a reference bit. For example, assume that Δ equals 10,000 references and that we can cause a timer interrupt every 5,000 references. When we get a timer interrupt, we copy and clear the reference-bit values for each page. Thus, if a page fault occurs, we can examine the current reference bit and two in-memory bits to determine whether a page was used within the last 10,000 to 15,000 references. If it was used, at least one of these bits will be on. If it has not been used, these bits will be off. Pages with at least one bit on will be considered to be in the working set.

Note that this arrangement is not entirely accurate, because we cannot tell where, within an interval of 5,000, a reference occurred. We can reduce the uncertainty by increasing the number of history bits and the frequency of interrupts (for example, 10 bits and interrupts every 1,000 references). However, the cost to service these more frequent interrupts will be correspondingly higher.

8.6.3 Page-Fault Frequency

The working-set model is successful, and knowledge of the working set can be useful for prepaging (Section 8.9.1), but it seems a clumsy way to control thrashing. A strategy that uses the **page-fault frequency** (PFF) takes a more direct approach.

The specific problem is how to prevent thrashing. Thrashing has a high page-fault rate. Thus, we want to control the page-fault rate. When it is too high, we know that the process needs more frames. Conversely, if the page-fault rate is too low, then the process may have too many frames. We can establish upper and lower bounds on the desired page-fault rate (Figure 8.21). If the actual page-fault rate exceeds the upper limit, we allocate the process another

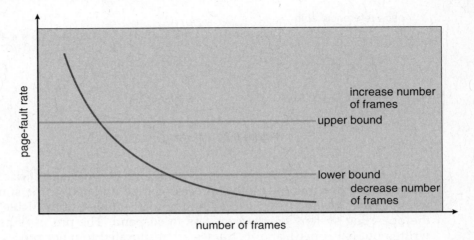

Figure 8.21   Page-fault frequency.

frame. If the page-fault rate falls below the lower limit, we remove a frame from the process. Thus, we can directly measure and control the page-fault rate to prevent thrashing.

As with the working-set strategy, we may have to swap out a process. If the page-fault rate increases and no free frames are available, we must select some process and swap it out to backing store. The freed frames are then distributed to processes with high page-fault rates.

8.6.4 Concluding Remarks

Practically speaking, thrashing and the resulting swapping have a disagreeably large impact on performance. The current best practice in implementing a computer facility is to include enough physical memory, whenever possible, to avoid thrashing and swapping. From smartphones through mainframes, providing enough memory to keep all working sets in memory concurrently, except under extreme conditions, gives the best user experience.

8.7   Memory-Mapped Files

Consider a sequential read of a file on disk using the standard system calls `open()`, `read()`, and `write()`. Each file access requires a system call and disk access. Alternatively, we can use the virtual memory techniques discussed so far to treat file I/O as routine memory accesses. This approach, known as memory mapping a file, allows a part of the virtual address space to be logically associated with the file. As we shall see, this can lead to significant performance increases.

8.7.1   Basic Mechanism

Memory mapping a file is accomplished by mapping a disk block to a page (or pages) in memory. Initial access to the file proceeds through ordinary demand paging, resulting in a page fault. However, a page-sized portion of the file is read from the file system into a physical page (some systems may opt to read

WORKING SETS AND PAGE-FAULT RATES

There is a direct relationship between the working set of a process and its page-fault rate. Typically, as shown in Figure 8.20, the working set of a process changes over time as references to data and code sections move from one locality to another. Assuming there is sufficient memory to store the working set of a process (that is, the process is not thrashing), the page-fault rate of the process will transition between peaks and valleys over time. This general behavior is shown below:

A peak in the page-fault rate occurs when we begin demand-paging a new locality. However, once the working set of this new locality is in memory, the page-fault rate falls. When the process moves to a new working set, the page-fault rate rises toward a peak once again, returning to a lower rate once the new working set is loaded into memory. The span of time between the start of one peak and the start of the next peak represents the transition from one working set to another.

in more than a page-sized chunk of memory at a time). Subsequent reads and writes to the file are handled as routine memory accesses. Manipulating files through memory rather than incurring the overhead of using the read() and write() system calls simplifies and speeds up file access and usage.

Note that writes to the file mapped in memory are not necessarily immediate (synchronous) writes to the file on disk. Some systems may choose to update the physical file when the operating system periodically checks whether the page in memory has been modified. When the file is closed, all the memory-mapped data are written back to disk and removed from the virtual memory of the process.

Some operating systems provide memory mapping only through a specific system call and use the standard system calls to perform all other file I/O. However, some systems choose to memory-map a file regardless of whether the file was specified as memory-mapped. Let's take Solaris as an example. If a file is specified as memory-mapped (using the mmap() system call), Solaris maps the file into the address space of the process. If a file is opened and accessed using ordinary system calls, such as open(), read(), and write(),

Figure 8.22 Memory-mapped files.

Solaris still memory-maps the file; however, the file is mapped to the kernel address space. Regardless of how the file is opened, then, Solaris treats all file I/O as memory-mapped, allowing file access to take place via the efficient memory subsystem.

Multiple processes may be allowed to map the same file concurrently, to allow sharing of data. Writes by any of the processes modify the data in virtual memory and can be seen by all others that map the same section of the file. Given our earlier discussions of virtual memory, it should be clear how the sharing of memory-mapped sections of memory is implemented: the virtual memory map of each sharing process points to the same page of physical memory—the page that holds a copy of the disk block. This memory sharing is illustrated in Figure 8.22. The memory-mapping system calls can also support copy-on-write functionality, allowing processes to share a file in read-only mode but to have their own copies of any data they modify. So that access to the shared data is coordinated, the processes involved might use one of the mechanisms for achieving mutual exclusion described in Chapter 5.

Quite often, shared memory is in fact implemented by memory mapping files. Under this scenario, processes can communicate using shared memory by having the communicating processes memory-map the same file into their virtual address spaces. The memory-mapped file serves as the region of shared memory between the communicating processes (Figure 8.23). We have already seen this in Section 3.4.1, where a POSIX shared memory object is created and each communicating process memory-maps the object into its address space. In the following section, we illustrate support in the Windows API for shared memory using memory-mapped files.

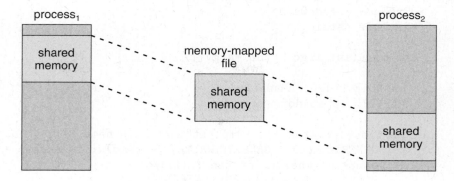

Figure 8.23 Shared memory using memory-mapped I/O.

8.7.2 Shared Memory in the Windows API

The general outline for creating a region of shared memory using memory-mapped files in the Windows API involves first creating a **file mapping** for the file to be mapped and then establishing a **view** of the mapped file in a process's virtual address space. A second process can then open and create a view of the mapped file in its virtual address space. The mapped file represents the shared-memory object that will enable communication to take place between the processes.

We next illustrate these steps in more detail. In this example, a producer process first creates a shared-memory object using the memory-mapping features available in the Windows API. The producer then writes a message to shared memory. After that, a consumer process opens a mapping to the shared-memory object and reads the message written by the consumer.

To establish a memory-mapped file, a process first opens the file to be mapped with the `CreateFile()` function, which returns a HANDLE to the opened file. The process then creates a mapping of this file HANDLE using the `CreateFileMapping()` function. Once the file mapping is established, the process then establishes a view of the mapped file in its virtual address space with the `MapViewOfFile()` function. The view of the mapped file represents the portion of the file being mapped in the virtual address space of the process —the entire file or only a portion of it may be mapped. We illustrate this sequence in the program shown in Figure 8.24. (We eliminate much of the error checking for code brevity.)

The call to `CreateFileMapping()` creates a **named shared-memory object** called `SharedObject`. The consumer process will communicate using this shared-memory segment by creating a mapping to the same named object. The producer then creates a view of the memory-mapped file in its virtual address space. By passing the last three parameters the value 0, it indicates that the mapped view is the entire file. It could instead have passed values specifying an offset and size, thus creating a view containing only a subsection of the file. (It is important to note that the entire mapping may not be loaded into memory when the mapping is established. Rather, the mapped file may be demand-paged, thus bringing pages into memory only as they are accessed.) The `MapViewOfFile()` function returns a pointer to the shared-memory object; any accesses to this memory location are thus accesses to the memory-mapped

```
#include <windows.h>
#include <stdio.h>

int main(int argc, char *argv[])
{
   HANDLE hFile, hMapFile;
   LPVOID lpMapAddress;

   hFile = CreateFile("temp.txt", /* file name */
      GENERIC_READ | GENERIC_WRITE, /* read/write access */
      0, /* no sharing of the file */
      NULL, /* default security */
      OPEN_ALWAYS, /* open new or existing file */
      FILE_ATTRIBUTE_NORMAL, /* routine file attributes */
      NULL); /* no file template */

   hMapFile = CreateFileMapping(hFile, /* file handle */
      NULL, /* default security */
      PAGE_READWRITE, /* read/write access to mapped pages */
      0, /* map entire file */
      0,
      TEXT("SharedObject")); /* named shared memory object */

   lpMapAddress = MapViewOfFile(hMapFile, /* mapped object handle */
      FILE_MAP_ALL_ACCESS, /* read/write access */
      0, /* mapped view of entire file */
      0,
      0);

   /* write to shared memory */
   sprintf(lpMapAddress,"Shared memory message");

   UnmapViewOfFile(lpMapAddress);
   CloseHandle(hFile);
   CloseHandle(hMapFile);
}
```

Figure 8.24 Producer writing to shared memory using the Windows API.

file. In this instance, the producer process writes the message "Shared memory message" to shared memory.

A program illustrating how the consumer process establishes a view of the named shared-memory object is shown in Figure 8.25. This program is somewhat simpler than the one shown in Figure 8.24, as all that is necessary is for the process to create a mapping to the existing named shared-memory object. The consumer process must also create a view of the mapped file, just as the producer process did in the program in Figure 8.24. The consumer then reads from shared memory the message "Shared memory message" that was written by the producer process.

```
#include <windows.h>
#include <stdio.h>

int main(int argc, char *argv[])
{
    HANDLE hMapFile;
    LPVOID lpMapAddress;

    hMapFile = OpenFileMapping(FILE_MAP_ALL_ACCESS, /* R/W access */
        FALSE, /* no inheritance */
        TEXT("SharedObject")); /* name of mapped file object */

    lpMapAddress = MapViewOfFile(hMapFile, /* mapped object handle */
        FILE_MAP_ALL_ACCESS, /* read/write access */
        0, /* mapped view of entire file */
        0,
        0);

    /* read from shared memory */
    printf("Read message %s", lpMapAddress);

    UnmapViewOfFile(lpMapAddress);
    CloseHandle(hMapFile);
}
```

Figure 8.25 Consumer reading from shared memory using the Windows API.

Finally, both processes remove the view of the mapped file with a call to UnmapViewOfFile(). We provide a programming exercise at the end of this chapter using shared memory with memory mapping in the Windows API.

8.7.3 Memory-Mapped I/O

In the case of I/O, as mentioned in Section 1.2.1, each I/O controller includes registers to hold commands and the data being transferred. Usually, special I/O instructions allow data transfers between these registers and system memory. To allow more convenient access to I/O devices, many computer architectures provide **memory-mapped** I/O. In this case, ranges of memory addresses are set aside and are mapped to the device registers. Reads and writes to these memory addresses cause the data to be transferred to and from the device registers. This method is appropriate for devices that have fast response times, such as video controllers. In the IBM PC, each location on the screen is mapped to a memory location. Displaying text on the screen is almost as easy as writing the text into the appropriate memory-mapped locations.

Memory-mapped I/O is also convenient for other devices, such as the serial and parallel ports used to connect modems and printers to a computer. The CPU transfers data through these kinds of devices by reading and writing a few device registers, called an I/O **port**. To send out a long string of bytes through a memory-mapped serial port, the CPU writes one data byte to the data register and sets a bit in the control register to signal that the byte is available. The device takes the data byte and then clears the bit in the control register to signal that it is ready for the next byte. Then the CPU can transfer the next byte. If the CPU uses polling to watch the control bit, constantly looping to see whether the device is ready, this method of operation is called **programmed I/O** (PIO). If the CPU does not poll the control bit, but instead receives an interrupt when the device is ready for the next byte, the data transfer is said to be **interrupt driven**.

8.8   Allocating Kernel Memory

When a process running in user mode requests additional memory, pages are allocated from the list of free page frames maintained by the kernel. This list is typically populated using a page-replacement algorithm such as those discussed in Section 8.4 and most likely contains free pages scattered throughout physical memory, as explained earlier. Remember, too, that if a user process requests a single byte of memory, internal fragmentation will result, as the process will be granted an entire page frame.

Kernel memory is often allocated from a free-memory pool different from the list used to satisfy ordinary user-mode processes. There are two primary reasons for this:

1. The kernel requests memory for data structures of varying sizes, some of which are less than a page in size. As a result, the kernel must use memory conservatively and attempt to minimize waste due to fragmentation. This is especially important because many operating systems do not subject kernel code or data to the paging system.

2. Pages allocated to user-mode processes do not necessarily have to be in contiguous physical memory. However, certain hardware devices interact directly with physical memory—without the benefit of a virtual memory interface—and consequently may require memory residing in physically contiguous pages.

In the following sections, we examine two strategies for managing free memory that is assigned to kernel processes: the "buddy system" and slab allocation.

8.8.1   Buddy System

The buddy system allocates memory from a fixed-size segment consisting of physically contiguous pages. Memory is allocated from this segment using a **power-of-2 allocator**, which satisfies requests in units sized as a power of 2 (4 KB, 8 KB, 16 KB, and so forth). A request in units not appropriately sized is rounded up to the next highest power of 2. For example, a request for 11 KB is satisfied with a 16-KB segment.

Let's consider a simple example. Assume the size of a memory segment is initially 256 KB and the kernel requests 21 KB of memory. The segment is initially divided into two **buddies**—which we will call A_L and A_R—each 128 KB in size. One of these buddies is further divided into two 64-KB buddies— B_L and B_R. However, the next-highest power of 2 from 21 KB is 32 KB so either B_L or B_R is again divided into two 32-KB buddies, C_L and C_R. One of these

physically contiguous pages

Figure 8.26 Buddy system allocation.

buddies is used to satisfy the 21-KB request. This scheme is illustrated in Figure 8.26, where C_L is the segment allocated to the 21-KB request.

An advantage of the buddy system is how quickly adjacent buddies can be combined to form larger segments using a technique known as **coalescing**. In Figure 8.26, for example, when the kernel releases the C_L unit it was allocated, the system can coalesce C_L and C_R into a 64-KB segment. This segment, B_L, can in turn be coalesced with its buddy B_R to form a 128-KB segment. Ultimately, we can end up with the original 256-KB segment.

The obvious drawback to the buddy system is that rounding up to the next highest power of 2 is very likely to cause fragmentation within allocated segments. For example, a 33-KB request can only be satisfied with a 64-KB segment. In fact, we cannot guarantee that less than 50 percent of the allocated unit will be wasted due to internal fragmentation. In the following section, we explore a memory allocation scheme where no space is lost due to fragmentation.

8.8.2 Slab Allocation

A second strategy for allocating kernel memory is known as **slab allocation**. A **slab** is made up of one or more physically contiguous pages. A **cache** consists of one or more slabs. There is a single cache for each unique kernel data structure —for example, a separate cache for the data structure representing process descriptors, a separate cache for file objects, a separate cache for semaphores, and so forth. Each cache is populated with **objects** that are instantiations of the kernel data structure the cache represents. For example, the cache representing semaphores stores instances of semaphore objects, the cache representing process descriptors stores instances of process descriptor objects, and so forth. The relationship among slabs, caches, and objects is shown in Figure 8.27. The figure shows two kernel objects 3 KB in size and three objects 7 KB in size, each stored in a separate cache.

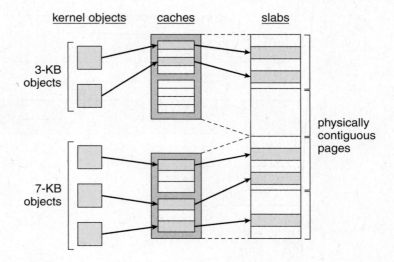

kernel objects   caches   slabs

physically
contiguous
pages

Figure 8.27 Slab allocation.

The slab-allocation algorithm uses caches to store kernel objects. When a cache is created, a number of objects—which are initially marked as free—are allocated to the cache. The number of objects in the cache depends on the size of the associated slab. For example, a 12-KB slab (made up of three continuous 4-KB pages) could store six 2-KB objects. Initially, all objects in the cache are marked as free. When a new object for a kernel data structure is needed, the allocator can assign any free object from the cache to satisfy the request. The object assigned from the cache is marked as used.

Let's consider a scenario in which the kernel requests memory from the slab allocator for an object representing a process descriptor. In Linux systems, a process descriptor is of the type struct task_struct, which requires approximately 1.7 KB of memory. When the Linux kernel creates a new task, it requests the necessary memory for the struct task_struct object from its cache. The cache will fulfill the request using a struct task_struct object that has already been allocated in a slab and is marked as free.

In Linux, a slab may be in one of three possible states:

1. **Full**. All objects in the slab are marked as used.

2. **Empty**. All objects in the slab are marked as free.

3. **Partial**. The slab consists of both used and free objects.

The slab allocator first attempts to satisfy the request with a free object in a partial slab. If none exists, a free object is assigned from an empty slab. If no empty slabs are available, a new slab is allocated from contiguous physical pages and assigned to a cache; memory for the object is allocated from this slab.

The slab allocator provides two main benefits:

1. No memory is wasted due to fragmentation. Fragmentation is not an issue because each unique kernel data structure has an associated cache, and each cache is made up of one or more slabs that are divided into

chunks the size of the objects being represented. Thus, when the kernel requests memory for an object, the slab allocator returns the exact amount of memory required to represent the object.

2. Memory requests can be satisfied quickly. The slab allocation scheme is thus particularly effective for managing memory when objects are frequently allocated and deallocated, as is often the case with requests from the kernel. The act of allocating—and releasing—memory can be a time-consuming process. However, objects are created in advance and thus can be quickly allocated from the cache. Furthermore, when the kernel has finished with an object and releases it, it is marked as free and returned to its cache, thus making it immediately available for subsequent requests from the kernel.

The slab allocator first appeared in the Solaris 2.4 kernel. Because of its general-purpose nature, this allocator is now also used for certain user-mode memory requests in Solaris. Linux originally used the buddy system; however, beginning with Version 2.2, the Linux kernel adopted the slab allocator.

Recent distributions of Linux now include two other kernel memory allocators—the SLOB and SLUB allocators. (Linux refers to its slab implementation as SLAB.)

The SLOB allocator is designed for systems with a limited amount of memory, such as embedded systems. SLOB (which stands for Simple List of Blocks) works by maintaining three lists of objects: *small* (for objects less than 256 bytes), *medium* (for objects less than 1,024 bytes), and *large* (for objects less than 1,024 bytes). Memory requests are allocated from an object on an appropriately sized list using a first-fit policy.

Beginning with Version 2.6.24, the SLUB allocator replaced SLAB as the default allocator for the Linux kernel. SLUB addresses performance issues with slab allocation by reducing much of the overhead required by the SLAB allocator. One change is to move the metadata that is stored with each slab under SLAB allocation to the page structure the Linux kernel uses for each page. Additionally, SLUB removes the per-CPU queues that the SLAB allocator maintains for objects in each cache. For systems with a large number of processors, the amount of memory allocated to these queues was not insignificant. Thus, SLUB provides better performance as the number of processors on a system increases.

8.9 Other Considerations

The major decisions that we make for a paging system are the selections of a replacement algorithm and an allocation policy, which we discussed earlier in this chapter. There are many other considerations as well, and we discuss several of them here.

8.9.1 Prepaging

An obvious property of pure demand paging is the large number of page faults that occur when a process is started. This situation results from trying to get the initial locality into memory. The same situation may arise at other times. For instance, when a swapped-out process is restarted, all its pages are on the disk, and each must be brought in by its own page fault. **Prepaging** is an attempt to prevent this high level of initial paging. The strategy is to bring into memory at one time all the pages that will be needed. Some operating systems—notably Solaris—prepage the page frames for small files.

In a system using the working-set model, for example, we could keep with each process a list of the pages in its working set. If we must suspend a process (due to an I/O wait or a lack of free frames), we remember the working set for that process. When the process is to be resumed (because I/O has finished or enough free frames have become available), we automatically bring back into memory its entire working set before restarting the process.

Prepaging may offer an advantage in some cases. The question is simply whether the cost of using prepaging is less than the cost of servicing the corresponding page faults. It may well be the case that many of the pages brought back into memory by prepaging will not be used.

Assume that s pages are prepaged and a fraction α of these s pages is actually used ($0 \le \alpha \le 1$). The question is whether the cost of the $s * \alpha$ saved page faults is greater or less than the cost of prepaging $s * (1 - \alpha)$ unnecessary pages. If α is close to 0, prepaging loses; if α is close to 1, prepaging wins.

8.9.2   Page Size

The designers of an operating system for an existing machine seldom have a choice concerning the page size. However, when new machines are being designed, a decision regarding the best page size must be made. As you might expect, there is no single best page size. Rather, there is a set of factors that support various sizes. Page sizes are invariably powers of 2, generally ranging from 4,096 (2^{12}) to 4,194,304 (2^{22}) bytes.

How do we select a page size? One concern is the size of the page table. For a given virtual memory space, decreasing the page size increases the number of pages and hence the size of the page table. For a virtual memory of 4 MB (2^{22}), for example, there would be 4,096 pages of 1,024 bytes but only 512 pages of 8,192 bytes. Because each active process must have its own copy of the page table, a large page size is desirable.

Memory is better utilized with smaller pages, however. If a process is allocated memory starting at location 00000 and continuing until it has as much as it needs, it probably will not end exactly on a page boundary. Thus, a part of the final page must be allocated (because pages are the units of allocation) but will be unused (creating internal fragmentation). Assuming independence of process size and page size, we can expect that, on the average, half of the final page of each process will be wasted. This loss is only 256 bytes for a page of 512 bytes but is 4,096 bytes for a page of 8,192 bytes. To minimize internal fragmentation, then, we need a small page size.

Another problem is the time required to read or write a page. I/O time is composed of seek, latency, and transfer times. Transfer time is proportional to the amount transferred (that is, the page size)—a fact that would seem to argue for a small page size. However, as we shall see in Section 9.1.1, latency and seek time normally dwarf transfer time. At a transfer rate of 2 MB per second, it takes only 0.2 milliseconds to transfer 512 bytes. Latency time, though, is perhaps 8 milliseconds, and seek time 20 milliseconds. Of the total I/O time

(28.2 milliseconds), therefore, only 1 percent is attributable to the actual transfer. Doubling the page size increases I/O time to only 28.4 milliseconds. It takes 28.4 milliseconds to read a single page of 1,024 bytes but 56.4 milliseconds to read the same amount as two pages of 512 bytes each. Thus, a desire to minimize I/O time argues for a larger page size.

With a smaller page size, though, total I/O should be reduced, since locality will be improved. A smaller page size allows each page to match program locality more accurately. For example, consider a process 200 KB in size, of which only half (100 KB) is actually used in an execution. If we have only one large page, we must bring in the entire page, a total of 200 KB transferred and allocated. If instead we had pages of only 1 byte, then we could bring in only the 100 KB that are actually used, resulting in only 100 KB transferred and allocated. With a smaller page size, then, we have better **resolution**, allowing us to isolate only the memory that is actually needed. With a larger page size, we must allocate and transfer not only what is needed but also anything else that happens to be in the page, whether it is needed or not. Thus, a smaller page size should result in less I/O and less total allocated memory.

But did you notice that with a page size of 1 byte, we would have a page fault for *each* byte? A process of 200 KB that used only half of that memory would generate only one page fault with a page size of 200 KB but 102,400 page faults with a page size of 1 byte. Each page fault generates the large amount of overhead needed for processing the interrupt, saving registers, replacing a page, queueing for the paging device, and updating tables. To minimize the number of page faults, we need to have a large page size.

Other factors must be considered as well (such as the relationship between page size and sector size on the paging device). The problem has no best answer. As we have seen, some factors (internal fragmentation, locality) argue for a small page size, whereas others (table size, I/O time) argue for a large page size. Nevertheless, the historical trend is toward larger page sizes, even for mobile systems. Indeed, the first edition of *Operating System Concepts* (1983) used 4,096 bytes as the upper bound on page sizes, and this value was the most common page size in 1990. Modern systems may now use much larger page sizes, as we will see in the following section.

8.9.3   TLB Reach

In Chapter 7, we introduced the **hit ratio** of the TLB. Recall that the hit ratio for the TLB refers to the percentage of virtual address translations that are resolved in the TLB rather than the page table. Clearly, the hit ratio is related to the number of entries in the TLB, and the way to increase the hit ratio is by increasing the number of entries in the TLB. This, however, does not come cheaply, as the associative memory used to construct the TLB is both expensive and power hungry.

Related to the hit ratio is a similar metric: the **TLB reach**. The TLB reach refers to the amount of memory accessible from the TLB and is simply the number of entries multiplied by the page size. Ideally, the working set for a process is stored in the TLB. If it is not, the process will spend a considerable amount of time resolving memory references in the page table rather than the TLB. If we double the number of entries in the TLB, we double the TLB reach. However, for some memory-intensive applications, this may still prove insufficient for storing the working set.

Another approach for increasing the TLB reach is to either increase the size of the page or provide multiple page sizes. If we increase the page size —say, from 8 KB to 32 KB—we quadruple the TLB reach. However, this may lead to an increase in fragmentation for some applications that do not require such a large page size. Alternatively, an operating system may provide several different page sizes. For example, the UltraSPARC supports page sizes of 8 KB, 64 KB, 512 KB, and 4 MB. Of these available pages sizes, Solaris uses both 8-KB and 4-MB page sizes. And with a 64-entry TLB, the TLB reach for Solaris ranges from 512 KB with 8-KB pages to 256 MB with 4-MB pages. For the majority of applications, the 8-KB page size is sufficient, although Solaris maps the first 4 MB of kernel code and data with two 4-MB pages. Solaris also allows applications —such as databases—to take advantage of the large 4-MB page size.

Providing support for multiple page sizes requires the operating system —not hardware—to manage the TLB. For example, one of the fields in a TLB entry must indicate the size of the page frame corresponding to the TLB entry. Managing the TLB in software and not hardware comes at a cost in performance. However, the increased hit ratio and TLB reach offset the performance costs. Indeed, recent trends indicate a move toward software-managed TLBs and operating-system support for multiple page sizes.

8.9.4   Inverted Page Tables

Section 7.6.3 introduced the concept of the inverted page table. The purpose of this form of page management is to reduce the amount of physical memory needed to track virtual-to-physical address translations. We accomplish this savings by creating a table that has one entry per page of physical memory, indexed by the pair <process-id, page-number>.

Because they keep information about which virtual memory page is stored in each physical frame, inverted page tables reduce the amount of physical memory needed to store this information. However, the inverted page table no longer contains complete information about the logical address space of a process, and that information is required if a referenced page is not currently in memory. Demand paging requires this information to process page faults. For the information to be available, an external page table (one per process) must be kept. Each such table looks like the traditional per-process page table and contains information on where each virtual page is located.

But do external page tables negate the utility of inverted page tables? Since these tables are referenced only when a page fault occurs, they do not need to be available quickly. Instead, they are themselves paged in and out of memory as necessary. Unfortunately, a page fault may now cause the virtual memory manager to generate another page fault as it pages in the external page table it needs to locate the virtual page on the backing store. This special case requires careful handling in the kernel and a delay in the page-lookup processing.

8.9.5   Program Structure

Demand paging is designed to be transparent to the user program. In many cases, the user is completely unaware of the paged nature of memory. In other cases, however, system performance can be improved if the user (or compiler) has an awareness of the underlying demand paging.

Let's look at a contrived but informative example. Assume that pages are 128 words in size. Consider a C program whose function is to initialize to 0 each element of a 128-by-128 array. The following code is typical:

```
int i, j;
int[128][128] data;

for (j = 0; j < 128; j++)
    for (i = 0; i < 128; i++)
        data[i][j] = 0;
```

Notice that the array is stored row major; that is, the array is stored data[0][0], data[0][1], ···, data[0][127], data[1][0], data[1][1], ···, data[127][127]. For pages of 128 words, each row takes one page. Thus, the preceding code zeros one word in each page, then another word in each page, and so on. If the operating system allocates fewer than 128 frames to the entire program, then its execution will result in $128 \times 128 = 16,384$ page faults. In contrast, suppose we change the code to

```
int i, j;
int[128][128] data;

for (i = 0; i < 128; i++)
    for (j = 0; j < 128; j++)
        data[i][j] = 0;
```

This code zeros all the words on one page before starting the next page, reducing the number of page faults to 128.

Careful selection of data structures and programming structures can increase locality and hence lower the page-fault rate and the number of pages in the working set. For example, a stack has good locality, since access is always made to the top. A hash table, in contrast, is designed to scatter references, producing bad locality. Of course, locality of reference is just one measure of the efficiency of the use of a data structure. Other heavily weighted factors include search speed, total number of memory references, and total number of pages touched.

At a later stage, the compiler and loader can have a significant effect on paging. Separating code and data and generating reentrant code means that code pages can be read-only and hence will never be modified. Clean pages do not have to be paged out to be replaced. The loader can avoid placing routines across page boundaries, keeping each routine completely in one page. Routines that call each other many times can be packed into the same page. This packaging is a variant of the bin-packing problem of operations research: try to pack the variable-sized load segments into the fixed-sized pages so that interpage references are minimized. Such an approach is particularly useful for large page sizes.

8.9.6 I/O Interlock and Page Locking

When demand paging is used, we sometimes need to allow some of the pages to be **locked** in memory. One such situation occurs when I/O is done to or from user (virtual) memory. I/O is often implemented by a separate I/O processor. For example, a controller for a USB storage device is generally given the number of bytes to transfer and a memory address for the buffer (Figure 8.28). When the transfer is complete, the CPU is interrupted.

We must be sure the following sequence of events does not occur: A process issues an I/O request and is put in a queue for that I/O device. Meanwhile, the CPU is given to other processes. These processes cause page faults, and one of them, using a global replacement algorithm, replaces the page containing the memory buffer for the waiting process. The pages are paged out. Some time later, when the I/O request advances to the head of the device queue, the I/O occurs to the specified address. However, this frame is now being used for a different page belonging to another process.

There are two common solutions to this problem. One solution is never to execute I/O to user memory. Instead, data are always copied between system memory and user memory. I/O takes place only between system memory and the I/O device. To write a block on tape, we first copy the block to system memory and then write it to tape. This extra copying may result in unacceptably high overhead.

Another solution is to allow pages to be locked into memory. Here, a lock bit is associated with every frame. If the frame is locked, it cannot be selected for replacement. Under this approach, to write a block on tape, we lock into memory the pages containing the block. The system can then continue as usual. Locked pages cannot be replaced. When the I/O is complete, the pages are unlocked.

Figure 8.28 The reason why frames used for I/O must be in memory.

Lock bits are used in various situations. Frequently, some or all of the operating-system kernel is locked into memory. Many operating systems cannot tolerate a page fault caused by the kernel or by a specific kernel module, including the one performing memory management. User processes may also need to lock pages into memory. A database process may want to manage a chunk of memory, for example, moving blocks between disk and memory itself because it has the best knowledge of how it is going to use its data. Such pinning of pages in memory is fairly common, and most operating systems have a system call allowing an application to request that a region of its logical address space be pinned. Note that this feature could be abused and could cause stress on the memory-management algorithms. Therefore, an application frequently requires special privileges to make such a request.

Another use for a lock bit involves normal page replacement. Consider the following sequence of events: A low-priority process faults. Selecting a replacement frame, the paging system reads the necessary page into memory. Ready to continue, the low-priority process enters the ready queue and waits for the CPU. Since it is a low-priority process, it may not be selected by the CPU scheduler for a time. While the low-priority process waits, a high-priority process faults. Looking for a replacement, the paging system sees a page that is in memory but has not been referenced or modified: it is the page that the low-priority process just brought in. This page looks like a perfect replacement: it is clean and will not need to be written out, and it apparently has not been used for a long time.

Whether the high-priority process should be able to replace the low-priority process is a policy decision. After all, we are simply delaying the low-priority process for the benefit of the high-priority process. However, we are wasting the effort spent to bring in the page for the low-priority process. If we decide to prevent replacement of a newly brought-in page until it can be used at least once, then we can use the lock bit to implement this mechanism. When a page is selected for replacement, its lock bit is turned on. It remains on until the faulting process is again dispatched.

Using a lock bit can be dangerous: the lock bit may get turned on but never turned off. Should this situation occur (because of a bug in the operating system, for example), the locked frame becomes unusable. On a single-user system, the overuse of locking would hurt only the user doing the locking. Multiuser systems must be less trusting of users. For instance, Solaris allows locking "hints," but it is free to disregard these hints if the free-frame pool becomes too small or if an individual process requests that too many pages be locked in memory.

8.10 Operating-System Examples

In this section, we describe how Windows and Solaris implement virtual memory.

8.10.1 Windows

Windows implements virtual memory using demand paging with clustering. Clustering handles page faults by bringing in not only the faulting page but also several pages following the faulting page. When a process is first created, it is assigned a working-set minimum and maximum. The **working-set minimum** is the minimum number of pages the process is guaranteed to have in memory. If sufficient memory is available, a process may be assigned as many pages as its **working-set maximum**. (In some circumstances, a process may be allowed to exceed its working-set maximum.) The virtual memory manager maintains a list of free page frames. Associated with this list is a threshold value that is used to indicate whether sufficient free memory is available. If a page fault occurs for a process that is below its working-set maximum, the virtual memory manager allocates a page from this list of free pages. If a process that is at its working-set maximum incurs a page fault, it must select a page for replacement using a local LRU page-replacement policy.

When the amount of free memory falls below the threshold, the virtual memory manager uses a tactic known as **automatic working-set trimming** to restore the value above the threshold. Automatic working-set trimming works by evaluating the number of pages allocated to processes. If a process has been allocated more pages than its working-set minimum, the virtual memory manager removes pages until the process reaches its working-set minimum. A process that is at its working-set minimum may be allocated pages from the free-page-frame list once sufficient free memory is available. Windows performs working-set trimming on both user mode and system processes.

8.10.2 Solaris

In Solaris, when a thread incurs a page fault, the kernel assigns a page to the faulting thread from the list of free pages it maintains. Therefore, it is imperative that the kernel keep a sufficient amount of free memory available. Associated with this list of free pages is a parameter—`lotsfree`—that represents a threshold to begin paging. The `lotsfree` parameter is typically set to 1/64 the size of the physical memory. Four times per second, the kernel checks whether the amount of free memory is less than `lotsfree`. If the number of free pages falls below `lotsfree`, a process known as a **pageout** starts up. The pageout process is similar to the second-chance algorithm described in Section 8.4.5.2, except that it uses two hands while scanning pages, rather than one.

The pageout process works as follows: The front hand of the clock scans all pages in memory, setting the reference bit to 0. Later, the back hand of the clock examines the reference bit for the pages in memory, appending each page whose reference bit is still set to 0 to the free list and writing to disk its contents if modified. Solaris maintains a cache list of pages that have been "freed" but have not yet been overwritten. The free list contains frames that have invalid contents. Pages can be reclaimed from the cache list if they are accessed before being moved to the free list.

The pageout algorithm uses several parameters to control the rate at which pages are scanned (known as the `scanrate`). The scanrate is expressed in pages per second and ranges from `slowscan` to `fastscan`. When free memory falls below `lotsfree`, scanning occurs at `slowscan` pages per second and progresses to `fastscan`, depending on the amount of free memory available. The default value of `slowscan` is 100 pages per second. `Fastscan` is typically set to the value (total physical pages)/2 pages per second, with a maximum of

8,192 pages per second. This is shown in Figure 8.29 (with `fastscan` set to the maximum).

The distance (in pages) between the hands of the clock is determined by a system parameter, `handspread`. The amount of time between the front hand's clearing a bit and the back hand's investigating its value depends on the `scanrate` and the `handspread`. If `scanrate` is 100 pages per second and `handspread` is 1,024 pages, 10 seconds can pass between the time a bit is set by the front hand and the time it is checked by the back hand. However, because of the demands placed on the memory system, a `scanrate` of several thousand is not uncommon. This means that the amount of time between clearing and investigating a bit is often a few seconds.

As mentioned above, the pageout process checks memory four times per second. However, if free memory falls below the value of `desfree` (Figure 8.29), pageout will run a hundred times per second with the intention of keeping at least `desfree` free memory available. If the pageout process is unable to keep the amount of free memory at `desfree` for a 30-second average, the kernel begins swapping processes, thereby freeing all pages allocated to swapped processes. In general, the kernel looks for processes that have been idle for long periods of time. If the system is unable to maintain the amount of free memory at `minfree`, the pageout process is called for every request for a new page.

Recent releases of the Solaris kernel have provided enhancements of the paging algorithm. One such enhancement involves recognizing pages from shared libraries. Pages belonging to libraries that are being shared by several processes—even if they are eligible to be claimed by the scanner— are skipped during the page-scanning process. Another enhancement concerns distinguishing pages that have been allocated to processes from pages allocated to regular files. This is known as **priority paging** and is covered in Section 11.6.2.

Figure 8.29 Solaris page scanner.

8.11 Summary

It is desirable to be able to execute a process whose logical address space is larger than the available physical address space. Virtual memory is a technique that enables us to map a large logical address space onto a smaller physical memory. Virtual memory allows us to run extremely large processes and to raise the degree of multiprogramming, increasing CPU utilization. Further, it frees application programmers from worrying about memory availability. In addition, with virtual memory, several processes can share system libraries and memory. With virtual memory, we can also use an efficient type of process creation known as copy-on-write, wherein parent and child processes share actual pages of memory.

Virtual memory is commonly implemented by demand paging. Pure demand paging never brings in a page until that page is referenced. The first reference causes a page fault to the operating system. The operating-system kernel consults an internal table to determine where the page is located on the backing store. It then finds a free frame and reads the page in from the backing store. The page table is updated to reflect this change, and the instruction that caused the page fault is restarted. This approach allows a process to run even though its entire memory image is not in main memory at once. As long as the page-fault rate is reasonably low, performance is acceptable.

We can use demand paging to reduce the number of frames allocated to a process. This arrangement can increase the degree of multiprogramming (allowing more processes to be available for execution at one time) and—in theory, at least—the CPU utilization of the system. It also allows processes to be run even though their memory requirements exceed the total available physical memory. Such processes run in virtual memory.

If total memory requirements exceed the capacity of physical memory, then it may be necessary to replace pages from memory to free frames for new pages. Various page-replacement algorithms are used. FIFO page replacement is easy to program but suffers from Belady's anomaly. Optimal page replacement requires future knowledge. LRU replacement is an approximation of optimal page replacement, but even it may be difficult to implement. Most page-replacement algorithms, such as the second-chance algorithm, are approximations of LRU replacement.

In addition to a page-replacement algorithm, a frame-allocation policy is needed. Allocation can be fixed, suggesting local page replacement, or dynamic, suggesting global replacement. The working-set model assumes that processes execute in localities. The working set is the set of pages in the current locality. Accordingly, each process should be allocated enough frames for its current working set. If a process does not have enough memory for its working set, it will thrash. Providing enough frames to each process to avoid thrashing may require process swapping and scheduling.

Most operating systems provide features for memory mapping files, thus allowing file I/O to be treated as routine memory access. The Win32 API implements shared memory through memory mapping of files.

Kernel processes typically require memory to be allocated using pages that are physically contiguous. The buddy system allocates memory to kernel processes in units sized according to a power of 2, which often results in fragmentation. Slab allocators assign kernel data structures to caches associated with slabs, which are made up of one or more physically contiguous pages. With slab allocation, no memory is wasted due to fragmentation, and memory requests can be satisfied quickly.

In addition to requiring us to solve the major problems of page replacement and frame allocation, the proper design of a paging system requires that we consider prepaging, page size, TLB reach, inverted page tables, program structure, I/O interlock and page locking, and other issues.

Review Questions

Review questions for this chapter can be accessed by visiting our website.

Practice Exercises

Answers for the Practice Exercises can be accceed by visiting our website.

8.1 Under what circumstances do page faults occur? Describe the actions taken by the operating system when a page fault occurs.

8.2 Assume that you have a page-reference string for a process with m frames (initially all empty). The page-reference string has length p, and n distinct page numbers occur in it. Answer these questions for any page-replacement algorithms:

   a. What is a lower bound on the number of page faults?

   b. What is an upper bound on the number of page faults?

8.3 Consider the page table shown in Figure 8.30 for a system with 12-bit virtual and physical addresses and with 256-byte pages. The list of free

Page	Page Frame
0	–
1	2
2	C
3	A
4	–
5	4
6	3
7	–
8	B
9	0

Figure 8.30 Page table for Exercise 8.3.

page frames is D, E, F (that is, D is at the head of the list, E is second, and F is last).

Convert the following virtual addresses to their equivalent physical addresses in hexadecimal. All numbers are given in hexadecimal. (A dash for a page frame indicates that the page is not in memory.)

- 9EF
- 111
- 700
- 0FF

8.4 Consider the following page-replacement algorithms. Rank these algorithms on a five-point scale from "bad" to "perfect" according to their page-fault rate. Separate those algorithms that suffer from Belady's anomaly from those that do not.

    a.   LRU replacement

    b.   FIFO replacement

    c.   Optimal replacement

    d.   Second-chance replacement

8.5 Discuss the hardware support required to support demand paging.

8.6 An operating system supports a paged virtual memory. The central processor has a cycle time of 1 microsecond. It costs an additional 1 microsecond to access a page other than the current one. Pages have 1,000 words, and the paging device is a drum that rotates at 3,000 revolutions per minute and transfers 1 million words per second. The following statistical measurements were obtained from the system:

- One percent of all instructions executed accessed a page other than the current page.
- Of the instructions that accessed another page, 80 percent accessed a page already in memory.
- When a new page was required, the replaced page was modified 50 percent of the time.

Calculate the effective instruction time on this system, assuming that the system is running one process only and that the processor is idle during drum transfers.

8.7 Consider the two-dimensional array A:

```
int A[][] = new int[100][100];
```

where A[0][0] is at location 200 in a paged memory system with pages of size 200. A small process that manipulates the matrix resides in page 0 (locations 0 to 199). Thus, every instruction fetch will be from page 0.

For three page frames, how many page faults are generated by the following array-initialization loops? Use LRU replacement, and assume that page frame 1 contains the process and the other two are initially empty.

a.
```
for (int j = 0; j < 100; j++)
    for (int i = 0; i < 100; i++)
        A[i][j] = 0;
```

b.
```
for (int i = 0; i < 100; i++)
    for (int j = 0; j < 100; j++)
        A[i][j] = 0;
```

8.8 Consider the following page reference string:

$$1, 2, 3, 4, 2, 1, 5, 6, 2, 1, 2, 3, 7, 6, 3, 2, 1, 2, 3, 6.$$

How many page faults would occur for the following replacement algorithms, assuming one, two, three, four, five, six, and seven frames? Remember that all frames are initially empty, so your first unique pages will cost one fault each.

- LRU replacement
- FIFO replacement
- Optimal replacement

8.9 Suppose that you want to use a paging algorithm that requires a reference bit (such as second-chance replacement or working-set model), but the hardware does not provide one. Sketch how you could simulate a reference bit even if one were not provided by the hardware, or explain why it is not possible to do so. If it is possible, calculate what the cost would be.

8.10 You have devised a new page-replacement algorithm that you think may be optimal. In some contorted test cases, Belady's anomaly occurs. Is the new algorithm optimal? Explain your answer.

8.11 Segmentation is similar to paging but uses variable-sized "pages." Define two segment-replacement algorithms, one based on the FIFO page-replacement scheme and the other on the LRU page-replacement scheme. Remember that since segments are not the same size, the segment that is chosen for replacement may be too small to leave enough consecutive locations for the needed segment. Consider strategies for systems where segments cannot be relocated and strategies for systems where they can.

8.12 Consider a demand-paged computer system where the degree of multiprogramming is currently fixed at four. The system was recently measured to determine utilization of the CPU and the paging disk. Three alternative results are shown below. For each case, what is happening? Can the degree of multiprogramming be increased to increase the CPU utilization? Is the paging helping?

a. CPU utilization 13 percent; disk utilization 97 percent

b.   CPU utilization 87 percent; disk utilization 3 percent

c.   CPU utilization 13 percent; disk utilization 3 percent

8.13   We have an operating system for a machine that uses base and limit registers, but we have modified the machine to provide a page table. Can the page tables be set up to simulate base and limit registers? How can they be, or why can they not be?

Exercises

8.14   Assume that a program has just referenced an address in virtual memory. Describe a scenario in which each of the following can occur. (If no such scenario can occur, explain why.)

- TLB miss with no page fault
- TLB miss and page fault
- TLB hit and no page fault
- TLB hit and page fault

8.15   A simplified view of thread states is *Ready*, *Running*, and *Blocked*, where a thread is either ready and waiting to be scheduled, is running on the processor, or is blocked (for example, waiting for I/O). This is illustrated in Figure 8.31. Assuming a thread is in the Running state, answer the following questions, and explain your answer:

a.   Will the thread change state if it incurs a page fault? If so, to what state will it change?

b.   Will the thread change state if it generates a TLB miss that is resolved in the page table? If so, to what state will it change?

c.   Will the thread change state if an address reference is resolved in the page table? If so, to what state will it change?

8.16   Consider a system that uses pure demand paging.

a.   When a process first starts execution, how would you characterize the page-fault rate?

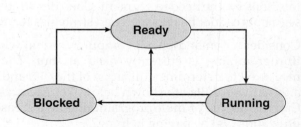

Figure 8.31   Thread state diagram for Exercise 8.15.

b. Once the working set for a process is loaded into memory, how would you characterize the page-fault rate?

c. Assume that a process changes its locality and the size of the new working set is too large to be stored in available free memory. Identify some options system designers could choose from to handle this situation.

8.17 What is the copy-on-write feature, and under what circumstances is its use beneficial? What hardware support is required to implement this feature?

8.18 A certain computer provides its users with a virtual memory space of 2^{32} bytes. The computer has 2^{22} bytes of physical memory. The virtual memory is implemented by paging, and the page size is 4,096 bytes. A user process generates the virtual address 11123456. Explain how the system establishes the corresponding physical location. Distinguish between software and hardware operations.

8.19 Assume that we have a demand-paged memory. The page table is held in registers. It takes 8 milliseconds to service a page fault if an empty frame is available or if the replaced page is not modified and 20 milliseconds if the replaced page is modified. Memory-access time is 100 nanoseconds.

Assume that the page to be replaced is modified 70 percent of the time. What is the maximum acceptable page-fault rate for an effective access time of no more than 200 nanoseconds?

8.20 When a page fault occurs, the process requesting the page must block while waiting for the page to be brought from disk into physical memory. Assume that there exists a process with five user-level threads and that the mapping of user threads to kernel threads is one to one. If one user thread incurs a page fault while accessing its stack, would the other user threads belonging to the same process also be affected by the page fault—that is, would they also have to wait for the faulting page to be brought into memory? Explain.

8.21 Consider the following page reference string:

$$7, 2, 3, 1, 2, 5, 3, 4, 6, 7, 7, 1, 0, 5, 4, 6, 2, 3, 0, 1.$$

Assuming demand paging with three frames, how many page faults would occur for the following replacement algorithms?

- LRU replacement
- FIFO replacement
- Optimal replacement

8.22 The page table shown in Figure 8.32 is for a system with 16-bit virtual and physical addresses and with 4,096-byte pages. The reference bit is set to 1 when the page has been referenced. Periodically, a thread zeroes out all values of the reference bit. A dash for a page frame indicates the page is not in memory. The page-replacement algorithm is localized LRU, and all numbers are provided in decimal.

Page	Page Frame	Reference Bit
0	9	0
1	1	0
2	14	0
3	10	0
4	–	0
5	13	0
6	8	0
7	15	0
8	–	0
9	0	0
10	5	0
11	4	0
12	–	0
13	–	0
14	3	0
15	2	0

Figure 8.32   Page table for Exercise 8.22.

a. Convert the following virtual addresses (in hexadecimal) to the equivalent physical addresses. You may provide answers in either hexadecimal or decimal. Also set the reference bit for the appropriate entry in the page table.

- 0xE12C
- 0x3A9D
- 0xA9D9
- 0x7001
- 0xACA1

b. Using the above addresses as a guide, provide an example of a logical address (in hexadecimal) that results in a page fault.

c. From what set of page frames will the LRU page-replacement algorithm choose in resolving a page fault?

8.23 Assume that you are monitoring the rate at which the pointer in the clock algorithm moves. (The pointer indicates the candidate page for replacement.) What can you say about the system if you notice the following behavior:

a. Pointer is moving fast.

b. Pointer is moving slow.

8.24 Discuss situations in which the least frequently used (LFU) page-replacement algorithm generates fewer page faults than the least recently used (LRU) page-replacement algorithm. Also discuss under what circumstances the opposite holds.

8.25 Discuss situations in which the most frequently used (MFU) page-replacement algorithm generates fewer page faults than the least recently used (LRU) page-replacement algorithm. Also discuss under what circumstances the opposite holds.

8.26 The VAX/VMS system uses a FIFO replacement algorithm for resident pages and a free-frame pool of recently used pages. Assume that the free-frame pool is managed using the LRU replacement policy. Answer the following questions:

    a.   If a page fault occurs and the page does not exist in the free-frame pool, how is free space generated for the newly requested page?

    b.   If a page fault occurs and the page exists in the free-frame pool, how is the resident page set and the free-frame pool managed to make space for the requested page?

    c.   What does the system degenerate to if the number of resident pages is set to one?

    d.   What does the system degenerate to if the number of pages in the free-frame pool is zero?

8.27 Consider a demand-paging system with the following time-measured utilizations:

CPU utilization	20%
Paging disk	97.7%
Other I/O devices	5%

For each of the following, indicate whether it will (or is likely to) improve CPU utilization. Explain your answers.

    a.   Install a faster CPU.

    b.   Install a bigger paging disk.

    c.   Increase the degree of multiprogramming.

    d.   Decrease the degree of multiprogramming.

    e.   Install more main memory.

    f.   Install a faster hard disk or multiple controllers with multiple hard disks.

    g.   Add prepaging to the page-fetch algorithms.

    h.   Increase the page size.

8.28 Suppose that a machine provides instructions that can access memory locations using the one-level indirect addressing scheme. What sequence of page faults is incurred when all of the pages of a program are currently nonresident and the first instruction of the program is an indirect memory-load operation? What happens when the operating system is using a per-process frame allocation technique and only two pages are allocated to this process?

8.29 Suppose that your replacement policy (in a paged system) is to examine each page regularly and to discard that page if it has not been used since the last examination. What would you gain and what would you lose by using this policy rather than LRU or second-chance replacement?

8.30 A page-replacement algorithm should minimize the number of page faults. We can achieve this minimization by distributing heavily used pages evenly over all of memory, rather than having them compete for a small number of page frames. We can associate with each page frame a counter of the number of pages associated with that frame. Then, to replace a page, we can search for the page frame with the smallest counter.

    a.   Define a page-replacement algorithm using this basic idea. Specifically address these problems:

       i.   What is the initial value of the counters?

      ii.   When are counters increased?

     iii.   When are counters decreased?

     iv.   How is the page to be replaced selected?

    b.   How many page faults occur for your algorithm for the following reference string with four page frames?

$$1, 2, 3, 4, 5, 3, 4, 1, 6, 7, 8, 7, 8, 9, 7, 8, 9, 5, 4, 5, 4, 2.$$

    c.   What is the minimum number of page faults for an optimal page-replacement strategy for the reference string in part b with four page frames?

8.31 Consider a demand-paging system with a paging disk that has an average access and transfer time of 20 milliseconds. Addresses are translated through a page table in main memory, with an access time of 1 microsecond per memory access. Thus, each memory reference through the page table takes two accesses. To improve this time, we have added an associative memory that reduces access time to one memory reference if the page-table entry is in the associative memory.

Assume that 80 percent of the accesses are in the associative memory and that, of those remaining, 10 percent (or 2 percent of the total) cause page faults. What is the effective memory access time?

8.32 What is the cause of thrashing? How does the system detect thrashing? Once it detects thrashing, what can the system do to eliminate this problem?

8.33 Is it possible for a process to have two working sets, one representing data and another representing code? Explain.

8.34 Consider the parameter Δ used to define the working-set window in the working-set model. When Δ is set to a small value, what is the effect on the page-fault frequency and the number of active (nonsuspended) processes currently executing in the system? What is the effect when Δ is set to a very high value?

8.35 In a 1,024-KB segment, memory is allocated using the buddy system. Using Figure 8.26 as a guide, draw a tree illustrating how the following memory requests are allocated:

- Request 6-KB
- Request 250 bytes
- Request 900 bytes
- Request 1,500 bytes
- Request 7-KB

Next, modify the tree for the following releases of memory. Perform coalescing whenever possible:

- Release 250 bytes
- Release 900 bytes
- Release 1,500 bytes

8.36 A system provides support for user-level and kernel-level threads. The mapping in this system is one to one (there is a corresponding kernel thread for each user thread). Does a multithreaded process consist of (a) a working set for the entire process or (b) a working set for each thread? Explain

8.37 The slab-allocation algorithm uses a separate cache for each different object type. Assuming there is one cache per object type, explain why this scheme doesn't scale well with multiple CPUs. What could be done to address this scalability issue?

8.38 Consider a system that allocates pages of different sizes to its processes. What are the advantages of such a paging scheme? What modifications to the virtual memory system provide this functionality?

Programming Problems

8.39 Write a program that implements the FIFO, LRU, and optimal page-replacement algorithms presented in this chapter. First, generate a random page-reference string where page numbers range from 0 to 9. Apply the random page-reference string to each algorithm, and record the number of page faults incurred by each algorithm. Implement the replacement algorithms so that the number of page frames can vary from 1 to 7. Assume that demand paging is used.

8.40 Repeat Exercise 3.22, this time using Windows shared memory. In particular, using the producer—consumer strategy, design two programs that communicate with shared memory using the Windows API as outlined in Section 8.7.2. The producer will generate the numbers specified in the Collatz conjecture and write them to a shared memory object. The consumer will then read and output the sequence of numbers from shared memory.

In this instance, the producer will be passed an integer parameter on the command line specifying how many numbers to produce (for example, providing 5 on the command line means the producer process will generate the first five numbers).

Programming Projects

Designing a Virtual Memory Manager

This project consists of writing a program that translates logical to physical addresses for a virtual address space of size $2^{16} = 65{,}536$ bytes. Your program will read from a file containing logical addresses and, using a TLB as well as a page table, will translate each logical address to its corresponding physical address and output the value of the byte stored at the translated physical address. The goal behind this project is to simulate the steps involved in translating logical to physical addresses.

Specifics

Your program will read a file containing several 32-bit integer numbers that represent logical addresses. However, you need only be concerned with 16-bit addresses, so you must mask the rightmost 16 bits of each logical address. These 16 bits are divided into (1) an 8-bit page number and (2) 8-bit page offset. Hence, the addresses are structured as shown in Figure 8.33.

Other specifics include the following:

- 2^8 entries in the page table

- Page size of 2^8 bytes

- 16 entries in the TLB

- Frame size of 2^8 bytes

- 256 frames

- Physical memory of 65,536 bytes (256 frames × 256-byte frame size)

Additionally, your program need only be concerned with reading logical addresses and translating them to their corresponding physical addresses. You do not need to support writing to the logical address space.

Figure 8.33 Address structure.

Address Translation

Your program will translate logical to physical addresses using a TLB and page table as outlined in Section 7.5. First, the page number is extracted from the logical address, and the TLB is consulted. In the case of a TLB-hit, the frame number is obtained from the TLB. In the case of a TLB-miss, the page table must be consulted. In the latter case, either the frame number is obtained from the page table or a page fault occurs. A visual representation of the address-translation process appears in Figure 8.34.

Handling Page Faults

Your program will implement demand paging as described in Section 8.2. The backing store is represented by the file BACKING_STORE.bin, a binary file of size 65,536 bytes. When a page fault occurs, you will read in a 256-byte page from the file BACKING_STORE and store it in an available page frame in physical memory. For example, if a logical address with page number 15 resulted in a page fault, your program would read in page 15 from BACKING_STORE (remember that pages begin at 0 and are 256 bytes in size) and store it in a page frame in physical memory. Once this frame is stored (and the page table and TLB are updated), subsequent accesses to page 15 will be resolved by either the TLB or the page table.

You will need to treat BACKING_STORE.bin as a random-access file so that you can randomly seek to certain positions of the file for reading. We suggest

Figure 8.34 A representation of the address-translation process.

using the standard C library functions for performing I/O, including `fopen()`, `fread()`, `fseek()`, and `fclose()`.

The size of physical memory is the same as the size of the virtual address space—65,536 bytes—so you do not need to be concerned about page replacements during a page fault. Later, we describe a modification to this project using a smaller amount of physical memory; at that point, a page-replacement strategy will be required.

Test File

We provide the file `addresses.txt`, which contains integer values representing logical addresses ranging from 0 − 65535 (the size of the virtual address space). Your program will open this file, read each logical address and translate it to its corresponding physical address, and output the value of the signed byte at the physical address.

How to Begin

First, write a simple program that extracts the page number and offset (based on Figure 8.33) from the following integer numbers:

> 1, 256, 32768, 32769, 128, 65534, 33153

Perhaps the easiest way to do this is by using the operators for bit-masking and bit-shifting. Once you can correctly establish the page number and offset from an integer number, you are ready to begin.

Initially, we suggest that you bypass the TLB and use only a page table. You can integrate the TLB once your page table is working properly. Remember, address translation can work without a TLB; the TLB just makes it faster. When you are ready to implement the TLB, recall that it has only 16 entries, so you will need to use a replacement strategy when you update a full TLB. You may use either a FIFO or an LRU policy for updating your TLB.

How to Run Your Program

Your program should run as follows:

> `./a.out addresses.txt`

Your program will read in the file `addresses.txt`, which contains 1,000 logical addresses ranging from 0 to 65535. Your program is to translate each logical address to a physical address and determine the contents of the signed byte stored at the correct physical address. (Recall that in the C language, the `char` data type occupies a byte of storage, so we suggest using `char` values.)

Your program is to output the following values:

1. The logical address being translated (the integer value being read from `addresses.txt`).

2. The corresponding physical address (what your program translates the logical address to).

3. The signed byte value stored at the translated physical address.

We also provide the file `correct.txt`, which contains the correct output values for the file `addresses.txt`. You should use this file to determine if your program is correctly translating logical to physical addresses.

Statistics

After completion, your program is to report the following statistics:

1. Page-fault rate—The percentage of address references that resulted in page faults.

2. TLB hit rate—The percentage of address references that were resolved in the TLB.

Since the logical addresses in `addresses.txt` were generated randomly and do not reflect any memory access locality, do not expect to have a high TLB hit rate.

Modifications

This project assumes that physical memory is the same size as the virtual address space. In practice, physical memory is typically much smaller than a virtual address space. A suggested modification is to use a smaller physical address space. We recommend using 128 page frames rather than 256. This change will require modifying your program so that it keeps track of free page frames as well as implementing a page-replacement policy using either FIFO or LRU (Section 8.4).

Bibliographical Notes

Demand paging was first used in the Atlas system, implemented on the Manchester University MUSE computer around 1960 ([Kilburn et al. (1961)]). Another early demand-paging system was MULTICS, implemented on the GE 645 system ([Organick (1972)]). Virtual memory was added to Unix in 1979 [Babaoglu and Joy (1981)]

[Belady et al. (1969)] were the first researchers to observe that the FIFO replacement strategy may produce the anomaly that bears Belady's name. [Mattson et al. (1970)] demonstrated that stack algorithms are not subject to Belady's anomaly.

The optimal replacement algorithm was presented by [Belady (1966)] and was proved to be optimal by [Mattson et al. (1970)]. Belady's optimal algorithm is for a fixed allocation; [Prieve and Fabry (1976)] presented an optimal algorithm for situations in which the allocation can vary.

The enhanced clock algorithm was discussed by [Carr and Hennessy (1981)].

The working-set model was developed by [Denning (1968)]. Discussions concerning the working-set model were presented by [Denning (1980)].

The scheme for monitoring the page-fault rate was developed by [Wulf (1969)], who successfully applied this technique to the Burroughs B5500 computer system.

Buddy system memory allocators were described in [Knowlton (1965)], [Peterson and Norman (1977)], and [Purdom, Jr. and Stigler (1970)]. [Bonwick (1994)] discussed the slab allocator, and [Bonwick and Adams (2001)] extended the discussion to multiple processors. Other memory-fitting algorithms can be found in [Stephenson (1983)], [Bays (1977)], and [Brent (1989)]. A survey of memory-allocation strategies can be found in [Wilson et al. (1995)].

[Solomon and Russinovich (2000)] and [Russinovich and Solomon (2005)] described how Windows implements virtual memory. [McDougall and Mauro (2007)] discussed virtual memory in Solaris. Virtual memory techniques in Linux and FreeBSD were described by [Love (2010)] and [McKusick and Neville-Neil (2005)], respectively. [Ganapathy and Schimmel (1998)] and [Navarro et al. (2002)] discussed operating system support for multiple page sizes.

Bibliography

[Babaoglu and Joy (1981)]   O. Babaoglu and W. Joy, "Converting a Swap-Based System to Do Paging in an Architecture Lacking Page-Reference Bits", *Proceedings of the ACM Symposium on Operating Systems Principles* (1981), pages 78–86.

[Bays (1977)]   C. Bays, "A Comparison of Next-Fit, First-Fit and Best-Fit", *Communications of the ACM*, Volume 20, Number 3 (1977), pages 191–192.

[Belady (1966)]   L. A. Belady, "A Study of Replacement Algorithms for a Virtual-Storage Computer", *IBM Systems Journal*, Volume 5, Number 2 (1966), pages 78–101.

[Belady et al. (1969)]   L. A. Belady, R. A. Nelson, and G. S. Shedler, "An Anomaly in Space-Time Characteristics of Certain Programs Running in a Paging Machine", *Communications of the ACM*, Volume 12, Number 6 (1969), pages 349–353.

[Bonwick (1994)]   J. Bonwick, "The Slab Allocator: An Object-Caching Kernel Memory Allocator", *USENIX Summer* (1994), pages 87–98.

[Bonwick and Adams (2001)]   J. Bonwick and J. Adams, "Magazines and Vmem: Extending the Slab Allocator to Many CPUs and Arbitrary Resources", *Proceedings of the 2001 USENIX Annual Technical Conference* (2001).

[Brent (1989)]   R. Brent, "Efficient Implementation of the First-Fit Strategy for Dynamic Storage Allocation", *ACM Transactions on Programming Languages and Systems*, Volume 11, Number 3 (1989), pages 388–403.

[Carr and Hennessy (1981)]   W. R. Carr and J. L. Hennessy, "WSClock—A Simple and Effective Algorithm for Virtual Memory Management", *Proceedings of the ACM Symposium on Operating Systems Principles* (1981), pages 87–95.

[Denning (1968)]   P. J. Denning, "The Working Set Model for Program Behavior", *Communications of the ACM*, Volume 11, Number 5 (1968), pages 323–333.

[Denning (1980)]   P. J. Denning, "Working Sets Past and Present", *IEEE Transactions on Software Engineering*, Volume SE-6, Number 1 (1980), pages 64–84.

[Ganapathy and Schimmel (1998)]   N. Ganapathy and C. Schimmel, "General Purpose Operating System Support for Multiple Page Sizes", *Proceedings of the USENIX Technical Conference* (1998).

[Kilburn et al. (1961)]   T. Kilburn, D. J. Howarth, R. B. Payne, and F. H. Sumner, "The Manchester University Atlas Operating System, Part I: Internal Organization", *Computer Journal*, Volume 4, Number 3 (1961), pages 222–225.

[Knowlton (1965)]   K. C. Knowlton, "A Fast Storage Allocator", *Communications of the ACM*, Volume 8, Number 10 (1965), pages 623–624.

[Love (2010)]   R. Love, *Linux Kernel Development*, Third Edition, Developer's Library (2010).

[Mattson et al. (1970)]   R. L. Mattson, J. Gecsei, D. R. Slutz, and I. L. Traiger, "Evaluation Techniques for Storage Hierarchies", *IBM Systems Journal*, Volume 9, Number 2 (1970), pages 78–117.

[McDougall and Mauro (2007)]   R. McDougall and J. Mauro, *Solaris Internals*, Second Edition, Prentice Hall (2007).

[McKusick and Neville-Neil (2005)]   M. K. McKusick and G. V. Neville-Neil, *The Design and Implementation of the FreeBSD UNIX Operating System*, Addison Wesley (2005).

[Navarro et al. (2002)]   J. Navarro, S. Lyer, P. Druschel, and A. Cox, "Practical, Transparent Operating System Support for Superpages", *Proceedings of the USENIX Symposium on Operating Systems Design and Implementation* (2002).

[Organick (1972)]   E. I. Organick, *The Multics System: An Examination of Its Structure*, MIT Press (1972).

[Peterson and Norman (1977)]   J. L. Peterson and T. A. Norman, "Buddy Systems", *Communications of the ACM*, Volume 20, Number 6 (1977), pages 421–431.

[Prieve and Fabry (1976)]   B. G. Prieve and R. S. Fabry, "VMIN—An Optimal Variable Space Page-Replacement Algorithm", *Communications of the ACM*, Volume 19, Number 5 (1976), pages 295–297.

[Purdom, Jr. and Stigler (1970)]   P. W. Purdom, Jr. and S. M. Stigler, "Statistical Properties of the Buddy System", *J. ACM*, Volume 17, Number 4 (1970), pages 683–697.

[Russinovich and Solomon (2005)]   M. E. Russinovich and D. A. Solomon, *Microsoft Windows Internals*, Fourth Edition, Microsoft Press (2005).

[Solomon and Russinovich (2000)]   D. A. Solomon and M. E. Russinovich, *Inside Microsoft Windows 2000*, Third Edition, Microsoft Press (2000).

[Stephenson (1983)]   C. J. Stephenson, "Fast Fits: A New Method for Dynamic Storage Allocation", *Proceedings of the Ninth Symposium on Operating Systems Principles* (1983), pages 30–32.

[Wilson et al. (1995)]   P. R. Wilson, M. S. Johnstone, M. Neely, and D. Boles, "Dynamic Storage Allocation: A Survey and Critical Review", *Proceedings of the International Workshop on Memory Management* (1995), pages 1–116.

[Wulf (1969)]   W. A. Wulf, "Performance Monitors for Multiprogramming Systems", *Proceedings of the ACM Symposium on Operating Systems Principles* (1969), pages 175–181.

Part Four

Storage Management

Since main memory is usually too small to accommodate all the data and programs permanently, the computer system must provide secondary storage to back up main memory. Modern computer systems use disks as the primary on-line storage medium for information (both programs and data). The file system provides the mechanism for on-line storage of and access to both data and programs residing on the disks. A file is a collection of related information defined by its creator. The files are mapped by the operating system onto physical devices. Files are normally organized into directories for ease of use.

The devices that attach to a computer vary in many aspects. Some devices transfer a character or a block of characters at a time. Some can be accessed only sequentially, others randomly. Some transfer data synchronously, others asynchronously. Some are dedicated, some shared. They can be read-only or read–write. They vary greatly in speed. In many ways, they are also the slowest major component of the computer.

Because of all this device variation, the operating system needs to provide a wide range of functionality to applications, to allow them to control all aspects of the devices. One key goal of an operating system's I/O subsystem is to provide the simplest interface possible to the rest of the system. Because devices are a performance bottleneck, another key is to optimize I/O for maximum concurrency.

CHAPTER

Mass-Storage Structure

The file system can be viewed logically as consisting of three parts. In Chapter 10, we examine the user and programmer interface to the file system. In Chapter 11, we describe the internal data structures and algorithms used by the operating system to implement this interface. In this chapter, we begin a discussion of file systems at the lowest level: the structure of secondary storage. We first describe the physical structure of hard disks and magnetic tapes. We then describe disk-scheduling algorithms, which schedule the order of disk I/Os to maximize performance. Next, we discuss disk formatting and management of boot blocks, damaged blocks, and swap space. We conclude with an examination of the structure of RAID systems.

CHAPTER OBJECTIVES

- To describe the physical structure of secondary storage devices and its effects on the uses of the devices.
- To explain the performance characteristics of mass-storage devices.
- To evaluate disk scheduling algorithms.
- To discuss operating-system services provided for mass storage, including RAID.

9.1 Overview of Mass-Storage Structure

In this section, we present a general overview of the physical structure of secondary and tertiary storage devices.

9.1.1 Hard Disks

Hard disks provide the bulk of secondary storage for modern computer systems. Conceptually, disks are relatively simple (Figure 9.1). Each disk platter has a flat circular shape, like a CD. Common platter diameters range from 1.8 to 3.5 inches. The two surfaces of a platter are covered with a magnetic material. We store information by recording it magnetically on the platters.

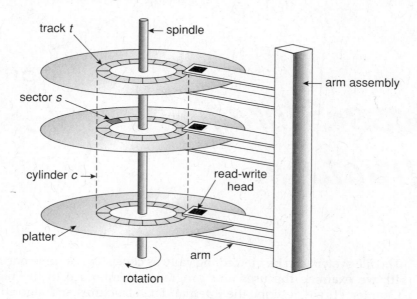

Figure 9.1   Moving-head disk mechanism.

A read–write head "flies" just above each surface of every platter. The heads are attached to a **disk arm** that moves all the heads as a unit. The surface of a platter is logically divided into circular **tracks**, which are subdivided into **sectors**. The set of tracks that are at one arm position makes up a **cylinder**. There may be thousands of concentric cylinders in a disk drive, and each track may contain hundreds of sectors. The storage capacity of common disk drives is measured in gigabytes.

When the disk is in use, a drive motor spins it at high speed. Most drives rotate 60 to 250 times per second, specified in terms of rotations per minute (**RPM**). Common drives spin at 5,400, 7,200, 10,000, and 15,000 RPM. Disk speed has two parts. The **transfer rate** is the rate at which data flow between the drive and the computer. The **positioning time**, or **random-access time**, consists of two parts: the time necessary to move the disk arm to the desired cylinder, called the **seek time**, and the time necessary for the desired sector to rotate to the disk head, called the **rotational latency**. Typical disks can transfer several megabytes of data per second, and they have seek times and rotational latencies of several milliseconds.

Because the disk head flies on an extremely thin cushion of air (measured in microns), there is a danger that the head will make contact with the disk surface. Although the disk platters are coated with a thin protective layer, the head will sometimes damage the magnetic surface. This accident is called a **head crash**. A head crash normally cannot be repaired; the entire disk must be replaced.

A disk can be **removable**, allowing different disks to be mounted as needed. Removable hard disks generally consist of one platter, held in a plastic case to prevent damage while not in the disk drive. Other forms of removable disks include CDs, DVDs, and Blu-ray discs as well as removable flash-memory devices known as **flash drives** (which are a type of solid-state drive).

A disk drive is attached to a computer by a set of wires called an I/O bus. Several kinds of buses are available, including advanced technology attachment (ATA), serial ATA (SATA), eSATA, universal serial bus (USB), and fibre channel (FC). The data transfers on a bus are carried out by special electronic processors called controllers. The host controller is the controller at the computer end of the bus. A disk controller is built into each disk drive. To perform a disk I/O operation, the computer places a command into the host controller, typically using memory-mapped I/O ports, as described in Section 8.7.3. The host controller then sends the command via messages to the disk controller, and the disk controller operates the disk-drive hardware to carry out the command. Disk controllers usually have a built-in cache. Data transfer at the disk drive happens between the cache and the disk surface, and data transfer to the host, at fast electronic speeds, occurs between the cache and the host controller.

9.1.2 Solid-State Disks

Sometimes old technologies are used in new ways as economics change or the technologies evolve. An example is the growing importance of solid-state disks, or SSDs. Simply described, an SSD is nonvolatile memory that is used like a hard drive. There are many variations of this technology, from DRAM with a battery to allow it to maintain its state in a power failure through flash-memory technologies like single-level cell (SLC) and multilevel cell (MLC) chips.

SSDs have the same characteristics as traditional hard disks but can be more reliable because they have no moving parts and faster because they have no seek time or latency. In addition, they consume less power. However, they are more expensive per megabyte than traditional hard disks, have less capacity than the larger hard disks, and may have shorter life spans than hard disks, so their uses are somewhat limited. One use for SSDs is in storage arrays, where they hold file-system metadata that require high performance. SSDs are also used in some laptop computers to make them smaller, faster, and more energy-efficient.

Because SSDs can be much faster than hard disk drives, standard bus interfaces can cause a major limit on throughput. Some SSDs are designed to connect directly to the system bus (PCI, for example). SSDs are changing other traditional aspects of computer design as well. Some systems use them as a direct replacement for disk drives, while others use them as a new cache tier, moving data between hard disks, SSDs, and memory to optimize performance.

In the remainder of this chapter, some sections pertain to SSDs, while others do not. For example, because SSDs have no disk head, disk-scheduling algorithms largely do not apply. Throughput and formatting, however, do apply.

9.1.3 Magnetic Tapes

Magnetic tape was used as an early secondary-storage medium. Although it is relatively permanent and can hold large quantities of data, its access time is slow compared with that of main memory and hard disk. In addition, random access to magnetic tape is about a thousand times slower than random access to hard disk, so tapes are not very useful for secondary storage. Tapes are

---

DISK TRANSFER RATES

As with many aspects of computing, published performance numbers for disks are not the same as real-world performance numbers. Stated transfer rates are always lower than effective transfer rates, for example. The transfer rate may be the rate at which bits can be read from the magnetic media by the disk head, but that is different from the rate at which blocks are delivered to the operating system.

---

used mainly for backup, for storage of infrequently used information, and as a medium for transferring information from one system to another.

A tape is kept in a spool and is wound or rewound past a read–write head. Moving to the correct spot on a tape can take minutes, but once positioned, tape drives can write data at speeds comparable to disk drives. Tape capacities vary greatly, depending on the particular kind of tape drive, with current capacities exceeding several terabytes. Some tapes have built-in compression that can more than double the effective storage. Tapes and their drivers are usually categorized by width, including 4, 8, and 19 millimeters and 1/4 and 1/2 inch. Some are named according to technology, such as LTO-5 and SDLT.

9.2 Disk Structure

Modern hard disk drives are addressed as large one-dimensional arrays of logical blocks, where the logical block is the smallest unit of transfer. The size of a logical block is usually 512 bytes, although some disks can be low-level formatted to have a different logical block size, such as 1,024 bytes. This option is described in Section 9.5.1. The one-dimensional array of logical blocks is mapped onto the sectors of the disk sequentially. Sector 0 is the first sector of the first track on the outermost cylinder. The mapping proceeds in order through that track, then through the rest of the tracks in that cylinder, and then through the rest of the cylinders from outermost to innermost.

By using this mapping, we can—at least in theory—convert a logical block number into an old-style disk address that consists of a cylinder number, a track number within that cylinder, and a sector number within that track. In practice, it is difficult to perform this translation, for two reasons. First, most disks have some defective sectors, but the mapping hides this by substituting spare sectors from elsewhere on the disk. Second, the number of sectors per track is not a constant on some drives.

Let's look more closely at the second reason. On media that use constant linear velocity (CLV), the density of bits per track is uniform. The farther a track is from the center of the disk, the greater its length, so the more sectors it can hold. As we move from outer zones to inner zones, the number of sectors per track decreases. Tracks in the outermost zone typically hold 40 percent more sectors than do tracks in the innermost zone. The drive increases its rotation speed as the head moves from the outer to the inner tracks to keep the same rate of data moving under the head. This method is used in CD-ROM and DVD-ROM drives. Alternatively, the disk rotation speed can stay constant; in this case, the density of bits decreases from inner tracks to outer tracks to keep the data rate constant. This method is used in hard disks and is known as constant angular velocity (CAV).

The number of sectors per track has been increasing as disk technology improves, and the outer zone of a disk usually has several hundred sectors per track. Similarly, the number of cylinders per disk has been increasing; large disks have tens of thousands of cylinders.

9.3 Disk Attachment

Computers access disk storage in two ways. One way is via I/O ports (or host-attached storage); this is common on small systems. The other way is via a remote host in a distributed file system; this is referred to as network-attached storage.

9.3.1 Host-Attached Storage

Host-attached storage is storage accessed through local I/O ports. These ports use several technologies. The typical desktop PC uses an I/O bus architecture called IDE or ATA. This architecture supports a maximum of two drives per I/O bus. A newer, similar protocol that has simplified cabling is SATA.

High-end workstations and servers generally use more sophisticated I/O architectures such as fibre channel (FC), a high-speed serial architecture that can operate over optical fiber or over a four-conductor copper cable. It has two variants. One is a large switched fabric having a 24-bit address space. This variant is expected to dominate in the future and is the basis of storage-area networks (SANs), discussed in Section 9.3.3. Because of the large address space and the switched nature of the communication, multiple hosts and storage devices can attach to the fabric, allowing great flexibility in I/O communication. The other FC variant is an arbitrated loop (FC-AL) that can address 126 devices (drives and controllers).

A wide variety of storage devices are suitable for use as host-attached storage. Among these are hard disk drives, RAID arrays, and CD, DVD, and tape drives. The I/O commands that initiate data transfers to a host-attached storage device are reads and writes of logical data blocks directed to specifically identified storage units (such as bus ID or target logical unit).

9.3.2 Network-Attached Storage

A network-attached storage (NAS) device is a special-purpose storage system that is accessed remotely over a data network (Figure 9.2). Clients access network-attached storage via a remote-procedure-call interface such as NFS for UNIX systems or CIFS for Windows machines. The remote procedure calls (RPCs) are carried via TCP or UDP over an IP network—usually the same local-area network (LAN) that carries all data traffic to the clients. Thus, it may be easiest to think of NAS as simply another storage-access protocol. The network-attached storage unit is usually implemented as a RAID array with software that implements the RPC interface.

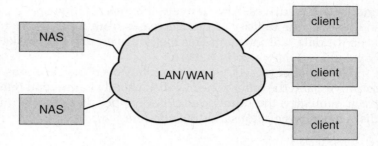

Figure 9.2   Network-attached storage.

Network-attached storage provides a convenient way for all the computers on a LAN to share a pool of storage with the same ease of naming and access enjoyed with local host-attached storage. However, it tends to be less efficient and have lower performance than some direct-attached storage options.

iSCSI is the latest network-attached storage protocol. In essence, it uses the IP network protocol to carry the SCSI protocol. Thus, networks—rather than SCSI cables—can be used as the interconnects between hosts and their storage. As a result, hosts can treat their storage as if it were directly attached, even if the storage is distant from the host.

9.3.3   Storage-Area Network

One drawback of network-attached storage systems is that the storage I/O operations consume bandwidth on the data network, thereby increasing the latency of network communication. This problem can be particularly acute in large client–server installations—the communication between servers and clients competes for bandwidth with the communication among servers and storage devices.

A storage-area network (SAN) is a private network (using storage protocols rather than networking protocols) connecting servers and storage units, as shown in Figure 9.3. The power of a SAN lies in its flexibility. Multiple hosts and multiple storage arrays can attach to the same SAN, and storage can be dynamically allocated to hosts. A SAN switch allows or prohibits access between the hosts and the storage. As one example, if a host is running low on disk space, the SAN can be configured to allocate more storage to that host. SANs make it possible for clusters of servers to share the same storage and for storage arrays to include multiple direct host connections. SANs typically have more ports—as well as more expensive ports—than storage arrays.

FC is the most common SAN interconnect, although the simplicity of iSCSI is increasing its use. Another SAN interconnect is InfiniBand — a special-purpose bus architecture that provides hardware and software support for high-speed interconnection networks for servers and storage units.

9.4   Disk Scheduling

One of the responsibilities of the operating system is to use the hardware efficiently. For the disk drives, meeting this responsibility entails having fast

Figure 9.3 Storage-area network.

access time and large disk bandwidth. For hard disks, the access time has two major components, as mentioned in Section 9.1.1. The **seek time** is the time for the disk arm to move the heads to the cylinder containing the desired sector. The **rotational latency** is the additional time for the disk to rotate the desired sector to the disk head. The disk **bandwidth** is the total number of bytes transferred, divided by the total time between the first request for service and the completion of the last transfer. We can improve both the access time and the bandwidth by managing the order in which disk I/O requests are serviced.

Whenever a process needs I/O to or from the disk, it issues a system call to the operating system. The request specifies several pieces of information:

- Whether this operation is input or output
- What the disk address for the transfer is
- What the memory address for the transfer is
- What the number of sectors to be transferred is

If the desired disk drive and controller are available, the request can be serviced immediately. If the drive or controller is busy, any new requests for service will be placed in the queue of pending requests for that drive. For a multiprogramming system with many processes, the disk queue may often have several pending requests. Thus, when one request is completed, the operating system chooses which pending request to service next. How does the operating system make this choice? Any one of several disk-scheduling algorithms can be used, and we discuss them next.

9.4.1 FCFS Scheduling

The simplest form of disk scheduling is, of course, the first-come, first-served (FCFS) algorithm. This algorithm is intrinsically fair, but it generally does not provide the fastest service. Consider, for example, a disk queue with requests for I/O to blocks on cylinders

98, 183, 37, 122, 14, 124, 65, 67,

Figure 9.4   FCFS disk scheduling.

in that order. If the disk head is initially at cylinder 53, it will first move from 53 to 98, then to 183, 37, 122, 14, 124, 65, and finally to 67, for a total head movement of 640 cylinders. This schedule is diagrammed in Figure 9.4.

The wild swing from 122 to 14 and then back to 124 illustrates the problem with this schedule. If the requests for cylinders 37 and 14 could be serviced together, before or after the requests for 122 and 124, the total head movement could be decreased substantially, and performance could be thereby improved.

9.4.2   SSTF Scheduling

It seems reasonable to service all the requests close to the current head position before moving the head far away to service other requests. This assumption is the basis for the **shortest-seek-time-first (SSTF) algorithm**. The SSTF algorithm selects the request with the least seek time from the current head position. In other words, SSTF chooses the pending request closest to the current head position.

For our example request queue, the closest request to the initial head position (53) is at cylinder 65. Once we are at cylinder 65, the next closest request is at cylinder 67. From there, the request at cylinder 37 is closer than the one at 98, so 37 is served next. Continuing, we service the request at cylinder 14, then 98, 122, 124, and finally 183 (Figure 9.5). This scheduling method results in a total head movement of only 236 cylinders—little more than one-third of the distance needed for FCFS scheduling of this request queue. Clearly, this algorithm gives a substantial improvement in performance.

SSTF scheduling is essentially a form of shortest-job-first (SJF) scheduling; and like SJF scheduling, it may cause starvation of some requests. Remember that requests may arrive at any time. Suppose that we have two requests in the queue, for cylinders 14 and 186, and while the request from 14 is being serviced, a new request near 14 arrives. This new request will be serviced next, making the request at 186 wait. While this request is being serviced, another request close to 14 could arrive. In theory, a continual stream of requests near one another could cause the request for cylinder 186 to wait indefinitely.

Figure 9.5 SSTF disk scheduling.

This scenario becomes increasingly likely as the pending-request queue grows longer.

Although the SSTF algorithm is a substantial improvement over the FCFS algorithm, it is not optimal. In the example, we can do better by moving the head from 53 to 37, even though the latter is not closest, and then to 14, before turning around to service 65, 67, 98, 122, 124, and 183. This strategy reduces the total head movement to 208 cylinders.

9.4.3 SCAN Scheduling

In the SCAN algorithm, the disk arm starts at one end of the disk and moves toward the other end, servicing requests as it reaches each cylinder, until it gets to the other end of the disk. At the other end, the direction of head movement is reversed, and servicing continues. The head continuously scans back and forth across the disk. The SCAN algorithm is sometimes called the **elevator algorithm**, since the disk arm behaves just like an elevator in a building, first servicing all the requests going up and then reversing to service requests the other way.

Let's return to our example to illustrate. Before applying SCAN to schedule the requests on cylinders 98, 183, 37, 122, 14, 124, 65, and 67, we need to know the direction of head movement in addition to the head's current position. Assuming that the disk arm is moving toward 0 and that the initial head position is again 53, the head will next service 37 and then 14. At cylinder 0, the arm will reverse and will move toward the other end of the disk, servicing the requests at 65, 67, 98, 122, 124, and 183 (Figure 9.6). If a request arrives in the queue just in front of the head, it will be serviced almost immediately; a request arriving just behind the head will have to wait until the arm moves to the end of the disk, reverses direction, and comes back.

Assuming a uniform distribution of requests for cylinders, consider the density of requests when the head reaches one end and reverses direction. At this point, relatively few requests are immediately in front of the head, since these cylinders have recently been serviced. The heaviest density of requests

queue = 98, 183, 37, 122, 14, 124, 65, 67
head starts at 53

Figure 9.6   SCAN disk scheduling.

is at the other end of the disk. These requests have also waited the longest, so why not go there first? That is the idea of the next algorithm.

9.4.4   C-SCAN Scheduling

Circular SCAN (C-SCAN) scheduling is a variant of SCAN designed to provide a more uniform wait time. Like SCAN, C-SCAN moves the head from one end of the disk to the other, servicing requests along the way. When the head reaches the other end, however, it immediately returns to the beginning of the disk without servicing any requests on the return trip (Figure 9.7). The C-SCAN scheduling algorithm essentially treats the cylinders as a circular list that wraps around from the final cylinder to the first one.

queue = 98, 183, 37, 122, 14, 124, 65, 67
head starts at 53

Figure 9.7   C-SCAN disk scheduling.

9.4.5 LOOK Scheduling

As we described them, both SCAN and C-SCAN move the disk arm across the full width of the disk. In practice, neither algorithm is often implemented this way. More commonly, the arm goes only as far as the final request in each direction. Then, it reverses direction immediately, without going all the way to the end of the disk. Versions of SCAN and C-SCAN that follow this pattern are called LOOK and C-LOOK scheduling, because they *look* for a request before continuing to move in a given direction (Figure 9.8).

9.4.6 Selection of a Disk-Scheduling Algorithm

Given so many disk-scheduling algorithms, how do we choose the best one? SSTF is common and has a natural appeal because it increases performance over FCFS. SCAN and C-SCAN perform better for systems that place a heavy load on the disk, because they are less likely to cause a starvation problem. For any particular list of requests, we can define an optimal order of retrieval, but the computation needed to find an optimal schedule may not justify the savings over SSTF or SCAN. With any scheduling algorithm, however, performance depends heavily on the number and types of requests. For instance, suppose that the queue usually has just one outstanding request. Then, all scheduling algorithms behave the same, because they have only one choice of where to move the disk head: they all behave like FCFS scheduling.

Requests for disk service can be greatly influenced by the file-allocation method. A program reading a contiguously allocated file will generate several requests that are close together on the disk, resulting in limited head movement. A linked or indexed file, in contrast, may include blocks that are widely scattered on the disk, resulting in greater head movement.

The location of directories and index blocks is also important. Since every file must be opened to be used, and opening a file requires searching the directory structure, the directories will be accessed frequently. Suppose that a directory entry is on the first cylinder and a file's data are on the final cylinder. In this case, the disk head has to move the entire width of the disk. If the directory

Figure 9.8   C-LOOK disk scheduling.

DISK SCHEDULING and SSDs

The disk-scheduling algorithms discussed in this section focus primarily on minimizing the amount of disk head movement in hard disk drives. SSDs—which do not contain moving disk heads—commonly use a simple FCFS policy. For example, the Linux **Noop** scheduler uses an FCFS policy but modifies it to merge adjacent requests. The observed behavior of SSDs indicates that the time required to service reads is uniform but that, because of the properties of flash memory, write service time is not uniform. Some SSD schedulers have exploited this property and merge only adjacent write requests, servicing all read requests in FCFS order.

---

entry were on the middle cylinder, the head would have to move only one-half the width. Caching the directories and index blocks in main memory can also help to reduce disk-arm movement, particularly for read requests.

Because of these complexities, the disk-scheduling algorithm should be written as a separate module of the operating system, so that it can be replaced with a different algorithm if necessary. Either SSTF or LOOK is a reasonable choice for the default algorithm.

The scheduling algorithms described here consider only the seek distances. For modern disks, the rotational latency can be nearly as large as the average seek time. It is difficult for the operating system to schedule for improved rotational latency, though, because modern disks do not disclose the physical location of logical blocks. Disk manufacturers have been alleviating this problem by implementing disk-scheduling algorithms in the controller hardware built into the disk drive. If the operating system sends a batch of requests to the controller, the controller can queue them and then schedule them to improve both the seek time and the rotational latency.

If I/O performance were the only consideration, the operating system would gladly turn over the responsibility of disk scheduling to the disk hardware. In practice, however, the operating system may have other constraints on the service order for requests. For instance, demand paging may take priority over application I/O, and writes are more urgent than reads if the cache is running out of free pages. Also, it may be desirable to guarantee the order of a set of disk writes to make the file system robust in the face of system crashes. Consider what could happen if the operating system allocated a disk page to a file and the application wrote data into that page before the operating system had a chance to flush the file system metadata back to disk. To accommodate such requirements, an operating system may choose to do its own disk scheduling and to spoon-feed the requests to the disk controller, one by one, for some types of I/O.

9.5 Disk Management

The operating system is responsible for several other aspects of disk management, too. Here we discuss disk initialization, booting from disk, and bad-block recovery.

9.5.1 Disk Formatting

A new hard disk is a blank slate: it is just a platter of a magnetic recording material. Before a disk can store data, it must be divided into sectors that the disk controller can read and write. This process is called **low-level formatting**, or **physical formatting**. Low-level formatting fills the disk with a special data structure for each sector. The data structure for a sector typically consists of a header, a data area (usually 512 bytes in size), and a trailer. The header and trailer contain information used by the disk controller, such as a sector number and an **error-correcting code** (ECC). When the controller writes a sector of data during normal I/O, the ECC is updated with a value calculated from all the bytes in the data area. When the sector is read, the ECC is recalculated and compared with the stored value. If the stored and calculated numbers are different, this mismatch indicates that the data area of the sector has become corrupted and that the disk sector may be bad (Section 9.5.3). The ECC is an error-correcting code because it contains enough information, if only a few bits of data have been corrupted, to enable the controller to identify which bits have changed and calculate what their correct values should be. It then reports a recoverable **soft error**. The controller automatically does the ECC processing whenever a sector is read or written.

Most hard disks are low-level-formatted at the factory as a part of the manufacturing process. This formatting enables the manufacturer to test the disk and to initialize the mapping from logical block numbers to defect-free sectors on the disk. For many hard disks, when the disk controller is instructed to low-level-format the disk, it can also be told how many bytes of data space to leave between the header and trailer of all sectors. It is usually possible to choose among a few sizes, such as 256, 512, and 1,024 bytes. Formatting a disk with a larger sector size means that fewer sectors can fit on each track; but it also means that fewer headers and trailers are written on each track and more space is available for user data. Some operating systems can handle only a sector size of 512 bytes.

Before it can use a disk to hold files, the operating system still needs to record its own data structures on the disk. It does so in two steps. The first step is to **partition** the disk into one or more groups of cylinders. The operating system can treat each partition as though it were a separate disk. For instance, one partition can hold a copy of the operating system's executable code, while another holds user files. The second step is **logical formatting**, or creation of a file system. In this step, the operating system stores the initial file-system data structures onto the disk. These data structures may include maps of free and allocated space and an initial empty directory.

To increase efficiency, most file systems group blocks together into larger chunks, frequently called **clusters**. Disk I/O is done via blocks, but file system I/O is done via clusters, effectively assuring that I/O has more sequential-access and fewer random-access characteristics.

Some operating systems give special programs the ability to use a disk partition as a large sequential array of logical blocks, without any file-system data structures. This array is sometimes called the **raw disk,** and I/O to this array is termed *raw I/O.* For example, some database systems prefer raw I/O because it enables them to control the exact disk location where each database record is stored. Raw I/O bypasses all the file-system services, such as the buffer cache, file locking, prefetching, space allocation, file names, and directories. We can make certain applications more efficient by allowing them to implement their own special-purpose storage services on a raw partition, but most applications perform better when they use the regular file-system services.

9.5.2 Boot Block

For a computer to start running—for instance, when it is powered up or rebooted—it must have an initial program to run. This initial **bootstrap** program tends to be simple. It initializes all aspects of the system, from CPU registers to device controllers and the contents of main memory, and then starts the operating system. To do its job, the bootstrap program finds the operating-system kernel on disk, loads that kernel into memory, and jumps to an initial address to begin the operating-system execution.

For most computers, the bootstrap is stored in **read-only memory** (ROM). This location is convenient, because ROM needs no initialization and is at a fixed location that the processor can start executing when powered up or reset. And, since ROM is read only, it cannot be infected by a computer virus. The problem is that changing this bootstrap code requires changing the ROM hardware chips. For this reason, most systems store a tiny bootstrap loader program in the boot ROM whose only job is to bring in a full bootstrap program from disk. The full bootstrap program can be changed easily: a new version is simply written onto the disk. The full bootstrap program is stored in the "boot blocks" at a fixed location on the disk. A disk that has a boot partition is called a **boot disk** or **system disk**.

The code in the boot ROM instructs the disk controller to read the boot blocks into memory (no device drivers are loaded at this point) and then starts executing that code. The full bootstrap program is more sophisticated than the bootstrap loader in the boot ROM. It is able to load the entire operating system from a non-fixed location on disk and to start the operating system running. Even so, the full bootstrap code may be small.

Let's consider as an example the boot process in Windows. First, note that Windows allows a hard disk to be divided into partitions, and one partition —identified as the **boot partition**—contains the operating system and device drivers. The Windows system places its boot code in the first sector on the hard disk, which it terms the **master boot record**, or **MBR**. Booting begins by running code that is resident in the system's ROM memory. This code directs the system to read the boot code from the MBR. In addition to containing boot code, the MBR contains a table listing the partitions for the hard disk and a flag indicating which partition the system is to be booted from, as illustrated in Figure 9.9. Once the system identifies the boot partition, it reads the first sector from that partition (which is called the **boot sector**) and continues with the remainder of the boot process, which includes loading the various subsystems and system services.

9.5.3 Bad Blocks

Because disks have moving parts and small tolerances (recall that the disk head flies just above the disk surface), they are prone to failure. Sometimes the failure is complete; in this case, the disk needs to be replaced and its contents

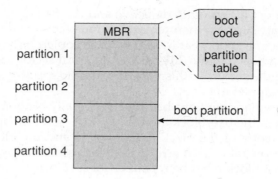

Figure 9.9 Booting from disk in Windows.

restored from backup media to the new disk. More frequently, one or more sectors become defective. Most disks even come from the factory with **bad blocks**. Depending on the disk and controller in use, these blocks are handled in a variety of ways.

On simple disks, such as some disks with IDE controllers, bad blocks are handled manually. One strategy is to scan the disk to find bad blocks while the disk is being formatted. Any bad blocks that are discovered are flagged as unusable so that the file system does not allocate them. If blocks go bad during normal operation, a special program (such as the Linux `badblocks` command) must be run manually to search for the bad blocks and to lock them away. Data that resided on the bad blocks usually are lost.

More sophisticated disks are smarter about bad-block recovery. The controller maintains a list of bad blocks on the disk. The list is initialized during the low-level formatting at the factory and is updated over the life of the disk. Low-level formatting also sets aside spare sectors not visible to the operating system. The controller can be told to replace each bad sector logically with one of the spare sectors. This scheme is known as **sector sparing** or **forwarding**.

A typical bad-sector transaction might be as follows:

- The operating system tries to read logical block 87.

- The controller calculates the ECC and finds that the sector is bad. It reports this finding to the operating system.

- The next time the system is rebooted, a special command is run to tell the controller to replace the bad sector with a spare.

- After that, whenever the system requests logical block 87, the request is translated into the replacement sector's address by the controller.

Note that such a redirection by the controller could invalidate any optimization by the operating system's disk-scheduling algorithm! For this reason, most disks are formatted to provide a few spare sectors in each cylinder and a spare cylinder as well. When a bad block is remapped, the controller uses a spare sector from the same cylinder, if possible.

As an alternative to sector sparing, some controllers can be instructed to replace a bad block by **sector slipping**. Here is an example: Suppose that logical block 17 becomes defective and the first available spare follows sector 202. Sector slipping then remaps all the sectors from 17 to 202, moving them all down one spot. That is, sector 202 is copied into the spare, then sector 201 into 202, then 200 into 201, and so on, until sector 18 is copied into sector 19. Slipping the sectors in this way frees up the space of sector 18 so that sector 17 can be mapped to it.

The replacement of a bad block generally is not totally automatic, because the data in the bad block are usually lost. Soft errors may trigger a process in which a copy of the block data is made and the block is spared or slipped. An unrecoverable **hard error**, however, results in lost data. Whatever file was using that block must be repaired (for instance, by restoration from a backup tape), and that requires manual intervention.

9.6   Swap-Space Management

Swapping was first presented in Section 7.2, where we discussed moving entire processes between disk and main memory. Swapping in that setting occurs when the amount of physical memory reaches a critically low point and processes are moved from memory to swap space to free available memory. In practice, very few modern operating systems implement swapping in this fashion. Rather, systems now combine swapping with virtual memory techniques (Chapter 8) and swap pages, not necessarily entire processes. In fact, some systems now use the terms "swapping" and "paging" interchangeably, reflecting the merging of these two concepts.

Swap-space management is another low-level task of the operating system. Virtual memory uses disk space as an extension of main memory. Since disk access is much slower than memory access, using swap space significantly decreases system performance. The main goal for the design and implementation of swap space is to provide the best throughput for the virtual memory system. In this section, we discuss how swap space is used, where swap space is located on disk, and how swap space is managed.

9.6.1 Swap-Space Use

Swap space is used in various ways by different operating systems, depending on the memory-management algorithms in use. For instance, systems that implement swapping may use swap space to hold an entire process image, including the code and data segments. Paging systems may simply store pages that have been pushed out of main memory. The amount of swap space needed on a system can therefore vary from a few megabytes of disk space to gigabytes, depending on the amount of physical memory, the amount of virtual memory it is backing, and the way in which the virtual memory is used.

Note that it may be safer to overestimate than to underestimate the amount of swap space required, because if a system runs out of swap space it may be forced to abort processes or may crash entirely. Overestimation wastes disk space that could otherwise be used for files, but it does no other harm. Some systems recommend the amount to be set aside for swap space. Solaris, for example, suggests setting swap space equal to the amount by which virtual memory exceeds pageable physical memory. In the past, Linux has suggested setting swap space to double the amount of physical memory. Today, that limitation is gone, and most Linux systems use considerably less swap space.

Some operating systems—including Linux—allow the use of multiple swap spaces, including both files and dedicated swap partitions. These swap spaces are usually placed on separate disks so that the load placed on the I/O system by paging and swapping can be spread over the system's I/O bandwidth.

9.6.2 Swap-Space Location

A swap space can reside in one of two places: it can be carved out of the normal file system, or it can be in a separate disk partition. If the swap space is simply a large file within the file system, normal file-system routines can be used to create it, name it, and allocate its space. This approach, though easy to implement, is inefficient. Navigating the directory structure and the disk-allocation data structures takes time and (possibly) extra disk accesses. External fragmentation can greatly increase swapping times by forcing multiple seeks during reading or writing of a process image. We can improve performance by caching the block location information in physical memory and by using special tools to allocate physically contiguous blocks for the swap file, but the cost of traversing the file-system data structures remains.

Alternatively, swap space can be created in a separate raw partition. No file system or directory structure is placed in this space. Rather, a separate swap-space storage manager is used to allocate and deallocate the blocks from the raw partition. This manager uses algorithms optimized for speed rather than for storage efficiency, because swap space is accessed much more frequently than file systems (when it is used). Internal fragmentation may increase, but this trade-off is acceptable because the life of data in the swap space generally is much shorter than that of files in the file system. Since swap space is reinitialized at boot time, any fragmentation is short-lived. The raw-partition approach creates a fixed amount of swap space during disk partitioning. Adding more swap space requires either repartitioning the disk (which involves moving the other file-system partitions or destroying them and restoring them from backup) or adding another swap space elsewhere.

Some operating systems are flexible and can swap both in raw partitions and in file-system space. Linux is an example: the policy and implementation are separate, allowing the machine's administrator to decide which type of swapping to use. The trade-off is between the convenience of allocation and management in the file system and the performance of swapping in raw partitions.

9.6.3 Swap-Space Management: An Example

We can illustrate how swap space is used by following the evolution of swapping and paging in various UNIX systems. The traditional UNIX kernel started with an implementation of swapping that copied entire processes between contiguous disk regions and memory. UNIX later evolved to a combination of swapping and paging as paging hardware became available.

In Solaris 1 (SunOS), the designers changed standard UNIX methods to improve efficiency and reflect technological developments. When a process executes, text-segment pages containing code are brought in from the file

Figure 9.10   The data structures for swapping on Linux systems.

system, accessed in main memory, and thrown away if selected for pageout. It is more efficient to reread a page from the file system than to write it to swap space and then reread it from there. Swap space is only used as a backing store for pages of **anonymous** memory, which includes memory allocated for the stack, heap, and uninitialized data of a process.

More changes were made in later versions of Solaris. The biggest change is that Solaris now allocates swap space only when a page is forced out of physical memory, rather than when the virtual memory page is first created. This scheme gives better performance on modern computers, which have more physical memory than older systems and tend to page less.

Linux is similar to Solaris in that swap space is used only for anonymous memory—that is, memory not backed by any file. Linux allows one or more swap areas to be established. A swap area may be in either a swap file on a regular file system or a dedicated swap partition. Each swap area consists of a series of 4-KB **page slots**, which are used to hold swapped pages. Associated with each swap area is a **swap map**—an array of integer counters, each corresponding to a page slot in the swap area. If the value of a counter is 0, the corresponding page slot is available. Values greater than 0 indicate that the page slot is occupied by a swapped page. The value of the counter indicates the number of mappings to the swapped page. For example, a value of 3 indicates that the swapped page is mapped to three different processes (which can occur if the swapped page is storing a region of memory shared by three processes). The data structures for swapping on Linux systems are shown in Figure 9.10.

9.7   RAID Structure

Disk drives have continued to get smaller and cheaper, so it is now economically feasible to attach many disks to a computer system. Having a large number of disks in a system presents opportunities for improving the rate at which data can be read or written, if the disks are operated in parallel. Furthermore, this setup offers the potential for improving the reliability of data storage, because redundant information can be stored on multiple disks. Thus, failure of one disk does not lead to loss of data. A variety of disk-organization techniques, collectively called **redundant arrays of independent disks** (RAID), are commonly used to address the performance and reliability issues.

In the past, RAIDs composed of small, cheap disks were viewed as a cost-effective alternative to large, expensive disks. Today, RAIDs are used for

STRUCTURING RAID

RAID storage can be structured in a variety of ways. For example, a system can have disks directly attached to its buses. In this case, the operating system or system software can implement RAID functionality. Alternatively, an intelligent host controller can control multiple attached disks and can implement RAID on those disks in hardware. Finally, a storage array, or RAID array, can be used. A RAID array is a standalone unit with its own controller, cache (usually), and disks. It is attached to the host via one or more standard controllers (for example, FC). This common setup allows an operating system or software without RAID functionality to have RAID-protected disks. It is even used on systems that do have RAID software layers because of its simplicity and flexibility.

their higher reliability and higher data-transfer rate, rather than for economic reasons. Hence, the *I* in *RAID*, which once stood for "inexpensive," now stands for "independent."

9.7.1   Improvement of Reliability via Redundancy

Let's first consider the reliability of RAIDs. The chance that some disk out of a set of N disks will fail is much higher than the chance that a specific single disk will fail. Suppose that the mean time to failure of a single disk is 100,000 hours. Then the mean time to failure of some disk in an array of 100 disks will be $100,000/100 = 1,000$ hours, or 41.66 days, which is not long at all! If we store only one copy of the data, then each disk failure will result in loss of a significant amount of data—and such a high rate of data loss is unacceptable.

The solution to the problem of reliability is to introduce redundancy; we store extra information that is not normally needed but that can be used in the event of failure of a disk to rebuild the lost information. Thus, even if a disk fails, data are not lost.

The simplest (but most expensive) approach to introducing redundancy is to duplicate every disk. This technique is called mirroring. With mirroring, a logical disk consists of two physical disks, and every write is carried out on both disks. The result is called a mirrored volume. If one of the disks in the volume fails, the data can be read from the other. Data will be lost only if the second disk fails before the first failed disk is replaced.

The mean time to failure of a mirrored volume—where failure is the loss of data—depends on two factors. One is the mean time to failure of the individual disks. The other is the mean time to repair, which is the time it takes (on average) to replace a failed disk and to restore the data on it. Suppose that the failures of the two disks are independent; that is, the failure of one disk is not connected to the failure of the other. Then, if the mean time to failure of a single disk is 100,000 hours and the mean time to repair is 10 hours, the mean time to data loss of a mirrored disk system is $100,000^2/(2*10) = 500*10^6$ hours, or 57,000 years!

You should be aware that we cannot really assume that disk failures will be independent. Power failures and natural disasters, such as earthquakes, fires, and floods, may result in damage to both disks at the same time. Also, manufacturing defects in a batch of disks can cause correlated failures. As disks age, the probability of failure grows, increasing the chance that a second disk will fail while the first is being repaired. In spite of all these considerations, however, mirrored-disk systems offer much higher reliability than do single-disk systems.

Power failures are a particular source of concern, since they occur far more frequently than do natural disasters. Even with mirroring of disks, if writes are in progress to the same block in both disks, and power fails before both blocks are fully written, the two blocks can be in an inconsistent state. One solution to this problem is to write one copy first, then the next. Another is to add a solid-state nonvolatile RAM (NVRAM) cache to the RAID array. This write-back cache is protected from data loss during power failures, so the write can be considered complete at that point, assuming the NVRAM has some kind of error protection and correction, such as ECC or mirroring.

9.7.2 Improvement in Performance via Parallelism

Now let's consider how parallel access to multiple disks improves performance. With disk mirroring, the rate at which read requests can be handled is doubled, since read requests can be sent to either disk (as long as both disks in a pair are functional, as is almost always the case). The transfer rate of each read is the same as in a single-disk system, but the number of reads per unit time has doubled.

With multiple disks, we can improve the transfer rate as well (or instead) by striping data across the disks. In its simplest form, data striping consists of splitting the bits of each byte across multiple disks; such striping is called bit-level striping. For example, if we have an array of eight disks, we write bit i of each byte to disk i. The array of eight disks can be treated as a single disk with sectors that are eight times the normal size and, more important, that have eight times the access rate. Every disk participates in every access (read or write); so the number of accesses that can be processed per second is about the same as on a single disk, but each access can read eight times as many data in the same time as on a single disk.

Bit-level striping can be generalized to include a number of disks that either is a multiple of 8 or divides 8. For example, if we use an array of four disks, bits i and $4 + i$ of each byte go to disk i. Further, striping need not occur at the bit level. In block-level striping, for instance, blocks of a file are striped across multiple disks; with n disks, block i of a file goes to disk $(i \bmod n) + 1$. Other levels of striping, such as bytes of a sector or sectors of a block, also are possible. Block-level striping is the most common.

Parallelism in a disk system, as achieved through striping, has two main goals:

1. Increase the throughput of multiple small accesses (that is, page accesses) by load balancing.

2. Reduce the response time of large accesses.

9.7.3 RAID Levels

Mirroring provides high reliability, but it is expensive. Striping provides high data-transfer rates, but it does not improve reliability. Numerous schemes to provide redundancy at lower cost by using disk striping combined with "parity" bits (which we describe shortly) have been proposed. These schemes have different cost–performance trade-offs and are classified according to levels called RAID levels. We describe the various levels here; Figure 9.11 shows them pictorially (in the figure, P indicates error-correcting bits and C indicates a second copy of the data). In all cases depicted in the figure, four disks' worth of data are stored, and the extra disks are used to store redundant information for failure recovery.

(a) RAID 0: non-redundant striping.

(b) RAID 1: mirrored disks.

(c) RAID 2: memory-style error-correcting codes.

(d) RAID 3: bit-interleaved parity.

(e) RAID 4: block-interleaved parity.

(f) RAID 5: block-interleaved distributed parity.

(g) RAID 6: P + Q redundancy.

Figure 9.11 RAID levels.

- **RAID level 0**. RAID level 0 refers to disk arrays with striping at the level of blocks but without any redundancy (such as mirroring or parity bits), as shown in Figure 9.11(a).

- **RAID level 1**. RAID level 1 refers to disk mirroring. Figure 9.11(b) shows a mirrored organization.

- **RAID level 2**. RAID level 2 is also known as memory-style error-correcting-code (ECC) organization. Memory systems have long detected certain errors by using parity bits. Each byte in a memory system may have a parity bit associated with it that records whether the number of bits in the byte set to 1 is even (parity = 0) or odd (parity = 1). If one of the bits in the byte is damaged (either a 1 becomes a 0, or a 0 becomes a 1), the parity of the byte changes and thus does not match the stored parity. Similarly, if the stored parity bit is damaged, it does not match the computed parity. Thus, all single-bit errors are detected by the memory system. Error-correcting schemes store two or more extra bits and can reconstruct the data if a single bit is damaged.

  The idea of ECC can be used directly in disk arrays via striping of bytes across disks. For example, the first bit of each byte can be stored in disk 1, the second bit in disk 2, and so on until the eighth bit is stored in disk 8; the error-correction bits are stored in further disks. This scheme is shown in Figure 9.11(c), where the disks labeled P store the error-correction bits. If one of the disks fails, the remaining bits of the byte and the associated error-correction bits can be read from other disks and used to reconstruct the damaged data. Note that RAID level 2 requires only three disks' overhead for four disks of data, unlike RAID level 1, which requires four disks' overhead.

- **RAID level 3**. RAID level 3, or bit-interleaved parity organization, improves on level 2 by taking into account the fact that, unlike memory systems, disk controllers can detect whether a sector has been read correctly, so a single parity bit can be used for error correction as well as for detection. The idea is as follows: If one of the sectors is damaged, we know exactly which sector it is, and we can figure out whether any bit in the sector is a 1 or a 0 by computing the parity of the corresponding bits from sectors in the other disks. If the parity of the remaining bits is equal to the stored parity, the missing bit is 0; otherwise, it is 1. RAID level 3 is as good as level 2 but is less expensive in the number of extra disks required (it has only a one-disk overhead), so level 2 is not used in practice. Level 3 is shown pictorially in Figure 9.11(d).

  RAID level 3 has two advantages over level 1. First, the storage overhead is reduced because only one parity disk is needed for several regular disks, whereas one mirror disk is needed for every disk in level 1. Second, since reads and writes of a byte are spread out over multiple disks with N-way striping of data, the transfer rate for reading or writing a single block is N times as fast as with RAID level 1. On the negative side, RAID level 3 supports fewer I/Os per second, since every disk has to participate in every I/O request.

  A further performance problem with RAID 3—and with all parity-based RAID levels—is the expense of computing and writing the parity.

This overhead results in significantly slower writes than with non-parity RAID arrays. To moderate this performance penalty, many RAID storage arrays include a hardware controller with dedicated parity hardware. This controller offloads the parity computation from the CPU to the array. The array has an NVRAM cache as well, to store the blocks while the parity is computed and to buffer the writes from the controller to the spindles. This combination can make parity RAID almost as fast as non-parity. In fact, a caching array doing parity RAID can outperform a non-caching non-parity RAID.

- **RAID level 4**. RAID level 4, or block-interleaved parity organization, uses block-level striping, as in RAID 0, and in addition keeps a parity block on a separate disk for corresponding blocks from N other disks. This scheme is diagrammed in Figure 9.11(e). If one of the disks fails, the parity block can be used with the corresponding blocks from the other disks to restore the blocks of the failed disk.

  A block read accesses only one disk, allowing other requests to be processed by the other disks. Thus, the data-transfer rate for each access is slower, but multiple read accesses can proceed in parallel, leading to a higher overall I/O rate. The transfer rates for large reads are high, since all the disks can be read in parallel. Large writes also have high transfer rates, since the data and parity can be written in parallel.

  Small independent writes cannot be performed in parallel. An operating-system write of data smaller than a block requires that the block be read, modified with the new data, and written back. The parity block has to be updated as well. This is known as the **read-modify-write cycle**. Thus, a single write requires four disk accesses: two to read the two old blocks and two to write the two new blocks.

  WAFL (which we cover in Chapter 11) uses RAID level 4 because this RAID level allows disks to be added to a RAID set seamlessly. If the added disks are initialized with blocks containing only zeros, then the parity value does not change, and the RAID set is still correct.

- **RAID level 5**. RAID level 5, or block-interleaved distributed parity, differs from level 4 in that it spreads data and parity among all $N+1$ disks, rather than storing data in N disks and parity in one disk. For each block, one of the disks stores the parity and the others store data. For example, with an array of five disks, the parity for the nth block is stored in disk $(n \bmod 5)+1$. The nth blocks of the other four disks store actual data for that block. This setup is shown in Figure 9.11(f), where the Ps are distributed across all the disks. A parity block cannot store parity for blocks in the same disk, because a disk failure would result in loss of data as well as of parity, and hence the loss would not be recoverable. By spreading the parity across all the disks in the set, RAID 5 avoids potential overuse of a single parity disk, which can occur with RAID 4. RAID 5 is the most common parity RAID system.

- **RAID level 6**. RAID level 6, also called the **P + Q redundancy scheme**, is much like RAID level 5 but stores extra redundant information to guard against multiple disk failures. Instead of parity, error-correcting codes such as the **Reed–Solomon codes** are used. In the scheme shown in Figure

9.11(g), 2 bits of redundant data are stored for every 4 bits of data—compared with 1 parity bit in level 5—and the system can tolerate two disk failures.

- **RAID levels 0 + 1 and 1 + 0**. RAID level 0 + 1 refers to a combination of RAID levels 0 and 1. RAID 0 provides the performance, while RAID 1 provides the reliability. Generally, this level provides better performance than RAID 5. It is common in environments where both performance and reliability are important. Unfortunately, like RAID 1, it doubles the number of disks needed for storage, so it is also relatively expensive. In RAID 0 + 1, a set of disks are striped, and then the stripe is mirrored to another, equivalent stripe.

  Another RAID option that is becoming available commercially is RAID level 1 + 0, in which disks are mirrored in pairs and then the resulting mirrored pairs are striped. This scheme has some theoretical advantages over RAID 0 + 1. For example, if a single disk fails in RAID 0 + 1, an entire stripe is inaccessible, leaving only the other stripe. With a failure in RAID 1 + 0, a single disk is unavailable, but the disk that mirrors it is still available, as are all the rest of the disks (Figure 9.12).

Numerous variations have been proposed to the basic RAID schemes described here. As a result, some confusion may exist about the exact definitions of the different RAID levels.

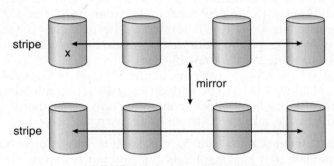

a) RAID 0 + 1 with a single disk failure.

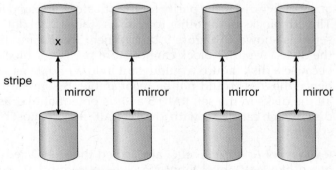

b) RAID 1 + 0 with a single disk failure.

Figure 9.12   RAID 0 + 1 and 1 + 0.

The implementation of RAID is another area of variation. Consider the following layers at which RAID can be implemented.

- Volume-management software can implement RAID within the kernel or at the system software layer. In this case, the storage hardware can provide minimal features and still be part of a full RAID solution. Parity RAID is fairly slow when implemented in software, so typically RAID 0, 1, or 0 + 1 is used.

- RAID can be implemented in the host bus-adapter (HBA) hardware. Only the disks directly connected to the HBA can be part of a given RAID set. This solution is low in cost but not very flexible.

- RAID can be implemented in the hardware of the storage array. The storage array can create RAID sets of various levels and can even slice these sets into smaller volumes, which are then presented to the operating system. The operating system need only implement the file system on each of the volumes. Arrays can have multiple connections available or can be part of a SAN, allowing multiple hosts to take advantage of the array's features.

- RAID can be implemented in the SAN interconnect layer by disk virtualization devices. In this case, a device sits between the hosts and the storage. It accepts commands from the servers and manages access to the storage. It could provide mirroring, for example, by writing each block to two separate storage devices.

Other features, such as snapshots and replication, can be implemented at each of these levels as well. A **snapshot** is a view of the file system before the last update took place. (Snapshots are covered more fully in Chapter 11.) **Replication** involves the automatic duplication of writes between separate sites for redundancy and disaster recovery. Replication can be synchronous or asynchronous. In synchronous replication, each block must be written locally and remotely before the write is considered complete, whereas in asynchronous replication, the writes are grouped together and written periodically. Asynchronous replication can result in data loss if the primary site fails, but it is faster and has no distance limitations.

The implementation of these features differs depending on the layer at which RAID is implemented. For example, if RAID is implemented in software, then each host may need to carry out and manage its own replication. If replication is implemented in the storage array or in the SAN interconnect, however, then whatever the host operating system or its features, the host's data can be replicated.

One other aspect of most RAID implementations is a hot spare disk or disks. A **hot spare** is not used for data but is configured to be used as a replacement in case of disk failure. For instance, a hot spare can be used to rebuild a mirrored pair should one of the disks in the pair fail. In this way, the RAID level can be reestablished automatically, without waiting for the failed disk to be replaced. Allocating more than one hot spare allows more than one failure to be repaired without human intervention.

9.7.4 Selecting a RAID Level

Given the many choices they have, how do system designers choose a RAID level? One consideration is rebuild performance. If a disk fails, the time needed to rebuild its data can be significant. This may be an important factor if a continuous supply of data is required, as it is in high-performance or interactive database systems. Furthermore, rebuild performance influences the mean time to failure.

Rebuild performance varies with the RAID level used. Rebuilding is easiest for RAID level 1, since data can be copied from another disk. For the other levels, we need to access all the other disks in the array to rebuild data in a failed disk. Rebuild times can be hours for RAID 5 rebuilds of large disk sets.

RAID level 0 is used in high-performance applications where data loss is not critical. RAID level 1 is popular for applications that require high reliability with fast recovery. RAID 0 + 1 and 1 + 0 are used where both performance and reliability are important—for example, for small databases. Due to RAID 1's high space overhead, RAID 5 is often preferred for storing large volumes of data. Level 6 is not supported currently by many RAID implementations, but it should offer better reliability than level 5.

RAID system designers and administrators of storage have to make several other decisions as well. For example, how many disks should be in a given RAID set? How many bits should be protected by each parity bit? If more disks are in an array, data-transfer rates are higher, but the system is more expensive. If more bits are protected by a parity bit, the space overhead due to parity bits is lower, but the chance that a second disk will fail before the first failed disk is repaired is greater, and that will result in data loss.

9.7.5 Extensions

The concepts of RAID have been generalized to other storage devices, including arrays of tapes, and even to the broadcast of data over wireless systems. When applied to arrays of tapes, RAID structures are able to recover data even if one of the tapes in an array is damaged. When applied to broadcast of data, a block of data is split into short units and is broadcast along with a parity unit. If one of the units is not received for any reason, it can be reconstructed from the other units. Commonly, tape-drive robots containing multiple tape drives will stripe data across all the drives to increase throughput and decrease backup time.

9.7.6 Problems with RAID

Unfortunately, RAID does not always assure that data are available for the operating system and its users. A pointer to a file could be wrong, for example, or pointers within the file structure could be wrong. Incomplete writes, if not properly recovered, could result in corrupt data. Some other process could accidentally write over a file system's structures, too. RAID protects against physical media errors, but not other hardware and software errors. As large as is the landscape of software and hardware bugs, that is how numerous are the potential perils for data on a system.

The **Solaris** ZFS file system takes an innovative approach to solving these problems through the use of **checksums**—a technique used to verify the

THE InServ STORAGE ARRAY

Innovation, in an effort to provide better, faster, and less expensive solutions, frequently blurs the lines that separated previous technologies. Consider the InServ storage array from 3Par. Unlike most other storage arrays, InServ does not require that a set of disks be configured at a specific RAID level. Rather, each disk is broken into 256-MB "chunklets." RAID is then applied at the chunklet level. A disk can thus participate in multiple and various RAID levels as its chunklets are used for multiple volumes.

InServ also provides snapshots similar to those created by the WAFL file system. The format of InServ snapshots can be read–write as well as read–only, allowing multiple hosts to mount copies of a given file system without needing their own copies of the entire file system. Any changes a host makes in its own copy are copy-on-write and so are not reflected in the other copies.

A further innovation is **utility storage**. Some file systems do not expand or shrink. On these systems, the original size is the only size, and any change requires copying data. An administrator can configure InServ to provide a host with a large amount of logical storage that initially occupies only a small amount of physical storage. As the host starts using the storage, unused disks are allocated to the host, up to the original logical level. The host thus can believe that it has a large fixed storage space, create its file systems there, and so on. Disks can be added or removed from the file system by InServ without the file system's noticing the change. This feature can reduce the number of drives needed by hosts, or at least delay the purchase of disks until they are really needed.

integrity of data. ZFS maintains internal checksums of all blocks, including data and metadata. These checksums are not kept with the block that is being checksummed. Rather, they are stored with the pointer to that block. (See Figure 9.13.) Consider an **inode** — a data structure for storing file system metadata — with pointers to its data. Within the inode is the checksum of each block of data. If there is a problem with the data, the checksum will be incorrect, and the file system will know about it. If the data are mirrored, and there is a block with a correct checksum and one with an incorrect checksum, ZFS will automatically update the bad block with the good one. Similarly, the directory entry that points to the inode has a checksum for the inode. Any problem in the inode is detected when the directory is accessed. This checksumming takes places throughout all ZFS structures, providing a much higher level of consistency, error detection, and error correction than is found in RAID disk sets or standard file systems. The extra overhead that is created by the checksum calculation and extra block read-modify-write cycles is not noticeable because the overall performance of ZFS is very fast.

Another issue with most RAID implementations is lack of flexibility. Consider a storage array with twenty disks divided into four sets of five disks. Each set of five disks is a RAID level 5 set. As a result, there are four separate volumes, each holding a file system. But what if one file system is too large to fit on a five-disk RAID level 5 set? And what if another file system needs very little space? If such factors are known ahead of time, then the disks and volumes

Figure 9.13   ZFS checksums all metadata and data.

can be properly allocated. Very frequently, however, disk use and requirements change over time.

Even if the storage array allowed the entire set of twenty disks to be created as one large RAID set, other issues could arise. Several volumes of various sizes could be built on the set. But some volume managers do not allow us to change a volume's size. In that case, we would be left with the same issue described above—mismatched file-system sizes. Some volume managers allow size changes, but some file systems do not allow for file-system growth or shrinkage. The volumes could change sizes, but the file systems would need to be recreated to take advantage of those changes.

ZFS combines file-system management and volume management into a unit providing greater functionality than the traditional separation of those functions allows. Disks, or partitions of disks, are gathered together via RAID sets into **pools** of storage. A pool can hold one or more ZFS file systems. The entire pool's free space is available to all file systems within that pool. ZFS uses the memory model of `malloc()` and `free()` to allocate and release storage for each file system as blocks are used and freed within the file system. As a result, there are no artificial limits on storage use and no need to relocate file systems between volumes or resize volumes. ZFS provides quotas to limit the size of a file system and reservations to assure that a file system can grow by a specified amount, but those variables can be changed by the file-system owner at any time. Figure 9.14(a) depicts traditional volumes and file systems, and Figure 9.14(b) shows the ZFS model.

9.8   Stable-Storage Implementation

In Chapter 5, we introduced the write-ahead log, which requires the availability of stable storage. By definition, information residing in stable storage is never lost. To implement such storage, we need to replicate the required information

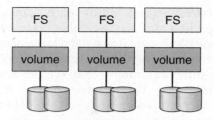

(a) Traditional volumes and file systems.

(b) ZFS and pooled storage.

Figure 9.14 (a) Traditional volumes and file systems. (b) A ZFS pool and file systems.

on multiple storage devices (usually disks) with independent failure modes. We also need to coordinate the writing of updates in a way that guarantees that a failure during an update will not leave all the copies in a damaged state and that, when we are recovering from a failure, we can force all copies to a consistent and correct value, even if another failure occurs during the recovery. In this section, we discuss how to meet these needs.

A disk write results in one of three outcomes:

1. **Successful completion**. The data were written correctly on disk.

2. **Partial failure**. A failure occurred in the midst of transfer, so only some of the sectors were written with the new data, and the sector being written during the failure may have been corrupted.

3. **Total failure**. The failure occurred before the disk write started, so the previous data values on the disk remain intact.

Whenever a failure occurs during writing of a block, the system needs to detect it and invoke a recovery procedure to restore the block to a consistent state. To do that, the system must maintain two physical blocks for each logical block. An output operation is executed as follows:

1. Write the information onto the first physical block.

2. When the first write completes successfully, write the same information onto the second physical block.

3. Declare the operation complete only after the second write completes successfully.

During recovery from a failure, each pair of physical blocks is examined. If both are the same and no detectable error exists, then no further action is necessary. If one block contains a detectable error then we replace its contents with the value of the other block. If neither block contains a detectable error, but the blocks differ in content, then we replace the content of the first block with that of the second. This recovery procedure ensures that a write to stable storage either succeeds completely or results in no change.

We can extend this procedure easily to allow the use of an arbitrarily large number of copies of each block of stable storage. Although having a large number of copies further reduces the probability of a failure, it is usually reasonable to simulate stable storage with only two copies. The data in stable storage are guaranteed to be safe unless a failure destroys all the copies.

Because waiting for disk writes to complete (synchronous I/O) is time consuming, many storage arrays add NVRAM as a cache. Since the memory is nonvolatile (it usually has battery power to back up the unit's power), it can be trusted to store the data en route to the disks. It is thus considered part of the stable storage. Writes to it are much faster than to disk, so performance is greatly improved.

9.9   Summary

Disk drives are the major secondary storage I/O devices on most computers. Most secondary storage devices are either hard disks or magnetic tapes, although solid-state disks are growing in importance. Modern disk drives are structured as large one-dimensional arrays of logical disk blocks. Generally, these logical blocks are 512 bytes in size. Disks may be attached to a computer system in one of two ways: (1) through the local I/O ports on the host computer or (2) through a network connection.

Requests for disk I/O are generated by the file system and by the virtual memory system. Each request specifies the address on the disk to be referenced, in the form of a logical block number. Disk-scheduling algorithms can improve the effective bandwidth, the average response time, and the variance in response time. Algorithms such as SSTF, SCAN, C-SCAN, LOOK, and C-LOOK are designed to make such improvements through strategies for disk-queue ordering. Performance of disk-scheduling algorithms can vary greatly on hard disks. In contrast, because solid-state disks have no moving parts, performance varies little among algorithms, and quite often a simple FCFS strategy is used.

Performance can be harmed by external fragmentation. Some systems have utilities that scan the file system to identify fragmented files; they then move blocks around to decrease the fragmentation. Defragmenting a badly fragmented file system can significantly improve performance, but the system may have reduced performance while the defragmentation is in progress. Sophisticated file systems, such as the UNIX Fast File System, incorporate many strategies to control fragmentation during space allocation so that disk reorganization is not needed.

The operating system manages the disk blocks. First, a disk must be low-level-formatted to create the sectors on the raw hardware—new disks usually come preformatted. Then, the disk is partitioned, file systems are created, and boot blocks are allocated to store the system's bootstrap program. Finally, when a block is corrupted, the system must have a way to lock out that block or to replace it logically with a spare.

Because an efficient swap space is a key to good performance, systems usually bypass the file system and use raw-disk access for paging I/O. Some systems dedicate a raw-disk partition to swap space, and others use a file within the file system instead. Still other systems allow the user or system administrator to make the decision by providing both options.

Because of the amount of storage required on large systems, disks are frequently made redundant via RAID algorithms. These algorithms allow more than one disk to be used for a given operation and allow continued operation and even automatic recovery in the face of a disk failure. RAID algorithms are organized into different levels; each level provides some combination of reliability and high transfer rates.

Review Questions

Review questions for this chapter can be accessed by visiting our website.

Practice Exercises

Answers for the Practice Exercises can be accceed by visiting our website.

9.1 Is disk scheduling, other than FCFS scheduling, useful in a single-user environment? Explain your answer.

9.2 Explain why SSTF scheduling tends to favor middle cylinders over the innermost and outermost cylinders.

9.3 Why is rotational latency usually not considered in disk scheduling? How would you modify SSTF, SCAN, and C-SCAN to include latency optimization?

9.4 Why is it important to balance file-system I/O among the disks and controllers on a system in a multitasking environment?

9.5 What are the tradeoffs involved in rereading code pages from the file system versus using swap space to store them?

9.6 Is there any way to implement truly stable storage? Explain your answer.

9.7 It is sometimes said that tape is a sequential-access medium, whereas a hard disk is a random-access medium. In fact, the suitability of a storage device for random access depends on the transfer size. The term "streaming transfer rate" denotes the rate for a data transfer that is underway, excluding the effect of access latency. In contrast, the "effective transfer rate" is the ratio of total bytes per total seconds, including overhead time such as access latency.

Suppose we have a computer with the following characteristics: the level-2 cache has an access latency of 8 nanoseconds and a streaming transfer rate of 800 megabytes per second, the main memory has an access latency of 60 nanoseconds and a streaming transfer rate of 80 megabytes per second, the hard disk has an access latency of 15 milliseconds and a streaming transfer rate of 5 megabytes per second, and a tape drive has an access latency of 60 seconds and a streaming transfer rate of 2 megabytes per second.

a. Random access causes the effective transfer rate of a device to decrease, because no data are transferred during the access time. For the disk described, what is the effective transfer rate if an average access is followed by a streaming transfer of (1) 512 bytes, (2) 8 kilobytes, (3) 1 megabyte, and (4) 16 megabytes?

b. The utilization of a device is the ratio of effective transfer rate to streaming transfer rate. Calculate the utilization of the disk drive for each of the four transfer sizes given in part a.

c. Suppose that a utilization of 25 percent (or higher) is considered acceptable. Using the performance figures given, compute the smallest transfer size for disk that gives acceptable utilization.

d. Complete the following sentence: A disk is a random-access device for transfers larger than _____ bytes and is a sequential-access device for smaller transfers.

e. Compute the minimum transfer sizes that give acceptable utilization for cache, memory, and tape.

f. When is a tape a random-access device, and when is it a sequential-access device?

9.8   Could a RAID level 1 organization achieve better performance for read requests than a RAID level 0 organization (with nonredundant striping of data)? If so, how?

Exercises

9.9   None of the disk-scheduling disciplines, except FCFS, is truly fair (starvation may occur).

a. Explain why this assertion is true.

b. Describe a way to modify algorithms such as SCAN to ensure fairness.

c. Explain why fairness is an important goal in a time-sharing system.

d. Give three or more examples of circumstances in which it is important that the operating system be unfair in serving I/O requests.

9.10   Explain why SSDs often use an FCFS disk-scheduling algorithm.

9.11   Suppose that a disk drive has 5,000 cylinders, numbered 0 to 4,999. The drive is currently serving a request at cylinder 2,150, and the previous request was at cylinder 1,805. The queue of pending requests, in FIFO order, is:

2,069, 1,212, 2,296, 2,800, 544, 1,618, 356, 1,523, 4,965, 3681

Starting from the current head position, what is the total distance (in cylinders) that the disk arm moves to satisfy all the pending requests for each of the following disk-scheduling algorithms?

a.   FCFS

b.   SSTF

c.   SCAN

d.   LOOK

e.   C-SCAN

f.   C-LOOK

9.12   Elementary physics states that when an object is subjected to a constant acceleration a, the relationship between distance d and time t is given by $d = \frac{1}{2}at^2$. Suppose that, during a seek, the disk in Exercise 9.11 accelerates the disk arm at a constant rate for the first half of the seek, then decelerates the disk arm at the same rate for the second half of the seek. Assume that the disk can perform a seek to an adjacent cylinder in 1 millisecond and a full-stroke seek over all 5,000 cylinders in 18 milliseconds.

a.   The distance of a seek is the number of cylinders over which the head moves. Explain why the seek time is proportional to the square root of the seek distance.

b.   Write an equation for the seek time as a function of the seek distance. This equation should be of the form $t = x + y\sqrt{L}$, where t is the time in milliseconds and L is the seek distance in cylinders.

c.   Calculate the total seek time for each of the schedules in Exercise 9.11. Determine which schedule is the fastest (has the smallest total seek time).

d.   The **percentage speedup** is the time saved divided by the original time. What is the percentage speedup of the fastest schedule over FCFS?

9.13   Suppose that the disk in Exercise 9.12 rotates at 7,200 RPM.

a.   What is the average rotational latency of this disk drive?

b.   What seek distance can be covered in the time that you found for part a?

9.14   Describe some advantages and disadvantages of using SSDs as a caching tier and as a disk-drive replacement compared with using only hard disks.

9.15   Compare the performance of C-SCAN and SCAN scheduling, assuming a uniform distribution of requests. Consider the average response time (the time between the arrival of a request and the completion of that request's service), the variation in response time, and the effective bandwidth. How does performance depend on the relative sizes of seek time and rotational latency?

9.16   Requests are not usually uniformly distributed. For example, we can expect a cylinder containing the file-system metadata to be accessed more frequently than a cylinder containing only files. Suppose you know that 50 percent of the requests are for a small, fixed number of cylinders.

   a.   Would any of the scheduling algorithms discussed in this chapter be particularly good for this case? Explain your answer.

   b.   Propose a disk-scheduling algorithm that gives even better performance by taking advantage of this "hot spot" on the disk.

9.17   Consider a RAID level 5 organization comprising five disks, with the parity for sets of four blocks on four disks stored on the fifth disk. How many blocks are accessed in order to perform the following?

   a.   A write of one block of data

   b.   A write of seven continuous blocks of data

9.18   Compare the throughput achieved by a RAID level 5 organization with that achieved by a RAID level 1 organization for the following:

   a.   Read operations on single blocks

   b.   Read operations on multiple contiguous blocks

9.19   Compare the performance of write operations achieved by a RAID level 5 organization with that achieved by a RAID level 1 organization.

9.20   Assume that you have a mixed configuration comprising disks organized as RAID level 1 and RAID level 5 disks. Assume that the system has flexibility in deciding which disk organization to use for storing a particular file. Which files should be stored in the RAID level 1 disks and which in the RAID level 5 disks in order to optimize performance?

9.21   The reliability of a hard-disk drive is typically described in terms of a quantity called **mean time between failures** (MTBF). Although this quantity is called a "time," the MTBF actually is measured in drive-hours per failure.

   a.   If a system contains 1,000 disk drives, each of which has a 750,000-hour MTBF, which of the following best describes how often a drive failure will occur in that disk farm: once per thousand years, once per century, once per decade, once per year, once per month, once per week, once per day, once per hour, once per minute, or once per second?

   b.   Mortality statistics indicate that, on the average, a U.S. resident has about 1 chance in 1,000 of dying between the ages of 20 and 21. Deduce the MTBF hours for 20-year-olds. Convert this figure from hours to years. What does this MTBF tell you about the expected lifetime of a 20-year-old?

c. The manufacturer guarantees a 1-million-hour MTBF for a certain model of disk drive. What can you conclude about the number of years for which one of these drives is under warranty?

9.22 Discuss the relative advantages and disadvantages of sector sparing and sector slipping.

9.23 Discuss the reasons why the operating system might require accurate information on how blocks are stored on a disk. How could the operating system improve file-system performance with this knowledge?

Programming Problems

9.24 Write a program that implements the following disk-scheduling algorithms:

a. FCFS

b. SSTF

c. SCAN

d. C-SCAN

e. LOOK

f. C-LOOK

Your program will service a disk with 5,000 cylinders numbered 0 to 4,999. The program will generate a random series of 1,000 cylinder requests and service them according to each of the algorithms listed above. The program will be passed the initial position of the disk head (as a parameter on the command line) and report the total amount of head movement required by each algorithm.

Bibliographical Notes

[Services (2012)] provides an overview of data storage in a variety of modern computing environments. [Teorey and Pinkerton (1972)] present an early comparative analysis of disk-scheduling algorithms using simulations that model a disk for which seek time is linear in the number of cylinders crossed. Scheduling optimizations that exploit disk idle times are discussed in [Lumb et al. (2000)]. [Kim et al. (2009)] discusses disk-scheduling algorithms for SSDs.

Discussions of redundant arrays of independent disks (RAIDs) are presented by [Patterson et al. (1988)].

[Russinovich and Solomon (2009)], [McDougall and Mauro (2007)], and [Love (2010)] discuss file system details in Windows, Solaris, and Linux, respectively.

The I/O size and randomness of the workload influence disk performance considerably. [Ousterhout et al. (1985)] and [Ruemmler and Wilkes (1993)] report numerous interesting workload characteristics—for example, most files are small, most newly created files are deleted soon thereafter, most files that are opened for reading are read sequentially in their entirety, and most seeks are short.

The concept of a storage hierarchy has been studied for more than forty years. For instance, a 1970 paper by [Mattson et al. (1970)] describes a mathematical approach to predicting the performance of a storage hierarchy.

Bibliography

[Kim et al. (2009)]   J. Kim, Y. Oh, E. Kim, J. C. D. Lee, and S. Noh, "Disk Schedulers for Solid State Drivers" (2009), pages 295–304.

[Love (2010)]   R. Love, *Linux Kernel Development*, Third Edition, Developer's Library (2010).

[Lumb et al. (2000)]   C. Lumb, J. Schindler, G. R. Ganger, D. F. Nagle, and E. Riedel, "Towards Higher Disk Head Utilization: Extracting Free Bandwidth From Busy Disk Drives", *Symposium on Operating Systems Design and Implementation* (2000), pages 87–102.

[Mattson et al. (1970)]   R. L. Mattson, J. Gecsei, D. R. Slutz, and I. L. Traiger, "Evaluation Techniques for Storage Hierarchies", *IBM Systems Journal*, Volume 9, Number 2 (1970), pages 78–117.

[McDougall and Mauro (2007)]   R. McDougall and J. Mauro, *Solaris Internals*, Second Edition, Prentice Hall (2007).

[Ousterhout et al. (1985)]   J. K. Ousterhout, H. D. Costa, D. Harrison, J. A. Kunze, M. Kupfer, and J. G. Thompson, "A Trace-Driven Analysis of the UNIX 4.2 BSD File System", *Proceedings of the ACM Symposium on Operating Systems Principles* (1985), pages 15–24.

[Patterson et al. (1988)]   D. A. Patterson, G. Gibson, and R. H. Katz, "A Case for Redundant Arrays of Inexpensive Disks (RAID)", *Proceedings of the ACM SIGMOD International Conference on the Management of Data* (1988), pages 109–116.

[Ruemmler and Wilkes (1993)]   C. Ruemmler and J. Wilkes, "Unix Disk Access Patterns", *Proceedings of the Winter USENIX Conference* (1993), pages 405–420.

[Russinovich and Solomon (2009)]   M. E. Russinovich and D. A. Solomon, *Windows Internals: Including Windows Server 2008 and Windows Vista*, Fifth Edition, Microsoft Press (2009).

[Services (2012)]   E. E. Services, *Information Storage and Management: Storing, Managing, and Protecting Digital Information in Classic, Virtualized, and Cloud Environments*, Wiley (2012).

[Teorey and Pinkerton (1972)]   T. J. Teorey and T. B. Pinkerton, "A Comparative Analysis of Disk Scheduling Policies", *Communications of the ACM*, Volume 15, Number 3 (1972), pages 177–184.

File-System Interface

For most users, the file system is the most visible aspect of an operating system. It provides the mechanism for on-line storage of and access to both data and programs of the operating system and all the users of the computer system. The file system consists of two distinct parts: a collection of files, each storing related data, and a directory structure, which organizes and provides information about all the files in the system. File systems live on devices, which we described in the preceding chapter and will continue to discuss in the following one. In this chapter, we consider the various aspects of files and the major directory structures. We also discuss the semantics of sharing files among multiple processes, users, and computers. Finally, we discuss ways to handle file protection, necessary when we have multiple users and we want to control who may access files and how files may be accessed.

CHAPTER OBJECTIVES

- To explain the function of file systems.
- To describe the interfaces to file systems.
- To discuss file-system design tradeoffs, including access methods, file sharing, file locking, and directory structures.
- To explore file-system protection.

10.1 File Concept

Computers can store information on various storage media, such as hard disks, magnetic tapes, and optical disks. So that the computer system will be convenient to use, the operating system provides a uniform logical view of stored information. The operating system abstracts from the physical properties of its storage devices to define a logical storage unit, the file. Files are mapped by the operating system onto physical devices. These storage devices are usually nonvolatile, so the contents are persistent between system reboots.

A file is a named collection of related information that is recorded on secondary storage. From a user's perspective, a file is the smallest allotment of logical secondary storage; that is, data cannot be written to secondary storage unless they are within a file. Commonly, files represent programs (both source and object forms) and data. Data files may be numeric, alphabetic, alphanumeric, or binary. Files may be free form, such as text files, or may be formatted rigidly. In general, a file is a sequence of bits, bytes, lines, or records, the meaning of which is defined by the file's creator and user. The concept of a file is thus extremely general.

The information in a file is defined by its creator. Many different types of information may be stored in a file—source or executable programs, numeric or text data, photos, music, video, and so on. A file has a certain defined structure, which depends on its type. A text file is a sequence of characters organized into lines (and possibly pages). A source file is a sequence of functions, each of which is further organized as declarations followed by executable statements. An executable file is a series of code sections that the loader can bring into memory and execute.

10.1.1 File Attributes

A file is named, for the convenience of its human users, and is referred to by its name. A name is usually a string of characters, such as example.c. Some systems differentiate between uppercase and lowercase characters in names, whereas other systems do not. When a file is named, it becomes independent of the process, the user, and even the system that created it. For instance, one user might create the file example.c, and another user might edit that file by specifying its name. The file's owner might write the file to a USB disk, send it as an e-mail attachment, or copy it across a network, and it could still be called example.c on the destination system.

A file's attributes vary from one operating system to another but typically consist of these:

- **Name**. The symbolic file name is the only information kept in human-readable form.

- **Identifier**. This unique tag, usually a number, identifies the file within the file system; it is the non-human-readable name for the file.

- **Type**. This information is needed for systems that support different types of files.

- **Location**. This information is a pointer to a device and to the location of the file on that device.

- **Size**. The current size of the file (in bytes, words, or blocks) and possibly the maximum allowed size are included in this attribute.

- **Protection**. Access-control information determines who can do reading, writing, executing, and so on.

- **Time, date, and user identification**. This information may be kept for creation, last modification, and last use. These data can be useful for protection, security, and usage monitoring.

Some newer file systems also support **extended file attributes**, including character encoding of the file and security features such as a file checksum. Figure 10.1 illustrates a **file info window** on Mac OS X, which displays a file's attributes.

The information about all files is kept in the directory structure, which also resides on secondary storage. Typically, a directory entry consists of the file's name and its unique identifier. The identifier in turn locates the other

Figure 10.1   A file info window on Mac OS X.

file attributes. It may take more than a kilobyte to record this information for each file. In a system with many files, the size of the directory itself may be megabytes. Because directories, like files, must be nonvolatile, they must be stored on the device and brought into memory piecemeal, as needed.

10.1.2   File Operations

A file is an abstract data type. To define a file properly, we need to consider the operations that can be performed on files. The operating system can provide system calls to create, write, read, reposition, delete, and truncate files. Let's examine what the operating system must do to perform each of these six basic file operations. It should then be easy to see how other similar operations, such as renaming a file, can be implemented.

- **Creating a file**. Two steps are necessary to create a file. First, space in the file system must be found for the file. We discuss how to allocate space for the file in Chapter 11. Second, an entry for the new file must be made in the directory.

- **Writing a file**. To write a file, we make a system call specifying both the name of the file and the information to be written to the file. Given the name of the file, the system searches the directory to find the file's location. The system must keep a **write pointer** to the location in the file where the next write is to take place. The write pointer must be updated whenever a write occurs.

- **Reading a file**. To read from a file, we use a system call that specifies the name of the file and where (in memory) the next block of the file should be put. Again, the directory is searched for the associated entry, and the system needs to keep a **read pointer** to the location in the file where the next read is to take place. Once the read has taken place, the read pointer is updated. Because a process is usually either reading from or writing to a file, the current operation location can be kept as a per-process **current-file-position pointer**. Both the read and write operations use this same pointer, saving space and reducing system complexity.

- **Repositioning within a file**. The directory is searched for the appropriate entry, and the current-file-position pointer is repositioned to a given value. Repositioning within a file need not involve any actual I/O. This file operation is also known as a file **seek**.

- **Deleting a file**. To delete a file, we search the directory for the named file. Having found the associated directory entry, we release all file space, so that it can be reused by other files, and erase the directory entry.

- **Truncating a file**. The user may want to erase the contents of a file but keep its attributes. Rather than forcing the user to delete the file and then recreate it, this function allows all attributes to remain unchanged—except for file length—but lets the file be reset to length zero and its file space released.

These six basic operations comprise the minimal set of required file operations. Other common operations include appending new information to the end of an existing file and renaming an existing file. These primitive operations can then be combined to perform other file operations. For instance, we can create a copy of a file—or copy the file to another I/O device, such as a printer or a display—by creating a new file and then reading from the old and writing to the new. We also want to have operations that allow a user to get and set the various attributes of a file. For example, we may want to have operations that allow a user to determine the status of a file, such as the file's length, and to set file attributes, such as the file's owner.

Most of the file operations mentioned involve searching the directory for the entry associated with the named file. To avoid this constant searching, many systems require that an open() system call be made before a file is first used. The operating system keeps a table, called the **open-file table**, containing information about all open files. When a file operation is requested, the file is specified via an index into this table, so no searching is required. When the file is no longer being actively used, it is closed by the process, and the operating system removes its entry from the open-file table. create() and delete() are system calls that work with closed rather than open files.

Some systems implicitly open a file when the first reference to it is made. The file is automatically closed when the job or program that opened the file terminates. Most systems, however, require that the programmer open a file explicitly with the open() system call before that file can be used. The open() operation takes a file name and searches the directory, copying the directory entry into the open-file table. The open() call can also accept access-mode information—create, read-only, read–write, append-only, and so on. This mode is checked against the file's permissions. If the request mode is allowed, the file is opened for the process. The open() system call typically returns a pointer to the entry in the open-file table. This pointer, not the actual file name, is used in all I/O operations, avoiding any further searching and simplifying the system-call interface.

The implementation of the open() and close() operations is more complicated in an environment where several processes may open the file simultaneously. This may occur in a system where several different applications open the same file at the same time. Typically, the operating system uses two levels of internal tables: a per-process table and a system-wide table. The per-process table tracks all files that a process has open. Stored in this table is information regarding the process's use of the file. For instance, the current file pointer for each file is found here. Access rights to the file and accounting information can also be included.

Each entry in the per-process table in turn points to a system-wide open-file table. The system-wide table contains process-independent information, such as the location of the file on disk, access dates, and file size. Once a file has been opened by one process, the system-wide table includes an entry for the file. When another process executes an open() call, a new entry is simply added to the process's open-file table pointing to the appropriate entry in the system-wide table. Typically, the open-file table also has an **open count** associated with each file to indicate how many processes have the file open. Each close() decreases this open count, and when the open count reaches zero, the file is no longer in use, and the file's entry is removed from the open-file table.

In summary, several pieces of information are associated with an open file.

- **File pointer**. On systems that do not include a file offset as part of the read() and write() system calls, the system must track the last read–write location as a current-file-position pointer. This pointer is unique to each process operating on the file and therefore must be kept separate from the on-disk file attributes.

- **File-open count**. As files are closed, the operating system must reuse its open-file table entries, or it could run out of space in the table. Multiple processes may have opened a file, and the system must wait for the last file to close before removing the open-file table entry. The file-open count tracks the number of opens and closes and reaches zero on the last close. The system can then remove the entry.

- **Disk location of the file**. Most file operations require the system to modify data within the file. The information needed to locate the file on disk is kept in memory so that the system does not have to read it from disk for each operation.

- **Access rights**. Each process opens a file in an access mode. This information is stored on the per-process table so the operating system can allow or deny subsequent I/O requests.

Some operating systems provide facilities for locking an open file (or sections of a file). File locks allow one process to lock a file and prevent other processes from gaining access to it. File locks are useful for files that are shared by several processes—for example, a system log file that can be accessed and modified by a number of processes in the system.

File locks provide functionality similar to reader–writer locks, covered in Section 5.7.2. A shared lock is akin to a reader lock in that several processes can acquire the lock concurrently. An exclusive lock behaves like a writer lock; only one process at a time can acquire such a lock. It is important to note that not all operating systems provide both types of locks: some systems only provide exclusive file locking.

FILE LOCKING IN JAVA

In the Java API, acquiring a lock requires first obtaining the FileChannel for the file to be locked. The lock() method of the FileChannel is used to acquire the lock. The API of the lock() method is

    FileLock lock(long begin, long end, boolean shared)

where begin and end are the beginning and ending positions of the region being locked. Setting shared to true is for shared locks; setting shared to false acquires the lock exclusively. The lock is released by invoking the release() of the FileLock returned by the lock() operation.

The program in Figure 10.2 illustrates file locking in Java. This program acquires two locks on the file file.txt. The first half of the file is acquired as an exclusive lock; the lock for the second half is a shared lock.

FILE LOCKING IN JAVA (Continued)

```java
import java.io.*;
import java.nio.channels.*;

public class LockingExample {
  public static final boolean EXCLUSIVE = false;
  public static final boolean SHARED = true;

  public static void main(String args[]) throws IOException {
    FileLock sharedLock = null;
    FileLock exclusiveLock = null;

    try {
    RandomAccessFile raf = new RandomAccessFile("file.txt","rw");

    // get the channel for the file
    FileChannel ch = raf.getChannel();

    // this locks the first half of the file - exclusive
    exclusiveLock = ch.lock(0, raf.length()/2, EXCLUSIVE);

    /** Now modify the data . . . */

    // release the lock
    exclusiveLock.release();

    // this locks the second half of the file - shared
    sharedLock = ch.lock(raf.length()/2+1,raf.length(),SHARED);

    /** Now read the data . . . */

    // release the lock
    sharedLock.release();
    } catch (java.io.IOException ioe) {
    System.err.println(ioe);
    }
    finally {
    if (exclusiveLock != null)
        exclusiveLock.release();
    if (sharedLock != null)
        sharedLock.release();
    }
  }
}
```

Figure 10.2 File-locking example in Java.

Furthermore, operating systems may provide either **mandatory** or **advisory** file-locking mechanisms. If a lock is mandatory, then once a process acquires an exclusive lock, the operating system will prevent any other process from accessing the locked file. For example, assume a process acquires an exclusive lock on the file system.log. If we attempt to open system.log from another process—for example, a text editor—the operating system will prevent access until the exclusive lock is released. This occurs even if the text editor is not written explicitly to acquire the lock. Alternatively, if the lock is advisory, then the operating system will not prevent the text editor from acquiring access to system.log. Rather, the text editor must be written so that it manually acquires the lock before accessing the file. In other words, if the locking scheme is mandatory, the operating system ensures locking integrity. For advisory locking, it is up to software developers to ensure that locks are appropriately acquired and released. As a general rule, Windows operating systems adopt mandatory locking, and UNIX systems employ advisory locks.

The use of file locks requires the same precautions as ordinary process synchronization. For example, programmers developing on systems with mandatory locking must be careful to hold exclusive file locks only while they are accessing the file. Otherwise, they will prevent other processes from accessing the file as well. Furthermore, some measures must be taken to ensure that two or more processes do not become involved in a deadlock while trying to acquire file locks.

10.1.3   File Types

When we design a file system—indeed, an entire operating system—we always consider whether the operating system should recognize and support file types. If an operating system recognizes the type of a file, it can then operate on the file in reasonable ways. For example, a common mistake occurs when a user tries to output the binary-object form of a program. This attempt normally produces garbage; however, the attempt can succeed if the operating system has been told that the file is a binary-object program.

A common technique for implementing file types is to include the type as part of the file name. The name is split into two parts—a name and an extension, usually separated by a period (Figure 10.3). In this way, the user and the operating system can tell from the name alone what the type of a file is. Most operating systems allow users to specify a file name as a sequence of characters followed by a period and terminated by an extension made up of additional characters. Examples include resume.docx, server.c, and ReaderThread.cpp.

The system uses the extension to indicate the type of the file and the type of operations that can be done on that file. Only a file with a .com, .exe, or .sh extension can be executed, for instance. The .com and .exe files are two forms of binary executable files, whereas the .sh file is a shell script containing, in ASCII format, commands to the operating system. Application programs also use extensions to indicate file types in which they are interested. For example, Java compilers expect source files to have a .java extension, and the Microsoft Word word processor expects its files to end with a .doc or .docx extension. These extensions are not always required, so a user may specify a file without the extension (to save typing), and the application will look for a file with the given name and the extension it expects. Because these extensions are not supported by the operating system, they can be considered "hints" to the applications that operate on them.

file type	usual extension	function
executable	exe, com, bin or none	ready-to-run machine-language program
object	obj, o	compiled, machine language, not linked
source code	c, cc, java, perl, asm	source code in various languages
batch	bat, sh	commands to the command interpreter
markup	xml, html, tex	textual data, documents
word processor	xml, rtf, docx	various word-processor formats
library	lib, a, so, dll	libraries of routines for programmers
print or view	gif, pdf, jpg	ASCII or binary file in a format for printing or viewing
archive	rar, zip, tar	related files grouped into one file, sometimes compressed, for archiving or storage
multimedia	mpeg, mov, mp3, mp4, avi	binary file containing audio or A/V information

Figure 10.3   Common file types.

Consider, too, the Mac OS X operating system. In this system, each file has a type, such as .app (for application). Each file also has a creator attribute containing the name of the program that created it. This attribute is set by the operating system during the create() call, so its use is enforced and supported by the system. For instance, a file produced by a word processor has the word processor's name as its creator. When the user opens that file, by double-clicking the mouse on the icon representing the file, the word processor is invoked automatically and the file is loaded, ready to be edited.

The UNIX system uses a crude magic number stored at the beginning of some files to indicate roughly the type of the file—executable program, shell script, PDF file, and so on. Not all files have magic numbers, so system features cannot be based solely on this information. UNIX does not record the name of the creating program, either. UNIX does allow file-name-extension hints, but these extensions are neither enforced nor depended on by the operating system; they are meant mostly to aid users in determining what type of contents the file contains. Extensions can be used or ignored by a given application, but that is up to the application's programmer.

10.1.4   File Structure

File types also can be used to indicate the internal structure of the file. As mentioned in Section 10.1.3, source and object files have structures that match the expectations of the programs that read them. Further, certain files must conform to a required structure that is understood by the operating system. For example, the operating system requires that an executable file have a specific structure so that it can determine where in memory to load the file and what the location of the first instruction is. Some operating systems extend this idea into a set of system-supported file structures, with sets of special operations for manipulating files with those structures.

This point brings us to one of the disadvantages of having the operating system support multiple file structures: the resulting size of the operating system is cumbersome. If the operating system defines five different file structures, it needs to contain the code to support these file structures. In addition, it may be necessary to define every file as one of the file types supported by the operating system. When new applications require information structured in ways not supported by the operating system, severe problems may result.

For example, assume that a system supports two types of files: text files (composed of ASCII characters separated by a carriage return and line feed) and executable binary files. Now, if we (as users) want to define an encrypted file to protect the contents from being read by unauthorized people, we may find neither file type to be appropriate. The encrypted file is not ASCII text lines but rather is (apparently) random bits. Although it may appear to be a binary file, it is not executable. As a result, we may have to circumvent or misuse the operating system's file-type mechanism or abandon our encryption scheme.

Some operating systems impose (and support) a minimal number of file structures. This approach has been adopted in UNIX, Windows, and others. UNIX considers each file to be a sequence of 8-bit bytes; no interpretation of these bits is made by the operating system. This scheme provides maximum flexibility but little support. Each application program must include its own code to interpret an input file as to the appropriate structure. However, all operating systems must support at least one structure—that of an executable file—so that the system is able to load and run programs.

10.1.5 Internal File Structure

Internally, locating an offset within a file can be complicated for the operating system. Disk systems typically have a well-defined block size determined by the size of a sector. All disk I/O is performed in units of one block (physical record), and all blocks are the same size. It is unlikely that the physical record size will exactly match the length of the desired logical record. Logical records may even vary in length. Packing a number of logical records into physical blocks is a common solution to this problem.

For example, the UNIX operating system defines all files to be simply streams of bytes. Each byte is individually addressable by its offset from the beginning (or end) of the file. In this case, the logical record size is 1 byte. The file system automatically packs and unpacks bytes into physical disk blocks— say, 512 bytes per block—as necessary.

The logical record size, physical block size, and packing technique determine how many logical records are in each physical block. The packing can be done either by the user's application program or by the operating system. In either case, the file may be considered a sequence of blocks. All the basic I/O

Figure 10.4   Sequential-access file.

functions operate in terms of blocks. The conversion from logical records to physical blocks is a relatively simple software problem.

Because disk space is always allocated in blocks, some portion of the last block of each file is generally wasted. If each block were 512 bytes, for example, then a file of 1,949 bytes would be allocated four blocks (2,048 bytes); the last 99 bytes would be wasted. The waste incurred to keep everything in units of blocks (instead of bytes) is internal fragmentation. All file systems suffer from internal fragmentation; the larger the block size, the greater the internal fragmentation.

10.2   Access Methods

Files store information. When it is used, this information must be accessed and read into computer memory. The information in the file can be accessed in several ways. Some systems provide only one access method for files. while others support many access methods, and choosing the right one for a particular application is a major design problem.

10.2.1   Sequential Access

The simplest access method is **sequential access**. Information in the file is processed in order, one record after the other. This mode of access is by far the most common; for example, editors and compilers usually access files in this fashion.

Reads and writes make up the bulk of the operations on a file. A read operation—`read_next()`—reads the next portion of the file and automatically advances a file pointer, which tracks the I/O location. Similarly, the write operation—`write_next()`—appends to the end of the file and advances to the end of the newly written material (the new end of file). Such a file can be reset to the beginning, and on some systems, a program may be able to skip forward or backward n records for some integer n—perhaps only for $n = 1$. Sequential access, which is depicted in Figure 10.4, is based on a tape model of a file and works as well on sequential-access devices as it does on random-access ones.

10.2.2   Direct Access

Another method is **direct access** (or **relative access**). Here, a file is made up of fixed-length **logical records** that allow programs to read and write records rapidly in no particular order. The direct-access method is based on a disk model of a file, since disks allow random access to any file block. For direct access, the file is viewed as a numbered sequence of blocks or records. Thus, we may read block 14, then read block 53, and then write block 7. There are no restrictions on the order of reading or writing for a direct-access file.

Direct-access files are of great use for immediate access to large amounts of information. Databases are often of this type. When a query concerning a particular subject arrives, we compute which block contains the answer and then read that block directly to provide the desired information.

As a simple example, on an airline-reservation system, we might store all the information about a particular flight (for example, flight 713) in the block identified by the flight number. Thus, the number of available seats for flight 713 is stored in block 713 of the reservation file. To store information about a larger set, such as people, we might compute a hash function on the people's names or search a small in-memory index to determine a block to read and search.

For the direct-access method, the file operations must be modified to include the block number as a parameter. Thus, we have read(n), where n is the block number, rather than read_next(), and write(n) rather than write_next(). An alternative approach is to retain read_next() and write_next(), as with sequential access, and to add an operation position_file(n) where n is the block number. Then, to effect a read(n), we would position_file(n) and then read_next().

The block number provided by the user to the operating system is normally a **relative block number**. A relative block number is an index relative to the beginning of the file. Thus, the first relative block of the file is 0, the next is 1, and so on, even though the absolute disk address may be 14703 for the first block and 3192 for the second. The use of relative block numbers allows the operating system to decide where the file should be placed (called the **allocation problem**, as we discuss in Chapter 11) and helps to prevent the user from accessing portions of the file system that may not be part of her file. Some systems start their relative block numbers at 0; others start at 1.

How, then, does the system satisfy a request for record N in a file? Assuming we have a logical record length L, the request for record N is turned into an I/O request for L bytes starting at location $L * (N)$ within the file (assuming the first record is $N = 0$). Since logical records are of a fixed size, it is also easy to read, write, or delete a record.

Not all operating systems support both sequential and direct access for files. Some systems allow only sequential file access; others allow only direct access. Some systems require that a file be defined as sequential or direct when it is created. Such a file can be accessed only in a manner consistent with its declaration. We can easily simulate sequential access on a direct-access file by simply keeping a variable cp that defines our current position, as shown in Figure 10.5. Simulating a direct-access file on a sequential-access file, however, is extremely inefficient and clumsy.

10.2.3 Other Access Methods

Other access methods can be built on top of a direct-access method. These methods generally involve the construction of an index for the file. The index, like an index in the back of a book, contains pointers to the various blocks. To

sequential access	implementation for direct access
reset	cp = 0;
read_next	read cp ; cp = cp + 1;
write_next	write cp; cp = cp + 1;

Figure 10.5 Simulation of sequential access on a direct-access file.

find a record in the file, we first search the index and then use the pointer to access the file directly and to find the desired record.

For example, a retail-price file might list the universal product codes (UPCs) for items, with the associated prices. Each record consists of a 10-digit UPC and a 6-digit price, for a 16-byte record. If our disk has 1,024 bytes per block, we can store 64 records per block. A file of 120,000 records would occupy about 2,000 blocks (2 million bytes). By keeping the file sorted by UPC, we can define an index consisting of the first UPC in each block. This index would have 2,000 entries of 10 digits each, or 20,000 bytes, and thus could be kept in memory. To find the price of a particular item, we can make a binary search of the index. From this search, we learn exactly which block contains the desired record and access that block. This structure allows us to search a large file doing little I/O.

With large files, the index file itself may become too large to be kept in memory. One solution is to create an index for the index file. The primary index file contains pointers to secondary index files, which point to the actual data items.

For example, IBM's indexed sequential-access method (ISAM) uses a small master index that points to disk blocks of a secondary index. The secondary index blocks point to the actual file blocks. The file is kept sorted on a defined key. To find a particular item, we first make a binary search of the master index, which provides the block number of the secondary index. This block is read in, and again a binary search is used to find the block containing the desired record. Finally, this block is searched sequentially. In this way, any record can be located from its key by at most two direct-access reads. Figure 10.6 shows a similar situation as implemented by VMS index and relative files.

10.3 Directory and Disk Structure

Next, we consider how to store files. Certainly, no general-purpose computer stores just one file. There are typically thousands, millions, even billions of files within a computer. Files are stored on random-access storage devices, including hard disks, optical disks, and solid-state (memory-based) disks.

A storage device can be used in its entirety for a file system. It can also be subdivided for finer-grained control. For example, a disk can be **partitioned** into quarters, and each quarter can hold a separate file system. Storage devices can also be collected together into RAID sets that provide protection from the failure of a single disk (as described in Section 9.7). Sometimes, disks are subdivided and also collected into RAID sets.

Figure 10.6   Example of index and relative files.

Partitioning is useful for limiting the sizes of individual file systems, putting multiple file-system types on the same device, or leaving part of the device available for other uses, such as swap space or unformatted (raw) disk space. A file system can be created on each of these parts of the disk. Any entity containing a file system is generally known as a **volume**. The volume may be a subset of a device, a whole device, or multiple devices linked together into a RAID set. Each volume can be thought of as a virtual disk. Volumes can also store multiple operating systems, allowing a system to boot and run more than one operating system.

Each volume that contains a file system must also contain information about the files in the system. This information is kept in entries in a **device directory** or **volume table of contents**. The device directory (more commonly known simply as the **directory**) records information—such as name, location, size, and type—for all files on that volume. Figure 10.7 shows a typical file-system organization.

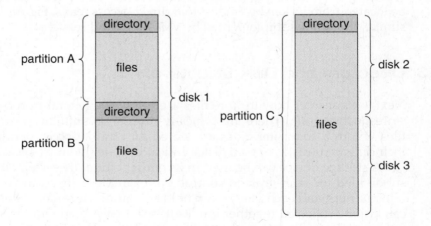

Figure 10.7   A typical file-system organization.

/	ufs
/devices	devfs
/dev	dev
/system/contract	ctfs
/proc	proc
/etc/mnttab	mntfs
/etc/svc/volatile	tmpfs
/system/object	objfs
/lib/libc.so.1	lofs
/dev/fd	fd
/var	ufs
/tmp	tmpfs
/var/run	tmpfs
/opt	ufs
/zpbge	zfs
/zpbge/backup	zfs
/export/home	zfs
/var/mail	zfs
/var/spool/mqueue	zfs
/zpbg	zfs
/zpbg/zones	zfs

Figure 10.8 Solaris file systems.

10.3.1 Storage Structure

As we have just seen, a general-purpose computer system has multiple storage devices, and those devices can be sliced up into volumes that hold file systems. Computer systems may have zero or more file systems, and the file systems may be of varying types. For example, a typical Solaris system may have dozens of file systems of a dozen different types, as shown in the file system list in Figure 10.8.

In this book, we consider only general-purpose file systems. It is worth noting, though, that there are many special-purpose file systems. Consider the types of file systems in the Solaris example mentioned above:

- **tmpfs**—a "temporary" file system that is created in volatile main memory and has its contents erased if the system reboots or crashes

- **objfs**—a "virtual" file system (essentially an interface to the kernel that looks like a file system) that gives debuggers access to kernel symbols

- **ctfs**—a virtual file system that maintains "contract" information to manage which processes start when the system boots and must continue to run during operation

- **lofs**—a "loop back" file system that allows one file system to be accessed in place of another one

- **procfs**—a virtual file system that presents information on all processes as a file system

- **ufs, zfs**—general-purpose file systems

The file systems of computers, then, can be extensive. Even within a file system, it is useful to segregate files into groups and manage and act on those groups. This organization involves the use of directories. In the remainder of this section, we explore the topic of directory structure.

10.3.2   Directory Overview

The directory can be viewed as a symbol table that translates file names into their directory entries. If we take such a view, we see that the directory itself can be organized in many ways. The organization must allow us to insert entries, to delete entries, to search for a named entry, and to list all the entries in the directory. In this section, we examine several schemes for defining the logical structure of the directory system.

When considering a particular directory structure, we need to keep in mind the operations that are to be performed on a directory:

- **Search for a file**. We need to be able to search a directory structure to find the entry for a particular file. Since files have symbolic names, and similar names may indicate a relationship among files, we may want to be able to find all files whose names match a particular pattern.

- **Create a file**. New files need to be created and added to the directory.

- **Delete a file**. When a file is no longer needed, we want to be able to remove it from the directory.

- **List a directory**. We need to be able to list the files in a directory and the contents of the directory entry for each file in the list.

- **Rename a file**. Because the name of a file represents its contents to its users, we must be able to change the name when the contents or use of the file changes. Renaming a file may also allow its position within the directory structure to be changed.

- **Traverse the file system**. We may wish to access every directory and every file within a directory structure. For reliability, it is a good idea to save the contents and structure of the entire file system at regular intervals. Often, we do this by copying all files to magnetic tape. This technique provides a backup copy in case of system failure. In addition, if a file is no longer in use, the file can be copied to tape and the disk space of that file released for reuse by another file.

In the following sections, we describe the most common schemes for defining the logical structure of a directory.

10.3.3   Single-Level Directory

The simplest directory structure is the single-level directory. All files are contained in the same directory, which is easy to support and understand (Figure 10.9).

A single-level directory has significant limitations, however, when the number of files increases or when the system has more than one user. Since all files are in the same directory, they must have unique names. If two users call

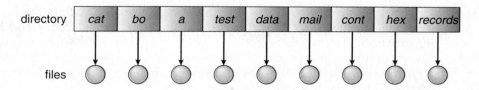

Figure 10.9   Single-level directory.

their data file `test.txt`, then the unique-name rule is violated. For example, in one programming class, 23 students called the program for their second assignment `prog2.c`; another 11 called it `assign2.c`. Fortunately, most file systems support file names of up to 255 characters, so it is relatively easy to select unique file names.

Even a single user on a single-level directory may find it difficult to remember the names of all the files as the number of files increases. It is not uncommon for a user to have hundreds of files on one computer system and an equal number of additional files on another system. Keeping track of so many files is a daunting task.

10.3.4 Two-Level Directory

As we have seen, a single-level directory often leads to confusion of file names among different users. The standard solution is to create a separate directory for each user.

In the two-level directory structure, each user has his own **user file directory (UFD)**. The UFDs have similar structures, but each lists only the files of a single user. When a user job starts or a user logs in, the system's **master file directory (MFD)** is searched. The MFD is indexed by user name or account number, and each entry points to the UFD for that user (Figure 10.10).

When a user refers to a particular file, only his own UFD is searched. Thus, different users may have files with the same name, as long as all the file names within each UFD are unique. To create a file for a user, the operating system searches only that user's UFD to ascertain whether another file of that name exists. To delete a file, the operating system confines its search to the local UFD; thus, it cannot accidentally delete another user's file that has the same name.

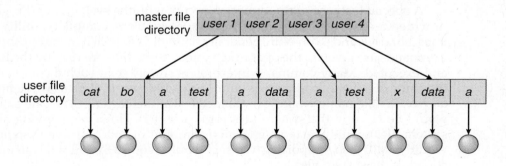

Figure 10.10   Two-level directory structure.

The user directories themselves must be created and deleted as necessary. A special system program is run with the appropriate user name and account information. The program creates a new UFD and adds an entry for it to the MFD. The execution of this program might be restricted to system administrators. The allocation of disk space for user directories can be handled with the techniques discussed in Chapter 11 for files themselves.

Although the two-level directory structure solves the name-collision problem, it still has disadvantages. This structure effectively isolates one user from another. Isolation is an advantage when the users are completely independent but is a disadvantage when the users want to cooperate on some task and to access one another's files. Some systems simply do not allow local user files to be accessed by other users.

If access is to be permitted, one user must have the ability to name a file in another user's directory. To name a particular file uniquely in a two-level directory, we must give both the user name and the file name. A two-level directory can be thought of as a tree, or an inverted tree, of height 2. The root of the tree is the MFD. Its direct descendants are the UFDs. The descendants of the UFDs are the files themselves. The files are the leaves of the tree. Specifying a user name and a file name defines a path in the tree from the root (the MFD) to a leaf (the specified file). Thus, a user name and a file name define a path name. Every file in the system has a path name. To name a file uniquely, a user must know the path name of the file desired.

For example, if user A wishes to access her own test file named test.txt, she can simply refer to test.txt. To access the file named test.txt of user B (with directory-entry name userb), however, she might have to refer to /userb/test.txt. Every system has its own syntax for naming files in directories other than the user's own.

Additional syntax is needed to specify the volume of a file. For instance, in Windows a volume is specified by a letter followed by a colon. Thus, a file specification might be C:\userb\test. Some systems go even further and separate the volume, directory name, and file name parts of the specification. In VMS, for instance, the file login.com might be specified as: u:[sst.jdeck]login.com;1, where u is the name of the volume, sst is the name of the directory, jdeck is the name of the subdirectory, and 1 is the version number. Other systems—such as UNIX and Linux—simply treat the volume name as part of the directory name. The first name given is that of the volume, and the rest is the directory and file. For instance, /u/pbg/test might specify volume u, directory pbg, and file test.

A special instance of this situation occurs with the system files. Programs provided as part of the system—loaders, assemblers, compilers, utility routines, libraries, and so on—are generally defined as files. When the appropriate commands are given to the operating system, these files are read by the loader and executed. Many command interpreters simply treat such a command as the name of a file to load and execute. In the directory system as we defined it above, this file name would be searched for in the current UFD. One solution would be to copy the system files into each UFD. However, copying all the system files would waste an enormous amount of space. (If the system files require 5 MB, then supporting 12 users would require $5 \times 12 = 60$ MB just for copies of the system files.)

The standard solution is to complicate the search procedure slightly. A special user directory is defined to contain the system files (for example, user 0). Whenever a file name is given to be loaded, the operating system first searches the local UFD. If the file is found, it is used. If it is not found, the system automatically searches the special user directory that contains the system files. The sequence of directories searched when a file is named is called the **search path**. The search path can be extended to contain an unlimited list of directories to search when a command name is given. This method is the one most used in UNIX and Windows. Systems can also be designed so that each user has his own search path.

10.3.5   Tree-Structured Directories

Once we have seen how to view a two-level directory as a two-level tree, the natural generalization is to extend the directory structure to a tree of arbitrary height (Figure 10.11). This generalization allows users to create their own subdirectories and to organize their files accordingly. A tree is the most common directory structure. The tree has a root directory, and every file in the system has a unique path name.

A directory (or subdirectory) contains a set of files or subdirectories. A directory is simply another file, but it is treated in a special way. All directories have the same internal format. One bit in each directory entry defines the entry as a file (0) or as a subdirectory (1). Special system calls are used to create and delete directories.

In normal use, each process has a current directory. The **current directory** should contain most of the files that are of current interest to the process. When reference is made to a file, the current directory is searched. If a file is needed that is not in the current directory, then the user usually must

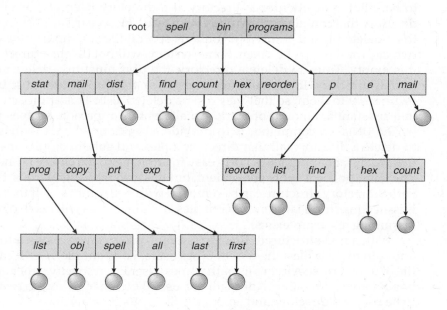

Figure 10.11   Tree-structured directory structure.

either specify a path name or change the current directory to be the directory holding that file. To change directories, a system call is provided that takes a directory name as a parameter and uses it to redefine the current directory. Thus, the user can change her current directory whenever she wants. From one change_directory() system call to the next, all open() system calls search the current directory for the specified file. Note that the search path may or may not contain a special entry that stands for "the current directory."

The initial current directory of a user's login shell is designated when the user job starts or the user logs in. The operating system searches the accounting file (or some other predefined location) to find an entry for this user (for accounting purposes). In the accounting file is a pointer to (or the name of) the user's initial directory. This pointer is copied to a local variable for this user that specifies the user's initial current directory. From that shell, other processes can be spawned. The current directory of any subprocess is usually the current directory of the parent when it was spawned.

Path names can be of two types: absolute and relative. An **absolute path name** begins at the root and follows a path down to the specified file, giving the directory names on the path. A **relative path name** defines a path from the current directory. For example, in the tree-structured file system of Figure 10.11, if the current directory is root/spell/mail, then the relative path name prt/first refers to the same file as does the absolute path name root/spell/mail/prt/first.

Allowing a user to define her own subdirectories permits her to impose a structure on her files. This structure might result in separate directories for files associated with different topics (for example, a subdirectory was created to hold the text of this book) or different forms of information (for example, the directory programs may contain source programs; the directory bin may store all the binaries).

An interesting policy decision in a tree-structured directory concerns how to handle the deletion of a directory. If a directory is empty, its entry in the directory that contains it can simply be deleted. However, suppose the directory to be deleted is not empty but contains several files or subdirectories. One of two approaches can be taken. Some systems will not delete a directory unless it is empty. Thus, to delete a directory, the user must first delete all the files in that directory. If any subdirectories exist, this procedure must be applied recursively to them, so that they can be deleted also. This approach can result in a substantial amount of work. An alternative approach, such as that taken by the UNIX rm command, is to provide an option: when a request is made to delete a directory, all that directory's files and subdirectories are also to be deleted. Either approach is fairly easy to implement; the choice is one of policy. The latter policy is more convenient, but it is also more dangerous, because an entire directory structure can be removed with one command. If that command is issued in error, a large number of files and directories will need to be restored (assuming a backup exists).

With a tree-structured directory system, users can be allowed to access, in addition to their files, the files of other users. For example, user B can access a file of user A by specifying its path names. User B can specify either an absolute or a relative path name. Alternatively, user B can change her current directory to be user A's directory and access the file by its file names.

10.3.6 Acyclic-Graph Directories

Consider two programmers who are working on a joint project. The files associated with that project can be stored in a subdirectory, separating them from other projects and files of the two programmers. But since both programmers are equally responsible for the project, both want the subdirectory to be in their own directories. In this situation, the common subdirectory should be *shared.* A shared directory or file exists in the file system in two (or more) places at once.

A tree structure prohibits the sharing of files or directories. An **acyclic graph** —that is, a graph with no cycles—allows directories to share subdirectories and files (Figure 10.12). The same file or subdirectory may be in two different directories. The acyclic graph is a natural generalization of the tree-structured directory scheme.

It is important to note that a shared file (or directory) is not the same as two copies of the file. With two copies, each programmer can view the copy rather than the original, but if one programmer changes the file, the changes will not appear in the other's copy. With a shared file, only one actual file exists, so any changes made by one person are immediately visible to the other. Sharing is particularly important for subdirectories; a new file created by one person will automatically appear in all the shared subdirectories.

When people are working as a team, all the files they want to share can be put into one directory. The UFD of each team member will contain this directory of shared files as a subdirectory. Even in the case of a single user, the user's file organization may require that some file be placed in different subdirectories. For example, a program written for a particular project should be both in the directory of all programs and in the directory for that project.

Shared files and subdirectories can be implemented in several ways. A common way, exemplified by many of the UNIX systems, is to create a new directory entry called a link. A **link** is effectively a pointer to another file

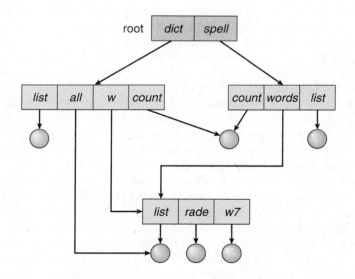

Figure 10.12 Acyclic-graph directory structure.

or subdirectory. For example, a link may be implemented as an absolute or a relative path name. When a reference to a file is made, we search the directory. If the directory entry is marked as a link, then the name of the real file is included in the link information. We **resolve** the link by using that path name to locate the real file. Links are easily identified by their format in the directory entry (or by having a special type on systems that support types) and are effectively indirect pointers. The operating system ignores these links when traversing directory trees to preserve the acyclic structure of the system.

Another common approach to implementing shared files is simply to duplicate all information about them in both sharing directories. Thus, both entries are identical and equal. Consider the difference between this approach and the creation of a link. The link is clearly different from the original directory entry; thus, the two are not equal. Duplicate directory entries, however, make the original and the copy indistinguishable. A major problem with duplicate directory entries is maintaining consistency when a file is modified.

An acyclic-graph directory structure is more flexible than a simple tree structure, but it is also more complex. Several problems must be considered carefully. A file may now have multiple absolute path names. Consequently, distinct file names may refer to the same file. This situation is similar to the aliasing problem for programming languages. If we are trying to traverse the entire file system—to find a file, to accumulate statistics on all files, or to copy all files to backup storage—this problem becomes significant, since we do not want to traverse shared structures more than once.

Another problem involves deletion. When can the space allocated to a shared file be deallocated and reused? One possibility is to remove the file whenever anyone deletes it, but this action may leave dangling pointers to the now-nonexistent file. Worse, if the remaining file pointers contain actual disk addresses, and the space is subsequently reused for other files, these dangling pointers may point into the middle of other files.

In a system where sharing is implemented by symbolic links, this situation is somewhat easier to handle. The deletion of a link need not affect the original file; only the link is removed. If the file entry itself is deleted, the space for the file is deallocated, leaving the links dangling. We can search for these links and remove them as well, but unless a list of the associated links is kept with each file, this search can be expensive. Alternatively, we can leave the links until an attempt is made to use them. At that time, we can determine that the file of the name given by the link does not exist and can fail to resolve the link name; the access is treated just as with any other illegal file name. (In this case, the system designer should consider carefully what to do when a file is deleted and another file of the same name is created, before a symbolic link to the original file is used.) In the case of UNIX, symbolic links are left when a file is deleted, and it is up to the user to realize that the original file is gone or has been replaced. Microsoft Windows uses the same approach.

Another approach to deletion is to preserve the file until all references to it are deleted. To implement this approach, we must have some mechanism for determining that the last reference to the file has been deleted. We could keep a list of all references to a file (directory entries or symbolic links). When a link or a copy of the directory entry is established, a new entry is added to the file-reference list. When a link or directory entry is deleted, we remove its entry on the list. The file is deleted when its file-reference list is empty.

The trouble with this approach is the variable and potentially large size of the file-reference list. However, we really do not need to keep the entire list—we need to keep only a count of the number of references. Adding a new link or directory entry increments the reference count. Deleting a link or entry decrements the count. When the count is 0, the file can be deleted; there are no remaining references to it. The UNIX operating system uses this approach for nonsymbolic links (or **hard links**), keeping a reference count in the file information block (or inode; see Section A.7.2). By effectively prohibiting multiple references to directories, we maintain an acyclic-graph structure.

To avoid problems such as the ones just discussed, some systems simply do not allow shared directories or links.

10.3.7   General Graph Directory

A serious problem with using an acyclic-graph structure is ensuring that there are no cycles. If we start with a two-level directory and allow users to create subdirectories, a tree-structured directory results. It should be fairly easy to see that simply adding new files and subdirectories to an existing tree-structured directory preserves the tree-structured nature. However, when we add links, the tree structure is destroyed, resulting in a simple graph structure (Figure 10.13).

The primary advantage of an acyclic graph is the relative simplicity of the algorithms to traverse the graph and to determine when there are no more references to a file. We want to avoid traversing shared sections of an acyclic graph twice, mainly for performance reasons. If we have just searched a major shared subdirectory for a particular file without finding it, we want to avoid searching that subdirectory again; the second search would be a waste of time.

If cycles are allowed to exist in the directory, we likewise want to avoid searching any component twice, for reasons of correctness as well as performance. A poorly designed algorithm might result in an infinite loop continually searching through the cycle and never terminating. One solution

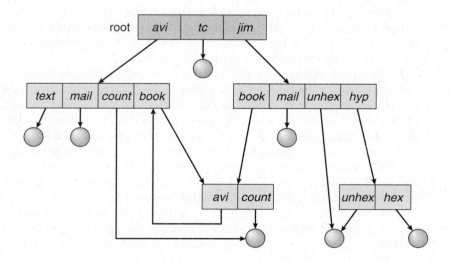

Figure 10.13   General graph directory.

is to limit arbitrarily the number of directories that will be accessed during a search.

A similar problem exists when we are trying to determine when a file can be deleted. With acyclic-graph directory structures, a value of 0 in the reference count means that there are no more references to the file or directory, and the file can be deleted. However, when cycles exist, the reference count may not be 0 even when it is no longer possible to refer to a directory or file. This anomaly results from the possibility of self-referencing (or a cycle) in the directory structure. In this case, we generally need to use a **garbage collection** scheme to determine when the last reference has been deleted and the disk space can be reallocated. Garbage collection involves traversing the entire file system, marking everything that can be accessed. Then, a second pass collects everything that is not marked onto a list of free space. (A similar marking procedure can be used to ensure that a traversal or search will cover everything in the file system once and only once.) Garbage collection for a disk-based file system, however, is extremely time consuming and is thus seldom attempted.

Garbage collection is necessary only because of possible cycles in the graph. Thus, an acyclic-graph structure is much easier to work with. The difficulty is to avoid cycles as new links are added to the structure. How do we know when a new link will complete a cycle? There are algorithms to detect cycles in graphs; however, they are computationally expensive, especially when the graph is on disk storage. A simpler algorithm in the special case of directories and links is to bypass links during directory traversal. Cycles are avoided, and no extra overhead is incurred.

10.4 File-System Mounting

Just as a file must be opened before it is used, a file system must be mounted before it can be available to processes on the system. More specifically, the directory structure may be built out of multiple volumes, which must be mounted to make them available within the file-system name space.

The mount procedure is straightforward. The operating system is given the name of the device and the **mount point**—the location within the file structure where the file system is to be attached. Some operating systems require that a file system type be provided, while others inspect the structures of the device and determine the type of file system. Typically, a mount point is an empty directory. For instance, on a UNIX system, a file system containing a user's home directories might be mounted as /home; then, to access the directory structure within that file system, we could precede the directory names with /home, as in /home/jane. Mounting that file system under /users would result in the path name /users/jane, which we could use to reach the same directory.

Next, the operating system verifies that the device contains a valid file system. It does so by asking the device driver to read the device directory and verifying that the directory has the expected format. Finally, the operating system notes in its directory structure that a file system is mounted at the specified mount point. This scheme enables the operating system to traverse its directory structure, switching among file systems, and even file systems of varying types, as appropriate.

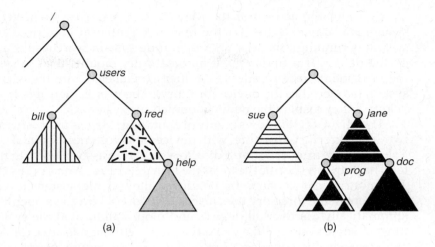

Figure 10.14   File system. (a) Existing system. (b) Unmounted volume.

To illustrate file mounting, consider the file system depicted in Figure 10.14, where the triangles represent subtrees of directories that are of interest. Figure 10.14(a) shows an existing file system, while Figure 10.14(b) shows an unmounted volume residing on /device/dsk. At this point, only the files on the existing file system can be accessed. Figure 10.15 shows the effects of mounting the volume residing on /device/dsk over /users. If the volume is unmounted, the file system is restored to the situation depicted in Figure 10.14.

Systems impose semantics to clarify functionality. For example, a system may disallow a mount over a directory that contains files; or it may make the mounted file system available at that directory and obscure the directory's existing files until the file system is unmounted, terminating the use of the file system and allowing access to the original files in that directory. As another example, a system may allow the same file system to be mounted repeatedly, at different mount points; or it may only allow one mount per file system.

Figure 10.15   Mount point.

Consider the actions of the Mac OS X operating system. Whenever the system encounters a disk for the first time (either at boot time or while the system is running), the Mac OS X operating system searches for a file system on the device. If it finds one, it automatically mounts the file system under the /Volumes directory, adding a folder icon labeled with the name of the file system (as stored in the device directory). The user is then able to click on the icon and thus display the newly mounted file system.

The Microsoft Windows family of operating systems maintains an extended two-level directory structure, with devices and volumes assigned drive letters. Volumes have a general graph directory structure associated with the drive letter. The path to a specific file takes the form of drive-letter:\path\to\file. The more recent versions of Windows allow a file system to be mounted anywhere in the directory tree, just as UNIX does. Windows operating systems automatically discover all devices and mount all located file systems at boot time. In some systems, like UNIX, the mount commands are explicit. A system configuration file contains a list of devices and mount points for automatic mounting at boot time, but other mounts may be executed manually.

Issues concerning file system mounting are further discussed in Section 11.2.2 and in Section A.7.5.

10.5 File Sharing

In the previous sections, we explored the motivation for file sharing and some of the difficulties involved in allowing users to share files. Such file sharing is very desirable for users who want to collaborate and to reduce the effort required to achieve a computing goal. Therefore, user-oriented operating systems must accommodate the need to share files in spite of the inherent difficulties.

In this section, we examine more aspects of file sharing. We begin by discussing general issues that arise when multiple users share files. Once multiple users are allowed to share files, the challenge is to extend sharing to multiple file systems, including remote file systems; we discuss that challenge as well. Finally, we consider what to do about conflicting actions occurring on shared files. For instance, if multiple users are writing to a file, should all the writes be allowed to occur, or should the operating system protect the users' actions from one another?

10.5.1 Multiple Users

When an operating system accommodates multiple users, the issues of file sharing, file naming, and file protection become preeminent. Given a directory structure that allows files to be shared by users, the system must mediate the file sharing. The system can either allow a user to access the files of other users by default or require that a user specifically grant access to the files. These are the issues of access control and protection, which are covered in Section 10.6.

To implement sharing and protection, the system must maintain more file and directory attributes than are needed on a single-user system. Although many approaches have been taken to meet this requirement, most systems have evolved to use the concepts of file (or directory) owner (or user) and group. The owner is the user who can change attributes and grant access and who has the most control over the file. The group attribute defines a subset of users who can share access to the file. For example, the owner of a file on a UNIX system can issue all operations on a file, while members of the file's group can execute one subset of those operations, and all other users can execute another subset of operations. Exactly which operations can be executed by group members and other users is definable by the file's owner. More details on permission attributes are included in the next section.

The owner and group IDs of a given file (or directory) are stored with the other file attributes. When a user requests an operation on a file, the user ID can be compared with the owner attribute to determine if the requesting user is the owner of the file. Likewise, the group IDs can be compared. The result indicates which permissions are applicable. The system then applies those permissions to the requested operation and allows or denies it.

Many systems have multiple local file systems, including volumes of a single disk or multiple volumes on multiple attached disks. In these cases, the ID checking and permission matching are straightforward, once the file systems are mounted.

10.5.2 Remote File Systems

With the advent of networks, communication among remote computers became possible. Networking allows the sharing of resources spread across a campus or even around the world. One obvious resource to share is data in the form of files.

Through the evolution of network and file technology, remote file-sharing methods have changed. The first implemented method involves manually transferring files between machines via programs like ftp. The second major method uses a **distributed file system (DFS)** in which remote directories are visible from a local machine. In some ways, the third method, the **World Wide Web**, is a reversion to the first. A browser is needed to gain access to the remote files, and separate operations (essentially a wrapper for ftp) are used to transfer files. Increasingly, cloud computing (Section 1.11.7) is being used for file sharing as well.

ftp is used for both anonymous and authenticated access. **Anonymous access** allows a user to transfer files without having an account on the remote system. The World Wide Web uses anonymous file exchange almost exclusively. DFS involves a much tighter integration between the machine that is accessing the remote files and the machine providing the files. This integration adds complexity, as we describe in this section.

10.5.2.1 The Client–Server Model

Remote file systems allow a computer to mount one or more file systems from one or more remote machines. In this case, the machine containing the files is the **server**, and the machine seeking access to the files is the **client**. The client–server relationship is common with networked machines. Generally, the server declares that a resource is available to clients and specifies exactly which resource (in this case, which files) and exactly which clients. A server can serve multiple clients, and a client can use multiple servers, depending on the implementation details of a given client–server facility.

The server usually specifies the available files on a volume or directory level. Client identification is more difficult. A client can be specified by a network name or other identifier, such as an IP address, but these can be spoofed, or imitated. As a result of spoofing, an unauthorized client could be allowed access to the server. More secure solutions include secure authentication of the client via encrypted keys. Unfortunately, with security come many challenges, including ensuring compatibility of the client and server (they must use the same encryption algorithms) and security of key exchanges (intercepted keys could again allow unauthorized access). Because of the difficulty of solving these problems, unsecure authentication methods are most commonly used.

In the case of UNIX and its network file system (NFS), authentication takes place via the client networking information, by default. In this scheme, the user's IDs on the client and server must match. If they do not, the server will be unable to determine access rights to files. Consider the example of a user who has an ID of 1000 on the client and 2000 on the server. A request from the client to the server for a specific file will not be handled appropriately, as the server will determine if user 1000 has access to the file rather than basing the determination on the real user ID of 2000. Access is thus granted or denied based on incorrect authentication information. The server must trust the client to present the correct user ID. Note that the NFS protocols allow many-to-many relationships. That is, many servers can provide files to many clients. In fact, a given machine can be both a server to some NFS clients and a client of other NFS servers.

Once the remote file system is mounted, file operation requests are sent on behalf of the user across the network to the server via the DFS protocol. Typically, a file-open request is sent along with the ID of the requesting user. The server then applies the standard access checks to determine if the user has credentials to access the file in the mode requested. The request is either allowed or denied. If it is allowed, a file handle is returned to the client application, and the application then can perform read, write, and other operations on the file. The client closes the file when access is completed. The operating system may apply semantics similar to those for a local file-system mount or may use different semantics.

10.5.2.2   Distributed Information Systems

To make client–server systems easier to manage, **distributed information systems**, also known as **distributed naming services**, provide unified access to the information needed for remote computing. The **domain name system (DNS)** provides host-name-to-network-address translations for the entire Internet. Before DNS became widespread, files containing the same information were sent via e-mail or `ftp` between all networked hosts. Obviously, this methodology was not scalable!

Other distributed information systems provide *user name/password/user ID/group ID* space for a distributed facility. UNIX systems have employed a wide variety of distributed information methods. Sun Microsystems (now part of Oracle Corporation) introduced **yellow pages** (since renamed **network information service**, or NIS), and most of the industry adopted its use. It centralizes storage of user names, host names, printer information, and the like.

Unfortunately, it uses unsecure authentication methods, including sending user passwords unencrypted (in clear text) and identifying hosts by IP address. Sun's NIS+ was a much more secure replacement for NIS but was much more complicated and was not widely adopted.

In the case of Microsoft's **common Internet file system** (CIFS), network information is used in conjunction with user authentication (user name and password) to create a network login that the server uses to decide whether to allow or deny access to a requested file system. For this authentication to be valid, the user names must match from machine to machine (as with NFS). Microsoft uses **active directory** as a distributed naming structure to provide a single name space for users. Once established, the distributed naming facility is used by all clients and servers to authenticate users.

The industry is moving toward use of the **lightweight directory-access protocol** (LDAP) as a secure distributed naming mechanism. In fact, active directory is based on LDAP. Oracle Solaris and most other major operating systems include LDAP and allow it to be employed for user authentication as well as system-wide retrieval of information, such as availability of printers. Conceivably, one distributed LDAP directory could be used by an organization to store all user and resource information for all the organization's computers. The result would be secure single sign-on for users, who would enter their authentication information once for access to all computers within the organization. It would also ease system-administration efforts by combining, in one location, information that is currently scattered in various files on each system or in different distributed information services.

10.5.2.3 Failure Modes

Local file systems can fail for a variety of reasons, including failure of the disk containing the file system, corruption of the directory structure or other disk-management information (collectively called **metadata**), disk-controller failure, cable failure, and host-adapter failure. User or system-administrator failure can also cause files to be lost or entire directories or volumes to be deleted. Many of these failures will cause a host to crash and an error condition to be displayed, and human intervention will be required to repair the damage.

Remote file systems have even more failure modes. Because of the complexity of network systems and the required interactions between remote machines, many more problems can interfere with the proper operation of remote file systems. In the case of networks, the network can be interrupted between two hosts. Such interruptions can result from hardware failure, poor hardware configuration, or networking implementation issues. Although some networks have built-in resiliency, including multiple paths between hosts, many do not. Any single failure can thus interrupt the flow of DFS commands.

Consider a client in the midst of using a remote file system. It has files open from the remote host; among other activities, it may be performing directory lookups to open files, reading or writing data to files, and closing files. Now consider a partitioning of the network, a crash of the server, or even a scheduled shutdown of the server. Suddenly, the remote file system is no longer reachable. This scenario is rather common, so it would not be appropriate for the client system to act as it would if a local file system were lost. Rather, the system can either terminate all operations to the lost server or delay operations until the server is again reachable. These failure semantics are defined and implemented as part of the remote-file-system protocol. Termination of all operations can result in users' losing data—and patience. Thus, most DFS protocols either enforce or allow delaying of file-system operations to remote hosts, with the hope that the remote host will become available again.

To implement this kind of recovery from failure, some kind of **state information** may be maintained on both the client and the server. If both server and client maintain knowledge of their current activities and open files, then they can seamlessly recover from a failure. In the situation where the server crashes but must recognize that it has remotely mounted exported file systems and opened files, NFS takes a simple approach, implementing a **stateless** DFS. In essence, it assumes that a client request for a file read or write would not have occurred unless the file system had been remotely mounted and the file had been previously open. The NFS protocol carries all the information needed to locate the appropriate file and perform the requested operation. Similarly, it does not track which clients have the exported volumes mounted, again assuming that if a request comes in, it must be legitimate. While this stateless approach makes NFS resilient and rather easy to implement, it also makes it unsecure. For example, forged read or write requests could be allowed by an NFS server. These issues are addressed in the industry standard NFS Version 4, in which NFS is made stateful to improve its security, performance, and functionality.

10.5.3 Consistency Semantics

Consistency semantics represent an important criterion for evaluating any file system that supports file sharing. These semantics specify how multiple users of a system are to access a shared file simultaneously. In particular, they specify when modifications of data by one user will be observable by other users. These semantics are typically implemented as code with the file system.

Consistency semantics are directly related to the process synchronization algorithms of Chapter 5. However, the complex algorithms of that chapter tend not to be implemented in the case of file I/O because of the great latencies and slow transfer rates of disks and networks. For example, performing an atomic transaction to a remote disk could involve several network communications, several disk reads and writes, or both. Systems that attempt such a full set of functionalities tend to perform poorly. A successful implementation of complex sharing semantics can be found in the Andrew file system.

For the following discussion, we assume that a series of file accesses (that is, reads and writes) attempted by a user to the same file is always enclosed between the open() and close() operations. The series of accesses between the open() and close() operations makes up a **file session**. To illustrate the concept, we sketch several prominent examples of consistency semantics.

10.5.3.1 UNIX Semantics

The UNIX file system uses the following consistency semantics:

- Writes to an open file by a user are visible immediately to other users who have this file open.

- One mode of sharing allows users to share the pointer of current location into the file. Thus, the advancing of the pointer by one user affects all sharing users. Here, a file has a single image that interleaves all accesses, regardless of their origin.

In the UNIX semantics, a file is associated with a single physical image that is accessed as an exclusive resource. Contention for this single image causes delays in user processes.

10.5.3.2   Session Semantics

The Andrew file system (OpenAFS) uses the following consistency semantics:

- Writes to an open file by a user are not visible immediately to other users that have the same file open.

- Once a file is closed, the changes made to it are visible only in sessions starting later. Already open instances of the file do not reflect these changes.

According to these semantics, a file may be associated temporarily with several (possibly different) images at the same time. Consequently, multiple users are allowed to perform both read and write accesses concurrently on their images of the file, without delay. Almost no constraints are enforced on scheduling accesses.

10.5.3.3   Immutable-Shared-Files Semantics

A unique approach is that of **immutable shared files**. Once a file is declared as shared by its creator, it cannot be modified. An immutable file has two key properties: its name may not be reused, and its contents may not be altered. Thus, the name of an immutable file signifies that the contents of the file are fixed. The implementation of these semantics in a distributed system is simple, because the sharing is disciplined (read-only).

10.6   Protection

When information is stored in a computer system, we want to keep it safe from physical damage (the issue of reliability) and improper access (the issue of protection).

Reliability is generally provided by duplicate copies of files. Many computers have systems programs that automatically (or through computer-operator intervention) copy disk files to tape at regular intervals (once per day or week or month) to maintain a copy should a file system be accidentally destroyed. File systems can be damaged by hardware problems (such as errors in reading or writing), power surges or failures, head crashes, dirt, temperature extremes, and vandalism. Files may be deleted accidentally. Bugs in the file-system software can also cause file contents to be lost. Reliability is covered in more detail in Chapter 9.

Protection can be provided in many ways. For a single-user laptop system, we might provide protection by locking the computer in a desk drawer or file cabinet. In a larger multiuser system, however, other mechanisms are needed.

10.6.1 Types of Access

The need to protect files is a direct result of the ability to access files. Systems that do not permit access to the files of other users do not need protection. Thus, we could provide complete protection by prohibiting access. Alternatively, we could provide free access with no protection. Both approaches are too extreme for general use. What is needed is controlled access.

Protection mechanisms provide controlled access by limiting the types of file access that can be made. Access is permitted or denied depending on several factors, one of which is the type of access requested. Several different types of operations may be controlled:

- **Read**. Read from the file.
- **Write**. Write or rewrite the file.
- **Execute**. Load the file into memory and execute it.
- **Append**. Write new information at the end of the file.
- **Delete**. Delete the file and free its space for possible reuse.
- **List**. List the name and attributes of the file.

Other operations, such as renaming, copying, and editing the file, may also be controlled. For many systems, however, these higher-level functions may be implemented by a system program that makes lower-level system calls. Protection is provided at only the lower level. For instance, copying a file may be implemented simply by a sequence of read requests. In this case, a user with read access can also cause the file to be copied, printed, and so on.

Many protection mechanisms have been proposed. Each has advantages and disadvantages and must be appropriate for its intended application. A small computer system that is used by only a few members of a research group, for example, may not need the same types of protection as a large corporate computer that is used for research, finance, and personnel operations. We discuss some approaches to protection in the following sections and present a more complete treatment in Chapter 13.

10.6.2 Access Control

The most common approach to the protection problem is to make access dependent on the identity of the user. Different users may need different types of access to a file or directory. The most general scheme to implement identity-dependent access is to associate with each file and directory an **access-control list** (ACL) specifying user names and the types of access allowed for each user. When a user requests access to a particular file, the operating system checks the access list associated with that file. If that user is listed for the requested access, the access is allowed. Otherwise, a protection violation occurs, and the user job is denied access to the file.

This approach has the advantage of enabling complex access methodologies. The main problem with access lists is their length. If we want to allow everyone to read a file, we must list all users with read access. This technique has two undesirable consequences:

- Constructing such a list may be a tedious and unrewarding task, especially if we do not know in advance the list of users in the system.

- The directory entry, previously of fixed size, now must be of variable size, resulting in more complicated space management.

These problems can be resolved by use of a condensed version of the access list.

To condense the length of the access-control list, many systems recognize three classifications of users in connection with each file:

- **Owner**. The user who created the file is the owner.

- **Group**. A set of users who are sharing the file and need similar access is a group, or work group.

- **Universe**. All other users in the system constitute the universe.

The most common recent approach is to combine access-control lists with the more general (and easier to implement) owner, group, and universe access-control scheme just described. For example, Solaris uses the three categories of access by default but allows access-control lists to be added to specific files and directories when more fine-grained access control is desired.

To illustrate, consider a person, Sara, who is writing a new book. She has hired three graduate students (Jim, Dawn, and Jill) to help with the project. The text of the book is kept in a file named book.tex. The protection associated with this file is as follows:

- Sara should be able to invoke all operations on the file.

- Jim, Dawn, and Jill should be able only to read and write the file; they should not be allowed to delete the file.

- All other users should be able to read, but not write, the file. (Sara is interested in letting as many people as possible read the text so that she can obtain feedback.)

To achieve such protection, we must create a new group—say, text—with members Jim, Dawn, and Jill. The name of the group, text, must then be associated with the file book.tex, and the access rights must be set in accordance with the policy we have outlined.

Now consider a visitor to whom Sara would like to grant temporary access to Chapter 1. The visitor cannot be added to the text group because that would give him access to all chapters. Because a file can be in only one group, Sara cannot add another group to Chapter 1. With the addition of access-control-list functionality, though, the visitor can be added to the access control list of Chapter 1.

PERMISSIONS IN A UNIX SYSTEM

In the UNIX system, directory protection and file protection are handled similarly. Associated with each subdirectory are three fields—owner, group, and universe—each consisting of the three bits rwx. Thus, a user can list the content of a subdirectory only if the r bit is set in the appropriate field. Similarly, a user can change his current directory to another current directory (say, foo) only if the x bit associated with the foo subdirectory is set in the appropriate field.

A sample directory listing from a UNIX environment is shown in below:

```
-rw-rw-r--    1 pbg   staff      31200   Sep 3 08:30   intro.ps
drwx------    5 pbg   staff        512   Jul 8 09.33   private/
drwxrwxr-x    2 pbg   staff        512   Jul 8 09:35   doc/
drwxrwx---    2 jwg   student      512   Aug 3 14:13   student-proj/
-rw-r--r--    1 pbg   staff       9423   Feb 24 2012   program.c
-rwxr-xr-x    1 pbg   staff      20471   Feb 24 2012   program
drwx--x--x    4 tag   faculty      512   Jul 31 10:31  lib/
drwx------    3 pbg   staff       1024   Aug 29 06:52  mail/
drwxrwxrwx    3 pbg   staff        512   Jul 8 09:35   test/
```

The first field describes the protection of the file or directory. A d as the first character indicates a subdirectory. Also shown are the number of links to the file, the owner's name, the group's name, the size of the file in bytes, the date of last modification, and finally the file's name (with optional extension).

For this scheme to work properly, permissions and access lists must be controlled tightly. This control can be accomplished in several ways. For example, in the UNIX system, groups can be created and modified only by the manager of the facility (or by any superuser). Thus, control is achieved through human interaction. Access lists are discussed further in Section 13.5.2.

With the more limited protection classification, only three fields are needed to define protection. Often, each field is a collection of bits, and each bit either allows or prevents the access associated with it. For example, the UNIX system defines three fields of 3 bits each—rwx, where r controls read access, w controls write access, and x controls execution. A separate field is kept for the file owner, for the file's group, and for all other users. In this scheme, 9 bits per file are needed to record protection information. Thus, for our example, the protection fields for the file book.tex are as follows: for the owner Sara, all bits are set; for the group text, the r and w bits are set; and for the universe, only the r bit is set.

One difficulty in combining approaches comes in the user interface. Users must be able to tell when the optional ACL permissions are set on a file. In the Solaris example, a "+" is appended to the regular permissions, as in:

```
19 -rw-r--r--+ 1 jim staff 130 May 25 22:13 file1
```

A separate set of commands, setfacl and getfacl, is used to manage the ACLs.

Figure 10.16 Windows 7 ® access-control list management.

Windows users typically manage access-control lists via the GUI. Figure 10.16 shows a file-permission window on Windows 7 NTFS file system. In this example, user "guest" is specifically denied access to the file ListPanel.java.

Another difficulty is assigning precedence when permission and ACLs conflict. For example, if Joe is in a file's group, which has read permission, but the file has an ACL granting Joe read and write permission, should a write by Joe be granted or denied? Solaris gives ACLs precedence (as they are more fine-grained and are not assigned by default). This follows the general rule that specificity should have priority.

10.6.3 Other Protection Approaches

Another approach to the protection problem is to associate a password with each file. Just as access to the computer system is often controlled by a password, access to each file can be controlled in the same way. If the passwords are chosen randomly and changed often, this scheme may be effective in limiting access to a file. The use of passwords has a few disadvantages, however. First, the number of passwords that a user needs to remember may become large, making the scheme impractical. Second, if only one password is used for all the files, then once it is discovered, all files are accessible; protection is on an all-or-none basis. Some systems allow a user to associate a password with a subdirectory, rather than with an individual file, to address this problem.

In a multilevel directory structure, we need to protect not only individual files but also collections of files in subdirectories; that is, we need to provide a mechanism for directory protection. The directory operations that must be protected are somewhat different from the file operations. We want to control the creation and deletion of files in a directory. In addition, we probably want to control whether a user can determine the existence of a file in a directory. Sometimes, knowledge of the existence and name of a file is significant in itself. Thus, listing the contents of a directory must be a protected operation. Similarly, if a path name refers to a file in a directory, the user must be allowed access to both the directory and the file. In systems where files may have numerous path names (such as acyclic and general graphs), a given user may have different access rights to a particular file, depending on the path name used.

10.7 Summary

A file is an abstract data type defined and implemented by the operating system. It is a sequence of logical records. A logical record may be a byte, a line (of fixed or variable length), or a more complex data item. The operating system may specifically support various record types or may leave that support to the application program.

The major task for the operating system is to map the logical file concept onto physical storage devices such as hard disk or tape. Since the physical record size of the device may not be the same as the logical record size, it may be necessary to order logical records into physical records. Again, this task may be supported by the operating system or left for the application program.

Each device in a file system keeps a volume table of contents or a device directory listing the location of the files on the device. In addition, it is useful to create directories to allow files to be organized. A single-level directory in a multiuser system causes naming problems, since each file must have a unique name. A two-level directory solves this problem by creating a separate directory for each user's files. The directory lists the files by name and includes the file's location on the disk, length, type, owner, time of creation, time of last use, and so on.

The natural generalization of a two-level directory is a tree-structured directory. A tree-structured directory allows a user to create subdirectories to organize files. Acyclic-graph directory structures enable users to share subdirectories and files but complicate searching and deletion. A general graph structure allows complete flexibility in the sharing of files and directories but sometimes requires garbage collection to recover unused disk space.

Disks are segmented into one or more volumes, each containing a file system or left "raw." File systems may be mounted into the system's naming structures to make them available. The naming scheme varies by operating system. Once mounted, the files within the volume are available for use. File systems may be unmounted to disable access or for maintenance.

File sharing depends on the semantics provided by the system. Files may have multiple readers, multiple writers, or limits on sharing. Distributed file systems allow client hosts to mount volumes or directories from servers, as long as they can access each other across a network. Remote file systems present challenges in reliability, performance, and security. Distributed information systems maintain user, host, and access information so that clients and servers can share state information to manage use and access.

Since files are the main information-storage mechanism in most computer systems, file protection is needed. Access to files can be controlled separately for each type of access—read, write, execute, append, delete, list directory, and so on. File protection can be provided by access lists, passwords, or other techniques.

Review Questions

Review questions for this chapter can be accessed by visiting our website.

Practice Exercises

Answers for the Practice Exercises can be accceed by visiting our website.

10.1 Some systems automatically delete all user files when a user logs off or a job terminates, unless the user explicitly requests that they be kept. Other systems keep all files unless the user explicitly deletes them. Discuss the relative merits of each approach.

10.2 Why do some systems keep track of the type of a file, while others leave it to the user and others simply do not implement multiple file types? Which system is "better"?

10.3 Similarly, some systems support many types of structures for a file's data, while others simply support a stream of bytes. What are the advantages and disadvantages of each approach?

10.4 Could you simulate a multilevel directory structure with a single-level directory structure in which arbitrarily long names can be used? If your answer is yes, explain how you can do so, and contrast this scheme with the multilevel directory scheme. If your answer is no, explain what prevents your simulation's success. How would your answer change if file names were limited to seven characters?

10.5 Explain the purpose of the open() and close() operations.

10.6 In some systems, a subdirectory can be read and written by an authorized user, just as ordinary files can be.

   a. Describe the protection problems that could arise.

b.   Suggest a scheme for dealing with each of these protection problems.

10.7   Consider a system that supports 5,000 users. Suppose that you want to allow 4,990 of these users to be able to access one file.

a.   How would you specify this protection scheme in UNIX?

b.   Can you suggest another protection scheme that can be used more effectively for this purpose than the scheme provided by UNIX?

10.8   Researchers have suggested that, instead of having an access list associated with each file (specifying which users can access the file, and how), we should have a **user control list** associated with each user (specifying which files a user can access, and how). Discuss the relative merits of these two schemes.

Exercises

10.9   Consider a file system in which a file can be deleted and its disk space reclaimed while links to that file still exist. What problems may occur if a new file is created in the same storage area or with the same absolute path name? How can these problems be avoided?

10.10   The open-file table is used to maintain information about files that are currently open. Should the operating system maintain a separate table for each user or maintain just one table that contains references to files that are currently being accessed by all users? If the same file is being accessed by two different programs or users, should there be separate entries in the open-file table? Explain.

10.11   What are the advantages and disadvantages of providing mandatory locks instead of advisory locks whose use is left to users' discretion?

10.12   Provide examples of applications that typically access files according to the following methods:

- Sequential
- Random

10.13   Some systems automatically open a file when it is referenced for the first time and close the file when the job terminates. Discuss the advantages and disadvantages of this scheme compared with the more traditional one, where the user has to open and close the file explicitly.

10.14   If the operating system knew that a certain application was going to access file data in a sequential manner, how could it exploit this information to improve performance?

10.15   Give an example of an application that could benefit from operating-system support for random access to indexed files.

10.16 Discuss the advantages and disadvantages of supporting links to files that cross mount points (that is, the file link refers to a file that is stored in a different volume).

10.17 Some systems provide file sharing by maintaining a single copy of a file. Other systems maintain several copies, one for each of the users sharing the file. Discuss the relative merits of each approach.

10.18 Discuss the advantages and disadvantages of associating with remote file systems (stored on file servers) a set of failure semantics different from that associated with local file systems.

10.19 What are the implications of supporting UNIX consistency semantics for shared access to files stored on remote file systems?

Bibliographical Notes

Database systems and their file structures are described in full in [Silberschatz et al. (2010)].

A multilevel directory structure was first implemented on the MULTICS system ([Organick (1972)]). Most operating systems now implement multilevel directory structures. These include Linux ([Love (2010)]), Mac OS X ([Singh (2007)]), Solaris ([McDougall and Mauro (2007)]), and all versions of Windows ([Russinovich and Solomon (2005)]).

The network file system (NFS), designed by Sun Microsystems, allows directory structures to be spread across networked computer systems. NFS Version 4 is described in RFC3505 (http://www.ietf.org/rfc/rfc3530.txt). A general discussion of Solaris file systems is found in the Sun *System Administration Guide: Devices and File Systems* (http://docs.sun.com/app/docs/doc/817-5093).

DNS was first proposed by [Su (1982)] and has gone through several revisions since. LDAP, also known as X.509, is a derivative subset of the X.500 distributed directory protocol. It was defined by [Yeong et al. (1995)] and has been implemented on many operating systems.

Bibliography

[Love (2010)]   R. Love, *Linux Kernel Development*, Third Edition, Developer's Library (2010).

[McDougall and Mauro (2007)]   R. McDougall and J. Mauro, *Solaris Internals*, Second Edition, Prentice Hall (2007).

[Organick (1972)]   E. I. Organick, *The Multics System: An Examination of Its Structure*, MIT Press (1972).

[Russinovich and Solomon (2005)]   M. E. Russinovich and D. A. Solomon, *Microsoft Windows Internals*, Fourth Edition, Microsoft Press (2005).

[Silberschatz et al. (2010)]   A. Silberschatz, H. F. Korth, and S. Sudarshan, *Database System Concepts*, Sixth Edition, McGraw-Hill (2010).

[Singh (2007)]   A. Singh, *Mac OS X Internals: A Systems Approach*, Addison-Wesley (2007).

[Su (1982)]   Z. Su, "A Distributed System for Internet Name Service", *Network Working Group, Request for Comments: 830* (1982).

[Yeong et al. (1995)]   W. Yeong, T. Howes, and S. Kille, "Lightweight Directory Access Protocol", *Network Working Group, Request for Comments: 1777* (1995).

File-System Implementation

As we saw in Chapter 10, the file system provides the mechanism for on-line storage and access to file contents, including data and programs. The file system resides permanently on secondary storage, which is designed to hold a large amount of data permanently. This chapter is primarily concerned with issues surrounding file storage and access on the most common secondary-storage medium, the disk. We explore ways to structure file use, to allocate disk space, to recover freed space, to track the locations of data, and to interface other parts of the operating system to secondary storage. Performance issues are considered throughout the chapter.

CHAPTER OBJECTIVES

- To describe the details of implementing local file systems and directory structures.
- To describe the implementation of remote file systems.
- To discuss block allocation and free-block algorithms and trade-offs.

11.1 File-System Structure

Disks provide most of the secondary storage on which file systems are maintained. Two characteristics make them convenient for this purpose:

1. A disk can be rewritten in place; it is possible to read a block from the disk, modify the block, and write it back into the same place.

2. A disk can access directly any block of information it contains. Thus, it is simple to access any file either sequentially or randomly, and switching from one file to another requires only moving the read–write heads and waiting for the disk to rotate.

We discuss disk structure in great detail in Chapter 9.

To improve I/O efficiency, I/O transfers between memory and disk are performed in units of **blocks**. Each block has one or more sectors. Depending on the disk drive, sector size varies from 32 bytes to 4,096 bytes; the usual size is 512 bytes.

File systems provide efficient and convenient access to the disk by allowing data to be stored, located, and retrieved easily. A file system poses two quite different design problems. The first problem is defining how the file system should look to the user. This task involves defining a file and its attributes, the operations allowed on a file, and the directory structure for organizing files. The second problem is creating algorithms and data structures to map the logical file system onto the physical secondary-storage devices.

The file system itself is generally composed of many different levels. The structure shown in Figure 11.1 is an example of a layered design. Each level in the design uses the features of lower levels to create new features for use by higher levels.

The I/O **control** level consists of device drivers and interrupt handlers to transfer information between the main memory and the disk system. A device driver can be thought of as a translator. Its input consists of high-level commands such as "retrieve block 123." Its output consists of low-level, hardware-specific instructions that are used by the hardware controller, which interfaces the I/O device to the rest of the system. The device driver usually writes specific bit patterns to special locations in the I/O controller's memory to tell the controller which device location to act on and what actions to take. The details of device drivers and the I/O infrastructure are covered in Chapter 12.

The **basic file system** needs only to issue generic commands to the appropriate device driver to read and write physical blocks on the disk. Each physical block is identified by its numeric disk address (for example, drive 1, cylinder 73, track 2, sector 10). This layer also manages the memory buffers and caches that hold various file-system, directory, and data blocks. A block in the buffer is allocated before the transfer of a disk block can occur. When the buffer is full, the buffer manager must find more buffer memory or free

Figure 11.1 Layered file system.

up buffer space to allow a requested I/O to complete. Caches are used to hold frequently used file-system metadata to improve performance, so managing their contents is critical for optimum system performance.

The **file-organization module** knows about files and their logical blocks, as well as physical blocks. By knowing the type of file allocation used and the location of the file, the file-organization module can translate logical block addresses to physical block addresses for the basic file system to transfer. Each file's logical blocks are numbered from 0 (or 1) through N. Since the physical blocks containing the data usually do not match the logical numbers, a translation is needed to locate each block. The file-organization module also includes the free-space manager, which tracks unallocated blocks and provides these blocks to the file-organization module when requested.

Finally, the **logical file system** manages metadata information. Metadata includes all of the file-system structure except the actual data (or contents of the files). The logical file system manages the directory structure to provide the file-organization module with the information the latter needs, given a symbolic file name. It maintains file structure via file-control blocks. A **file-control block (FCB)** (an **inode** in UNIX file systems) contains information about the file, including ownership, permissions, and location of the file contents. The logical file system is also responsible for protection, as discussed in Chapters 10 and 13.

When a layered structure is used for file-system implementation, duplication of code is minimized. The I/O control and sometimes the basic file-system code can be used by multiple file systems. Each file system can then have its own logical file-system and file-organization modules. Unfortunately, layering can introduce more operating-system overhead, which may result in decreased performance. The use of layering, including the decision about how many layers to use and what each layer should do, is a major challenge in designing new systems.

Many file systems are in use today, and most operating systems support more than one. For example, most CD-ROMs are written in the ISO 9660 format, a standard format agreed on by CD-ROM manufacturers. In addition to removable-media file systems, each operating system has one or more disk-based file systems. UNIX uses the **UNIX file system (UFS)**, which is based on the Berkeley Fast File System (FFS). Windows supports disk file-system formats of FAT, FAT32, and NTFS (or Windows NT File System), as well as CD-ROM and DVD file-system formats. Although Linux supports over forty different file systems, the standard Linux file system is known as the **extended file system**, with the most common versions being ext3 and ext4. There are also distributed file systems in which a file system on a server is mounted by one or more client computers across a network.

File-system research continues to be an active area of operating-system design and implementation. Google created its own file system to meet the company's specific storage and retrieval needs, which include high-performance access from many clients across a very large number of disks. Another interesting project is the FUSE file system, which provides flexibility in file-system development and use by implementing and executing file systems as user-level rather than kernel-level code. Using FUSE, a user can add a new file system to a variety of operating systems and can use that file system to manage her files.

11.2 File-System Implementation

As was described in Section 10.1.2, operating systems implement open()
and close() systems calls for processes to request access to file contents.
In this section, we delve into the structures and operations used to implement
file-system operations.

11.2.1 Overview

Several on-disk and in-memory structures are used to implement a file system.
These structures vary depending on the operating system and the file system,
but some general principles apply.

   On disk, the file system may contain information about how to boot an
operating system stored there, the total number of blocks, the number and
location of free blocks, the directory structure, and individual files. Many of
these structures are detailed throughout the remainder of this chapter. Here,
we describe them briefly:

- A **boot control block** (per volume) can contain information needed by the
  system to boot an operating system from that volume. If the disk does not
  contain an operating system, this block can be empty. It is typically the
  first block of a volume. In UFS, it is called the **boot block**. In NTFS, it is the
  partition boot sector.

- A **volume control block** (per volume) contains volume (or partition)
  details, such as the number of blocks in the partition, the size of the blocks,
  a free-block count and free-block pointers, and a free-FCB count and FCB
  pointers. In UFS, this is called a **superblock**. In NTFS, it is stored in the
  master file table.

- A directory structure (per file system) is used to organize the files. In UFS,
  this includes file names and associated inode numbers. In NTFS, it is stored
  in the master file table.

- A per-file FCB contains many details about the file. It has a unique
  identifier number to allow association with a directory entry. In NTFS,
  this information is actually stored within the master file table, which uses
  a relational database structure, with a row per file.

   The in-memory information is used for both file-system management and
performance improvement via caching. The data are loaded at mount time,
updated during file-system operations, and discarded at dismount. Several
types of structures may be included.

- An in-memory **mount table** contains information about each mounted
  volume.

- An in-memory directory-structure cache holds the directory information
  of recently accessed directories. (For directories at which volumes are
  mounted, it can contain a pointer to the volume table.)

- The **system-wide open-file table** contains a copy of the FCB of each open
  file, as well as other information.

| file permissions |
| file dates (create, access, write) |
| file owner, group, ACL |
| file size |
| file data blocks or pointers to file data blocks |

Figure 11.2 A typical file-control block.

- The **per-process open-file table** contains a pointer to the appropriate entry in the system-wide open-file table, as well as other information.
- Buffers hold file-system blocks when they are being read from disk or written to disk.

To create a new file, an application program calls the logical file system. The logical file system knows the format of the directory structures. To create a new file, it allocates a new FCB. (Alternatively, if the file-system implementation creates all FCBs at file-system creation time, an FCB is allocated from the set of free FCBs.) The system then reads the appropriate directory into memory, updates it with the new file name and FCB, and writes it back to the disk. A typical FCB is shown in Figure 11.2.

Some operating systems, including UNIX, treat a directory exactly the same as a file—one with a "type" field indicating that it is a directory. Other operating systems, including Windows, implement separate system calls for files and directories and treat directories as entities separate from files. Whatever the larger structural issues, the logical file system can call the file-organization module to map the directory I/O into disk-block numbers, which are passed on to the basic file system and I/O control system.

Now that a file has been created, it can be used for I/O. First, though, it must be opened. The open() call passes a file name to the logical file system. The open() system call first searches the system-wide open-file table to see if the file is already in use by another process. If it is, a per-process open-file table entry is created pointing to the existing system-wide open-file table. This algorithm can save substantial overhead. If the file is not already open, the directory structure is searched for the given file name. Parts of the directory structure are usually cached in memory to speed directory operations. Once the file is found, the FCB is copied into a system-wide open-file table in memory. This table not only stores the FCB but also tracks the number of processes that have the file open.

Next, an entry is made in the per-process open-file table, with a pointer to the entry in the system-wide open-file table and some other fields. These other fields may include a pointer to the current location in the file (for the next read() or write() operation) and the access mode in which the file is open. The open() call returns a pointer to the appropriate entry in the per-process

Figure 11.3 In-memory file-system structures. (a) File open. (b) File read.

file-system table. All file operations are then performed via this pointer. The file name may not be part of the open-file table, as the system has no use for it once the appropriate FCB is located on disk. It could be cached, though, to save time on subsequent opens of the same file. The name given to the entry varies. UNIX systems refer to it as a **file descriptor**; Windows refers to it as a **file handle**.

When a process closes the file, the per-process table entry is removed, and the system-wide entry's open count is decremented. When all users that have opened the file close it, any updated metadata is copied back to the disk-based directory structure, and the system-wide open-file table entry is removed.

Some systems complicate this scheme further by using the file system as an interface to other system aspects, such as networking. For example, in UFS, the system-wide open-file table holds the inodes and other information for files and directories. It also holds similar information for network connections and devices. In this way, one mechanism can be used for multiple purposes.

The caching aspects of file-system structures should not be overlooked. Most systems keep all information about an open file, except for its actual data blocks, in memory. The BSD UNIX system is typical in its use of caches wherever disk I/O can be saved. Its average cache hit rate of 85 percent shows that these techniques are well worth implementing. The BSD UNIX system is described fully in Appendix A.

The operating structures of a file-system implementation are summarized in Figure 11.3.

11.2.2 Partitions and Mounting

The layout of a disk can have many variations, depending on the operating system. A disk can be sliced into multiple partitions, or a volume can span multiple partitions on multiple disks. The former layout is discussed here, while the latter, which is more appropriately considered a form of RAID, is covered in Section 9.7.

Each partition can be either "raw," containing no file system, or "cooked," containing a file system. Raw disk is used where no file system is appropriate. UNIX swap space can use a raw partition, for example, since it uses its own format on disk and does not use a file system. Likewise, some databases use raw disk and format the data to suit their needs. Raw disk can also hold information needed by disk RAID systems, such as bit maps indicating which blocks are mirrored and which have changed and need to be mirrored. Similarly, raw disk can contain a miniature database holding RAID configuration information, such as which disks are members of each RAID set. Raw disk use is discussed in Section 9.5.1.

Boot information can be stored in a separate partition, as described in Section 9.5.2. Again, it has its own format, because at boot time the system does not have the file-system code loaded and therefore cannot interpret the file-system format. Rather, boot information is usually a sequential series of blocks, loaded as an image into memory. Execution of the image starts at a predefined location, such as the first byte. This boot loader in turn knows enough about the file-system structure to be able to find and load the kernel and start it executing. It can contain more than the instructions for how to boot a specific operating system. For instance, many systems can be dual-booted, allowing us to install multiple operating systems on a single system. How does the system know which one to boot? A boot loader that understands multiple file systems and multiple operating systems can occupy the boot space. Once loaded, it can boot one of the operating systems available on the disk. The disk can have multiple partitions, each containing a different type of file system and a different operating system.

The root partition, which contains the operating-system kernel and sometimes other system files, is mounted at boot time. Other volumes can be automatically mounted at boot or manually mounted later, depending on the operating system. As part of a successful mount operation, the operating system verifies that the device contains a valid file system. It does so by asking the device driver to read the device directory and verifying that the directory has the expected format. If the format is invalid, the partition must have its consistency checked and possibly corrected, either with or without user intervention. Finally, the operating system notes in its in-memory mount table that a file system is mounted, along with the type of the file system. The details of this function depend on the operating system.

Microsoft Windows–based systems mount each volume in a separate name space, denoted by a letter and a colon. To record that a file system is mounted at F:, for example, the operating system places a pointer to the file system in a field of the device structure corresponding to F:. When a process specifies the driver letter, the operating system finds the appropriate file-system pointer and traverses the directory structures on that device to find the specified file or directory. Later versions of Windows can mount a file system at any point within the existing directory structure.

On UNIX, file systems can be mounted at any directory. Mounting is implemented by setting a flag in the in-memory copy of the inode for that directory. The flag indicates that the directory is a mount point. A field then points to an entry in the mount table, indicating which device is mounted there. The mount table entry contains a pointer to the superblock of the file system on that device. This scheme enables the operating system to traverse its directory structure, switching seamlessly among file systems of varying types.

11.2.3 Virtual File Systems

The previous section makes it clear that modern operating systems must concurrently support multiple types of file systems. But how does an operating system allow multiple types of file systems to be integrated into a directory structure? And how can users seamlessly move between file-system types as they navigate the file-system space? We now discuss some of these implementation details.

An obvious but suboptimal method of implementing multiple types of file systems is to write directory and file routines for each type. Instead, however, most operating systems, including UNIX, use object-oriented techniques to simplify, organize, and modularize the implementation. The use of these methods allows very dissimilar file-system types to be implemented within the same structure, including network file systems, such as NFS. Users can access files contained within multiple file systems on the local disk or even on file systems available across the network.

Data structures and procedures are used to isolate the basic system-call functionality from the implementation details. Thus, the file-system implementation consists of three major layers, as depicted schematically in Figure 11.4. The first layer is the file-system interface, based on the open(), read(), write(), and close() calls and on file descriptors.

The second layer is called the **virtual file system** (VFS) layer. The VFS layer serves two important functions:

1. It separates file-system-generic operations from their implementation by defining a clean VFS interface. Several implementations for the VFS interface may coexist on the same machine, allowing transparent access to different types of file systems mounted locally.

2. It provides a mechanism for uniquely representing a file throughout a network. The VFS is based on a file-representation structure, called a **vnode**, that contains a numerical designator for a network-wide unique file. (UNIX inodes are unique within only a single file system.) This network-wide uniqueness is required for support of network file systems. The kernel maintains one vnode structure for each active node (file or directory).

Thus, the VFS distinguishes local files from remote ones, and local files are further distinguished according to their file-system types.

The VFS activates file-system-specific operations to handle local requests according to their file-system types and calls the NFS protocol procedures for

Figure 11.4   Schematic view of a virtual file system.

remote requests. File handles are constructed from the relevant vnodes and are passed as arguments to these procedures. The layer implementing the file-system type or the remote-file-system protocol is the third layer of the architecture.

Let's briefly examine the VFS architecture in Linux. The four main object types defined by the Linux VFS are:

- The **inode object**, which represents an individual file
- The **file object**, which represents an open file
- The **superblock object**, which represents an entire file system
- The **dentry object**, which represents an individual directory entry

For each of these four object types, the VFS defines a set of operations that may be implemented. Every object of one of these types contains a pointer to a function table. The function table lists the addresses of the actual functions that implement the defined operations for that particular object. For example, an abbreviated API for some of the operations for the file object includes:

- `int open(. . .)`—Open a file.
- `int close(. . .)`—Close an already-open file.
- `ssize_t read(. . .)`—Read from a file.
- `ssize_t write(. . .)`—Write to a file.
- `int mmap(. . .)`—Memory-map a file.

An implementation of the file object for a specific file type is required to implement each function specified in the definition of the file object. (The complete definition of the file object is specified in the struct file_operations, which is located in the file /usr/include/linux/fs.h.)

Thus, the VFS software layer can perform an operation on one of these objects by calling the appropriate function from the object's function table, without having to know in advance exactly what kind of object it is dealing with. The VFS does not know, or care, whether an inode represents a disk file, a directory file, or a remote file. The appropriate function for that file's read() operation will always be at the same place in its function table, and the VFS software layer will call that function without caring how the data are actually read.

11.3   Directory Implementation

The selection of directory-allocation and directory-management algorithms significantly affects the efficiency, performance, and reliability of the file system. In this section, we discuss the trade-offs involved in choosing one of these algorithms.

11.3.1   Linear List

The simplest method of implementing a directory is to use a linear list of file names with pointers to the data blocks. This method is simple to program but time-consuming to execute. To create a new file, we must first search the directory to be sure that no existing file has the same name. Then, we add a new entry at the end of the directory. To delete a file, we search the directory for the named file and then release the space allocated to it. To reuse the directory entry, we can do one of several things. We can mark the entry as unused (by assigning it a special name, such as an all-blank name, or by including a used–unused bit in each entry), or we can attach it to a list of free directory entries. A third alternative is to copy the last entry in the directory into the freed location and to decrease the length of the directory. A linked list can also be used to decrease the time required to delete a file.

The real disadvantage of a linear list of directory entries is that finding a file requires a linear search. Directory information is used frequently, and users will notice if access to it is slow. In fact, many operating systems implement a software cache to store the most recently used directory information. A cache hit avoids the need to constantly reread the information from disk. A sorted list allows a binary search and decreases the average search time. However, the requirement that the list be kept sorted may complicate creating and deleting files, since we may have to move substantial amounts of directory information to maintain a sorted directory. A more sophisticated tree data structure, such as a balanced tree, might help here. An advantage of the sorted list is that a sorted directory listing can be produced without a separate sort step.

11.3.2   Hash Table

Another data structure used for a file directory is a hash table. Here, a linear list stores the directory entries, but a hash data structure is also used. The hash table takes a value computed from the file name and returns a pointer to the file name in the linear list. Therefore, it can greatly decrease the directory search time. Insertion and deletion are also fairly straightforward, although some provision must be made for collisions—situations in which two file names hash to the same location.

The major difficulties with a hash table are its generally fixed size and the dependence of the hash function on that size. For example, assume that we make a linear-probing hash table that holds 64 entries. The hash function converts file names into integers from 0 to 63 (for instance, by using the remainder of a division by 64). If we later try to create a 65th file, we must enlarge the directory hash table—say, to 128 entries. As a result, we need a new hash function that must map file names to the range 0 to 127, and we must reorganize the existing directory entries to reflect their new hash-function values.

Alternatively, we can use a chained-overflow hash table. Each hash entry can be a linked list instead of an individual value, and we can resolve collisions by adding the new entry to the linked list. Lookups may be somewhat slowed, because searching for a name might require stepping through a linked list of colliding table entries. Still, this method is likely to be much faster than a linear search through the entire directory.

11.4   Allocation Methods

The direct-access nature of disks gives us flexibility in the implementation of files. In almost every case, many files are stored on the same disk. The main problem is how to allocate space to these files so that disk space is utilized effectively and files can be accessed quickly. Three major methods of allocating disk space are in wide use: contiguous, linked, and indexed. Each method has advantages and disadvantages. Although some systems support all three, it is more common for a system to use one method for all files within a file-system type.

11.4.1   Contiguous Allocation

Contiguous allocation requires that each file occupy a set of contiguous blocks on the disk. Disk addresses define a linear ordering on the disk. With this ordering, assuming that only one job is accessing the disk, accessing block $b + 1$ after block b normally requires no head movement. When head movement is needed (from the last sector of one cylinder to the first sector of the next cylinder), the head need only move from one track to the next. Thus, the number of disk seeks required for accessing contiguously allocated files is minimal, as is seek time when a seek is finally needed.

Contiguous allocation of a file is defined by the disk address of the first block and length (in block units) of the file. If the file is n blocks long and starts at location b, then it occupies blocks $b, b + 1, b + 2, ..., b + n - 1$. The directory entry for each file indicates the address of the starting block and the length of the area allocated for this file (Figure 11.5).

Accessing a file that has been allocated contiguously is easy. For sequential access, the file system remembers the disk address of the last block referenced and, when necessary, reads the next block. For direct access to block i of a

Figure 11.5   Contiguous allocation of disk space.

file that starts at block *b,* we can immediately access block *b* + *i.* Thus, both sequential and direct access can be supported by contiguous allocation.

Contiguous allocation has some problems, however. One difficulty is finding space for a new file. The system chosen to manage free space determines how this task is accomplished; these management systems are discussed in Section 11.5. Any management system can be used, but some are slower than others.

The contiguous-allocation problem can be seen as a particular application of the general **dynamic storage-allocation** problem discussed in Section 7.3, which involves how to satisfy a request of size *n* from a list of free holes. First fit and best fit are the most common strategies used to select a free hole from the set of available holes. Simulations have shown that both first fit and best fit are more efficient than worst fit in terms of both time and storage utilization. Neither first fit nor best fit is clearly best in terms of storage utilization, but first fit is generally faster.

All these algorithms suffer from the problem of **external fragmentation**. As files are allocated and deleted, the free disk space is broken into little pieces. External fragmentation exists whenever free space is broken into chunks. It becomes a problem when the largest contiguous chunk is insufficient for a request; storage is fragmented into a number of holes, none of which is large enough to store the data. Depending on the total amount of disk storage and the average file size, external fragmentation may be a minor or a major problem.

One strategy for preventing loss of significant amounts of disk space to external fragmentation is to copy an entire file system onto another disk. The original disk is then freed completely, creating one large contiguous free space. We then copy the files back onto the original disk by allocating contiguous space from this one large hole. This scheme effectively **compacts** all free space into one contiguous space, solving the fragmentation problem. The cost of this compaction is time, however, and the cost can be particularly high for large hard disks. Compacting these disks may take hours and may be necessary on a weekly basis. Some systems require that this function be done **off-line**, with the file system unmounted. During this **down time**, normal system operation generally cannot be permitted, so such compaction is avoided at all costs on production machines. Most modern systems that need defragmentation can perform it **on-line** during normal system operations, but the performance penalty can be substantial.

Another problem with contiguous allocation is determining how much space is needed for a file. When the file is created, the total amount of space it will need must be found and allocated. How does the creator (program or person) know the size of the file to be created? In some cases, this determination may be fairly simple (copying an existing file, for example). In general, however, the size of an output file may be difficult to estimate.

If we allocate too little space to a file, we may find that the file cannot be extended. Especially with a best-fit allocation strategy, the space on both sides of the file may be in use. Hence, we cannot make the file larger in place. Two possibilities then exist. First, the user program can be terminated, with an appropriate error message. The user must then allocate more space and run the program again. These repeated runs may be costly. To prevent them, the user will normally overestimate the amount of space needed, resulting in considerable wasted space. The other possibility is to find a larger hole, copy the contents of the file to the new space, and release the previous space. This series of actions can be repeated as long as space exists, although it can be time consuming. The user need never be informed explicitly about what is happening, however; the system continues despite the problem, although more and more slowly.

Even if the total amount of space needed for a file is known in advance, preallocation may be inefficient. A file that will grow slowly over a long period (months or years) must be allocated enough space for its final size, even though much of that space will be unused for a long time. The file therefore has a large amount of internal fragmentation.

To minimize these drawbacks, some operating systems use a modified contiguous-allocation scheme. Here, a contiguous chunk of space is allocated initially. Then, if that amount proves not to be large enough, another chunk of contiguous space, known as an **extent**, is added. The location of a file's blocks is then recorded as a location and a block count, plus a link to the first block of the next extent. On some systems, the owner of the file can set the extent size, but this setting results in inefficiencies if the owner is incorrect. Internal fragmentation can still be a problem if the extents are too large, and external fragmentation can become a problem as extents of varying sizes are allocated and deallocated. The commercial Veritas file system uses extents to optimize performance. Veritas is a high-performance replacement for the standard UNIX UFS.

11.4.2 Linked Allocation

Linked allocation solves all problems of contiguous allocation. With linked allocation, each file is a linked list of disk blocks; the disk blocks may be scattered anywhere on the disk. The directory contains a pointer to the first

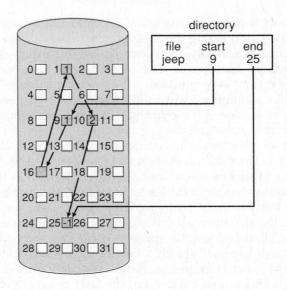

Figure 11.6   Linked allocation of disk space.

and last blocks of the file. For example, a file of five blocks might start at block 9 and continue at block 16, then block 1, then block 10, and finally block 25 (Figure 11.6). Each block contains a pointer to the next block. These pointers are not made available to the user. Thus, if each block is 512 bytes in size, and a disk address (the pointer) requires 4 bytes, then the user sees blocks of 508 bytes.

To create a new file, we simply create a new entry in the directory. With linked allocation, each directory entry has a pointer to the first disk block of the file. This pointer is initialized to null (the end-of-list pointer value) to signify an empty file. The size field is also set to 0. A write to the file causes the free-space management system to find a free block, and this new block is written to and is linked to the end of the file. To read a file, we simply read blocks by following the pointers from block to block. There is no external fragmentation with linked allocation, and any free block on the free-space list can be used to satisfy a request. The size of a file need not be declared when the file is created. A file can continue to grow as long as free blocks are available. Consequently, it is never necessary to compact disk space.

Linked allocation does have disadvantages, however. The major problem is that it can be used effectively only for sequential-access files. To find the ith block of a file, we must start at the beginning of that file and follow the pointers until we get to the ith block. Each access to a pointer requires a disk read, and some require a disk seek. Consequently, it is inefficient to support a direct-access capability for linked-allocation files.

Another disadvantage is the space required for the pointers. If a pointer requires 4 bytes out of a 512-byte block, then 0.78 percent of the disk is being used for pointers, rather than for information. Each file requires slightly more space than it would otherwise.

The usual solution to this problem is to collect blocks into multiples, called **clusters**, and to allocate clusters rather than blocks. For instance, the file system may define a cluster as four blocks and operate on the disk only in cluster units. Pointers then use a much smaller percentage of the file's disk space. This method allows the logical-to-physical block mapping to remain simple but improves disk throughput (because fewer disk-head seeks are required) and decreases the space needed for block allocation and free-list management. The cost of this approach is an increase in internal fragmentation, because more space is wasted when a cluster is partially full than when a block is partially full. Clusters can be used to improve the disk-access time for many other algorithms as well, so they are used in most file systems.

Yet another problem of linked allocation is reliability. Recall that the files are linked together by pointers scattered all over the disk, and consider what would happen if a pointer were lost or damaged. A bug in the operating-system software or a disk hardware failure might result in picking up the wrong pointer. This error could in turn result in linking into the free-space list or into another file. One partial solution is to use doubly linked lists, and another is to store the file name and relative block number in each block. However, these schemes require even more overhead for each file.

An important variation on linked allocation is the use of a **file-allocation table** (FAT). This simple but efficient method of disk-space allocation was used by the MS-DOS operating system. A section of disk at the beginning of each volume is set aside to contain the table. The table has one entry for each disk block and is indexed by block number. The FAT is used in much the same way as a linked list. The directory entry contains the block number of the first block of the file. The table entry indexed by that block number contains the block number of the next block in the file. This chain continues until it reaches the last block, which has a special end-of-file value as the table entry. An unused block is indicated by a table value of 0. Allocating a new block to a file is a simple matter of finding the first 0-valued table entry and replacing the previous end-of-file value with the address of the new block. The 0 is then replaced with the end-of-file value. An illustrative example is the FAT structure shown in Figure 11.7 for a file consisting of disk blocks 217, 618, and 339.

The FAT allocation scheme can result in a significant number of disk head seeks, unless the FAT is cached. The disk head must move to the start of the volume to read the FAT and find the location of the block in question, then move to the location of the block itself. In the worst case, both moves occur for each of the blocks. A benefit is that random-access time is improved, because the disk head can find the location of any block by reading the information in the FAT.

11.4.3 Indexed Allocation

Linked allocation solves the external-fragmentation and size-declaration problems of contiguous allocation. However, in the absence of a FAT, linked allocation cannot support efficient direct access, since the pointers to the blocks are scattered with the blocks themselves all over the disk and must be retrieved in order. Indexed allocation solves this problem by bringing all the pointers together into one location: the **index block**.

Each file has its own index block, which is an array of disk-block addresses. The ith entry in the index block points to the ith block of the file. The directory

Figure 11.7 File-allocation table.

contains the address of the index block (Figure 11.8). To find and read the ith block, we use the pointer in the ith index-block entry. This scheme is similar to the paging scheme described in Section 7.5.

When the file is created, all pointers in the index block are set to null. When the ith block is first written, a block is obtained from the free-space manager, and its address is put in the ith index-block entry.

Indexed allocation supports direct access, without suffering from external fragmentation, because any free block on the disk can satisfy a request for more space. Indexed allocation does suffer from wasted space, however. The pointer

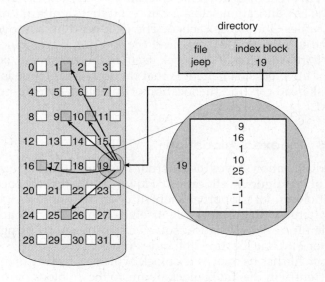

Figure 11.8 Indexed allocation of disk space.

overhead of the index block is generally greater than the pointer overhead of linked allocation. Consider a common case in which we have a file of only one or two blocks. With linked allocation, we lose the space of only one pointer per block. With indexed allocation, an entire index block must be allocated, even if only one or two pointers will be non-null.

This point raises the question of how large the index block should be. Every file must have an index block, so we want the index block to be as small as possible. If the index block is too small, however, it will not be able to hold enough pointers for a large file, and a mechanism will have to be available to deal with this issue. Mechanisms for this purpose include the following:

- **Linked scheme**. An index block is normally one disk block. Thus, it can be read and written directly by itself. To allow for large files, we can link together several index blocks. For example, an index block might contain a small header giving the name of the file and a set of the first 100 disk-block addresses. The next address (the last word in the index block) is null (for a small file) or is a pointer to another index block (for a large file).

- **Multilevel index**. A variant of linked representation uses a first-level index block to point to a set of second-level index blocks, which in turn point to the file blocks. To access a block, the operating system uses the first-level index to find a second-level index block and then uses that block to find the desired data block. This approach could be continued to a third or fourth level, depending on the desired maximum file size. With 4,096-byte blocks, we could store 1,024 four-byte pointers in an index block. Two levels of indexes allow 1,048,576 data blocks and a file size of up to 4 GB.

- **Combined scheme**. Another alternative, used in UNIX-based file systems, is to keep the first, say, 15 pointers of the index block in the file's inode. The first 12 of these pointers point to **direct blocks**; that is, they contain addresses of blocks that contain data of the file. Thus, the data for small files (of no more than 12 blocks) do not need a separate index block. If the block size is 4 KB, then up to 48 KB of data can be accessed directly. The next three pointers point to **indirect blocks**. The first points to a **single indirect block**, which is an index block containing not data but the addresses of blocks that do contain data. The second points to a **double indirect block**, which contains the address of a block that contains the addresses of blocks that contain pointers to the actual data blocks. The last pointer contains the address of a **triple indirect block**. (A UNIX inode is shown in Figure 11.9.)

  Under this method, the number of blocks that can be allocated to a file exceeds the amount of space addressable by the 4-byte file pointers used by many operating systems. A 32-bit file pointer reaches only 2^{32} bytes, or 4 GB. Many UNIX and Linux implementations now support 64-bit file pointers, which allows files and file systems to be several exbibytes in size. The ZFS file system supports 128-bit file pointers.

Indexed-allocation schemes suffer from some of the same performance problems as does linked allocation. Specifically, the index blocks can be cached in memory, but the data blocks may be spread all over a volume.

Figure 11.9   The UNIX inode.

11.4.4 Performance

The allocation methods that we have discussed vary in their storage efficiency and data-block access times. Both are important criteria in selecting the proper method or methods for an operating system to implement.

Before selecting an allocation method, we need to determine how the systems will be used. A system with mostly sequential access should not use the same method as a system with mostly random access.

For any type of access, contiguous allocation requires only one access to get a disk block. Since we can easily keep the initial address of the file in memory, we can calculate immediately the disk address of the ith block (or the next block) and read it directly.

For linked allocation, we can also keep the address of the next block in memory and read it directly. This method is fine for sequential access; for direct access, however, an access to the ith block might require i disk reads. This problem indicates why linked allocation should not be used for an application requiring direct access.

As a result, some systems support direct-access files by using contiguous allocation and sequential-access files by using linked allocation. For these systems, the type of access to be made must be declared when the file is created. A file created for sequential access will be linked and cannot be used for direct access. A file created for direct access will be contiguous and can support both direct access and sequential access, but its maximum length must be declared when it is created. In this case, the operating system must have appropriate data structures and algorithms to support both allocation methods. Files can be converted from one type to another by the creation of a new file of the desired type, into which the contents of the old file are copied. The old file may then be deleted and the new file renamed.

Indexed allocation is more complex. If the index block is already in memory, then the access can be made directly. However, keeping the index block in memory requires considerable space. If this memory space is not available, then we may have to read first the index block and then the desired data block. For a two-level index, two index-block reads might be necessary. For an extremely large file, accessing a block near the end of the file would require reading in all the index blocks before the needed data block finally could be read. Thus, the performance of indexed allocation depends on the index structure, on the size of the file, and on the position of the block desired.

Some systems combine contiguous allocation with indexed allocation by using contiguous allocation for small files (up to three or four blocks) and automatically switching to an indexed allocation if the file grows large. Since most files are small, and contiguous allocation is efficient for small files, average performance can be quite good.

Many other optimizations are in use. Given the disparity between CPU speed and disk speed, it is not unreasonable to add thousands of extra instructions to the operating system to save just a few disk-head movements. Furthermore, this disparity is increasing over time, to the point where hundreds of thousands of instructions could reasonably be used to optimize head movements.

11.5   Free-Space Management

Since disk space is limited, we need to reuse the space from deleted files for new files, if possible. (Write-once optical disks allow only one write to any given sector, and thus reuse is not physically possible.) To keep track of free disk space, the system maintains a **free-space list**. The free-space list records all free disk blocks—those not allocated to some file or directory. To create a file, we search the free-space list for the required amount of space and allocate that space to the new file. This space is then removed from the free-space list. When a file is deleted, its disk space is added to the free-space list. The free-space list, despite its name, may not be implemented as a list, as we discuss next.

11.5.1   Bit Vector

Frequently, the free-space list is implemented as a **bit map** or **bit vector**. Each block is represented by 1 bit. If the block is free, the bit is 1; if the block is allocated, the bit is 0.

For example, consider a disk where blocks 2, 3, 4, 5, 8, 9, 10, 11, 12, 13, 17, 18, 25, 26, and 27 are free and the rest of the blocks are allocated. The free-space bit map would be

0011110011111100011000000111000000 ...

The main advantage of this approach is its relative simplicity and its efficiency in finding the first free block or n consecutive free blocks on the disk. Indeed, many computers supply bit-manipulation instructions that can be used effectively for that purpose. One technique for finding the first free block on a system that uses a bit-vector to allocate disk space is to sequentially check each word in the bit map to see whether that value is not 0, since a

0-valued word contains only 0 bits and represents a set of allocated blocks. The first non-0 word is scanned for the first 1 bit, which is the location of the first free block. The calculation of the block number is

(number of bits per word) × (number of 0-value words) + offset of first 1 bit.

Again, we see hardware features driving software functionality. Unfortunately, bit vectors are inefficient unless the entire vector is kept in main memory (and is written to disk occasionally for recovery needs). Keeping it in main memory is possible for smaller disks but not necessarily for larger ones. A 1.3-GB disk with 512-byte blocks would need a bit map of over 332 KB to track its free blocks, although clustering the blocks in groups of four reduces this number to around 83 KB per disk. A 1-TB disk with 4-KB blocks requires 32 MB ($2^{40} / 2^{12} = 2^{28}$ bits $= 2^{25}$ bytes $= 2^5$ MB) to store its bit map. Given that disk size constantly increases, the problem with bit vectors will continue to escalate as well.

11.5.2 Linked List

Another approach to free-space management is to link together all the free disk blocks, keeping a pointer to the first free block in a special location on the disk and caching it in memory. This first block contains a pointer to the next free disk block, and so on. Recall our earlier example (Section 11.5.1), in which blocks 2, 3, 4, 5, 8, 9, 10, 11, 12, 13, 17, 18, 25, 26, and 27 were free and the rest of the blocks were allocated. In this situation, we would keep a pointer to block 2 as the first free block. Block 2 would contain a pointer to block 3, which would point to block 4, which would point to block 5, which would point to block 8, and so on (Figure 11.10). This scheme is not efficient; to traverse the list, we must read each block, which requires substantial I/O time. Fortunately,

Figure 11.10   Linked free-space list on disk.

however, traversing the free list is not a frequent action. Usually, the operating system simply needs a free block so that it can allocate that block to a file, so the first block in the free list is used. The FAT method incorporates free-block accounting into the allocation data structure. No separate method is needed.

11.5.3 Grouping

A modification of the free-list approach stores the addresses of n free blocks in the first free block. The first $n-1$ of these blocks are actually free. The last block contains the addresses of another n free blocks, and so on. The addresses of a large number of free blocks can now be found quickly, unlike the situation when the standard linked-list approach is used.

11.5.4 Counting

Another approach takes advantage of the fact that, generally, several contiguous blocks may be allocated or freed simultaneously, particularly when space is allocated with the contiguous-allocation algorithm or through clustering. Thus, rather than keeping a list of n free disk addresses, we can keep the address of the first free block and the number (n) of free contiguous blocks that follow the first block. Each entry in the free-space list then consists of a disk address and a count. Although each entry requires more space than would a simple disk address, the overall list is shorter, as long as the count is generally greater than 1. Note that this method of tracking free space is similar to the extent method of allocating blocks. These entries can be stored in a balanced tree, rather than a linked list, for efficient lookup, insertion, and deletion.

11.5.5 Space Maps

Oracle's ZFS file system (found in Solaris and other operating systems) was designed to encompass huge numbers of files, directories, and even file systems (in ZFS, we can create file-system hierarchies). On these scales, metadata I/O can have a large performance impact. Consider, for example, that if the free-space list is implemented as a bit map, bit maps must be modified both when blocks are allocated and when they are freed. Freeing 1 GB of data on a 1-TB disk could cause thousands of blocks of bit maps to be updated, because those data blocks could be scattered over the entire disk. Clearly, the data structures for such a system could be large and inefficient.

In its management of free space, ZFS uses a combination of techniques to control the size of data structures and minimize the I/O needed to manage those structures. First, ZFS creates **metaslabs** to divide the space on the device into chunks of manageable size. A given volume may contain hundreds of metaslabs. Each metaslab has an associated space map. ZFS uses the counting algorithm to store information about free blocks. Rather than write counting structures to disk, it uses log-structured file-system techniques to record them. The space map is a log of all block activity (allocating and freeing), in time order, in counting format. When ZFS decides to allocate or free space from a metaslab, it loads the associated space map into memory in a balanced-tree structure (for very efficient operation), indexed by offset, and replays the log into that structure. The in-memory space map is then an accurate representation of the allocated and free space in the metaslab. ZFS also condenses the map as much as possible by combining contiguous free blocks into a single entry. Finally, the free-space list is updated on disk as part of the transaction-oriented operations of ZFS. During the collection and sorting phase, block requests can still occur, and ZFS satisfies these requests from the log. In essence, the log plus the balanced tree *is* the free list.

11.6 Efficiency and Performance

Now that we have discussed various block-allocation and directory-management options, we can further consider their effect on performance and efficient disk use. Disks tend to represent a major bottleneck in system performance, since they are the slowest main computer component. In this section, we discuss a variety of techniques used to improve the efficiency and performance of secondary storage.

11.6.1 Efficiency

The efficient use of disk space depends heavily on the disk-allocation and directory algorithms in use. For instance, UNIX inodes are preallocated on a volume. Even an empty disk has a percentage of its space lost to inodes. However, by preallocating the inodes and spreading them across the volume, we improve the file system's performance. This improved performance results from the UNIX allocation and free-space algorithms, which try to keep a file's data blocks near that file's inode block to reduce seek time.

As another example, let's reconsider the clustering scheme discussed in Section 11.4, which improves file-seek and file-transfer performance at the cost of internal fragmentation. To reduce this fragmentation, BSD UNIX varies the cluster size as a file grows. Large clusters are used where they can be filled, and small clusters are used for small files and the last cluster of a file. This system is described in Appendix A.

The types of data normally kept in a file's directory (or inode) entry also require consideration. Commonly, a "last write date" is recorded to supply information to the user and to determine whether the file needs to be backed up. Some systems also keep a "last access date," so that a user can determine when the file was last read. The result of keeping this information is that, whenever the file is read, a field in the directory structure must be written to. That means the block must be read into memory, a section changed, and the block written back out to disk, because operations on disks occur only in block (or cluster) chunks. So any time a file is opened for reading, its directory entry must be read and written as well. This requirement can be inefficient for frequently accessed files, so we must weigh its benefit against its performance cost when designing a file system. Generally, every data item associated with a file needs to be considered for its effect on efficiency and performance.

Consider, for instance, how efficiency is affected by the size of the pointers used to access data. Most systems use either 32-bit or 64-bit pointers throughout the operating system. Using 32-bit pointers limits the size of a file to 2^{32}, or 4 GB. Using 64-bit pointers allows very large file sizes, but 64-bit pointers require more space to store. As a result, the allocation and free-space-management methods (linked lists, indexes, and so on) use more disk space.

One of the difficulties in choosing a pointer size—or, indeed, any fixed allocation size within an operating system—is planning for the effects of changing technology. Consider that the IBM PC XT had a 10-MB hard drive and an MS-DOS file system that could support only 32 MB. (Each FAT entry was 12 bits, pointing to an 8-KB cluster.) As disk capacities increased, larger disks had to be split into 32-MB partitions, because the file system could not track blocks beyond 32 MB. As hard disks with capacities of over 100 MB became common, the disk data structures and algorithms in MS-DOS had to be modified to allow larger file systems. (Each FAT entry was expanded to 16 bits and later to 32 bits.) The initial file-system decisions were made for efficiency reasons; however, with the advent of MS-DOS Version 4, millions of computer users were inconvenienced when they had to switch to the new, larger file system. Solaris' ZFS file system uses 128-bit pointers, which theoretically should never need to be extended. (The minimum mass of a device capable of storing 2^{128} bytes using atomic-level storage would be about 272 trillion kilograms.)

As another example, consider the evolution of the Solaris operating system. Originally, many data structures were of fixed length, allocated at system startup. These structures included the process table and the open-file table. When the process table became full, no more processes could be created. When the file table became full, no more files could be opened. The system would fail to provide services to users. Table sizes could be increased only by recompiling the kernel and rebooting the system. With later releases of Solaris, almost all kernel structures were allocated dynamically, eliminating these artificial limits on system performance. Of course, the algorithms that manipulate these tables are more complicated, and the operating system is a little slower because it must dynamically allocate and deallocate table entries; but that price is the usual one for more general functionality.

11.6.2 Performance

Even after the basic file-system algorithms have been selected, we can still improve performance in several ways. As will be discussed in Chapter 12, most disk controllers include local memory to form an on-board cache that is large enough to store entire tracks at a time. Once a seek is performed, the track is read into the disk cache starting at the sector under the disk head (reducing latency time). The disk controller then transfers any sector requests to the operating system. Once blocks make it from the disk controller into main memory, the operating system may cache the blocks there.

Some systems maintain a separate section of main memory for a **buffer cache**, where blocks are kept under the assumption that they will be used again shortly. Other systems cache file data using a **page cache**. The page cache uses virtual memory techniques to cache file data as pages rather than as file-system-oriented blocks. Caching file data using virtual addresses is far more efficient than caching through physical disk blocks, as accesses interface with virtual memory rather than the file system. Several systems—including Solaris, Linux, and Windows —use page caching to cache both process pages and file data. This is known as **unified virtual memory**.

Figure 11.11   I/O without a unified buffer cache.

Some versions of UNIX and Linux provide a **unified buffer cache**. To illustrate the benefits of the unified buffer cache, consider the two alternatives for opening and accessing a file. One approach is to use memory mapping (Section 8.7); the second is to use the standard system calls `read()` and `write()`. Without a unified buffer cache, we have a situation similar to Figure 11.11. Here, the `read()` and `write()` system calls go through the buffer cache. The memory-mapping call, however, requires using two caches—the page cache and the buffer cache. A memory mapping proceeds by reading in disk blocks from the file system and storing them in the buffer cache. Because the virtual memory system does not interface with the buffer cache, the contents of the file in the buffer cache must be copied into the page cache. This situation, known as **double caching**, requires caching file-system data twice. Not only does it waste memory but it also wastes significant CPU and I/O cycles due to the extra data movement within system memory. In addition, inconsistencies between the two caches can result in corrupt files. In contrast, when a unified buffer cache is provided, both memory mapping and the `read()` and `write()` system calls use the same page cache. This has the benefit of avoiding double caching, and it allows the virtual memory system to manage file-system data. The unified buffer cache is shown in Figure 11.12.

Regardless of whether we are caching disk blocks or pages (or both), LRU (Section 8.4.4) seems a reasonable general-purpose algorithm for block or page replacement. However, the evolution of the Solaris page-caching algorithms reveals the difficulty in choosing an algorithm. Solaris allows processes and the page cache to share unused memory. Versions earlier than Solaris 2.5.1 made no distinction between allocating pages to a process and allocating them to the page cache. As a result, a system performing many I/O operations used most of the available memory for caching pages. Because of the high rates of I/O, the page scanner (Section 8.10.2) reclaimed pages from processes—rather than from the page cache—when free memory ran low. Solaris 2.6 and Solaris 7 optionally implemented priority paging, in which the page scanner gives

Figure 11.12 I/O using a unified buffer cache.

priority to process pages over the page cache. Solaris 8 applied a fixed limit to process pages and the file-system page cache, preventing either from forcing the other out of memory. Solaris 9 and 10 again changed the algorithms to maximize memory use and minimize thrashing.

Another issue that can affect the performance of I/O is whether writes to the file system occur synchronously or asynchronously. **Synchronous writes** occur in the order in which the disk subsystem receives them, and the writes are not buffered. Thus, the calling routine must wait for the data to reach the disk drive before it can proceed. In an **asynchronous write**, the data are stored in the cache, and control returns to the caller. Most writes are asynchronous. However, metadata writes, among others, can be synchronous. Operating systems frequently include a flag in the open system call to allow a process to request that writes be performed synchronously. For example, databases use this feature for atomic transactions, to assure that data reach stable storage in the required order.

Some systems optimize their page cache by using different replacement algorithms, depending on the access type of the file. A file being read or written sequentially should not have its pages replaced in LRU order, because the most recently used page will be used last, or perhaps never again. Instead, sequential access can be optimized by techniques known as free-behind and read-ahead. **Free-behind** removes a page from the buffer as soon as the next page is requested. The previous pages are not likely to be used again and waste buffer space. With **read-ahead**, a requested page and several subsequent pages are read and cached. These pages are likely to be requested after the current page is processed. Retrieving these data from the disk in one transfer and caching them saves a considerable amount of time. One might think that a track cache on the controller would eliminate the need for read-ahead on a multiprogrammed system. However, because of the high latency and overhead involved in making many small transfers from the track cache to main memory, performing a read-ahead remains beneficial.

The page cache, the file system, and the disk drivers have some interesting interactions. When data are written to a disk file, the pages are buffered in the cache, and the disk driver sorts its output queue according to disk address. These two actions allow the disk driver to minimize disk-head seeks and to write data at times optimized for disk rotation. Unless synchronous writes are required, a process writing to disk simply writes into the cache, and the system asynchronously writes the data to disk when convenient. The user process sees very fast writes. When data are read from a disk file, the block I/O system does some read-ahead; however, writes are much more nearly asynchronous than are reads. Thus, output to the disk through the file system is often faster than is input for large transfers, counter to intuition.

11.7   Recovery

Files and directories are kept both in main memory and on disk, and care must be taken to ensure that a system failure does not result in loss of data or in data inconsistency. We deal with these issues in this section. We also consider how a system can recover from such a failure.

A system crash can cause inconsistencies among on-disk file-system data structures, such as directory structures, free-block pointers, and free FCB pointers. Many file systems apply changes to these structures in place. A typical operation, such as creating a file, can involve many structural changes within the file system on the disk. Directory structures are modified, FCBs are allocated, data blocks are allocated, and the free counts for all of these blocks are decreased. These changes can be interrupted by a crash, and inconsistencies among the structures can result. For example, the free FCB count might indicate that an FCB had been allocated, but the directory structure might not point to the FCB. Compounding this problem is the caching that operating systems do to optimize I/O performance. Some changes may go directly to disk, while others may be cached. If the cached changes do not reach disk before a crash occurs, more corruption is possible.

In addition to crashes, bugs in file-system implementation, disk controllers, and even user applications can corrupt a file system. File systems have varying methods to deal with corruption, depending on the file-system data structures and algorithms. We deal with these issues next.

11.7.1   Consistency Checking

Whatever the cause of corruption, a file system must first detect the problems and then correct them. For detection, a scan of all the metadata on each file system can confirm or deny the consistency of the system. Unfortunately, this scan can take minutes or hours and should occur every time the system boots. Alternatively, a file system can record its state within the file-system metadata. At the start of any metadata change, a status bit is set to indicate that the metadata is in flux. If all updates to the metadata complete successfully, the file system can clear that bit. If, however, the status bit remains set, a consistency checker is run.

The **consistency checker**—a systems program such as `fsck` in UNIX— compares the data in the directory structure with the data blocks on disk and tries to fix any inconsistencies it finds. The allocation and free-space-management algorithms dictate what types of problems the checker can find and how successful it will be in fixing them. For instance, if linked allocation is used and there is a link from any block to its next block, then the entire file can be reconstructed from the data blocks, and the directory structure can be recreated. In contrast, the loss of a directory entry on an indexed allocation system can be disastrous, because the data blocks have no knowledge of one another. For this reason, UNIX caches directory entries for reads; but any write that results in space allocation, or other metadata changes, is done synchronously, before the corresponding data blocks are written. Of course, problems can still occur if a synchronous write is interrupted by a crash.

11.7.2 Log-Structured File Systems

Computer scientists often find that algorithms and technologies originally used in one area are equally useful in other areas. Such is the case with the database log-based recovery algorithms. These logging algorithms have been applied successfully to the problem of consistency checking. The resulting implementations are known as **log-based transaction-oriented** (or **journaling**) file systems.

Note that with the consistency-checking approach discussed in the preceding section, we essentially allow structures to break and repair them on recovery. However, there are several problems with this approach. One is that the inconsistency may be irreparable. The consistency check may not be able to recover the structures, resulting in loss of files and even entire directories. Consistency checking can require human intervention to resolve conflicts, and that is inconvenient if no human is available. The system can remain unavailable until the human tells it how to proceed. Consistency checking also takes system and clock time. To check terabytes of data, hours of clock time may be required.

The solution to this problem is to apply log-based recovery techniques to file-system metadata updates. Both NTFS and the Veritas file system use this method, and it is included in recent versions of UFS on Solaris. In fact, it is becoming common on many operating systems.

Fundamentally, all metadata changes are written sequentially to a log. Each set of operations for performing a specific task is a **transaction**. Once the changes are written to this log, they are considered to be committed, and the system call can return to the user process, allowing it to continue execution. Meanwhile, these log entries are replayed across the actual file-system structures. As the changes are made, a pointer is updated to indicate which actions have completed and which are still incomplete. When an entire committed transaction is completed, it is removed from the log file, which is actually a circular buffer. A **circular buffer** writes to the end of its space and then continues at the beginning, overwriting older values as it goes. We would not want the buffer to write over data that had not yet been saved, so that scenario is avoided. The log may be in a separate section of the file system or even on a separate disk spindle. It is more efficient, but more complex, to have it under separate read and write heads, thereby decreasing head contention and seek times.

If the system crashes, the log file will contain zero or more transactions. Any transactions it contains were not completed to the file system, even though they were committed by the operating system, so they must now be completed. The transactions can be executed from the pointer until the work is complete so that the file-system structures remain consistent. The only problem occurs when a transaction was aborted—that is, was not committed before the system crashed. Any changes from such a transaction that were applied to the file system must be undone, again preserving the consistency of the file system. This recovery is all that is needed after a crash, eliminating any problems with consistency checking.

A side benefit of using logging on disk metadata updates is that those updates proceed much faster than when they are applied directly to the on-disk data structures. The reason is found in the performance advantage of sequential I/O over random I/O. The costly synchronous random metadata writes are turned into much less costly synchronous sequential writes to the log-structured file system's logging area. Those changes, in turn, are replayed asynchronously via random writes to the appropriate structures. The overall result is a significant gain in performance of metadata-oriented operations, such as file creation and deletion.

11.7.3   Other Solutions

Another alternative to consistency checking is employed by Network Appliance's WAFL file system and the Solaris ZFS file system. These systems never overwrite blocks with new data. Rather, a transaction writes all data and meta-data changes to new blocks. When the transaction is complete, the metadata structures that pointed to the old versions of these blocks are updated to point to the new blocks. The file system can then remove the old pointers and the old blocks and make them available for reuse. If the old pointers and blocks are kept, a snapshot is created; the snapshot is a view of the file system before the last update took place. This solution should require no consistency checking if the pointer update is done atomically. WAFL does have a consistency checker, however, so some failure scenarios can still cause metadata corruption. (See Section 11.9 for details of the WAFL file system.)

ZFS takes an even more innovative approach to disk consistency. It never overwrites blocks, just like WAFL. However, ZFS goes further and provides checksumming of all metadata and data blocks. This solution (when combined with RAID) assures that data are always correct. ZFS therefore has no consistency checker. (More details on ZFS are found in Section 9.7.6.)

11.7.4   Backup and Restore

Magnetic disks sometimes fail, and care must be taken to ensure that the data lost in such a failure are not lost forever. To this end, system programs can be used to back up data from disk to another storage device, such as a magnetic tape or other hard disk. Recovery from the loss of an individual file, or of an entire disk, may then be a matter of restoring the data from backup.

To minimize the copying needed, we can use information from each file's directory entry. For instance, if the backup program knows when the last backup of a file was done, and the file's last write date in the directory indicates that the file has not changed since that date, then the file does not need to be copied again. A typical backup schedule may then be as follows:

- **Day 1**. Copy to a backup medium all files from the disk. This is called a full backup.

- **Day** 2. Copy to another medium all files changed since day 1. This is an incremental backup.

- **Day** 3. Copy to another medium all files changed since day 2.

  .
  .
  .

- **Day** N. Copy to another medium all files changed since day $N-1$. Then go back to day 1.

The new cycle can have its backup written over the previous set or onto a new set of backup media.

Using this method, we can restore an entire disk by starting restores with the full backup and continuing through each of the incremental backups. Of course, the larger the value of N, the greater the number of media that must be read for a complete restore. An added advantage of this backup cycle is that we can restore any file accidentally deleted during the cycle by retrieving the deleted file from the backup of the previous day.

The length of the cycle is a compromise between the amount of backup medium needed and the number of days covered by a restore. To decrease the number of tapes that must be read to do a restore, an option is to perform a full backup and then each day back up all files that have changed since the full backup. In this way, a restore can be done via the most recent incremental backup and the full backup, with no other incremental backups needed. The trade-off is that more files will be modified each day, so each successive incremental backup involves more files and more backup media.

A user may notice that a particular file is missing or corrupted long after the damage was done. For this reason, we usually plan to take a full backup from time to time that will be saved "forever." It is a good idea to store these permanent backups far away from the regular backups to protect against hazard, such as a fire that destroys the computer and all the backups too. And if the backup cycle reuses media, we must take care not to reuse the media too many times—if the media wear out, it might not be possible to restore any data from the backups.

11.8 NFS

Network file systems are commonplace. They are typically integrated with the overall directory structure and interface of the client system. NFS is a good example of a widely used, well implemented client–server network file system. Here, we use it as an example to explore the implementation details of network file systems.

NFS is both an implementation and a specification of a software system for accessing remote files across LANs (or even WANs). NFS is part of ONC+, which most UNIX vendors and some PC operating systems support. The implementation described here is part of the Solaris operating system, which is a modified version of UNIX SVR4. It uses either the TCP or UDP/IP protocol (depending on

Figure 11.13   Three independent file systems.

the interconnecting network). The specification and the implementation are intertwined in our description of NFS. Whenever detail is needed, we refer to the Solaris implementation; whenever the description is general, it applies to the specification also.

There are multiple versions of NFS, with the latest being Version 4. Here, we describe Version 3, as that is the one most commonly deployed.

11.8.1   Overview

NFS views a set of interconnected workstations as a set of independent machines with independent file systems. The goal is to allow some degree of sharing among these file systems (on explicit request) in a transparent manner. Sharing is based on a client–server relationship. A machine may be, and often is, both a client and a server. Sharing is allowed between any pair of machines. To ensure machine independence, sharing of a remote file system affects only the client machine and no other machine.

So that a remote directory will be accessible in a transparent manner from a particular machine—say, from *M1*—a client of that machine must first carry out a mount operation. The semantics of the operation involve mounting a remote directory over a directory of a local file system. Once the mount operation is completed, the mounted directory looks like an integral subtree of the local file system, replacing the subtree descending from the local directory. The local directory becomes the name of the root of the newly mounted directory. Specification of the remote directory as an argument for the mount operation is not done transparently; the location (or host name) of the remote directory has to be provided. However, from then on, users on machine *M1* can access files in the remote directory in a totally transparent manner.

To illustrate file mounting, consider the file system depicted in Figure 11.13, where the triangles represent subtrees of directories that are of interest. The figure shows three independent file systems of machines named *U*, *S1*, and *S2*. At this point, on each machine, only the local files can be accessed. Figure 11.14(a) shows the effects of mounting S1:/usr/shared over U:/usr/local. This figure depicts the view users on *U* have of their file system. After the mount is complete, they can access any file within the dir1 directory using the

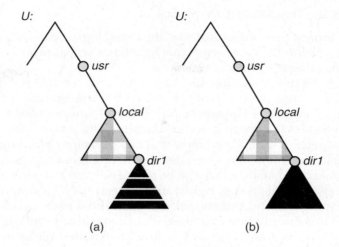

Figure 11.14   Mounting in NFS. (a) Mounts. (b) Cascading mounts.

prefix /usr/local/dir1. The original directory /usr/local on that machine is no longer visible.

Subject to access-rights accreditation, any file system, or any directory within a file system, can be mounted remotely on top of any local directory. Diskless workstations can even mount their own roots from servers. Cascading mounts are also permitted in some NFS implementations. That is, a file system can be mounted over another file system that is remotely mounted, not local. A machine is affected by only those mounts that it has itself invoked. Mounting a remote file system does not give the client access to other file systems that were, by chance, mounted over the former file system. Thus, the mount mechanism does not exhibit a transitivity property.

In Figure 11.14(b), we illustrate cascading mounts. The figure shows the result of mounting S2:/usr/dir2 over U:/usr/local/dir1, which is already remotely mounted from *S1*. Users can access files within dir2 on *U* using the prefix /usr/local/dir1. If a shared file system is mounted over a user's home directories on all machines in a network, the user can log into any workstation and get their home environment. This property permits user mobility.

One of the design goals of NFS was to operate in a heterogeneous environment of different machines, operating systems, and network architectures. The NFS specification is independent of these media. This independence is achieved through the use of RPC primitives built on top of an external data representation (XDR) protocol used between two implementation-independent interfaces. Hence, if the system's heterogeneous machines and file systems are properly interfaced to NFS, file systems of different types can be mounted both locally and remotely.

The NFS specification distinguishes between the services provided by a mount mechanism and the actual remote-file-access services. Accordingly, two separate protocols are specified for these services: a mount protocol and a protocol for remote file accesses, the NFS **protocol**. The protocols are specified as sets of RPCs. These RPCs are the building blocks used to implement transparent remote file access.

11.8.2   The Mount Protocol

The **mount protocol** establishes the initial logical connection between a server and a client. In Solaris, each machine has a server process, outside the kernel, performing the protocol functions.

A mount operation includes the name of the remote directory to be mounted and the name of the server machine storing it. The mount request is mapped to the corresponding RPC and is forwarded to the mount server running on the specific server machine. The server maintains an **export list** that specifies local file systems that it exports for mounting, along with names of machines that are permitted to mount them. (In Solaris, this list is the /etc/dfs/dfstab, which can be edited only by a superuser.) The specification can also include access rights, such as read only. To simplify the maintenance of export lists and mount tables, a distributed naming scheme can be used to hold this information and make it available to appropriate clients.

Recall that any directory within an exported file system can be mounted remotely by an accredited machine. A component unit is such a directory. When the server receives a mount request that conforms to its export list, it returns to the client a file handle that serves as the key for further accesses to files within the mounted file system. The file handle contains all the information that the server needs to distinguish an individual file it stores. In UNIX terms, the file handle consists of a file-system identifier and an inode number to identify the exact mounted directory within the exported file system.

The server also maintains a list of the client machines and the corresponding currently mounted directories. This list is used mainly for administrative purposes—for instance, for notifying all clients that the server is going down. Only through addition and deletion of entries in this list can the server state be affected by the mount protocol.

Usually, a system has a static mounting preconfiguration that is established at boot time (/etc/vfstab in Solaris); however, this layout can be modified. In addition to the actual mount procedure, the mount protocol includes several other procedures, such as unmount and return export list.

11.8.3   The NFS Protocol

The NFS protocol provides a set of RPCs for remote file operations. The procedures support the following operations:

- Searching for a file within a directory
- Reading a set of directory entries
- Manipulating links and directories
- Accessing file attributes
- Reading and writing files

These procedures can be invoked only after a file handle for the remotely mounted directory has been established.

The omission of open and close operations is intentional. A prominent feature of NFS servers is that they are stateless. Servers do not maintain information about their clients from one access to another. No parallels to

UNIX's open-files table or file structures exist on the server side. Consequently, each request has to provide a full set of arguments, including a unique file identifier and an absolute offset inside the file for the appropriate operations. The resulting design is robust; no special measures need be taken to recover a server after a crash. File operations must be idempotent for this purpose, that is, the same operation performed multiple times has the same effect as if it were only performed once. To achieve idempotence, every NFS request has a sequence number, allowing the server to determine if a request has been duplicated or if any are missing.

Maintaining the list of clients that we mentioned seems to violate the statelessness of the server. However, this list is not essential for the correct operation of the client or the server, and hence it does not need to be restored after a server crash. Consequently, it may include inconsistent data and is treated as only a hint.

A further implication of the stateless-server philosophy and a result of the synchrony of an RPC is that modified data (including indirection and status blocks) must be committed to the server's disk before results are returned to the client. That is, a client can cache write blocks, but when it flushes them to the server, it assumes that they have reached the server's disks. The server must write all NFS data synchronously. Thus, a server crash and recovery will be invisible to a client; all blocks that the server is managing for the client will be intact. The resulting performance penalty can be large, because the advantages of caching are lost. Performance can be increased by using storage with its own nonvolatile cache (usually battery-backed-up memory). The disk controller acknowledges the disk write when the write is stored in the nonvolatile cache. In essence, the host sees a very fast synchronous write. These blocks remain intact even after a system crash and are written from this stable storage to disk periodically.

A single NFS write procedure call is guaranteed to be atomic and is not intermixed with other write calls to the same file. The NFS protocol, however, does not provide concurrency-control mechanisms. A write() system call may be broken down into several RPC writes, because each NFS write or read call can contain up to 8 KB of data and UDP packets are limited to 1,500 bytes. As a result, two users writing to the same remote file may get their data intermixed. The claim is that, because lock management is inherently stateful, a service outside the NFS should provide locking (and Solaris does). Users are advised to coordinate access to shared files using mechanisms outside the scope of NFS.

NFS is integrated into the operating system via a VFS. As an illustration of the architecture, let's trace how an operation on an already-open remote file is handled (follow the example in Figure 11.15). The client initiates the operation with a regular system call. The operating-system layer maps this call to a VFS operation on the appropriate vnode. The VFS layer identifies the file as a remote one and invokes the appropriate NFS procedure. An RPC call is made to the NFS service layer at the remote server. This call is reinjected to the VFS layer on the remote system, which finds that it is local and invokes the appropriate file-system operation. This path is retraced to return the result. An advantage of this architecture is that the client and the server are identical; thus, a machine may be a client, or a server, or both. The actual service on each server is performed by kernel threads.

Figure 11.15 Schematic view of the NFS architecture.

11.8.4 Path-Name Translation

Path-name translation in NFS involves the parsing of a path name such as /usr/local/dir1/file.txt into separate directory entries, or components: (1) usr, (2) local, and (3) dir1. Path-name translation is done by breaking the path into component names and performing a separate NFS lookup call for every pair of component name and directory vnode. Once a mount point is crossed, every component lookup causes a separate RPC to the server. This expensive path-name-traversal scheme is needed, since the layout of each client's logical name space is unique, dictated by the mounts the client has performed. It would be much more efficient to hand a server a path name and receive a target vnode once a mount point is encountered. At any point, however, there might be another mount point for the particular client of which the stateless server is unaware.

So that lookup is fast, a directory-name-lookup cache on the client side holds the vnodes for remote directory names. This cache speeds up references to files with the same initial path name. The directory cache is discarded when attributes returned from the server do not match the attributes of the cached vnode.

Recall that some implementations of NFS allow mounting a remote file system on top of another already-mounted remote file system (a cascading mount). When a client has a cascading mount, more than one server can be involved in a path-name traversal. However, when a client does a lookup on a directory on which the server has mounted a file system, the client sees the underlying directory instead of the mounted directory.

11.8.5   Remote Operations

With the exception of opening and closing files, there is an almost one-to-one correspondence between the regular UNIX system calls for file operations and the NFS protocol RPCs. Thus, a remote file operation can be translated directly to the corresponding RPC. Conceptually, NFS adheres to the remote-service paradigm; but in practice, buffering and caching techniques are employed for the sake of performance. No direct correspondence exists between a remote operation and an RPC. Instead, file blocks and file attributes are fetched by the RPCs and are cached locally. Future remote operations use the cached data, subject to consistency constraints.

There are two caches: the file-attribute (inode-information) cache and the file-blocks cache. When a file is opened, the kernel checks with the remote server to determine whether to fetch or revalidate the cached attributes. The cached file blocks are used only if the corresponding cached attributes are up to date. The attribute cache is updated whenever new attributes arrive from the server. Cached attributes are, by default, discarded after 60 seconds. Both read-ahead and delayed-write techniques are used between the server and the client. Clients do not free delayed-write blocks until the server confirms that the data have been written to disk. Delayed-write is retained even when a file is opened concurrently, in conflicting modes. Hence, UNIX semantics (Section 10.5.3.1) are not preserved.

Tuning the system for performance makes it difficult to characterize the consistency semantics of NFS. New files created on a machine may not be visible elsewhere for 30 seconds. Furthermore, writes to a file at one site may or may not be visible at other sites that have this file open for reading. New opens of a file observe only the changes that have already been flushed to the server. Thus, NFS provides neither strict emulation of UNIX semantics nor the session semantics of Andrew (Section 10.5.3.2). In spite of these drawbacks, the utility and good performance of the mechanism make it the most widely used multi-vendor-distributed system in operation.

11.9   Example: The WAFL File System

Because disk I/O has such a huge impact on system performance, file-system design and implementation command quite a lot of attention from system designers. Some file systems are general purpose, in that they can provide reasonable performance and functionality for a wide variety of file sizes, file types, and I/O loads. Others are optimized for specific tasks in an attempt to provide better performance in those areas than general-purpose file systems. The **write-anywhere file layout (WAFL)** from Network Appliance is an example of this sort of optimization. WAFL is a powerful, elegant file system optimized for random writes.

WAFL is used exclusively on network file servers produced by Network Appliance and is meant for use as a distributed file system. It can provide files to clients via the NFS, CIFS, ftp, and http protocols, although it was designed just for NFS and CIFS. When many clients use these protocols to talk to a file server, the server may see a very large demand for random reads and an even larger demand for random writes. The NFS and CIFS protocols cache data from read operations, so writes are of the greatest concern to file-server creators.

WAFL is used on file servers that include an NVRAM cache for writes. The WAFL designers took advantage of running on a specific architecture to optimize the file system for random I/O, with a stable-storage cache in front. Ease of use is one of the guiding principles of WAFL. Its creators also designed it to include a new snapshot functionality that creates multiple read-only copies of the file system at different points in time, as we shall see.

The file system is similar to the Berkeley Fast File System, with many modifications. It is block-based and uses inodes to describe files. Each inode contains 16 pointers to blocks (or indirect blocks) belonging to the file described by the inode. Each file system has a root inode. All of the metadata lives in files. All inodes are in one file, the free-block map in another, and the free-inode map in a third, as shown in Figure 11.16. Because these are standard files, the data blocks are not limited in location and can be placed anywhere. If a file system is expanded by addition of disks, the lengths of the metadata files are automatically expanded by the file system.

Thus, a WAFL file system is a tree of blocks with the root inode as its base. To take a snapshot, WAFL creates a copy of the root inode. Any file or metadata updates after that go to new blocks rather than overwriting their existing blocks. The new root inode points to metadata and data changed as a result of these writes. Meanwhile, the snapshot (the old root inode) still points to the old blocks, which have not been updated. It therefore provides access to the file system just as it was at the instant the snapshot was made—and takes very little disk space to do so. In essence, the extra disk space occupied by a snapshot consists of just the blocks that have been modified since the snapshot was taken.

An important change from more standard file systems is that the free-block map has more than one bit per block. It is a bitmap with a bit set for each snapshot that is using the block. When all snapshots that have been using the block are deleted, the bit map for that block is all zeros, and the block is free to be reused. Used blocks are never overwritten, so writes are very fast, because a write can occur at the free block nearest the current head location. There are many other performance optimizations in WAFL as well.

Many snapshots can exist simultaneously, so one can be taken each hour of the day and each day of the month. A user with access to these snapshots can access files as they were at any of the times the snapshots were taken. The snapshot facility is also useful for backups, testing, versioning, and so on.

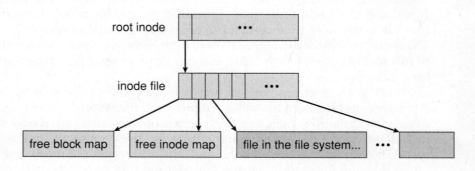

Figure 11.16 The WAFL file layout.

(a) Before a snapshot.

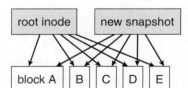

(b) After a snapshot, before any blocks change.

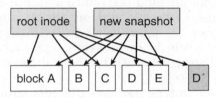

(c) After block D has changed to D´.

Figure 11.17   Snapshots in WAFL.

WAFL's snapshot facility is very efficient in that it does not even require that copy-on-write copies of each data block be taken before the block is modified. Other file systems provide snapshots, but frequently with less efficiency. WAFL snapshots are depicted in Figure 11.17.

Newer versions of WAFL actually allow read–write snapshots, known as **clones**. Clones are also efficient, using the same techniques as shapshots. In this case, a read-only snapshot captures the state of the file system, and a clone refers back to that read-only snapshot. Any writes to the clone are stored in new blocks, and the clone's pointers are updated to refer to the new blocks. The original snapshot is unmodified, still giving a view into the file system as it was before the clone was updated. Clones can also be promoted to replace the original file system; this involves throwing out all of the old pointers and any associated old blocks. Clones are useful for testing and upgrades, as the original version is left untouched and the clone deleted when the test is done or if the upgrade fails.

Another feature that naturally results from the WAFL file system implementation is **replication**, the duplication and synchronization of a set of data over a network to another system. First, a snapshot of a WAFL file system is duplicated to another system. When another snapshot is taken on the source system, it is relatively easy to update the remote system just by sending over all blocks contained in the new snapshot. These blocks are the ones that have changed between the times the two snapshots were taken. The remote system adds these blocks to the file system and updates its pointers, and the new system then is a duplicate of the source system as of the time of the second snapshot. Repeating this process maintains the remote system as a nearly up-to-date copy of the first system. Such replication is used for disaster recovery. Should the first system be destroyed, most of its data are available for use on the remote system.

Finally, we should note that the ZFS file system supports similarly efficient snapshots, clones, and replication.

11.10 Summary

The file system resides permanently on secondary storage, which is designed to hold a large amount of data permanently. The most common secondary-storage medium is the disk.

Physical disks may be segmented into partitions to control media use and to allow multiple, possibly varying, file systems on a single spindle. These file systems are mounted onto a logical file system architecture to make them available for use. File systems are often implemented in a layered or modular structure. The lower levels deal with the physical properties of storage devices. Upper levels deal with symbolic file names and logical properties of files. Intermediate levels map the logical file concepts into physical device properties.

Any file-system type can have different structures and algorithms. A VFS layer allows the upper layers to deal with each file-system type uniformly. Even remote file systems can be integrated into the system's directory structure and acted on by standard system calls via the VFS interface.

The various files can be allocated space on the disk in three ways: through contiguous, linked, or indexed allocation. Contiguous allocation can suffer from external fragmentation. Direct access is very inefficient with linked allocation. Indexed allocation may require substantial overhead for its index block. These algorithms can be optimized in many ways. Contiguous space can be enlarged through extents to increase flexibility and to decrease external fragmentation. Indexed allocation can be done in clusters of multiple blocks to increase throughput and to reduce the number of index entries needed. Indexing in large clusters is similar to contiguous allocation with extents.

Free-space allocation methods also influence the efficiency of disk-space use, the performance of the file system, and the reliability of secondary storage. The methods used include bit vectors and linked lists. Optimizations include grouping, counting, and the FAT, which places the linked list in one contiguous area.

Directory-management routines must consider efficiency, performance, and reliability. A hash table is a commonly used method, as it is fast and efficient. Unfortunately, damage to the table or a system crash can result in inconsistency between the directory information and the disk's contents. A consistency checker can be used to repair the damage. Operating-system backup tools allow disk data to be copied to tape, enabling the user to recover from data or even disk loss due to hardware failure, operating system bug, or user error.

Network file systems, such as NFS, use client–server methodology to allow users to access files and directories from remote machines as if they were on local file systems. System calls on the client are translated into network protocols and retranslated into file-system operations on the server. Networking and multiple-client access create challenges in the areas of data consistency and performance.

Due to the fundamental role that file systems play in system operation, their performance and reliability are crucial. Techniques such as log structures and caching help improve performance, while log structures and RAID improve reliability. The WAFL file system is an example of optimization of performance to match a specific I/O load.

Review Questions

Review questions for this chapter can be accessed by visiting our website.

Practice Exercises

Answers for the Practice Exercises can be accceed by visiting our website.

11.1 Consider a file currently consisting of 100 blocks. Assume that the file-control block (and the index block, in the case of indexed allocation) is already in memory. Calculate how many disk I/O operations are required for contiguous, linked, and indexed (single-level) allocation strategies, if, for one block, the following conditions hold. In the contiguous-allocation case, assume that there is no room to grow at the beginning but there is room to grow at the end. Also assume that the block information to be added is stored in memory.

    a.   The block is added at the beginning.

    b.   The block is added in the middle.

    c.   The block is added at the end.

    d.   The block is removed from the beginning.

    e.   The block is removed from the middle.

    f.   The block is removed from the end.

11.2 What problems could occur if a system allowed a file system to be mounted simultaneously at more than one location?

11.3 Why must the bit map for file allocation be kept on mass storage, rather than in main memory?

11.4 Consider a system that supports the strategies of contiguous, linked, and indexed allocation. What criteria should be used in deciding which strategy is best utilized for a particular file?

11.5 One problem with contiguous allocation is that the user must preallocate enough space for each file. If the file grows to be larger than the space allocated for it, special actions must be taken. One solution to this problem is to define a file structure consisting of an initial contiguous area (of a specified size). If this area is filled, the operating system automatically defines an overflow area that is linked to the initial contiguous area. If the overflow area is filled, another overflow area is allocated. Compare this implementation of a file with the standard contiguous and linked implementations.

11.6   How do caches help improve performance? Why do systems not use more or larger caches if they are so useful?

11.7   Why is it advantageous to the user for an operating system to dynamically allocate its internal tables? What are the penalties to the operating system for doing so?

11.8   Explain how the VFS layer allows an operating system to support multiple types of file systems easily.

Exercises

11.9   Consider a file system that uses a modifed contiguous-allocation scheme with support for extents. A file is a collection of extents, with each extent corresponding to a contiguous set of blocks. A key issue in such systems is the degree of variability in the size of the extents. What are the advantages and disadvantages of the following schemes?

    a.   All extents are of the same size, and the size is predetermined.

    b.   Extents can be of any size and are allocated dynamically.

    c.   Extents can be of a few fixed sizes, and these sizes are predetermined.

11.10   Contrast the performance of the three techniques for allocating disk blocks (contiguous, linked, and indexed) for both sequential and random file access.

11.11   What are the advantages of the variant of linked allocation that uses a FAT to chain together the blocks of a file?

11.12   Consider a system where free space is kept in a free-space list.

    a.   Suppose that the pointer to the free-space list is lost. Can the system reconstruct the free-space list? Explain your answer.

    b.   Consider a file system similar to the one used by UNIX with indexed allocation. How many disk I/O operations might be required to read the contents of a small local file at /a/b/c? Assume that none of the disk blocks is currently being cached.

    c.   Suggest a scheme to ensure that the pointer is never lost as a result of memory failure.

11.13   Some file systems allow disk storage to be allocated at different levels of granularity. For instance, a file system could allocate 4 KB of disk space as a single 4-KB block or as eight 512-byte blocks. How could we take advantage of this flexibility to improve performance? What modifications would have to be made to the free-space management scheme in order to support this feature?

11.14 Discuss how performance optimizations for file systems might result in difficulties in maintaining the consistency of the systems in the event of computer crashes.

11.15 Consider a file system on a disk that has both logical and physical block sizes of 512 bytes. Assume that the information about each file is already in memory. For each of the three allocation strategies (contiguous, linked, and indexed), answer these questions:

    a. How is the logical-to-physical address mapping accomplished in this system? (For the indexed allocation, assume that a file is always less than 512 blocks long.)

    b. If we are currently at logical block 10 (the last block accessed was block 10) and want to access logical block 4, how many physical blocks must be read from the disk?

11.16 Consider a file system that uses inodes to represent files. Disk blocks are 8 KB in size, and a pointer to a disk block requires 4 bytes. This file system has 12 direct disk blocks, as well as single, double, and triple indirect disk blocks. What is the maximum size of a file that can be stored in this file system?

11.17 Fragmentation on a storage device can be eliminated by recompaction of the information. Typical disk devices do not have relocation or base registers (such as those used when memory is to be compacted), so how can we relocate files? Give three reasons why recompacting and relocation of files are often avoided.

11.18 Assume that in a particular augmentation of a remote-file-access protocol, each client maintains a name cache that caches translations from file names to corresponding file handles. What issues should we take into account in implementing the name cache?

11.19 Explain why logging metadata updates ensures recovery of a file system after a file-system crash.

11.20 Consider the following backup scheme:

- **Day 1**. Copy to a backup medium all files from the disk.
- **Day 2**. Copy to another medium all files changed since day 1.
- **Day 3**. Copy to another medium all files changed since day 1.

This differs from the schedule given in Section 11.7.4 by having all subsequent backups copy all files modified since the first full backup. What are the benefits of this system over the one in Section 11.7.4? What are the drawbacks? Are restore operations made easier or more difficult? Explain your answer.

Programming Problems

The following exercise examines the relationship between files and inodes on a UNIX or Linux system. On these systems, files are represented with inodes. That is, an inode is a file (and vice versa). You can complete this exercise on the Linux virtual machine that is provided with this text. You can also complete the exercise on any Linux, UNIX, or Mac OS X system, but it will require creating two simple text files named `file1.txt` and `file3.txt` whose contents are unique sentences.

11.21 In the source code available with this text, open `file1.txt` and examine its contents. Next, obtain the inode number of this file with the command

```
ls -li file1.txt
```

This will produce output similar to the following:

```
16980 -rw-r--r-- 2 os os 22 Sep 14 16:13 file1.txt
```

where the inode number is boldfaced. (The inode number of `file1.txt` is likely to be different on your system.)

The UNIX `ln` command creates a link between a source and target file. This command works as follows:

```
ln [-s] <source file> <target file>
```

UNIX provides two types of links: (1) **hard links** and (2) **soft links**. A hard link creates a separate target file that has the same inode as the source file. Enter the following command to create a hard link between `file1.txt` and `file2.txt`:

```
ln file1.txt file2.txt
```

What are the inode values of `file1.txt` and `file2.txt`? Are they the same or different? Do the two files have the same—or different—contents?

Next, edit `file2.txt` and change its contents. After you have done so, examine the contents of `file1.txt`. Are the contents of `file1.txt` and `file2.txt` the same or different?

Next, enter the following command which removes `file1.txt`:

```
rm file1.txt
```

Does `file2.txt` still exist as well?

Now examine the man pages for both the `rm` and `unlink` commands. Afterwards, remove `file2.txt` by entering the command

```
strace rm file2.txt
```

The `strace` command traces the execution of system calls as the command `rm file2.txt` is run. What system call is used for removing `file2.txt`?

A soft link (or symbolic link) creates a new file that "points" to the name of the file it is linking to. In the source code available with this text, create a soft link to file3.txt by entering the following command:

```
ln -s file3.txt file4.txt
```

After you have done so, obtain the inode numbers of file3.txt and file4.txt using the command

```
ls -li file*.txt
```

Are the inodes the same, or is each unique? Next, edit the contents of file4.txt. Have the contents of file3.txt been altered as well? Last, delete file3.txt. After you have done so, explain what happens when you attempt to edit file4.txt.

Bibliographical Notes

The MS-DOS FAT system is explained in [Norton and Wilton (1988)]. The internals of the BSD UNIX system are covered in full in [McKusick and Neville-Neil (2005)]. Details concerning file systems for Linux can be found in [Love (2010)]. The Google file system is described in [Ghemawat et al. (2003)]. FUSE can be found at http://fuse.sourceforge.net.

Log-structured file organizations for enhancing both performance and consistency are discussed in [Rosenblum and Ousterhout (1991)], [Seltzer et al. (1993)], and [Seltzer et al. (1995)]. Algorithms such as balanced trees (and much more) are covered by [Knuth (1998)] and [Cormen et al. (2009)]. [Silvers (2000)] discusses implementing the page cache in the NetBSD operating system. The ZFS source code for space maps can be found at http://src.opensolaris.org/source/xref/onnv/onnv-gate/usr/src/uts/common/fs/zfs/space_map.c.

The network file system (NFS) is discussed in [Callaghan (2000)]. NFS Version 4 is a standard described at http://www.ietf.org/rfc/rfc3530.txt. [Ousterhout (1991)] discusses the role of distributed state in networked file systems. Log-structured designs for networked file systems are proposed in [Hartman and Ousterhout (1995)] and [Thekkath et al. (1997)]. NFS and the UNIX file system (UFS) are described in [Vahalia (1996)] and [Mauro and McDougall (2007)]. The NTFS file system is explained in [Solomon (1998)]. The Ext3 file system used in Linux is described in [Mauerer (2008)] and the WAFL file system is covered in [Hitz et al. (1995)]. ZFS documentation can be found at http://www.opensolaris.org/os/community/ZFS/docs.

Bibliography

[Callaghan (2000)]   B. Callaghan, *NFS Illustrated*, Addison-Wesley (2000).

[Cormen et al. (2009)]   T. H. Cormen, C. E. Leiserson, R. L. Rivest, and C. Stein, *Introduction to Algorithms,* Third Edition, MIT Press (2009).

[Ghemawat et al. (2003)]   S. Ghemawat, H. Gobioff, and S.-T. Leung, "The Google File System", *Proceedings of the ACM Symposium on Operating Systems Principles* (2003).

[Hartman and Ousterhout (1995)] J. H. Hartman and J. K. Ousterhout, "The Zebra Striped Network File System", *ACM Transactions on Computer Systems*, Volume 13, Number 3 (1995), pages 274–310.

[Hitz et al. (1995)] D. Hitz, J. Lau, and M. Malcolm, "File System Design for an NFS File Server Appliance", Technical report, NetApp (1995).

[Knuth (1998)] D. E. Knuth, *The Art of Computer Programming, Volume 3: Sorting and Searching*, Second Edition, Addison-Wesley (1998).

[Love (2010)] R. Love, *Linux Kernel Development*, Third Edition, Developer's Library (2010).

[Mauerer (2008)] W. Mauerer, *Professional Linux Kernel Architecture*, John Wiley and Sons (2008).

[Mauro and McDougall (2007)] J. Mauro and R. McDougall, *Solaris Internals: Core Kernel Architecture*, Prentice Hall (2007).

[McKusick and Neville-Neil (2005)] M. K. McKusick and G. V. Neville-Neil, *The Design and Implementation of the FreeBSD UNIX Operating System*, Addison Wesley (2005).

[Norton and Wilton (1988)] P. Norton and R. Wilton, *The New Peter Norton Programmer's Guide to the IBM PC & PS/2*, Microsoft Press (1988).

[Ousterhout (1991)] J. Ousterhout. "The Role of Distributed State". *In CMU Computer Science: a 25th Anniversary Commemorative*, R. F. Rashid, Ed., Addison-Wesley (1991).

[Rosenblum and Ousterhout (1991)] M. Rosenblum and J. K. Ousterhout, "The Design and Implementation of a Log-Structured File System", *Proceedings of the ACM Symposium on Operating Systems Principles* (1991), pages 1–15.

[Seltzer et al. (1993)] M. I. Seltzer, K. Bostic, M. K. McKusick, and C. Staelin, "An Implementation of a Log-Structured File System for UNIX", *USENIX Winter* (1993), pages 307–326.

[Seltzer et al. (1995)] M. I. Seltzer, K. A. Smith, H. Balakrishnan, J. Chang, S. McMains, and V. N. Padmanabhan, "File System Logging Versus Clustering: A Performance Comparison", *USENIX Winter* (1995), pages 249–264.

[Silvers (2000)] C. Silvers, "UBC: An Efficient Unified I/O and Memory Caching Subsystem for NetBSD", *USENIX Annual Technical Conference—FREENIX Track* (2000).

[Solomon (1998)] D. A. Solomon, *Inside Windows NT*, Second Edition, Microsoft Press (1998).

[Thekkath et al. (1997)] C. A. Thekkath, T. Mann, and E. K. Lee, "Frangipani: A Scalable Distributed File System", *Symposium on Operating Systems Principles* (1997), pages 224–237.

[Vahalia (1996)] U. Vahalia, *Unix Internals: The New Frontiers*, Prentice Hall (1996).

CHAPTER 12

I/O Systems

The two main jobs of a computer are I/O and processing. In many cases, the main job is I/O, and the processing is merely incidental. For instance, when we browse a web page or edit a file, our immediate interest is to read or enter some information, not to compute an answer.

The role of the operating system in computer I/O is to manage and control I/O operations and I/O devices. Although related topics appear in other chapters, here we bring together the pieces to paint a complete picture of I/O. First, we describe the basics of I/O hardware, because the nature of the hardware interface places constraints on the internal facilities of the operating system. Next, we discuss the I/O services provided by the operating system and the embodiment of these services in the application I/O interface. Then, we explain how the operating system bridges the gap between the hardware interface and the application interface. We also discuss the UNIX System V STREAMS mechanism, which enables an application to assemble pipelines of driver code dynamically. Finally, we discuss the performance aspects of I/O and the principles of operating-system design that improve I/O performance.

CHAPTER OBJECTIVES

- To explore the structure of an operating system's I/O subsystem.
- To discuss the principles and complexities of I/O hardware.
- To explain the performance aspects of I/O hardware and software.

12.1 Overview

The control of devices connected to the computer is a major concern of operating-system designers. Because I/O devices vary so widely in their function and speed (consider a mouse, a hard disk, and a tape robot), varied methods are needed to control them. These methods form the I/O subsystem of the kernel, which separates the rest of the kernel from the complexities of managing I/O devices.

I/O-device technology exhibits two conflicting trends. On the one hand, we see increasing standardization of software and hardware interfaces. This trend helps us to incorporate improved device generations into existing computers and operating systems. On the other hand, we see an increasingly broad variety of I/O devices. Some new devices are so unlike previous devices that it is a challenge to incorporate them into our computers and operating systems. This challenge is met by a combination of hardware and software techniques. The basic I/O hardware elements, such as ports, buses, and device controllers, accommodate a wide variety of I/O devices. To encapsulate the details and oddities of different devices, the kernel of an operating system is structured to use device-driver modules. The **device drivers** present a uniform device-access interface to the I/O subsystem, much as system calls provide a standard interface between the application and the operating system.

12.2   I/O Hardware

Computers operate a great many kinds of devices. Most fit into the general categories of storage devices (disks, tapes), transmission devices (network connections, Bluetooth), and human-interface devices (screen, keyboard, mouse, audio in and out). Other devices are more specialized, such as those involved in the steering of a jet. In these aircraft, a human gives input to the flight computer via a joystick and foot pedals, and the computer sends output commands that cause motors to move rudders and flaps and fuels to the engines. Despite the incredible variety of I/O devices, though, we need only a few concepts to understand how the devices are attached and how the software can control the hardware.

A device communicates with a computer system by sending signals over a cable or even through the air. The device communicates with the machine via a connection point, or **port**—for example, a serial port. If devices share a common set of wires, the connection is called a bus. A **bus** is a set of wires and a rigidly defined protocol that specifies a set of messages that can be sent on the wires. In terms of the electronics, the messages are conveyed by patterns of electrical voltages applied to the wires with defined timings. When device *A* has a cable that plugs into device *B,* and device *B* has a cable that plugs into device *C,* and device *C* plugs into a port on the computer, this arrangement is called a **daisy chain**. A daisy chain usually operates as a bus.

Buses are used widely in computer architecture and vary in their signaling methods, speed, throughput, and connection methods. A typical PC bus structure appears in Figure 12.1. In the figure, a **PCI bus** (the common PC system bus) connects the processor–memory subsystem to fast devices, and an **expansion bus** connects relatively slow devices, such as the keyboard and serial and USB ports. In the upper-right portion of the figure, four disks are connected together on a **Small Computer System Interface** (SCSI) bus plugged into a SCSI controller. Other common buses used to interconnect main parts of a computer include **PCI Express** (**PCIe**), with throughput of up to 16 GB per second, and **HyperTransport**, with throughput of up to 25 GB per second.

A **controller** is a collection of electronics that can operate a port, a bus, or a device. A serial-port controller is a simple device controller. It is a single chip (or portion of a chip) in the computer that controls the signals on the

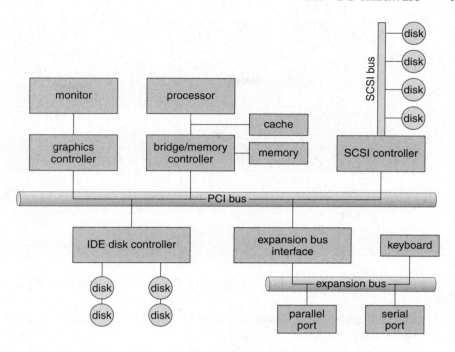

Figure 12.1   A typical PC bus structure.

wires of a serial port. By contrast, a SCSI bus controller is not simple. Because the SCSI protocol is complex, the SCSI bus controller is often implemented as a separate circuit board (or a **host adapter**) that plugs into the computer. It typically contains a processor, microcode, and some private memory to enable it to process the SCSI protocol messages. Some devices have their own built-in controllers. If you look at a disk drive, you will see a circuit board attached to one side. This board is the disk controller. It implements the disk side of the protocol for some kind of connection—SCSI or **Serial Advanced Technology Attachment (SATA)**, for instance. It has microcode and a processor to do many tasks, such as bad-sector mapping, prefetching, buffering, and caching.

How can the processor give commands and data to a controller to accomplish an I/O transfer? The short answer is that the controller has one or more registers for data and control signals. The processor communicates with the controller by reading and writing bit patterns in these registers. One way in which this communication can occur is through the use of special I/O instructions that specify the transfer of a byte or word to an I/O port address. The I/O instruction triggers bus lines to select the proper device and to move bits into or out of a device register. Alternatively, the device controller can support **memory-mapped** I/O. In this case, the device-control registers are mapped into the address space of the processor. The CPU executes I/O requests using the standard data-transfer instructions to read and write the device-control registers at their mapped locations in physical memory.

Some systems use both techniques. For instance, PCs use I/O instructions to control some devices and memory-mapped I/O to control others. Figure 12.2 shows the usual I/O port addresses for PCs. The graphics controller has I/O ports for basic control operations, but the controller has a large memory-

I/O address range (hexadecimal)	device
000–00F	DMA controller
020–021	interrupt controller
040–043	timer
200–20F	game controller
2F8–2FF	serial port (secondary)
320–32F	hard-disk controller
378–37F	parallel port
3D0–3DF	graphics controller
3F0–3F7	diskette-drive controller
3F8–3FF	serial port (primary)

Figure 12.2   Device I/O port locations on PCs (partial).

mapped region to hold screen contents. The process sends output to the screen by writing data into the memory-mapped region. The controller generates the screen image based on the contents of this memory. This technique is simple to use. Moreover, writing millions of bytes to the graphics memory is faster than issuing millions of I/O instructions. But the ease of writing to a memory-mapped I/O controller is offset by a disadvantage. Because a common type of software fault is a write through an incorrect pointer to an unintended region of memory, a memory-mapped device register is vulnerable to accidental modification. Of course, protected memory helps to reduce this risk.

An I/O port typically consists of four registers, called the status, control, data-in, and data-out registers.

- The **data-in register** is read by the host to get input.

- The **data-out register** is written by the host to send output.

- The **status register** contains bits that can be read by the host. These bits indicate states, such as whether the current command has completed, whether a byte is available to be read from the data-in register, and whether a device error has occurred.

- The **control register** can be written by the host to start a command or to change the mode of a device. For instance, a certain bit in the control register of a serial port chooses between full-duplex and half-duplex communication, another bit enables parity checking, a third bit sets the word length to 7 or 8 bits, and other bits select one of the speeds supported by the serial port.

The data registers are typically 1 to 4 bytes in size. Some controllers have FIFO chips that can hold several bytes of input or output data to expand the capacity of the controller beyond the size of the data register. A FIFO chip can hold a small burst of data until the device or host is able to receive those data.

12.2.1 Polling

The complete protocol for interaction between the host and a controller can be intricate, but the basic handshaking notion is simple. We explain handshaking with an example. Assume that 2 bits are used to coordinate the producer–consumer relationship between the controller and the host. The controller indicates its state through the busy bit in the `status` register. (Recall that to *set* a bit means to write a 1 into the bit and to *clear* a bit means to write a 0 into it.) The controller sets the busy bit when it is busy working and clears the busy bit when it is ready to accept the next command. The host signals its wishes via the `command-ready` bit in the `command` register. The host sets the `command-ready` bit when a command is available for the controller to execute. For this example, the host writes output through a port, coordinating with the controller by handshaking as follows.

1. The host repeatedly reads the busy bit until that bit becomes clear.

2. The host sets the `write` bit in the `command` register and writes a byte into the `data-out` register.

3. The host sets the `command-ready` bit.

4. When the controller notices that the `command-ready` bit is set, it sets the busy bit.

5. The controller reads the command register and sees the `write` command. It reads the `data-out` register to get the byte and does the I/O to the device.

6. The controller clears the `command-ready` bit, clears the `error` bit in the status register to indicate that the device I/O succeeded, and clears the busy bit to indicate that it is finished.

This loop is repeated for each byte.

In step 1, the host is **busy-waiting** or **polling**: it is in a loop, reading the `status` register over and over until the busy bit becomes clear. If the controller and device are fast, this method is a reasonable one. But if the wait may be long, the host should probably switch to another task. How, then, does the host know when the controller has become idle? For some devices, the host must service the device quickly, or data will be lost. For instance, when data are streaming in on a serial port or from a keyboard, the small buffer on the controller will overflow and data will be lost if the host waits too long before returning to read the bytes.

In many computer architectures, three CPU-instruction cycles are sufficient to poll a device: `read` a device register, `logical`-- and to extract a status bit, and `branch` if not zero. Clearly, the basic polling operation is efficient. But polling becomes inefficient when it is attempted repeatedly yet rarely finds a device ready for service, while other useful CPU processing remains undone. In such instances, it may be more efficient to arrange for the hardware controller to notify the CPU when the device becomes ready for service, rather than to require the CPU to poll repeatedly for an I/O completion. The hardware mechanism that enables a device to notify the CPU is called an **interrupt**.

CPU

I/O controller

Figure 12.3   Interrupt-driven I/O cycle.

12.2.2 Interrupts

The basic interrupt mechanism works as follows. The CPU hardware has a wire called the **interrupt-request line** that the CPU senses after executing every instruction. When the CPU detects that a controller has asserted a signal on the interrupt-request line, the CPU performs a state save and jumps to the **interrupt-handler routine** at a fixed address in memory. The interrupt handler determines the cause of the interrupt, performs the necessary processing, performs a state restore, and executes a `return from interrupt` instruction to return the CPU to the execution state prior to the interrupt. We say that the device controller *raises* an interrupt by asserting a signal on the interrupt request line, the CPU *catches* the interrupt and *dispatches* it to the interrupt handler, and the handler *clears* the interrupt by servicing the device. Figure 12.3 summarizes the interrupt-driven I/O cycle. We stress interrupt management in this chapter because even single-user modern systems manage hundreds of interrupts per second and servers hundreds of thousands per second.

The basic interrupt mechanism just described enables the CPU to respond to an asynchronous event, as when a device controller becomes ready for service. In a modern operating system, however, we need more sophisticated interrupt-handling features.

1. We need the ability to defer interrupt handling during critical processing.

2. We need an efficient way to dispatch to the proper interrupt handler for a device without first polling all the devices to see which one raised the interrupt.

3. We need multilevel interrupts, so that the operating system can distinguish between high- and low-priority interrupts and can respond with the appropriate degree of urgency.

In modern computer hardware, these three features are provided by the CPU and by the **interrupt-controller hardware**.

Most CPUs have two interrupt request lines. One is the **nonmaskable interrupt**, which is reserved for events such as unrecoverable memory errors. The second interrupt line is **maskable**: it can be turned off by the CPU before the execution of critical instruction sequences that must not be interrupted. The maskable interrupt is used by device controllers to request service.

The interrupt mechanism accepts an **address**—a number that selects a specific interrupt-handling routine from a small set. In most architectures, this address is an offset in a table called the **interrupt vector**. This vector contains the memory addresses of specialized interrupt handlers. The purpose of a vectored interrupt mechanism is to reduce the need for a single interrupt handler to search all possible sources of interrupts to determine which one needs service. In practice, however, computers have more devices (and, hence, interrupt handlers) than they have address elements in the interrupt vector. A common way to solve this problem is to use **interrupt chaining**, in which each element in the interrupt vector points to the head of a list of interrupt handlers. When an interrupt is raised, the handlers on the corresponding list are called one by one, until one is found that can service the request. This structure is a compromise between the overhead of a huge interrupt table and the inefficiency of dispatching to a single interrupt handler.

Figure 12.4 illustrates the design of the interrupt vector for the Intel Pentium processor. The events from 0 to 31, which are nonmaskable, are used to signal various error conditions. The events from 32 to 255, which are maskable, are used for purposes such as device-generated interrupts.

The interrupt mechanism also implements a system of **interrupt priority levels**. These levels enable the CPU to defer the handling of low-priority interrupts without masking all interrupts and makes it possible for a high-priority interrupt to preempt the execution of a low-priority interrupt.

A modern operating system interacts with the interrupt mechanism in several ways. At boot time, the operating system probes the hardware buses to determine what devices are present and installs the corresponding interrupt handlers into the interrupt vector. During I/O, the various device controllers raise interrupts when they are ready for service. These interrupts signify that output has completed, or that input data are available, or that a failure has been detected. The interrupt mechanism is also used to handle a wide variety of **exceptions**, such as dividing by 0, accessing a protected or nonexistent memory address, or attempting to execute a privileged instruction from user mode. The events that trigger interrupts have a common property: they are occurrences that induce the operating system to execute an urgent, self-contained routine.

vector number	description
0	divide error
1	debug exception
2	null interrupt
3	breakpoint
4	INTO-detected overflow
5	bound range exception
6	invalid opcode
7	device not available
8	double fault
9	coprocessor segment overrun (reserved)
10	invalid task state segment
11	segment not present
12	stack fault
13	general protection
14	page fault
15	(Intel reserved, do not use)
16	floating-point error
17	alignment check
18	machine check
19–31	(Intel reserved, do not use)
32–255	maskable interrupts

Figure 12.4   Intel Pentium processor event-vector table.

An operating system has other good uses for an efficient hardware and software mechanism that saves a small amount of processor state and then calls a privileged routine in the kernel. For example, many operating systems use the interrupt mechanism for virtual memory paging. A page fault is an exception that raises an interrupt. The interrupt suspends the current process and jumps to the page-fault handler in the kernel. This handler saves the state of the process, moves the process to the wait queue, performs page-cache management, schedules an I/O operation to fetch the page, schedules another process to resume execution, and then returns from the interrupt.

Another example is found in the implementation of system calls. Usually, a program uses library calls to issue system calls. The library routines check the arguments given by the application, build a data structure to convey the arguments to the kernel, and then execute a special instruction called a software interrupt, or trap. This instruction has an operand that identifies the desired kernel service. When a process executes the trap instruction, the interrupt hardware saves the state of the user code, switches to kernel mode, and dispatches to the kernel routine that implements the requested service. The trap is given a relatively low interrupt priority compared with those assigned to device interrupts—executing a system call on behalf of an application is less urgent than servicing a device controller before its FIFO queue overflows and loses data.

Interrupts can also be used to manage the flow of control within the kernel. For example, consider one example of the processing required to complete a disk read. One step is to copy data from kernel space to the user buffer. This copying is time consuming but not urgent—it should not block other high-priority interrupt handling. Another step is to start the next pending I/O for that disk drive. This step has higher priority. If the disks are to be used efficiently, we need to start the next I/O as soon as the previous one completes. Consequently, a pair of interrupt handlers implements the kernel code that completes a disk read. The high-priority handler records the I/O status, clears the device interrupt, starts the next pending I/O, and raises a low-priority interrupt to complete the work. Later, when the CPU is not occupied with high-priority work, the low-priority interrupt will be dispatched. The corresponding handler completes the user-level I/O by copying data from kernel buffers to the application space and then calling the scheduler to place the application on the ready queue.

A threaded kernel architecture is well suited to implement multiple interrupt priorities and to enforce the precedence of interrupt handling over background processing in kernel and application routines. We illustrate this point with the Solaris kernel. In Solaris, interrupt handlers are executed as kernel threads. A range of high priorities is reserved for these threads. These priorities give interrupt handlers precedence over application code and kernel housekeeping and implement the priority relationships among interrupt handlers. The priorities cause the Solaris thread scheduler to preempt low-priority interrupt handlers in favor of higher-priority ones, and the threaded implementation enables multiprocessor hardware to run several interrupt handlers concurrently. We describe the interrupt architecture of UNIX in Appendix A.

In summary, interrupts are used throughout modern operating systems to handle asynchronous events and to trap to supervisor-mode routines in the kernel. To enable the most urgent work to be done first, modern computers use a system of interrupt priorities. Device controllers, hardware faults, and system calls all raise interrupts to trigger kernel routines. Because interrupts are used so heavily for time-sensitive processing, efficient interrupt handling is required for good system performance.

12.2.3 Direct Memory Access

For a device that does large transfers, such as a disk drive, it seems wasteful to use an expensive general-purpose processor to watch status bits and to feed data into a controller register one byte at a time—a process termed programmed I/O (PIO). Many computers avoid burdening the main CPU with PIO by offloading some of this work to a special-purpose processor called a direct-memory-access (DMA) controller. To initiate a DMA transfer, the host writes a DMA command block into memory. This block contains a pointer to the source of a transfer, a pointer to the destination of the transfer, and a count of the number of bytes to be transferred. The CPU writes the address of this command block to the DMA controller, then goes on with other work. The DMA controller proceeds to operate the memory bus directly, placing addresses on the bus to perform transfers without the help of the main CPU. A simple DMA controller is a standard component in all modern computers, from smartphones to mainframes.

Handshaking between the DMA controller and the device controller is performed via a pair of wires called **DMA-request** and **DMA-acknowledge**. The device controller places a signal on the DMA-request wire when a word of data is available for transfer. This signal causes the DMA controller to seize the memory bus, place the desired address on the memory-address wires, and place a signal on the DMA-acknowledge wire. When the device controller receives the DMA-acknowledge signal, it transfers the word of data to memory and removes the DMA-request signal.

When the entire transfer is finished, the DMA controller interrupts the CPU. This process is depicted in Figure 12.5. When the DMA controller seizes the memory bus, the CPU is momentarily prevented from accessing main memory, although it can still access data items in its primary and secondary caches. Although this **cycle stealing** can slow down the CPU computation, offloading the data-transfer work to a DMA controller generally improves the total system performance. Some computer architectures use physical memory addresses for DMA, but others perform **direct virtual memory access (DVMA)**, using virtual addresses that undergo translation to physical addresses. DVMA can perform a transfer between two memory-mapped devices without the intervention of the CPU or the use of main memory.

On protected-mode kernels, the operating system generally prevents processes from issuing device commands directly. This discipline protects data from access-control violations and also protects the system from erroneous use of device controllers that could cause a system crash. Instead, the operating system exports functions that a sufficiently privileged process can use to access low-level operations on the underlying hardware. On kernels without memory protection, processes can access device controllers directly. This direct access can be used to achieve high performance, since it can avoid kernel communication, context switches, and layers of kernel software. Unfortunately,

Figure 12.5   Steps in a DMA transfer.

it interferes with system security and stability. The trend in general-purpose operating systems is to protect memory and devices so that the system can try to guard against erroneous or malicious applications.

12.2.4 I/O Hardware Summary

Although the hardware aspects of I/O are complex when considered at the level of detail of electronics-hardware design, the concepts that we have just described are sufficient to enable us to understand many I/O features of operating systems. Let's review the main concepts:

- A bus
- A controller
- An I/O port and its registers
- The handshaking relationship between the host and a device controller
- The execution of this handshaking in a polling loop or via interrupts
- The offloading of this work to a DMA controller for large transfers

We gave a basic example of the handshaking that takes place between a device controller and the host earlier in this section. In reality, the wide variety of available devices poses a problem for operating-system implementers. Each kind of device has its own set of capabilities, control-bit definitions, and protocols for interacting with the host—and they are all different. How can the operating system be designed so that we can attach new devices to the computer without rewriting the operating system? And when the devices vary so widely, how can the operating system give a convenient, uniform I/O interface to applications? We address those questions next.

12.3 Application I/O Interface

In this section, we discuss structuring techniques and interfaces for the operating system that enable I/O devices to be treated in a standard, uniform way. We explain, for instance, how an application can open a file on a disk without knowing what kind of disk it is and how new disks and other devices can be added to a computer without disruption of the operating system.

Like other complex software-engineering problems, the approach here involves abstraction, encapsulation, and software layering. Specifically, we can abstract away the detailed differences in I/O devices by identifying a few general kinds. Each general kind is accessed through a standardized set of functions—an **interface**. The differences are encapsulated in kernel modules called device drivers that internally are custom-tailored to specific devices but that export one of the standard interfaces. Figure 12.6 illustrates how the I/O-related portions of the kernel are structured in software layers.

The purpose of the device-driver layer is to hide the differences among device controllers from the I/O subsystem of the kernel, much as the I/O system calls encapsulate the behavior of devices in a few generic classes that hide hardware differences from applications. Making the I/O subsystem

Figure 12.6 A kernel I/O structure.

independent of the hardware simplifies the job of the operating-system developer. It also benefits the hardware manufacturers. They either design new devices to be compatible with an existing host controller interface (such as SATA), or they write device drivers to interface the new hardware to popular operating systems. Thus, we can attach new peripherals to a computer without waiting for the operating-system vendor to develop support code.

Unfortunately for device-hardware manufacturers, each type of operating system has its own standards for the device-driver interface. A given device may ship with multiple device drivers—for instance, drivers for Windows, Linux, AIX, and Mac OS X. Devices vary on many dimensions, as illustrated in Figure 12.7.

- **Character-stream or block**. A character-stream device transfers bytes one by one, whereas a block device transfers a block of bytes as a unit.

- **Sequential or random access**. A sequential device transfers data in a fixed order determined by the device, whereas the user of a random-access device can instruct the device to seek to any of the available data storage locations.

- **Synchronous or asynchronous**. A synchronous device performs data transfers with predictable response times, in coordination with other aspects of the system. An asynchronous device exhibits irregular or unpredictable response times not coordinated with other computer events.

- **Sharable or dedicated**. A sharable device can be used concurrently by several processes or threads; a dedicated device cannot.

aspect	variation	example
data-transfer mode	character block	terminal disk
access method	sequential random	modem CD-ROM
transfer schedule	synchronous asynchronous	tape keyboard
sharing	dedicated sharable	tape keyboard
device speed	latency seek time transfer rate delay between operations	
I/O direction	read only write only read–write	CD-ROM graphics controller disk

Figure 12.7 Characteristics of I/O devices.

- **Speed of operation**. Device speeds range from a few bytes per second to a few gigabytes per second.

- **Read–write, read only, or write only**. Some devices perform both input and output, but others support only one data transfer direction.

For the purpose of application access, many of these differences are hidden by the operating system, and the devices are grouped into a few conventional types. The resulting styles of device access have been found to be useful and broadly applicable. Although the exact system calls may differ across operating systems, the device categories are fairly standard. The major access conventions include block I/O, character-stream I/O, memory-mapped file access, and network sockets. Operating systems also provide special system calls to access a few additional devices, such as a time-of-day clock and a timer. Some operating systems provide a set of system calls for graphical display, video, and audio devices.

Most operating systems also have an escape (or back door) that transparently passes arbitrary commands from an application to a device driver. In UNIX, this system call is ioctl() (for "I/O control"). The ioctl() system call enables an application to access any functionality that can be implemented by any device driver, without the need to invent a new system call. The ioctl() system call has three arguments. The first is a file descriptor that connects the application to the driver by referring to a hardware device managed by that driver. The second is an integer that selects one of the commands implemented in the driver. The third is a pointer to an arbitrary data structure in memory that enables the application and driver to communicate any necessary control information or data.

12.3.1 Block and Character Devices

The **block-device interface** captures all the aspects necessary for accessing disk drives and other block-oriented devices. The device is expected to understand commands such as `read()` and `write()`. If it is a random-access device, it is also expected to have a `seek()` command to specify which block to transfer next. Applications normally access such a device through a file-system interface. We can see that `read()`, `write()`, and `seek()` capture the essential behaviors of block-storage devices, so that applications are insulated from the low-level differences among those devices.

The operating system itself, as well as special applications such as database-management systems, may prefer to access a block device as a simple linear array of blocks. This mode of access is sometimes called **raw I/O**. If the application performs its own buffering, then using a file system would cause extra, unneeded buffering. Likewise, if an application provides its own locking of file blocks or regions, then any operating-system locking services would be redundant at the least and contradictory at the worst. To avoid these conflicts, raw-device access passes control of the device directly to the application, letting the operating system step out of the way. Unfortunately, no operating-system services are then performed on this device. A compromise that is becoming common is for the operating system to allow a mode of operation on a file that disables buffering and locking. In the UNIX world, this is called **direct I/O**.

Memory-mapped file access can be layered on top of block-device drivers. Rather than offering read and write operations, a memory-mapped interface provides access to disk storage via an array of bytes in main memory. The system call that maps a file into memory returns the virtual memory address that contains a copy of the file. The actual data transfers are performed only when needed to satisfy access to the memory image. Because the transfers are handled by the same mechanism as that used for demand-paged virtual memory access, memory-mapped I/O is efficient. Memory mapping is also convenient for programmers—access to a memory-mapped file is as simple as reading from and writing to memory. Operating systems that offer virtual memory commonly use the mapping interface for kernel services. For instance, to execute a program, the operating system maps the executable into memory and then transfers control to the entry address of the executable. The mapping interface is also commonly used for kernel access to swap space on disk.

A keyboard is an example of a device that is accessed through a **character-stream interface**. The basic system calls in this interface enable an application to `get()` or `put()` one character. On top of this interface, libraries can be built that offer line-at-a-time access, with buffering and editing services (for example, when a user types a backspace, the preceding character is removed from the input stream). This style of access is convenient for input devices such as keyboards, mice, and modems that produce data for input "spontaneously" —that is, at times that cannot necessarily be predicted by the application. This access style is also good for output devices such as printers and audio boards, which naturally fit the concept of a linear stream of bytes.

12.3.2 Network Devices

Because the performance and addressing characteristics of network I/O differ significantly from those of disk I/O, most operating systems provide a network

I/O interface that is different from the read()–write()–seek() interface used for disks. One interface available in many operating systems, including UNIX and Windows, is the network socket interface.

Think of a wall socket for electricity: any electrical appliance can be plugged in. By analogy, the system calls in the socket interface enable an application to create a socket, to connect a local socket to a remote address (which plugs this application into a socket created by another application), to listen for any remote application to plug into the local socket, and to send and receive packets over the connection. To support the implementation of servers, the socket interface also provides a function called select() that manages a set of sockets. A call to select() returns information about which sockets have a packet waiting to be received and which sockets have room to accept a packet to be sent. The use of select() eliminates the polling and busy waiting that would otherwise be necessary for network I/O. These functions encapsulate the essential behaviors of networks, greatly facilitating the creation of distributed applications that can use any underlying network hardware and protocol stack.

Many other approaches to interprocess communication and network communication have been implemented. For instance, Windows provides one interface to the network interface card and a second interface to the network protocols. In UNIX, which has a long history as a proving ground for network technology, we find half-duplex pipes, full-duplex FIFOs, full-duplex STREAMS, message queues, and sockets. Information on UNIX networking is given in Section A.9.

12.3.3 Clocks and Timers

Most computers have hardware clocks and timers that provide three basic functions:

- Give the current time.
- Give the elapsed time.
- Set a timer to trigger operation X at time T.

These functions are used heavily by the operating system, as well as by time-sensitive applications. Unfortunately, the system calls that implement these functions are not standardized across operating systems.

The hardware to measure elapsed time and to trigger operations is called a **programmable interval timer**. It can be set to wait a certain amount of time and then generate an interrupt, and it can be set to do this once or to repeat the process to generate periodic interrupts. The scheduler uses this mechanism to generate an interrupt that will preempt a process at the end of its time slice. The disk I/O subsystem uses it to invoke the periodic flushing of dirty cache buffers to disk, and the network subsystem uses it to cancel operations that are proceeding too slowly because of network congestion or failures. The operating system may also provide an interface for user processes to use timers. The operating system can support more timer requests than the number of timer hardware channels by simulating virtual clocks. To do so, the kernel (or the timer device driver) maintains a list of interrupts wanted by its own routines and by user requests, sorted in earliest-time-first order. It sets the timer for the earliest time. When the timer interrupts, the kernel signals the requester and reloads the timer with the next earliest time.

On many computers, the interrupt rate generated by the hardware clock is between 18 and 60 ticks per second. This resolution is coarse, since a modern computer can execute hundreds of millions of instructions per second. The precision of triggers is limited by the coarse resolution of the timer, together with the overhead of maintaining virtual clocks. Furthermore, if the timer ticks are used to maintain the system time-of-day clock, the system clock can drift. In most computers, the hardware clock is constructed from a high-frequency counter. In some computers, the value of this counter can be read from a device register, in which case the counter can be considered a high-resolution clock. Although this clock does not generate interrupts, it offers accurate measurements of time intervals.

12.3.4 Nonblocking and Asynchronous I/O

Another aspect of the system-call interface relates to the choice between blocking I/O and nonblocking I/O. When an application issues a **blocking** system call, the execution of the application is suspended. The application is moved from the operating system's run queue to a wait queue. After the system call completes, the application is moved back to the run queue, where it is eligible to resume execution. When it resumes execution, it will receive the values returned by the system call. The physical actions performed by I/O devices are generally asynchronous—they take a varying or unpredictable amount of time. Nevertheless, most operating systems use blocking system calls for the application interface, because blocking application code is easier to understand than nonblocking application code.

Some user-level processes need **nonblocking** I/O. One example is a user interface that receives keyboard and mouse input while processing and displaying data on the screen. Another example is a video application that reads frames from a file on disk while simultaneously decompressing and displaying the output on the display.

One way an application writer can overlap execution with I/O is to write a multithreaded application. Some threads can perform blocking system calls, while others continue executing. Some operating systems provide nonblocking I/O system calls. A nonblocking call does not halt the execution of the application for an extended time. Instead, it returns quickly, with a return value that indicates how many bytes were transferred.

An alternative to a nonblocking system call is an asynchronous system call. An asynchronous call returns immediately, without waiting for the I/O to complete. The application continues to execute its code. The completion of the I/O at some future time is communicated to the application, either through the setting of some variable in the address space of the application or through the triggering of a signal or software interrupt or a call-back routine that is executed outside the linear control flow of the application. The difference between nonblocking and asynchronous system calls is that a nonblocking read() returns immediately with whatever data are available—the full number of bytes requested, fewer, or none at all. An asynchronous read() call requests a transfer that will be performed in its entirety but will complete at some future time. These two I/O methods are shown in Figure 12.8.

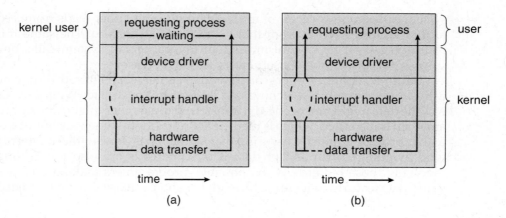

Figure 12.8 Two I/O methods: (a) synchronous and (b) asynchronous.

Asynchronous activities occur throughout modern operating systems. Frequently, they are not exposed to users or applications but rather are contained within the operating-system operation. Disk and network I/O are useful examples. By default, when an application issues a network send request or a disk write request, the operating system notes the request, buffers the I/O, and returns to the application. When possible, to optimize overall system performance, the operating system completes the request. If a system failure occurs in the interim, the application will lose any "in-flight" requests. Therefore, operating systems usually put a limit on how long they will buffer a request. Some versions of UNIX flush their disk buffers every 30 seconds, for example, or each request is flushed within 30 seconds of its occurrence. Data consistency within applications is maintained by the kernel, which reads data from its buffers before issuing I/O requests to devices, assuring that data not yet written are nevertheless returned to a requesting reader. Note that multiple threads performing I/O to the same file might not receive consistent data, depending on how the kernel implements its I/O. In this situation, the threads may need to use locking protocols. Some I/O requests need to be performed immediately, so I/O system calls usually have a way to indicate that a given request, or I/O to a specific device, should be performed synchronously.

A good example of nonblocking behavior is the `select()` system call for network sockets. This system call takes an argument that specifies a maximum waiting time. By setting it to 0, an application can poll for network activity without blocking. But using `select()` introduces extra overhead, because the `select()` call only checks whether I/O is possible. For a data transfer, `select()` must be followed by some kind of `read()` or `write()` command. A variation on this approach, found in Mach, is a blocking multiple-read call. It specifies desired reads for several devices in one system call and returns as soon as any one of them completes.

12.3.5 Vectored I/O

Some operating systems provide another major variation of I/O via their applications interfaces. Vectored I/O allows one system call to perform multiple I/O operations involving multiple locations. For example, the UNIX `readv` system call accepts a vector of multiple buffers and either reads from a source to that vector or writes from that vector to a destination. The same transfer could be caused by several individual invocations of system calls, but this scatter–gather method is useful for a variety of reasons.

Multiple separate buffers can have their contents transferred via one system call, avoiding context-switching and system-call overhead. Without vectored I/O, the data might first need to be transferred to a larger buffer in the right order and then transmitted, which is inefficient. In addition, some versions of scatter–gather provide atomicity, assuring that all the I/O is done without interruption (and avoiding corruption of data if other threads are also performing I/O involving those buffers). When possible, programmers make use of scatter–gather I/O features to increase throughput and decrease system overhead.

12.4 Kernel I/O Subsystem

Kernels provide many services related to I/O. Several services—scheduling, buffering, caching, spooling, device reservation, and error handling—are provided by the kernel's I/O subsystem and build on the hardware and device-driver infrastructure. The I/O subsystem is also responsible for protecting itself from errant processes and malicious users.

12.4.1   I/O Scheduling

To schedule a set of I/O requests means to determine a good order in which to execute them. The order in which applications issue system calls rarely is the best choice. Scheduling can improve overall system performance, can share device access fairly among processes, and can reduce the average waiting time for I/O to complete. Here is a simple example to illustrate. Suppose that a disk arm is near the beginning of a disk and that three applications issue blocking read calls to that disk. Application 1 requests a block near the end of the disk, application 2 requests one near the beginning, and application 3 requests one in the middle of the disk. The operating system can reduce the distance that the disk arm travels by serving the applications in the order 2, 3, 1. Rearranging the order of service in this way is the essence of I/O scheduling.

Operating-system developers implement scheduling by maintaining a wait queue of requests for each device. When an application issues a blocking I/O system call, the request is placed on the queue for that device. The I/O scheduler rearranges the order of the queue to improve the overall system efficiency and the average response time experienced by applications. The operating system may also try to be fair, so that no one application receives especially poor service, or it may give priority service for delay-sensitive requests. For instance, requests from the virtual memory subsystem may take priority over application requests. Several scheduling algorithms for disk I/O are detailed in Section 9.4.

When a kernel supports asynchronous I/O, it must be able to keep track of many I/O requests at the same time. For this purpose, the operating system might attach the wait queue to a device-status table. The kernel manages this table, which contains an entry for each I/O device, as shown in Figure 12.9. Each table entry indicates the device's type, address, and state (not functioning,

Figure 12.9   Device-status table.

idle, or busy). If the device is busy with a request, the type of request and other parameters will be stored in the table entry for that device.

Scheduling I/O operations is one way in which the I/O subsystem improves the efficiency of the computer. Another way is by using storage space in main memory or on disk via buffering, caching, and spooling.

12.4.2   Buffering

A **buffer**, of course, is a memory area that stores data being transferred between two devices or between a device and an application. Buffering is done for three reasons. One reason is to cope with a speed mismatch between the producer and consumer of a data stream. Suppose, for example, that a file is being received via modem for storage on the hard disk. The modem is about a thousand times slower than the hard disk. So a buffer is created in main memory to accumulate the bytes received from the modem. When an entire buffer of data has arrived, the buffer can be written to disk in a single operation. Since the disk write is not instantaneous and the modem still needs a place to store additional incoming data, two buffers are used. After the modem fills the first buffer, the disk write is requested. The modem then starts to fill the second buffer while the first buffer is written to disk. By the time the modem has filled the second buffer, the disk write from the first one should have completed, so the modem can switch back to the first buffer while the disk writes the second one. This **double buffering** decouples the producer of data from the consumer, thus relaxing timing requirements between them. The need for this decoupling is illustrated in Figure 12.10, which lists the enormous differences in device speeds for typical computer hardware.

A second use of buffering is to provide adaptations for devices that have different data-transfer sizes. Such disparities are especially common in computer networking, where buffers are used widely for fragmentation and reassembly of messages. At the sending side, a large message is fragmented into small network packets. The packets are sent over the network, and the

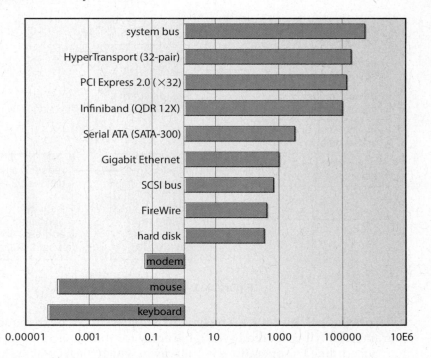

Figure 12.10 Sun Enterprise 6000 device-transfer rates (logarithmic).

receiving side places them in a reassembly buffer to form an image of the source data.

A third use of buffering is to support copy semantics for application I/O. An example will clarify the meaning of "copy semantics." Suppose that an application has a buffer of data that it wishes to write to disk. It calls the write() system call, providing a pointer to the buffer and an integer specifying the number of bytes to write. After the system call returns, what happens if the application changes the contents of the buffer? With **copy semantics**, the version of the data written to disk is guaranteed to be the version at the time of the application system call, independent of any subsequent changes in the application's buffer. A simple way in which the operating system can guarantee copy semantics is for the write() system call to copy the application data into a kernel buffer before returning control to the application. The disk write is performed from the kernel buffer, so that subsequent changes to the application buffer have no effect. Copying of data between kernel buffers and application data space is common in operating systems, despite the overhead that this operation introduces, because of the clean semantics. The same effect can be obtained more efficiently by clever use of virtual memory mapping and copy-on-write page protection.

12.4.3 Caching

A **cache** is a region of fast memory that holds copies of data. Access to the cached copy is more efficient than access to the original. For instance, the instructions of the currently running process are stored on disk, cached in physical memory, and copied again in the CPU's secondary and primary caches. The difference between a buffer and a cache is that a buffer may hold the only existing copy of a data item, whereas a cache, by definition, holds a copy on faster storage of an item that resides elsewhere.

Caching and buffering are distinct functions, but sometimes a region of memory can be used for both purposes. For instance, to preserve copy semantics and to enable efficient scheduling of disk I/O, the operating system uses buffers in main memory to hold disk data. These buffers are also used as a cache, to improve the I/O efficiency for files that are shared by applications or that are being written and reread rapidly. When the kernel receives a file I/O request, the kernel first accesses the buffer cache to see whether that region of the file is already available in main memory. If it is, a physical disk I/O can be avoided or deferred. Also, disk writes are accumulated in the buffer cache for several seconds, so that large transfers are gathered to allow efficient write schedules.

12.4.4 Spooling and Device Reservation

A **spool** is a buffer that holds output for a device, such as a printer, that cannot accept interleaved data streams. Although a printer can serve only one job at a time, several applications may wish to print their output concurrently, without having their output mixed together. The operating system solves this problem by intercepting all output to the printer. Each application's output is spooled to a separate disk file. When an application finishes printing, the spooling system queues the corresponding spool file for output to the printer. The spooling system copies the queued spool files to the printer one at a time. In some operating systems, spooling is managed by a system daemon process. In others, it is handled by an in-kernel thread. In either case, the operating system provides a control interface that enables users and system administrators to display the queue, remove unwanted jobs before those jobs print, suspend printing while the printer is serviced, and so on.

Some devices, such as tape drives and printers, cannot usefully multiplex the I/O requests of multiple concurrent applications. Spooling is one way operating systems can coordinate concurrent output. Another way to deal with concurrent device access is to provide explicit facilities for coordination. Some operating systems (including VMS) provide support for exclusive device access by enabling a process to allocate an idle device and to deallocate that device when it is no longer needed. Other operating systems enforce a limit of one open file handle to such a device. Many operating systems provide functions that enable processes to coordinate exclusive access among themselves. For instance, Windows provides system calls to wait until a device object becomes available. It also has a parameter to the OpenFile() system call that declares the types of access to be permitted to other concurrent threads. On these systems, it is up to the applications to avoid deadlock.

12.4.5 Error Handling

An operating system that uses protected memory can guard against many kinds of hardware and application errors, so that a complete system failure is not the usual result of each minor mechanical malfunction. Devices and I/O transfers can fail in many ways, either for transient reasons, as when a network becomes overloaded, or for "permanent" reasons, as when a disk controller becomes defective. Operating systems can often compensate effectively for transient failures. For instance, a disk read() failure results in a read() retry, and a network send() error results in a resend(), if the protocol so specifies. Unfortunately, if an important component experiences a permanent failure, the operating system is unlikely to recover.

As a general rule, an I/O system call will return one bit of information about the status of the call, signifying either success or failure. In the UNIX operating system, an additional integer variable named errno is used to return an error code—one of about a hundred values—indicating the general nature of the failure (for example, argument out of range, bad pointer, or file not open). By contrast, some hardware can provide highly detailed error information, although many current operating systems are not designed to convey this information to the application. For instance, a failure of a SCSI device is reported by the SCSI protocol in three levels of detail: a **sense key** that identifies the general nature of the failure, such as a hardware error or an illegal request; an **additional sense code** that states the category of failure, such as a bad command parameter or a self-test failure; and an **additional sense-code qualifier** that gives even more detail, such as which command parameter was in error or which hardware subsystem failed its self-test. Further, many SCSI devices maintain internal pages of error-log information that can be requested by the host—but seldom are.

12.4.6 I/O Protection

Errors are closely related to the issue of protection. A user process may accidentally or purposely attempt to disrupt the normal operation of a system by attempting to issue illegal I/O instructions. We can use various mechanisms to ensure that such disruptions cannot take place in the system.

To prevent users from performing illegal I/O, we define all I/O instructions to be privileged instructions. Thus, users cannot issue I/O instructions directly; they must do it through the operating system. To do I/O, a user program executes a system call to request that the operating system perform I/O on its behalf (Figure 12.11). The operating system, executing in monitor mode, checks that the request is valid and, if it is, does the I/O requested. The operating system then returns to the user.

In addition, any memory-mapped and I/O port memory locations must be protected from user access by the memory-protection system. Note that a kernel cannot simply deny all user access. Most graphics games and video editing and playback software need direct access to memory-mapped graphics controller memory to speed the performance of the graphics, for example. The kernel might in this case provide a locking mechanism to allow a section of graphics memory (representing a window on screen) to be allocated to one process at a time.

12.4.7 Kernel Data Structures

The kernel needs to keep state information about the use of I/O components. It does so through a variety of in-kernel data structures, such as the open-file table structure from Section 11.1. The kernel uses many similar structures to

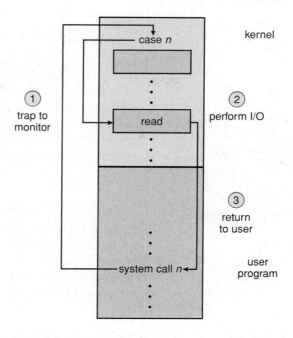

Figure 12.11 Use of a system call to perform I/O.

track network connections, character-device communications, and other I/O activities.

UNIX provides file-system access to a variety of entities, such as user files, raw devices, and the address spaces of processes. Although each of these entities supports a read() operation, the semantics differ. For instance, to read a user file, the kernel needs to probe the buffer cache before deciding whether to perform a disk I/O. To read a raw disk, the kernel needs to ensure that the request size is a multiple of the disk sector size and is aligned on a sector boundary. To read a process image, it is merely necessary to copy data from memory. UNIX encapsulates these differences within a uniform structure by using an object-oriented technique. The open-file record, shown in Figure 12.12, contains a dispatch table that holds pointers to the appropriate routines, depending on the type of file.

Some operating systems use object-oriented methods even more extensively. For instance, Windows uses a message-passing implementation for I/O. An I/O request is converted into a message that is sent through the kernel to the I/O manager and then to the device driver, each of which may change the message contents. For output, the message contains the data to be written. For input, the message contains a buffer to receive the data. The message-passing approach can add overhead, by comparison with procedural techniques that use shared data structures, but it simplifies the structure and design of the I/O system and adds flexibility.

12.4.8 Power Management

Computers residing in data centers may seem far removed from the concerns of power use, but as power costs increase and the world becomes increasingly

Figure 12.12   UNIX I/O kernel structure.

concerned with the long term effects of greenhouse gas emissions, datacenters have become a cause of concern and a target for increased efficiencies. Electricity use generates heat, and computer components can fail due to high temperatures, so cooling is part of the equation as well. Consider that the cooling of a modern datacenter may use twice as much electricity as powering the equipment does. Many approaches to datacenter power optimization are in use, ranging from interchanging datacenter air without side air, chilling with natural sources such as lake water, and solar panels.

Operating systems play a role in power use (and therefore heat generation and cooling). In cloud computing environments, processing loads can be adjusted by monitoring and management tools to evacuate all user processes from systems, idling those systems and powering them off until the load requires their power on and resource use. An operating system could analyze its load, and if sufficiently low and hardware-enabled, power off components such as CPUs and external I/O devices.

In mobile computing, power management becomes a first class operating system aspect. Minimizing power use and therefore maximizing battery life increases the usability of a device and helps a device compete with alternative devices. Today's mobile devices offer the functionality of yesterday's high-end desktop, yet are powered by batteries and are small enough to fit in your pocket. In order to provide satisfactory battery life, modern mobile operating systems are designed from the ground up with power management as a key feature. Let's examine in detail three major features that enable the popular Android mobile system to maximize battery life: power collapse, component-level power management, and wake locks.

Power collapse is the ability to put a device into a very deep sleep state, where it uses only marginally more power than if it were fully powered off, yet is still able to respond to external stimuli such as the user pressing a button, at which time it quickly powers back on. This is achieved by powering off many of the individual components within a device–such as the screen, speakers, and I/O subsystem–such that they consume no power. The operating system then places the CPU in its lowest sleep state. A modern ARM CPU might consume hundreds of milliwatts per core under typical load yet only a handful of milliwatts in its lowest sleep state. In such a state, the CPU is idle, yet is able to receive an interrupt, wake up, and resume its previous activity very quickly. Thus an idle Android phone in your pocket uses very little power, yet is able to spring to life when it receives a phone call.

How is Android able to turn off the individual components of a phone? How does it know when it is safe to power off the flash storage and how does it know to do that before powering down the overall I/O subsystem? The answer is component-level power management, which is the infrastructure to understand the relationship between components and whether each component is in use. To understand the relationship between components, Android builds a device tree that represents the physical device topology of a phone. For example, in such a topology flash and USB storage would be sub-nodes of the I/O subsystem, which is a sub-node of the system bus, which in turn connects to the CPU. To understand usage, each component is associated with its device driver and the driver tracks whether the component is in use–for example, if there is I/O pending to flash or if an application has an open reference to the audio subsystem. With this information, Android can manage the power of the individual components in a phone: If a component is unused, it is turned off. If all of the components on, say, the system bus are unused, the system bus is turned off. And if all of the components in the entire device tree are unused, the system may enter power collapse.

With these technologies, Android can aggressively manage its power consumption. But a final piece of the solution is missing: The ability for applications to temporarily prevent the system from entering power collapse. Consider a user playing a game, watching a video, or waiting for a webpage to render. In all of these cases, the application desires a way, at least temporarily, to keep the device awake. Wake locks enable this functionality. Applications acquire and release wake locks as needed. While an application holds a wake lock, the kernel will prevent the system from entering power collapse. For example, while the Android Market is updating an application, it will hold a wake lock to ensure that the system does not go to sleep until the update is complete. Once complete, the Android Market will release the wake lock, allowing the system to enter power collapse.

Modern mobile devices juggle the need to provide extensive features and high performance with the limited power capacity of today's batteries. Aggressive powering down of components, called power collapse, coupled with component-level power management and wake locks, allow the Android system to optimize its power consumption.

12.4.9 Kernel I/O Subsystem Summary

In summary, the I/O subsystem coordinates an extensive collection of services that are available to applications and to other parts of the kernel. The I/O subsystem supervises these procedures:

- Management of the name space for files and devices
- Access control to files and devices
- Operation control (for example, a modem cannot seek())
- File-system space allocation
- Device allocation
- Buffering, caching, and spooling
- I/O scheduling
- Device-status monitoring, error handling, and failure recovery
- Device-driver configuration and initialization
- Power management if I/O devices

The upper levels of the I/O subsystem access devices via the uniform interface provided by the device drivers.

12.5 Transforming I/O Requests to Hardware Operations

Earlier, we described the handshaking between a device driver and a device controller, but we did not explain how the operating system connects an application request to a set of network wires or to a specific disk sector. Consider, for example, reading a file from disk. The application refers to the data by a file name. Within a disk, the file system maps from the file name through the file-system directories to obtain the space allocation of the file. For instance, in MS-DOS, the name maps to a number that indicates an entry in the file-access table, and that table entry tells which disk blocks are allocated to the file. In UNIX, the name maps to an inode number, and the corresponding inode contains the space-allocation information. But how is the connection made from the file name to the disk controller (the hardware port address or the memory-mapped controller registers)?

One method is that used by MS-DOS, a relatively simple operating system. The first part of an MS-DOS file name, preceding the colon, is a string that identifies a specific hardware device. For example, C: is the first part of every file name on the primary hard disk. The fact that C: represents the primary hard disk is built into the operating system; C: is mapped to a specific port address through a device table. Because of the colon separator, the device name space is separate from the file-system name space. This separation makes it easy for the operating system to associate extra functionality with each device. For instance, it is easy to invoke spooling on any files written to the printer.

If, instead, the device name space is incorporated in the regular file-system name space, as it is in UNIX, the normal file-system name services are provided automatically. If the file system provides ownership and access control to all file names, then devices have owners and access control. Since files are stored on devices, such an interface provides access to the I/O system at two levels. Names can be used to access the devices themselves or to access the files stored on the devices.

UNIX represents device names in the regular file-system name space. Unlike an MS-DOS file name, which has a colon separator, a UNIX path name has no clear separation of the device portion. In fact, no part of the path name is the name of a device. UNIX has a **mount table** that associates prefixes of path names with specific device names. To resolve a path name, UNIX looks up the name in the mount table to find the longest matching prefix; the corresponding entry in the mount table gives the device name. This device name also has the form of a name in the file-system name space. When UNIX looks up this name in the file-system directory structures, it finds not an inode number but a <major, minor> device number. The major device number identifies a device driver that should be called to handle I/O to this device. The minor device number is passed to the device driver to index into a device table. The corresponding device-table entry gives the port address or the memory-mapped address of the device controller.

Modern operating systems gain significant flexibility from the multiple stages of lookup tables in the path between a request and a physical device controller. The mechanisms that pass requests between applications and drivers are general. Thus, we can introduce new devices and drivers into a computer without recompiling the kernel. In fact, some operating systems have the ability to load device drivers on demand. At boot time, the system first probes the hardware buses to determine what devices are present. It then loads in the necessary drivers, either immediately or when first required by an I/O request.

We next describe the typical life cycle of a blocking read request, as depicted in Figure 12.13. The figure suggests that an I/O operation requires a great many steps that together consume a tremendous number of CPU cycles.

1. A process issues a blocking `read()` system call to a file descriptor of a file that has been opened previously.

2. The system-call code in the kernel checks the parameters for correctness. In the case of input, if the data are already available in the buffer cache, the data are returned to the process, and the I/O request is completed.

3. Otherwise, a physical I/O must be performed. The process is removed from the run queue and is placed on the wait queue for the device, and the I/O request is scheduled. Eventually, the I/O subsystem sends the request to the device driver. Depending on the operating system, the request is sent via a subroutine call or an in-kernel message.

4. The device driver allocates kernel buffer space to receive the data and schedules the I/O. Eventually, the driver sends commands to the device controller by writing into the device-control registers.

Figure 12.13 The life cycle of an I/O request.

5. The device controller operates the device hardware to perform the data transfer.

6. The driver may poll for status and data, or it may have set up a DMA transfer into kernel memory. We assume that the transfer is managed by a DMA controller, which generates an interrupt when the transfer completes.

7. The correct interrupt handler receives the interrupt via the interrupt-vector table, stores any necessary data, signals the device driver, and returns from the interrupt.

8. The device driver receives the signal, determines which I/O request has completed, determines the request's status, and signals the kernel I/O subsystem that the request has been completed.

9. The kernel transfers data or return codes to the address space of the requesting process and moves the process from the wait queue back to the ready queue.

10. Moving the process to the ready queue unblocks the process. When the scheduler assigns the process to the CPU, the process resumes execution at the completion of the system call.

12.6 STREAMS

UNIX System V has an interesting mechanism, called STREAMS, that enables an application to assemble pipelines of driver code dynamically. A stream is a full-duplex connection between a device driver and a user-level process. It consists of a **stream head** that interfaces with the user process, a **driver end** that controls the device, and zero or more **stream modules** between the stream head and the driver end. Each of these components contains a pair of queues —a read queue and a write queue. Message passing is used to transfer data between queues. The STREAMS structure is shown in Figure 12.14.

Modules provide the functionality of STREAMS processing; they are *pushed* onto a stream by use of the `ioctl()` system call. For example, a process can open a serial-port device via a stream and can push on a module to handle

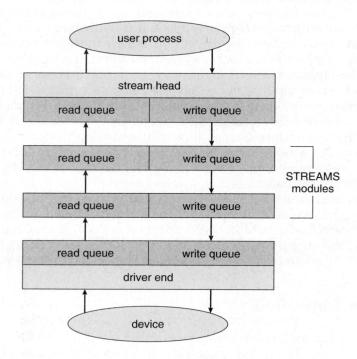

Figure 12.14 The STREAMS structure.

input editing. Because messages are exchanged between queues in adjacent modules, a queue in one module may overflow an adjacent queue. To prevent this from occurring, a queue may support **flow control**. Without flow control, a queue accepts all messages and immediately sends them on to the queue in the adjacent module without buffering them. A queue that supports flow control buffers messages and does not accept messages without sufficient buffer space. This process involves exchanges of control messages between queues in adjacent modules.

A user process writes data to a device using either the `write()` or `putmsg()` system call. The `write()` system call writes raw data to the stream, whereas `putmsg()` allows the user process to specify a message. Regardless of the system call used by the user process, the stream head copies the data into a message and delivers it to the queue for the next module in line. This copying of messages continues until the message is copied to the driver end and hence the device. Similarly, the user process reads data from the stream head using either the `read()` or `getmsg()` system call. If `read()` is used, the stream head gets a message from its adjacent queue and returns ordinary data (an unstructured byte stream) to the process. If `getmsg()` is used, a message is returned to the process.

STREAMS I/O is asynchronous (or nonblocking) except when the user process communicates with the stream head. When writing to the stream, the user process will block, assuming the next queue uses flow control, until there is room to copy the message. Likewise, the user process will block when reading from the stream until data are available.

As mentioned, the driver end—like the stream head and modules—has a read and write queue. However, the driver end must respond to interrupts, such as one triggered when a frame is ready to be read from a network. Unlike the stream head, which may block if it is unable to copy a message to the next queue in line, the driver end must handle all incoming data. Drivers must support flow control as well. However, if a device's buffer is full, the device typically resorts to dropping incoming messages. Consider a network card whose input buffer is full. The network card must simply drop further messages until there is enough buffer space to store incoming messages.

The benefit of using STREAMS is that it provides a framework for a modular and incremental approach to writing device drivers and network protocols. Modules may be used by different streams and hence by different devices. For example, a networking module may be used by both an Ethernet network card and a 802.11 wireless network card. Furthermore, rather than treating character-device I/O as an unstructured byte stream, STREAMS allows support for message boundaries and control information when communicating between modules. Most UNIX variants support STREAMS, and it is the preferred method for writing protocols and device drivers. For example, System V UNIX and Solaris implement the socket mechanism using STREAMS.

12.7 Performance

I/O is a major factor in system performance. It places heavy demands on the CPU to execute device-driver code and to schedule processes fairly and efficiently as they block and unblock. The resulting context switches stress the CPU and its hardware caches. I/O also exposes any inefficiencies in the interrupt-handling mechanisms in the kernel. In addition, I/O loads down the memory bus during data copies between controllers and physical memory and again during copies between kernel buffers and application data space. Coping gracefully with all these demands is one of the major concerns of a computer architect.

Although modern computers can handle many thousands of interrupts per second, interrupt handling is a relatively expensive task. Each interrupt causes the system to perform a state change, to execute the interrupt handler, and then to restore state. Programmed I/O can be more efficient than interrupt-driven I/O, if the number of cycles spent in busy waiting is not excessive. An I/O completion typically unblocks a process, leading to the full overhead of a context switch.

Network traffic can also cause a high context-switch rate. Consider, for instance, a remote login from one machine to another. Each character typed on the local machine must be transported to the remote machine. On the local machine, the character is typed; a keyboard interrupt is generated; and the character is passed through the interrupt handler to the device driver, to the kernel, and then to the user process. The user process issues a network I/O system call to send the character to the remote machine. The character then flows into the local kernel, through the network layers that construct a network packet, and into the network device driver. The network device driver transfers the packet to the network controller, which sends the character and generates an interrupt. The interrupt is passed back up through the kernel to cause the network I/O system call to complete.

Now, the remote system's network hardware receives the packet, and an interrupt is generated. The character is unpacked from the network protocols and is given to the appropriate network daemon. The network daemon identifies which remote login session is involved and passes the packet to the appropriate subdaemon for that session. Throughout this flow, there are context switches and state switches (Figure 12.15). Usually, the receiver echoes the character back to the sender; that approach doubles the work.

To eliminate the context switches involved in moving each character between daemons and the kernel, the Solaris developers reimplemented the `telnet` daemon using in-kernel threads. Sun estimated that this improvement increased the maximum number of network logins from a few hundred to a few thousand on a large server.

Other systems use separate **front-end processors** for terminal I/O to reduce the interrupt burden on the main CPU. For instance, a **terminal concentrator** can multiplex the traffic from hundreds of remote terminals into one port on a large computer. An **I/O channel** is a dedicated, special-purpose CPU found in mainframes and in other high-end systems. The job of a channel is to offload I/O work from the main CPU. The idea is that the channels keep the data flowing smoothly, while the main CPU remains free to process the data. Like the device controllers and DMA controllers found in smaller computers, a channel can process more general and sophisticated programs, so channels can be tuned for particular workloads.

We can employ several principles to improve the efficiency of I/O:

- Reduce the number of context switches.

- Reduce the number of times that data must be copied in memory while passing between device and application.

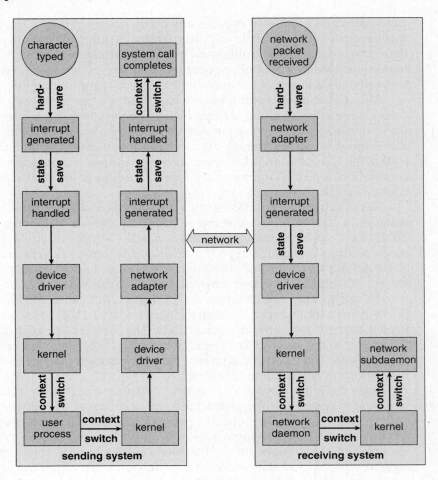

Figure 12.15   Intercomputer communications.

- Reduce the frequency of interrupts by using large transfers, smart controllers, and polling (if busy waiting can be minimized).

- Increase concurrency by using DMA-knowledgeable controllers or channels to offload simple data copying from the CPU.

- Move processing primitives into hardware, to allow their operation in device controllers to be concurrent with CPU and bus operation.

- Balance CPU, memory subsystem, bus, and I/O performance, because an overload in any one area will cause idleness in others.

I/O devices vary greatly in complexity. For instance, a mouse is simple. The mouse movements and button clicks are converted into numeric values that are passed from hardware, through the mouse device driver, to the application. By contrast, the functionality provided by the Windows disk device driver is complex. It not only manages individual disks but also implements RAID arrays (Section 9.7). To do so, it converts an application's read or write request into a coordinated set of disk I/O operations. Moreover, it implements sophisticated error-handling and data-recovery algorithms and takes many steps to optimize disk performance.

Where should the I/O functionality be implemented—in the device hardware, in the device driver, or in application software? Sometimes we observe the progression depicted in Figure 12.16.

- Initially, we implement experimental I/O algorithms at the application level, because application code is flexible and application bugs are unlikely to cause system crashes. Furthermore, by developing code at the application level, we avoid the need to reboot or reload device drivers after every change to the code. An application-level implementation can be inefficient, however, because of the overhead of context switches and because the application cannot take advantage of internal kernel data structures and kernel functionality (such as efficient in-kernel messaging, threading, and locking).

- When an application-level algorithm has demonstrated its worth, we may reimplement it in the kernel. This can improve performance, but the development effort is more challenging, because an operating-system kernel is a large, complex software system. Moreover, an in-kernel implementation must be thoroughly debugged to avoid data corruption and system crashes.

- The highest performance may be obtained through a specialized implementation in hardware, either in the device or in the controller. The disadvantages of a hardware implementation include the difficulty and expense of making further improvements or of fixing bugs, the increased development time (months rather than days), and the decreased flexibility. For instance, a hardware RAID controller may not provide any means for the kernel to influence the order or location of individual block reads and

Figure 12.16 Device functionality progression.

writes, even if the kernel has special information about the workload that would enable it to improve the I/O performance.

12.8 Summary

The basic hardware elements involved in I/O are buses, device controllers, and the devices themselves. The work of moving data between devices and main memory is performed by the CPU as programmed I/O or is offloaded to a DMA controller. The kernel module that controls a device is a device driver. The system-call interface provided to applications is designed to handle several basic categories of hardware, including block devices, character devices, memory-mapped files, network sockets, and programmed interval timers. The system calls usually block the processes that issue them, but nonblocking and asynchronous calls are used by the kernel itself and by applications that must not sleep while waiting for an I/O operation to complete.

The kernel's I/O subsystem provides numerous services. Among these are I/O scheduling, buffering, caching, spooling, device reservation, error handling. Another service, name translation, makes the error handling, and power management. Another service, name translation, makes the error handling, and power management. Another service, name translation, makes the connections between hardware devices and the symbolic file names used by applications. It involves several levels of mapping that translate from character-string names, to specific device drivers and device addresses, and then to physical addresses of I/O ports or bus controllers. This mapping may occur within the file-system name space, as it does in UNIX, or in a separate device name space, as it does in MS-DOS.

STREAMS is an implementation and methodology that provides a framework for a modular and incremental approach to writing device drivers and network protocols. Through streams, drivers can be stacked, with data passing through them sequentially and bidirectionally for processing.

I/O system calls are costly in terms of CPU consumption because of the many layers of software between a physical device and an application. These layers imply overhead from several sources: context switching to cross the kernel's protection boundary, signal and interrupt handling to service the I/O devices, and the load on the CPU and memory system to copy data between kernel buffers and application space.

Review Questions

Review questions for this chapter can be accessed by visiting our website.

Practice Exercises

Answers for the Practice Exercises can be accceed by visiting our website.

12.1   State three advantages of placing functionality in a device controller, rather than in the kernel. State three disadvantages.

12.2   The example of handshaking in Section 12.2 used two bits: a busy bit and a command-ready bit. Is it possible to implement this handshaking with only one bit? If it is, describe the protocol. If it is not, explain why one bit is insufficient.

12.3   Why might a system use interrupt-driven I/O to manage a single serial port and polling I/O to manage a front-end processor, such as a terminal concentrator?

12.4   Polling for an I/O completion can waste a large number of CPU cycles if the processor iterates a busy-waiting loop many times before the I/O completes. But if the I/O device is ready for service, polling can be much more efficient than is catching and dispatching an interrupt. Describe a hybrid strategy that combines polling, sleeping, and interrupts for I/O device service. For each of these three strategies (pure polling, pure interrupts, hybrid), describe a computing environment in which that strategy is more efficient than is either of the others.

12.5   How does DMA increase system concurrency? How does it complicate hardware design?

12.6   Why is it important to scale up system-bus and device speeds as CPU speed increases?

12.7   Distinguish between a STREAMS driver and a STREAMS module.

Exercises

12.8   When multiple interrupts from different devices appear at about the same time, a priority scheme could be used to determine the order in which the interrupts would be serviced. Discuss what issues need to be considered in assigning priorities to different interrupts.

12.9   What are the advantages and disadvantages of supporting memory-mapped I/O to device control registers?

12.10   Consider the following I/O scenarios on a single-user PC:

a.   A mouse used with a graphical user interface

b.   A tape drive on a multitasking operating system (with no device preallocation available)

c.   A disk drive containing user files

d.   A graphics card with direct bus connection, accessible through memory-mapped I/O

For each of these scenarios, would you design the operating system to use buffering, spooling, caching, or a combination? Would you use polled I/O or interrupt-driven I/O? Give reasons for your choices.

12.11   In most multiprogrammed systems, user programs access memory through virtual addresses, while the operating system uses raw physical addresses to access memory. What are the implications of this design for the initiation of I/O operations by the user program and their execution by the operating system?

12.12 What are the various kinds of performance overhead associated with servicing an interrupt?

12.13 Describe three circumstances under which blocking I/O should be used. Describe three circumstances under which nonblocking I/O should be used. Why not just implement nonblocking I/O and have processes busy-wait until their devices are ready?

12.14 Typically, at the completion of a device I/O, a single interrupt is raised and appropriately handled by the host processor. In certain settings, however, the code that is to be executed at the completion of the I/O can be broken into two separate pieces. The first piece executes immediately after the I/O completes and schedules a second interrupt for the remaining piece of code to be executed at a later time. What is the purpose of using this strategy in the design of interrupt handlers?

12.15 Some DMA controllers support direct virtual memory access, where the targets of I/O operations are specified as virtual addresses and a translation from virtual to physical address is performed during the DMA. How does this design complicate the design of the DMA controller? What are the advantages of providing such functionality?

12.16 UNIX coordinates the activities of the kernel I/O components by manipulating shared in-kernel data structures, whereas Windows uses object-oriented message passing between kernel I/O components. Discuss three pros and three cons of each approach.

12.17 Write (in pseudocode) an implementation of virtual clocks, including the queueing and management of timer requests for the kernel and applications. Assume that the hardware provides three timer channels.

12.18 Discuss the advantages and disadvantages of guaranteeing reliable transfer of data between modules in the STREAMS abstraction.

Bibliographical Notes

[Vahalia (1996)] provides a good overview of I/O and networking in UNIX. [McKusick and Neville-Neil (2005)] detail the I/O structures and methods employed in FreeBSD. The use and programming of the various interprocess-communication and network protocols in UNIX are explored in [Stevens (1992)]. [Hart (2005)] covers Windows programming.

[Intel (2011)] provides a good source for Intel processors. [Rago (1993)] provides a good discussion of STREAMS. [Hennessy and Patterson (2012)] describe multiprocessor systems and cache-consistency issues.

Bibliography

[Hart (2005)]   J. M. Hart, *Windows System Programming,* Third Edition, Addison-Wesley (2005).

[Hennessy and Patterson (2012)]   J. Hennessy and D. Patterson, *Computer Architecture: A Quantitative Approach*, Fifth Edition, Morgan Kaufmann (2012).

[Intel (2011)]   *Intel 64 and IA-32 Architectures Software Developer's Manual, Combined Volumes: 1, 2A, 2B, 3A and 3B*. Intel Corporation (2011).

[McKusick and Neville-Neil (2005)]   M. K. McKusick and G. V. Neville-Neil, *The Design and Implementation of the FreeBSD UNIX Operating System*, Addison Wesley (2005).

[Rago (1993)]   S. Rago, *UNIX System V Network Programming*, Addison-Wesley (1993).

[Stevens (1992)]   R. Stevens, *Advanced Programming in the UNIX Environment*, Addison-Wesley (1992).

[Vahalia (1996)]   U. Vahalia, *Unix Internals: The New Frontiers*, Prentice Hall (1996).

Part Five

Protection and Security

Protection mechanisms control access to a system by limiting the types of file access permitted to users. In addition, protection must ensure that only processes that have gained proper authorization from the operating system can operate on memory segments, the CPU, and other resources.

Protection is provided by a mechanism that controls the access of programs, processes, or users to the resources defined by a computer system. This mechanism must provide a means for specifying the controls to be imposed, together with a means of enforcing them.

Security ensures the authentication of system users to protect the integrity of the information stored in the system (both data and code), as well as the physical resources of the computer system. The security system prevents unauthorized access, malicious destruction or alteration of data, and accidental introduction of inconsistency.

Protection

The processes in an operating system must be protected from one another's activities. To provide such protection, we can use various mechanisms to ensure that only processes that have gained proper authorization from the operating system can operate on the files, memory segments, CPU, and other resources of a system.

Protection refers to a mechanism for controlling the access of programs, processes, or users to the resources defined by a computer system. This mechanism must provide a means for specifying the controls to be imposed, together with a means of enforcement. We distinguish between protection and security, which is a measure of confidence that the integrity of a system and its data will be preserved. In this chapter, we focus on protection. Security assurance is a much broader topic, and we address it in Chapter 14.

CHAPTER OBJECTIVES

- To discuss the goals and principles of protection in a modern computer system.
- To explain how protection domains, combined with an access matrix, are used to specify the resources a process may access.
- To examine capability- and language-based protection systems.

13.1 Goals of Protection

As computer systems have become more sophisticated and pervasive in their applications, the need to protect their integrity has also grown. Protection was originally conceived as an adjunct to multiprogramming operating systems, so that untrustworthy users might safely share a common logical name space, such as a directory of files, or share a common physical name space, such as memory. Modern protection concepts have evolved to increase the reliability of any complex system that makes use of shared resources.

We need to provide protection for several reasons. The most obvious is the need to prevent the mischievous, intentional violation of an access restriction by a user. Of more general importance, however, is the need to ensure that each program component active in a system uses system resources only in ways consistent with stated policies. This requirement is an absolute one for a reliable system.

Protection can improve reliability by detecting latent errors at the interfaces between component subsystems. Early detection of interface errors can often prevent contamination of a healthy subsystem by a malfunctioning subsystem. Also, an unprotected resource cannot defend against use (or misuse) by an unauthorized or incompetent user. A protection-oriented system provides means to distinguish between authorized and unauthorized usage.

The role of protection in a computer system is to provide a mechanism for the enforcement of the policies governing resource use. These policies can be established in a variety of ways. Some are fixed in the design of the system, while others are formulated by the management of a system. Still others are defined by the individual users to protect their own files and programs. A protection system must have the flexibility to enforce a variety of policies.

Policies for resource use may vary by application, and they may change over time. For these reasons, protection is no longer the concern solely of the designer of an operating system. The application programmer needs to use protection mechanisms as well, to guard resources created and supported by an application subsystem against misuse. In this chapter, we describe the protection mechanisms the operating system should provide, but application designers can use them as well in designing their own protection software.

Note that *mechanisms* are distinct from *policies*. Mechanisms determine *how* something will be done; policies decide *what* will be done. The separation of policy and mechanism is important for flexibility. Policies are likely to change from place to place or time to time. In the worst case, every change in policy would require a change in the underlying mechanism. Using general mechanisms enables us to avoid such a situation.

13.2 Principles of Protection

Frequently, a guiding principle can be used throughout a project, such as the design of an operating system. Following this principle simplifies design decisions and keeps the system consistent and easy to understand. A key, time-tested guiding principle for protection is the **principle of least privilege**. It dictates that programs, users, and even systems be given just enough privileges to perform their tasks.

Consider the analogy of a security guard with a passkey. If this key allows the guard into just the public areas that she guards, then misuse of the key will result in minimal damage. If, however, the passkey allows access to all areas, then damage from its being lost, stolen, misused, copied, or otherwise compromised will be much greater.

An operating system following the principle of least privilege implements its features, programs, system calls, and data structures so that failure or compromise of a component does the minimum damage and allows the minimum damage to be done. The overflow of a buffer in a system daemon might cause the daemon process to fail, for example, but should not allow the execution of code from the daemon process's stack that would enable a remote user to gain maximum privileges and access to the entire system (as happens too often today).

Such an operating system also provides system calls and services that allow applications to be written with fine-grained access controls. It provides mechanisms to enable privileges when they are needed and to disable them when they are not needed. Also beneficial is the creation of audit trails for all privileged function access. The audit trail allows the programmer, system administrator, or law-enforcement officer to trace all protection and security activities on the system.

Managing users with the principle of least privilege entails creating a separate account for each user, with just the privileges that the user needs. An operator who needs to mount tapes and back up files on the system has access to just those commands and files needed to accomplish the job. Some systems implement role-based access control (RBAC) to provide this functionality.

Computers implemented in a computing facility under the principle of least privilege can be limited to running specific services, accessing specific remote hosts via specific services, and doing so during specific times. Typically, these restrictions are implemented through enabling or disabling each service and through using access control lists, as described in Section 10.6.2 and in Section 13.6.

The principle of least privilege can help produce a more secure computing environment. Unfortunately, it frequently does not. For example, Windows 2000 has a complex protection scheme at its core and yet has many security holes. By comparison, Solaris is considered relatively secure, even though it is a variant of UNIX, which historically was designed with little protection in mind. One reason for the difference may be that Windows 2000 has more lines of code and more services than Solaris and thus has more to secure and protect. Another reason could be that the protection scheme in Windows 2000 is incomplete or protects the wrong aspects of the operating system, leaving other areas vulnerable.

13.3 Domain of Protection

A computer system is a collection of processes and objects. By *objects,* we mean both hardware objects (such as the CPU, memory segments, printers, disks, and tape drives) and software objects (such as files, programs, and semaphores). Each object has a unique name that differentiates it from all other objects in the system, and each can be accessed only through well-defined and meaningful operations. Objects are essentially abstract data types.

The operations that are possible may depend on the object. For example, on a CPU, we can only execute. Memory segments can be read and written, whereas a CD-ROM or DVD-ROM can only be read. Tape drives can be read, written, and rewound. Data files can be created, opened, read, written, closed, and deleted; program files can be read, written, executed, and deleted.

A process should be allowed to access only those resources for which it has authorization. Furthermore, at any time, a process should be able to access only those resources that it currently requires to complete its task. This second requirement, commonly referred to as the need-to-know principle, is useful in limiting the amount of damage a faulty process can cause in the system.

For example, when process p invokes procedure $A()$, the procedure should be allowed to access only its own variables and the formal parameters passed to it; it should not be able to access all the variables of process p. Similarly, consider the case in which process p invokes a compiler to compile a particular file. The compiler should not be able to access files arbitrarily but should have access only to a well-defined subset of files (such as the source file, listing file, and so on) related to the file to be compiled. Conversely, the compiler may have private files used for accounting or optimization purposes that process p should not be able to access. The need-to-know principle is similar to the principle of least privilege discussed in Section 13.2 in that the goals of protection are to minimize the risks of possible security violations.

13.3.1 Domain Structure

To facilitate the scheme just described, a process operates within a **protection domain**, which specifies the resources that the process may access. Each domain defines a set of objects and the types of operations that may be invoked on each object. The ability to execute an operation on an object is an **access right**. A domain is a collection of access rights, each of which is an ordered pair <object-name, rights-set>. For example, if domain D has the access right <file F, {read,write}>, then a process executing in domain D can both read and write file F. It cannot, however, perform any other operation on that object.

Domains may share access rights. For example, in Figure 13.1, we have three domains: D_1, D_2, and D_3. The access right <O_4, {print}> is shared by D_2 and D_3, implying that a process executing in either of these two domains can print object O_4. Note that a process must be executing in domain D_1 to read and write object O_1, while only processes in domain D_3 may execute object O_1.

The association between a process and a domain may be either **static**, if the set of resources available to the process is fixed throughout the process's lifetime, or **dynamic**. As might be expected, establishing dynamic protection domains is more complicated than establishing static protection domains.

If the association between processes and domains is fixed, and we want to adhere to the need-to-know principle, then a mechanism must be available to change the content of a domain. The reason stems from the fact that a process may execute in two different phases and may, for example, need read access in one phase and write access in another. If a domain is static, we must define the domain to include both read and write access. However, this arrangement provides more rights than are needed in each of the two phases, since we have read access in the phase where we need only write access, and vice versa.

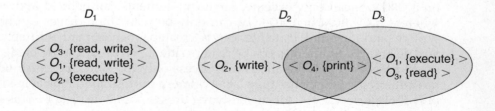

Figure 13.1 System with three protection domains.

Thus, the need-to-know principle is violated. We must allow the contents of a domain to be modified so that the domain always reflects the minimum necessary access rights.

If the association is dynamic, a mechanism is available to allow **domain switching**, enabling the process to switch from one domain to another. We may also want to allow the content of a domain to be changed. If we cannot change the content of a domain, we can provide the same effect by creating a new domain with the changed content and switching to that new domain when we want to change the domain content.

A domain can be realized in a variety of ways:

- Each *user* may be a domain. In this case, the set of objects that can be accessed depends on the identity of the user. Domain switching occurs when the user is changed—generally when one user logs out and another user logs in.

- Each *process* may be a domain. In this case, the set of objects that can be accessed depends on the identity of the process. Domain switching occurs when one process sends a message to another process and then waits for a response.

- Each *procedure* may be a domain. In this case, the set of objects that can be accessed corresponds to the local variables defined within the procedure. Domain switching occurs when a procedure call is made.

We discuss domain switching in greater detail in Section 13.4.

Consider the standard dual-mode (monitor–user mode) model of operating-system execution. When a process executes in monitor mode, it can execute privileged instructions and thus gain complete control of the computer system. In contrast, when a process executes in user mode, it can invoke only nonprivileged instructions. Consequently, it can execute only within its predefined memory space. These two modes protect the operating system (executing in monitor domain) from the user processes (executing in user domain). In a multiprogrammed operating system, two protection domains are insufficient, since users also want to be protected from one another. Therefore, a more elaborate scheme is needed. We illustrate such a scheme by examining two influential operating systems—UNIX and MULTICS —to see how they implement these concepts.

13.3.2   An Example: UNIX

In the UNIX operating system, a domain is associated with the user. Switching the domain corresponds to changing the user identification temporarily. This change is accomplished through the file system as follows. An owner identification and a domain bit (known as the **setuid bit**) are associated with each file. When the setuid bit is on, and a user executes that file, the userID is set to that of the owner of the file. When the bit is off, however, the userID does not change. For example, when a user A (that is, a user with userID = A) starts executing a file owned by B, whose associated domain bit is off, the userID of the process is set to A. When the setuid bit is on, the userID is set to that of the owner of the file: B. When the process exits, this temporary userID change ends.

Other methods are used to change domains in operating systems in which userIDs are used for domain definition, because almost all systems need to provide such a mechanism. This mechanism is used when an otherwise privileged facility needs to be made available to the general user population. For instance, it might be desirable to allow users to access a network without letting them write their own networking programs. In such a case, on a UNIX system, the setuid bit on a networking program would be set, causing the userID to change when the program was run. The userID would change to that of a user with network access privilege (such as root, the most powerful userID). One problem with this method is that if a user manages to create a file with userID root and with its setuid bit on, that user can become root and do anything and everything on the system. The setuid mechanism is discussed further in Appendix A.

An alternative to this method used in some other operating systems is to place privileged programs in a special directory. The operating system is designed to change the userID of any program run from this directory, either to the equivalent of root or to the userID of the owner of the directory. This eliminates one security problem, which occurs when intruders create programs to manipulate the setuid feature and hide the programs in the system for later use (using obscure file or directory names). This method is less flexible than that used in UNIX, however.

Even more restrictive, and thus more protective, are systems that simply do not allow a change of userID. In these instances, special techniques must be used to allow users access to privileged facilities. For instance, a **daemon process** may be started at boot time and run as a special userID. Users then run a separate program, which sends requests to this process whenever they need to use the facility. This method is used by the TOPS-20 operating system.

In any of these systems, great care must be taken in writing privileged programs. Any oversight can result in a total lack of protection on the system. Generally, these programs are the first to be attacked by people trying to break into a system. Unfortunately, the attackers are frequently successful. For example, security has been breached on many UNIX systems because of the setuid feature. We discuss security in Chapter 14.

13.3.3   An Example: MULTICS

In the MULTICS system, the protection domains are organized hierarchically into a ring structure. Each ring corresponds to a single domain (Figure 13.2). The rings are numbered from 0 to 7. Let D_i and D_j be any two domain rings. If $j < i$, then D_i is a subset of D_j. That is, a process executing in domain D_j has more privileges than does a process executing in domain D_i. A process executing in domain D_0 has the most privileges. If only two rings exist, this scheme is equivalent to the monitor–user mode of execution, where monitor mode corresponds to D_0 and user mode corresponds to D_1.

MULTICS has a segmented address space; each segment is a file, and each segment is associated with one of the rings. A segment description includes an entry that identifies the ring number. In addition, it includes three access bits

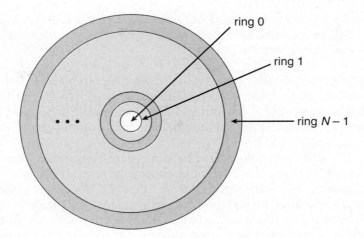

Figure 13.2   MULTICS ring structure.

to control reading, writing, and execution. The association between segments and rings is a policy decision with which we are not concerned here.

A current-ring-number counter is associated with each process, identifying the ring in which the process is executing currently. When a process is executing in ring i, it cannot access a segment associated with ring j ($j < i$). It can access a segment associated with ring k ($k \geq i$). The type of access, however, is restricted according to the access bits associated with that segment.

Domain switching in MULTICS occurs when a process crosses from one ring to another by calling a procedure in a different ring. Obviously, this switch must be done in a controlled manner; otherwise, a process could start executing in ring 0, and no protection would be provided. To allow controlled domain switching, we modify the ring field of the segment descriptor to include the following:

- **Access bracket**. A pair of integers, $b1$ and $b2$, such that $b1 \leq b2$.

- **Limit**. An integer $b3$ such that $b3 > b2$.

- **List of gates**. Identifies the entry points (or **gates**) at which the segments may be called.

If a process executing in ring i calls a procedure (or segment) with access bracket ($b1,b2$), then the call is allowed if $b1 \leq i \leq b2$, and the current ring number of the process remains i. Otherwise, a trap to the operating system occurs, and the situation is handled as follows:

- If $i < b1$, then the call is allowed to occur, because we have a transfer to a ring (or domain) with fewer privileges. However, if parameters are passed that refer to segments in a lower ring (that is, segments not accessible to the called procedure), then these segments must be copied into an area that can be accessed by the called procedure.

- If $i > b2$, then the call is allowed to occur only if $b3$ is greater than or equal to i and the call has been directed to one of the designated entry points in the list of gates. This scheme allows processes with limited access rights to call procedures in lower rings that have more access rights, but only in a carefully controlled manner.

The main disadvantage of the ring (or hierarchical) structure is that it does not allow us to enforce the need-to-know principle. In particular, if an object must be accessible in domain D_j but not accessible in domain D_i, then we must have $j < i$. But this requirement means that every segment accessible in D_i is also accessible in D_j.

The MULTICS protection system is generally more complex and less efficient than are those used in current operating systems. If protection interferes with the ease of use of the system or significantly decreases system performance, then its use must be weighed carefully against the purpose of the system. For instance, we would want to have a complex protection system on a computer used by a university to process students' grades and also used by students for classwork. A similar protection system would not be suited to a computer being used for number crunching, in which performance is of utmost importance. We would prefer to separate the mechanism from the protection policy, allowing the same system to have complex or simple protection depending on the needs of its users. To separate mechanism from policy, we require a more general model of protection.

13.4   Access Matrix

Our general model of protection can be viewed abstractly as a matrix, called an **access matrix**. The rows of the access matrix represent domains, and the columns represent objects. Each entry in the matrix consists of a set of access rights. Because the column defines objects explicitly, we can omit the object name from the access right. The entry access(i,j) defines the set of operations that a process executing in domain D_i can invoke on object O_j.

To illustrate these concepts, we consider the access matrix shown in Figure 13.3. There are four domains and four objects—three files (F_1, F_2, F_3) and one laser printer. A process executing in domain D_1 can read files F_1 and F_3. A process executing in domain D_4 has the same privileges as one executing in

object domain	F_1	F_2	F_3	printer
D_1	read		read	
D_2				print
D_3		read	execute	
D_4	read write		read write	

Figure 13.3 Access matrix.

domain D_1; but in addition, it can also write onto files F_1 and F_3. The laser printer can be accessed only by a process executing in domain D_2.

The access-matrix scheme provides us with the mechanism for specifying a variety of policies. The mechanism consists of implementing the access matrix and ensuring that the semantic properties we have outlined hold. More specifically, we must ensure that a process executing in domain D_i can access only those objects specified in row i, and then only as allowed by the access-matrix entries.

The access matrix can implement policy decisions concerning protection. The policy decisions involve which rights should be included in the $(i, j)^{th}$ entry. We must also decide the domain in which each process executes. This last policy is usually decided by the operating system.

The users normally decide the contents of the access-matrix entries. When a user creates a new object O_j, the column O_j is added to the access matrix with the appropriate initialization entries, as dictated by the creator. The user may decide to enter some rights in some entries in column j and other rights in other entries, as needed.

The access matrix provides an appropriate mechanism for defining and implementing strict control for both static and dynamic association between processes and domains. When we switch a process from one domain to another, we are executing an operation (switch) on an object (the domain). We can control domain switching by including domains among the objects of the access matrix. Similarly, when we change the content of the access matrix, we are performing an operation on an object: the access matrix. Again, we can control these changes by including the access matrix itself as an object. Actually, since each entry in the access matrix can be modified individually, we must consider each entry in the access matrix as an object to be protected. Now, we need to consider only the operations possible on these new objects (domains and the access matrix) and decide how we want processes to be able to execute these operations.

Processes should be able to switch from one domain to another. Switching from domain D_i to domain D_j is allowed if and only if the access right switch $\in$ access(i, j). Thus, in Figure 13.4, a process executing in domain D_2 can switch to domain D_3 or to domain D_4. A process in domain D_4 can switch to D_1, and one in domain D_1 can switch to D_2.

object domain	F_1	F_2	F_3	laser printer	D_1	D_2	D_3	D_4
D_1	read		read			switch		
D_2				print			switch	switch
D_3		read	execute					
D_4	read write		read write		switch			

Figure 13.4 Access matrix of Figure 13.3 with domains as objects.

Allowing controlled change in the contents of the access-matrix entries requires three additional operations: copy, owner, and control. We examine these operations next.

The ability to copy an access right from one domain (or row) of the access matrix to another is denoted by an asterisk (*) appended to the access right. The copy right allows the access right to be copied only within the column (that is, for the object) for which the right is defined. For example, in Figure 13.5(a), a process executing in domain D_2 can copy the read operation into any entry associated with file F_2. Hence, the access matrix of Figure 13.5(a) can be modified to the access matrix shown in Figure 13.5(b).

This scheme has two additional variants:

1. A right is copied from access(i, j) to access(k, j); it is then removed from access(i, j). This action is a transfer of a right, rather than a copy.

2. Propagation of the copy right may be limited. That is, when the right R^* is copied from access(i, j) to access(k, j), only the right R (not R^*) is created. A process executing in domain D_k cannot further copy the right R.

A system may select only one of these three copy rights, or it may provide all three by identifying them as separate rights: copy, transfer, and limited copy.

We also need a mechanism to allow addition of new rights and removal of some rights. The owner right controls these operations. If access(i, j) includes the owner right, then a process executing in domain D_i can add and remove any right in any entry in column j. For example, in Figure 13.6(a), domain D_1 is the owner of F_1 and thus can add and delete any valid right in column F_1.

object / domain	F_1	F_2	F_3
D_1	execute		write*
D_2	execute	read*	execute
D_3	execute		

(a)

object / domain	F_1	F_2	F_3
D_1	execute		write*
D_2	execute	read*	execute
D_3	execute	read	

(b)

Figure 13.5 Access matrix with *copy* rights.

object domain	F_1	F_2	F_3
D_1	owner execute		write
D_2		read* owner	read* owner write
D_3	execute		

(a)

object domain	F_1	F_2	F_3
D_1	owner execute		write
D_2		owner read* write*	read* owner write
D_3		write	write

(b)

Figure 13.6 Access matrix with owner rights.

Similarly, domain D_2 is the owner of F_2 and F_3 and thus can add and remove any valid right within these two columns. Thus, the access matrix of Figure 13.6(a) can be modified to the access matrix shown in Figure 13.6(b).

The copy and owner rights allow a process to change the entries in a column. A mechanism is also needed to change the entries in a row. The control right is applicable only to domain objects. If access(i, j) includes the control right, then a process executing in domain D_i can remove any access right from row j. For example, suppose that, in Figure 13.4, we include the control right in access(D_2, D_4). Then, a process executing in domain D_2 could modify domain D_4, as shown in Figure 13.7.

The copy and owner rights provide us with a mechanism to limit the propagation of access rights. However, they do not give us the appropriate tools for preventing the propagation (or disclosure) of information. The problem of guaranteeing that no information initially held in an object can migrate outside of its execution environment is called the **confinement problem**. This problem is in general unsolvable (see the bibliographical notes at the end of the chapter).

These operations on the domains and the access matrix are not in themselves important, but they illustrate the ability of the access-matrix model to allow us to implement and control dynamic protection requirements. New objects and new domains can be created dynamically and included in the access-matrix model. However, we have shown only that the basic mechanism

object domain	F_1	F_2	F_3	laser printer	D_1	D_2	D_3	D_4
D_1	read		read			switch		
D_2				print			switch	switch control
D_3		read	execute					
D_4	write		write		switch			

Figure 13.7   Modified access matrix of Figure 13.4.

exists. System designers and users must make the policy decisions concerning which domains are to have access to which objects in which ways.

13.5   Implementation of the Access Matrix

How can the access matrix be implemented effectively? In general, the matrix will be sparse; that is, most of the entries will be empty. Although data-structure techniques are available for representing sparse matrices, they are not particularly useful for this application, because of the way in which the protection facility is used. Here, we first describe several methods of implementing the access matrix and then compare the methods.

13.5.1   Global Table

The simplest implementation of the access matrix is a global table consisting of a set of ordered triples <domain, object, rights-set>. Whenever an operation M is executed on an object O_j within domain D_i, the global table is searched for a triple $<D_i, O_j, R_k>$, with $M \in R_k$. If this triple is found, the operation is allowed to continue; otherwise, an exception (or error) condition is raised.

This implementation suffers from several drawbacks. The table is usually large and thus cannot be kept in main memory, so additional I/O is needed. Virtual memory techniques are often used for managing this table. In addition, it is difficult to take advantage of special groupings of objects or domains. For example, if everyone can read a particular object, this object must have a separate entry in every domain.

13.5.2   Access Lists for Objects

Each column in the access matrix can be implemented as an access list for one object, as described in Section 10.6.2. Obviously, the empty entries can be discarded. The resulting list for each object consists of ordered pairs <domain, rights-set>, which define all domains with a nonempty set of access rights for that object.

This approach can be extended easily to define a list plus a *default* set of access rights. When an operation M on an object O_j is attempted in domain D_i, we search the access list for object O_j, looking for an entry $<D_i, R_k>$ with

$M \in R_k$. If the entry is found, we allow the operation; if it is not, we check the default set. If M is in the default set, we allow the access. Otherwise, access is denied, and an exception condition occurs. For efficiency, we may check the default set first and then search the access list.

13.5.3 Capability Lists for Domains

Rather than associating the columns of the access matrix with the objects as access lists, we can associate each row with its domain. A **capability list** for a domain is a list of objects together with the operations allowed on those objects. An object is often represented by its physical name or address, called a **capability**. To execute operation M on object O_j, the process executes the operation M, specifying the capability (or pointer) for object O_j as a parameter. Simple **possession** of the capability means that access is allowed.

The capability list is associated with a domain, but it is never directly accessible to a process executing in that domain. Rather, the capability list is itself a protected object, maintained by the operating system and accessed by the user only indirectly. Capability-based protection relies on the fact that the capabilities are never allowed to migrate into any address space directly accessible by a user process (where they could be modified). If all capabilities are secure, the object they protect is also secure against unauthorized access.

Capabilities were originally proposed as a kind of secure pointer, to meet the need for resource protection that was foreseen as multiprogrammed computer systems came of age. The idea of an inherently protected pointer provides a foundation for protection that can be extended up to the application level.

To provide inherent protection, we must distinguish capabilities from other kinds of objects, and they must be interpreted by an abstract machine on which higher-level programs run. Capabilities are usually distinguished from other data in one of two ways:

- Each object has a **tag** to denote whether it is a capability or accessible data. The tags themselves must not be directly accessible by an application program. Hardware or firmware support may be used to enforce this restriction. Although only one bit is necessary to distinguish between capabilities and other objects, more bits are often used. This extension allows all objects to be tagged with their types by the hardware. Thus, the hardware can distinguish integers, floating-point numbers, pointers, Booleans, characters, instructions, capabilities, and uninitialized values by their tags.

- Alternatively, the address space associated with a program can be split into two parts. One part is accessible to the program and contains the program's normal data and instructions. The other part, containing the capability list, is accessible only by the operating system. A segmented memory space (Section 7.4) is useful to support this approach.

Several capability-based protection systems have been developed; we describe them briefly in Section 13.8. The Mach operating system also uses a version of capability-based protection; it is described in Appendix B.

13.5.4 A Lock–Key Mechanism

The lock–key scheme is a compromise between access lists and capability lists. Each object has a list of unique bit patterns, called locks. Similarly, each domain has a list of unique bit patterns, called keys. A process executing in a domain can access an object only if that domain has a key that matches one of the locks of the object.

As with capability lists, the list of keys for a domain must be managed by the operating system on behalf of the domain. Users are not allowed to examine or modify the list of keys (or locks) directly.

13.5.5 Comparison

As you might expect, choosing a technique for implementing an access matrix involves various trade-offs. Using a global table is simple; however, the table can be quite large and often cannot take advantage of special groupings of objects or domains. Access lists correspond directly to the needs of users. When a user creates an object, he can specify which domains can access the object, as well as what operations are allowed. However, because access-right information for a particular domain is not localized, determining the set of access rights for each domain is difficult. In addition, every access to the object must be checked, requiring a search of the access list. In a large system with long access lists, this search can be time consuming.

Capability lists do not correspond directly to the needs of users, but they are useful for localizing information for a given process. The process attempting access must present a capability for that access. Then, the protection system needs only to verify that the capability is valid. Revocation of capabilities, however, may be inefficient (Section 13.7).

The lock–key mechanism, as mentioned, is a compromise between access lists and capability lists. The mechanism can be both effective and flexible, depending on the length of the keys. The keys can be passed freely from domain to domain. In addition, access privileges can be effectively revoked by the simple technique of changing some of the locks associated with the object (Section 13.7).

Most systems use a combination of access lists and capabilities. When a process first tries to access an object, the access list is searched. If access is denied, an exception condition occurs. Otherwise, a capability is created and attached to the process. Additional references use the capability to demonstrate swiftly that access is allowed. After the last access, the capability is destroyed. This strategy is used in the MULTICS system and in the CAL system.

As an example of how such a strategy works, consider a file system in which each file has an associated access list. When a process opens a file, the directory structure is searched to find the file, access permission is checked, and buffers are allocated. All this information is recorded in a new entry in a file table associated with the process. The operation returns an index into this table for the newly opened file. All operations on the file are made by specification of the index into the file table. The entry in the file table then points to the file and its buffers. When the file is closed, the file-table entry is deleted. Since the file table is maintained by the operating system, the user cannot accidentally corrupt it. Thus, the user can access only those files that have been opened.

Since access is checked when the file is opened, protection is ensured. This strategy is used in the UNIX system.

The right to access must still be checked on each access, and the file-table entry has a capability only for the allowed operations. If a file is opened for reading, then a capability for read access is placed in the file-table entry. If an attempt is made to write onto the file, the system identifies this protection violation by comparing the requested operation with the capability in the file-table entry.

13.6 Access Control

In Section 10.6.2, we described how access controls can be used on files within a file system. Each file and directory is assigned an owner, a group, or possibly a list of users, and for each of those entities, access-control information is assigned. A similar function can be added to other aspects of a computer system. A good example of this is found in Solaris 10.

Solaris 10 advances the protection available in the operating system by explicitly adding the principle of least privilege via **role-based access control (RBAC)**. This facility revolves around privileges. A privilege is the right to execute a system call or to use an option within that system call (such as opening a file with write access). Privileges can be assigned to processes, limiting them to exactly the access they need to perform their work. Privileges and programs can also be assigned to **roles**. Users are assigned roles or can take roles based on passwords to the roles. In this way, a user can take a role that enables a privilege, allowing the user to run a program to accomplish a specific task, as depicted in Figure 13.8. This implementation of privileges decreases the security risk associated with superusers and setuid programs.

Figure 13.8 Role-based access control in Solaris 10.

Notice that this facility is similar to the access matrix described in Section 13.4. This relationship is further explored in the exercises at the end of the chapter.

13.7 Revocation of Access Rights

In a dynamic protection system, we may sometimes need to revoke access rights to objects shared by different users. Various questions about revocation may arise:

* **Immediate versus delayed**. Does revocation occur immediately, or is it delayed? If revocation is delayed, can we find out when it will take place?

* **Selective versus general**. When an access right to an object is revoked, does it affect all the users who have an access right to that object, or can we specify a select group of users whose access rights should be revoked?

* **Partial versus total**. Can a subset of the rights associated with an object be revoked, or must we revoke all access rights for this object?

* **Temporary versus permanent**. Can access be revoked permanently (that is, the revoked access right will never again be available), or can access be revoked and later be obtained again?

With an access-list scheme, revocation is easy. The access list is searched for any access rights to be revoked, and they are deleted from the list. Revocation is immediate and can be general or selective, total or partial, and permanent or temporary.

Capabilities, however, present a much more difficult revocation problem, as mentioned earlier. Since the capabilities are distributed throughout the system, we must find them before we can revoke them. Schemes that implement revocation for capabilities include the following:

* **Reacquisition**. Periodically, capabilities are deleted from each domain. If a process wants to use a capability, it may find that that capability has been deleted. The process may then try to reacquire the capability. If access has been revoked, the process will not be able to reacquire the capability.

* **Back-pointers**. A list of pointers is maintained with each object, pointing to all capabilities associated with that object. When revocation is required, we can follow these pointers, changing the capabilities as necessary. This scheme was adopted in the MULTICS system. It is quite general, but its implementation is costly.

* **Indirection**. The capabilities point indirectly, not directly, to the objects. Each capability points to a unique entry in a global table, which in turn points to the object. We implement revocation by searching the global table for the desired entry and deleting it. Then, when an access is attempted, the capability is found to point to an illegal table entry. Table entries can be reused for other capabilities without difficulty, since both the capability and the table entry contain the unique name of the object. The object for a

capability and its table entry must match. This scheme was adopted in the CAL system. It does not allow selective revocation.

- **Keys**. A key is a unique bit pattern that can be associated with a capability. This key is defined when the capability is created, and it can be neither modified nor inspected by the process that owns the capability. A **master key** is associated with each object; it can be defined or replaced with the set-key operation. When a capability is created, the current value of the master key is associated with the capability. When the capability is exercised, its key is compared with the master key. If the keys match, the operation is allowed to continue; otherwise, an exception condition is raised. Revocation replaces the master key with a new value via the set-key operation, invalidating all previous capabilities for this object.

  This scheme does not allow selective revocation, since only one master key is associated with each object. If we associate a list of keys with each object, then selective revocation can be implemented. Finally, we can group all keys into one global table of keys. A capability is valid only if its key matches some key in the global table. We implement revocation by removing the matching key from the table. With this scheme, a key can be associated with several objects, and several keys can be associated with each object, providing maximum flexibility.

  In key-based schemes, the operations of defining keys, inserting them into lists, and deleting them from lists should not be available to all users. In particular, it would be reasonable to allow only the owner of an object to set the keys for that object. This choice, however, is a policy decision that the protection system can implement but should not define.

13.8 Capability-Based Systems

In this section, we survey two capability-based protection systems. These systems differ in their complexity and in the types of policies that can be implemented on them. Neither system is widely used, but both provide interesting proving grounds for protection theories.

13.8.1   An Example: Hydra

Hydra is a capability-based protection system that provides considerable flexibility. The system implements a fixed set of possible access rights, including such basic forms of access as the right to read, write, or execute a memory segment. In addition, a user (of the protection system) can declare other rights. The interpretation of user-defined rights is performed solely by the user's program, but the system provides access protection for the use of these rights, as well as for the use of system-defined rights. These facilities constitute a significant development in protection technology.

Operations on objects are defined procedurally. The procedures that implement such operations are themselves a form of object, and they are accessed indirectly by capabilities. The names of user-defined procedures must be identified to the protection system if it is to deal with objects of the user-defined type. When the definition of an object is made known to Hydra, the names of operations on the type become **auxiliary rights**. Auxiliary rights can be described in a capability for an instance of the type. For a process to perform an operation on a typed object, the capability it holds for that object must contain the name of the operation being invoked among its auxiliary rights. This restriction enables discrimination of access rights to be made on an instance-by-instance and process-by-process basis.

Hydra also provides rights amplification. This scheme allows a procedure to be certified as *trustworthy* to act on a formal parameter of a specified type on behalf of any process that holds a right to execute the procedure. The rights held by a trustworthy procedure are independent of, and may exceed, the rights held by the calling process. However, such a procedure must not be regarded as universally trustworthy (the procedure is not allowed to act on other types, for instance), and the trustworthiness must not be extended to any other procedures or program segments that might be executed by a process.

Amplification allows implementation procedures access to the representation variables of an abstract data type. If a process holds a capability to a typed object A, for instance, this capability may include an auxiliary right to invoke some operation P but does not include any of the so-called kernel rights, such as read, write, or execute, on the segment that represents A. Such a capability gives a process a means of indirect access (through the operation P) to the representation of A, but only for specific purposes.

When a process invokes the operation P on an object A, however, the capability for access to A may be amplified as control passes to the code body of P. This amplification may be necessary to allow P the right to access the storage segment representing A so as to implement the operation that P defines on the abstract data type. The code body of P may be allowed to read or to write to the segment of A directly, even though the calling process cannot. On return from P, the capability for A is restored to its original, unamplified state. This case is a typical one in which the rights held by a process for access to a protected segment must change dynamically, depending on the task to be performed. The dynamic adjustment of rights is performed to guarantee consistency of a programmer-defined abstraction. Amplification of rights can be stated explicitly in the declaration of an abstract type to the Hydra operating system.

When a user passes an object as an argument to a procedure, we may need to ensure that the procedure cannot modify the object. We can implement this restriction readily by passing an access right that does not have the modification (write) right. However, if amplification may occur, the right to modify may be reinstated. Thus, the user-protection requirement can be circumvented. In general, of course, a user may trust that a procedure performs its task correctly. This assumption is not always correct, however, because of hardware or software errors. Hydra solves this problem by restricting amplifications.

The procedure-call mechanism of Hydra was designed as a direct solution to the *problem of mutually suspicious subsystems*. This problem is defined as follows. Suppose that a program can be invoked as a service by a number of different users (for example, a sort routine, a compiler, a game). When users invoke this service program, they take the risk that the program will malfunction and will either damage the given data or retain some access right to the data to be used (without authority) later. Similarly, the service program may have some private files (for accounting purposes, for example) that should not be accessed directly by the calling user program. Hydra provides mechanisms for directly dealing with this problem.

A Hydra subsystem is built on top of its protection kernel and may require protection of its own components. A subsystem interacts with the kernel through calls on a set of kernel-defined primitives that define access rights to resources defined by the subsystem. The subsystem designer can define policies for use of these resources by user processes, but the policies are enforced by use of the standard access protection provided by the capability system.

Programmers can make direct use of the protection system after acquainting themselves with its features in the appropriate reference manual. Hydra provides a large library of system-defined procedures that can be called by user programs. Programmers can explicitly incorporate calls on these system procedures into their program code or can use a program translator that has been interfaced to Hydra.

13.8.2 An Example: Cambridge CAP System

A different approach to capability-based protection has been taken in the design of the Cambridge CAP system. CAP's capability system is simpler and superficially less powerful than that of Hydra. However, closer examination shows that it, too, can be used to provide secure protection of user-defined objects. CAP has two kinds of capabilities. The ordinary kind is called a data capability. It can be used to provide access to objects, but the only rights provided are the standard read, write, and execute of the individual storage segments associated with the object. Data capabilities are interpreted by microcode in the CAP machine.

The second kind of capability is the so-called software capability, which is protected, but not interpreted, by the CAP microcode. It is interpreted by a *protected* (that is, privileged) procedure, which may be written by an application programmer as part of a subsystem. A particular kind of rights amplification is associated with a protected procedure. When executing the code body of such a procedure, a process temporarily acquires the right to read or write the contents of a software capability itself. This specific kind of rights amplification corresponds to an implementation of the seal and unseal primitives on capabilities. Of course, this privilege is still subject to type verification to ensure that only software capabilities for a specified abstract type are passed to any such procedure. Universal trust is not placed in any code other than the CAP machine's microcode. (See the bibliographical notes at the end of the chapter for references.)

The interpretation of a software capability is left completely to the subsystem, through the protected procedures it contains. This scheme allows a variety of protection policies to be implemented. Although programmers can define their own protected procedures (any of which might be incorrect), the security of the overall system cannot be compromised. The basic protection system will not allow an unverified, user-defined, protected procedure access to any storage segments (or capabilities) that do not belong to the protection environment in which it resides. The most serious consequence of an insecure protected procedure is a protection breakdown of the subsystem for which that procedure has responsibility.

The designers of the CAP system have noted that the use of software capabilities allowed them to realize considerable economies in formulating and implementing protection policies commensurate with the requirements of abstract resources. However, subsystem designers who want to make use of this facility cannot simply study a reference manual, as is the case with Hydra. Instead, they must learn the principles and techniques of protection, since the system provides them with no library of procedures.

13.9 Language-Based Protection

To the degree that protection is provided in existing computer systems, it is usually achieved through an operating-system kernel, which acts as a security agent to inspect and validate each attempt to access a protected resource. Since comprehensive access validation may be a source of considerable overhead, either we must give it hardware support to reduce the cost of each validation, or we must allow the system designer to compromise the goals of protection. Satisfying all these goals is difficult if the flexibility to implement protection policies is restricted by the support mechanisms provided or if protection environments are made larger than necessary to secure greater operational efficiency.

As operating systems have become more complex, and particularly as they have attempted to provide higher-level user interfaces, the goals of protection have become much more refined. The designers of protection systems have drawn heavily on ideas that originated in programming languages and especially on the concepts of abstract data types and objects. Protection systems are now concerned not only with the identity of a resource to which access is attempted but also with the functional nature of that access. In the newest protection systems, concern for the function to be invoked extends beyond a set of system-defined functions, such as standard file-access methods, to include functions that may be user-defined as well.

Policies for resource use may also vary, depending on the application, and they may be subject to change over time. For these reasons, protection can no longer be considered a matter of concern only to the designer of an operating system. It should also be available as a tool for use by the application designer, so that resources of an application subsystem can be guarded against tampering or the influence of an error.

13.9.1 Compiler-Based Enforcement

At this point, programming languages enter the picture. Specifying the desired control of access to a shared resource in a system is making a declarative statement about the resource. This kind of statement can be integrated into a language by an extension of its typing facility. When protection is declared along with data typing, the designer of each subsystem can specify its requirements for protection, as well as its need for use of other resources in a system. Such a specification should be given directly as a program is composed, and in the language in which the program itself is stated. This approach has several significant advantages:

1. Protection needs are simply declared, rather than programmed as a sequence of calls on procedures of an operating system.

2. Protection requirements can be stated independently of the facilities provided by a particular operating system.

3. The means for enforcement need not be provided by the designer of a subsystem.

4. A declarative notation is natural because access privileges are closely related to the linguistic concept of data type.

A variety of techniques can be provided by a programming-language implementation to enforce protection, but any of these must depend on some degree of support from an underlying machine and its operating system. For example, suppose a language is used to generate code to run on the Cambridge CAP system. On this system, every storage reference made on the underlying hardware occurs indirectly through a capability. This restriction prevents any process from accessing a resource outside of its protection environment at any time. However, a program may impose arbitrary restrictions on how a resource can be used during execution of a particular code segment. We can implement such restrictions most readily by using the software capabilities provided by CAP. A language implementation might provide standard protected procedures to interpret software capabilities that would realize the protection policies that could be specified in the language. This scheme puts policy specification at the disposal of the programmers, while freeing them from implementing its enforcement.

Even if a system does not provide a protection kernel as powerful as those of Hydra or CAP, mechanisms are still available for implementing protection specifications given in a programming language. The principal distinction is that the *security* of this protection will not be as great as that supported by a protection kernel, because the mechanism must rely on more assumptions about the operational state of the system. A compiler can separate references for which it can certify that no protection violation could occur from those for which a violation might be possible, and it can treat them differently. The security provided by this form of protection rests on the assumption that the code generated by the compiler will not be modified prior to or during its execution.

What, then, are the relative merits of enforcement based solely on a kernel, as opposed to enforcement provided largely by a compiler?

- **Security**. Enforcement by a kernel provides a greater degree of security of the protection system itself than does the generation of protection-checking code by a compiler. In a compiler-supported scheme, security rests on correctness of the translator, on some underlying mechanism of storage management that protects the segments from which compiled code is executed, and, ultimately, on the security of files from which a program is loaded. Some of these considerations also apply to a software-supported protection kernel, but to a lesser degree, since the kernel may reside in fixed physical storage segments and may be loaded only from a designated file. With a tagged-capability system, in which all address computation is performed either by hardware or by a fixed microprogram, even greater security is possible. Hardware-supported protection is also relatively immune to protection violations that might occur as a result of either hardware or system software malfunction.

- **Flexibility**. There are limits to the flexibility of a protection kernel in implementing a user-defined policy, although it may supply adequate facilities for the system to provide enforcement of its own policies. With a programming language, protection policy can be declared and enforcement provided as needed by an implementation. If a language does not provide sufficient flexibility, it can be extended or replaced with less disturbance than would be caused by the modification of an operating-system kernel.

- **Efficiency**. The greatest efficiency is obtained when enforcement of protection is supported directly by hardware (or microcode). Insofar as software support is required, language-based enforcement has the advantage that static access enforcement can be verified off-line at compile time. Also, since an intelligent compiler can tailor the enforcement mechanism to meet the specified need, the fixed overhead of kernel calls can often be avoided.

In summary, the specification of protection in a programming language allows the high-level description of policies for the allocation and use of resources. A language implementation can provide software for protection enforcement when automatic hardware-supported checking is unavailable. In addition, it can interpret protection specifications to generate calls on whatever protection system is provided by the hardware and the operating system.

One way of making protection available to the application program is through the use of a software capability that could be used as an object of computation. Inherent in this concept is the idea that certain program components might have the privilege of creating or examining these software capabilities. A capability-creating program would be able to execute a primitive operation that would seal a data structure, rendering the latter's contents inaccessible to any program components that did not hold either the seal or the unseal privilege. Such components might copy the data structure or pass its address to other program components, but they could not gain access to its contents. The reason for introducing such software capabilities is to bring a protection mechanism into the programming language. The only problem with the concept as proposed is that the use of the seal and unseal operations takes a procedural approach to specifying protection. A nonprocedural or declarative notation seems a preferable way to make protection available to the application programmer.

What is needed is a safe, dynamic access-control mechanism for distributing capabilities to system resources among user processes. To contribute to the overall reliability of a system, the access-control mechanism should be safe to use. To be useful in practice, it should also be reasonably efficient. This requirement has led to the development of a number of language constructs that allow the programmer to declare various restrictions on the use of a specific managed resource. (See the bibliographical notes for appropriate references.) These constructs provide mechanisms for three functions:

1. Distributing capabilities safely and efficiently among customer processes. In particular, mechanisms ensure that a user process will use the managed resource only if it was granted a capability to that resource.

2. Specifying the type of operations that a particular process may invoke on an allocated resource (for example, a reader of a file should be allowed only to read the file, whereas a writer should be able both to read and to write). It should not be necessary to grant the same set of rights to every user process, and it should be impossible for a process to enlarge its set of access rights, except with the authorization of the access-control mechanism.

3. Specifying the order in which a particular process may invoke the various operations of a resource (for example, a file must be opened before it can be read). It should be possible to give two processes different restrictions on the order in which they can invoke the operations of the allocated resource.

The incorporation of protection concepts into programming languages, as a practical tool for system design, is in its infancy. Protection will likely become a matter of greater concern to the designers of new systems with distributed architectures and increasingly stringent requirements on data security. Then the importance of suitable language notations in which to express protection requirements will be recognized more widely.

13.9.2 Protection in Java

Because Java was designed to run in a distributed environment, the Java virtual machine—or JVM—has many built-in protection mechanisms. Java programs are composed of **classes**, each of which is a collection of data fields and functions (called **methods**) that operate on those fields. The JVM loads a class in response to a request to create instances (or objects) of that class. One of the most novel and useful features of Java is its support for dynamically loading untrusted classes over a network and for executing mutually distrusting classes within the same JVM.

Because of these capabilities, protection is a paramount concern. Classes running in the same JVM may be from different sources and may not be equally trusted. As a result, enforcing protection at the granularity of the JVM process is insufficient. Intuitively, whether a request to open a file should be allowed will generally depend on which class has requested the open. The operating system lacks this knowledge.

Thus, such protection decisions are handled within the JVM. When the JVM loads a class, it assigns the class to a protection domain that gives the permissions of that class. The protection domain to which the class is assigned depends on the URL from which the class was loaded and any digital signatures on the class file. (Digital signatures are covered in Section 14.4.1.3.) A configurable policy file determines the permissions granted to the domain (and its classes). For example, classes loaded from a trusted server might be placed in a protection domain that allows them to access files in the user's home directory, whereas classes loaded from an untrusted server might have no file access permissions at all.

It can be complicated for the JVM to determine what class is responsible for a request to access a protected resource. Accesses are often performed indirectly, through system libraries or other classes. For example, consider a class that is not allowed to open network connections. It could call a system library to request the load of the contents of a URL. The JVM must decide whether or not to open a network connection for this request. But which class should be used to determine if the connection should be allowed, the application or the system library?

The philosophy adopted in Java is to require the library class to explicitly permit a network connection. More generally, in order to access a protected resource, some method in the calling sequence that resulted in the request must explicitly assert the privilege to access the resource. By doing so, this method *takes responsibility* for the request. Presumably, it will also perform whatever checks are necessary to ensure the safety of the request. Of course, not every method is allowed to assert a privilege; a method can assert a privilege only if its class is in a protection domain that is itself allowed to exercise the privilege.

This implementation approach is called **stack inspection**. Every thread in the JVM has an associated stack of its ongoing method invocations. When a caller may not be trusted, a method executes an access request within a doPrivileged block to perform the access to a protected resource directly or indirectly. doPrivileged() is a static method in the AccessController class that is passed a class with a run() method to invoke. When the doPrivileged block is entered, the stack frame for this method is annotated to indicate this fact. Then, the contents of the block are executed. When an access to a protected resource is subsequently requested, either by this method or a method it calls, a call to checkPermissions() is used to invoke stack inspection to determine if the request should be allowed. The inspection examines stack frames on the calling thread's stack, starting from the most recently added frame and working toward the oldest. If a stack frame is first found that has the doPrivileged() annotation, then checkPermissions() returns immediately and silently, allowing the access. If a stack frame is first found for which access is disallowed based on the protection domain of the method's class, then checkPermissions() throws an AccessControlException. If the stack inspection exhausts the stack without finding either type of frame, then whether access is allowed depends on the implementation (for example, some implementations of the JVM may allow access, while other implementations may not).

Stack inspection is illustrated in Figure 13.9. Here, the gui() method of a class in the *untrusted applet* protection domain performs two operations, first a get() and then an open(). The former is an invocation of the get() method of a class in the *URL loader* protection domain, which is permitted to open() sessions to sites in the lucent.com domain, in particular a proxy server proxy.lucent.com for retrieving URLs. For this reason, the untrusted applet's get() invocation will succeed: the checkPermissions() call in the networking library encounters the stack frame of the get() method, which performed its open() in a doPrivileged block. However, the untrusted applet's open() invocation will result in an exception, because the checkPermissions() call finds no doPrivileged annotation before encountering the stack frame of the gui() method.

protection domain:	untrusted applet	URL loader	networking
socket permission:	none	*.lucent.com:80, connect	any

class:	gui:
	   ...
	   get(url);
	   open(addr);
	   ...
		get(URL u):
		   ...
		   doPrivileged {
		     open('proxy.lucent.com:80');
		   }
		   <request u from proxy>
		   ...
			open(Addr a):
			   ...
			   checkPermission
			   (a, connect);
			   connect (a);
			   ...

Figure 13.9 Stack inspection.

Of course, for stack inspection to work, a program must be unable to modify the annotations on its own stack frame or to otherwise manipulate stack inspection. This is one of the most important differences between Java and many other languages (including C++). A Java program cannot directly access memory; it can manipulate only an object for which it has a reference. References cannot be forged, and manipulations are made only through well-defined interfaces. Compliance is enforced through a sophisticated collection of load-time and run-time checks. As a result, an object cannot manipulate its run-time stack, because it cannot get a reference to the stack or other components of the protection system.

More generally, Java's load-time and run-time checks enforce **type safety** of Java classes. Type safety ensures that classes cannot treat integers as pointers, write past the end of an array, or otherwise access memory in arbitrary ways. Rather, a program can access an object only via the methods defined on that object by its class. This is the foundation of Java protection, since it enables a class to effectively **encapsulate** and protect its data and methods from other classes loaded in the same JVM. For example, a variable can be defined as private so that only the class that contains it can access it or protected so that it can be accessed only by the class that contains it, subclasses of that class, or classes in the same package. Type safety ensures that these restrictions can be enforced.

13.10 Summary

Computer systems contain many objects, and they need to be protected from misuse. Objects may be hardware (such as memory, CPU time, and I/O devices) or software (such as files, programs, and semaphores). An access right is permission to perform an operation on an object. A domain is a set of access rights. Processes execute in domains and may use any of the access rights in the domain to access and manipulate objects. During its lifetime, a process may be either bound to a protection domain or allowed to switch from one domain to another.

The access matrix is a general model of protection that provides a mechanism for protection without imposing a particular protection policy on the system or its users. The separation of policy and mechanism is an important design property.

The access matrix is sparse. It is normally implemented either as access lists associated with each object or as capability lists associated with each domain. We can include dynamic protection in the access-matrix model by considering domains and the access matrix itself as objects. Revocation of access rights in a dynamic protection model is typically easier to implement with an access-list scheme than with a capability list.

Real systems are much more limited than the general model and tend to provide protection only for files. UNIX is representative, providing read, write, and execution protection separately for the owner, group, and general public for each file. MULTICS uses a ring structure in addition to file access. Hydra, the Cambridge CAP system, and Mach are capability systems that extend protection to user-defined software objects. Solaris 10 implements the principle of least privilege via role-based access control, a form of the access matrix.

Language-based protection provides finer-grained arbitration of requests and privileges than the operating system is able to provide. For example, a single Java JVM can run several threads, each in a different protection class. It enforces the resource requests through sophisticated stack inspection and via the type safety of the language.

Review Questions

Review questions for this chapter can be accessed by visiting our website.

Practice Exercises

Answers for the Practice Exercises can be accceed by visiting our website.

13.1 What are the main differences between capability lists and access lists?

13.2 A Burroughs B7000/B6000 MCP file can be tagged as sensitive data. When such a file is deleted, its storage area is overwritten by some random bits. For what purpose would such a scheme be useful?

13.3 In a ring-protection system, level 0 has the greatest access to objects, and level n (where $n > 0$) has fewer access rights. The access rights of a program at a particular level in the ring structure are considered a set of capabilities. What is the relationship between the capabilities of a domain at level j and a domain at level i to an object (for $j > i$)?

13.4 The RC 4000 system, among others, has defined a tree of processes (called a process tree) such that all the descendants of a process can be given resources (objects) and access rights by their ancestors only. Thus, a descendant can never have the ability to do anything that its ancestors cannot do. The root of the tree is the operating system, which has the ability to do anything. Assume that the set of access rights is represented by an access matrix, A. $A(x,y)$ defines the access rights of process x to object y. If x is a descendant of z, what is the relationship between $A(x,y)$ and $A(z,y)$ for an arbitrary object y?

13.5 What protection problems may arise if a shared stack is used for parameter passing?

13.6 Consider a computing environment where a unique number is associated with each process and each object in the system. Suppose that we allow a process with number n to access an object with number m only if $n > m$. What type of protection structure do we have?

13.7 Consider a computing environment where a process is given the privilege of accessing an object only n times. Suggest a scheme for implementing this policy.

13.8 If all the access rights to an object are deleted, the object can no longer be accessed. At this point, the object should also be deleted, and the space it occupies should be returned to the system. Suggest an efficient implementation of this scheme.

13.9 Why is it difficult to protect a system in which users are allowed to do their own I/O?

13.10 Capability lists are usually kept within the address space of the user. How does the system ensure that the user cannot modify the contents of the list?

Exercises

13.11 Consider the ring-protection scheme in MULTICS. If we were to implement the system calls of a typical operating system and store them in a segment associated with ring 0, what should be the values stored in the ring field of the segment descriptor? What happens during a system call when a process executing in a higher-numbered ring invokes a procedure in ring 0?

13.12 The access-control matrix can be used to determine whether a process can switch from, say, domain A to domain B and enjoy the access privileges of domain B. Is this approach equivalent to including the access privileges of domain B in those of domain A?

13.13 Consider a computer system in which computer games can be played by students only between 10 P.M. and 6 A.M., by faculty members between 5 P.M. and 8 A.M., and by the computer center staff at all times. Suggest a scheme for implementing this policy efficiently.

13.14 What hardware features does a computer system need for efficient capability manipulation? Can these features be used for memory protection?

13.15 Discuss the strengths and weaknesses of implementing an access matrix using access lists that are associated with objects.

13.16   Discuss the strengths and weaknesses of implementing an access matrix using capabilities that are associated with domains.

13.17   Explain why a capability-based system such as Hydra provides greater flexibility than the ring-protection scheme in enforcing protection policies.

13.18   Discuss the need for rights amplification in Hydra. How does this practice compare with the cross-ring calls in a ring-protection scheme?

13.19   What is the need-to-know principle? Why is it important for a protection system to adhere to this principle?

13.20   Discuss which of the following systems allow module designers to enforce the need-to-know principle.

    a.   The MULTICS ring-protection scheme

    b.   Hydra's capabilities

    c.   JVM's stack-inspection scheme

13.21   Describe how the Java protection model would be compromised if a Java program were allowed to directly alter the annotations of its stack frame.

13.22   How are the access-matrix facility and the role-based access-control facility similar? How do they differ?

13.23   How does the principle of least privilege aid in the creation of protection systems?

13.24   How can systems that implement the principle of least privilege still have protection failures that lead to security violations?

Bibliographical Notes

The access-matrix model of protection between domains and objects was developed by [Lampson (1969)] and [Lampson (1971)]. [Popek (1974)] and [Saltzer and Schroeder (1975)] provided excellent surveys on the subject of protection. [Harrison et al. (1976)] used a formal version of the access-matrix model to enable them to prove properties of a protection system mathematically.

The concept of a capability evolved from Iliffe's and Jodeit's *codewords*, which were implemented in the Rice University computer ([Iliffe and Jodeit (1962)]). The term *capability* was introduced by [Dennis and Horn (1966)].

The Hydra system was described by [Wulf et al. (1981)]. The CAP system was described by [Needham and Walker (1977)]. [Organick (1972)] discussed the MULTICS ring-protection system.

Revocation was discussed by [Redell and Fabry (1974)], [Cohen and Jefferson (1975)], and [Ekanadham and Bernstein (1979)]. The principle of separation of policy and mechanism was advocated by the designer of Hydra ([Levin et al. (1975)]). The confinement problem was first discussed by [Lampson (1973)] and was further examined by [Lipner (1975)].

The use of higher-level languages for specifying access control was suggested first by [Morris (1973)], who proposed the use of the seal and unseal operations discussed in Section 13.9. [Kieburtz and Silberschatz (1978)], [Kieburtz and Silberschatz (1983)], and [McGraw and Andrews (1979)] proposed various language constructs for dealing with general dynamic-resource-management schemes. [Jones and Liskov (1978)] considered how a static access-control scheme can be incorporated in a programming language that supports abstract data types. The use of minimal operating-system support to enforce protection was advocated by the Exokernel Project ([Ganger et al. (2002)], [Kaashoek et al. (1997)]). Extensibility of system code through language-based protection mechanisms was discussed in [Bershad et al. (1995)]. Other techniques for enforcing protection include sandboxing ([Goldberg et al. (1996)]) and software fault isolation ([Wahbe et al. (1993)]). The issues of lowering the overhead associated with protection costs and enabling user-level access to networking devices were discussed in [McCanne and Jacobson (1993)] and [Basu et al. (1995)].

More detailed analyses of stack inspection, including comparisons with other approaches to Java security, can be found in [Wallach et al. (1997)] and [Gong et al. (1997)].

Bibliography

[Basu et al. (1995)]   A. Basu, V. Buch, W. Vogels, and T. von Eicken, "U-Net: A User-Level Network Interface for Parallel and Distributed Computing", *Proceedings of the ACM Symposium on Operating Systems Principles* (1995), pages 40–53.

[Bershad et al. (1995)]   B. N. Bershad, S. Savage, P. Pardyak, E. G. Sirer, M. Fiuczynski, D. Becker, S. Eggers, and C. Chambers, "Extensibility, Safety and Performance in the SPIN Operating System", *Proceedings of the ACM Symposium on Operating Systems Principles* (1995), pages 267–284.

[Cohen and Jefferson (1975)]   E. S. Cohen and D. Jefferson, "Protection in the Hydra Operating System", *Proceedings of the ACM Symposium on Operating Systems Principles* (1975), pages 141–160.

[Dennis and Horn (1966)]   J. B. Dennis and E. C. V. Horn, "Programming Semantics for Multiprogrammed Computations", *Communications of the ACM*, Volume 9, Number 3 (1966), pages 143–155.

[Ekanadham and Bernstein (1979)]   K. Ekanadham and A. J. Bernstein, "Conditional Capabilities", *IEEE Transactions on Software Engineering*, Volume SE-5, Number 5 (1979), pages 458–464.

[Ganger et al. (2002)]   G. R. Ganger, D. R. Engler, M. F. Kaashoek, H. M. Briceno, R. Hunt, and T. Pinckney, "Fast and Flexible Application-Level Networking on Exokernel Systems", *ACM Transactions on Computer Systems*, Volume 20, Number 1 (2002), pages 49–83.

[Goldberg et al. (1996)]   I. Goldberg, D. Wagner, R. Thomas, and E. A. Brewer, "A Secure Environment for Untrusted Helper Applications", *Proceedings of the 6th Usenix Security Symposium* (1996).

[Gong et al. (1997)]   L. Gong, M. Mueller, H. Prafullchandra, and R. Schemers, "Going Beyond the Sandbox: An Overview of the New Security Architecture in the Java Development Kit 1.2", *Proceedings of the USENIX Symposium on Internet Technologies and Systems* (1997).

[Harrison et al. (1976)]   M. A. Harrison, W. L. Ruzzo, and J. D. Ullman, "Protection in Operating Systems", *Communications of the ACM*, Volume 19, Number 8 (1976), pages 461–471.

[Iliffe and Jodeit (1962)]   J. K. Iliffe and J. G. Jodeit, "A Dynamic Storage Allocation System", *Computer Journal*, Volume 5, Number 3 (1962), pages 200–209.

[Jones and Liskov (1978)]   A. K. Jones and B. H. Liskov, "A Language Extension for Expressing Constraints on Data Access", *Communications of the ACM*, Volume 21, Number 5 (1978), pages 358–367.

[Kaashoek et al. (1997)]   M. F. Kaashoek, D. R. Engler, G. R. Ganger, H. M. Briceno, R. Hunt, D. Mazieres, T. Pinckney, R. Grimm, J. Jannotti, and K. Mackenzie, "Application Performance and Flexibility on Exokernel Systems", *Proceedings of the ACM Symposium on Operating Systems Principles* (1997), pages 52–65.

[Kieburtz and Silberschatz (1978)]   R. B. Kieburtz and A. Silberschatz, "Capability Managers", *IEEE Transactions on Software Engineering*, Volume SE-4, Number 6 (1978), pages 467–477.

[Kieburtz and Silberschatz (1983)]   R. B. Kieburtz and A. Silberschatz, "Access Right Expressions", *ACM Transactions on Programming Languages and Systems*, Volume 5, Number 1 (1983), pages 78–96.

[Lampson (1969)]   B. W. Lampson, "Dynamic Protection Structures", *Proceedings of the AFIPS Fall Joint Computer Conference* (1969), pages 27–38.

[Lampson (1971)]   B. W. Lampson, "Protection", *Proceedings of the Fifth Annual Princeton Conference on Information Systems Science* (1971), pages 437–443.

[Lampson (1973)]   B. W. Lampson, "A Note on the Confinement Problem", *Communications of the ACM*, Volume 10, Number 16 (1973), pages 613–615.

[Levin et al. (1975)]   R. Levin, E. S. Cohen, W. M. Corwin, F. J. Pollack, and W. A. Wulf, "Policy/Mechanism Separation in Hydra", *Proceedings of the ACM Symposium on Operating Systems Principles* (1975), pages 132–140.

[Lipner (1975)]   S. Lipner, "A Comment on the Confinement Problem", *Operating System Review*, Volume 9, Number 5 (1975), pages 192–196.

[McCanne and Jacobson (1993)]   S. McCanne and V. Jacobson, "The BSD Packet Filter: A New Architecture for User-level Packet Capture", *USENIX Winter* (1993), pages 259–270.

[McGraw and Andrews (1979)]   J. R. McGraw and G. R. Andrews, "Access Control in Parallel Programs", *IEEE Transactions on Software Engineering*, Volume SE-5, Number 1 (1979), pages 1–9.

[Morris (1973)]   J. H. Morris, "Protection in Programming Languages", *Communications of the ACM*, Volume 16, Number 1 (1973), pages 15–21.

[Needham and Walker (1977)]   R. M. Needham and R. D. H. Walker, "The Cambridge CAP Computer and Its Protection System", *Proceedings of the Sixth Symposium on Operating System Principles* (1977), pages 1–10.

[Organick (1972)]   E. I. Organick, *The Multics System: An Examination of Its Structure*, MIT Press (1972).

[Popek (1974)]   G. J. Popek, "Protection Structures", *Computer*, Volume 7, Number 6 (1974), pages 22–33.

[Redell and Fabry (1974)]   D. D. Redell and R. S. Fabry, "Selective Revocation of Capabilities", *Proceedings of the IRIA International Workshop on Protection in Operating Systems* (1974), pages 197–210.

[Saltzer and Schroeder (1975)]   J. H. Saltzer and M. D. Schroeder, "The Protection of Information in Computer Systems", *Proceedings of the IEEE* (1975), pages 1278–1308.

[Wahbe et al. (1993)]   R. Wahbe, S. Lucco, T. E. Anderson, and S. L. Graham, "Efficient Software-Based Fault Isolation", *ACM SIGOPS Operating Systems Review*, Volume 27, Number 5 (1993), pages 203–216.

[Wallach et al. (1997)]   D. S. Wallach, D. Balfanz, D. Dean, and E. W. Felten, "Extensible Security Architectures for Java", *Proceedings of the ACM Symposium on Operating Systems Principles* (1997), pages 116–128.

[Wulf et al. (1981)]   W. A. Wulf, R. Levin, and S. P. Harbison, *Hydra/C.mmp: An Experimental Computer System*, McGraw-Hill (1981).

CHAPTER *14*

Security

Protection, as we discussed in Chapter 13, is strictly an *internal* problem: How do we provide controlled access to programs and data stored in a computer system? **Security**, on the other hand, requires not only an adequate protection system but also consideration of the *external* environment within which the system operates. A protection system is ineffective if user authentication is compromised or a program is run by an unauthorized user.

Computer resources must be guarded against unauthorized access, malicious destruction or alteration, and accidental introduction of inconsistency. These resources include information stored in the system (both data and code), as well as the CPU, memory, disks, tapes, and networking that are the computer. In this chapter, we start by examining ways in which resources may be accidentally or purposely misused. We then explore a key security enabler —cryptography. Finally, we look at mechanisms to guard against or detect attacks.

CHAPTER OBJECTIVES

- To discuss security threats and attacks.
- To explain the fundamentals of encryption, authentication, and hashing.
- To examine the uses of cryptography in computing.
- To describe various countermeasures to security attacks.

14.1 The Security Problem

In many applications, ensuring the security of the computer system is worth considerable effort. Large commercial systems containing payroll or other financial data are inviting targets to thieves. Systems that contain data pertaining to corporate operations may be of interest to unscrupulous competitors. Furthermore, loss of such data, whether by accident or fraud, can seriously impair the ability of the corporation to function.

In Chapter 13, we discussed mechanisms that the operating system can provide (with appropriate aid from the hardware) that allow users to protect

633

their resources, including programs and data. These mechanisms work well only as long as the users conform to the intended use of and access to these resources. We say that a system is secure if its resources are used and accessed as intended under all circumstances. Unfortunately, total security cannot be achieved. Nonetheless, we must have mechanisms to make security breaches a rare occurrence, rather than the norm.

Security violations (or misuse) of the system can be categorized as intentional (malicious) or accidental. It is easier to protect against accidental misuse than against malicious misuse. For the most part, protection mechanisms are the core of protection from accidents. The following list includes several forms of accidental and malicious security violations. We should note that in our discussion of security, we use the terms intruder and cracker for those attempting to breach security. In addition, a threat is the potential for a security violation, such as the discovery of a vulnerability, whereas an attack is the attempt to break security.

- **Breach of confidentiality**. This type of violation involves unauthorized reading of data (or theft of information). Typically, a breach of confidentiality is the goal of an intruder. Capturing secret data from a system or a data stream, such as credit-card information or identity information for identity theft, can result directly in money for the intruder.

- **Breach of integrity**. This violation involves unauthorized modification of data. Such attacks can, for example, result in passing of liability to an innocent party or modification of the source code of an important commercial application.

- **Breach of availability**. This violation involves unauthorized destruction of data. Some crackers would rather wreak havoc and gain status or bragging rights than gain financially. Website defacement is a common example of this type of security breach.

- **Theft of service**. This violation involves unauthorized use of resources. For example, an intruder (or intrusion program) may install a daemon on a system that acts as a file server.

- **Denial of service**. This violation involves preventing legitimate use of the system. Denial-of-service (DOS) attacks are sometimes accidental. The original Internet worm turned into a DOS attack when a bug failed to delay its rapid spread. We discuss DOS attacks further in Section 14.3.3.

Attackers use several standard methods in their attempts to breach security. The most common is masquerading, in which one participant in a communication pretends to be someone else (another host or another person). By masquerading, attackers breach authentication, the correctness of identification; they can then gain access that they would not normally be allowed or escalate their privileges—obtain privileges to which they would not normally be entitled. Another common attack is to replay a captured exchange of data. A replay attack consists of the malicious or fraudulent repeat of a valid data transmission. Sometimes the replay comprises the entire attack—for example, in a repeat of a request to transfer money. But frequently it is done along with message modification, again to escalate privileges. Consider

Figure 14.1 Standard security attacks.

the damage that could be done if a request for authentication had a legitimate user's information replaced with an unauthorized user's. Yet another kind of attack is the **man-in-the-middle attack**, in which an attacker sits in the data flow of a communication, masquerading as the sender to the receiver, and vice versa. In a network communication, a man-in-the-middle attack may be preceded by a **session hijacking**, in which an active communication session is intercepted. Several attack methods are depicted in Figure 14.1.

As we have already suggested, absolute protection of the system from malicious abuse is not possible, but the cost to the perpetrator can be made sufficiently high to deter most intruders. In some cases, such as a denial-of-service attack, it is preferable to prevent the attack but sufficient to detect the attack so that countermeasures can be taken.

To protect a system, we must take security measures at four levels:

1. **Physical**. The site or sites containing the computer systems must be physically secured against armed or surreptitious entry by intruders. Both the machine rooms and the terminals or workstations that have access to the machines must be secured.

2. **Human**. Authorization must be done carefully to assure that only appropriate users have access to the system. Even authorized users, however, may be "encouraged" to let others use their access (in exchange for a bribe, for example). They may also be tricked into allowing access via **social engineering**. One type of social-engineering attack is **phishing**. Here, a legitimate-looking e-mail or web page misleads a user into entering confidential information. Another technique is **dumpster diving**, a general term for attempting to gather information in order to gain unauthorized access to the computer (by looking through trash, finding phone books, or finding notes containing passwords, for example). These security problems are management and personnel issues, not problems pertaining to operating systems.

3. **Operating system**. The system must protect itself from accidental or purposeful security breaches. A runaway process could constitute an accidental denial-of-service attack. A query to a service could reveal passwords. A stack overflow could allow the launching of an unauthorized process. The list of possible breaches is almost endless.

4. **Network**. Much computer data in modern systems travels over private leased lines, shared lines like the Internet, wireless connections, or dial-up lines. Intercepting these data could be just as harmful as breaking into a computer, and interruption of communications could constitute a remote denial-of-service attack, diminishing users' use of and trust in the system.

Security at the first two levels must be maintained if operating-system security is to be ensured. A weakness at a high level of security (physical or human) allows circumvention of strict low-level (operating-system) security measures. Thus, the old adage that a chain is only as strong as its weakest link is especially true of system security. All of these aspects must be addressed for security to be maintained.

Furthermore, the system must provide protection (Chapter 13) to allow the implementation of security features. Without the ability to authorize users and processes, to control their access, and to log their activities, it would be impossible for an operating system to implement security measures or to run securely. Hardware protection features are needed to support an overall protection scheme. For example, a system without memory protection cannot be secure. New hardware features are allowing systems to be made more secure, as we shall discuss.

Unfortunately, little in security is straightforward. As intruders exploit security vulnerabilities, security countermeasures are created and deployed. This causes intruders to become more sophisticated in their attacks. For example, recent security incidents include the use of spyware to provide a conduit for spam through innocent systems (we discuss this practice in Section 14.2). This cat-and-mouse game is likely to continue, with more security tools needed to block the escalating intruder techniques and activities.

In the remainder of this chapter, we address security at the network and operating-system levels. Security at the physical and human levels, although important, is for the most part beyond the scope of this text. Security within the operating system and between operating systems is implemented in several ways, ranging from passwords for authentication through guarding against viruses to detecting intrusions. We start with an exploration of security threats.

14.2   Program Threats

Processes, along with the kernel, are the only means of accomplishing work on a computer. Therefore, writing a program that creates a breach of security, or causing a normal process to change its behavior and create a breach, is a common goal of crackers. In fact, even most nonprogram security events have as their goal causing a program threat. For example, while it is useful to log in to a system without authorization, it is quite a lot more useful to leave behind a **back-door** daemon that provides information or allows easy access even if the original exploit is blocked. In this section, we describe common methods by which programs cause security breaches. Note that there is considerable variation in the naming conventions for security holes and that we use the most common or descriptive terms.

14.2.1   Trojan Horse

Many systems have mechanisms for allowing programs written by users to be executed by other users. If these programs are executed in a domain that provides the access rights of the executing user, the other users may misuse these rights. A text-editor program, for example, may include code to search the file to be edited for certain keywords. If any are found, the entire file may be copied to a special area accessible to the creator of the text editor. A code segment that misuses its environment is called a **Trojan horse**. Long search paths, such as are common on UNIX systems, exacerbate the Trojan-horse problem. The search path lists the set of directories to search when an ambiguous program name is given. The path is searched for a file of that name, and the file is executed. All the directories in such a search path must be secure, or a Trojan horse could be slipped into the user's path and executed accidentally.

For instance, consider the use of the "." character in a search path. The "." tells the shell to include the current directory in the search. Thus, if a user has "." in her search path, has set her current directory to a friend's directory, and enters the name of a normal system command, the command may be executed from the friend's directory. The program will run within the user's domain, allowing the program to do anything that the user is allowed to do, including deleting the user's files, for instance.

A variation of the Trojan horse is a program that emulates a login program. An unsuspecting user starts to log in at a terminal and notices that he has apparently mistyped his password. He tries again and is successful. What has happened is that his authentication key and password have been stolen by the login emulator, which was left running on the terminal by the thief. The emulator stored away the password, printed out a login error message, and exited; the user was then provided with a genuine login prompt. This type of attack can be defeated by having the operating system print a usage message at the end of an interactive session or by a nontrappable key sequence, such as the `control-alt-delete` combination used by all modern Windows operating systems.

Another variation on the Trojan horse is spyware. Spyware sometimes accompanies a program that the user has chosen to install. Most frequently, it comes along with freeware or shareware programs, but sometimes it is included with commercial software. The goal of spyware is to download ads to display on the user's system, create pop-up browser windows when certain sites are visited, or capture information from the user's system and return it to a central site. This latter practice is an example of a general category of attacks known as covert channels, in which surreptitious communication occurs. For example, the installation of an innocuous-seeming program on a Windows system could result in the loading of a spyware daemon. The spyware could contact a central site, be given a message and a list of recipient addresses, and deliver a spam message to those users from the Windows machine. This process continues until the user discovers the spyware. Frequently, the spyware is not discovered. In 2010, it was estimated that 90 percent of spam was being delivered by this method. This theft of service is not even considered a crime in most countries!

Spyware is a micro example of a macro problem: violation of the principle of least privilege. Under most circumstances, a user of an operating system does not need to install network daemons. Such daemons are installed via two mistakes. First, a user may run with more privileges than necessary (for example, as the administrator), allowing programs that she runs to have more access to the system than is necessary. This is a case of human error—a common security weakness. Second, an operating system may allow by default more privileges than a normal user needs. This is a case of poor operating-system design decisions. An operating system (and, indeed, software in general) should allow fine-grained control of access and security, but it must also be easy to manage and understand. Inconvenient or inadequate security measures are bound to be circumvented, causing an overall weakening of the security they were designed to implement.

14.2.2 Trap Door

The designer of a program or system might leave a hole in the software that only she is capable of using. This type of security breach (or trap door) was shown in the movie *War Games*. For instance, the code might check for a specific user ID or password, and it might circumvent normal security procedures. Programmers have been arrested for embezzling from banks by including rounding errors in their code and having the occasional half-cent credited to their accounts. This account crediting can add up to a large amount of money, considering the number of transactions that a large bank executes.

A clever trap door could be included in a compiler. The compiler could generate standard object code as well as a trap door, regardless of the source code being compiled. This activity is particularly nefarious, since a search of the source code of the program will not reveal any problems. Only the source code of the compiler would contain the information.

Trap doors pose a difficult problem because, to detect them, we have to analyze all the source code for all components of a system. Given that software systems may consist of millions of lines of code, this analysis is not done frequently, and frequently it is not done at all!

14.2.3 Logic Bomb

Consider a program that initiates a security incident only under certain circumstances. It would be hard to detect because under normal operations, there would be no security hole. However, when a predefined set of parameters was met, the security hole would be created. This scenario is known as a logic bomb. A programmer, for example, might write code to detect whether he was still employed; if that check failed, a daemon could be spawned to allow remote access, or code could be launched to cause damage to the site.

14.2.4 Stack and Buffer Overflow

The stack- or buffer-overflow attack is the most common way for an attacker outside the system, on a network or dial-up connection, to gain unauthorized access to the target system. An authorized user of the system may also use this exploit for privilege escalation.

Essentially, the attack exploits a bug in a program. The bug can be a simple case of poor programming, in which the programmer neglected to code bounds checking on an input field. In this case, the attacker sends more data than the program was expecting. By using trial and error, or by examining the source code of the attacked program if it is available, the attacker determines the vulnerability and writes a program to do the following:

1. Overflow an input field, command-line argument, or input buffer—for example, on a network daemon—until it writes into the stack.

2. Overwrite the current return address on the stack with the address of the exploit code loaded in step 3.

3. Write a simple set of code for the next space in the stack that includes the commands that the attacker wishes to execute—for instance, spawn a shell.

The result of this attack program's execution will be a root shell or other privileged command execution.

For instance, if a web-page form expects a user name to be entered into a field, the attacker could send the user name, plus extra characters to overflow the buffer and reach the stack, plus a new return address to load onto the stack, plus the code the attacker wants to run. When the buffer-reading subroutine returns from execution, the return address is the exploit code, and the code is run.

Let's look at a buffer-overflow exploit in more detail. Consider the simple C program shown in Figure 14.2. This program creates a character array of size BUFFER_SIZE and copies the contents of the parameter provided on the command line—argv[1]. As long as the size of this parameter is less than BUFFER_SIZE (we need one byte to store the null terminator), this program works properly. But consider what happens if the parameter provided on the command line is longer than BUFFER_SIZE. In this scenario, the strcpy() function will begin copying from argv[1] until it encounters a null terminator (\0) or until the program crashes. Thus, this program suffers from a potential buffer-overflow problem in which copied data overflow the buffer array.

```
#include <stdio.h>
#define BUFFER_SIZE 256

int main(int argc, char *argv[])
{
   char buffer[BUFFER_SIZE];

   if (argc < 2)
      return -1;
   else {
      strcpy(buffer,argv[1]);
      return 0;
   }
}
```

Figure 14.2   C program with buffer-overflow condition.

Note that a careful programmer could have performed bounds checking on the size of argv[1] by using the strncpy() function rather than strcpy(), replacing the line "strcpy(buffer, argv[1]);" with "strncpy(buffer, argv[1], sizeof(buffer)-1);". Unfortunately, good bounds checking is the exception rather than the norm.

Furthermore, lack of bounds checking is not the only possible cause of the behavior of the program in Figure 14.2. The program could instead have been carefully designed to compromise the integrity of the system. We now consider the possible security vulnerabilities of a buffer overflow.

When a function is invoked in a typical computer architecture, the variables defined locally to the function (sometimes known as **automatic variables**), the parameters passed to the function, and the address to which control returns once the function exits are stored in a *stack frame*. The layout for a typical stack frame is shown in Figure 14.3. Examining the stack frame from top to bottom, we first see the parameters passed to the function, followed by any automatic variables declared in the function. We next see the *frame pointer*, which is the address of the beginning of the stack frame. Finally, we have the return

Figure 14.3   The layout for a typical stack frame.

address, which specifies where to return control once the function exits. The frame pointer must be saved on the stack, as the value of the stack pointer can vary during the function call. The saved frame pointer allows relative access to parameters and automatic variables.

Given this standard memory layout, a cracker could execute a buffer-overflow attack. Her goal is to replace the return address in the stack frame so that it now points to the code segment containing the attacking program.

The programmer first writes a short code segment such as the following:

```
#include <stdio.h>

int main(int argc, char *argv[])
{
    execvp(''\bin\sh'',''\bin \sh'', NULL);
    return 0;
}
```

Using the execvp() system call, this code segment creates a shell process. If the program being attacked runs with system-wide permissions, this newly created shell will gain complete access to the system. Of course, the code segment could do anything allowed by the privileges of the attacked process. This code segment is then compiled so that the assembly language instructions can be modified. The primary modification is to remove unnecessary features in the code, thereby reducing the code size so that it can fit into a stack frame. This assembled code fragment is now a binary sequence that will be at the heart of the attack.

Refer again to the program shown in Figure 14.2. Let's assume that when the main() function is called in that program, the stack frame appears as shown in Figure 14.4(a). Using a debugger, the programmer then finds the

Figure 14.4 Hypothetical stack frame for Figure 14.2, (a) before and (b) after.

address of buffer[0] in the stack. That address is the location of the code the attacker wants executed. The binary sequence is appended with the necessary amount of NO-OP instructions (for NO-OPeration) to fill the stack frame up to the location of the return address, and the location of buffer[0], the new return address, is added. The attack is complete when the attacker gives this constructed binary sequence as input to the process. The process then copies the binary sequence from argv[1] to position buffer[0] in the stack frame. Now, when control returns from main(), instead of returning to the location specified by the old value of the return address, we return to the modified shell code, which runs with the access rights of the attacked process! Figure 14.4(b) contains the modified shell code.

There are many ways to exploit potential buffer-overflow problems. In this example, we considered the possibility that the program being attacked— the code shown in Figure 14.2—ran with system-wide permissions. However, the code segment that runs once the value of the return address has been modified might perform any type of malicious act, such as deleting files, opening network ports for further exploitation, and so on.

This example buffer-overflow attack reveals that considerable knowledge and programming skill are needed to recognize exploitable code and then to exploit it. Unfortunately, it does not take great programmers to launch security attacks. Rather, one cracker can determine the bug and then write an exploit. Anyone with rudimentary computer skills and access to the exploit— a so-called **script kiddie**—can then try to launch the attack at target systems.

The buffer-overflow attack is especially pernicious because it can be run between systems and can travel over allowed communication channels. Such attacks can occur within protocols that are expected to be used to communicate with the target machine, and they can therefore be hard to detect and prevent. They can even bypass the security added by firewalls (Section 14.7).

One solution to this problem is for the CPU to have a feature that disallows execution of code in a stack section of memory. Recent versions of Sun's SPARC chip include this setting, and recent versions of Solaris enable it. The return address of the overflowed routine can still be modified; but when the return address is within the stack and the code there attempts to execute, an exception is generated, and the program is halted with an error.

Recent versions of AMD and Intel x86 chips include the NX feature to prevent this type of attack. The use of the feature is supported in several x86 operating systems, including Linux and Windows XP SP2. The hardware implementation involves the use of a new bit in the page tables of the CPUs. This bit marks the associated page as nonexecutable, so that instructions cannot be read from it and executed. As this feature becomes more prevalent, buffer-overflow attacks should greatly diminish.

14.2.5 Viruses

Another form of program threat is a **virus**. A virus is a fragment of code embedded in a legitimate program. Viruses are self-replicating and are designed to "infect" other programs. They can wreak havoc in a system by modifying or destroying files and causing system crashes and program malfunctions. As with most penetration attacks, viruses are very specific to architectures, operating systems, and applications. Viruses are a particular problem for users of

PCs. UNIX and other multiuser operating systems generally are not susceptible to viruses because the executable programs are protected from writing by the operating system. Even if a virus does infect such a program, its powers usually are limited because other aspects of the system are protected.

Viruses are usually borne via e-mail, with spam the most common vector. They can also spread when users download viral programs from Internet file-sharing services or exchange infected disks.

Another common form of virus transmission uses Microsoft Office files, such as Microsoft Word documents. These documents can contain *macros* (or Visual Basic programs) that programs in the Office suite (Word, PowerPoint, and Excel) will execute automatically. Because these programs run under the user's own account, the macros can run largely unconstrained (for example, deleting user files at will). Commonly, the virus will also e-mail itself to others in the user's contact list. Here is a code sample that shows how simple it is to write a Visual Basic macro that a virus could use to format the hard drive of a Windows computer as soon as the file containing the macro was opened:

```
Sub AutoOpen()
Dim oFS
    Set oFS = CreateObject(''Scripting.FileSystemObject'')
    vs = Shell(''c: command.com /k format c:'',vbHide)
End Sub
```

How do viruses work? Once a virus reaches a target machine, a program known as a **virus dropper** inserts the virus into the system. The virus dropper is usually a Trojan horse, executed for other reasons but installing the virus as its core activity. Once installed, the virus may do any one of a number of things. There are literally thousands of viruses, but they fall into several main categories. Note that many viruses belong to more than one category.

- **File**. A standard file virus infects a system by appending itself to a file. It changes the start of the program so that execution jumps to its code. After it executes, it returns control to the program so that its execution is not noticed. File viruses are sometimes known as parasitic viruses, as they leave no full files behind and leave the host program still functional.

- **Boot**. A boot virus infects the boot sector of the system, executing every time the system is booted and before the operating system is loaded. It watches for other bootable media and infects them. These viruses are also known as memory viruses, because they do not appear in the file system. Figure 14.5 shows how a boot virus works.

- **Macro**. Most viruses are written in a low-level language, such as assembly or C. Macro viruses are written in a high-level language, such as Visual Basic. These viruses are triggered when a program capable of executing the macro is run. For example, a macro virus could be contained in a spreadsheet file.

- **Source code**. A source code virus looks for source code and modifies it to include the virus and to help spread the virus.

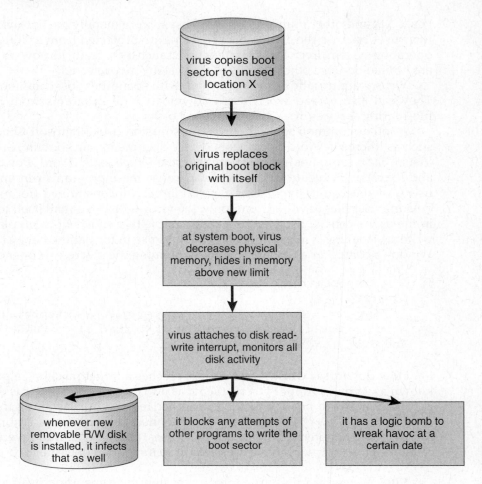

Figure 14.5   A boot-sector computer virus.

- **Polymorphic**. A polymorphic virus changes each time it is installed to avoid detection by antivirus software. The changes do not affect the virus's functionality but rather change the virus's signature. A **virus signature** is a pattern that can be used to identify a virus, typically a series of bytes that make up the virus code.

- **Encrypted**. An encrypted virus includes decryption code along with the encrypted virus, again to avoid detection. The virus first decrypts and then executes.

- **Stealth**. This tricky virus attempts to avoid detection by modifying parts of the system that could be used to detect it. For example, it could modify the read system call so that if the file it has modified is read, the original form of the code is returned rather than the infected code.

- **Tunneling**. This virus attempts to bypass detection by an antivirus scanner by installing itself in the interrupt-handler chain. Similar viruses install themselves in device drivers.

- **Multipartite**. A virus of this type is able to infect multiple parts of a system, including boot sectors, memory, and files. This makes it difficult to detect and contain.

- **Armored**. An armored virus is coded to make it hard for antivirus researchers to unravel and understand. It can also be compressed to avoid detection and disinfection. In addition, virus droppers and other full files that are part of a virus infestation are frequently hidden via file attributes or unviewable file names.

This vast variety of viruses has continued to grow. For example, in 2004 a new and widespread virus was detected. It exploited three separate bugs for its operation. This virus started by infecting hundreds of Windows servers (including many trusted sites) running Microsoft Internet Information Server (IIS). Any vulnerable Microsoft Explorer web browser visiting those sites received a browser virus with any download. The browser virus installed several back-door programs, including a **keystroke logger**, which records everything entered on the keyboard (including passwords and credit-card numbers). It also installed a daemon to allow unlimited remote access by an intruder and another that allowed an intruder to route spam through the infected desktop computer.

Generally, viruses are the most disruptive security attacks, and because they are effective, they will continue to be written and to spread. An active security-related debate within the computing community concerns the existence of a **monoculture**, in which many systems run the same hardware, operating system, and application software. This monoculture supposedly consists of Microsoft products. One question is whether such a monoculture even exists today. Another question is whether, if it does, it increases the threat of and damage caused by viruses and other security intrusions.

14.3 System and Network Threats

Program threats typically use a breakdown in the protection mechanisms of a system to attack programs. In contrast, system and network threats involve the abuse of services and network connections. System and network threats create a situation in which operating-system resources and user files are misused. Sometimes, a system and network attack is used to launch a program attack, and vice versa.

The more *open* an operating system is—the more services it has enabled and the more functions it allows—the more likely it is that a bug is available to exploit. Increasingly, operating systems strive to be **secure by default**. For example, Solaris 10 moved from a model in which many services (FTP, telnet, and others) were enabled by default when the system was installed to a model in which almost all services are disabled at installation time and must specifically be enabled by system administrators. Such changes reduce the system's **attack surface**—the set of ways in which an attacker can try to break into the system.

In the remainder of this section, we discuss some examples of system and network threats, including worms, port scanning, and denial-of-service attacks. It is important to note that masquerading and replay attacks are also commonly launched over networks between systems. In fact, these attacks are more effective and harder to counter when multiple systems are involved. For example, within a computer, the operating system usually can determine the sender and receiver of a message. Even if the sender changes to the ID of someone else, there may be a record of that ID change. When multiple systems are involved, especially systems controlled by attackers, then such tracing is much more difficult.

In general, we can say that sharing secrets (to prove identity and as keys to encryption) is required for authentication and encryption, and sharing secrets is easier in environments (such as a single operating system) in which secure sharing methods exist. These methods include shared memory and interprocess communications. Creating secure communication and authentication is discussed in Section 14.4 and in Section 14.5.

14.3.1 Worms

A **worm** is a process that uses the **spawn** mechanism to duplicate itself. The worm spawns copies of itself, using up system resources and perhaps locking out all other processes. On computer networks, worms are particularly potent, since they may reproduce themselves among systems and thus shut down an entire network. Such an event occurred in 1988 to UNIX systems on the Internet, causing the loss of system and system-administrator time worth millions of dollars.

At the close of the workday on November 2, 1988, Robert Tappan Morris, Jr., a first-year Cornell graduate student, unleashed a worm program on one or more hosts connected to the Internet. Targeting Sun Microsystems' Sun 3 workstations and VAX computers running variants of Version 4 BSD UNIX, the worm quickly spread over great distances. Within a few hours of its release, it had consumed system resources to the point of bringing down the infected machines.

Although Morris designed the self-replicating program for rapid reproduction and distribution, some of the features of the UNIX networking environment provided the means to propagate the worm throughout the system. It is likely that Morris chose for initial infection an Internet host left open for and accessible to outside users. From there, the worm program exploited flaws in the UNIX operating system's security routines and took advantage of UNIX utilities that simplify resource sharing in local-area networks to gain unauthorized access to thousands of other connected sites. Morris's methods of attack are outlined next.

The worm was made up of two programs, a **grappling hook** (also called a **bootstrap** or **vector**) program and the main program. Named 11.c, the grappling hook consisted of 99 lines of C code compiled and run on each machine it accessed. Once established on the computer system under attack, the grappling hook connected to the machine where it originated and uploaded a copy of the main worm onto the *hooked* system (Figure 14.6). The main program proceeded to search for other machines to which the newly infected system could connect easily. In these actions, Morris exploited the UNIX networking utility rsh for easy remote task execution. By setting up special files that list host–login name pairs, users can omit entering a password each time

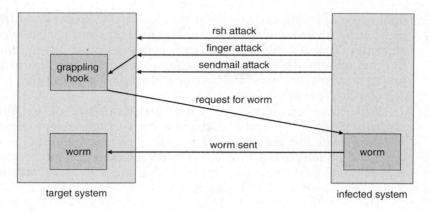

Figure 14.6 The Morris Internet worm.

they access a remote account on the paired list. The worm searched these special files for site names that would allow remote execution without a password. Where remote shells were established, the worm program was uploaded and began executing anew.

The attack via remote access was one of three infection methods built into the worm. The other two methods involved operating-system bugs in the UNIX `finger` and `sendmail` programs.

The `finger` utility functions as an electronic telephone directory. The command

```
finger user-name@hostname
```

returns a person's real and login names along with other information that the user may have provided, such as office and home address and telephone number, research plan, or clever quotation. Finger runs as a background process (or daemon) at each BSD site and responds to queries throughout the Internet. The worm executed a buffer-overflow attack on `finger`. The program queried `finger` with a 536-byte string crafted to exceed the buffer allocated for input and to overwrite the stack frame. Instead of returning to the `main` routine where it resided before Morris's call, the `finger` daemon was routed to a procedure within the invading 536-byte string now residing on the stack. The new procedure executed `/bin/sh`, which, if successful, gave the worm a remote shell on the machine under attack.

The bug exploited in `sendmail` also involved using a daemon process for malicious entry. `sendmail` sends, receives, and routes electronic mail. Debugging code in the utility permits testers to verify and display the state of the mail system. The debugging option was useful to system administrators and was often left on. Morris included in his attack arsenal a call to `debug` that —instead of specifying a user address, as would be normal in testing—issued a set of commands that mailed and executed a copy of the grappling-hook program.

Once in place, the main worm systematically attempted to discover user passwords. It began by trying simple cases of no password or passwords constructed of account–user-name combinations, then used comparisons with an internal dictionary of 432 favorite password choices, and then went to the final stage of trying each word in the standard UNIX on-line dictionary as a possible password. This elaborate and efficient three-stage password-cracking algorithm enabled the worm to gain access to other user accounts on the infected system. The worm then searched for rsh data files in these newly broken accounts and used them as described previously to gain access to user accounts on remote systems.

With each new access, the worm program searched for already active copies of itself. If it found one, the new copy exited, except in every seventh instance. Had the worm exited on all duplicate sightings, it might have remained undetected. Allowing every seventh duplicate to proceed (possibly to confound efforts to stop its spread by baiting with "fake" worms) created a wholesale infestation of Sun and VAX systems on the Internet.

The very features of the UNIX network environment that assisted in the worm's propagation also helped to stop its advance. Ease of electronic communication, mechanisms to copy source and binary files to remote machines, and access to both source code and human expertise allowed cooperative efforts to develop solutions quickly. By the evening of the next day, November 3, methods of halting the invading program were circulated to system administrators via the Internet. Within days, specific software patches for the exploited security flaws were available.

Why did Morris unleash the worm? The action has been characterized as both a harmless prank gone awry and a serious criminal offense. Based on the complexity of the attack, it is unlikely that the worm's release or the scope of its spread was unintentional. The worm program took elaborate steps to cover its tracks and to repel efforts to stop its spread. Yet the program contained no code aimed at damaging or destroying the systems on which it ran. The author clearly had the expertise to include such commands; in fact, data structures were present in the bootstrap code that could have been used to transfer Trojan-horse or virus programs. The behavior of the program may lead to interesting observations, but it does not provide a sound basis for inferring motive. What is not open to speculation, however, is the legal outcome: a federal court convicted Morris and handed down a sentence of three years' probation, 400 hours of community service, and a $10,000 fine. Morris's legal costs probably exceeded $100,000.

Security experts continue to evaluate methods to decrease or eliminate worms. A more recent event, though, shows that worms are still a fact of life on the Internet. It also shows that as the Internet grows, the damage that even "harmless" worms can do also grows and can be significant. This example occurred during August 2003. The fifth version of the "Sobig" worm, .more properly known as "W32.Sobig.F@mm," was released by persons at this time unknown. It was the fastest-spreading worm released to date, at its peak infecting hundreds of thousands of computers and one in seventeen e-mail messages on the Internet. It clogged e-mail inboxes, slowed networks, and took a huge number of hours to clean up.

Sobig.F was launched by being uploaded to a pornography newsgroup via an account created with a stolen credit card. It was disguised as a photo. The virus targeted Microsoft Windows systems and used its own SMTP engine to e-mail itself to all the addresses found on an infected system. It used a variety of subject lines to help avoid detection, including "Thank You!" "Your details," and "Re: Approved." It also used a random address on the host as the "From:" address, making it difficult to determine from the message which machine was the infected source. Sobig.F included an attachment for the target e-mail reader to click on, again with a variety of names. If this payload was executed, it stored a program called WINPPR32.EXE in the default Windows directory, along with a text file. It also modified the Windows registry.

The code included in the attachment was also programmed to periodically attempt to connect to one of twenty servers and download and execute a program from them. Fortunately, the servers were disabled before the code could be downloaded. The content of the program from these servers has not yet been determined. If the code was malevolent, untold damage to a vast number of machines could have resulted.

14.3.2   Port Scanning

Port scanning is not an attack but rather a means for a cracker to detect a system's vulnerabilities to attack. Port scanning typically is automated, involving a tool that attempts to create a TCP/IP connection to a specific port or a range of ports. For example, suppose there is a known vulnerability (or bug) in sendmail. A cracker could launch a port scanner to try to connect, say, to port 25 of a particular system or to a range of systems. If the connection was successful, the cracker (or tool) could attempt to communicate with the answering service to determine if the service was indeed sendmail and, if so, if it was the version with the bug.

Now imagine a tool in which each bug of every service of every operating system was encoded. The tool could attempt to connect to every port of one or more systems. For every service that answered, it could try to use each known bug. Frequently, the bugs are buffer overflows, allowing the creation of a privileged command shell on the system. From there, of course, the cracker could install Trojan horses, back-door programs, and so on.

There is no such tool, but there are tools that perform subsets of that functionality. For example, nmap (from http://www.insecure.org/nmap/) is a very versatile open-source utility for network exploration and security auditing. When pointed at a target, it will determine what services are running, including application names and versions. It can identify the host operating system. It can also provide information about defenses, such as what firewalls are defending the target. It does not exploit any known bugs.

Because port scans are detectable (Section 14.6.3), they frequently are launched from **zombie systems**. Such systems are previously compromised, independent systems that are serving their owners while being used for nefarious purposes, including denial-of-service attacks and spam relay. Zombies make crackers particularly difficult to prosecute because determining the source of the attack and the person that launched it is challenging. This is one of many reasons for securing "inconsequential" systems, not just systems containing "valuable" information or services.

14.3.3   Denial of Service

As mentioned earlier, denial-of-service attacks are aimed not at gaining information or stealing resources but rather at disrupting legitimate use of a system or facility. Most such attacks involve systems that the attacker has not penetrated. Launching an attack that prevents legitimate use is frequently easier than breaking into a machine or facility.

Denial-of-service attacks are generally network based. They fall into two categories. Attacks in the first category use so many facility resources that, in essence, no useful work can be done. For example, a website click could download a Java applet that proceeds to use all available CPU time or to pop up windows infinitely. The second category involves disrupting the network of the facility. There have been several successful denial-of-service attacks of this kind against major websites. These attacks result from abuse of some of the fundamental functionality of TCP/IP. For instance, if the attacker sends the part of the protocol that says "I want to start a TCP connection," but never follows with the standard "The connection is now complete," the result can be partially started TCP sessions. If enough of these sessions are launched, they can eat up all the network resources of the system, disabling any further legitimate TCP connections. Such attacks, which can last hours or days, have caused partial or full failure of attempts to use the target facility. The attacks are usually stopped at the network level until the operating systems can be updated to reduce their vulnerability.

Generally, it is impossible to prevent denial-of-service attacks. The attacks use the same mechanisms as normal operation. Even more difficult to prevent and resolve are distributed denial-of-service (DDOS) attacks. These attacks are launched from multiple sites at once, toward a common target, typically by zombies. DDOS attacks have become more common and are sometimes associated with blackmail attempts. A site comes under attack, and the attackers offer to halt the attack in exchange for money.

Sometimes a site does not even know it is under attack. It can be difficult to determine whether a system slowdown is an attack or just a surge in system use. Consider that a successful advertising campaign that greatly increases traffic to a site could be considered a DDOS.

There are other interesting aspects of DOS attacks. For example, if an authentication algorithm locks an account for a period of time after several incorrect attempts to access the account, then an attacker could cause all authentication to be blocked by purposely making incorrect attempts to access all accounts. Similarly, a firewall that automatically blocks certain kinds of traffic could be induced to block that traffic when it should not. These examples suggest that programmers and systems managers need to fully understand the algorithms and technologies they are deploying. Finally, computer science classes are notorious sources of accidental system DOS attacks. Consider the first programming exercises in which students learn to create subprocesses or threads. A common bug involves spawning subprocesses infinitely. The system's free memory and CPU resources don't stand a chance.

14.4 Cryptography as a Security Tool

There are many defenses against computer attacks, running the gamut from methodology to technology. The broadest tool available to system designers and users is cryptography. In this section, we discuss cryptography and its use in computer security. Note that the cryptography discussed here has been simplified for educational purposes; readers are cautioned against using any of the schemes described here in the real world. Good cryptography libraries are widely available and would make a good basis for production applications.

In an isolated computer, the operating system can reliably determine the sender and recipient of all interprocess communication, since it controls all communication channels in the computer. In a network of computers, the situation is quite different. A networked computer receives bits "from the wire" with no immediate and reliable way of determining what machine or application sent those bits. Similarly, the computer sends bits onto the network with no way of knowing who might eventually receive them. Additionally, when either sending or receiving, the system has no way of knowing if an eavesdropper listened to the communication.

Commonly, network addresses are used to infer the potential senders and receivers of network messages. Network packets arrive with a source address, such as an IP address. And when a computer sends a message, it names the intended receiver by specifying a destination address. However, for applications where security matters, we are asking for trouble if we assume that the source or destination address of a packet reliably determines who sent or received that packet. A rogue computer can send a message with a falsified source address, and numerous computers other than the one specified by the destination address can (and typically do) receive a packet. For example, all of the routers on the way to the destination will receive the packet, too. How, then, is an operating system to decide whether to grant a request when it cannot trust the named source of the request? And how is it supposed to provide protection for a request or data when it cannot determine who will receive the response or message contents it sends over the network?

It is generally considered infeasible to build a network of any scale in which the source and destination addresses of packets can be *trusted* in this sense. Therefore, the only alternative is somehow to eliminate the need to trust the network. This is the job of cryptography. Abstractly, **cryptography** is used to constrain the potential senders and/or receivers of a message. Modern cryptography is based on secrets called **keys** that are selectively distributed to computers in a network and used to process messages. Cryptography enables a recipient of a message to verify that the message was created by some computer possessing a certain key. Similarly, a sender can encode its message so that only a computer with a certain key can decode the message. Unlike network addresses, however, keys are designed so that it is not computationally feasible to derive them from the messages they were used to generate or from any other public information. Thus, they provide a much more trustworthy means of constraining senders and receivers of messages. Note that cryptography is a field of study unto itself, with large and small complexities and subtleties. Here, we explore the most important aspects of the parts of cryptography that pertain to operating systems.

14.4.1 Encryption

Because it solves a wide variety of communication security problems, **encryption** is used frequently in many aspects of modern computing. It is used to send messages securely across across a network, as well as to protect database data, files, and even entire disks from having their contents read by unauthorized entities. An encryption algorithm enables the sender of a message to ensure that only a computer possessing a certain key can read the message, or ensure that the writer of data is the only reader of that data. Encryption of messages is an ancient practice, of course, and there have been many encryption algorithms, dating back to ancient times. In this section, we describe important modern encryption principles and algorithms.

An encryption algorithm consists of the following components:

- A set K of keys.

- A set M of messages.

- A set C of ciphertexts.

- An encrypting function $E : K \rightarrow (M \rightarrow C)$. That is, for each $k \in K$, E_k is a function for generating ciphertexts from messages. Both E and E_k for any k should be efficiently computable functions. Generally, E_k is a randomized mapping from messages to ciphertexts.

- A decrypting function $D : K \rightarrow (C \rightarrow M)$. That is, for each $k \in K$, D_k is a function for generating messages from ciphertexts. Both D and D_k for any k should be efficiently computable functions.

An encryption algorithm must provide this essential property: given a ciphertext $c \in C$, a computer can compute m such that $E_k(m) = c$ only if it possesses k. Thus, a computer holding k can decrypt ciphertexts to the plaintexts used to produce them, but a computer not holding k cannot decrypt ciphertexts. Since ciphertexts are generally exposed (for example, sent on a network), it is important that it be infeasible to derive k from the ciphertexts.

There are two main types of encryption algorithms: symmetric and asymmetric. We discuss both types in the following sections.

14.4.1.1   Symmetric Encryption

In a **symmetric encryption algorithm**, the same key is used to encrypt and to decrypt. Therefore, the secrecy of k must be protected. Figure 14.7 shows an example of two users communicating securely via symmetric encryption over an insecure channel. Note that the key exchange can take place directly between the two parties or via a trusted third party (that is, a certificate authority), as discussed in Section 14.4.1.4.

For the past several decades, the most commonly used symmetric encryption algorithm in the United States for civilian applications has been the **data-encryption standard (DES)** cipher adopted by the National Institute of Standards and Technology (NIST). DES works by taking a 64-bit value and a 56-bit key and performing a series of transformations that are based on substitution and permutation operations. Because DES works on a block of bits at a time, is known as a **block cipher**, and its transformations are typical of block ciphers. With block ciphers, if the same key is used for encrypting an extended amount of data, it becomes vulnerable to attack.

DES is now considered insecure for many applications because its keys can be exhaustively searched with moderate computing resources. (Note, though, that it is still frequently used.) Rather than giving up on DES, NIST created a modification called **triple DES**, in which the DES algorithm is repeated three times (two encryptions and one decryption) on the same plaintext using two

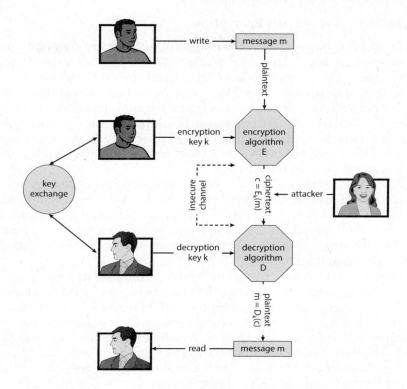

Figure 14.7   A secure communication over an insecure medium.

or three keys—for example, $c = E_{k3}(D_{k2}(E_{k1}(m)))$. When three keys are used, the effective key length is 168 bits. Triple DES is in widespread use today.

In 2001, NIST adopted a new block cipher, called the **advanced encryption standard (AES)**, to replace DES. AES is another block cipher. It can use key lengths of 128, 192, or 256 bits and works on 128-bit blocks. Generally, the algorithm is compact and efficient.

Block ciphers are not in themselves secure encryption schemes. In particular, they do not directly handle messages longer than their required block sizes. However, there are many **modes of encryption** that are based on stream ciphers, which can be used to securely encrypt longer messages.

RC4 is perhaps the most common stream cipher. A **stream cipher** is designed to encrypt and decrypt a stream of bytes or bits rather than a block. This is useful when the length of a communication would make a block cipher too slow. The key is input into a pseudo–random-bit generator, which is an algorithm that attempts to produce random bits. The output of the generator when fed a key is a keystream. A **keystream** is an infinite set of bits that can be used to encrypt a plaintext stream by simply XORing it with the plaintext. (XOR, for "eXclusive OR" is an operation that compares two input bits and generates one output bit. If the bits are the same, the result is 0. If the bits are different, the result is 1.) RC4 is used in encrypting steams of data, such as in WEP, the wireless LAN protocol. Unfortunately, RC4 as used in WEP (IEEE standard 802.11) has been found to be breakable in a reasonable amount of computer time. In fact, RC4 itself has vulnerabilities.

14.4.1.2   Asymmetric Encryption

In an **asymmetric encryption algorithm**, there are different encryption and decryption keys. An entity preparing to receive encrypted communication creates two keys and makes one of them (called the public key) available to anyone who wants it. Any sender can use that key to encrypt a communication, but only the key creator can decrypt the communication. This scheme, known as **public-key encryption**, was a breakthrough in cryptography. No longer must a key be kept secret and delivered securely. Instead, anyone can encrypt a message to the receiving entity, and no matter who else is listening, only that entity can decrypt the message.

As an example of how public-key encryption works, we describe an algorithm known as RSA, after its inventors, Rivest, Shamir, and Adleman. RSA is the most widely used asymmetric encryption algorithm. (Asymmetric algorithms based on elliptic curves are gaining ground, however, because the key length of such an algorithm can be shorter for the same amount of cryptographic strength.)

In RSA, k_e is the **public key**, and k_d is the **private key**. N is the product of two large, randomly chosen prime numbers p and q (for example, p and q are 512 bits each). It must be computationally infeasible to derive $k_{d,N}$ from $k_{e,N}$, so that k_e need not be kept secret and can be widely disseminated. The encryption algorithm is $E_{k_e,N}(m) = m^{k_e} \bmod N$, where k_e satisfies $k_e k_d \bmod (p-1)(q-1) = 1$. The decryption algorithm is then $D_{k_d,N}(c) = c^{k_d} \bmod N$.

An example using small values is shown in Figure 14.8. In this example, we make $p = 7$ and $q = 13$. We then calculate $N = 7*13 = 91$ and $(p-1)(q-1) = 72$. We next select k_e relatively prime to 72 and < 72, yielding 5. Finally, we calculate k_d such that $k_e k_d \bmod 72 = 1$, yielding 29. We now have our keys: the public key, $k_{e,N} = 5, 91$, and the private key, $k_{d,N} = 29, 91$. Encrypting the message 69 with the public key results in the message 62, which is then decoded by the receiver via the private key.

The use of asymmetric encryption begins with the publication of the public key of the destination. For bidirectional communication, the source also must publish its public key. "Publication" can be as simple as handing over an electronic copy of the key, or it can be more complex. The private key (or "secret key") must be zealously guarded, as anyone holding that key can decrypt any message created by the matching public key.

We should note that the seemingly small difference in key use between asymmetric and symmetric cryptography is quite large in practice. Asymmetric cryptography is much more computationally expensive to execute. It is much faster for a computer to encode and decode ciphertext by using the usual symmetric algorithms than by using asymmetric algorithms. Why, then, use an asymmetric algorithm? In truth, these algorithms are not used for general-purpose encryption of large amounts of data. However, they are used not only for encryption of small amounts of data but also for authentication, confidentiality, and key distribution, as we show in the following sections.

14.4.1.3   Authentication

We have seen that encryption offers a way of constraining the set of possible receivers of a message. Constraining the set of potential senders of a message is called **authentication**. Authentication is thus complementary to encryption.

Figure 14.8 Encryption and decryption using RSA asymmetric cryptography.

Authentication is also useful for proving that a message has not been modified. In this section, we discuss authentication as a constraint on possible senders of a message. Note that this sort of authentication is similar to but distinct from user authentication, which we discuss in Section 14.5.

An authentication algorithm using symmetric keys consists of the following components:

- A set K of keys.

- A set M of messages.

- A set A of authenticators.

- A function $S : K \rightarrow (M \rightarrow A)$. That is, for each $k \in K$, S_k is a function for generating authenticators from messages. Both S and S_k for any k should be efficiently computable functions.

- A function $V : K \rightarrow (M \times A \rightarrow \{\texttt{true}, \texttt{false}\})$. That is, for each $k \in K$, V_k is a function for verifying authenticators on messages. Both V and V_k for any k should be efficiently computable functions.

The critical property that an authentication algorithm must possess is this: for a message m, a computer can generate an authenticator $a \in A$ such that $V_k(m, a) = \texttt{true}$ only if it possesses k. Thus, a computer holding k can generate authenticators on messages so that any computer possessing k can verify them. However, a computer not holding k cannot generate authenticators on messages that can be verified using V_k. Since authenticators are generally exposed (for example, sent on a network with the messages themselves), it must not be feasible to derive k from the authenticators. Practically, if $V_k(m, a)$ = true, then we know that m has not been modified, and that the sender of the message has k. If we share k with only one entity, then we know that the message originated from k.

Just as there are two types of encryption algorithms, there are two main varieties of authentication algorithms. The first step in understanding these algorithms is to explore hash functions. A **hash function** $H(m)$ creates a small, fixed-sized block of data, known as a **message digest** or **hash value**, from a message m. Hash functions work by taking a message, splitting it into blocks, and processing the blocks to produce an n-bit hash. H must be collision resistant —that is, it must be infeasible to find an $m' \neq m$ such that $H(m) = H(m')$. Now, if $H(m) = H(m')$, we know that $m = m'$—that is, we know that the message has not been modified. Common message-digest functions include MD5, now considered insecure, which produces a 128-bit hash, and SHA-1, which outputs a 160-bit hash. Message digests are useful for detecting changed messages but are not useful as authenticators. For example, $H(m)$ can be sent along with a message; but if H is known, then someone could modify m to m' and recompute $H(m')$, and the message modification would not be detected. Therefore, we must authenticate $H(m)$.

The first main type of authentication algorithm uses symmetric encryption. In a **message-authentication code (MAC)**, a cryptographic checksum is generated from the message using a secret key. A MAC provides a way to securely authenticate short values. If we use it to authenticate $H(m)$ for an H that is collision resistant, then we obtain a way to securely authenticate long messages by hashing them first. Note that k is needed to compute both S_k and V_k, so anyone able to compute one can compute the other.

The second main type of authentication algorithm is a **digital-signature algorithm**, and the authenticators thus produced are called **digital signatures**. Digital signatures are very useful in that they enable *anyone* to verify the authenticity of the message. In a digital-signature algorithm, it is computationally infeasible to derive k_s from k_v. Thus, k_v is the public key, and k_s is the private key.

Consider as an example the RSA digital-signature algorithm. It is similar to the RSA encryption algorithm, but the key use is reversed. The digital signature of a message is derived by computing $S_{ks}(m) = H(m)^{k_s} \bmod N$. The key k_s again is a pair $\langle d, N \rangle$, where N is the product of two large, randomly chosen prime numbers p and q. The verification algorithm is then $V_{kv}(m, a) \overset{?}{=} a^{k_v} \bmod N = H(m))$, where k_v satisfies $k_v k_s \bmod (p-1)(q-1) = 1$.

Note that encryption and authentication may be used together or separately. Sometimes, for instance, we want authentication but not confidentiality. For example, a company could provide a software patch and could "sign" that patch to prove that it came from the company and that it hasn't been modified.

Authentication is a component of many aspects of security. For example, digital signatures are the core of **nonrepudiation**, which supplies proof that an entity performed an action. A typical example of nonrepudiation involves the filling out of electronic forms as an alternative to the signing of paper contracts. Nonrepudiation assures that a person filling out an electronic form cannot deny that he did so.

14.4.1.4   Key Distribution

Certainly, a good part of the battle between cryptographers (those inventing ciphers) and cryptanalysts (those trying to break them) involves keys. With symmetric algorithms, both parties need the key, and no one else should have it. The delivery of the symmetric key is a huge challenge. Sometimes it is performed **out-of-band**—say, via a paper document or a conversation. These methods do not scale well, however. Also consider the key-management challenge. Suppose a user wanted to communicate with N other users privately. That user would need N keys and, for more security, would need to change those keys frequently.

These are the very reasons for efforts to create asymmetric key algorithms. Not only can the keys be exchanged in public, but a given user needs only one private key, no matter how many other people she wants to communicate with. There is still the matter of managing a public key for each recipient of the communication, but since public keys need not be secured, simple storage can be used for that **key ring**.

Unfortunately, even the distribution of public keys requires some care. Consider the man-in-the-middle attack shown in Figure 14.9. Here, the person who wants to receive an encrypted message sends out his public key, but an attacker also sends her "bad" public key (which matches her private key). The person who wants to send the encrypted message knows no better and so uses the bad key to encrypt the message. The attacker then happily decrypts it.

The problem is one of authentication—what we need is proof of who (or what) owns a public key. One way to solve that problem involves the use of digital certificates. A **digital certificate** is a public key digitally signed by a trusted party. The trusted party receives proof of identification from some entity and certifies that the public key belongs to that entity. But how do we know we can trust the certifier? These **certificate authorities** have their public keys included within web browsers (and other consumers of certificates) before they are distributed. The certificate authorities can then vouch for other authorities (digitally signing the public keys of these other authorities), and so on, creating a web of trust. The certificates can be distributed in a standard X.509 digital certificate format that can be parsed by computer. This scheme is used for secure web communication, as we discuss in Section 14.4.3.

14.4.2   Implementation of Cryptography

Network protocols are typically organized in **layers**, like an onion or a parfait, with each layer acting as a client of the one below it. That is, when one protocol generates a message to send to its protocol peer on another machine, it hands its message to the protocol below it in the network-protocol stack for delivery to its peer on that machine. For example, in an IP network, TCP (a *transport-layer* protocol) acts as a client of IP (a *network-layer* protocol): TCP packets are passed down to IP for delivery to the IP peer at the other end of the connection. IP encapsulates the TCP packet in an IP packet, which it similarly passes down to the *data-link layer* to be transmitted across the network to its peer on the

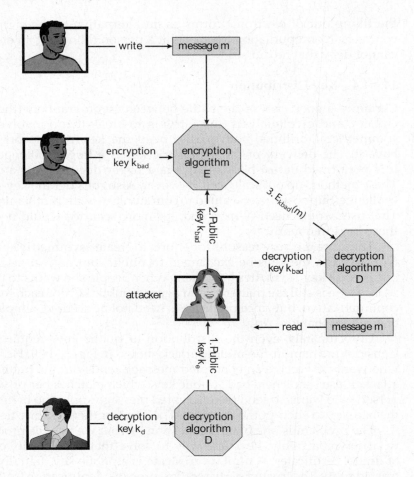

write ─→ message m

encryption key k_{bad} ─→ encryption algorithm E

2. Public key k_{bad}

3. $E_{kbad}(m)$

decryption key k_{bad} ─ decryption algorithm D

attacker

1. Public key k_e

read ─→ message m

decryption key k_d ─→ decryption algorithm D

Figure 14.9 A man-in-the-middle attack on asymmetric cryptography.

destination computer. This IP peer then delivers the TCP packet up to the TCP peer on that machine.

Cryptography can be inserted at almost any layer in the OSI model. SSL (Section 14.4.3), for example, provides security at the transport layer. Network-layer security generally has been standardized on **IPSec**, which defines IP packet formats that allow the insertion of authenticators and the encryption of packet contents. IPSec uses symmetric encryption and uses the **Internet Key Exchange (IKE)** protocol for key exchange. IKE is based on pubic-key encryption. IPSec is becoming widely used as the basis for **virtual private networks (VPNs)**, in which all traffic between two IPSec endpoints is encrypted to make a private network out of one that may otherwise be public. Numerous protocols also have been developed for use by applications, such as PGP for encrypting e-mail, but then the applications themselves must be coded to implement security.

Where is cryptographic protection best placed in a protocol stack? In general, there is no definitive answer. On the one hand, more protocols benefit from protections placed lower in the stack. For example, since IP packets encapsulate TCP packets, encryption of IP packets (using IPSec, for example) also hides the contents of the encapsulated TCP packets. Similarly, authenticators on IP packets detect the modification of contained TCP header information.

On the other hand, protection at lower layers in the protocol stack may give insufficient protection to higher-layer protocols. For example, an application server that accepts connections encrypted with IPSec might be able to authenticate the client computers from which requests are received. However, to authenticate a user at a client computer, the server may need to use an application-level protocol—the user may be required to type a password. Also consider the problem of e-mail. E-mail delivered via the industry-standard SMTP protocol is stored and forwarded, frequently multiple times, before it is delivered. Each of these transmissions could go over a secure or an insecure network. For e-mail to be secure, the e-mail message needs to be encrypted so that its security is independent of the transports that carry it.

14.4.3   An Example: SSL

SSL 3.0 is a cryptographic protocol that enables two computers to communicate securely—that is, so that each can limit the sender and receiver of messages to the other. It is perhaps the most commonly used cryptographic protocol on the Internet today, since it is the standard protocol by which web browsers communicate securely with web servers. For completeness, we should note that SSL was designed by Netscape and that it evolved into the industry- standard TLS protocol. In this discussion, we use SSL to mean both SSL and TLS.

SSL is a complex protocol with many options. Here, we present only a single variation of it. Even then, we describe it in a very simplified and abstract form, so as to maintain focus on its use of cryptographic primitives. What we are about to see is a complex dance in which asymmetric cryptography is used so that a client and a server can establish a secure **session key** that can be used for symmetric encryption of the session between the two—all of this while avoiding man-in-the-middle and replay attacks. For added cryptographic strength, the session keys are forgotten once a session is completed. Another communication between the two will require generation of new session keys.

The SSL protocol is initiated by a client c to communicate securely with a server. Prior to the protocol's use, the server s is assumed to have obtained a certificate, denoted cert$_s$, from certification authority CA. This certificate is a structure containing the following:

- Various attributes (attrs) of the server, such as its unique *distinguished* name and its *common* (DNS) name

- The identity of a asymmetric encryption algorithm $E()$ for the server

- The public key k_e of this server

- A validity interval (interval) during which the certificate should be considered valid

- A digital signature a on the above information made by the CA—that is, $a = S_{kCA}(\langle\ attrs, E_{ke}, interval\ \rangle)$

In addition, prior to the protocol's use, the client is presumed to have obtained the public verification algorithm V_{kCA} for CA. In the case of the Web, the user's browser is shipped from its vendor containing the verification algorithms and public keys of certain certification authorities. The user can add or delete these as she chooses.

When c connects to s, it sends a 28-byte random value n_c to the server, which responds with a random value n_s of its own, plus its certificate $cert_s$. The client verifies that $V_{kCA}(\langle$ attrs, E_{ke}, interval$\rangle$, a$)$ = true and that the current time is in the validity interval interval. If both of these tests are satisfied, the server has proved its identity. Then the client generates a random 46-byte **premaster secret** pms and sends cpms = E_{ke}(pms) to the server. The server recovers pms = D_{kd}(cpms). Now both the client and the server are in possession of n_c, n_s, and pms, and each can compute a shared 48-byte **master secret** ms = $H(n_c, n_s,$ pms). Only the server and client can compute ms, since only they know pms. Moreover, the dependence of ms on n_c and n_s ensures that ms is a *fresh* value —that is, a session key that has not been used in a previous communication. At this point, the client and the server both compute the following keys from the ms:

- A symmetric encryption key k_{cs}^{crypt} for encrypting messages from the client to the server

- A symmetric encryption key k_{sc}^{crypt} for encrypting messages from the server to the client

- A MAC generation key k_{cs}^{mac} for generating authenticators on messages from the client to the server

- A MAC generation key k_{sc}^{mac} for generating authenticators on messages from the server to the client

To send a message m to the server, the client sends

$$c = E_{k_{cs}^{crypt}}(\langle m, S_{k_{cs}^{mac}}(m)\rangle).$$

Upon receiving c, the server recovers

$$\langle m, a \rangle = D_{k_{cs}^{crypt}}(c)$$

and accepts m if $V_{k_{cs}^{mac}}(m, a)$ = true. Similarly, to send a message m to the client, the server sends

$$c = E_{k_{sc}^{crypt}}(\langle m, S_{k_{sc}^{mac}}(m)\rangle)$$

and the client recovers

$$\langle m, a \rangle = D_{k_{sc}^{crypt}}(c)$$

and accepts m if $V_{k_{sc}^{mac}}(m, a)$ = true.

This protocol enables the server to limit the recipients of its messages to the client that generated pms and to limit the senders of the messages it accepts to that same client. Similarly, the client can limit the recipients of the messages it sends and the senders of the messages it accepts to the party that knows k_d (that is, the party that can decrypt cpms). In many applications, such as web transactions, the client needs to verify the identity of the party that knows k_d. This is one purpose of the certificate $cert_s$. In particular, the attrs field contains information that the client can use to determine the identity—for example, the domain name—of the server with which it is communicating. For applications in which the server also needs information about the client, SSL supports an option by which a client can send a certificate to the server.

In addition to its use on the Internet, SSL is being used for a wide variety of tasks. For example, IPSec VPNs now have a competitor in SSL VPNs. IPSec is good for point-to-point encryption of traffic—say, between two company offices. SSL VPNs are more flexible but not as efficient, so they might be used between an individual employee working remotely and the corporate office.

14.5   User Authentication

Our earlier discussion of authentication involves messages and sessions. But what about users? If a system cannot authenticate a user, then authenticating that a message came from that user is pointless. Thus, a major security problem for operating systems is **user authentication**. The protection system depends on the ability to identify the programs and processes currently executing, which in turn depends on the ability to identify each user of the system. Users normally identify themselves. How do we determine whether a user's identity is authentic? Generally, user authentication is based on one or more of three things: the user's possession of something (a key or card), the user's knowledge of something (a user identifier and password), or an attribute of the user (fingerprint, retina pattern, or signature).

14.5.1   Passwords

The most common approach to authenticating a user identity is the use of **passwords**. When the user identifies herself by user ID or account name, she is asked for a password. If the user-supplied password matches the password stored in the system, the system assumes that the account is being accessed by the owner of that account.

Passwords are often used to protect objects in the computer system, in the absence of more complete protection schemes. They can be considered a special case of either keys or capabilities. For instance, a password may be associated with each resource (such as a file). Whenever a request is made to use the resource, the password must be given. If the password is correct, access is granted. Different passwords may be associated with different access rights. For example, different passwords may be used for reading files, appending files, and updating files.

In practice, most systems require only one password for a user to gain full rights. Although more passwords theoretically would be more secure, such systems tend not to be implemented due to the classic trade-off between security and convenience. If security makes something inconvenient, then the security is frequently bypassed or otherwise circumvented.

14.5.2   Password Vulnerabilities

Passwords are extremely common because they are easy to understand and use. Unfortunately, passwords can often be guessed, accidentally exposed, sniffed (read by an eavesdropper), or illegally transferred from an authorized user to an unauthorized one, as we show next.

There are two common ways to guess a password. One way is for the intruder (either human or program) to know the user or to have information about the user. All too frequently, people use obvious information (such as the names of their cats or spouses) as their passwords. The other way is to use brute force, trying enumeration—or all possible combinations of valid password characters (letters, numbers, and punctuation on some systems)—until the password is found. Short passwords are especially vulnerable to this method. For example, a four-character password provides only 10,000 variations. On average, guessing 5,000 times would produce a correct hit. A program that could try a password every millisecond would take only about 5 seconds to guess a four-character password. Enumeration is less successful where systems allow longer passwords that include both uppercase and lowercase letters, along with numbers and all punctuation characters. Of course, users must take advantage of the large password space and must not, for example, use only lowercase letters.

In addition to being guessed, passwords can be exposed as a result of visual or electronic monitoring. An intruder can look over the shoulder of a user (**shoulder surfing**) when the user is logging in and can learn the password easily by watching the keyboard. Alternatively, anyone with access to the network on which a computer resides can seamlessly add a network monitor, allowing him to **sniff**, or watch, all data being transferred on the network, including user IDs and passwords. Encrypting the data stream containing the password solves this problem. Even such a system could have passwords stolen, however. For example, if a file is used to contain the passwords, it could be copied for off-system analysis. Or consider a Trojan-horse program installed on the system that captures every keystroke before sending it on to the application.

Exposure is a particularly severe problem if the password is written down where it can be read or lost. Some systems force users to select hard-to-remember or long passwords, or to change their password frequently, which may cause a user to record the password or to reuse it. As a result, such systems provide much less security than systems that allow users to select easy passwords!

The final type of password compromise, illegal transfer, is the result of human nature. Most computer installations have a rule that forbids users to share accounts. This rule is sometimes implemented for accounting reasons but is often aimed at improving security. For instance, suppose one user ID is shared by several users, and a security breach occurs from that user ID. It is impossible to know who was using the ID at the time the break occurred or even whether the user was an authorized one. With one user per user ID, any user can be questioned directly about use of the account; in addition, the user might notice something different about the account and detect the break-in. Sometimes, users break account-sharing rules to help friends or to circumvent accounting, and this behavior can result in a system's being accessed by unauthorized users —possibly harmful ones.

Passwords can be either generated by the system or selected by a user. System-generated passwords may be difficult to remember, and thus users may write them down. As mentioned, however, user-selected passwords are often easy to guess (the user's name or favorite car, for example). Some systems will check a proposed password for ease of guessing or cracking before accepting it. Some systems also *age* passwords, forcing users to change their passwords at regular intervals (every three months, for instance). This method is not foolproof either, because users can easily toggle between two passwords. The solution, as implemented on some systems, is to record a password history for each user. For instance, the system could record the last N passwords and not allow their reuse.

Several variants on these simple password schemes can be used. For example, the password can be changed more frequently. At the extreme, the password is changed from session to session. A new password is selected (either by the system or by the user) at the end of each session, and that password must be used for the next session. In such a case, even if a password is used by an unauthorized person, that person can use it only once. When the legitimate user tries to use a now-invalid password at the next session, he discovers the security violation. Steps can then be taken to repair the breached security.

14.5.3 Securing Passwords

One problem with all these approaches is the difficulty of keeping the password secret within the computer. How can the system store a password securely yet allow its use for authentication when the user presents her password? The UNIX system uses secure hashing to avoid the necessity of keeping its password list secret. Because the list is hashed rather than encrypted, it is impossible for the system to decrypt the stored value and determine the original password.

Here's how this system works. Each user has a password. The system contains a function that is extremely difficult—the designers hope impossible —to invert but is simple to compute. That is, given a value x, it is easy to compute the hash function value $f(x)$. Given a function value $f(x)$, however, it is impossible to compute x. This function is used to encode all passwords. Only encoded passwords are stored. When a user presents a password, it is hashed and compared against the stored encoded password. Even if the stored encoded password is seen, it cannot be decoded, so the password cannot be determined. Thus, the password file does not need to be kept secret.

The flaw in this method is that the system no longer has control over the passwords. Although the passwords are hashed, anyone with a copy of the password file can run fast hash routines against it—hashing each word in a dictionary, for instance, and comparing the results against the passwords. If the user has selected a password that is also a word in the dictionary, the password is cracked. On sufficiently fast computers, or even on clusters of slow computers, such a comparison may take only a few hours. Furthermore, because UNIX systems use a well-known hashing algorithm, a cracker might keep a cache of passwords that have been cracked previously. For these reasons, systems include a "salt," or recorded random number, in the hashing algorithm. The salt value is added to the password to ensure that if two plaintext passwords are the same, they result in different hash values. In addition, the salt value makes hashing a dictionary ineffective, because each dictionary term would need to be combined with each salt value for comparison to the stored passwords. Newer versions of UNIX also store the hashed password entries in a file readable only by the superuser. The programs that compare the hash to the stored value are run `setuid` to root, so they can read this file, but other users cannot.

Another weakness in the UNIX password methods is that many UNIX systems treat only the first eight characters as significant. It is therefore extremely important for users to take advantage of the available password space. Complicating the issue further is the fact that some systems do not allow the use of dictionary words as passwords. A good technique is to generate your password by using the first letter of each word of an easily remembered phrase using both upper and lower characters with a number or punctuation mark thrown in for good measure. For example, the phrase "My mother's name is Katherine" might yield the password "Mmn.isK!". The password is hard to crack but easy for the user to remember. A more secure system would allow more characters in its passwords. Indeed, a system might also allow passwords to include the space character, so that a user could create a **passphrase**.

14.5.4 One-Time Passwords

To avoid the problems of password sniffing and shoulder surfing, a system can use a set of **paired passwords**. When a session begins, the system randomly selects and presents one part of a password pair; the user must supply the other part. In this system, the user is **challenged** and must **respond** with the correct answer to that challenge.

This approach can be generalized to the use of an algorithm as a password. Such algorithmic passwords are not susceptible to reuse. That is, a user can type in a password, and no entity intercepting that password will be able to reuse it. In this scheme, the system and the user share a symmetric password. The password pw is never transmitted over a medium that allows exposure. Rather, the password is used as input to the function, along with a **challenge** ch presented by the system. The user then computes the function $H(pw, ch)$. The result of this function is transmitted as the authenticator to the computer. Because the computer also knows pw and ch, it can perform the same computation. If the results match, the user is authenticated. The next time the user needs to be authenticated, another ch is generated, and the same steps ensue. This time, the authenticator is different. This **one-time password** system is one of only a few ways to prevent improper authentication due to password exposure.

One-time password systems are implemented in various ways. Commercial implementations use hardware calculators with a display or a display and numeric keypad. These calculators generally take the shape of a credit card, a key-chain dongle, or a USB device. Software running on computers or smartphones provides the user with $H(pw, ch)$; pw can be input by the user or generated by the calculator in synchronization with the computer. Sometimes, pw is just a **personal identification number** (PIN). The output of any of these systems shows the one-time password. A one-time password generator that requires input by the user involves **two-factor authentication**. Two different types of components are needed in this case—for example, a one-time password generator that generates the correct response only if the PIN is valid. Two-factor authentication offers far better authentication protection than single-factor authentication because it requires "something you have" as well as "something you know."

Another variation on one-time passwords uses a **code book,** or **one-time pad,** which is a list of single-use passwords. Each password on the list is used once and then is crossed out or erased. The commonly used S/Key system uses either a software calculator or a code book based on these calculations as a source of one-time passwords. Of course, the user must protect his code book, and it is helpful if the code book does not identify the system to which the codes are authenticators.

14.5.5   Biometrics

Yet another variation on the use of passwords for authentication involves the use of biometric measures. Palm- or hand-readers are commonly used to secure physical access—for example, access to a data center. These readers match stored parameters against what is being read from hand-reader pads. The parameters can include a temperature map, as well as finger length, finger width, and line patterns. These devices are currently too large and expensive to be used for normal computer authentication.

Fingerprint readers have become accurate and cost-effective and should become more common in the future. These devices read finger ridge patterns and convert them into a sequence of numbers. Over time, they can store a set of sequences to adjust for the location of the finger on the reading pad and other factors. Software can then scan a finger on the pad and compare its features with these stored sequences to determine if they match. Of course, multiple users can have profiles stored, and the scanner can differentiate among them. A very accurate two-factor authentication scheme can result from requiring a password as well as a user name and fingerprint scan. If this information is encrypted in transit, the system can be very resistant to spoofing or replay attack.

Multifactor authentication is better still. Consider how strong authentication can be with a USB device that must be plugged into the system, a PIN, and a fingerprint scan. Except for having to place ones finger on a pad and plug the USB into the system, this authentication method is no less convenient than that using normal passwords. Recall, though, that strong authentication by itself is not sufficient to guarantee the ID of the user. An authenticated session can still be hijacked if it is not encrypted.

14.6   Implementing Security Defenses

Just as there are myriad threats to system and network security, there are many security solutions. The solutions range from improved user education, through technology, to writing bug-free software. Most security professionals subscribe to the theory of **defense in depth,** which states that more layers of defense are better than fewer layers. Of course, this theory applies to any kind of security. Consider the security of a house without a door lock, with a door lock, and with a lock and an alarm. In this section, we look at the major methods, tools, and techniques that can be used to improve resistance to threats.

14.6.1   Security Policy

The first step toward improving the security of any aspect of computing is to have a **security policy.** Policies vary widely but generally include a statement of what is being secured. For example, a policy might state that all outside-accessible applications must have a code review before being deployed, or that users should not share their passwords, or that all connection points between a company and the outside must have port scans run every six months. Without a policy in place, it is impossible for users and administrators to know what is permissible, what is required, and what is not allowed. The policy is a road map to security, and if a site is trying to move from less secure to more secure, it needs a map to know how to get there.

Once the security policy is in place, the people it affects should know it well. It should be their guide. The policy should also be a living document that is reviewed and updated periodically to ensure that it is still pertinent and still followed.

14.6.2 Vulnerability Assessment

How can we determine whether a security policy has been correctly implemented? The best way is to execute a vulnerability assessment. Such assessments can cover broad ground, from social engineering through risk assessment to port scans. Risk assessment, for example, attempts to value the assets of the entity in question (a program, a management team, a system, or a facility) and determine the odds that a security incident will affect the entity and decrease its value. When the odds of suffering a loss and the amount of the potential loss are known, a value can be placed on trying to secure the entity.

The core activity of most vulnerability assessments is a penetration test, in which the entity is scanned for known vulnerabilities. Because this book is concerned with operating systems and the software that runs on them, we concentrate on those aspects of vulnerability assessment.

Vulnerability scans typically are done at times when computer use is relatively low, to minimize their impact. When appropriate, they are done on test systems rather than production systems, because they can induce unhappy behavior from the target systems or network devices.

A scan within an individual system can check a variety of aspects of the system:

- Short or easy-to-guess passwords
- Unauthorized privileged programs, such as setuid programs
- Unauthorized programs in system directories
- Unexpectedly long-running processes
- Improper directory protections on user and system directories
- Improper protections on system data files, such as the password file, device drivers, or the operating-system kernel itself
- Dangerous entries in the program search path (for example, the Trojan horse discussed in Section 14.2.1)
- Changes to system programs detected with checksum values
- Unexpected or hidden network daemons

Any problems found by a security scan can be either fixed automatically or reported to the managers of the system.

Networked computers are much more susceptible to security attacks than are standalone systems. Rather than attacks from a known set of access points, such as directly connected terminals, we face attacks from an unknown and large set of access points—a potentially severe security problem. To a lesser extent, systems connected to telephone lines via modems are also more exposed.

In fact, the U.S. government considers a system to be only as secure as its most far-reaching connection. For instance, a top-secret system may be accessed only from within a building also considered top-secret. The system loses its top-secret rating if any form of communication can occur outside that environment. Some government facilities take extreme security precautions. The connectors that plug a terminal into the secure computer are locked in a safe in the office when the terminal is not in use. A person must have proper ID to gain access to the building and her office, must know a physical lock combination, and must know authentication information for the computer itself to gain access to the computer—an example of multifactor authentication.

Unfortunately for system administrators and computer-security professionals, it is frequently impossible to lock a machine in a room and disallow all remote access. For instance, the Internet currently connects millions of computers and has become a mission-critical, indispensable resource for many companies and individuals. If you consider the Internet a club, then, as in any club with millions of members, there are many good members and some bad members. The bad members have many tools they can use to attempt to gain access to the interconnected computers, just as Morris did with his worm.

Vulnerability scans can be applied to networks to address some of the problems with network security. The scans search a network for ports that respond to a request. If services are enabled that should not be, access to them can be blocked, or they can be disabled. The scans then determine the details of the application listening on that port and try to determine if it has any known vulnerabilities. Testing those vulnerabilities can determine if the system is misconfigured or lacks needed patches.

Finally, though, consider the use of port scanners in the hands of a cracker rather than someone trying to improve security. These tools could help crackers find vulnerabilities to attack. (Fortunately, it is possible to detect port scans through anomaly detection, as we discuss next.) It is a general challenge to security that the same tools can be used for good and for harm. In fact, some people advocate security through obscurity, stating that no tools should be written to test security, because such tools can be used to find (and exploit) security holes. Others believe that this approach to security is not a valid one, pointing out, for example, that crackers could write their own tools. It seems reasonable that security through obscurity be considered one of the layers of security only so long as it is not the only layer. For example, a company could publish its entire network configuration, but keeping that information secret makes it harder for intruders to know what to attack or to determine what might be detected. Even here, though, a company assuming that such information will remain a secret has a false sense of security.

14.6.3   Intrusion Detection

Securing systems and facilities is intimately linked to intrusion detection. **Intrusion detection**, as its name suggests, strives to detect attempted or successful intrusions into computer systems and to initiate appropriate responses to the intrusions. Intrusion detection encompasses a wide array of techniques that vary on a number of axes, including the following:

- The time at which detection occurs. Detection can occur in real time (while the intrusion is occurring) or after the fact.

- The types of inputs examined to detect intrusive activity. These may include user-shell commands, process system calls, and network packet headers or contents. Some forms of intrusion might be detected only by correlating information from several such sources.

- The range of response capabilities. Simple forms of response include alerting an administrator to the potential intrusion or somehow halting the potentially intrusive activity—for example, killing a process engaged in such activity. In a sophisticated form of response, a system might transparently divert an intruder's activity to a **honeypot**—a false resource exposed to the attacker. The resource appears real to the attacker and enables the system to monitor and gain information about the attack.

These degrees of freedom in the design space for detecting intrusions have yielded a wide range of solutions, known as **intrusion-detection systems** (**IDSs**) and **intrusion-prevention systems** (**IDPs**). IDS systems raise an alarm when an intrusion is detected, while IDP systems act as routers, passing traffic unless an intrusion is detected (at which point that traffic is blocked).

But just what constitutes an intrusion? Defining a suitable specification of intrusion turns out to be quite difficult, and thus automatic IDSs and IDPs today typically settle for one of two less ambitious approaches. In the first, called **signature-based detection**, system input or network traffic is examined for specific behavior patterns (or **signatures**) known to indicate attacks. A simple example of signature-based detection is scanning network packets for the string /etc/passwd/ targeted for a UNIX system. Another example is virus-detection software, which scans binaries or network packets for known viruses.

The second approach, typically called **anomaly detection**, attempts through various techniques to detect anomalous behavior within computer systems. Of course, not all anomalous system activity indicates an intrusion, but the presumption is that intrusions often induce anomalous behavior. An example of anomaly detection is monitoring system calls of a daemon process to detect whether the system-call behavior deviates from normal patterns, possibly indicating that a buffer overflow has been exploited in the daemon to corrupt its behavior. Another example is monitoring shell commands to detect anomalous commands for a given user or detecting an anomalous login time for a user, either of which may indicate that an attacker has succeeded in gaining access to that user's account.

Signature-based detection and anomaly detection can be viewed as two sides of the same coin. Signature-based detection attempts to characterize dangerous behaviors and to detect when one of these behaviors occurs, whereas anomaly detection attempts to characterize normal (or nondangerous) behaviors and to detect when something other than these behaviors occurs.

These different approaches yield IDSs and IDPs with very different properties, however. In particular, anomaly detection can find previously unknown methods of intrusion (so-called **zero-day attacks**). Signature-based detection, in contrast, will identify only known attacks that can be codified in a recognizable pattern. Thus, new attacks that were not contemplated when the signatures were generated will evade signature-based detection. This problem is well known to vendors of virus-detection software, who must release new signatures with great frequency as new viruses are detected manually.

Anomaly detection is not necessarily superior to signature-based detection, however. Indeed, a significant challenge for systems that attempt anomaly detection is to benchmark "normal" system behavior accurately. If the system has already been penetrated when it is benchmarked, then the intrusive activity may be included in the "normal" benchmark. Even if the system is benchmarked cleanly, without influence from intrusive behavior, the benchmark must give a fairly complete picture of normal behavior. Otherwise, the number of **false positives** (false alarms) or, worse, **false negatives** (missed intrusions) will be excessive.

To illustrate the impact of even a marginally high rate of false alarms, consider an installation consisting of a hundred UNIX workstations from which security-relevant events are recorded for purposes of intrusion detection. A small installation such as this could easily generate a million audit records per day. Only one or two might be worthy of an administrator's investigation. If we suppose, optimistically, that each actual attack is reflected in ten audit records, we can roughly compute the rate of occurrence of audit records reflecting truly intrusive activity as follows:

$$\frac{2\frac{\text{intrusions}}{\text{day}} \cdot 10\frac{\text{records}}{\text{intrusion}}}{10^6 \frac{\text{records}}{\text{day}}} = 0.00002.$$

Interpreting this as a "probability of occurrence of intrusive records," we denote it as $P(I)$; that is, event I is the occurrence of a record reflecting truly intrusive behavior. Since $P(I) = 0.00002$, we also know that $P(\neg I) = 1 - P(I) = 0.99998$. Now we let A denote the raising of an alarm by an IDS. An accurate IDS should maximize both $P(I|A)$ and $P(\neg I|\neg A)$—that is, the probabilities that an alarm indicates an intrusion and that no alarm indicates no intrusion. Focusing on $P(I|A)$ for the moment, we can compute it using **Bayes' theorem**:

$$P(I|A) = \frac{P(I) \cdot P(A|I)}{P(I) \cdot P(A|I) + P(\neg I) \cdot P(A|\neg I)}$$

$$= \frac{0.00002 \cdot P(A|I)}{0.00002 \cdot P(A|I) + 0.99998 \cdot P(A|\neg I)}$$

Now consider the impact of the false-alarm rate $P(A|\neg I)$ on $P(I|A)$. Even with a very good true-alarm rate of $P(A|I) = 0.8$, a seemingly good false-alarm rate of $P(A|\neg I) = 0.0001$ yields $P(I|A) \approx 0.14$. That is, fewer than one in every seven alarms indicates a real intrusion! In systems where a security administrator investigates each alarm, a high rate of false alarms—called a "Christmas tree effect"—is exceedingly wasteful and will quickly teach the administrator to ignore alarms.

This example illustrates a general principle for IDSs and IDPs: for usability, they must offer an extremely low false-alarm rate. Achieving a sufficiently low false-alarm rate is an especially serious challenge for anomaly-detection systems, as mentioned, because of the difficulties of adequately benchmarking normal system behavior. However, research continues to improve anomaly-detection techniques. Intrusion detection software is evolving to implement signatures, anomaly algorithms, and other algorithms and to combine the results to arrive at a more accurate anomaly-detection rate.

14.6.4 Virus Protection

As we have seen, viruses can and do wreak havoc on systems. Protection from viruses thus is an important security concern. Antivirus programs are often used to provide this protection. Some of these programs are effective against only particular known viruses. They work by searching all the programs on a system for the specific pattern of instructions known to make up the virus. When they find a known pattern, they remove the instructions, disinfecting the program. Antivirus programs may have catalogs of thousands of viruses for which they search.

Both viruses and antivirus software continue to become more sophisticated. Some viruses modify themselves as they infect other software to avoid the basic pattern-match approach of antivirus programs. Antivirus programs in turn now look for families of patterns rather than a single pattern to identify a virus. In fact, some antivirus programs implement a variety of detection algorithms. They can decompress compressed viruses before checking for a signature. Some also look for process anomalies. A process opening an executable file for writing is suspicious, for example, unless it is a compiler. Another popular technique is to run a program in a sandbox, which is a controlled or emulated section of the system. The antivirus software analyzes the behavior of the code in the sandbox before letting it run unmonitored. Some antivirus programs also put up a complete shield rather than just scanning files within a file system. They search boot sectors, memory, inbound and outbound e-mail, files as they are downloaded, files on removable devices or media, and so on.

The best protection against computer viruses is prevention, or the practice of safe computing. Purchasing unopened software from vendors and avoiding free or pirated copies from public sources or disk exchange offer the safest route to preventing infection. However, even new copies of legitimate software applications are not immune to virus infection: in a few cases, disgruntled employees of a software company have infected the master copies of software programs to do economic harm to the company. For macro viruses, one defense is to exchange Microsoft Word documents in an alternative file format called rich text format (RTF). Unlike the native Word format, RTF does not include the capability to attach macros.

Another defense is to avoid opening any e-mail attachments from unknown users. Unfortunately, history has shown that e-mail vulnerabilities appear as fast as they are fixed. For example, in 2000, the *love bug* virus became very widespread by traveling in e-mail messages that pretended to be love notes sent by friends of the receivers. Once a receiver opened the attached Visual Basic script, the virus propagated by sending itself to the first addresses in the receiver's e-mail contact list. Fortunately, except for clogging e-mail systems

THE TRIPWIRE FILE SYSTEM

An example of an anomaly-detection tool is the Tripwire file system integrity-checking tool for UNIX, developed at Purdue University. Tripwire operates on the premise that many intrusions result in modification of system directories and files. For example, an attacker might modify the system programs, perhaps inserting copies with Trojan horses, or might insert new programs into directories commonly found in user-shell search paths. Or an intruder might remove system log files to cover his tracks. Tripwire is a tool to monitor file systems for added, deleted, or changed files and to alert system administrators to these modifications.

The operation of Tripwire is controlled by a configuration file tw.config that enumerates the directories and files to be monitored for changes, deletions, or additions. Each entry in this configuration file includes a selection mask to specify the file attributes (inode attributes) that will be monitored for changes. For example, the selection mask might specify that a file's permissions be monitored but its access time be ignored. In addition, the selection mask can instruct that the file be monitored for changes. Monitoring the hash of a file for changes is as good as monitoring the file itself, and storing hashes of files requires far less room than copying the files themselves.

When run initially, Tripwire takes as input the tw.config file and computes a signature for each file or directory consisting of its monitored attributes (inode attributes and hash values). These signatures are stored in a database. When run subsequently, Tripwire inputs both tw.config and the previously stored database, recomputes the signature for each file or directory named in tw.config, and compares this signature with the signature (if any) in the previously computed database. Events reported to an administrator include any monitored file or directory whose signature differs from that in the database (a changed file), any file or directory in a monitored directory for which a signature does not exist in the database (an added file), and any signature in the database for which the corresponding file or directory no longer exists (a deleted file).

Although effective for a wide class of attacks, Tripwire does have limitations. Perhaps the most obvious is the need to protect the Tripwire program and its associated files, especially the database file, from unauthorized modification. For this reason, Tripwire and its associated files should be stored on some tamper-proof medium, such as a write-protected disk or a secure server where logins can be tightly controlled. Unfortunately, this makes it less convenient to update the database after authorized updates to monitored directories and files. A second limitation is that some security-relevant files —for example, system log files—are *supposed* to change over time, and Tripwire does not provide a way to distinguish between an authorized and an unauthorized change. So, for example, an attack that modifies (without deleting) a system log that would normally change anyway would escape Tripwire's detection capabilities. The best Tripwire can do in this case is to detect certain obvious inconsistencies (for example, a shrinking log file). Free and commercial versions of Tripwire are available from http://tripwire.org and http://tripwire.com.

and users' inboxes, it was relatively harmless. It did, however, effectively negate the defensive strategy of opening attachments only from people known to the receiver. A more effective defense method is to avoid opening any e-mail attachment that contains executable code. Some companies now enforce this as policy by removing all incoming attachments to e-mail messages.

Another safeguard, although it does not prevent infection, does permit early detection. A user must begin by completely reformatting the hard disk, especially the boot sector, which is often targeted for viral attack. Only secure software is uploaded, and a signature of each program is taken via a secure message-digest computation. The resulting file name and associated message-digest list must then be kept free from unauthorized access. Periodically, or each time a program is run, the operating system recomputes the signature and compares it with the signature on the original list; any differences serve as a warning of possible infection. This technique can be combined with others. For example, a high-overhead antivirus scan, such as a sandbox, can be used; and if a program passes the test, a signature can be created for it. If the signatures match the next time the program is run, it does not need to be virus-scanned again.

14.6.5 Auditing, Accounting, and Logging

Auditing, accounting, and logging can decrease system performance, but they are useful in several areas, including security. Logging can be general or specific. All system-call executions can be logged for analysis of program behavior (or misbehavior). More typically, suspicious events are logged. Authentication failures and authorization failures can tell us quite a lot about break-in attempts.

Accounting is another potential tool in a security administrator's kit. It can be used to find performance changes, which in turn can reveal security problems. One of the early UNIX computer break-ins was detected by Cliff Stoll when he was examining accounting logs and spotted an anomaly.

14.7 Firewalling to Protect Systems and Networks

We turn next to the question of how a trusted computer can be connected safely to an untrustworthy network. One solution is the use of a firewall to separate trusted and untrusted systems. A **firewall** is a computer, appliance, or router that sits between the trusted and the untrusted. A network firewall limits network access between the two **security domains** and monitors and logs all connections. It can also limit connections based on source or destination address, source or destination port, or direction of the connection. For instance, web servers use HTTP to communicate with web browsers. A firewall therefore may allow only HTTP to pass from all hosts outside the firewall to the web server within the firewall. The Morris Internet worm used the finger protocol to break into computers, so finger would not be allowed to pass, for example.

In fact, a network firewall can separate a network into multiple domains. A common implementation has the Internet as the untrusted domain; a semitrusted and semisecure network, called the **demilitarized zone (DMZ)**, as another domain; and a company's computers as a third domain (Figure

Figure 14.10   Domain separation via firewall.

14.10). Connections are allowed from the Internet to the DMZ computers and from the company computers to the Internet but are not allowed from the Internet or DMZ computers to the company computers. Optionally, controlled communications may be allowed between the DMZ and one company computer or more. For instance, a web server on the DMZ may need to query a database server on the corporate network. With a firewall, however, access is contained, and any DMZ systems that are broken into still are unable to access the company computers.

Of course, a firewall itself must be secure and attack-proof. Otherwise, its ability to secure connections can be compromised. Furthermore, firewalls do not prevent attacks that **tunnel**, or travel within protocols or connections that the firewall allows. A buffer-overflow attack to a web server will not be stopped by the firewall, for example, because the HTTP connection is allowed; it is the contents of the HTTP connection that house the attack. Likewise, denial-of-service attacks can affect firewalls as much as any other machines. Another vulnerability of firewalls is **spoofing**, in which an unauthorized host pretends to be an authorized host by meeting some authorization criterion. For example, if a firewall rule allows a connection from a host and identifies that host by its IP address, then another host could send packets using that same address and be allowed through the firewall.

In addition to the most common network firewalls, there are other, newer kinds of firewalls, each with its pros and cons. A **personal firewall** is a software layer either included with the operating system or added as an application. Rather than limiting communication between security domains, it limits communication to (and possibly from) a given host. A user could add a personal firewall to her PC so that a Trojan horse would be denied access to the network to which the PC is connected, for example. An **application proxy firewall** understands the protocols that applications speak across the network. For example, SMTP is used for mail transfer. An application proxy accepts a connection just as an SMTP server would and then initiates a connection to the original destination SMTP server. It can monitor the traffic as it forwards the message, watching for and disabling illegal commands, attempts to exploit bugs, and so on. Some firewalls are designed for one specific protocol. An XML **firewall**, for example, has the specific purpose of analyzing XML traffic and blocking disallowed or malformed XML. **System-call firewalls** sit between applications and the kernel, monitoring system-call execution. For example, in Solaris 10, the "least privilege" feature implements a list of more than fifty system calls that processes may or may not be allowed to make. A process that does not need to spawn other processes can have that ability taken away, for instance.

14.8 Computer-Security Classifications

The U.S. Department of Defense Trusted Computer System Evaluation Criteria specify four security classifications in systems: A, B, C, and D. This specification is widely used to determine the security of a facility and to model security solutions, so we explore it here. The lowest-level classification is division D, or minimal protection. Division D includes only one class and is used for systems that have failed to meet the requirements of any of the other security classes. For instance, MS-DOS and Windows 3.1 are in division D.

Division C, the next level of security, provides discretionary protection and accountability of users and their actions through the use of audit capabilities. Division C has two levels: C1 and C2. A C1-class system incorporates some form of controls that allow users to protect private information and to keep other users from accidentally reading or destroying their data. A C1 environment is one in which cooperating users access data at the same levels of sensitivity. Most versions of UNIX are C1 class.

The total of all protection systems within a computer system (hardware, software, firmware) that correctly enforce a security policy is known as a **trusted computer base** (TCB). The TCB of a C1 system controls access between users and files by allowing the user to specify and control sharing of objects by named individuals or defined groups. In addition, the TCB requires that the users identify themselves before they start any activities that the TCB is expected to mediate. This identification is accomplished via a protected mechanism or password. The TCB protects the authentication data so that they are inaccessible to unauthorized users.

A C2-class system adds an individual-level access control to the requirements of a C1 system. For example, access rights of a file can be specified to the level of a single individual. In addition, the system administrator can selectively audit the actions of any one or more users based on individual identity. The TCB also protects itself from modification of its code or data structures. In addition, no information produced by a prior user is available to another user who accesses a storage object that has been released back to the system. Some special, secure versions of UNIX have been certified at the C2 level.

Division-B mandatory-protection systems have all the properties of a class-C2 system. In addition, they attach a sensitivity label to each object in the system. The B1-class TCB maintains these labels, which are used for decisions pertaining to mandatory access control. For example, a user at the confidential level could not access a file at the more sensitive secret level. The TCB also denotes the sensitivity level at the top and bottom of each page of any human-readable output. In addition to the normal user-name–password authentication information, the TCB also maintains the clearance and authorizations of individual users and will support at least two levels of security. These levels are hierarchical, so that a user may access any objects that carry sensitivity labels equal to or lower than his security clearance. For example, a secret-level user could access a file at the confidential level in the absence of other access controls. Processes are also isolated through the use of distinct address spaces.

A B2-class system extends the sensitivity labels to each system resource, such as storage objects. Physical devices are assigned minimum and maximum security levels that the system uses to enforce constraints imposed by the physical environments in which the devices are located. In addition, a B2 system supports covert channels and the auditing of events that could lead to the exploitation of a covert channel.

A B3-class system allows the creation of access-control lists that denote users or groups not granted access to a given named object. The TCB also contains a mechanism to monitor events that may indicate a violation of security policy. The mechanism notifies the security administrator and, if necessary, terminates the event in the least disruptive manner.

The highest-level classification is division A. Architecturally, a class-A1 system is functionally equivalent to a B3 system, but it uses formal design specifications and verification techniques, granting a high degree of assurance that the TCB has been implemented correctly. A system beyond class A1 might be designed and developed in a trusted facility by trusted personnel.

The use of a TCB merely ensures that the system can enforce aspects of a security policy; the TCB does not specify what the policy should be. Typically, a given computing environment develops a security policy for **certification** and has the plan **accredited** by a security agency, such as the National Computer Security Center. Certain computing environments may require other certification, such as that supplied by TEMPEST, which guards against electronic eavesdropping. For example, a TEMPEST-certified system has terminals that are shielded to prevent electromagnetic fields from escaping. This shielding ensures that equipment outside the room or building where the terminal is housed cannot detect what information is being displayed by the terminal.

14.9   An Example: Windows 7

Microsoft Windows 7 is a general-purpose operating system designed to support a variety of security features and methods. In this section, we examine features that Windows 7 uses to perform security functions.

The Windows 7 security model is based on the notion of **user accounts**. Windows 7 allows the creation of any number of user accounts, which can be grouped in any manner. Access to system objects can then be permitted or denied as desired. Users are identified to the system by a *unique* security ID. When a user logs on, Windows 7 creates a **security access token** that includes the security ID for the user, security IDs for any groups of which the user is a member, and a list of any special privileges that the user has. Examples of special privileges include backing up files and directories, shutting down the computer, logging on interactively, and changing the system clock. Every process that Windows 7 runs on behalf of a user will receive a copy of the access token. The system uses the security IDs in the access token to permit or deny access to system objects whenever the user, or a process on behalf of the user, attempts to access the object. Authentication of a user account is typically accomplished via a user name and password, although the modular design of Windows 7 allows the development of custom authentication packages. For example, a retinal (or eye) scanner might be used to verify that the user is who she says she is.

Windows 7 uses the idea of a subject to ensure that programs run by a user do not get greater access to the system than the user is authorized to have. A **subject** is used to track and manage permissions for each program that a user runs. It is composed of the user's access token and the program acting on behalf of the user. Since Windows 7 operates with a client–server model, two classes of subjects are used to control access: simple subjects and server subjects. An example of a **simple subject** is the typical application program that a user executes after she logs on. The simple subject is assigned a **security context** based on the security access token of the user. A **server subject** is a process implemented as a protected server that uses the security context of the client when acting on the client's behalf.

As mentioned in Section 14.7, auditing is a useful security technique. Windows 7 has built-in auditing that allows many common security threats to be monitored. Examples include failure auditing for login and logoff events to detect random password break-ins, success auditing for login and logoff events to detect login activity at strange hours, success and failure write-access auditing for executable files to track a virus outbreak, and success and failure auditing for file access to detect access to sensitive files.

Windows added mandatory integrity control, which works by assigning an **integrity label** to each securable object and subject. In order for a given subject to have access to an object, it must have the access requested in the discretionary access-control list, and its integrity label must be equal to or higher than that of the secured object (for the given operation). The integrity labels in Windows 7 are (in ascending order): untrusted, low, medium, high, and system. In addition, three access mask bits are permitted for integrity labels: NoReadUp, NoWriteUp, and NoExecuteUp. NoWriteUp is automatically enforced, so a lower-integrity subject cannot perform a write operation on a higher-integrity object. However, unless explictly blocked by the security descriptor, it can perform read or execute operations.

For securable objects without an explicit integrity label, a default label of medium is assigned. The label for a given subject is assigned during logon. For instance, a nonadministrative user will have an integrity label of medium. In addition to integrity labels, Windows Vista also added User Account Control (UAC), which represents an administrative account (not the built-in Administrators account) with two separate tokens. One, for normal usage, has the built-in Administrators group disabled and has an integrity label of medium. The other, for elevated usage, has the built-in Administrators group enabled and an integrity label of high.

Security attributes of an object in Windows 7 are described by a **security descriptor**. The security descriptor contains the security ID of the owner of the object (who can change the access permissions), a group security ID used only by the POSIX subsystem, a discretionary access-control list that identifies which users or groups are allowed (and which are explicitly denied) access, and a system access-control list that controls which auditing messages the system will generate. Optionally, the system access-control list can set the integrity of the object and identify which operations to block from lower-integrity subjects: read, write (always enforced), or execute. For example, the security descriptor of the file foo.bar might have owner avi and this discretionary access-control list:

- avi—all access

- group cs—read–write access

- user cliff—no access

In addition, it might have a system access-control list that tells the system to audit writes by everyone, along with an integrity label of medium that denies read, write, and execute to lower-integrity subjects.

An access-control list is composed of access-control entries that contain the security ID of the individual and an access mask that defines all possible actions on the object, with a value of AccessAllowed or AccessDenied for each action. Files in Windows 7 may have the following access types: Read-Data, WriteData, AppendData, Execute, ReadExtendedAttribute, Write-ExtendedAttribute, ReadAttributes, and WriteAttributes. We can see how this allows a fine degree of control over access to objects.

Windows 7 classifies objects as either container objects or noncontainer objects. **Container objects**, such as directories, can logically contain other objects. By default, when an object is created within a container object, the new object inherits permissions from the parent object. Similarly, if the user copies a file from one directory to a new directory, the file will inherit the permissions of the destination directory. **Noncontainer objects** inherit no other permissions. Furthermore, if a permission is changed on a directory, the new permissions do not automatically apply to existing files and subdirectories; the user may explicitly apply them if he so desires.

The system administrator can prohibit printing to a printer on the system for all or part of a day and can use the Windows 7 Performance Monitor to help her spot approaching problems. In general, Windows 7 does a good job of providing features to help ensure a secure computing environment. Many of these features are not enabled by default, however, which may be one reason for the myriad security breaches on Windows 7 systems. Another reason is the vast number of services Windows 7 starts at system boot time and the number of applications that typically are installed on a Windows 7 system. For a real multiuser environment, the system administrator should formulate a security plan and implement it, using the features that Windows 7 provides and other security tools.

14.10 Summary

Protection is an internal problem. Security, in contrast, must consider both the computer system and the environment—people, buildings, businesses, valuable objects, and threats—within which the system is used.

The data stored in the computer system must be protected from unauthorized access, malicious destruction or alteration, and accidental introduction of inconsistency. It is easier to protect against accidental loss of data consistency than to protect against malicious access to the data. Absolute protection of the information stored in a computer system from malicious abuse is not possible; but the cost to the perpetrator can be made sufficiently high to deter most, if not all, attempts to access that information without proper authority.

Several types of attacks can be launched against programs and against individual computers or the masses. Stack- and buffer-overflow techniques allow successful attackers to change their level of system access. Viruses and worms are self-perpetuating, sometimes infecting thousands of computers. Denial-of-service attacks prevent legitimate use of target systems.

Encryption limits the domain of receivers of data, while authentication limits the domain of senders. Encryption is used to provide confidentiality of data being stored or transferred. Symmetric encryption requires a shared key, while asymmetric encryption provides a public key and a private key. Authentication, when combined with hashing, can prove that data have not been changed.

User authentication methods are used to identify legitimate users of a system. In addition to standard user-name and password protection, several authentication methods are used. One-time passwords, for example, change from session to session to avoid replay attacks. Two-factor authentication requires two forms of authentication, such as a hardware calculator with an activation PIN. Multifactor authentication uses three or more forms. These methods greatly decrease the chance of authentication forgery.

Methods of preventing or detecting security incidents include intrusion-detection systems, antivirus software, auditing and logging of system events, monitoring of system software changes, system-call monitoring, and firewalls.

Review Questions

Review questions for this chapter can be accessed by visiting our website.

Practice Exercises

Answers for the Practice Exercises can be accceed by visiting our website.

Exercises

14.1 Buffer-overflow attacks can be avoided by adopting a better programming methodology or by using special hardware support. Discuss these solutions.

14.2 A password may become known to other users in a variety of ways. Is there a simple method for detecting that such an event has occurred? Explain your answer.

14.3 What is the purpose of using a "salt" along with the user-provided password? Where should the "salt" be stored, and how should it be used?

14.4 The list of all passwords is kept within the operating system. Thus, if a user manages to read this list, password protection is no longer provided. Suggest a scheme that will avoid this problem. (Hint: Use different internal and external representations.)

14.5 An experimental addition to UNIX allows a user to connect a **watchdog** program to a file. The watchdog is invoked whenever a program requests access to the file. The watchdog then either grants or denies access to the file. Discuss two pros and two cons of using watchdogs for security.

14.6 The UNIX program COPS scans a given system for possible security holes and alerts the user to possible problems. What are two potential hazards of using such a system for security? How can these problems be limited or eliminated?

14.7 Discuss a means by which managers of systems connected to the Internet could design their systems to limit or eliminate the damage done by worms. What are the drawbacks of making the change that you suggest?

14.8 Argue for or against the judicial sentence handed down against Robert Morris, Jr., for his creation and execution of the Internet worm discussed in Section 14.3.1.

14.9 Make a list of six security concerns for a bank's computer system. For each item on your list, state whether this concern relates to physical, human, or operating-system security.

14.10 What are two advantages of encrypting data stored in the computer system?

14.11 What commonly used computer programs are prone to man-in-the-middle attacks? Discuss solutions for preventing this form of attack.

14.12 Compare symmetric and asymmetric encryption schemes, and discuss the circumstances under which a distributed system would use one or the other.

14.13 Why doesn't $D_{kd,N}(E_{ke,N}(m))$ provide authentication of the sender? To what uses can such an encryption be put?

14.14 Discuss how the asymmetric encryption algorithm can be used to achieve the following goals.

    a. Authentication: the receiver knows that only the sender could have generated the message.

    b. Secrecy: only the receiver can decrypt the message.

    c. Authentication and secrecy: only the receiver can decrypt the message, and the receiver knows that only the sender could have generated the message.

14.15   Consider a system that generates 10 million audit records per day. Assume that, on average, there are 10 attacks per day on this system and each attack is reflected in 20 records. If the intrusion-detection system has a true-alarm rate of 0.6 and a false-alarm rate of 0.0005, what percentage of alarms generated by the system correspond to real intrusions?

Bibliographical Notes

General discussions concerning security are given by [Denning (1982)], [Pfleeger and Pfleeger (2006)] and [Tanenbaum (2010)]. Computer networking is discussed in [Kurose and Ross (2013)].

Issues concerning the design and verification of secure systems are discussed by [Rushby (1981)] and by [Silverman (1983)]. A security kernel for a multiprocessor microcomputer is described by [Schell (1983)]. A distributed secure system is described by [Rushby and Randell (1983)].

[Morris and Thompson (1979)] discuss password security. [Morshedian (1986)] presents methods to fight password pirates. Password authentication with insecure communications is considered by [Lamport (1981)]. The issue of password cracking is examined by [Seely (1989)]. Computer break-ins are discussed by [Lehmann (1987)] and by [Reid (1987)]. Issues related to trusting computer programs are discussed in [Thompson (1984)].

Discussions concerning UNIX security are offered by [Grampp and Morris (1984)], [Wood and Kochan (1985)], [Farrow (1986)], [Filipski and Hanko (1986)], [Hecht et al. (1988)], [Kramer (1988)], and [Garfinkel et al. (2003)]. [Bershad and Pinkerton (1988)] present the watchdog extension to BSD UNIX.

[Spafford (1989)] presents a detailed technical discussion of the Internet worm. The Spafford article appears with three others in a special section on the Morris Internet worm in *Communications of the ACM* (Volume 32, Number 6, June 1989).

Security problems associated with the TCP/IP protocol suite are described in [Bellovin (1989)]. The mechanisms commonly used to prevent such attacks are discussed in [Cheswick et al. (2003)]. Another approach to protecting networks from insider attacks is to secure topology or route discovery. [Kent et al. (2000)], [Hu et al. (2002)], [Zapata and Asokan (2002)], and [Hu and Perrig (2004)] present solutions for secure routing. [Savage et al. (2000)] examine the distributed denial-of-service attack and propose IP trace-back solutions to address the problem. [Perlman (1988)] proposes an approach to diagnose faults when the network contains malicious routers.

Information about various viruses and worms can be found at http://www.securelist.com, as well as in two books authored by [Ludwig (1998)] and [Ludwig (2002)]. Another website containing up-to-date security information is http://www.eeye.com/resources/security-center/research. A paper on the dangers of a computer monoculture can be found at http://cryptome.org/cyberinsecurity.htm.

[Diffie and Hellman (1976)] and [Diffie and Hellman (1979)] were the first researchers to propose the use of the public-key encryption scheme. The algorithm presented in Section 14.4.1 is based on the public-key encryption scheme; it was developed by [Rivest et al. (1978)]. [C. Kaufman (2002)] and

[Stallings and Brown (2011)] explore the use of cryptography in computer systems. Discussions concerning protection of digital signatures are offered by [Akl (1983)], [Davies (1983)], [Denning (1983)], and [Denning (1984)]. Complete cryptography information is presented in [Schneier (1996)] and [Katz and Lindell (2008)].

The RSA algorithm is presented in [Rivest et al. (1978)]. Information about NIST's AES activities can be found at http://www.nist.gov/aes; information about other cryptographic standards for the United States can also be found at that site. In 1999, SSL 3.0 was modified slightly and presented in an IETF Request for Comments (RFC) under the name TLS.

The example in Section 14.6.3 illustrating the impact of false-alarm rate on the effectiveness of IDSs is based on [Axelsson (1999)]. The description of Tripwire in Section 14.6.4 is based on [Kim and Spafford (1993)]. Research into system-call-based anomaly detection is described in [Forrest et al. (1996)].

The U.S. government is, of course, concerned about security. The **Department of Defense Trusted Computer System Evaluation Criteria** ([DoD (1985)]), known also as the **Orange Book**, describes a set of security levels and the features that an operating system must have to qualify for each security rating. Reading it is a good starting point for understanding security concerns. The **Microsoft Windows NT Workstation Resource Kit** ([Microsoft (1996)]) describes the security model of NT and how to use that model.

Bibliography

[Akl (1983)]   S. G. Akl, "Digital Signatures: A Tutorial Survey", *Computer*, Volume 16, Number 2 (1983), pages 15–24.

[Axelsson (1999)]   S. Axelsson, "The Base-Rate Fallacy and Its Implications for Intrusion Detection", *Proceedings of the ACM Conference on Computer and Communications Security* (1999), pages 1–7.

[Bellovin (1989)]   S. M. Bellovin, "Security Problems in the TCP/IP Protocol Suite", *Computer Communications Review*, Volume 19:2, (1989), pages 32–48.

[Bershad and Pinkerton (1988)]   B. N. Bershad and C. B. Pinkerton, "Watchdogs: Extending the Unix File System", *Proceedings of the Winter USENIX Conference*, Volume 1, Number 2 (1988), pages 169–188.

[C. Kaufman (2002)]   M. S. C. Kaufman, R. Perlman, *Network Security: Private Communication in a Public World*, Second Edition, Prentice Hall (2002).

[Cheswick et al. (2003)]   W. Cheswick, S. Bellovin, and A. Rubin, *Firewalls and Internet Security: Repelling the Wily Hacker*, Second Edition, Addison-Wesley (2003).

[Davies (1983)]   D. W. Davies, "Applying the RSA Digital Signature to Electronic Mail", *Computer*, Volume 16, Number 2 (1983), pages 55–62.

[Denning (1982)]   D. E. Denning, *Cryptography and Data Security*, Addison-Wesley (1982).

[Denning (1983)]   D. E. Denning, "Protecting Public Keys and Signature Keys", *Computer*, Volume 16, Number 2 (1983), pages 27–35.

[Denning (1984)]   D. E. Denning, "Digital Signatures with RSA and Other Public-Key Cryptosystems", *Communications of the ACM*, Volume 27, Number 4 (1984), pages 388–392.

[Diffie and Hellman (1976)]   W. Diffie and M. E. Hellman, "New Directions in Cryptography", *IEEE Transactions on Information Theory*, Volume 22, Number 6 (1976), pages 644–654.

[Diffie and Hellman (1979)]   W. Diffie and M. E. Hellman, "Privacy and Authentication", *Proceedings of the IEEE* (1979), pages 397–427.

[DoD (1985)]   *Trusted Computer System Evaluation Criteria.*   Department of Defense (1985).

[Farrow (1986)]   R. Farrow, "Security Issues and Strategies for Users", *UNIX World* (April 1986), pages 65–71.

[Filipski and Hanko (1986)]   A. Filipski and J. Hanko, "Making UNIX Secure", *Byte* (April 1986), pages 113–128.

[Forrest et al. (1996)]   S. Forrest, S. A. Hofmeyr, and T. A. Longstaff, "A Sense of Self for UNIX Processes", *Proceedings of the IEEE Symposium on Security and Privacy* (1996), pages 120–128.

[Garfinkel et al. (2003)]   S. Garfinkel, G. Spafford, and A. Schwartz, *Practical UNIX & Internet Security*, O'Reilly & Associates (2003).

[Grampp and Morris (1984)]   F. T. Grampp and R. H. Morris, "UNIX Operating-System Security", *AT&T Bell Laboratories Technical Journal*, Volume 63, Number 8 (1984), pages 1649–1672.

[Hecht et al. (1988)]   M. S. Hecht, A. Johri, R. Aditham, and T. J. Wei, "Experience Adding C2 Security Features to UNIX", *Proceedings of the Summer USENIX Conference* (1988), pages 133–146.

[Hu and Perrig (2004)]   Y.-C. Hu and A. Perrig, "SPV: A Secure Path Vector Routing Scheme for Securing BGP", *Proceedings of ACM SIGCOMM Conference on Data Communication* (2004).

[Hu et al. (2002)]   Y.-C. Hu, A. Perrig, and D. Johnson, "Ariadne: A Secure On-Demand Routing Protocol for Ad Hoc Networks", *Proceedings of the Annual International Conference on Mobile Computing and Networking* (2002).

[Katz and Lindell (2008)]   J. Katz and Y. Lindell, *Introduction to Modern Cryptography*, Chapman & Hall/CRC Press (2008).

[Kent et al. (2000)]   S. Kent, C. Lynn, and K. Seo, "Secure Border Gateway Protocol (Secure-BGP)", *IEEE Journal on Selected Areas in Communications*, Volume 18, Number 4 (2000), pages 582–592.

[Kim and Spafford (1993)]   G. H. Kim and E. H. Spafford, "The Design and Implementation of Tripwire: A File System Integrity Checker", Technical report, Purdue University (1993).

[Kramer (1988)]   S. M. Kramer, "Retaining SUID Programs in a Secure UNIX", *Proceedings of the Summer USENIX Conference* (1988), pages 107–118.

[Kurose and Ross (2013)]   J. Kurose and K. Ross, *Computer Networking—A Top–Down Approach*, Sixth Edition, Addison-Wesley (2013).

[Lamport (1981)]   L. Lamport, "Password Authentication with Insecure Communications", *Communications of the ACM*, Volume 24, Number 11 (1981), pages 770–772.

[Lehmann (1987)]   F. Lehmann, "Computer Break-Ins", *Communications of the ACM*, Volume 30, Number 7 (1987), pages 584–585.

[Ludwig (1998)]   M. Ludwig, *The Giant Black Book of Computer Viruses*, Second Edition, American Eagle Publications (1998).

[Ludwig (2002)]   M. Ludwig, *The Little Black Book of Email Viruses*, American Eagle Publications (2002).

[Microsoft (1996)]   *Microsoft Windows NT Workstation Resource Kit*. Microsoft Press (1996).

[Morris and Thompson (1979)]   R. Morris and K. Thompson, "Password Security: A Case History", *Communications of the ACM*, Volume 22, Number 11 (1979), pages 594–597.

[Morshedian (1986)]   D. Morshedian, "How to Fight Password Pirates", *Computer*, Volume 19, Number 1 (1986).

[Perlman (1988)]   R. Perlman, *Network Layer Protocols with Byzantine Robustness*. PhD thesis, Massachusetts Institute of Technology (1988).

[Pfleeger and Pfleeger (2006)]   C. Pfleeger and S. Pfleeger, *Security in Computing*, Fourth Edition, Prentice Hall (2006).

[Reid (1987)]   B. Reid, "Reflections on Some Recent Widespread Computer Break-Ins", *Communications of the ACM*, Volume 30, Number 2 (1987), pages 103–105.

[Rivest et al. (1978)]   R. L. Rivest, A. Shamir, and L. Adleman, "On Digital Signatures and Public Key Cryptosystems", *Communications of the ACM*, Volume 21, Number 2 (1978), pages 120–126.

[Rushby (1981)]   J. M. Rushby, "Design and Verification of Secure Systems", *Proceedings of the ACM Symposium on Operating Systems Principles* (1981), pages 12–21.

[Rushby and Randell (1983)]   J. Rushby and B. Randell, "A Distributed Secure System", *Computer*, Volume 16, Number 7 (1983), pages 55–67.

[Savage et al. (2000)]   S. Savage, D. Wetherall, A. R. Karlin, and T. Anderson, "Practical Network Support for IP Traceback", *Proceedings of ACM SIGCOMM Conference on Data Communication* (2000), pages 295–306.

[Schell (1983)]   R. R. Schell, "A Security Kernel for a Multiprocessor Microcomputer", *Computer* (1983), pages 47–53.

[Schneier (1996)]   B. Schneier, *Applied Cryptography*, Second Edition, John Wiley and Sons (1996).

[Seely (1989)]   D. Seely, "Password Cracking: A Game of Wits", *Communications of the ACM*, Volume 32, Number 6 (1989), pages 700–704.

[Silverman (1983)]   J. M. Silverman, "Reflections on the Verification of the Security of an Operating System Kernel", *Proceedings of the ACM Symposium on Operating Systems Principles* (1983), pages 143–154.

[Spafford (1989)]   E. H. Spafford, "The Internet Worm: Crisis and Aftermath", *Communications of the ACM*, Volume 32, Number 6 (1989), pages 678–687.

[Stallings and Brown (2011)]   W. Stallings and L. Brown, *Computer Security: Principles and Practice*, Second Edition, Prentice Hall (2011).

[Tanenbaum (2010)]   A. S. Tanenbaum, *Computer Networks*, Fifth Edition, Prentice Hall (2010).

[Thompson (1984)]   K. Thompson, "Reflections on Trusting Trust", *Communications of ACM*, Volume 27, Number 8 (1984), pages 761–763.

[Wood and Kochan (1985)]   P. Wood and S. Kochan, *UNIX System Security*, Hayden (1985).

[Zapata and Asokan (2002)]   M. Zapata and N. Asokan, "Securing Ad Hoc Routing Protocols", *Proc. 2002 ACM Workshop on Wireless Security* (2002), pages 1–10.

Part Six

Case Studies

In the final part of the book, we integrate the concepts described earlier by examining real operating systems. We cover in detail—Linux, for several reasons: it is popular, it is freely available, and it represents a full-featured UNIX system. This gives a student of operating systems an opportunity to read—and modify—*real* operating-system source code.

We also provide on-line coverage of two more systems: FreeBSD and Mach. The FreeBSD system is another UNIX system. However, whereas Linux combines features from several UNIX systems, FreeBSD is based on the BSD model. FreeBSD source code, like Linux source code, is freely available. Mach is a modern operating system that provides compatibility with BSD UNIX.

CHAPTER 15

The Linux System

Updated by Robert Love

This chapter presents an in-depth examination of the Linux operating system. By examining a complete, real system, we can see how the concepts we have discussed relate both to one another and to practice.

Linux is a variant of UNIX that has gained popularity over the last several decades, powering devices as small as mobile phones and as large as room-filling supercomputers. In this chapter, we look at the history and development of Linux and cover the user and programmer interfaces that Linux presents —interfaces that owe a great deal to the UNIX tradition. We also discuss the design and implementation of these interfaces. Linux is a rapidly evolving operating system. This chapter describes developments through the Linux 3.2 kernel, which was released in 2012.

CHAPTER OBJECTIVES

- To explore the history of the UNIX operating system from which Linux is derived and the principles upon which Linux's design is based.
- To examine the Linux process model and illustrate how Linux schedules processes and provides interprocess communication.
- To look at memory management in Linux.
- To explore how Linux implements file systems and manages I/O devices.

15.1 Linux History

Linux looks and feels much like any other UNIX system; indeed, UNIX compatibility has been a major design goal of the Linux project. However, Linux is much younger than most UNIX systems. Its development began in 1991, when a Finnish university student, Linus Torvalds, began developing a small but self-contained kernel for the 80386 processor, the first true 32-bit processor in Intel's range of PC-compatible CPUs.

687

Early in its development, the Linux source code was made available free—both at no cost and with minimal distributional restrictions—on the Internet. As a result, Linux's history has been one of collaboration by many developers from all around the world, corresponding almost exclusively over the Internet. From an initial kernel that partially implemented a small subset of the UNIX system services, the Linux system has grown to include all of the functionality expected of a modern UNIX system.

In its early days, Linux development revolved largely around the central operating-system kernel—the core, privileged executive that manages all system resources and interacts directly with the computer hardware. We need much more than this kernel, of course, to produce a full operating system. We thus need to make a distinction between the Linux kernel and a complete Linux system. The **Linux kernel** is an original piece of software developed from scratch by the Linux community. The **Linux system**, as we know it today, includes a multitude of components, some written from scratch, others borrowed from other development projects, and still others created in collaboration with other teams.

The basic Linux system is a standard environment for applications and user programming, but it does not enforce any standard means of managing the available functionality as a whole. As Linux has matured, a need has arisen for another layer of functionality on top of the Linux system. This need has been met by various Linux distributions. A **Linux distribution** includes all the standard components of the Linux system, plus a set of administrative tools to simplify the initial installation and subsequent upgrading of Linux and to manage installation and removal of other packages on the system. A modern distribution also typically includes tools for management of file systems, creation and management of user accounts, administration of networks, Web browsers, word processors, and so on.

15.1.1 The Linux Kernel

The first Linux kernel released to the public was version 0.01, dated May 14, 1991. It had no networking, ran only on 80386-compatible Intel processors and PC hardware, and had extremely limited device-driver support. The virtual memory subsystem was also fairly basic and included no support for memory-mapped files; however, even this early incarnation supported shared pages with copy-on-write and protected address spaces. The only file system supported was the Minix file system, as the first Linux kernels were cross-developed on a Minix platform.

The next milestone, Linux 1.0, was released on March 14, 1994. This release culminated three years of rapid development of the Linux kernel. Perhaps the single biggest new feature was networking: 1.0 included support for UNIX's standard TCP/IP networking protocols, as well as a BSD-compatible socket interface for networking programming. Device-driver support was added for running IP over Ethernet or (via the PPP or SLIP protocols) over serial lines or modems.

The 1.0 kernel also included a new, much enhanced file system without the limitations of the original Minix file system, and it supported a range of SCSI controllers for high-performance disk access. The developers extended the virtual memory subsystem to support paging to swap files and memory mapping of arbitrary files (but only read-only memory mapping was implemented in 1.0).

A range of extra hardware support was included in this release. Although still restricted to the Intel PC platform, hardware support had grown to include floppy-disk and CD-ROM devices, as well as sound cards, a range of mice, and international keyboards. Floating-point emulation was provided in the kernel for 80386 users who had no 80387 math coprocessor. System V UNIX-style **interprocess communication (IPC)**, including shared memory, semaphores, and message queues, was implemented.

At this point, development started on the 1.1 kernel stream, but numerous bug-fix patches were released subsequently for 1.0. A pattern was adopted as the standard numbering convention for Linux kernels. Kernels with an odd minor-version number, such as 1.1 or 2.5, are **development kernels**; even-numbered minor-version numbers are stable **production kernels**. Updates for the stable kernels are intended only as remedial versions, whereas the development kernels may include newer and relatively untested functionality. As we will see, this pattern remained in effect until version 3.

In March 1995, the 1.2 kernel was released. This release did not offer nearly the same improvement in functionality as the 1.0 release, but it did support a much wider variety of hardware, including the new PCI hardware bus architecture. Developers added another PC-specific feature—support for the 80386 CPU's virtual 8086 mode—to allow emulation of the DOS operating system for PC computers. They also updated the IP implementation with support for accounting and firewalling. Simple support for dynamically loadable and unloadable kernel modules was supplied as well.

The 1.2 kernel was the final PC-only Linux kernel. The source distribution for Linux 1.2 included partially implemented support for SPARC, Alpha, and MIPS CPUs, but full integration of these other architectures did not begin until after the 1.2 stable kernel was released.

The Linux 1.2 release concentrated on wider hardware support and more complete implementations of existing functionality. Much new functionality was under development at the time, but integration of the new code into the main kernel source code was deferred until after the stable 1.2 kernel was released. As a result, the 1.3 development stream saw a great deal of new functionality added to the kernel.

This work was released in June 1996 as Linux version 2.0. This release was given a major version-number increment because of two major new capabilities: support for multiple architectures, including a 64-bit native Alpha port, and symmetric multiprocessing (SMP) support. Additionally, the memory-management code was substantially improved to provide a unified cache for file-system data independent of the caching of block devices. As a result of this change, the kernel offered greatly increased file-system and virtual-memory performance. For the first time, file-system caching was extended to networked file systems, and writable memory-mapped regions were also supported. Other major improvements included the addition of internal kernel threads, a mechanism exposing dependencies between loadable modules, support for the automatic loading of modules on demand, file-system quotas, and POSIX-compatible real-time process-scheduling classes.

Improvements continued with the release of Linux 2.2 in 1999. A port to UltraSPARC systems was added. Networking was enhanced with more flexible firewalling, improved routing and traffic management, and support for TCP large window and selective acknowledgement. Acorn, Apple, and NT disks could now be read, and NFS was enhanced with a new kernel-mode NFS daemon. Signal handling, interrupts, and some I/O were locked at a finer level than before to improve symmetric multiprocessor (SMP) performance.

Advances in the 2.4 and 2.6 releases of the kernel included increased support for SMP systems, journaling file systems, and enhancements to the memory-management and block I/O systems. The process scheduler was modified in version 2.6, providing an efficient $O(1)$ scheduling algorithm. In addition, the 2.6 kernel was preemptive, allowing a process to be preempted even while running in kernel mode.

Linux kernel version 3.0 was released in July 2011. The major version bump from 2 to 3 occurred to commemorate the twentieth anniversary of Linux. New features include improved virtualization support, a new page write-back facility, improvements to the memory-management system, and yet another new process scheduler—the Completely Fair Scheduler (CFS). We focus on this newest kernel in the remainder of this chapter.

15.1.2 The Linux System

As we noted earlier, the Linux kernel forms the core of the Linux project, but other components make up a complete Linux operating system. Whereas the Linux kernel is composed entirely of code written from scratch specifically for the Linux project, much of the supporting software that makes up the Linux system is not exclusive to Linux but is common to a number of UNIX-like operating systems. In particular, Linux uses many tools developed as part of Berkeley's BSD operating system, MIT's X Window System, and the Free Software Foundation's GNU project.

This sharing of tools has worked in both directions. The main system libraries of Linux were originated by the GNU project, but the Linux community greatly improved the libraries by addressing omissions, inefficiencies, and bugs. Other components, such as the GNU C compiler (gcc), were already of sufficiently high quality to be used directly in Linux. The network administration tools under Linux were derived from code first developed for 4.3 BSD, but more recent BSD derivatives, such as FreeBSD, have borrowed code from Linux in return. Examples of this sharing include the Intel floating-point-emulation math library and the PC sound-hardware device drivers.

The Linux system as a whole is maintained by a loose network of developers collaborating over the Internet, with small groups or individuals having responsibility for maintaining the integrity of specific components. A small number of public Internet file-transfer-protocol (FTP) archive sites act as de facto standard repositories for these components. The File System Hierarchy Standard document is also maintained by the Linux community as a means of ensuring compatibility across the various system components. This standard specifies the overall layout of a standard Linux file system; it determines under which directory names configuration files, libraries, system binaries, and run-time data files should be stored.

15.1.3 Linux Distributions

In theory, anybody can install a Linux system by fetching the latest revisions of the necessary system components from the FTP sites and compiling them. In Linux's early days, this is precisely what a Linux user had to do. As Linux has matured, however, various individuals and groups have attempted to make this job less painful by providing standard, precompiled sets of packages for easy installation.

These collections, or distributions, include much more than just the basic Linux system. They typically include extra system-installation and management utilities, as well as precompiled and ready-to-install packages of many of the common UNIX tools, such as news servers, web browsers, text-processing and editing tools, and even games.

The first distributions managed these packages by simply providing a means of unpacking all the files into the appropriate places. One of the important contributions of modern distributions, however, is advanced package management. Today's Linux distributions include a package-tracking database that allows packages to be installed, upgraded, or removed painlessly.

The SLS distribution, dating back to the early days of Linux, was the first collection of Linux packages that was recognizable as a complete distribution. Although it could be installed as a single entity, SLS lacked the package-management tools now expected of Linux distributions. The **Slackware** distribution represented a great improvement in overall quality, even though it also had poor package management. In fact, it is still one of the most widely installed distributions in the Linux community.

Since Slackware's release, many commercial and noncommercial Linux distributions have become available. **Red Hat** and **Debian** are particularly popular distributions; the first comes from a commercial Linux support company and the second from the free-software Linux community. Other commercially supported versions of Linux include distributions from **Canonical** and **SuSE**, and others too numerous to list here. There are too many Linux distributions in circulation for us to list all of them here. The variety of distributions does not prevent Linux distributions from being compatible, however. The RPM package file format is used, or at least understood, by the majority of distributions, and commercial applications distributed in this format can be installed and run on any distribution that can accept RPM files.

15.1.4 Linux Licensing

The Linux kernel is distributed under version 2.0 of the GNU General Public License (GPL), the terms of which are set out by the Free Software Foundation. Linux is not public-domain software. **Public domain** implies that the authors have waived copyright rights in the software, but copyright rights in Linux code are still held by the code's various authors. Linux is *free* software, however, in the sense that people can copy it, modify it, use it in any manner they want, and give away (or sell) their own copies.

The main implication of Linux's licensing terms is that nobody using Linux, or creating a derivative of Linux (a legitimate exercise), can distribute the derivative without including the source code. Software released under the GPL cannot be redistributed as a binary-only product. If you release software that includes any components covered by the GPL, then, under the GPL, you must make source code available alongside any binary distributions. (This restriction does not prohibit making—or even selling—binary software distributions, as long as anybody who receives binaries is also given the opportunity to get the originating source code for a reasonable distribution charge.)

15.2 Design Principles

In its overall design, Linux resembles other traditional, nonmicrokernel UNIX implementations. It is a multiuser, preemptively multitasking system with a full set of UNIX-compatible tools. Linux's file system adheres to traditional UNIX semantics, and the standard UNIX networking model is fully implemented. The internal details of Linux's design have been influenced heavily by the history of this operating system's development.

Although Linux runs on a wide variety of platforms, it was originally developed exclusively on PC architecture. A great deal of that early development was carried out by individual enthusiasts rather than by well-funded development or research facilities, so from the start Linux attempted to squeeze as much functionality as possible from limited resources. Today, Linux can run happily on a multiprocessor machine with many gigabytes of main memory and many terabytes of disk space, but it is still capable of operating usefully in under 16 MB of RAM.

As PCs became more powerful and as memory and hard disks became cheaper, the original, minimalist Linux kernels grew to implement more UNIX functionality. Speed and efficiency are still important design goals, but much recent and current work on Linux has concentrated on a third major design goal: standardization. One of the prices paid for the diversity of UNIX implementations currently available is that source code written for one may not necessarily compile or run correctly on another. Even when the same system calls are present on two different UNIX systems, they do not necessarily behave in exactly the same way. The POSIX standards comprise a set of specifications for different aspects of operating-system behavior. There are POSIX documents for common operating-system functionality and for extensions such as process threads and real-time operations. Linux is designed to comply with the relevant POSIX documents, and at least two Linux distributions have achieved official POSIX certification.

Because it gives standard interfaces to both the programmer and the user, Linux presents few surprises to anybody familiar with UNIX. We do not detail these interfaces here. The sections on the programmer interface (Section A.3) and user interface (Section A.4) of BSD apply equally well to Linux. By default, however, the Linux programming interface adheres to SVR4 UNIX semantics, rather than to BSD behavior. A separate set of libraries is available to implement BSD semantics in places where the two behaviors differ significantly.

Many other standards exist in the UNIX world, but full certification of Linux with respect to these standards is sometimes slowed because certification is often available only for a fee, and the expense involved in certifying an operating system's compliance with most standards is substantial. However, supporting a wide base of applications is important for any operating system, so implementation of standards is a major goal for Linux development, even if the implementation is not formally certified. In addition to the basic POSIX standard, Linux currently supports the POSIX threading extensions—Pthreads —and a subset of the POSIX extensions for real-time process control.

15.2.1 Components of a Linux System

The Linux system is composed of three main bodies of code, in line with most traditional UNIX implementations:

1. **Kernel**. The kernel is responsible for maintaining all the important abstractions of the operating system, including such things as virtual memory and processes.

2. **System libraries**. The system libraries define a standard set of functions through which applications can interact with the kernel. These functions implement much of the operating-system functionality that does not need the full privileges of kernel code. The most important system library is the **C library**, known as `libc`. In addition to providing the standard C library, `libc` implements the user mode side of the Linux system call interface, as well as other critical system-level interfaces.

3. **System utilities**. The system utilities are programs that perform individual, specialized management tasks. Some system utilities are invoked just once to initialize and configure some aspect of the system. Others —known as **daemons** in UNIX terminology—run permanently, handling such tasks as responding to incoming network connections, accepting logon requests from terminals, and updating log files.

Figure 15.1 illustrates the various components that make up a full Linux system. The most important distinction here is between the kernel and everything else. All the kernel code executes in the processor's privileged mode with full access to all the physical resources of the computer. Linux refers to this privileged mode as **kernel mode**. Under Linux, no user code is built into the kernel. Any operating-system-support code that does not need to run in kernel mode is placed into the system libraries and runs in **user mode**. Unlike kernel mode, user mode has access only to a controlled subset of the system's resources.

system-management programs	user processes	user utility programs	compilers
system shared libraries			
Linux kernel			
loadable kernel modules			

Figure 15.1 Components of the Linux system.

Although various modern operating systems have adopted a message-passing architecture for their kernel internals, Linux retains UNIX's historical model: the kernel is created as a single, monolithic binary. The main reason is performance. Because all kernel code and data structures are kept in a single address space, no context switches are necessary when a process calls an operating-system function or when a hardware interrupt is delivered. Moreover, the kernel can pass data and make requests between various subsystems using relatively cheap C function invocation and not more complicated interprocess communication (IPC). This single address space contains not only the core scheduling and virtual memory code but all kernel code, including all device drivers, file systems, and networking code.

Even though all the kernel components share this same melting pot, there is still room for modularity. In the same way that user applications can load shared libraries at run time to pull in a needed piece of code, so the Linux kernel can load (and unload) modules dynamically at run time. The kernel does not need to know in advance which modules may be loaded—they are truly independent loadable components.

The Linux kernel forms the core of the Linux operating system. It provides all the functionality necessary to run processes, and it provides system services to give arbitrated and protected access to hardware resources. The kernel implements all the features required to qualify as an operating system. On its own, however, the operating system provided by the Linux kernel is not a complete UNIX system. It lacks much of the functionality and behavior of UNIX, and the features that it does provide are not necessarily in the format in which a UNIX application expects them to appear. The operating-system interface visible to running applications is not maintained directly by the kernel. Rather, applications make calls to the system libraries, which in turn call the operating-system services as necessary.

The system libraries provide many types of functionality. At the simplest level, they allow applications to make system calls to the Linux kernel. Making a system call involves transferring control from unprivileged user mode to privileged kernel mode; the details of this transfer vary from architecture to architecture. The libraries take care of collecting the system-call arguments and, if necessary, arranging those arguments in the special form necessary to make the system call.

The libraries may also provide more complex versions of the basic system calls. For example, the C language's buffered file-handling functions are all implemented in the system libraries, providing more advanced control of file I/O than the basic kernel system calls. The libraries also provide routines that do not correspond to system calls at all, such as sorting algorithms, mathematical functions, and string-manipulation routines. All the functions necessary to support the running of UNIX or POSIX applications are implemented in the system libraries.

The Linux system includes a wide variety of user-mode programs—both system utilities and user utilities. The system utilities include all the programs necessary to initialize and then administer the system, such as those to set up networking interfaces and to add and remove users from the system. User utilities are also necessary to the basic operation of the system but do not require elevated privileges to run. They include simple file-management utilities such as those to copy files, create directories, and edit text files. One of the most important user utilities is the **shell**, the standard command-line interface on UNIX systems. Linux supports many shells; the most common is the **bourne-again shell (bash)**.

15.3 Kernel Modules

The Linux kernel has the ability to load and unload arbitrary sections of kernel code on demand. These loadable kernel modules run in privileged kernel mode and as a consequence have full access to all the hardware capabilities of the machine on which they run. In theory, there is no restriction on what a kernel module is allowed to do. Among other things, a kernel module can implement a device driver, a file system, or a networking protocol.

Kernel modules are convenient for several reasons. Linux's source code is free, so anybody wanting to write kernel code is able to compile a modified kernel and to reboot into that new functionality. However, recompiling, relinking, and reloading the entire kernel is a cumbersome cycle to undertake when you are developing a new driver. If you use kernel modules, you do not have to make a new kernel to test a new driver—the driver can be compiled on its own and loaded into the already running kernel. Of course, once a new driver is written, it can be distributed as a module so that other users can benefit from it without having to rebuild their kernels.

This latter point has another implication. Because it is covered by the GPL license, the Linux kernel cannot be released with proprietary components added to it unless those new components are also released under the GPL and the source code for them is made available on demand. The kernel's module interface allows third parties to write and distribute, on their own terms, device drivers or file systems that could not be distributed under the GPL.

Kernel modules allow a Linux system to be set up with a standard minimal kernel, without any extra device drivers built in. Any device drivers that the user needs can be either loaded explicitly by the system at startup or loaded automatically by the system on demand and unloaded when not in use. For example, a mouse driver can be loaded when a USB mouse is plugged into the system and unloaded when the mouse is unplugged.

The module support under Linux has four components:

1. The **module-management system** allows modules to be loaded into memory and to communicate with the rest of the kernel.

2. The **module loader and unloader**, which are user-mode utilities, work with the module-management system to load a module into memory.

3. The **driver-registration system** allows modules to tell the rest of the kernel that a new driver has become available.

4. A **conflict-resolution mechanism** allows different device drivers to reserve hardware resources and to protect those resources from accidental use by another driver.

15.3.1 Module Management

Loading a module requires more than just loading its binary contents into kernel memory. The system must also make sure that any references the module makes to kernel symbols or entry points are updated to point to the correct locations in the kernel's address space. Linux deals with this reference updating by splitting the job of module loading into two separate sections: the management of sections of module code in kernel memory and the handling of symbols that modules are allowed to reference.

Linux maintains an internal symbol table in the kernel. This symbol table does not contain the full set of symbols defined in the kernel during the latter's compilation; rather, a symbol must be explicitly exported. The set of exported symbols constitutes a well-defined interface by which a module can interact with the kernel.

Although exporting symbols from a kernel function requires an explicit request by the programmer, no special effort is needed to import those symbols into a module. A module writer just uses the standard external linking of the C language. Any external symbols referenced by the module but not declared by it are simply marked as unresolved in the final module binary produced by the compiler. When a module is to be loaded into the kernel, a system utility first scans the module for these unresolved references. All symbols that still need to be resolved are looked up in the kernel's symbol table, and the correct addresses of those symbols in the currently running kernel are substituted into the module's code. Only then is the module passed to the kernel for loading. If the system utility cannot resolve all references in the module by looking them up in the kernel's symbol table, then the module is rejected.

The loading of the module is performed in two stages. First, the module-loader utility asks the kernel to reserve a continuous area of virtual kernel memory for the module. The kernel returns the address of the memory allocated, and the loader utility can use this address to relocate the module's machine code to the correct loading address. A second system call then passes the module, plus any symbol table that the new module wants to export, to the kernel. The module itself is now copied verbatim into the previously allocated space, and the kernel's symbol table is updated with the new symbols for possible use by other modules not yet loaded.

The final module-management component is the module requester. The kernel defines a communication interface to which a module-management program can connect. With this connection established, the kernel will inform the management process whenever a process requests a device driver, file system, or network service that is not currently loaded and will give the manager the opportunity to load that service. The original service request will complete once the module is loaded. The manager process regularly queries the kernel to see whether a dynamically loaded module is still in use and unloads that module when it is no longer actively needed.

15.3.2 Driver Registration

Once a module is loaded, it remains no more than an isolated region of memory until it lets the rest of the kernel know what new functionality it provides. The kernel maintains dynamic tables of all known drivers and provides a set of routines to allow drivers to be added to or removed from these tables at any time. The kernel makes sure that it calls a module's startup routine when that module is loaded and calls the module's cleanup routine before that module is unloaded. These routines are responsible for registering the module's functionality.

A module may register many types of functionality; it is not limited to only one type. For example, a device driver might want to register two separate mechanisms for accessing the device. Registration tables include, among others, the following items:

- **Device drivers**. These drivers include character devices (such as printers, terminals, and mice), block devices (including all disk drives), and network interface devices.

- **File systems**. The file system may be anything that implements Linux's virtual file system calling routines. It might implement a format for storing files on a disk, but it might equally well be a network file system, such as NFS, or a virtual file system whose contents are generated on demand, such as Linux's /proc file system.

- **Network protocols**. A module may implement an entire networking protocol, such as TCP or simply a new set of packet-filtering rules for a network firewall.

- **Binary format**. This format specifies a way of recognizing, loading, and executing a new type of executable file.

In addition, a module can register a new set of entries in the sysctl and /proc tables, to allow that module to be configured dynamically (Section 15.7.4).

15.3.3 Conflict Resolution

Commercial UNIX implementations are usually sold to run on a vendor's own hardware. One advantage of a single-supplier solution is that the software vendor has a good idea about what hardware configurations are possible. PC hardware, however, comes in a vast number of configurations, with large numbers of possible drivers for devices such as network cards and video display adapters. The problem of managing the hardware configuration becomes more severe when modular device drivers are supported, since the currently active set of devices becomes dynamically variable.

Linux provides a central conflict-resolution mechanism to help arbitrate access to certain hardware resources. Its aims are as follows:

- To prevent modules from clashing over access to hardware resources

- To prevent **autoprobes**—device-driver probes that auto-detect device configuration—from interfering with existing device drivers

- To resolve conflicts among multiple drivers trying to access the same hardware—as, for example, when both the parallel printer driver and the parallel line IP (PLIP) network driver try to talk to the parallel port

To these ends, the kernel maintains lists of allocated hardware resources. The PC has a limited number of possible I/O ports (addresses in its hardware I/O address space), interrupt lines, and DMA channels. When any device driver wants to access such a resource, it is expected to reserve the resource with the kernel database first. This requirement incidentally allows the system administrator to determine exactly which resources have been allocated by which driver at any given point.

A module is expected to use this mechanism to reserve in advance any hardware resources that it expects to use. If the reservation is rejected because the resource is not present or is already in use, then it is up to the module to decide how to proceed. It may fail in its initialization attempt and request that it be unloaded if it cannot continue, or it may carry on, using alternative hardware resources.

15.4   Process Management

A process is the basic context in which all user-requested activity is serviced within the operating system. To be compatible with other UNIX systems, Linux must use a process model similar to those of other versions of UNIX. Linux operates differently from UNIX in a few key places, however. In this section, we review the traditional UNIX process model (Section A.3.2) and introduce Linux's threading model.

15.4.1   The fork() and exec() Process Model

The basic principle of UNIX process management is to separate into two steps two operations that are usually combined into one: the creation of a new process and the running of a new program. A new process is created by the fork() system call, and a new program is run after a call to exec(). These are two distinctly separate functions. We can create a new process with fork() without running a new program—the new subprocess simply continues to execute exactly the same program, at exactly the same point, that the first (parent) process was running. In the same way, running a new program does not require that a new process be created first. Any process may call exec() at any time. A new binary object is loaded into the process's address space and the new executable starts executing in the context of the existing process.

This model has the advantage of great simplicity. It is not necessary to specify every detail of the environment of a new program in the system call that runs that program. The new program simply runs in its existing environment. If a parent process wishes to modify the environment in which a new program is to be run, it can fork and then, still running the original executable in a child process, make any system calls it requires to modify that child process before finally executing the new program.

Under UNIX, then, a process encompasses all the information that the operating system must maintain to track the context of a single execution of a single program. Under Linux, we can break down this context into a number of specific sections. Broadly, process properties fall into three groups: the process identity, environment, and context.

15.4.1.1   Process Identity

A process identity consists mainly of the following items:

- **Process ID (PID)**. Each process has a unique identifier. The PID is used to specify the process to the operating system when an application makes a system call to signal, modify, or wait for the process. Additional identifiers associate the process with a process group (typically, a tree of processes forked by a single user command) and login session.

- **Credentials**. Each process must have an associated user ID and one or more group IDs (user groups are discussed in Section 10.6.2) that determine the rights of a process to access system resources and files.

- **Personality**. Process personalities are not traditionally found on UNIX systems, but under Linux each process has an associated personality identifier that can slightly modify the semantics of certain system calls. Personalities are primarily used by emulation libraries to request that system calls be compatible with certain varieties of UNIX.

- **Namespace**. Each process is associated with a specific view of the file-system hierarchy, called its namespace. Most processes share a common namespace and thus operate on a shared file-system hierarchy. Processes and their children can, however, have different namespaces, each with a unique file-system hierarchy—their own root directory and set of mounted file systems.

Most of these identifiers are under the limited control of the process itself. The process group and session identifiers can be changed if the process wants to start a new group or session. Its credentials can be changed, subject to appropriate security checks. However, the primary PID of a process is unchangeable and uniquely identifies that process until termination.

15.4.1.2 Process Environment

A process's environment is inherited from its parent and is composed of two null-terminated vectors: the argument vector and the environment vector. The argument vector simply lists the command-line arguments used to invoke the running program; it conventionally starts with the name of the program itself. The environment vector is a list of "NAME=VALUE" pairs that associates named environment variables with arbitrary textual values. The environment is not held in kernel memory but is stored in the process's own user-mode address space as the first datum at the top of the process's stack.

The argument and environment vectors are not altered when a new process is created. The new child process will inherit the environment of its parent. However, a completely new environment is set up when a new program is invoked. On calling exec(), a process must supply the environment for the new program. The kernel passes these environment variables to the next program, replacing the process's current environment. The kernel otherwise leaves the environment and command-line vectors alone—their interpretation is left entirely to the user-mode libraries and applications.

The passing of environment variables from one process to the next and the inheriting of these variables by the children of a process provide flexible ways to pass information to components of the user-mode system software. Various important environment variables have conventional meanings to related parts of the system software. For example, the TERM variable is set up to name the type of terminal connected to a user's login session. Many programs use this variable to determine how to perform operations on the user's display, such as moving the cursor and scrolling a region of text. Programs with multilingual support use the LANG variable to determine the language in which to display system messages for programs that include multilingual support.

The environment-variable mechanism custom-tailors the operating system on a per-process basis. Users can choose their own languages or select their own editors independently of one another.

15.4.1.3   Process Context

The process identity and environment properties are usually set up when a process is created and not changed until that process exits. A process may choose to change some aspects of its identity if it needs to do so, or it may alter its environment. In contrast, process context is the state of the running program at any one time; it changes constantly. Process context includes the following parts:

- **Scheduling context**. The most important part of the process context is its scheduling context—the information that the scheduler needs to suspend and restart the process. This information includes saved copies of all the process's registers. Floating-point registers are stored separately and are restored only when needed. Thus, processes that do not use floating-point arithmetic do not incur the overhead of saving that state. The scheduling context also includes information about scheduling priority and about any outstanding signals waiting to be delivered to the process. A key part of the scheduling context is the process's kernel stack, a separate area of kernel memory reserved for use by kernel-mode code. Both system calls and interrupts that occur while the process is executing will use this stack.

- **Accounting**. The kernel maintains accounting information about the resources currently being consumed by each process and the total resources consumed by the process in its entire lifetime so far.

- **File table**. The file table is an array of pointers to kernel file structures representing open files. When making file-I/O system calls, processes refer to files by an integer, known as a **file descriptor (fd)**, that the kernel uses to index into this table.

- **File-system context**. Whereas the file table lists the existing open files, the file-system context applies to requests to open new files. The file-system context includes the process's root directory, current working directory, and namespace.

- **Signal-handler table**. UNIX systems can deliver asynchronous signals to a process in response to various external events. The signal-handler table defines the action to take in response to a specific signal. Valid actions include ignoring the signal, terminating the process, and invoking a routine in the process's address space.

- **Virtual memory context**. The virtual memory context describes the full contents of a process's private address space; we discuss it in Section 15.6.

15.4.2 Processes and Threads

Linux provides the `fork()` system call, which duplicates a process without loading a new executable image. Linux also provides the ability to create threads via the `clone()` system call. Linux does not distinguish between processes and threads, however. In fact, Linux generally uses the term *task* —rather than *process* or *thread*—when referring to a flow of control within a program. The `clone()` system call behaves identically to `fork()`, except that it accepts as arguments a set of flags that dictate what resources are shared between the parent and child (whereas a process created with `fork()` shares no resources with its parent). The flags include:

flag	meaning
CLONE_FS	File-system information is shared.
CLONE_VM	The same memory space is shared.
CLONE_SIGHAND	Signal handlers are shared.
CLONE_FILES	The set of open files is shared.

Thus, if `clone()` is passed the flags CLONE_FS, CLONE_VM, CLONE_SIGHAND, and CLONE_FILES, the parent and child tasks will share the same file-system information (such as the current working directory), the same memory space, the same signal handlers, and the same set of open files. Using `clone()` in this fashion is equivalent to creating a thread in other systems, since the parent task shares most of its resources with its child task. If none of these flags is set when `clone()` is invoked, however, the associated resources are not shared, resulting in functionality similar to that of the `fork()` system call.

The lack of distinction between processes and threads is possible because Linux does not hold a process's entire context within the main process data structure. Rather, it holds the context within independent subcontexts. Thus, a process's file-system context, file-descriptor table, signal-handler table, and virtual memory context are held in separate data structures. The process data structure simply contains pointers to these other structures, so any number of processes can easily share a subcontext by pointing to the same subcontext and incrementing a reference count.

The arguments to the `clone()` system call tell it which subcontexts to copy and which to share. The new process is always given a new identity and a new scheduling context—these are the essentials of a Linux process. According to the arguments passed, however, the kernel may either create new subcontext data structures initialized so as to be copies of the parent's or set up the new process to use the same subcontext data structures being used by the parent. The `fork()` system call is nothing more than a special case of `clone()` that copies all subcontexts, sharing none.

15.5 Scheduling

Scheduling is the job of allocating CPU time to different tasks within an operating system. Linux, like all UNIX systems, supports **preemptive multitasking**. In such a system, the process scheduler decides which process runs and when.

Making these decisions in a way that balances fairness and performance across many different workloads is one of the more complicated challenges in modern operating systems.

Normally, we think of scheduling as the running and interrupting of user processes, but another aspect of scheduling is also important to Linux: the running of the various kernel tasks. Kernel tasks encompass both tasks that are requested by a running process and tasks that execute internally on behalf of the kernel itself, such as tasks spawned by Linux's I/O subsystem.

15.5.1 Process Scheduling

Linux has two separate process-scheduling algorithms. One is a time-sharing algorithm for fair, preemptive scheduling among multiple processes. The other is designed for real-time tasks, where absolute priorities are more important than fairness.

The scheduling algorithm used for routine time-sharing tasks received a major overhaul with version 2.6 of the kernel. Earlier versions ran a variation of the traditional UNIX scheduling algorithm. This algorithm does not provide adequate support for SMP systems, does not scale well as the number of tasks on the system grows, and does not maintain fairness among interactive tasks, particularly on systems such as desktops and mobile devices. The process scheduler was first overhauled with version 2.5 of the kernel. Version 2.5 implemented a scheduling algorithm that selects which task to run in constant time—known as $O(1)$—regardless of the number of tasks or processors in the system. The new scheduler also provided increased support for SMP, including processor affinity and load balancing. These changes, while improving scalability, did not improve interactive performance or fairness—and, in fact, made these problems worse under certain workloads. Consequently, the process scheduler was overhauled a second time, with Linux kernel version 2.6. This version ushered in the **Completely Fair Scheduler (CFS)**.

The Linux scheduler is a preemptive, priority-based algorithm with two separate priority ranges: a **real-time** range from 0 to 99 and a `nice` **value** ranging from −20 to 19. Smaller `nice` values indicate higher priorities. Thus, by increasing the `nice` value, you are decreasing your priority and being "nice" to the rest of the system.

CFS is a significant departure from the traditional UNIX process scheduler. In the latter, the core variables in the scheduling algorithm are priority and time slice. The **time slice** is the length of time—the *slice* of the processor— that a process is afforded. Traditional UNIX systems give processes a fixed time slice, perhaps with a boost or penalty for high- or low-priority processes, respectively. A process may run for the length of its time slice, and higher-priority processes run before lower-priority processes. It is a simple algorithm that many non-UNIX systems employ. Such simplicity worked well for early time-sharing systems but has proved incapable of delivering good interactive performance and fairness on today's modern desktops and mobile devices.

CFS introduced a new scheduling algorithm called **fair scheduling** that eliminates time slices in the traditional sense. Instead of time slices, all processes are allotted a proportion of the processor's time. CFS calculates how long a process should run as a function of the total number of runnable processes.

To start, CFS says that if there are N runnable processes, then each should be afforded $1/N$ of the processor's time. CFS then adjusts this allotment by weighting each process's allotment by its `nice` value. Processes with the default `nice` value have a weight of 1—their priority is unchanged. Processes with a smaller `nice` value (higher priority) receive a higher weight, while processes with a larger `nice` value (lower priority) receive a lower weight. CFS then runs each process for a "time slice" proportional to the process's weight divided by the total weight of all runnable processes.

To calculate the actual length of time a process runs, CFS relies on a configurable variable called **target latency**, which is the interval of time during which every runnable task should run at least once. For example, assume that the target latency is 10 milliseconds. Further assume that we have two runnable processes of the same priority. Each of these processes has the same weight and therefore receives the same proportion of the processor's time. In this case, with a target latency of 10 milliseconds, the first process runs for 5 milliseconds, then the other process runs for 5 milliseconds, then the first process runs for 5 milliseconds again, and so forth. If we have 10 runnable processes, then CFS will run each for a millisecond before repeating.

But what if we had, say, 1,000 processes? Each process would run for 1 microsecond if we followed the procedure just described. Due to switching costs, scheduling processes for such short lengths of time is inefficient. CFS consequently relies on a second configurable variable, the **minimum granularity**, which is a minimum length of time any process is allotted the processor. All processes, regardless of the target latency, will run for at least the minimum granularity. In this manner, CFS ensures that switching costs do not grow unacceptably large when the number of runnable processes grows too large. In doing so, it violates its attempts at fairness. In the usual case, however, the number of runnable processes remains reasonable, and both fairness and switching costs are maximized.

With the switch to fair scheduling, CFS behaves differently from traditional UNIX process schedulers in several ways. Most notably, as we have seen, CFS eliminates the concept of a static time slice. Instead, each process receives a proportion of the processor's time. How long that allotment is depends on how many other processes are runnable. This approach solves several problems in mapping priorities to time slices inherent in preemptive, priority-based scheduling algorithms. It is possible, of course, to solve these problems in other ways without abandoning the classic UNIX scheduler. CFS, however, solves the problems with a simple algorithm that performs well on interactive workloads such as mobile devices without compromising throughput performance on the largest of servers.

15.5.2 Real-Time Scheduling

Linux's real-time scheduling algorithm is significantly simpler than the fair scheduling employed for standard time-sharing processes. Linux implements the two real-time scheduling classes required by POSIX.1b: first-come, first-served (FCFS) and round-robin (Section 6.3.1 and Section 6.3.4, respectively). In both cases, each process has a priority in addition to its scheduling class. The scheduler always runs the process with the highest priority. Among processes of equal priority, it runs the process that has been waiting longest. The only difference between FCFS and round-robin scheduling is that FCFS processes continue to run until they either exit or block, whereas a round-robin process will be preempted after a while and will be moved to the end of the scheduling queue, so round-robin processes of equal priority will automatically time-share among themselves.

Linux's real-time scheduling is soft—rather than hard—real time. The scheduler offers strict guarantees about the relative priorities of real-time processes, but the kernel does not offer any guarantees about how quickly a real-time process will be scheduled once that process becomes runnable. In contrast, a hard real-time system can guarantee a minimum latency between when a process becomes runnable and when it actually runs.

15.5.3 Kernel Synchronization

The way the kernel schedules its own operations is fundamentally different from the way it schedules processes. A request for kernel-mode execution can occur in two ways. A running program may request an operating-system service, either explicitly via a system call or implicitly—for example, when a page fault occurs. Alternatively, a device controller may deliver a hardware interrupt that causes the CPU to start executing a kernel-defined handler for that interrupt.

The problem for the kernel is that all these tasks may try to access the same internal data structures. If one kernel task is in the middle of accessing some data structure when an interrupt service routine executes, then that service routine cannot access or modify the same data without risking data corruption. This fact relates to the idea of critical sections—portions of code that access shared data and thus must not be allowed to execute concurrently. As a result, kernel synchronization involves much more than just process scheduling. A framework is required that allows kernel tasks to run without violating the integrity of shared data.

Prior to version 2.6, Linux was a nonpreemptive kernel, meaning that a process running in kernel mode could not be preempted—even if a higher-priority process became available to run. With version 2.6, the Linux kernel became fully preemptive. Now, a task can be preempted when it is running in the kernel.

The Linux kernel provides spinlocks and semaphores (as well as reader–writer versions of these two locks) for locking in the kernel. On SMP machines, the fundamental locking mechanism is a spinlock, and the kernel is designed so that spinlocks are held for only short durations. On single-processor machines, spinlocks are not appropriate for use and are replaced by enabling and disabling kernel preemption. That is, rather than holding a spinlock, the task disables kernel preemption. When the task would otherwise release the spinlock, it enables kernel preemption. This pattern is summarized below:

single processor	multiple processors
Disable kernel preemption.	Acquire spin lock.
Enable kernel preemption.	Release spin lock.

Linux uses an interesting approach to disable and enable kernel preemption. It provides two simple kernel interfaces—preempt_disable() and preempt_enable(). In addition, the kernel is not preemptible if a kernel-mode task is holding a spinlock. To enforce this rule, each task in the system has a thread-info structure that includes the field preempt_count, which is a counter indicating the number of locks being held by the task. The counter is incremented when a lock is acquired and decremented when a lock is released. If the value of preempt_count for the task currently running is greater than zero, it is not safe to preempt the kernel, as this task currently holds a lock. If the count is zero, the kernel can safely be interrupted, assuming there are no outstanding calls to preempt_disable().

Spinlocks—along with the enabling and disabling of kernel preemption—are used in the kernel only when the lock is held for short durations. When a lock must be held for longer periods, semaphores are used.

The second protection technique used by Linux applies to critical sections that occur in interrupt service routines. The basic tool is the processor's interrupt-control hardware. By disabling interrupts (or using spinlocks) during a critical section, the kernel guarantees that it can proceed without the risk of concurrent access to shared data structures.

However, there is a penalty for disabling interrupts. On most hardware architectures, interrupt enable and disable instructions are not cheap. More importantly, as long as interrupts remain disabled, all I/O is suspended, and any device waiting for servicing will have to wait until interrupts are reenabled; thus, performance degrades. To address this problem, the Linux kernel uses a synchronization architecture that allows long critical sections to run for their entire duration without having interrupts disabled. This ability is especially useful in the networking code. An interrupt in a network device driver can signal the arrival of an entire network packet, which may result in a great deal of code being executed to disassemble, route, and forward that packet within the interrupt service routine.

Linux implements this architecture by separating interrupt service routines into two sections: the top half and the bottom half. The **top half** is the standard interrupt service routine that runs with recursive interrupts disabled. Interrupts of the same number (or line) are disabled, but other interrupts may run. The **bottom half** of a service routine is run, with all interrupts enabled, by a miniature scheduler that ensures that bottom halves never interrupt themselves. The bottom-half scheduler is invoked automatically whenever an interrupt service routine exits.

This separation means that the kernel can complete any complex processing that has to be done in response to an interrupt without worrying about being interrupted itself. If another interrupt occurs while a bottom half is executing, then that interrupt can request that the same bottom half execute, but the execution will be deferred until the one currently running completes. Each execution of the bottom half can be interrupted by a top half but can never be interrupted by a similar bottom half.

The top-half/bottom-half architecture is completed by a mechanism for disabling selected bottom halves while executing normal, foreground kernel code. The kernel can code critical sections easily using this system. Interrupt handlers can code their critical sections as bottom halves; and when the foreground kernel wants to enter a critical section, it can disable any relevant

Figure 15.2   Interrupt protection levels.

bottom halves to prevent any other critical sections from interrupting it. At the end of the critical section, the kernel can reenable the bottom halves and run any bottom-half tasks that have been queued by top-half interrupt service routines during the critical section.

Figure 15.2 summarizes the various levels of interrupt protection within the kernel. Each level may be interrupted by code running at a higher level but will never be interrupted by code running at the same or a lower level. Except for user-mode code, user processes can always be preempted by another process when a time-sharing scheduling interrupt occurs.

15.5.4   Symmetric Multiprocessing

The Linux 2.0 kernel was the first stable Linux kernel to support **symmetric multiprocessor (**SMP**)** hardware, allowing separate processes to execute in parallel on separate processors. The original implementation of SMP imposed the restriction that only one processor at a time could be executing kernel code.

In version 2.2 of the kernel, a single kernel spinlock (sometimes termed BKL for "big kernel lock") was created to allow multiple processes (running on different processors) to be active in the kernel concurrently. However, the BKL provided a very coarse level of locking granularity, resulting in poor scalability to machines with many processors and processes. Later releases of the kernel made the SMP implementation more scalable by splitting this single kernel spinlock into multiple locks, each of which protects only a small subset of the kernel's data structures. Such spinlocks are described in Section 15.5.3. The 3.0 kernel provides additional SMP enhancements, including ever-finer locking, processor affinity, and load-balancing algorithms.

15.6   Memory Management

Memory management under Linux has two components. The first deals with allocating and freeing physical memory—pages, groups of pages, and small blocks of RAM. The second handles virtual memory, which is memory-mapped into the address space of running processes. In this section, we describe these two components and then examine the mechanisms by which the loadable components of a new program are brought into a process's virtual memory in response to an exec() system call.

15.6.1 Management of Physical Memory

Due to specific hardware constraints, Linux separates physical memory into four different zones, or regions:

- ZONE_DMA
- ZONE_DMA32
- ZONE_NORMAL
- ZONE_HIGHMEM

These zones are architecture specific. For example, on the Intel x86-32 architecture, certain ISA (industry standard architecture) devices can only access the lower 16 MB of physical memory using DMA. On these systems, the first 16 MB of physical memory comprise ZONE_DMA. On other systems, certain devices can only access the first 4 GB of physical memory, despite supporting 64-bit addresses. On such systems, the first 4 GB of physical memory comprise ZONE_DMA32. ZONE_HIGHMEM (for "high memory") refers to physical memory that is not mapped into the kernel address space. For example, on the 32-bit Intel architecture (where 2^{32} provides a 4-GB address space), the kernel is mapped into the first 896 MB of the address space; the remaining memory is referred to as high memory and is allocated from ZONE_HIGHMEM. Finally, ZONE_NORMAL comprises everything else—the normal, regularly mapped pages. Whether an architecture has a given zone depends on its constraints. A modern, 64-bit architecture such as Intel x86-64 has a small 16 MB ZONE_DMA (for legacy devices) and all the rest of its memory in ZONE_NORMAL, with no "high memory".

The relationship of zones and physical addresses on the Intel x86-32 architecture is shown in Figure 15.3. The kernel maintains a list of free pages for each zone. When a request for physical memory arrives, the kernel satisfies the request using the appropriate zone.

The primary physical-memory manager in the Linux kernel is the page allocator. Each zone has its own allocator, which is responsible for allocating and freeing all physical pages for the zone and is capable of allocating ranges of physically contiguous pages on request. The allocator uses a buddy system (Section 8.8.1) to keep track of available physical pages. In this scheme, adjacent units of allocatable memory are paired together (hence its name). Each allocatable memory region has an adjacent partner (or buddy). Whenever two allocated partner regions are freed up, they are combined to form a larger region—a buddy heap. That larger region also has a partner, with which it can combine to form a still larger free region. Conversely, if a small memory request

zone	physical memory
ZONE_DMA	< 16 MB
ZONE_NORMAL	16 .. 896 MB
ZONE_HIGHMEM	> 896 MB

Figure 15.3 Relationship of zones and physical addresses in Intel x86-32.

cannot be satisfied by allocation of an existing small free region, then a larger free region will be subdivided into two partners to satisfy the request. Separate linked lists are used to record the free memory regions of each allowable size. Under Linux, the smallest size allocatable under this mechanism is a single physical page. Figure 15.4 shows an example of buddy-heap allocation. A 4-KB region is being allocated, but the smallest available region is 16 KB. The region is broken up recursively until a piece of the desired size is available.

Ultimately, all memory allocations in the Linux kernel are made either statically, by drivers that reserve a contiguous area of memory during system boot time, or dynamically, by the page allocator. However, kernel functions do not have to use the basic allocator to reserve memory. Several specialized memory-management subsystems use the underlying page allocator to manage their own pools of memory. The most important are the virtual memory system, described in Section 15.6.2; the kmalloc() variable-length allocator; the slab allocator, used for allocating memory for kernel data structures; and the page cache, used for caching pages belonging to files.

Many components of the Linux operating system need to allocate entire pages on request, but often smaller blocks of memory are required. The kernel provides an additional allocator for arbitrary-sized requests, where the size of a request is not known in advance and may be only a few bytes. Analogous to the C language's malloc() function, this kmalloc() service allocates entire physical pages on demand but then splits them into smaller pieces. The kernel maintains lists of pages in use by the kmalloc() service. Allocating memory involves determining the appropriate list and either taking the first free piece available on the list or allocating a new page and splitting it up. Memory regions claimed by the kmalloc() system are allocated permanently until they are freed explicitly with a corresponding call to kfree(); the kmalloc() system cannot reallocate or reclaim these regions in response to memory shortages.

Another strategy adopted by Linux for allocating kernel memory is known as slab allocation. A **slab** is used for allocating memory for kernel data structures and is made up of one or more physically contiguous pages. A **cache** consists of one or more slabs. There is a single cache for each unique kernel data structure—for example, a cache for the data structure representing process descriptors, a cache for file objects, a cache for inodes, and so forth.

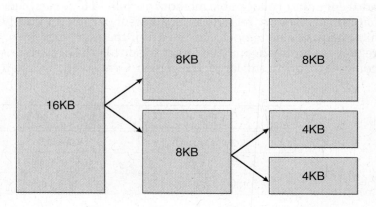

Figure 15.4 Splitting of memory in the buddy system.

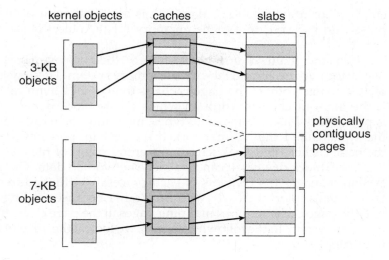

Figure 15.5 Slab allocator in Linux.

Each cache is populated with **objects** that are instantiations of the kernel data structure the cache represents. For example, the cache representing inodes stores instances of inode structures, and the cache representing process descriptors stores instances of process descriptor structures. The relationship among slabs, caches, and objects is shown in Figure 15.5. The figure shows two kernel objects 3 KB in size and three objects 7 KB in size. These objects are stored in the respective caches for 3-KB and 7-KB objects.

The slab-allocation algorithm uses caches to store kernel objects. When a cache is created, a number of objects are allocated to the cache. The number of objects in the cache depends on the size of the associated slab. For example, a 12-KB slab (made up of three contiguous 4-KB pages) could store six 2-KB objects. Initially, all the objects in the cache are marked as free. When a new object for a kernel data structure is needed, the allocator can assign any free object from the cache to satisfy the request. The object assigned from the cache is marked as used.

Let's consider a scenario in which the kernel requests memory from the slab allocator for an object representing a process descriptor. In Linux systems, a process descriptor is of the type struct task_struct, which requires approximately 1.7 KB of memory. When the Linux kernel creates a new task, it requests the necessary memory for the struct task_struct object from its cache. The cache will fulfill the request using a struct task_struct object that has already been allocated in a slab and is marked as free.

In Linux, a slab may be in one of three possible states:

1. **Full**. All objects in the slab are marked as used.

2. **Empty**. All objects in the slab are marked as free.

3. **Partial**. The slab consists of both used and free objects.

The slab allocator first attempts to satisfy the request with a free object in a partial slab. If none exists, a free object is assigned from an empty slab. If no empty slabs are available, a new slab is allocated from contiguous physical pages and assigned to a cache; memory for the object is allocated from this slab.

Two other main subsystems in Linux do their own management of physical pages: the page cache and the virtual memory system. These systems are closely related to each other. The **page cache** is the kernel's main cache for files and is the main mechanism through which I/O to block devices (Section 15.8.1) is performed. File systems of all types, including the native Linux disk-based file systems and the NFS networked file system, perform their I/O through the page cache. The page cache stores entire pages of file contents and is not limited to block devices. It can also cache networked data. The virtual memory system manages the contents of each process's virtual address space. These two systems interact closely with each other because reading a page of data into the page cache requires mapping pages in the page cache using the virtual memory system. In the following section, we look at the virtual memory system in greater detail.

15.6.2 Virtual Memory

The Linux virtual memory system is responsible for maintaining the address space accessible to each process. It creates pages of virtual memory on demand and manages loading those pages from disk and swapping them back out to disk as required. Under Linux, the virtual memory manager maintains two separate views of a process's address space: as a set of separate regions and as a set of pages.

The first view of an address space is the logical view, describing instructions that the virtual memory system has received concerning the layout of the address space. In this view, the address space consists of a set of nonoverlapping regions, each region representing a continuous, page-aligned subset of the address space. Each region is described internally by a single vm_area_struct structure that defines the properties of the region, including the process's read, write, and execute permissions in the region as well as information about any files associated with the region. The regions for each address space are linked into a balanced binary tree to allow fast lookup of the region corresponding to any virtual address.

The kernel also maintains a second, physical view of each address space. This view is stored in the hardware page tables for the process. The page-table entries identify the exact current location of each page of virtual memory, whether it is on disk or in physical memory. The physical view is managed by a set of routines, which are invoked from the kernel's software-interrupt handlers whenever a process tries to access a page that is not currently present in the page tables. Each vm_area_struct in the address-space description contains a field pointing to a table of functions that implement the key page-management functionality for any given virtual memory region. All requests to read or write an unavailable page are eventually dispatched to the appropriate handler in the function table for the vm_area_struct, so that the central memory-management routines do not have to know the details of managing each possible type of memory region.

15.6.2.1 Virtual Memory Regions

Linux implements several types of virtual memory regions. One property that characterizes virtual memory is the backing store for the region, which describes where the pages for the region come from. Most memory regions are backed either by a file or by nothing. A region backed by nothing is the simplest type of virtual memory region. Such a region represents **demand-zero memory**: when a process tries to read a page in such a region, it is simply given back a page of memory filled with zeros.

A region backed by a file acts as a viewport onto a section of that file. Whenever the process tries to access a page within that region, the page table is filled with the address of a page within the kernel's page cache corresponding to the appropriate offset in the file. The same page of physical memory is used by both the page cache and the process's page tables, so any changes made to the file by the file system are immediately visible to any processes that have mapped that file into their address space. Any number of processes can map the same region of the same file, and they will all end up using the same page of physical memory for the purpose.

A virtual memory region is also defined by its reaction to writes. The mapping of a region into the process's address space can be either *private* or *shared*. If a process writes to a privately mapped region, then the pager detects that a copy-on-write is necessary to keep the changes local to the process. In contrast, writes to a shared region result in updating of the object mapped into that region, so that the change will be visible immediately to any other process that is mapping that object.

15.6.2.2 Lifetime of a Virtual Address Space

The kernel creates a new virtual address space in two situations: when a process runs a new program with the exec() system call and when a new process is created by the fork() system call. The first case is easy. When a new program is executed, the process is given a new, completely empty virtual address space. It is up to the routines for loading the program to populate the address space with virtual memory regions.

The second case, creating a new process with fork(), involves creating a complete copy of the existing process's virtual address space. The kernel copies the parent process's vm_area_struct descriptors, then creates a new set of page tables for the child. The parent's page tables are copied directly into the child's, and the reference count of each page covered is incremented. Thus, after the fork, the parent and child share the same physical pages of memory in their address spaces.

A special case occurs when the copying operation reaches a virtual memory region that is mapped privately. Any pages to which the parent process has written within such a region are private, and subsequent changes to these pages by either the parent or the child must not update the page in the other process's address space. When the page-table entries for such regions are copied, they are set to be read only and are marked for copy-on-write. As long as neither process modifies these pages, the two processes share the same page of physical memory. However, if either process tries to modify a copy-on-write page, the reference count on the page is checked. If the page is still shared, then the process copies the page's contents to a brand-new page of physical memory and uses its copy instead. This mechanism ensures that private data pages are shared between processes whenever possible and copies are made only when absolutely necessary.

15.6.2.3   Swapping and Paging

An important task for a virtual memory system is to relocate pages of memory from physical memory out to disk when that memory is needed. Early UNIX systems performed this relocation by swapping out the contents of entire processes at once, but modern versions of UNIX rely more on paging—the movement of individual pages of virtual memory between physical memory and disk. Linux does not implement whole-process swapping; it uses the newer paging mechanism exclusively.

The paging system can be divided into two sections. First, the **policy algorithm** decides which pages to write out to disk and when to write them. Second, the **paging mechanism** carries out the transfer and pages data back into physical memory when they are needed again.

Linux's **pageout policy** uses a modified version of the standard clock (or second-chance) algorithm described in Section 8.4.5.2. Under Linux, a multiple-pass clock is used, and every page has an *age* that is adjusted on each pass of the clock. The age is more precisely a measure of the page's youthfulness, or how much activity the page has seen recently. Frequently accessed pages will attain a higher age value, but the age of infrequently accessed pages will drop toward zero with each pass. This age valuing allows the pager to select pages to page out based on a least frequently used (LFU) policy.

The paging mechanism supports paging both to dedicated swap devices and partitions and to normal files, although swapping to a file is significantly slower due to the extra overhead incurred by the file system. Blocks are allocated from the swap devices according to a bitmap of used blocks, which is maintained in physical memory at all times. The allocator uses a next-fit algorithm to try to write out pages to continuous runs of disk blocks for improved performance. The allocator records the fact that a page has been paged out to disk by using a feature of the page tables on modern processors: the page-table entry's page-not-present bit is set, allowing the rest of the page-table entry to be filled with an index identifying where the page has been written.

15.6.2.4   Kernel Virtual Memory

Linux reserves for its own internal use a constant, architecture-dependent region of the virtual address space of every process. The page-table entries that map to these kernel pages are marked as protected, so that the pages are not visible or modifiable when the processor is running in user mode. This kernel virtual memory area contains two regions. The first is a static area that contains page-table references to every available physical page of memory in the system, so that a simple translation from physical to virtual addresses occurs when kernel code is run. The core of the kernel, along with all pages allocated by the normal page allocator, resides in this region.

The remainder of the kernel's reserved section of address space is not reserved for any specific purpose. Page-table entries in this address range can be modified by the kernel to point to any other areas of memory. The kernel provides a pair of facilities that allow kernel code to use this virtual memory. The vmalloc() function allocates an arbitrary number of physical pages of memory that may not be physically contiguous into a single region of virtually contiguous kernel memory. The vremap() function maps a sequence of virtual addresses to point to an area of memory used by a device driver for memory-mapped I/O.

15.6.3 Execution and Loading of User Programs

The Linux kernel's execution of user programs is triggered by a call to the exec() system call. This exec() call commands the kernel to run a new program within the current process, completely overwriting the current execution context with the initial context of the new program. The first job of this system service is to verify that the calling process has permission rights to the file being executed. Once that matter has been checked, the kernel invokes a loader routine to start running the program. The loader does not necessarily load the contents of the program file into physical memory, but it does at least set up the mapping of the program into virtual memory.

There is no single routine in Linux for loading a new program. Instead, Linux maintains a table of possible loader functions, and it gives each such function the opportunity to try loading the given file when an exec() system call is made. The initial reason for this loader table was that, between the releases of the 1.0 and 1.2 kernels, the standard format for Linux's binary files was changed. Older Linux kernels understood the a.out format for binary files—a relatively simple format common on older UNIX systems. Newer Linux systems use the more modern ELF format, now supported by most current UNIX implementations. ELF has a number of advantages over a.out, including flexibility and extendability. New sections can be added to an ELF binary (for example, to add extra debugging information) without causing the loader routines to become confused. By allowing registration of multiple loader routines, Linux can easily support the ELF and a.out binary formats in a single running system.

In Section 15.6.3.1 and Section 15.6.3.2, we concentrate exclusively on the loading and running of ELF-format binaries. The procedure for loading a.out binaries is simpler but similar in operation.

15.6.3.1   Mapping of Programs into Memory

Under Linux, the binary loader does not load a binary file into physical memory. Rather, the pages of the binary file are mapped into regions of virtual memory. Only when the program tries to access a given page will a page fault result in the loading of that page into physical memory using demand paging.

It is the responsibility of the kernel's binary loader to set up the initial memory mapping. An ELF-format binary file consists of a header followed by several page-aligned sections. The ELF loader works by reading the header and mapping the sections of the file into separate regions of virtual memory.

Figure 15.6 shows the typical layout of memory regions set up by the ELF loader. In a reserved region at one end of the address space sits the kernel, in

Figure 15.6   Memory layout for ELF programs.

its own privileged region of virtual memory inaccessible to normal user-mode programs. The rest of virtual memory is available to applications, which can use the kernel's memory-mapping functions to create regions that map a portion of a file or that are available for application data.

The loader's job is to set up the initial memory mapping to allow the execution of the program to start. The regions that need to be initialized include the stack and the program's text and data regions.

The stack is created at the top of the user-mode virtual memory; it grows downward toward lower-numbered addresses. It includes copies of the arguments and environment variables given to the program in the exec() system call. The other regions are created near the bottom end of virtual memory. The sections of the binary file that contain program text or read-only data are mapped into memory as a write-protected region. Writable initialized data are mapped next; then any uninitialized data are mapped in as a private demand-zero region.

Directly beyond these fixed-sized regions is a variable-sized region that programs can expand as needed to hold data allocated at run time. Each process has a pointer, brk, that points to the current extent of this data region, and processes can extend or contract their brk region with a single system call —sbrk().

Once these mappings have been set up, the loader initializes the process's program-counter register with the starting point recorded in the ELF header, and the process can be scheduled.

15.6.3.2   Static and Dynamic Linking

Once the program has been loaded and has started running, all the necessary contents of the binary file have been loaded into the process's virtual address space. However, most programs also need to run functions from the system libraries, and these library functions must also be loaded. In the simplest case, the necessary library functions are embedded directly in the program's executable binary file. Such a program is statically linked to its libraries, and statically linked executables can commence running as soon as they are loaded.

The main disadvantage of static linking is that every program generated must contain copies of exactly the same common system library functions. It is much more efficient, in terms of both physical memory and disk-space usage, to load the system libraries into memory only once. Dynamic linking allows that to happen.

Linux implements dynamic linking in user mode through a special linker library. Every dynamically linked program contains a small, statically linked function that is called when the program starts. This static function just maps the link library into memory and runs the code that the function contains. The link library determines the dynamic libraries required by the program and the names of the variables and functions needed from those libraries by reading the information contained in sections of the ELF binary. It then maps the libraries into the middle of virtual memory and resolves the references to the symbols contained in those libraries. It does not matter exactly where in memory these shared libraries are mapped: they are compiled into **position-independent code (PIC)**, which can run at any address in memory.

15.7   File Systems

Linux retains UNIX's standard file-system model. In UNIX, a file does not have to be an object stored on disk or fetched over a network from a remote file server. Rather, UNIX files can be anything capable of handling the input or output of a stream of data. Device drivers can appear as files, and interprocess-communication channels or network connections also look like files to the user.

The Linux kernel handles all these types of files by hiding the implementation details of any single file type behind a layer of software, the virtual file system (VFS). Here, we first cover the virtual file system and then discuss the standard Linux file system—ext3.

15.7.1   The Virtual File System

The Linux VFS is designed around object-oriented principles. It has two components: a set of definitions that specify what file-system objects are allowed to look like and a layer of software to manipulate the objects. The VFS defines four main object types:

- An **inode object** represents an individual file.
- A **file object** represents an open file.
- A **superblock object** represents an entire file system.
- A **dentry object** represents an individual directory entry.

For each of these four object types, the VFS defines a set of operations. Every object of one of these types contains a pointer to a function table. The function table lists the addresses of the actual functions that implement the defined operations for that object. For example, an abbreviated API for some of the file object's operations includes:

- int open(. . .) — Open a file.

- ssize_t read(. . .) — Read from a file.

- ssize_t write(. . .) — Write to a file.

- int mmap(. . .) — Memory-map a file.

The complete definition of the file object is specified in the struct file_operations, which is located in the file /usr/include/linux/fs.h. An implementation of the file object (for a specific file type) is required to implement each function specified in the definition of the file object.

The VFS software layer can perform an operation on one of the file-system objects by calling the appropriate function from the object's function table, without having to know in advance exactly what kind of object it is dealing with. The VFS does not know, or care, whether an inode represents a networked file, a disk file, a network socket, or a directory file. The appropriate function for that file's read() operation will always be at the same place in its function table, and the VFS software layer will call that function without caring how the data are actually read.

The inode and file objects are the mechanisms used to access files. An inode object is a data structure containing pointers to the disk blocks that contain the actual file contents, and a file object represents a point of access to the data in an open file. A process cannot access an inode's contents without first obtaining a file object pointing to the inode. The file object keeps track of where in the file the process is currently reading or writing, to keep track of sequential file I/O. It also remembers the permissions (for example, read or write) requested when the file was opened and tracks the process's activity if necessary to perform adaptive read-ahead, fetching file data into memory before the process requests the data, to improve performance.

File objects typically belong to a single process, but inode objects do not. There is one file object for every instance of an open file, but always only a single inode object. Even when a file is no longer in use by any process, its inode object may still be cached by the VFS to improve performance if the file is used again in the near future. All cached file data are linked onto a list in the file's inode object. The inode also maintains standard information about each file, such as the owner, size, and time most recently modified.

Directory files are dealt with slightly differently from other files. The UNIX programming interface defines a number of operations on directories, such as creating, deleting, and renaming a file in a directory. The system calls for these directory operations do not require that the user open the files concerned, unlike the case for reading or writing data. The VFS therefore defines these directory operations in the inode object, rather than in the file object.

The superblock object represents a connected set of files that form a self-contained file system. The operating-system kernel maintains a single superblock object for each disk device mounted as a file system and for each networked file system currently connected. The main responsibility of the superblock object is to provide access to inodes. The VFS identifies every inode by a unique file-system/inode number pair, and it finds the inode corresponding to a particular inode number by asking the superblock object to return the inode with that number.

Finally, a dentry object represents a directory entry, which may include the name of a directory in the path name of a file (such as /usr) or the actual file (such as stdio.h). For example, the file /usr/include/stdio.h contains the directory entries (1) /, (2) usr, (3) include, and (4) stdio.h. Each of these values is represented by a separate dentry object.

As an example of how dentry objects are used, consider the situation in which a process wishes to open the file with the pathname /usr/include/stdio.h using an editor. Because Linux treats directory names as files, translating this path requires first obtaining the inode for the root— /. The operating system must then read through this file to obtain the inode for the file include. It must continue this process until it obtains the inode for the file stdio.h. Because path-name translation can be a time-consuming task, Linux maintains a cache of dentry objects, which is consulted during path-name translation. Obtaining the inode from the dentry cache is considerably faster than having to read the on-disk file.

15.7.2 The Linux ext3 File System

The standard on-disk file system used by Linux is called **ext3**, for historical reasons. Linux was originally programmed with a Minix-compatible file system, to ease exchanging data with the Minix development system, but that file system was severely restricted by 14-character file-name limits and a maximum file-system size of 64 MB. The Minix file system was superseded by a new file system, which was christened the **extended file system (extfs)**. A later redesign to improve performance and scalability and to add a few missing features led to the **second extended file system (ext2)**. Further development added journaling capabilities, and the system was renamed the **third extended file system (ext3)**. Linux kernel developers are working on augmenting ext3 with modern file-system features such as extents. This new file system is called the **fourth extended file system (ext4)**. The rest of this section discusses ext3, however, since it remains the most-deployed Linux file system. Most of the discussion applies equally to ext4.

Linux's ext3 has much in common with the BSD Fast File System (FFS) (Section A.7.7). It uses a similar mechanism for locating the data blocks belonging to a specific file, storing data-block pointers in indirect blocks throughout the file system with up to three levels of indirection. As in FFS, directory files are stored on disk just like normal files, although their contents are interpreted differently. Each block in a directory file consists of a linked list of entries. In turn, each entry contains the length of the entry, the name of a file, and the inode number of the inode to which that entry refers.

The main differences between ext3 and FFS lie in their disk-allocation policies. In FFS, the disk is allocated to files in blocks of 8 KB. These blocks are subdivided into fragments of 1 KB for storage of small files or partially filled blocks at the ends of files. In contrast, ext3 does not use fragments at all but performs all its allocations in smaller units. The default block size on ext3 varies as a function of the total size of the file system. Supported block sizes are 1, 2, 4, and 8 KB.

To maintain high performance, the operating system must try to perform I/O operations in large chunks whenever possible by clustering physically adjacent I/O requests. Clustering reduces the per-request overhead incurred by device drivers, disks, and disk-controller hardware. A block-sized I/O request size is too small to maintain good performance, so ext3 uses allocation policies designed to place logically adjacent blocks of a file into physically adjacent blocks on disk, so that it can submit an I/O request for several disk blocks as a single operation.

The ext3 allocation policy works as follows: As in FFS, an ext3 file system is partitioned into multiple segments. In ext3, these are called **block groups**. FFS uses the similar concept of **cylinder groups**, where each group corresponds to a single cylinder of a physical disk. (Note that modern disk-drive technology packs sectors onto the disk at different densities, and thus with different cylinder sizes, depending on how far the disk head is from the center of the disk. Therefore, fixed-sized cylinder groups do not necessarily correspond to the disk's geometry.)

When allocating a file, ext3 must first select the block group for that file. For data blocks, it attempts to allocate the file to the block group to which the file's inode has been allocated. For inode allocations, it selects the block group in which the file's parent directory resides for nondirectory files. Directory files are not kept together but rather are dispersed throughout the available block groups. These policies are designed not only to keep related information within the same block group but also to spread out the disk load among the disk's block groups to reduce the fragmentation of any one area of the disk.

Within a block group, ext3 tries to keep allocations physically contiguous if possible, reducing fragmentation if it can. It maintains a bitmap of all free blocks in a block group. When allocating the first blocks for a new file, it starts searching for a free block from the beginning of the block group. When extending a file, it continues the search from the block most recently allocated to the file. The search is performed in two stages. First, ext3 searches for an entire free byte in the bitmap; if it fails to find one, it looks for any free bit. The search for free bytes aims to allocate disk space in chunks of at least eight blocks where possible.

Once a free block has been identified, the search is extended backward until an allocated block is encountered. When a free byte is found in the bitmap, this backward extension prevents ext3 from leaving a hole between the most recently allocated block in the previous nonzero byte and the zero byte found. Once the next block to be allocated has been found by either bit or byte search, ext3 extends the allocation forward for up to eight blocks and preallocates these extra blocks to the file. This preallocation helps to reduce fragmentation during interleaved writes to separate files and also reduces the CPU cost of disk allocation by allocating multiple blocks simultaneously. The preallocated blocks are returned to the free-space bitmap when the file is closed.

Figure 15.7 illustrates the allocation policies. Each row represents a sequence of set and unset bits in an allocation bitmap, indicating used and free blocks on disk. In the first case, if we can find any free blocks sufficiently near the start of the search, then we allocate them no matter how fragmented

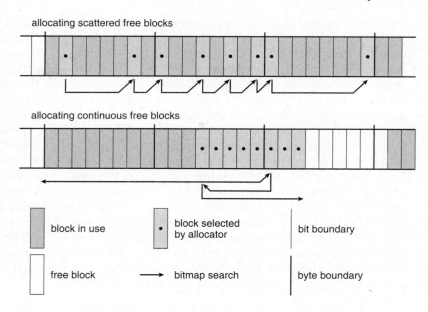

allocating scattered free blocks

allocating continuous free blocks

- block in use
- block selected by allocator
- bit boundary
- free block
- bitmap search
- byte boundary

Figure 15.7 ext3 block-allocation policies.

they may be. The fragmentation is partially compensated for by the fact that the blocks are close together and can probably all be read without any disk seeks. Furthermore, allocating them all to one file is better in the long run than allocating isolated blocks to separate files once large free areas become scarce on disk. In the second case, we have not immediately found a free block close by, so we search forward for an entire free byte in the bitmap. If we allocated that byte as a whole, we would end up creating a fragmented area of free space between it and the allocation preceding it. Thus, before allocating, we back up to make this allocation flush with the allocation preceding it, and then we allocate forward to satisfy the default allocation of eight blocks.

15.7.3 Journaling

The ext3 file system supports a popular feature called **journaling**, whereby modifications to the file system are written sequentially to a journal. A set of operations that performs a specific task is a **transaction**. Once a transaction is written to the journal, it is considered to be committed. Meanwhile, the journal entries relating to the transaction are replayed across the actual file-system structures. As the changes are made, a pointer is updated to indicate which actions have completed and which are still incomplete. When an entire committed transaction is completed, it is removed from the journal. The journal, which is actually a circular buffer, may be in a separate section of the file system, or it may even be on a separate disk spindle. It is more efficient, but more complex, to have it under separate read–write heads, thereby decreasing head contention and seek times.

If the system crashes, some transactions may remain in the journal. Those transactions were never completed to the file system even though they were committed by the operating system, so they must be completed once the system recovers. The transactions can be executed from the pointer until the work is complete, and the file-system structures remain consistent. The only problem occurs when a transaction has been aborted—that is, it was not committed before the system crashed. Any changes from those transactions that were applied to the file system must be undone, again preserving the consistency of the file system. This recovery is all that is needed after a crash, eliminating all problems with consistency checking.

Journaling file systems may perform some operations faster than non-journaling systems, as updates proceed much faster when they are applied to the in-memory journal rather than directly to the on-disk data structures. The reason for this improvement is found in the performance advantage of sequential I/O over random I/O. Costly synchronous random writes to the file system are turned into much less costly synchronous sequential writes to the file system's journal. Those changes, in turn, are replayed asynchronously via random writes to the appropriate structures. The overall result is a significant gain in performance of file-system metadata-oriented operations, such as file creation and deletion. Due to this performance improvement, ext3 can be configured to journal only metadata and not file data.

15.7.4 The Linux Process File System

The flexibility of the Linux VFS enables us to implement a file system that does not store data persistently at all but rather provides an interface to some other functionality. The Linux **process file system**, known as the /proc file system, is an example of a file system whose contents are not actually stored anywhere but are computed on demand according to user file I/O requests.

A /proc file system is not unique to Linux. SVR4 UNIX introduced a /proc file system as an efficient interface to the kernel's process debugging support. Each subdirectory of the file system corresponded not to a directory on any disk but rather to an active process on the current system. A listing of the file system reveals one directory per process, with the directory name being the ASCII decimal representation of the process's unique process identifier (PID).

Linux implements such a /proc file system but extends it greatly by adding a number of extra directories and text files under the file system's root directory. These new entries correspond to various statistics about the kernel and the associated loaded drivers. The /proc file system provides a way for programs to access this information as plain text files; the standard UNIX user environment provides powerful tools to process such files. For example, in the past, the traditional UNIX ps command for listing the states of all running processes has been implemented as a privileged process that reads the process state directly from the kernel's virtual memory. Under Linux, this command is implemented as an entirely unprivileged program that simply parses and formats the information from /proc.

The /proc file system must implement two things: a directory structure and the file contents within. Because a UNIX file system is defined as a set of file and directory inodes identified by their inode numbers, the /proc file system must define a unique and persistent inode number for each directory and the associated files. Once such a mapping exists, the file system can use this inode number to identify just what operation is required when a user tries to read from a particular file inode or to perform a lookup in a particular directory inode. When data are read from one of these files, the /proc file system will collect the appropriate information, format it into textual form, and place it into the requesting process's read buffer.

The mapping from inode number to information type splits the inode number into two fields. In Linux, a PID is 16 bits in size, but an inode number is 32 bits. The top 16 bits of the inode number are interpreted as a PID, and the remaining bits define what type of information is being requested about that process.

A PID of zero is not valid, so a zero PID field in the inode number is taken to mean that this inode contains global—rather than process-specific—information. Separate global files exist in /proc to report information such as the kernel version, free memory, performance statistics, and drivers currently running.

Not all the inode numbers in this range are reserved. The kernel can allocate new /proc inode mappings dynamically, maintaining a bitmap of allocated inode numbers. It also maintains a tree data structure of registered global /proc file-system entries. Each entry contains the file's inode number, file name, and access permissions, along with the special functions used to generate the file's contents. Drivers can register and deregister entries in this tree at any time, and a special section of the tree—appearing under the /proc/sys directory—is reserved for kernel variables. Files under this tree are managed by a set of common handlers that allow both reading and writing of these variables, so a system administrator can tune the value of kernel parameters simply by writing out the new desired values in ASCII decimal to the appropriate file.

To allow efficient access to these variables from within applications, the /proc/sys subtree is made available through a special system call, sysctl(), that reads and writes the same variables in binary, rather than in text, without the overhead of the file system. sysctl() is not an extra facility; it simply reads the /proc dynamic entry tree to identify the variables to which the application is referring.

15.8 Input and Output

To the user, the I/O system in Linux looks much like that in any UNIX system. That is, to the extent possible, all device drivers appear as normal files. Users can open an access channel to a device in the same way they open any other file—devices can appear as objects within the file system. The system administrator can create special files within a file system that contain references to a specific device driver, and a user opening such a file will be able to read from and write to the device referenced. By using the normal file-protection system, which determines who can access which file, the administrator can set access permissions for each device.

Linux splits all devices into three classes: block devices, character devices, and network devices. Figure 15.8 illustrates the overall structure of the device-driver system.

Block devices include all devices that allow random access to completely independent, fixed-sized blocks of data, including hard disks and floppy disks, CD-ROMs and Blu-ray discs, and flash memory. Block devices are typically used to store file systems, but direct access to a block device is also allowed so that programs can create and repair the file system that the device contains. Applications can also access these block devices directly if they wish. For example, a database application may prefer to perform its own fine-tuned layout of data onto a disk rather than using the general-purpose file system.

Character devices include most other devices, such as mice and keyboards. The fundamental difference between block and character devices is random access—block devices are accessed randomly, while character devices are accessed serially. For example, seeking to a certain position in a file might be supported for a DVD but makes no sense for a pointing device such as a mouse.

Network devices are dealt with differently from block and character devices. Users cannot directly transfer data to network devices. Instead, they must communicate indirectly by opening a connection to the kernel's networking subsystem. We discuss the interface to network devices separately in Section 15.10.

15.8.1   Block Devices

Block devices provide the main interface to all disk devices in a system. Performance is particularly important for disks, and the block-device system must provide functionality to ensure that disk access is as fast as possible. This functionality is achieved through the scheduling of I/O operations.

In the context of block devices, a block represents the unit with which the kernel performs I/O. When a block is read into memory, it is stored in a buffer. The **request manager** is the layer of software that manages the reading and writing of buffer contents to and from a block-device driver.

A separate list of requests is kept for each block-device driver. Traditionally, these requests have been scheduled according to a unidirectional-elevator (C-SCAN) algorithm that exploits the order in which requests are inserted in and removed from the lists. The request lists are maintained in sorted order of increasing starting-sector number. When a request is accepted for processing by a block-device driver, it is not removed from the list. It is removed only after the I/O is complete, at which point the driver continues with the next request in the list, even if new requests have been inserted in the list before the active

Figure 15.8   Device-driver block structure.

request. As new I/O requests are made, the request manager attempts to merge requests in the lists.

Linux kernel version 2.6 introduced a new I/O scheduling algorithm. Although a simple elevator algorithm remains available, the default I/O scheduler is now the **Completely Fair Queueing (CFQ)** scheduler. The CFQ I/O scheduler is fundamentally different from elevator-based algorithms. Instead of sorting requests into a list, CFQ maintains a set of lists—by default, one for each process. Requests originating from a process go in that process's list. For example, if two processes are issuing I/O requests, CFQ will maintain two separate lists of requests, one for each process. The lists are maintained according to the C-SCAN algorithm.

CFQ services the lists differently as well. Where a traditional C-SCAN algorithm is indifferent to a specific process, CFQ services each process's list round-robin. It pulls a configurable number of requests (by default, four) from each list before moving on to the next. This method results in fairness at the process level—each process receives an equal fraction of the disk's bandwidth. The result is beneficial with interactive workloads where I/O latency is important. In practice, however, CFQ performs well with most workloads.

15.8.2   Character Devices

A character-device driver can be almost any device driver that does not offer random access to fixed blocks of data. Any character-device drivers registered to the Linux kernel must also register a set of functions that implement the file I/O operations that the driver can handle. The kernel performs almost no preprocessing of a file read or write request to a character device. It simply passes the request to the device in question and lets the device deal with the request.

The main exception to this rule is the special subset of character-device drivers that implement terminal devices. The kernel maintains a standard interface to these drivers by means of a set of `tty_struct` structures. Each of these structures provides buffering and flow control on the data stream from the terminal device and feeds those data to a line discipline.

A **line discipline** is an interpreter for the information from the terminal device. The most common line discipline is the `tty` discipline, which glues the terminal's data stream onto the standard input and output streams of a user's running processes, allowing those processes to communicate directly with the user's terminal. This job is complicated by the fact that several such processes may be running simultaneously, and the `tty` line discipline is responsible for attaching and detaching the terminal's input and output from the various processes connected to it as those processes are suspended or awakened by the user.

Other line disciplines also are implemented that have nothing to do with I/O to a user process. The PPP and SLIP networking protocols are ways of encoding a networking connection over a terminal device such as a serial line. These protocols are implemented under Linux as drivers that at one end appear to the terminal system as line disciplines and at the other end appear to the networking system as network-device drivers. After one of these line disciplines has been enabled on a terminal device, any data appearing on that terminal will be routed directly to the appropriate network-device driver.

15.9 Interprocess Communication

Linux provides a rich environment for processes to communicate with each other. Communication may be just a matter of letting another process know that some event has occurred, or it may involve transferring data from one process to another.

15.9.1 Synchronization and Signals

The standard Linux mechanism for informing a process that an event has occurred is the **signal**. Signals can be sent from any process to any other process, with restrictions on signals sent to processes owned by another user. However, a limited number of signals are available, and they cannot carry information. Only the fact that a signal has occurred is available to a process. Signals are not generated only by processes. The kernel also generates signals internally. For example, it can send a signal to a server process when data arrive on a network channel, to a parent process when a child terminates, or to a waiting process when a timer expires.

Internally, the Linux kernel does not use signals to communicate with processes running in kernel mode. If a kernel-mode process is expecting an event to occur, it will not use signals to receive notification of that event. Rather, communication about incoming asynchronous events within the kernel takes place through the use of scheduling states and wait_queue structures. These mechanisms allow kernel-mode processes to inform one another about relevant events, and they also allow events to be generated by device drivers or by the networking system. Whenever a process wants to wait for some event to complete, it places itself on a wait queue associated with that event and tells the scheduler that it is no longer eligible for execution. Once the event has completed, every process on the wait queue will be awoken. This procedure allows multiple processes to wait for a single event. For example, if several processes are trying to read a file from a disk, then they will all be awakened once the data have been read into memory successfully.

Although signals have always been the main mechanism for communicating asynchronous events among processes, Linux also implements the semaphore mechanism of System V UNIX. A process can wait on a semaphore as easily as it can wait for a signal, but semaphores have two advantages: large numbers of semaphores can be shared among multiple independent processes, and operations on multiple semaphores can be performed atomically. Internally, the standard Linux wait queue mechanism synchronizes processes that are communicating with semaphores.

15.9.2 Passing of Data among Processes

Linux offers several mechanisms for passing data among processes. The standard UNIX **pipe** mechanism allows a child process to inherit a communication channel from its parent; data written to one end of the pipe can be read at the other. Under Linux, pipes appear as just another type of inode to virtual file system software, and each pipe has a pair of wait queues to synchronize the reader and writer. UNIX also defines a set of networking facilities that can send streams of data to both local and remote processes. Networking is covered in Section 15.10.

Another process communications method, shared memory, offers an extremely fast way to communicate large or small amounts of data. Any data written by one process to a shared memory region can be read immediately by any other process that has mapped that region into its address space. The main disadvantage of shared memory is that, on its own, it offers no synchronization. A process can neither ask the operating system whether a piece of shared memory has been written to nor suspend execution until such a write occurs. Shared memory becomes particularly powerful when used in conjunction with another interprocess-communication mechanism that provides the missing synchronization.

A shared-memory region in Linux is a persistent object that can be created or deleted by processes. Such an object is treated as though it were a small, independent address space. The Linux paging algorithms can elect to page shared-memory pages out to disk, just as they can page out a process's data pages. The shared-memory object acts as a backing store for shared-memory regions, just as a file can act as a backing store for a memory-mapped memory region. When a file is mapped into a virtual address space region, then any page faults that occur cause the appropriate page of the file to be mapped into virtual memory. Similarly, shared-memory mappings direct page faults to map in pages from a persistent shared-memory object. Also just as for files, shared-memory objects remember their contents even if no processes are currently mapping them into virtual memory.

15.10 Network Structure

Networking is a key area of functionality for Linux. Not only does Linux support the standard Internet protocols used for most UNIX-to-UNIX communications, but it also implements a number of protocols native to other, non-UNIX operating systems. In particular, since Linux was originally implemented primarily on PCs, rather than on large workstations or on server-class systems, it supports many of the protocols typically used on PC networks, such as AppleTalk and IPX.

Internally, networking in the Linux kernel is implemented by three layers of software:

1. The socket interface

2. Protocol drivers

3. Network-device drivers

User applications perform all networking requests through the socket interface. This interface is designed to look like the 4.3 BSD socket layer, so that any programs designed to make use of Berkeley sockets will run on Linux without any source-code changes. This interface is described in Section A.9.1. The BSD socket interface is sufficiently general to represent network addresses for a wide range of networking protocols. This single interface is used in Linux to access not just those protocols implemented on standard BSD systems but all the protocols supported by the system.

The next layer of software is the protocol stack, which is similar in organization to BSD's own framework. Whenever any networking data arrive at this layer, either from an application's socket or from a network-device driver, the data are expected to have been tagged with an identifier specifying which network protocol they contain. Protocols can communicate with one another if they desire; for example, within the Internet protocol set, separate protocols manage routing, error reporting, and reliable retransmission of lost data.

The protocol layer may rewrite packets, create new packets, split or reassemble packets into fragments, or simply discard incoming data. Ultimately, once the protocol layer has finished processing a set of packets, it passes them on, either upward to the socket interface if the data are destined for a local connection or downward to a device driver if the data need to be transmitted remotely. The protocol layer decides to which socket or device it will send the packet.

All communication between the layers of the networking stack is performed by passing single skbuff (socket buffer) structures. Each of these structures contains a set of pointers into a single continuous area of memory, representing a buffer inside which network packets can be constructed. The valid data in a skbuff do not need to start at the beginning of the skbuff's buffer, and they do not need to run to the end. The networking code can add data to or trim data from either end of the packet, as long as the result still fits into the skbuff. This capacity is especially important on modern microprocessors, where improvements in CPU speed have far outstripped the performance of main memory. The skbuff architecture allows flexibility in manipulating packet headers and checksums while avoiding any unnecessary data copying.

The most important set of protocols in the Linux networking system is the TCP/IP protocol suite. This suite comprises a number of separate protocols. The IP protocol implements routing between different hosts anywhere on the network. On top of the routing protocol are the UDP, TCP, and ICMP protocols. The UDP protocol carries arbitrary individual datagrams between hosts. The TCP protocol implements reliable connections between hosts with guaranteed in-order delivery of packets and automatic retransmission of lost data. The ICMP protocol carries various error and status messages between hosts.

Each packet (skbuff) arriving at the networking stack's protocol software is expected to be already tagged with an internal identifier indicating the protocol to which the packet is relevant. Different networking-device drivers encode the protocol type in different ways; thus, the protocol for incoming data must be identified in the device driver. The device driver uses a hash table of known networking-protocol identifiers to look up the appropriate protocol and passes the packet to that protocol. New protocols can be added to the hash table as kernel-loadable modules.

Incoming IP packets are delivered to the IP driver. The job of this layer is to perform routing. After deciding where the packet is to be sent, the IP driver forwards the packet to the appropriate internal protocol driver to be delivered locally or injects it back into a selected network-device-driver queue to be forwarded to another host. It performs the routing decision using two tables: the persistent forwarding information base (FIB) and a cache of recent routing decisions. The FIB holds routing-configuration information and can specify routes based either on a specific destination address or on a wildcard representing multiple destinations. The FIB is organized as a set of hash tables indexed by destination address; the tables representing the most specific routes are always searched first. Successful lookups from this table are added to the route-caching table, which caches routes only by specific destination. No wildcards are stored in the cache, so lookups can be made quickly. An entry in the route cache expires after a fixed period with no hits.

At various stages, the IP software passes packets to a separate section of code for **firewall management**—selective filtering of packets according to arbitrary criteria, usually for security purposes. The firewall manager maintains a number of separate **firewall chains** and allows a skbuff to be matched against any chain. Chains are reserved for separate purposes: one is used for forwarded packets, one for packets being input to this host, and one for data generated at this host. Each chain is held as an ordered list of rules, where a rule specifies one of a number of possible firewall-decision functions plus some arbitrary data for matching purposes.

Two other functions performed by the IP driver are disassembly and reassembly of large packets. If an outgoing packet is too large to be queued to a device, it is simply split up into smaller **fragments**, which are all queued to the driver. At the receiving host, these fragments must be reassembled. The IP driver maintains an ipfrag object for each fragment awaiting reassembly and an ipq for each datagram being assembled. Incoming fragments are matched against each known ipq. If a match is found, the fragment is added to it; otherwise, a new ipq is created. Once the final fragment has arrived for a ipq, a completely new skbuff is constructed to hold the new packet, and this packet is passed back into the IP driver.

Packets identified by the IP as destined for this host are passed on to one of the other protocol drivers. The UDP and TCP protocols share a means of associating packets with source and destination sockets: each connected pair of sockets is uniquely identified by its source and destination addresses and by the source and destination port numbers. The socket lists are linked to hash tables keyed on these four address and port values for socket lookup on incoming packets. The TCP protocol has to deal with unreliable connections, so it maintains ordered lists of unacknowledged outgoing packets to retransmit after a timeout and of incoming out-of-order packets to be presented to the socket when the missing data have arrived.

15.11 Security

Linux's security model is closely related to typical UNIX security mechanisms. The security concerns can be classified in two groups:

1. **Authentication**. Making sure that nobody can access the system without first proving that she has entry rights

2. **Access control**. Providing a mechanism for checking whether a user has the right to access a certain object and preventing access to objects as required

15.11.1 Authentication

Authentication in UNIX has typically been performed through the use of a publicly readable password file. A user's password is combined with a random "salt" value, and the result is encoded with a one-way transformation function and stored in the password file. The use of the one-way function means that the original password cannot be deduced from the password file except by trial and error. When a user presents a password to the system, the password is recombined with the salt value stored in the password file and passed through the same one-way transformation. If the result matches the contents of the password file, then the password is accepted.

Historically, UNIX implementations of this mechanism have had several drawbacks. Passwords were often limited to eight characters, and the number of possible salt values was so low that an attacker could easily combine a dictionary of commonly used passwords with every possible salt value and have a good chance of matching one or more passwords in the password file, gaining unauthorized access to any accounts compromised as a result. Extensions to the password mechanism have been introduced that keep the encrypted password secret in a file that is not publicly readable, that allow longer passwords, or that use more secure methods of encoding the password. Other authentication mechanisms have been introduced that limit the periods during which a user is permitted to connect to the system. Also, mechanisms exist to distribute authentication information to all the related systems in a network.

A new security mechanism has been developed by UNIX vendors to address authentication problems. The **pluggable authentication modules (PAM)** system is based on a shared library that can be used by any system component that needs to authenticate users. An implementation of this system is available under Linux. PAM allows authentication modules to be loaded on demand as specified in a system-wide configuration file. If a new authentication mechanism is added at a later date, it can be added to the configuration file, and all system components will immediately be able to take advantage of it. PAM modules can specify authentication methods, account restrictions, session-setup functions, and password-changing functions (so that, when users change their passwords, all the necessary authentication mechanisms can be updated at once).

15.11.2 Access Control

Access control under UNIX systems, including Linux, is performed through the use of unique numeric identifiers. A user identifier (UID) identifies a single user or a single set of access rights. A group identifier (GID) is an extra identifier that can be used to identify rights belonging to more than one user.

Access control is applied to various objects in the system. Every file available in the system is protected by the standard access-control mechanism. In addition, other shared objects, such as shared-memory sections and semaphores, employ the same access system.

Every object in a UNIX system under user and group access control has a single UID and a single GID associated with it. User processes also have a single

UID, but they may have more than one GID. If a process's UID matches the UID of an object, then the process has **user rights** or **owner rights** to that object. If the UIDs do not match but any GID of the process matches the object's GID, then **group rights** are conferred; otherwise, the process has **world rights** to the object.

Linux performs access control by assigning objects a **protection mask** that specifies which access modes—read, write, or execute—are to be granted to processes with owner, group, or world access. Thus, the owner of an object might have full read, write, and execute access to a file; other users in a certain group might be given read access but denied write access; and everybody else might be given no access at all.

The only exception is the privileged **root** UID. A process with this special UID is granted automatic access to any object in the system, bypassing normal access checks. Such processes are also granted permission to perform privileged operations, such as reading any physical memory or opening reserved network sockets. This mechanism allows the kernel to prevent normal users from accessing these resources: most of the kernel's key internal resources are implicitly owned by the root UID.

Linux implements the standard UNIX setuid mechanism described in Section A.3.2. This mechanism allows a program to run with privileges different from those of the user running the program. For example, the lpr program (which submits a job to a print queue) has access to the system's print queues even if the user running that program does not. The UNIX implementation of setuid distinguishes between a process's real and effective UID. The real UID is that of the user running the program; the effective UID is that of the file's owner.

Under Linux, this mechanism is augmented in two ways. First, Linux implements the POSIX specification's saved user-id mechanism, which allows a process to drop and reacquire its effective UID repeatedly. For security reasons, a program may want to perform most of its operations in a safe mode, waiving the privileges granted by its setuid status; but it may wish to perform selected operations with all its privileges. Standard UNIX implementations achieve this capacity only by swapping the real and effective UIDs. When this is done, the previous effective UID is remembered, but the program's real UID does not always correspond to the UID of the user running the program. Saved UIDs allow a process to set its effective UID to its real UID and then return to the previous value of its effective UID without having to modify the real UID at any time.

The second enhancement provided by Linux is the addition of a process characteristic that grants just a subset of the rights of the effective UID. The **fsuid** and **fsgid** process properties are used when access rights are granted to files. The appropriate property is set every time the effective UID or GID is set. However, the fsuid and fsgid can be set independently of the effective ids, allowing a process to access files on behalf of another user without taking on the identity of that other user in any other way. Specifically, server processes can use this mechanism to serve files to a certain user without becoming vulnerable to being killed or suspended by that user.

Finally, Linux provides a mechanism for flexible passing of rights from one program to another—a mechanism that has become common in modern versions of UNIX. When a local network socket has been set up between any two processes on the system, either of those processes may send to the other process a file descriptor for one of its open files; the other process receives a duplicate file descriptor for the same file. This mechanism allows a client to pass access to a single file selectively to some server process without granting that process any other privileges. For example, it is no longer necessary for a print server to be able to read all the files of a user who submits a new print job. The print client can simply pass the server file descriptors for any files to be printed, denying the server access to any of the user's other files.

15.12 Summary

Linux is a modern, free operating system based on UNIX standards. It has been designed to run efficiently and reliably on common PC hardware; it also runs on a variety of other platforms, such as mobile phones. It provides a programming interface and user interface compatible with standard UNIX systems and can run a large number of UNIX applications, including an increasing number of commercially supported applications.

Linux has not evolved in a vacuum. A complete Linux system includes many components that were developed independently of Linux. The core Linux operating-system kernel is entirely original, but it allows much existing free UNIX software to run, resulting in an entire UNIX-compatible operating system free from proprietary code.

The Linux kernel is implemented as a traditional monolithic kernel for performance reasons, but it is modular enough in design to allow most drivers to be dynamically loaded and unloaded at run time.

Linux is a multiuser system, providing protection between processes and running multiple processes according to a time-sharing scheduler. Newly created processes can share selective parts of their execution environment with their parent processes, allowing multithreaded programming. Interprocess communication is supported by both System V mechanisms—message queues, semaphores, and shared memory—and BSD's socket interface. Multiple networking protocols can be accessed simultaneously through the socket interface.

The memory-management system uses page sharing and copy-on-write to minimize the duplication of data shared by different processes. Pages are loaded on demand when they are first referenced and are paged back out to backing store according to an LFU algorithm if physical memory needs to be reclaimed.

To the user, the file system appears as a hierarchical directory tree that obeys UNIX semantics. Internally, Linux uses an abstraction layer to manage multiple file systems. Device-oriented, networked, and virtual file systems are supported. Device-oriented file systems access disk storage through a page cache that is unified with the virtual memory system.

Review Questions

Review questions for this chapter can be accessed by visiting our website.

Practice Exercises

Answers for the Practice Exercises can be accceed by visiting our website.

15.1 Dynamically loadable kernel modules give flexibility when drivers are added to a system, but do they have disadvantages too? Under what circumstances would a kernel be compiled into a single binary file, and when would it be better to keep it split into modules? Explain your answer.

15.2 Multithreading is a commonly used programming technique. Describe three different ways to implement threads, and compare these three methods with the Linux clone() mechanism. When might using each alternative mechanism be better or worse than using clones?

15.3 The Linux kernel does not allow paging out of kernel memory. What effect does this restriction have on the kernel's design? What are two advantages and two disadvantages of this design decision?

15.4 Discuss three advantages of dynamic (shared) linkage of libraries compared with static linkage. Describe two cases in which static linkage is preferable.

15.5 Compare the use of networking sockets with the use of shared memory as a mechanism for communicating data between processes on a single computer. What are the advantages of each method? When might each be preferred?

15.6 At one time, UNIX systems used disk-layout optimizations based on the rotation position of disk data, but modern implementations, including Linux, simply optimize for sequential data access. Why do they do so? Of what hardware characteristics does sequential access take advantage? Why is rotational optimization no longer so useful?

Exercises

15.7 What are the advantages and disadvantages of writing an operating system in a high-level language, such as C?

15.8 In what circumstances is the system-call sequence fork() exec() most appropriate? When is vfork() preferable?

15.9 What socket type should be used to implement an intercomputer file-transfer program? What type should be used for a program that periodically tests to see whether another computer is up on the network? Explain your answer.

15.10 Linux runs on a variety of hardware platforms. What steps must Linux developers take to ensure that the system is portable to different processors and memory-management architectures and to minimize the amount of architecture-specific kernel code?

15.11   What are the advantages and disadvantages of making only some of the symbols defined inside a kernel accessible to a loadable kernel module?

15.12   What are the primary goals of the conflict-resolution mechanism used by the Linux kernel for loading kernel modules?

15.13   Discuss how the clone() operation supported by Linux is used to support both processes and threads.

15.14   Would you classify Linux threads as user-level threads or as kernel-level threads? Support your answer with the appropriate arguments.

15.15   What extra costs are incurred in the creation and scheduling of a process, compared with the cost of a cloned thread?

15.16   How does Linux's Completely Fair Scheduler (CFS) provide improved fairness over a traditional UNIX process scheduler? When is the fairness guaranteed?

15.17   What are the two configurable variables of the Completely Fair Scheduler (CFS)? What are the pros and cons of setting each of them to very small and very large values?

15.18   The Linux scheduler implements "soft" real-time scheduling. What features necessary for certain real-time programming tasks are missing? How might they be added to the kernel? What are the costs (downsides) of such features?

15.19   Under what circumstances would a user process request an operation that results in the allocation of a demand-zero memory region?

15.20   What scenarios would cause a page of memory to be mapped into a user program's address space with the copy-on-write attribute enabled?

15.21   In Linux, shared libraries perform many operations central to the operating system. What is the advantage of keeping this functionality out of the kernel? Are there any drawbacks? Explain your answer.

15.22   What are the benefits of a journaling file system such as Linux's ext3? What are the costs? Why does ext3 provide the option to journal only metadata?

15.23   The directory structure of a Linux operating system could include files corresponding to several different file systems, including the Linux /proc file system. How might the need to support different file-system types affect the structure of the Linux kernel?

15.24   In what ways does the Linux setuid feature differ from the setuid feature SVR4?

15.25   The Linux source code is freely and widely available over the Internet and from CD-ROM vendors. What are three implications of this availability for the security of the Linux system?

Bibliographical Notes

The Linux system is a product of the Internet; as a result, much of the available documentation on Linux is available in some form on the Internet. The following key sites reference most of the useful information available:

- The *Linux Cross-Reference Page (LXR)* (http://lxr.linux.no) maintains current listings of the Linux kernel, browsable via the Web and fully cross-referenced.

- The *Kernel Hackers' Guide* provides a helpful overview of the Linux kernel components and internals and is located at http://tldp.org/LDP/tlk/tlk.html.

- The *Linux Weekly News (LWN)* (http://lwn.net) provides weekly Linux-related news, including a very well researched subsection on Linux kernel news.

Many mailing lists devoted to Linux are also available. The most important are maintained by a mailing-list manager that can be reached at the e-mail address majordomo@vger.rutgers.edu. Send e-mail to this address with the single line "help" in the mail's body for information on how to access the list server and to subscribe to any lists.

Finally, the Linux system itself can be obtained over the Internet. Complete Linux distributions are available from the home sites of the companies concerned, and the Linux community also maintains archives of current system components at several places on the Internet. The most important is ftp://ftp.kernel.org/pub/linux.

In addition to investigating Internet resources, you can read about the internals of the Linux kernel in [Mauerer (2008)] and [Love (2010)].

Bibliography

[Love (2010)]   R. Love, *Linux Kernel Development*, Third Edition, Developer's Library (2010).

[Mauerer (2008)]   W. Mauerer, *Professional Linux Kernel Architecture*, John Wiley and Sons (2008).

Index

M